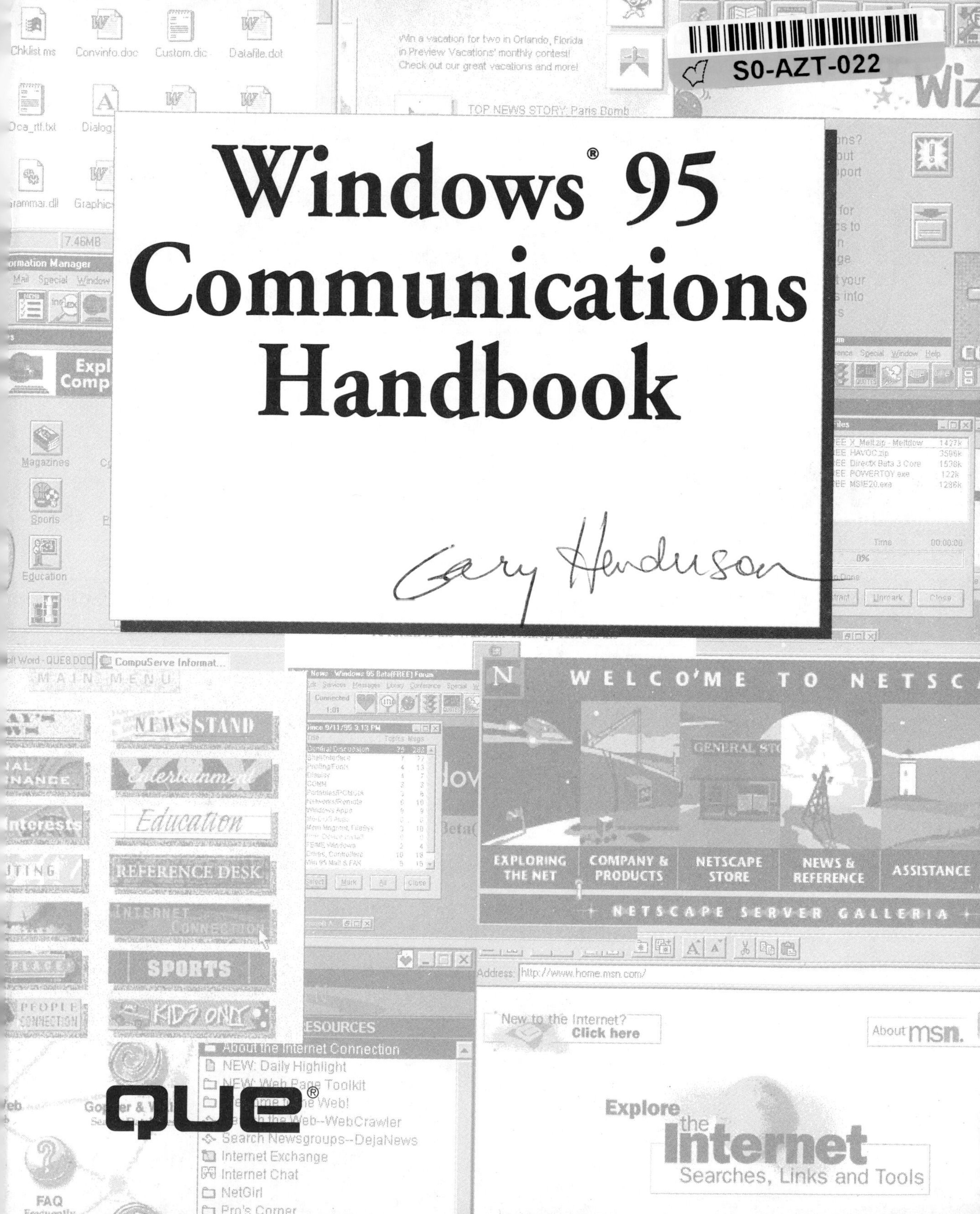
S0-AZT-022
Windows® 95
Communications
Handbook
Gary Henderson
que®

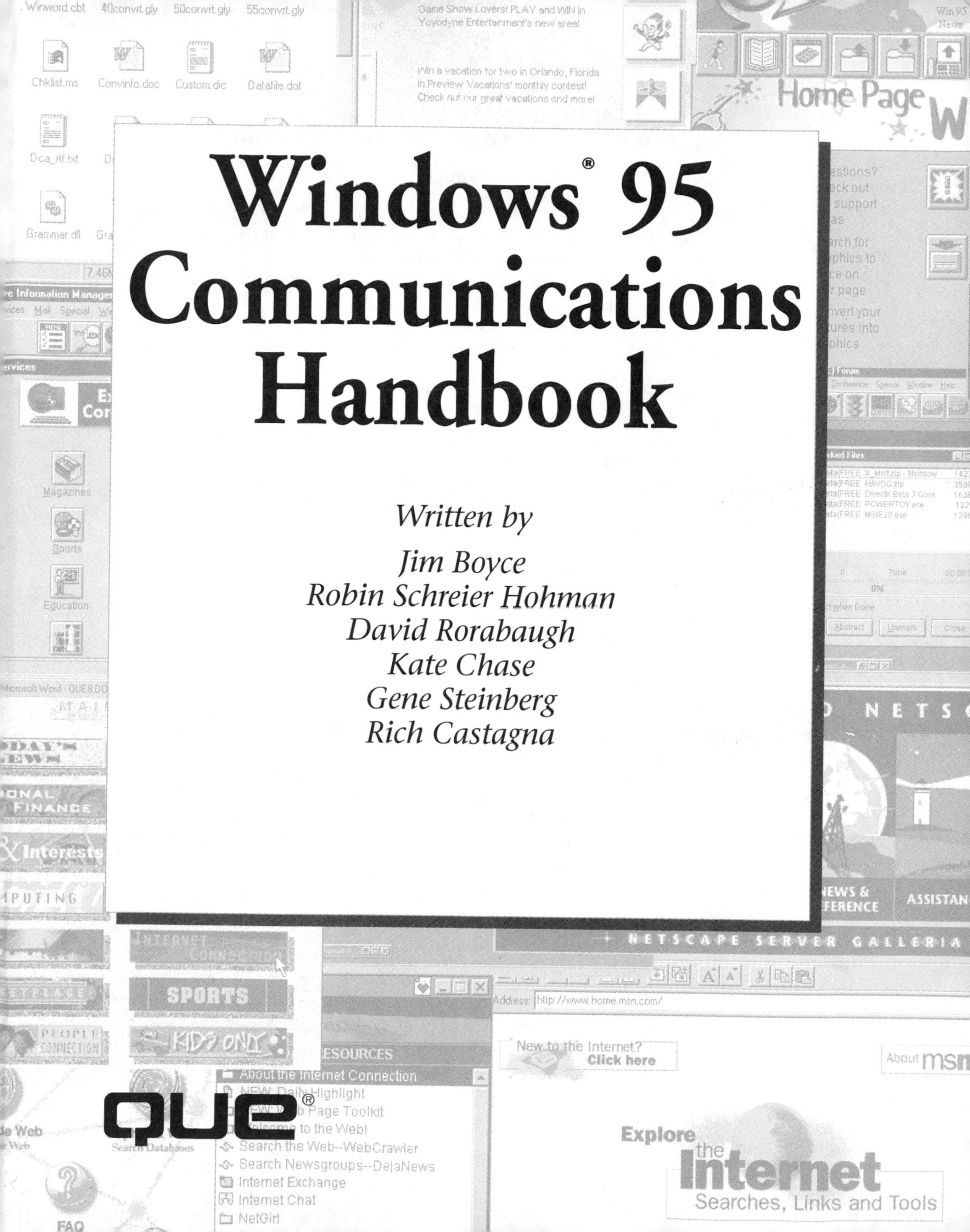
Windows® 95
Communications
Handbook
Written by
Jim Boyce
Robin Schreier Hohman
David Rorabaugh
Kate Chase
Gene Steinberg
Rich Castagna
que®

Windows 95 Communications Handbook

Library of Congress Catalog No.: 95-72577

ISBN: 0-7897-0675-X

While every effort has been made to supply complete and accurate information, this book is sold *as is*, without warranty of any kind, either express or implied, respecting the contents of this book, including but not limited to implied warranties for the book's quality, performance, merchantability, or fitness for any particular purpose. Neither Que Corporation, Windows Magazine, CMP Publications, Inc., nor Que's dealers or distributors shall be liable to the purchaser or any other person or entity with respect to any liability, loss, or damage caused or alleged to have been caused directly or indirectly by this book.

98 97 96 6 5 4 3 2 1

Interpretation of the printing code: the rightmost double-digit number is the year of the book's printing; the rightmost single-digit number, the number of the book's printing. For example, a printing code of 96-1 shows that the first printing of the book occurred in 1996.

All terms mentioned in this book that are known to be trademarks or service marks have been appropriately capitalized. Que cannot attest to the accuracy of this information. Use of a term in this book should not be regarded as affecting the validity of any trademark or service mark.

Windows is a trademark of Microsoft Corporation and is used by CMP Publications, Inc. under license from the owner. Windows Magazine is an independent publication not affiliated with Microsoft Corporation. Microsoft Corporation is not responsible in any way for the editorial policy or other contents of this publication.

Screen reproductions in this book were created using Collage Plus from Inner Media, Inc., Hollis, NH.

Composed in *Stone* and *MCPdigital* by Que Corporation.

Credits

President
Roland Elgey

Vice President and Publisher
Marie Butler-Knight

Publishing Director
Brad R. Koch

Editorial Services Director
Elizabeth Keaffaber

Managing Editor
Michael Cunningham

Director of Marketing
Lynn E. Zingraf

Senior Series Editor
Chris Nelson

Acquisitions Editors
Thomas E. Barich
Elizabeth A. South

Product Director
Lisa D. Wagner

Product Development Specialist
Joyce J. Nielsen

Production Editor
Thomas F. Hayes

Copy Editors
Geneil Breeze
Charles K. Bowles II
Julie McNamee
Rebecca Mounts

Assistant Product Marketing Manager
Kim Margolius

Technical Editor
Elske C. Petstock

Technical Specialist
Nadeem Muhammed

Acquisitions Coordinator
Tracey Williams

Operations Coordinator
Patty Brooks

Editorial Assistant
Carmen Krikorian

Book Designer
Kim Scott

Cover Designer
Kim Scott

Production Team
Brian Buschkill
Chad Dressler
Joan Evan
Jason Hand
Sonja Hart
John Hulse
Clint Lahnen
Bob LaRoche
Glenn Larsen
Michelle Lee
Laura Robbins
Bobbi Satterfield
Craig Small
Todd Wente

Indexer
Carol Sheehan

About the Authors

Jim Boyce, the lead author for *Windows 95 Communications Handbook*, is a contributing editor and columnist for *Windows* magazine, a columnist for *CADENCE* magazine, and a regular contributor to other computer publications. He has been involved with computers since the late seventies, and has used computers as a user, programmer, and systems manager in a variety of capacities. He has a wide range of experience in the DOS, Windows, and UNIX environments. Jim has authored and coauthored over two dozen books on computers and software. You can contact Jim at 76516.3403@compuserve.com.

Robin Schreier Hohman has been writing about computers and other subjects for more than 10 years. Her articles have appeared in newspapers, magazines, and books. She also survived a stint as a writer/producer in television news, and she refuses to be cowed by even the most obstinate computer software.

Kate Chase is a writer and columnist specializing in online services and the Internet. She spent five years as a technical forum leader with AOL before merging her two careers into computer journalism. Her work appears frequently in *I-Way*, *Maximize for Windows*, *DOS World*, and other magazines, and Kate writes a regular column covering cyberspace for the *L.A. Village View*, albeit from her home on a remote mountain in England. She would like to thank Chris and Alex for their unflinching support. She can be reached via Internet e-mail at katechase@aol.com.

Gene Steinberg is an inveterate desktop computer user who first joined America Online in 1989. He quickly became addicted to the new online service and finally earned positions on its computing forum staff. At present, he is Forum Leader of the service's Macintosh Multimedia Forum and curator of AOL Portrait Gallery, a library containing photos of America Online members and their families.

In his regular life, Gene has worked at several occupations. He first studied broadcasting in school and then worked for a number of years as a disc jockey and newscaster. Gene is now a full-time writer and computer software and systems consultant. His published work (in addition to the first editions of this book) includes *Special Edition Using America Online, Using America Onlne with Your Mac,* and *Special Edition Using the Macintosh* for Que Corporation, and feature articles and product reviews for Macworld.

Rich Castagna is a senior editor at *Windows* magazine, and formerly held the same position at *PC Sources* magazine. In these capacities, and as a freelance writer and editor, Castagna has been involved with personal computers for more than 10 years and has reviewed more than 100 hardware and software products.

David R. Rorabaugh is a Novell Certified NetWare Engineer and a Microsoft Certified Professional. He can be reached via e-mail on CompuServe at 76376,3423.

Acknowledgments

Many people helped in the creation of this book in one way or another. Jim Boyce offers his thanks to Roland Elgey and Brad Koch for their support and the opportunity to do this book.

Elizabeth South and Tom Barich for their valuable help in putting together the project and authoring team.

Lisa Wagner for her excellent suggestions about the content and structure of the book. Tom Hayes for an outstanding job of editing and fine-tuning the book.

We'd Like to Hear from You!

As part of our continuing effort to produce books of the highest possible quality, Que would like to hear your comments. To stay competitive, we *really* want you, as a computer book reader and user, to let us know what you like or dislike most about this book or other Que products.

You can mail comments, ideas, or suggestions for improving future editions to the address below, or send us a fax at (317) 581-4663. For the on-line inclined, Macmillan Computer Publishing has a forum on CompuServe (type **GO MACMILLAN** at any prompt) through which our staff and authors are available for questions and comments. The address of our Internet site, the Macmillan Information SuperLibrary is **http://www.mcp.com** (World Wide Web). Our Web site has received critical acclaim from many reviewers—be sure to check it out.

In addition to exploring our forums, please feel free to contact me personally to discuss your opinions of this book:

CompuServe:	**74404,3307**
America Online:	**ldw indy**
Internet:	**lwagner@que.mcp.com**

Thanks in advance—your comments will help us to continue publishing the best books available on computer topics in today's market.

Lisa D. Wagner
Product Director
Que Corporation
201 W. 103rd Street
Indianapolis, Indiana 46290 USA

Although we cannot provide general technical support, we're happy to help you resolve problems you encounter related to our books, disks, or other products. If you need such assistance, please contact our Tech Support department at 800-545-5914 ext. 3833.

To order other Que or Macmillan Computer Publishing books or products, please call our Customer Service department at 800-835-3202 ext. 666.

Contents at a Glance

Contents

III Using Online Services 147

8 Using CompuServe 149

9 Using America Online 179

IV Working with E-Mail and Faxes 281

22 Using FTP, Ping, and Other Internet Tools 471

VI Using Local and Remote Networking 493

23 Using Dial-Up Networking 495

24 Using Direct Cable Connection 519

Introduction

Just a few years ago, data communications fell mostly in the domains of the high-end "power" user and hard-core home computer user. Today, being connected is almost as commonplace as...well, computers. Whether you're interested in electronic mail (e-mail), using commercial information services like CompuServe, surfing the Internet, connecting your home PC to your office LAN, or just uploading a file to a friend's computer, you're treading in the world of data communications. It's not just for the wizards of techno-lore—even five-year-olds are getting in on the action, learning to surf the web before they learn to ride a bicycle.

What brought about the explosive growth in computer communications? Two things had the most impact—a change in the way we work and the availability of broadly appealing data content. To stay competitive, most companies have found they *must* provide data communications (e-mail, online services, etc.) not only for their employees, but also provide accessibility to their customers through a company BBS (Bulletin Board System) or Internet web site. And content—the types and breadth of data that now is available online—has come a very long way in the last year. Where a few years ago the content was directed primarily at special interests, today's content appeals to a much broader audience.

What This Book Is About

Windows 95 includes a number of features and utilities that make communications easy even for a novice user. These communications tools include improved support for high-speed communications, easy modem configuration, a simple communications program, an e-mail program, Internet support, and more. *Windows 95 Communications Handbook* leads you through these new features, helping you install, configure, and use them. In the book, you'll learn about everything from how to choose your communications hardware and software to setting up your own mini-network and enabling others to dial into your computer to share information.

As much as possible, *Windows 95 Communications Handbook* uses hands-on, step-by-step examples and plenty of illustrations to help you through the process of setting up and using Windows 95's communications features. The book focuses on practical application rather than theory, so you'll find lots of specific tips to help you make the most of your hardware and software in the shortest possible time.

The authors who have contributed to *Windows 95 Communications Handbook* are experts in their areas, but have the unique ability of explaining their subjects in ways that a layman can easily understand. Most important, the authors write from practical experience—the chapters about commercial online services (CompuServe, America Online, and Prodigy), for example, are written by authors who are dedicated users of these services and can lead you through the ins and outs of getting the most from these services under Windows 95.

Who This Book Is For

Windows 95 Communications Handbook is geared toward all Windows 95 users, new and experienced alike. Because the book focuses on tasks instead of concepts, you'll find the information you need in understandable terms, regardless of your Windows 95 experience level.

We do assume, however that you have some level of experience with Windows 95 and are able to use the Windows 95 interface. For example, you should know how to use the mouse, work with program menus and dialog boxes, and perform other common Windows 95 tasks. Tasks that are not quite so obvious, however, we spell out for you. For example, you'll find step-by-step instructions on how to set up your modem in Windows 95—we'll tell you what programs to start and what buttons to click, so all you have to do is follow the instructions.

How This Book Is Structured

Windows 95 Communications Handbook is divided into six parts that take you from basic hardware and software selection and configuration through more advanced topics such as using Dial-Up Networking. The chapters are written to stand alone, so you don't have to keep referring from one chapter to another to set up or use a particular communications feature in Windows 95. The following sections explain the parts of the book and what topics are covered in each one.

Part I: Getting Started

Part I contains four chapters that explore and explain basic communications topics. Chapter 1, "Communication Basics," introduces you to communications, providing an overview of online services, e-mail, the Internet, Bulletin Board Systems (BBS), and other communications topics. Chapter 2, "Getting Started," offers tips on choosing modems and other communication hardware and software that work well with Windows 95.

Chapter 3, "Configuring Modems and Ports," will help you understand how your PC's serial (COM) ports and modem work, and will help you install and configure the ports and modem. Chapter 4, "Configuring Parallel Ports," provides an overview of parallel (LPT) ports and explains how to configure your parallel ports for high-speed performance, and use parallel port communications devices.

Part II: Using Communications Programs

Part II helps you begin to explore the communications capabilities of Windows 95. In Chapter 5, "Using HyperTerminal," you learn how to install, configure, and connect to online services and other computers using HyperTerminal, the communications program that is bundled with Windows 95. Chapter 6, "Using Third-Party Communications Programs," explores some of the most popular Windows 95 communications programs available from sources other than Microsoft, and offers specific tips on getting the most from these programs. In Chapter 7, "Transferring Files," you learn everything you need to know to begin transferring files efficiently between your computer and other computers or online services.

Part III: Using Online Services

Part III introduces you to the rapidly expanding world of online services, offering tips on using Windows 95-based programs to access these services and pointing you to Windows 95-related topic areas on the online services. Chapter 8, "Using CompuServe," explains how to connect to CompuServe using CompuServe's new Windows 95 version of its CIM program, and also teaches you how you can reduce your online charges with the use of programs that process your email and messages offline. Chapter 9, "Using America Online," offers a similar overview of America Online, and Chapter 10, "Using Prodigy," provides the same type of information for Prodigy users. Chapter 11, "Using The Microsoft Network (MSN)," explores Microsoft's new information service (MSN) and teaches you how to work with the MSN software that is built into Windows 95. Chapter 12, "Using GNN," gives you a look at one of the hottest new information sources on the Internet, GNN.

Part IV: Working with E-Mail and Faxes

Electronic mail (e-mail) was, until a few years ago, used very little outside of the academic community, and fax machines were found in a relatively small number of businesses. Today, it seems like everyone has an e-mail address and a fax machine. Part IV explains how to configure and use the e-mail and fax features in Windows 95. Chapter 13, "Configuring Exchange," teaches you how to install and configure the email program included with Windows 95. Chapter 14, "Using Exchange with Microsoft Mail," teaches you how to use Exchange to send and receive e-mail to and from a Microsoft Mail postoffice. Chapter 15, "Using Exchange for Internet Mail," explains how to use the Internet Mail service provider included with Microsoft Plus! for Windows 95 to send and receive Internet mail. Chapter 16, "Using Exchange for CompuServe Mail," explains how to use the CompuServe Mail provider included on the Windows 95 CD to send and receive CompuServe e-mail through Exchange. Chapter 17, "Using Remote Mail," will help you understand how to use Exchange to send and retrieve e-mail to and from a remote mail provider. Chapter 18, "Using Microsoft Fax," closes Part IV by teaching you how to use the fax service provider in conjunction with Microsoft Exchange to send and receive faxes using your computer and a fax modem.

Part V: Using the Internet

Interest in and use of the Internet have exploded in recent years, driven by much easier access to the Internet and much better data content on the Internet. Part V will help you connect your computer to the Internet so you can begin taking advantage of Internet email, the World Wide Web, and other Internet resources. Chapter 19, "Configuring TCP/IP," explains the network protocol required by the Internet and shows you how to configure TCP/IP on your computer. Chapter 20, "Connecting to the Internet," explains the different options you have for connecting your computer to the Internet. Chapter 21, "Using Internet Resources," gives you a broad look at programs and techniques you can use to find and access resources on the Internet through tools included with Windows 95 and others available right on the Internet. Chapter 22, "Using FTP, Ping, and Other Internet Tools," shows you how to transfer files and use a selection of other Internet utility programs included with Windows 95.

Part VI: Using Local and Remote Networking

Part VI explores a number of topics relating to communicating with other computers and sharing data. Chapter 23, "Using Dial-Up Networking," teaches you how to use your PC to connect to a remote local area network (LAN) or other computer to use disks and printers at the remote site as if they were connected to your own PC. Chapter 23 also teaches you how to set up your Windows 95 PC as a Dial-Up Networking server, enabling other people to dial into your computer to access its resources.

Chapter 24, "Using Direct Cable Connection," explains the features in Windows 95 that enable you to connect together two computers using the computers' serial or parallel ports, creating an inexpensive, mini-network. In Chapter 25, "Using Remote Control Programs," you learn about Windows 95 features and programs that let you control a remote computer over a phone or network connection. Chapter 26, "Sharing Resources," helps tie together many of the other chapters in Part VI, showing you how to share the disks and printers on your system with other users, and how to access the resources shared by other users.

This book also contains two appendixes and an Index of Common Problems. Appendix A "Internet Resources for Windows 95," explains the resources available that link the Internet with Windows 95. Appendix B, "What's on the CD?," provides detailed information on the material available on the CD that ships with this book.

Special Features in the Book

Que has over a decade of experience writing and developing the most successful computer books available. With that experience, we've learned what special features help readers the most. Look for these special features throughout the book to enhance your learning experience.

Chapter Roadmaps

Near the beginning of each chapter is a list of topics to be covered in the chapter. This list serves as a roadmap to the chapter so you can tell at a glance what is covered. It also provides a useful outline of the key topics you'll be reading about.

Notes

Notes present interesting or useful information that isn't necessarily essential to the discussion. This secondary track of information enhances your understanding of Windows, but you can safely skip notes and not be in danger of missing crucial information. Notes look like this:

Note

An *information service* is a user-installed or user-activated utility or protocol that enables messaging applications to do one or more of the following: send and receive items; store items in folders; and, obtain addresses and directory information.

Tips

Tips present short advice on quick or often-overlooked procedures. These include shortcuts that save you time.

Tip

If you attach a binary document file to a fax and transmit the fax to someone who also is using Microsoft Fax, the document is transferred as a binary file, enabling the recipient to open and edit the document. You can turn off this option, however, which becomes necessary if the recipient does not have a program that will enable him or her to view or edit the document.

Cautions

Cautions serve to warn you about potential problems that a procedure may cause, unexpected results, and mistakes to avoid. Cautions look like this:

Caution

In general, you shouldn't mess with your system's IRQ settings unless you really need to. Changing a setting incorrectly could result in more than one device not working properly. Before you start changing settings, use the System object in the Control Panel to print a log of your system's IRQ assignments.

Troubleshooting

No matter how carefully you follow the steps in the book, you eventually come across something that just doesn't work the way you think it should. Troubleshooting sections anticipate these common errors or hidden pitfalls and present solutions. A troubleshooting section looks like this:

Troubleshooting

I've installed a new serial port adapter, but Windows 95 doesn't automatically recognize it.

You can install the port manually. Open the Control Panel and choose the Add New Hardware icon to start the Add New Hardware wizard. Choose No when the wizard prompts you to specify whether you want it to detect the new hardware. Follow the prompts provided by the wizard to manually select the serial port.

Index of Common Problems

This feature goes hand in hand with the Troubleshooting elements. If you are having a problem with Windows 95 and don't know where to look in the book for an answer, look to the Index of Common Problems, located near the back of the book, immediately preceding the index. Use the Index of Common Problems to find all the Troubleshooting sections in the book and other discussions of common problems and fixes.

Cross-References

Throughout the book in the margins, you see references to other sections and pages in the book, like the one next to this paragraph. These cross-references point you to related topics and discussions in other parts of the book.

▶ See "Installing the Internet Mail Provider," p. 344

In addition to these special features, there are several conventions used in this book to make it easier to read and understand. These conventions include the following.

Underlined Hot Keys, or Mnemonics

Hot keys in this book appear underlined, like they appear on-screen. For example, the F in File is a hot key, or shortcut for opening the File menu. In Windows, many menus, commands, buttons, and other options have these hot keys. To use a hot-key shortcut, press Alt and the key for the underlined character. For instance, to choose the Properties button, press Alt and then R.

Shortcut Key Combinations

In this book, shortcut key combinations are joined with plus signs (+). For example, Ctrl+V means hold down the Ctrl key, press the V key, and then release both keys (Ctrl+V is a shortcut for the Paste command).

Menu Commands

Instructions for choosing menu commands have this form:

> Choose File, New.

This example means open the File menu and select New, which in this case opens a new file.

Instructions involving the new Windows 95 Start menu are an exception. When you are to choose something through this menu, the form is

> Open the Start menu and choose Programs, Accessories, WordPad.

In this case, you open the WordPad word processing accessory. Notice that in the Start menu you simply drag the mouse pointer and point at the option or command you want to choose (even through a whole series of submenus); you don't need to click anything.

This book also has the following typeface enhancements to indicate special text, as shown in the following table.

Typeface	Description
Italic	Italics is used to indicate terms and variables in commands or addresses.
Boldface	Bold is used to indicate text you type, and Internet addresses and other locators in the online world.
`Computer type`	This command is used for on-screen messages and commands (such as DOS copy or UNIX commands).
MYFILE.DOC	File names and directories are set in all caps to distinguish them from regular text, as in MYFILE.DOC.

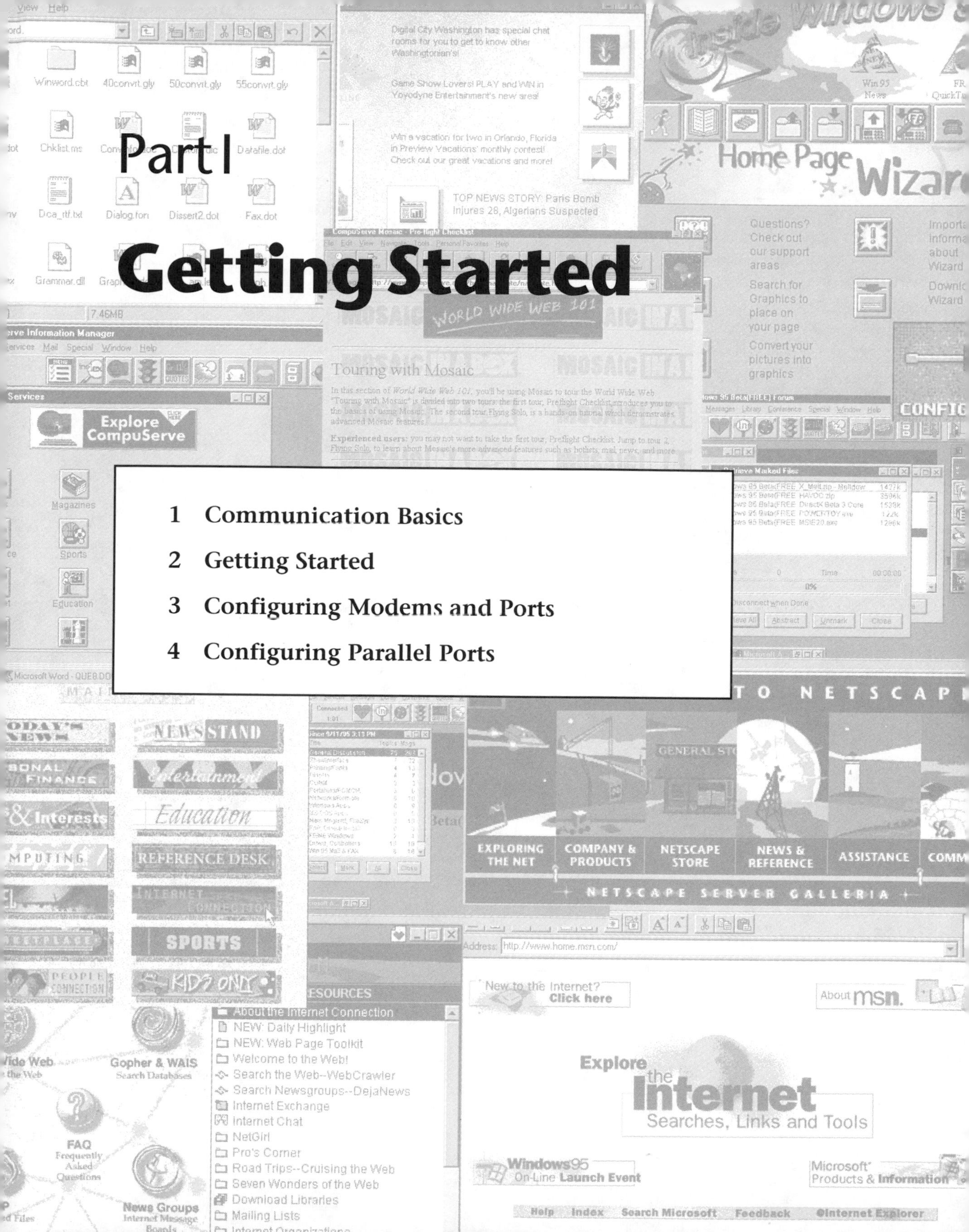

Part I

Getting Started

CHAPTER 1

Communication Basics

by Jim Boyce

Very few people have problems understanding the basic features of most word processing programs because the topic relates so closely to the types of work they do. Whether you're writing a letter at home or a report at work, you can easily make the mental connection between the document on your display and the printed page.

On the other hand, the different types of data communications often don't fit into a "traditional" framework, so you might not be familiar with the term *data communications*. In this chapter, you gain an understanding of

- E-mail and faxing
- Commercial online services
- The Internet
- Bulletin Board Systems (BBS)
- Dial-Up Networking
- Remote control programs
- Using the Briefcase
- Connection options

This information will help build a solid foundation for your particular applications of Windows 95's varied communications capabilities.

Understanding E-Mail and Faxing

Two of the most common examples of data communications today are *e-mail* and *faxing*. These two topics represent a large slice of the "communications pie," and are rapidly becoming the most prevalent way in which people exchange information using their PCs.

Understanding E-Mail

The term *e-mail* stands for *electronic mail*. Essentially, almost any form of information you send electronically to another person by computer is e-mail.

Where it might take weeks to deliver a written letter by conventional means, your e-mail message can arrive at its destination in hours or even minutes.

Note

During the Gulf War, I used a unique kind of e-mail to send messages to my brother, who was stationed in Saudi Arabia. I composed a message and mailed it to an address on CompuServe. The message was transferred electronically to the Middle East, then printed and delivered as a regular letter. This method allowed for a delivery time of about a week (slow for e-mail), compared to four or five weeks to send a postal letter.

Tip

In addition to speed, e-mail offers the advantage of lower cost. It is typically less expensive to send a message by e-mail than it is to send a message by surface delivery (post, or "snail mail") or even by phone.

And perhaps the most significant advantage to e-mail is its streamlined approach to sending and receiving messages. With regular mail, you have to write your message, then print it out, address an envelope, attach the proper postage, and take it to a mailbox. It's much easier to write and address an e-mail message and then click the Send button to let your computer deliver it for you. Return messages (replies) also are easier for you to handle—your e-mail program can be set to automatically collect and deliver your incoming messages.

E-Mail in Windows 95

Windows 95 includes an e-mail application called Microsoft Exchange for Windows. Exchange serves as a universal inbox for all of your electronic messages, including e-mail, faxes, and voice mail (see fig. 1.1). Also included is a set of *information service* protocols that allows Exchange to store and process messages routed through specific *service providers*. For example, there's a CompuServe Mail protocol that enables you to use Exchange to send messages via the CompuServe Information Service.

> **Note**
>
> An *information service* is a user-installed or user-activated utility or protocol that enables messaging applications to do one or more of the following: send and receive items; store items in folders; and, obtain addresses and directory information.

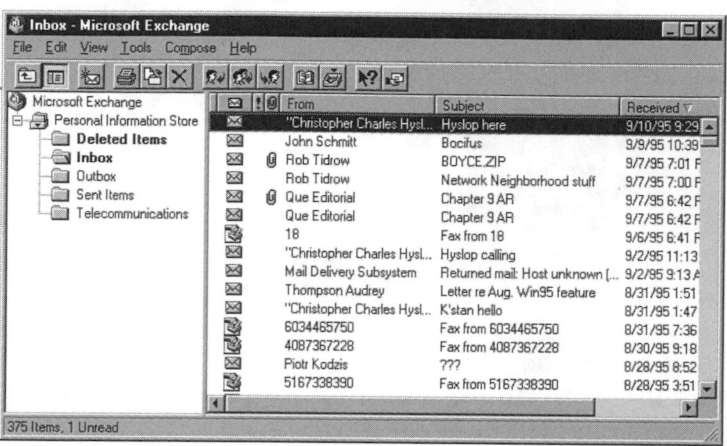

Fig. 1.1
This inbox contains default folders and a few user-created folders.

The basic Windows 95 software package also provides e-mail protocols for Microsoft Mail and The Microsoft Network. The Microsoft Mail provider enables you to send and receive e-mail on your LAN. The optional Microsoft Plus! for Windows 95 package includes the additional software you'll need if you want to use Exchange to send and receive mail via the Internet.

▶ See "Working with Microsoft Mail," p. 333

▶ See "Installing the Internet Mail Provider," p. 344

▶ See "Installing CompuServe Mail," p. 356

> **Note**
>
> Although Microsoft Exchange for Windows works only with those information service protocols described here, other e-mail service providers and program publishers will likely offer new or upgraded software that interface with Exchange.

Faxing in Windows 95

The Microsoft Fax service provider for Exchange enables you to send and receive faxes through a fax modem, using Exchange as an inbox and outbox for your faxes. Microsoft Fax monitors the fax modem, answering the call when a fax comes in. You can compose a fax of just text as you might an e-mail message, or you can attach documents to the fax. Microsoft Fax uses a special printer driver to "print" the document to the fax modem, sending the fax to its recipient.

▶ See "Installing Microsoft Fax," p. 378

Figure 1.2 shows the first part of the process of composing a fax—specifying the recipient. You can choose an existing fax address from your Personal Address Book (PAB) or enter a new address.

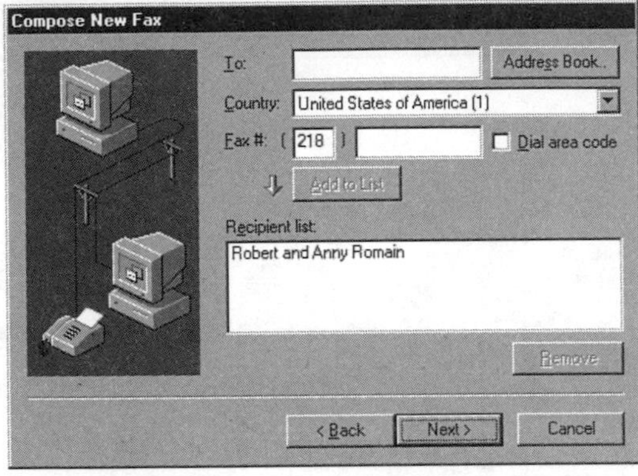

Fig. 1.2
You can compose faxes of text only or include binary document files.

After you specify the address, you can type some text to become the message body of the fax, or you can attach a file to the fax message, and Microsoft Fax will transmit the file as the body of the fax.

Tip

If you attach a binary document file to a fax and transmit the fax to someone who also is using Microsoft Fax, the document is transferred as a binary file, enabling the recipient to open and edit the document. You can turn off this option, however, which becomes necessary if the recipient does not have a program that will enable him or her to view or edit the document.

A reduction in physical paperwork is one of the primary advantages of using Exchange to send and receive faxes. Faxes are prepared and stored electronically, and you can view them on-screen without having to print them. When you do need a hard copy, you can print it to any printer.

The disadvantage of using a fax modem is that faxing a paper document that is not stored electronically on your PC requires a scanner to scan the document into an electronic form so it can be transmitted through the fax modem. If you seldom need to send paper faxes, however, using Exchange and a fax modem is a good option.

Microsoft Fax is not a full-featured fax program, however. Microsoft Fax includes only a limited number of cover page designs, although you can create your own cover pages and modify the designs included with Microsoft Fax.

The program also lacks the tools that would enable you to annotate or change a fax. These tools are included with other Windows 95-based fax programs.

Commercial Online Services

Online services offer one-stop access to a wide variety of information. You can retrieve news and other information, send and receive e-mail, interact with other users through special interest forums and chat areas, perform research, and enjoy access to games and other leisure activities. Most offer their own *front-end* programs that make it easy to navigate through the maze of resources available online today. Figure 1.3 shows CompuServe's front-end program, WinCIM.

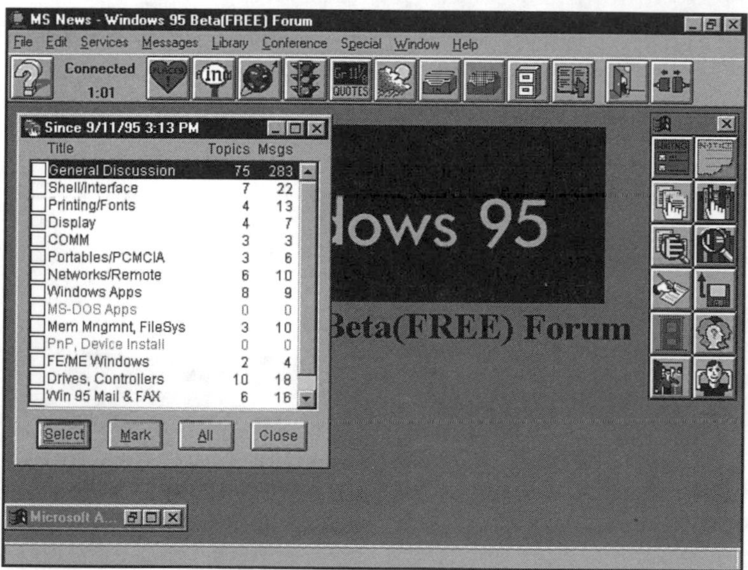

Fig. 1.3
WinCIM makes it easy to navigate CompuServe's many forums and other content areas.

> **Note**
>
> One of the newest online services is The Microsoft Network (MSN), opened by Microsoft in August of 1995 in conjunction with the first release of Windows 95. The most important feature about MSN is its tight integration into the Windows 95 interface—the software you need to connect to MSN is included with Windows 95.

▶ See "Using The Microsoft Network (MSN)," p. 233

Online services offer one-stop access to a wide variety of information: special interest forums, travel information, sports, news, multiplayer games, databases, and much more. You can retrieve news and other information, send and receive e-mail, interact with other users through special interest forums and chat areas, perform research, and enjoy access to games and other leisure activities.

Most online services also now include access to the Internet. Rather than gain access to the Internet through an Internet service provider, you can access the Internet directly from your online service. Figure 1.4 shows an Internet Web page being accessed through America Online.

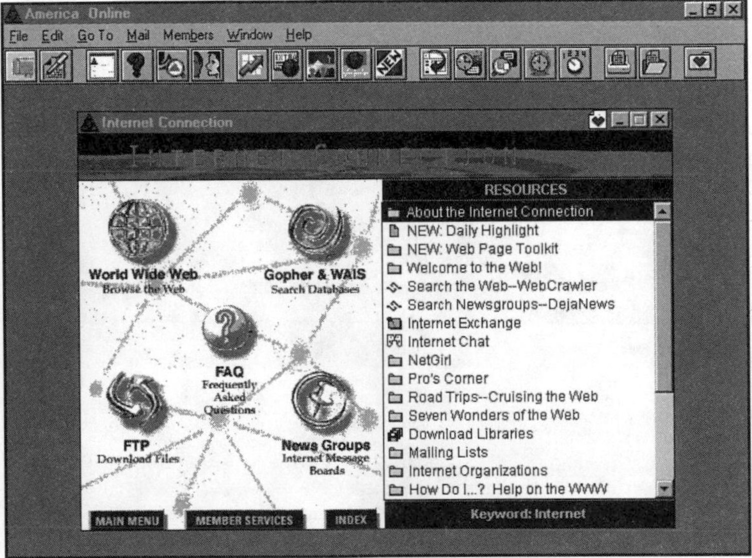

Fig. 1.4
Most online services now provide access to the Internet.

All commercial online services charge some type of fee for you to access the service. Most charge a flat monthly fee along with hourly connect-time rates. Some areas of the services carry additional access fees. Typically, you can send and receive a set number of e-mail messages (usually a relatively large number) for your basic monthly rate, and e-mail messages beyond that number are charged at a nominal rate according to the lengths of the messages.

The Internet

The Internet began as a network of computers developed primarily for the military. In the ensuing decades, the Internet has expanded to become a huge global network of computers also serving education, business, government, and individuals. The Internet also serves as a global e-mail delivery system, enabling people to communicate with one another almost instantly across the globe. In many ways, the Internet is similar to the online services described previously. The breadth of content available on the Internet has expanded dramatically, making the Internet a rich information source.

As explained previously, you can connect to the Internet through most commercial online services. Many *Internet service providers* also provide direct dial-up access to the Internet. For a flat monthly fee and/or hourly connect charges, you can dial into a local access number from most locations to connect to the Internet.

Windows 95 includes many features geared toward Internet support, such as a TCP/IP network protocol. Each computer on the Internet must use a common protocol that enables it to communicate with the other computers on the Internet. TCP/IP serves as that common protocol. Windows 95's Dial-Up Networking enables you to easily connect to an Internet service provider to gain access to the Internet.

If you install Microsoft Plus! for Windows 95, the Internet Explorer (see fig. 1.5) included with Plus! will enable you to browse the World Wide Web using a native Windows 95 Web browser. If you prefer, you can use a third-party Web browser such as Netscape (see fig. 1.6) or one of the many others that are available.

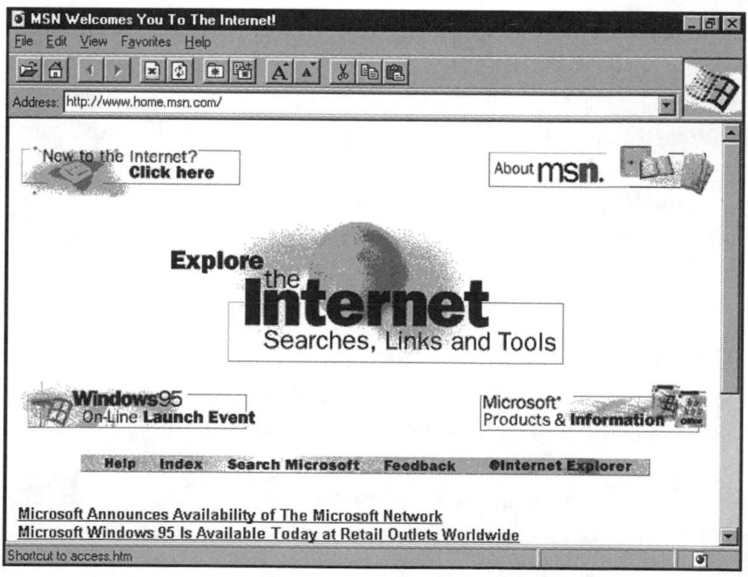

Fig. 1.5
Microsoft Plus! includes Internet Explorer, a Windows 95-based Web browser.

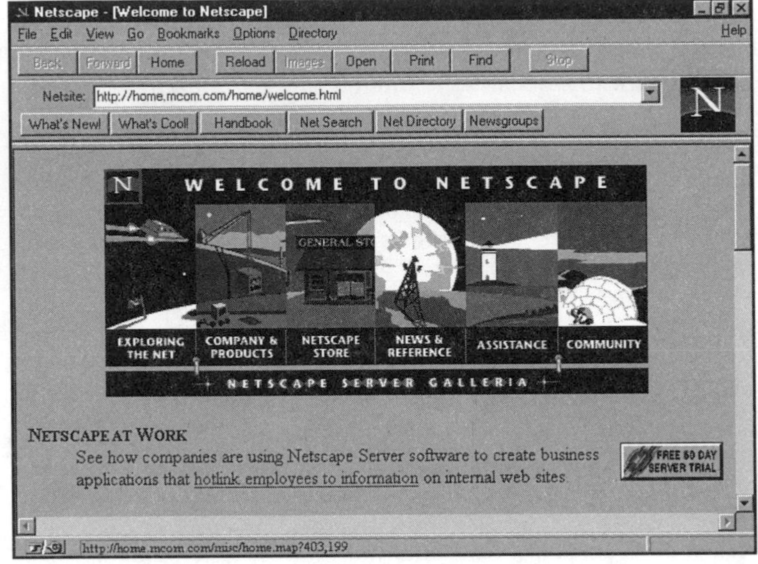

Fig. 1.6
You can use one of many third-party Windows 95-based Web browsers such as Netscape to browse the Web.

▶ See "Using FTP, Ping, and Other Internet Tools," p. 471

Also included with Windows 95 are a set of utilities to help you navigate and use the Internet. These tools include FTP for file transfer, Ping for testing network connections, Winipcfg for configuring your TCP/IP connection, route for manipulating Internet routing tables, and more.

Bulletin Board Systems (BBS)

For many years, Bulletin Board Systems (BBSs) have been the most common means, other than commercial online services, that people had to communicate and share data. Typically, a BBS is a microcomputer (often a PC) to which you can connect using a modem. The BBS typically contains files of interest to specific types of users, and message areas enabling BBS users to exchange messages on topics that interest them.

Many commercial and business-operated BBSs exist, as well. For example, many hardware and software companies maintain a BBS that enables their customers to download files, such as drivers, for their hardware and software. The BBS also serves as a means for customers to receive technical support—customers leave messages on the BBS, and the company's technical support staff respond to those questions. The next time the customer logs onto the BBS, he receives the reply to his message.

▶ See "Using HyperTerminal," p. 91

Windows 95 includes a few features that will enable you to connect to your favorite BBS sites. For example, Windows 95 includes a communications program called HyperTerminal that enables you to dial into a BBS (or almost any other computer) to access the BBS's content and message areas, and upload and download files. Figure 1.7 shows HyperTerminal connected to an online aviation weather information service.

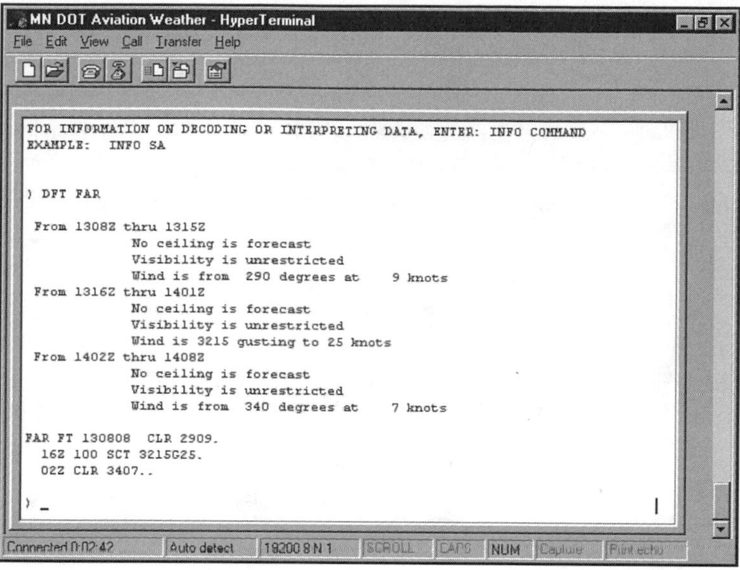

Fig. 1.7 You can use HyperTerminal to connect to a wide variety of information services, including commercial services.

In addition to connecting to BBS sites, you also can use HyperTerminal to connect to commercial online services such as CompuServe. Using HyperTerminal to connect to these services is not ideal, however, because the custom interface programs provided by these online services are significantly better than HyperTerminal, primarily because they are tailored specifically to each online service.

If you connect to BBS sites often, you should consider buying one of the many third-party communications programs available for Windows 95. These third-party programs provide much better file transfer and other features that make them preferable to HyperTerminal.

One-on-One Connections

Another type of data communications you might need or want to try is connecting your computer directly to a friend's or coworker's computer through a modem. With HyperTerminal or other communications program, you can dial another person's computer to connect and transfer files, exchange messages, or even play interactive games.

(continues)

(continued)

Although you can establish these one-to-one sessions using HyperTerminal, a much better alternative is to use Windows 95's Dial-Up Networking. Dial-Up Networking represents the easiest way to connect together two Windows 95 computers to share files or even printers across a modem link.

The client software you need to connect to a Windows 95, Windows NT, or NetWare server is included with Windows 95. The extra software needed to turn a Windows 95 PC into a Dial-Up Networking server is included on the Windows 95 CD. You can configure one of the computers in your one-to-one session as a Dial-Up Networking server (a two-minute task) and let the other computer connect to it through a modem.

After the two computers are connected, you can exchange files freely between the computers as if they were connected on a local LAN instead of by modem (see fig. 1.8). Even so, you still can protect the files on either system from unwanted browsing—only those folders that are specifically shared by one computer can be accessed by the other.

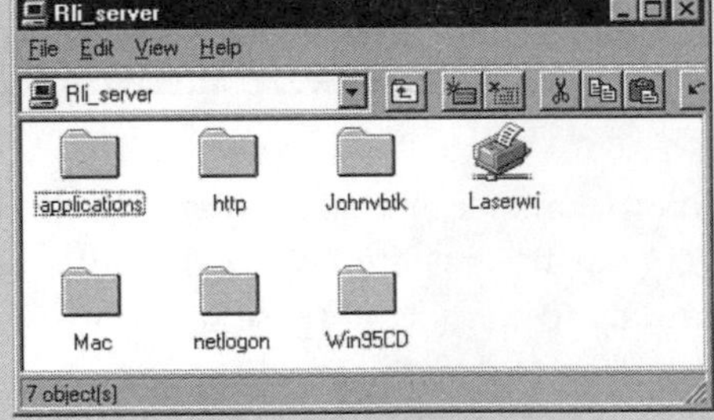

Fig. 1.8
The shared folders on a remote computer appear just like local folders.

Dial-Up Networking

▶ See "Understanding Dial-Up Networking," p. 495

▶ See "Configuring Exchange for Remote Mail," p. 363

Dial-Up Networking and its companion Scripting Tool utility are two of the most impressive communications features in Windows 95. They make possible connections that were impractical or that required third-party software—and often special hardware—to accomplish with previous versions of Windows.

Dial-Up Networking also provides an excellent means for you to connect to a friend's or coworker's computer. For example, you can use it to connect your notebook PC to your office LAN when you are traveling, enabling you to access files and printers on the LAN. Or, you can connect to the office LAN from your home PC, enabling you to work from home.

One of Dial-Up Networking's more useful features is its direct operational interface with other Windows 95 communications applications. Microsoft Exchange, for example, can make use of Dial-Up Networking to connect you to your office e-mail server while you are traveling. Best of all, the connection and the handling of incoming and outgoing messages can happen automatically—you simply set Exchange's scheduling function and it automatically uses a Dial-Up Networking connection to access the server and send and retrieve your waiting mail.

Direct Cable Connection

Another feature in Windows 95 that lets you easily connect two computers is Direct Cable Connection. With Direct Cable Connection, you can connect two Windows 95 computers using a null-modem serial cable or parallel cable. Once connected, the two computers can share files and printers as if they were connected by a typical LAN connection (network interface cards and cabling).

Direct Cable Connection also makes it possible for you to connect a PC to a computer that is already on a network. For example, if you use a notebook PC to work at home or while traveling, you can use Direct Cable Connection to connect the notebook to your office PC when you return to the office. Then, you can use either the regular network interface features in Windows 95 to transfer files between the systems, or use a Briefcase—another feature new in Windows 95—to synchronize the files.

▶ See "Using Direct Cable Connection," p. 519

Troubleshooting

I need to install some software from a CD to my notebook PC, but don't have a CD drive in my notebook. What should I do?

Connect your notebook to a desktop Windows 95 computer (assuming it has a CD) using Direct Cable Connection. Then, share the CD on the other computer and access it from your notebook, installing the software to your computer. You can use the same technique to install software from a floppy disk if one of the computers doesn't have the proper size disk drive.

Using a Briefcase

When you work with more than one PC, it can be difficult to keep track of which documents are current, particularly if you work on the same documents on both computers. Is the copy of the quarterly report on your desktop

PC the latest or is it the copy on your notebook? Another new feature in Windows 95 called the Briefcase goes a long way toward solving this problem.

The Briefcase appears like a normal folder (see fig. 1.9), but performs a very special function. The Briefcase tracks sets of documents or other files across multiple PCs, helping you determine which copy of a particular document is the most current. More important, however, is that the Briefcase will help you synchronize the files, replacing the older copy with the current version.

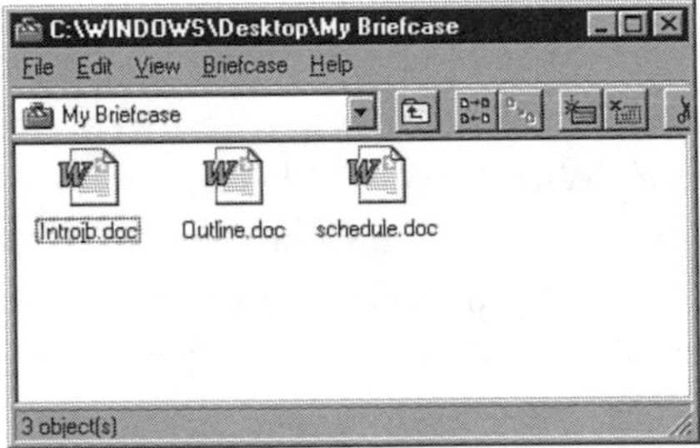

Fig. 1.10
You can use the Briefcase to synchronize files between two computers.

Although one of its main uses is to enable you to synchronize files between a notebook PC and your main office PC, you also can use a Briefcase to synchronize files with other users on the network. If you are working on a document with another user on the LAN, use a Briefcase to help you know when the other user's copy of the file is more or less current than your own.

Built-In Networking

Windows 95 includes extensive, integral support for peer-to-peer networking. Without buying any additional software, you can network Windows 95 PCs, enabling them to share files, printers, e-mail, fax modems, and other network resources. Windows 95 includes *network client software* that enables a Windows 95 PC to access Windows NT and NetWare servers. In addition, any Windows 95 PC can act as a server while still allowing the PC to be used as a regular workstation.

▶ See "Installing Dial-Up Networking," p. 498

The significant change in Windows 95's networking capability over previous versions of Windows is the tighter integration of the network into the Windows 95 interface. This integration makes it much easier for the average person to access and use resources shared by other users on the network. A special folder called the Network Neighborhood (see fig. 1.10) provides quick access to other PCs in your workgroup, as well as the entire network.

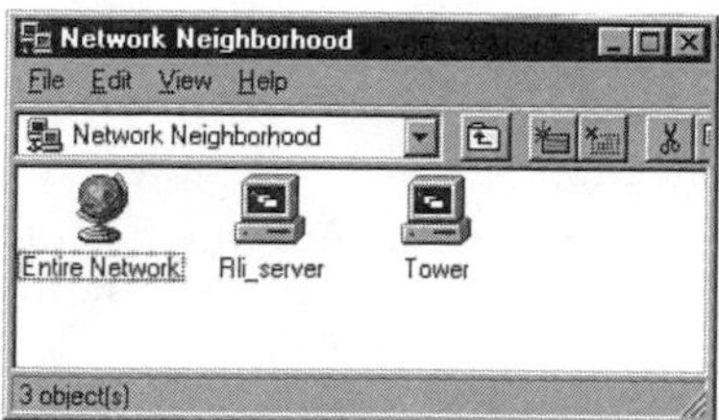

Fig. 1.10
The Network Neighborhood provides quick and easy access to shared network resources such as folders and printers.

Unlike Windows for Workgroups and other network operating systems that require you to associate a local drive letter with a remote network resource before you can use it, Windows 95 lets you use the remote folder directly. You simply drill down through the folders in the Network Neighborhood until you find the folder and files you need. Then, you can work with them as if they were located on your computer instead of on another PC across the network. Figure 1.11 shows a shared folder on a remote computer to illustrate that the remote files are as accessible as files on your local computer. The shared folder appears essentially the same as any local folder.

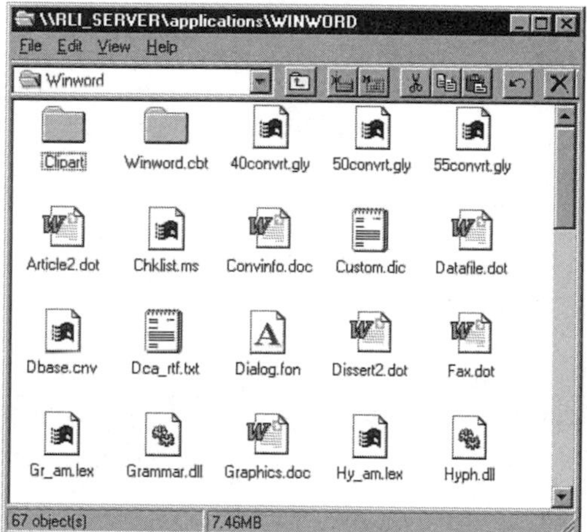

Fig. 1.11
Just double-click an item in a shared folder to use the item.

Remote Control

The ability to access a remote computer's files and printers through Dial-Up Networking is often as much control over a remote PC as a person needs. In some situations, however, you might want to exercise complete control over a remote PC, controlling it as if you were sitting at its keyboard.

▶ See "Using Remote Control Programs," p. 533

Third-party programs are available that let you do just that—control a PC remotely. Using such a program you can dial the remote PC and control it as if you were sitting in front of it. You can run programs on the remote PC and perform almost all other tasks you could perform if you had direct access to the remote computer. The input and output, however, happen at your local computer. Your keyboard entry, mouse movements, and other input travel through the modem (or LAN connection) to the other PC. The display appears on your monitor.

Remote control programs enable you to run programs on the remote PC without requiring a copy of those programs on your local PC. Remote control programs also are great support tools, enabling a technical support or help desk staff member to control your PC, resolving problems for you or showing you how to perform tasks with which you are unfamiliar.

Remote Management

In addition to supporting various third-party remote control programs, Windows 95 also supports remote registries and remote management. The Registry stores information about your PC's hardware, as well as custom user settings. These settings determine how your desktop appears and how your PC functions for you. Supporting remote registries, or the ability to log on to a Windows 95 machine using a Registry that is stored on a remote computer, enables your custom settings to follow you from PC to PC. If you log on to your network from different locations in your office, for example, you'll still see the same desktop, applications, and other settings, regardless of which computer you use to log on to the system. This gives you the freedom to roam the network without losing your custom settings.

Windows 95 also supports remote management. A network administrator can modify Registry settings and user policies in real time on a remote PC, enabling the administrator to control the PC's configuration and the user's access rights remotely. Windows 95 also provides a Simple Network Management Protocol (SNMP) agent, enabling system administrators to perform tasks such as distributing new versions of software automatically to users' PCs.

Getting Connected

Windows 95 includes most of the software you'll need to begin taking advantage of its data communications features, but you still might need some additional hardware and software. If you want to use an online service, the Internet, or a BBS; or use Dial-Up Networking, you'll have to have a modem for your computer.

▶ See "Choosing a Modem," 33

You also need to consider how you will link your computer to these services and other realms of the outside world. Most people, at least in a home setting, will find a standard phone connection more than sufficient. In an office setting, however, you might be able to take advantage of high-speed data circuits to access the Internet, commercial services, and other online resources.

You'll find tips in Chapter 2, "Getting Started," that will help you decide which connection services and equipment are right for you.

▶ See "Phone Lines and Other Connections," p. 35

Other types of connections will naturally require other special hardware. To take advantage of Direct Cable Connection, for example, you'll need a null-modem serial cable or parallel cable with the correct connectors at each end. You'll find tips on choosing or making your own cable in Chapter 24, "Using Direct Cable Connection." ❖

▶ See "Making Your Own Cable," p. 530

CHAPTER 2

Getting Started

by Dave Rorabaugh

Just as you don't need to know how a car's engine works to drive a car, you don't need to know how the communications hardware and software work in Windows 95 to use them. The more you know about your hardware and software, however, the more prepared you'll be to overcome problems when they arise. You'll also be able to get more efficient use out of your communications programs and hardware.

This chapter gives you an overview of key communications issues, both general and specific to Windows 95. In addition to explaining the workings of modems and Windows 95's communications components, this chapter also discusses different options you have for connecting your computer to the outside world.

In this chapter, you'll learn to

- Understand communications in Windows 95
- Recognize how modems work
- Choose a modem
- Work with phone lines and other connection options
- Choose your communications software

If you're not concerned with how your modem or the Windows 95 communications components work and want to begin using them immediately, turn to Chapter 3, "Configuring Modems and Ports," to begin the process of setting up your hardware and communications software. If you're interested in the inner workings of your computer's communications hardware and software, read on.

Understanding Communications in Windows 95

As you learned in Chapter 1, the term *communications* encompasses a broad spectrum of features. In Windows 3.x, communications fell into two fairly distinct categories: networking (LAN connections) and data communications (online services, communications programs, and so on). In Windows 95, however, that distinction has blurred. You can network your computer to others through your modem, and you can connect to information services through your network and the Internet.

This intertwining of features required that Microsoft make some very fundamental changes to the core communications technology in Windows 95 over previous versions of Windows. In addition to radically changing previous Windows 3.x features, Windows 95 introduces new features and capabilities, including its use of telephony features.

By separating the Windows communications functions between the communications and telephony APIs (Application Programming Interfaces), Windows 95 makes it easier for hardware manufacturers and developers to build in support for special hardware and features. This modular design also all but eliminates conflicts between different communications devices, because the hardware drivers can rely on the telephony and communications APIs to avoid potential conflicts and "referee" those that do occur. The Communications API is responsible for data transfer and manipulation, while the Telephony API (TAPI) is responsible for control and arbitration functions.

Communications with Windows 3.x Programs

Windows 3.x programs communicate with modems and other communications hardware in Windows 95 in much the same way they do in Windows 3.x. These programs use the 16-bit communications API and communicate through a device driver that is essentially the same as the one used in Windows 3.x. This gives precedence to Windows 95 communications programs. If a Windows 95 program such as Microsoft Fax is monitoring a port, a Windows 3.x program can't request control of the port.

If you try to connect to an online service with a Windows 3.x terminal program, for example, and Microsoft Fax is monitoring the modem for incoming faxes, your communications port will experience an error. Depending on the design of the program, the program will probably inform you that the communications port is not available (see fig. 2.1). These error messages will vary by program, but will usually tell you that the requested port is not available.

When Microsoft Fax is monitoring the port, Windows 3.x programs simply can't see it. To enable the Windows 3.x program to access the port, you must direct Microsoft Fax to stop monitoring for incoming calls. This releases the port, enabling the Windows 3.x program to gain access to it.

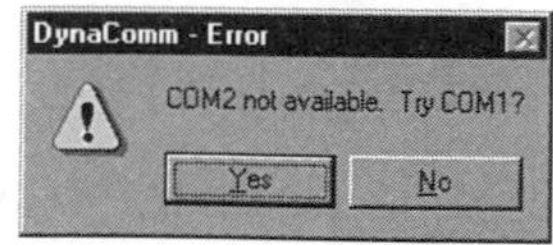

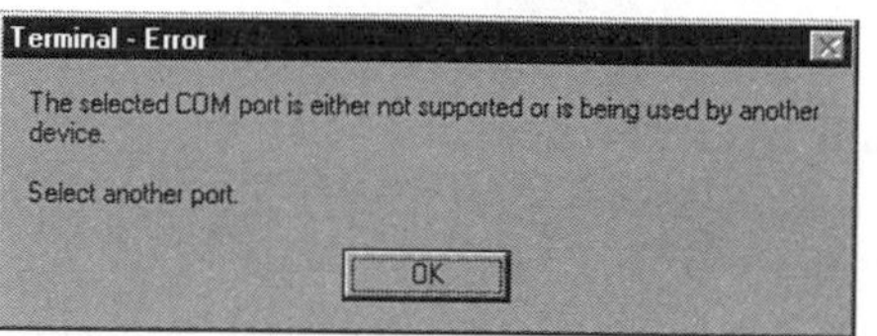

Fig. 2.1
Windows 3.x programs can't gain access to a port from a Windows 95 program that is monitoring the port.

This conflict between programs doesn't apply to Windows 95, because its programs use telephony functions to arbitrate access. A Windows 95 program, for example, would use telephony commands to request the port from Microsoft Fax. Assuming Microsoft Fax wasn't actively using the port to send or receive a fax, Microsoft Fax would relinquish control of the port. When the other program terminates, control of the port can be returned to Microsoft Fax.

Communications with DOS Programs

DOS-based communications programs don't interface with Windows-based communications programs. DOS programs use their own set of communications drivers, which communicate directly with the hardware. This lack of shared structure can lead to conflicts between DOS communications programs and Windows programs. For that reason, it's best to use Windows-based programs whenever possible, particularly Windows 95 programs.

The Network Connection

Many features in Windows 95 combine TAPI and modem-related services with networking features. Dial-Up Networking, for example, enables you to network your PC to another PC or to a LAN through a modem. Instead of transferring files with a terminal program, you use the network interface features provided in Windows 95, moving files around as if they were located on your LAN.

Direct Cable Connection provides another example of how Windows 95 combines communications ports and networking. Although the two computers are connected through a serial or parallel cable, they appear as if they are connected by a LAN, and you share information between them using the same methods you would use on a LAN. See Chapter 24 "Using Direct Cable Connection," for more information.

Providing a unified method of sharing files, printers, and other information—whether over a modem, cable, or LAN—makes it much easier to share those resources. When you've learned how to transfer files across the LAN, for example, you don't have to learn a new method to transfer files from your desktop computer to your notebook. This tight integration also means that the networking components in Windows 95 work in conjunction with TAPI and the other communications components. When Dial-Up Networking needs to establish a connection to a remote computer, for example, it does so through TAPI and the communications drivers. Dial-Up Networking Connections will be discussed in Chapter 23, "Using Dial-Up Networking."

Bringing It All Together

The communications and networking components in Windows 95 are just part of the communications picture. In most cases, you will also need a modem, phone connection, software, and other components to communicate with the outside world. The following sections of the chapter explain these items, giving you an understanding of how they work and tips on how to choose the options that are right for you.

Understanding Modems

The word *modem* is actually a compound acronym taken from the words MOdulator/DEModulator. A modem does just what its name implies: it modulates and demodulates signals. But, that doesn't mean very much to the average person. So in layman's terms, modems convert the bits of data coming from your computer into a form that can be transmitted across a phone line. Modems also convert the signals coming through the phone line back into bits that the computer can interpret. Modems, therefore, enable two computers to "talk" to each other, sending data back and forth along the phone line. The sending computer sends digital data to the sending modem, which modulates it into an analog signal that is sent across the phone line. The receiving modem demodulates this analog signal and converts it to digital data, which is transferred to the receiving modem.

Serial versus Parallel Modems

As it became clear that the old-style serial ports were no longer adequate for newer, high-speed communications devices, some manufacturers, notably Microcom, created modems that attached to a parallel port rather than to a serial port. Serial ports transmit data one bit at a time, while parallel ports transmit data eight bits (one byte) at a time. Parallel ports require much more wiring than serial ports, and transmit data for shorter distances, but generally achieve much faster transmission speeds.

Using the much higher data rates available on the parallel port, these modems were able to achieve much higher rates of throughput. Unfortunately, problems arose on two fronts. Parallel modems occasionally caused problems with attached printers, and few systems have more than one installed parallel port. Software vendors were also slow to accept parallel modems as viable, and even today, few software packages support this type of connection.

Windows 95, however, supports the parallel port modems directly, so any communications package "Designed for Windows 95" should support them. Parallel port modems offer significantly greater throughput than the old-style serial ports, and in most cases, better throughput than the newer style buffered serial ports. They are no match, however, for the high-speed intelligent serial ports offered by companies such as Hayes, Digiboard, and Arnet. If you are considering a parallel port modem, ask yourself: do you have a spare parallel port, does your software support this type of modem, and are there enough choices to keep your choice competitive?

Understanding Modem Standards

When shopping for a modem, there are a number of "standards" that various manufacturers will claim to support. A *standard* refers to a technical description of a set of capabilities and functions, how they operate, how they interoperate, and how they are to be implemented. Some of these are truly international, industry-wide standards, and some are proprietary and only supported by one or a small group of vendors. The process of establishing an official standard is lengthy, and often political. During this process, it's not uncommon for many manufacturers to start releasing new products which support the "draft" standard. These products often offer all the advantages of the new standard, but hit the market several months or more before the standard becomes official.

The problems arise in two areas: varying interpretations of the "draft" standard, and changes made to the draft before final ratification. In both cases, you usually need to upgrade (or even replace) the modem later to gain full compliance with the official standard. In the interim, you may experience problems interoperating with other modems that claim to adhere to the same "draft" standard or interoperating with other modems that comply with the final standard. When buying modems that support draft or proprietary standards, it's a good idea to know exactly what you are connecting to. In these cases, it's often necessary to purchase identical models, or at least similar models from the same manufacturer, in order to ensure that they will work together as advertised. These types of limitations make connecting a wide variety of different modems and systems impractical if not impossible in many cases. However, if you are in control of the entire communications loop, you may find the benefits too compelling to resist.

Today, it makes little sense to purchase anything less than a 14.4kbps modem. While slower modems may still be available, the newer, faster models are the easiest to find and the most widely supported. When shopping for modems, you'll see a number of references to modem standards. Here is a list of the standards that apply to 14.4kbps and faster modems:

- *V.32bis.* The first of the 14.4kbps standards, this was the second iteration of the original 9600bps V.32 standard. This is the foundation for *all* truly compatible 14.4kbps modems. This is the official CCITT 14.4kbps standard.
- *V.FAST.* This was the original designation of what would later become V.34, the final 28.8kbps standard. There were a number of companies that implemented V.FAST designs, but the majority were only compatible with other modems of the same model. V.FAST never gained widespread acceptance, since the only way to guarantee interoperability was to connect two identical modems.
- *V.FC.* V.FC, or Fast Class, was an attempt to standardize V.FAST, based on the draft standards that would become V.34. V.FC was mainly championed by Rockwell, who manufactured the chipsets upon which V.FC modems were based. This produced a much higher level of interoperability between different V.FC modems, although different vendors still implemented the spec in different ways. Some, but not all, V.FC modems can be upgraded to V.34.
- *V.34.* This is the final 28.8kbps modem standard. When buying a 28.8kbps modem, insist on full V.34 compatibility. This is the official CCITT 28.8kbps standard.

Choosing a Modem

There are several general considerations when choosing a modem: your budget, your applications, and your existing hardware.

Your budget will determine whether you purchase the latest and greatest leading-edge hot rod, a standard middle-of-the-road model, or a "bargain." Each category has its risks and rewards. The leading edge models may not have drivers available or be supported by newer software yet. They may also offer features that may not yet be standardized or even widely supported. The "bargains," usually sold solely on the basis of price, often suffer from poor quality or performance, and almost never have direct support from any major software vendors. In general, the safest choice is to look for a modem that complies with the current standards, is supported by a wide variety of software, and comes from an established company.

Your applications have a far greater impact on your decision than most people realize, or at least more than they realize *before* the purchase. Older DOS and Windows 3.1 communications software will usually come with a list of supported devices, and for best results, it's a good idea to choose a modem supported by the software you intend to use. Windows 95 brings much of this into the operating system level, and directly supports a wide variety of modems. With Windows 95 and "Designed for Windows 95" communications software, you need to make sure Windows supports your modem, or that a Windows 95 driver is available for the modem.

Software manufacturers frequently publish hardware compatibility lists for their products. While you may not find these printed on the outside of the packages in the store, you will probably be able to find them from the vendor's tech support, BBS, Web site, or CompuServe forum. Microsoft also publishes a hardware compatibility list for Windows. You should obtain and review these lists when shopping for software, to ensure that your modem is supported by either Windows or the third-party software.

In either case, the next level below direct application or operating system support is "compatibility." Many modems on the market, especially at the lower end of the market, simply mimic the command set and responses of a more widely accepted modem. "Hayes Compatible" is the most common designation, meaning that the modem is compatible with the standard Hayes command set. Windows 95 refers to this as a "standard modem." While this type of generic substitution or support may work effectively, it may not take advantage of many of the modem's more advanced features, and performance may suffer as a result.

Many buyers don't consider their current system and its existing configuration when purchasing a new modem. If you purchase a modem with a new system, your vendor should take care of setting all the system options necessary to accommodate the new device. However, if you are adding the modem on your own, there are several things you need to bear in mind. First, you need to make the choice between an internal modem and an external modem. Internal modems will usually be slightly less expensive than an equivalent external modem from the same manufacturer. External modems do not usually require that you open your computer's case and make changes inside, and are more easily moved between different systems. Both flavors have their own advantages and disadvantages, but they each also have a unique set of considerations.

Modems and Configuration Issues

Internal modems require an available slot in your computer, and require that you be familiar with the way the communication ports on your system are configured. Most new computers ship from the factory with two serial ports, COM1 and COM2. When installing an internal modem, one of these ports should be disabled—that function will be served by the new modem you are installing. When installing an internal modem, you should configure your modem for COM1 or COM2 and disable the corresponding internal port. On most newer systems, this is easily done within the computer's setup program. On older systems, it may require changing jumpers on an add-in card, and those settings will vary greatly between different systems.

Many modems will offer the option of configuring the modem as COM3 or COM4. This is not recommended, since the result has the modem sharing the same interrupt assignment as the existing COM1 or COM2 ports. Not all software supports interrupt sharing, and the easiest way to avoid problems is to ensure that your modem and serial ports are properly assigned.

External modems attach by a serial cable to one of the COM ports on your computer. This will almost always avoid the need to reconfigure your system's ports, or make changes inside your computer. However, the COM ports on your computer are now part of the discussion, since your computer uses them to communicate with the modem.

There are two types of serial ports that are common on standard systems. The first type is the old-style, standard serial port. These ports are usually implemented with 8250 or 16450 type circuits, and provide a straight serial interface. Especially under Windows, these older style ports are not suitable for use at higher modem speeds, and are not recommended for use with external modems that operate above 9600bps. The second type, common on most newer systems, is the high-performance serial port. These ports are usually implemented with 16550 type circuits, and include small 16-byte buffers for incoming and outgoing data to prevent data loss at higher speeds. Windows 95 automatically recognizes and enables the buffering on the 16550 type ports.

There is also a third type of serial port, which is commonly referred to as an intelligent serial port. Intelligent serial ports generally assign a much larger amount of buffer memory and/or a dedicated microprocessor to manage the port(s). Intelligent serial ports are usually sold with either one or two ports on a card, and these cards generally cost between $50 and $200. If your system uses the older, non-buffered type of serial ports, you should consider an internal modem or replacement serial ports.

Laptops

For laptops, your purchasing decisions are much simpler. With almost all new laptops, you have two choices: a proprietary internal modem from the laptop manufacturer, or a *PCMCIA* "credit-card" modem. Each has its advantages and disadvantages. One truth is universal though, if you need to purchase an internal card modem for your laptop, buy it from the laptop manufacturer.

PCMCIA modems come with their own unique considerations; among the most important are compatibility with your laptop's power-management features and physical compatibility with any other PCMCIA cards you may use. Too often, the jack port on a PCMCIA credit-card Ethernet adapter may block the jack port on a PCMCIA credit-card modem. If you are going to be using both, make sure the cable connections don't block each other, or buy a single card that serves both functions.

Phone Lines and Other Connections

To communicate with the outside world requires some form of communications hardware, such as a modem, and some form of connection medium, such as a phone line.

POTS

Plain Old Telephone Service (POTS) is ubiquitous, almost every household in America has one form or another of the standard two-wire phone line. POTS is an analog service, which uses AC and DC electrical signals for carrier and signaling. In most homes, these phone lines are terminated in modular RJ-11 jacks. In older homes, they may be terminated in older four-wire jacks, a large plug with four round pins arranged in a square pattern, or the phones may actually be hard-wired to screw-terminals. You will need some form of adapter (or a new or replacement jack) to connect a modem, which has modular RJ-11 jacks, to the older wiring systems, but the wiring itself hasn't changed much in several decades. In most cases, you'll be able to find these adapters at the same stores where you find other telephone jacks and cables. Your local electronics store or home center should have all the parts you'll need.

One thing that has changed, mostly during the 1960s and 1970s, is the conversion from pulse to tone dialing. Virtually the entire phone system in the United States is now capable of supporting touch tone dialing—only a few isolated localities still use equipment old enough to require pulse dialing.

When you place a call using POTS, your modem will take the line off-hook and listen for a dial-tone on the line. Your modem will then dial the number and initiate a call. When the modem on the other end answers, the two modems will handshake, negotiate, and establish a data connection. At that point, you have effectively established a digital connection over a circuit-switched analog line.

Leased Lines

Leased lines are similar to POTS in that they use the same phone company resources. The biggest differences are that leased lines use four wires instead of two, normally use specialized modems, and do *not* require dial-tone or dialing. In essence, a leased line is a permanently open circuit between two points. This type of line is often used to interconnect networks, or to connect a system or network to a remote site or service. For data use, leased lines are generally available in several different categories, usually classified by their transmission capacity.

ISDN

Integrated Services Digital Network (ISDN) is a newer, all-digital type of phone service that is becoming more and more popular. ISDN provides *much* greater capacity and far more features than POTS. Most ISDN circuits are Basic Rate Interface (BRI). While the wiring coming in from the phone company remains the same standard two-wire (tip and ring, single pair) as is used for POTS, BRI provides a total of three "channels" on the ISDN line, two 64kbps "B" bearer channels and one 16kbps "D" data channel. The bearer channels are used for transferring data, while the data channel is used for control signals. The other type of ISDN service, Primary Rate Interface, or PRI, is more commonly used by service providers and large businesses. PRI provides a total of twenty-four channels, twenty-three 64kbps "B" bearer channels and one 64kbps "D" data channel. PRI ISDN circuits require special wiring and circuitry, and are far more expensive to implement, and are normally only used by large businesses or service providers.

ISDN requires special connections and equipment. On the customer end, a minimum of two components are required for a data connection, a network termination, and a terminal adapter. The network termination (commonly referred to as an NT-1) is essentially the connection between any installed premises equipment and the outgoing ISDN line. The terminal adapter is functionally the equivalent of a communications port on your computer, and physically the equivalent of a modem. Some terminal adapters come in internal versions, which install inside your computer as an add-in card, while others are external, and connect to a COM port on your computer. For the internal models, the terminal adapters do not generally take the place of an existing COM port. For external terminal adapters, the COM port to which you connect the terminal adapter must be able to handle the high-speed connection, meaning that a 16550 style port is a minimum requirement. Recently, with ISDN gaining in popularity at a rapid pace, it's becoming common for many vendors to combine the NT-1 and the Terminal Adapter on a single device. This simplifies the connections and reduces the number of components.

Connecting with ISDN is very similar to connecting with a modem, but much faster. Where a high-speed modem may take 20-40 seconds to negotiate and establish a connection, ISDN will usually make the connection in 3-5 seconds. The high bandwidth (higher transmission speed and capacity), combined with this "instant on" accessibility, are major attractions of ISDN.

Recently, ISDN has been experiencing a high level of growth and expansion in the market. Not only are most regional phone companies beginning to aggressively market ISDN services to both business and residential customers, but equipment vendors, information services, and service providers are starting to jump on the bandwagon as well. 3Com, long a familiar name in networking, now offers a line of ISDN adapters, many combined with high-speed analog modems. Other vendors, such as Motorola, are making big splashes by entering the market with high-performance ISDN products at a fraction of the cost traditionally associated with ISDN service and hardware. PSI, one of the country's largest Internet Service Providers (ISPs), offers 64kbps ISDN service through every one of its points of presence (POPs) nationwide. Starting this fall, CompuServe plans to provide ISDN connections to its international network in ten U.S. cities, with more to follow as its network grows to accommodate the new connections.

WinSock Connections

Windows Sockets, or WinSock, is a standard method of communicating with a TCP/IP network, such as the Internet. Different TCP/IP software vendors may choose to implement their protocol stack differently, especially on different networks or operating systems. Windows Sockets was developed to give programmers a standard interface for communicating, regardless of which vendor provides the actual protocol stack. The WinSock API remains constant, and sits on top of the vendor's TCP/IP implementation. Calls made to the WinSock API are passed to the appropriate protocol module.

Windows 95 provides a complete TCP/IP protocol stack with full WinSock support. If you're going to use non-proprietary software over a standard connection, Windows 95 includes all you'll need. Different service providers may, however, require you to use their own TCP/IP software, or a custom implementation of WinSock that includes direct ties to their service. In these cases, you will be unable to use the standard Windows 95 services until your vendor provides a compatible update. You may be limited to the software provided by your vendor, depending on how proprietary its implementation is.

With different WinSock implementations, different functions may be included. The most common custom features involve making dial-up connections by triggering a communications module to connect to the service provider. Windows 95 provides the tools necessary to do this, but until all the third-party software vendors update their programs for Windows 95 compatibility, many still require the replacement of the standard Windows 95 WINSOCK.DLL with their own. Since Windows 95 installs the default DLL during its upgrade installation, you may need to go back and restore the original WINSOCK.DLL after your upgrade is complete, in order to restore your link to your service provider. Windows 95 renames WINSOCK.DLL to WINSOCK.OLD during installation, so this is a simple change to make.

Once you have a standard WinSock implementation, either from Windows 95 or from your service provider, you should be able to use any WinSock-compliant program over that connection. Unless your provider has a proprietary implementation, this opens up a huge variety of software, allowing you to pick and choose among dozens, if not hundreds, of different applications, many that are either available for free or at low cost. If you're not yet connected to the Internet, you'll also find a treasure trove of WinSock applications available on many local bulletin boards, as well as on the major information services. This is the true benefit of an open, standard implementation of WinSock.

Other Hardware

There are a number of accessory items you may use in communicating, especially in relation to working with phone lines. Accessories, such as fax switches, have become more common as we find more and more ways to communicate.

A common accessory is the electronic fax switch, to which you can connect several devices. By listening to the line, the switch can determine whether the incoming call is voice, fax, or data, and route it to the appropriate device. This allows you to use one line for three different purposes, sparing you the cost of additional phone lines.

Some modems go further, by building in hardware and firmware components that support various telephone company options. Distinctive ringing allows you to have a different ring and a separate number for a single phone line, so you can have a voice number and a fax number, which ring differently on the same line. Caller ID allows you to see the phone number from which an incoming call is being placed. Several modem manufacturers have implemented support for these features in their products.

As more and more people start to connect their phone lines to their computers, there is a rising level of concern for electrically isolating the phone line, so that any surges or spikes would not also damage the computer. To this end, line protectors that filter and regulate the phone line, sometimes in addition to filtering and regulating AC power, are becoming more common, and more popular. Many companies that offer surge protectors also offer models that include a loop for the phone line, providing more complete isolation for your computer system.

Since the phone companies have relinquished ownership of the wiring within our homes, more and more people are doing more and more of their own interior wiring. This, and the special needs of users who take portable or laptop computers with them when they travel, have created a number of interesting options and accessories. Couplers, extensions, and splitters have all become common, and are part of most "road warriors'" tool kits. A coupler will allow you to connect two phone cables end-to-end, normally for the purpose of making a longer cable or extension. *Couplers* come in two types: straight-through or reversed. In most cases, the reversed type is what you will want, since this is what's needed for a true extension. Straight-through couplers, normally marked with a straight arrow, are normally used for special purposes, and can cause problems if used in a system that can't handle polarity reversals. However, straight-through couplers can also be used to correct a flaw in premises wiring, by intentionally reversing the polarity of a miswired jack. *Splitters* simply allow more than one device to be connected to a single line, and are often combined with couplers or extensions.

One new accessory that is gaining in popularity with home, business, and mobile users alike, is a telephone headset that connects to your modem, allowing you to use your computer as a dialer and use the headset for voice calls. These are compact, and are often quite high in quality for a relatively low price. A number of users have discovered that they enjoy the portable, hands-free freedom of headset phones, and these models made for use with a modem are far less expensive, smaller, and lighter because they don't need to include any of the actual dialing mechanisms.

Choosing Communications Software

Your communications needs will determine what type or types of communications software you need. You may find one program that will communicate with everything, and you may end up with several different programs, or suites of programs, to communicate with different types of systems.

You may also find that you need to evaluate software carefully to ensure support for special features. Many new modems offer features that are not yet supported by every communications program. You may also have special interests that make one product a better choice than another. You may also find that, in certain applications, you don't have any choice of what software to use. There is a lot of variety, and a lot of both general purpose and application specific software available. Careful planning and evaluation will allow you to select the product, or mix of products, that will best serve your needs.

General Purpose Communications

Communicating with publicly accessible systems, such as Bulletin Board Systems (BBSs), normally requires a general purpose communications program. This is essentially a bundle of a dialer, a terminal emulator, and a file transfer program. Windows 95 includes HyperTerminal (see fig. 2.2), from Hilgraeve, which is a special, easy-to-use version of its more powerful HyperAccess product.

Note

HyperTerminal will be discussed in detail in Chapter 5, "Using HyperTerminal."

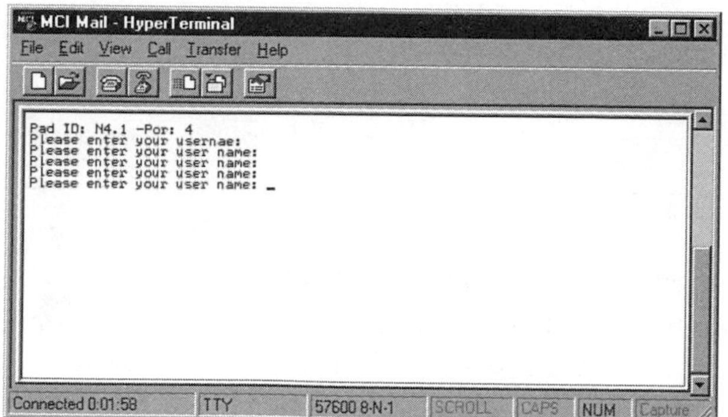

Fig. 2.2
Windows 95 HyperTerminal.

There are other products on the market, such as Datastorm's Procomm Plus or DCA's Crosstalk, which provide more advanced features than HyperTerminal. If you spend a lot of time on BBS calls, or have a need for advanced features, you should try several different packages to see which works best for you. Each has a different personality.

> **Note**
>
> Third-party communications software will be discussed in detail in Chapter 6, "Using Third-Party Communications Programs."

Remote Control

Many companies are now providing remote access to systems on their networks by using what is known as *remote control software*. Remote control is an application that will require custom software to match that on the system you're trying to control. One part of the software runs on the "host" system, usually at the office, which you wish to access from a "remote" system, usually either at home or on the road. The host and remote software may be sold separately, or in a combined package.

There are several different products on the market, such as Symantec's pcAnywhere, Stac's ReachOut, Microcom's Carbon Copy, Ocean Isle's Remotely Possible, and several others. The remote clients for almost any existing remote control product will work just fine under Windows 95, however, at this writing, a Windows 95 specific host product has not yet been shipped.

> **Note**
>
> Remote control software and applications will be discussed in detail in Chapter 26, "Sharing Resources."

Commercial Information Services

The big four information services (CompuServe, America Online, Prodigy, and Microsoft Network) all provide proprietary software to allow access to their services. With the exception of CompuServe, you have no choice—you *must* use the software the Information Service provides in order to access the service.

CompuServe allows access from a general-purpose communications program, such as HyperTerminal, or from third-party products, such as TAPCIS, OzCIS, and others. CompuServe provides CompuServe Information Manager (CIM) as a front-end to its service. Beginning with the 2.0 version of WinCIM, CompuServe includes its updated Spry Mosaic and Internet access tools. Version 2.0 is a 16-bit Windows 3.x application, but is written to be compatible with Windows 95. A full 32-bit implementation is due in mid-1996. CompuServe will be covered in detail in Chapter 8, "Using CompuServe."

America Online (AOL) aggressively distributes trial memberships bundled with copies of their access software. Most readers who subscribe to at least one computer-related magazine will already have received several copies.

> **Note**
>
> America Online will be covered in detail in Chapter 9, "Using America Online."

Prodigy provides new subscribers with a copy of its access software when you sign up.

> **Note**
>
> Prodigy will be covered in detail in Chapter 10, "Using Prodigy."

Microsoft has bundled the access software for Microsoft Network with Windows 95. At present, you *must* be running Windows 95 to access Microsoft Network, although a Macintosh client is planned.

> **Note**
>
> Microsoft Network will be covered in detail in Chapter 11, "Using The Microsoft Network (MSN)."

Internet Service Providers

To gain access to the Internet, you need some form of connection to an Internet Service Provider, or ISP. There are three ways to get connected;

- Directly to an ISP, such as PSI, Netcom, or UUNet
- Over an office, campus, or organizational network
- Through a bulletin board or information service

Most Internet Service Providers provide their own communications software in the form of a TCP/IP protocol stack, a dialer, and a suite of Internet applications. With Windows 95, you should be able to make the connection easily using the built-in TCP/IP software and dial-up networking features. This will often give you the option to use a wider variety of software.

In the office, where you have direct access to the Internet from your desktop, Windows 95 includes everything you'll need to get started, and even provides a wizard to help set it up for you. All you have to add is the client software, such as a Web browser. Anticipating this, Microsoft includes the Internet Explorer, a Windows 95 browser, in the Plus! pack, and it is also available for download from its FTP site.

The major commercial information services, and many larger bulletin boards, provide access to some or all Internet services. The information services all currently require that you use their own software to gain access to the Internet, while many bulletin boards will allow you a great deal of access using a general purpose communications program, such as HyperTerminal.

> **Note**
>
> Each method of connecting to the Internet will be discussed in detail in Chapter 20, "Connecting to the Internet."

CHAPTER 3

Configuring Modems and Ports

by Jim Boyce

In Chapter 2 you learned how modems work and explored the options available to you for connecting your PC to the outside world. This chapter helps you move from some of those theoretical topics to some hands-on experience. In this chapter you learn how to set up your PC's COM ports and get your modem working. You also learn how to begin using the modem and some of Windows 95's communications utilities to begin putting your modem to work.

In this chapter, you learn how to

- Understand and configure COM ports
- Install and configure modems
- Configure Telephony settings
- Use the Phone Dialer

Before you begin configuring your PC's COM ports, you should have a basic understanding of how the ports work. The next section explains the basic function of a COM port.

Understanding COM Ports

Your PC probably contains at least two serial ports. Because these ports typically are used for communications, they often are called COM ports. These ports are identified by number, such as COM1, COM2, COM3, and so on. Where are these ports? Often, the PC contains an *I/O adapter* that contains the COM ports, at least one parallel (LPT) port, and a game controller port. The adapter installs in one of the PC's bus slots beside its other adapters (such as the video adapter). The connectors for the ports stick out the back of the

PC. In many newer PC designs, the ports are built directly onto the PC's motherboard, and cables connect the ports from the motherboard to the port connectors on the back of the PC.

Regardless of its design, a typical PC contains either two or four COM ports, but it's possible to install special communications adapters in a PC to support many more COM ports. Generally, though, these multi-port adapters are used only in servers to enable multiple modems or terminals to connect to the server.

▶ See "Avoiding COM Port Conflicts," p. 61

Often, one COM port is used to connect a mouse or other pointing device to the PC. If your PC uses a PS/2-style or bus mouse, however, the mouse doesn't connect to the COM port, but instead uses a different type of connection. Some output devices, including some printers and most plotters, connect through COM ports.

▶ See "Configuring COM Ports," p. 55

Most PCs also use a COM port to connect a modem to the system. For example, you might have a mouse connected to COM1 and a modem connected to COM2. If your PC contains an internal modem, you must configure the modem as a specific COM port. If your PC has a mouse connected to COM1, for example, you might configure the modem as COM2.

Understanding Serial Communications

▶ See "How Bytes Are Broken into Bits," p. 51

Serial ports get their name from the fact that data flows through the port in *serial* fashion or one bit at a time. Unlike a parallel port that transfers data one byte at a time, a serial port has to break up each byte into its component bits and send the data out through the port one bit at a time. When data comes into the port, the serial port circuitry reconstructs the bits coming in the port back into their original bytes (see fig. 3.1). Fortunately, a PC's serial port circuitry can perform these byte-to-bit and bit-to-byte translations very quickly. Even so, being forced to move only one bit through the port at a time can become a bottleneck. In the section "UARTs and FIFO Buffers," you learn how you can minimize this bottleneck.

About Bits and Bytes

Bits and bytes are not really all that mysterious. A bit is the smallest unit of data a computer recognizes. Bits are represented by the computer as ones and zeroes. A one indicates the bit is on, and a zero indicates the bit is off. This on/off relationship lies at the core of all digital data storage. Even audio CDs store music as a series of on and off bits.

Computers need some means of storing complex data, and that's where the *byte* comes into the picture. A byte is a collection of eight bits. Specific patterns of bits in a byte represent letters and numbers to the computer (which are used to build more complex data). Although it takes the average person like you or me a lot of brain power and time to read a series of eight bits and decipher it into a letter or number, the computer can do it incredibly fast.

In typical data communications, bytes of data are broken into their component bits and transferred down a phone line. At the other end of the connection, the bits are reassembled into bytes. If you use a parallel device (such as Windows 95's Direct Cable Connection) to transfer information, those bytes don't have to be chopped into their component bits. Instead, the bytes can move through the parallel port *in parallel* or as an entire byte. That's why today's parallel ports offer better transfer rates than serial ports, and why you'll get the best performance from Windows 95's Direct Cable Connection if you use a parallel port connection instead of a serial port connection.

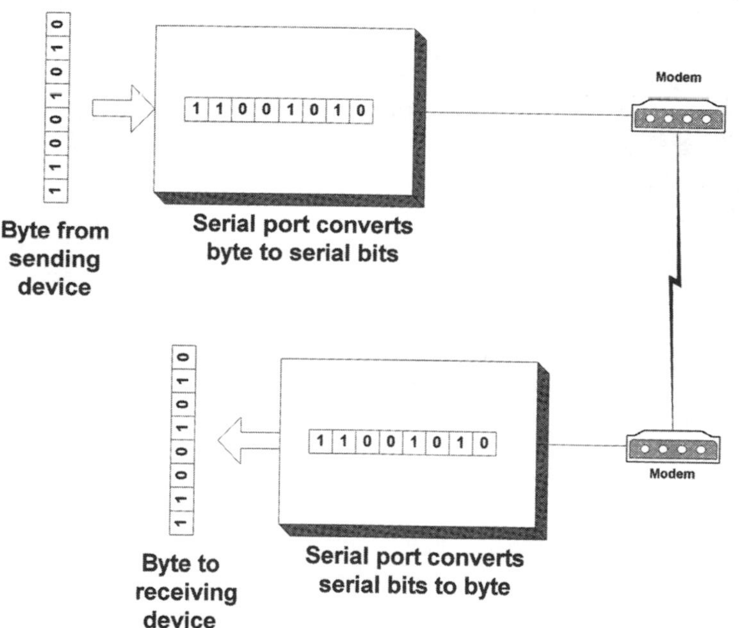

Fig. 3.1
Serial ports break bytes into bits for sending and reassemble incoming bits into bytes.

The serial port circuitry not only handles the translation of bits to bytes and vice versa, but also handles such tasks as *buffering* incoming and outgoing data. This means, for example, that incoming data is stored in a buffer until the port can process it. Outgoing data also is held in a buffer until the port can transmit it.

Fortunately, almost all of the work the serial ports perform is handled automatically by the computer. There are a few settings you can modify in Windows 95, however, that control how the serial ports do their jobs. Before you begin configuring these settings, you need to understand the other configuration settings for the ports, beginning with IRQ and base address settings.

Understanding IRQ and Base Address Settings

IRQ is an acronym taken from Interrupt ReQuest. Your PC contains interrupt request lines that devices can use to signal the CPU that the device needs the CPU's attention. If the serial port's buffer is full, for example, and needs to tell the CPU that it needs to process the data in the buffer, the serial port gets the CPU's attention through its IRQ line.

Many devices don't require an IRQ assignment, but some common devices do require them. Serial ports, parallel ports, disk controllers, sound cards, and other devices usually do require an IRQ assignment. Table 3.1 lists common IRQ assignments to help you identify available IRQ lines in your system.

Table 3.1 Common IRQ Assignments

IRQ Number	Typical Assignment
NMI	Non-Maskable Interrupt; reports parity errors
0	System timer
1	Keyboard
2	EGA/VGA and cascaded interrupt for second IRQ controller (IRQ9-15)
3	COM2, COM4
4	COM1, COM3
5	LPT2 (printer port 2)
6	Floppy disk controller
7	LPT1 (printer port 1)
8	Real-time clock
9	Software redirected to IRQ2
10	Available
11	Available
12	Available

IRQ Number	Typical Assignment
13	Math coprocessor
14	Hard disk controller or host adapter
15	Available or hard disk controller

It is unlikely that you will have to configure your serial ports' IRQ settings, because Windows 95 should automatically detect them and configure them for you. If you decide to change those IRQ values for some reason, such as to eliminate a conflict with another device, Table 3.1 will come in handy to help you determine the necessary settings. You learn later in the section "Configuring COM Ports" how to set the IRQ and other settings for a COM port if Windows 95 doesn't automatically detect the correct settings.

Caution

In general, you shouldn't mess with your system's IRQ settings unless you really need to. Changing a setting incorrectly could result in more than one device not working properly. Before you start changing settings, use the System object in the Control Panel to print a log of your system's IRQ assignments.

If you need to change your serial ports' IRQ settings, it's likely you'll have to do so by changing jumpers or switches on the serial port adapter—or in the case of a motherboard with built-in serial ports, on the motherboard. How you accomplish this depends entirely on the serial port adapter or motherboard design. To learn how to set each port for a specific IRQ setting, check the adapter's (or motherboard's) manual.

If you're installing an internal modem, you must configure the modem as a specific COM port and set its IRQ and base addresssettings (base address settings are explained later in this section). In general, the process of specifying these settings is the same for a serial port adapter or motherboard. Check the modem's manual to learn how to configure it for a particular COM port.

Tip

You can use the Device Manager in Control Panel's System object to print a list of all IRQ and base address assignments in your system. The section "Viewing and Printing Hardware Settings" tells you how to do this.

In addition to an IRQ line to signal the CPU for attention, many devices also require an *I/O base address*. The base address is a memory location through which the device can communicate with the CPU and vice versa. Often, a device uses a range of addresses, so you'll often see the base address referred to as the *input/output range*. Windows 95 uses the term input/output range to refer to I/O address settings and uses the term *resources* to refer to the combination of IRQ and I/O range settings for a particular device.

Serial ports by convention use specific IRQ and base I/O range settings. Table 3.2 lists these common settings.

Table 3.2 Common Serial Port Resource Settings

Port	IRQ	I/O Range
COM1	4	03F8-03FF
COM2	3	02F8-02FF
COM3	4	03E8-03EF
COM4	3	02E8-02EF

Although you can configure your ports in Windows 95 to use settings different from those shown in table 3.2, there usually is no reason to use settings other than the common default settings. The only reason to use different settings is if you have another device in the system that needs to use the settings commonly used by a COM port. Most hardware manufacturers follow standard conventions for their hardware, so it's unlikely that you will have a sound card or other device that needs to use the same IRQ or I/O range as your COM ports.

Baud and Bits-Per-Second (bps)

The term *baud* refers to the frequency at which the modem changes tone during each second. Early modems (300-baud modems, for example), typically sent one digital bit per baud. So, a 300-baud modem transmitted data at 300 bits-per-second, or 300bps. Today's modems transmit data much more rapidly by sending multiple bits per baud. So, the convention for identifying modem speed has changed over the years. Instead of referring to a modem as a 14,400-baud modem, the modem will be referred to as a 14,400bps modem, or 14.4kbps modem. kbps stands for *one thousand bits per second*, and 14.4kbps equals 14,400bps.

How Bytes Are Broken into Bits

In order for two computers to communicate with one another through a serial port, the two computers must agree on the same format for sending and receiving data. Because each byte of data comes through the port as a string of bits, each computer has to know where each byte stops and starts.

Most modems, and therefore most serial ports, function as *asynchronous* devices. This means that the data transfer is not synchronized, and the sending and receiving devices are not necessarily in step with one another. To ensure that the data flows between the two devices without getting lost in translation, the data must include some sort of markers so the two devices can interpret the data properly.

When data is transferred over a serial connection, the data is sent as a *word* made up of four to eight bits, with eight bits being the most common word length. The number of bits in each word is called the *word length.* Seven or eight bits is the most common word length used in the United States.

Start and Stop Bits

In order to determine where a data word ends and the next begins, *start bits* and *stop bits* are used. A start bit, a stop bit, a pair of stop bits, or some combination of start bits and stop bits frame the data word, enabling the sending and receiving devices to determine where one word stops and the next begins. Figure 3.2 illustrates the use of stop bits and start bits.

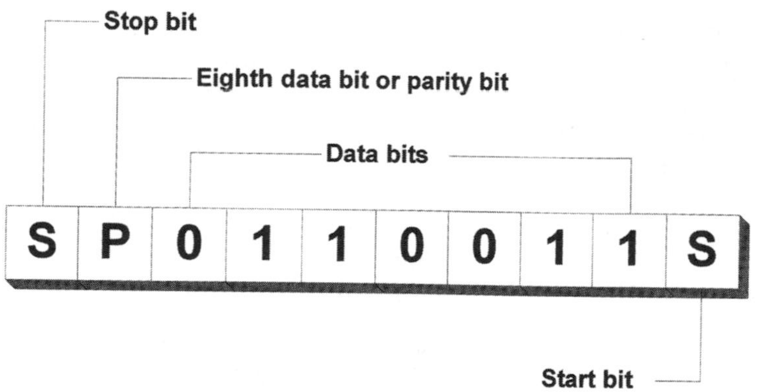

Fig. 3.2
Data, parity, start, and stop bits define the way data is transferred.

To understand how stop bits and start bits work, you need to understand that a serial port doesn't actually send anything down the line. Instead, the line is pulsed from a normal positive state to a negative state. To send a 0 (off bit), the line isn't pulsed; to send a 1 (on bit), the line is pulsed. Each negative pulse is interpreted as a 1 (on bit) at the other end of the connection.

Stop bits really are just timing values. If the line is pulsed for the same length of time as a single data bit, you have one stop bit. Pulse the line for the equivalent time of 1 1/2 data bits, and you have 1 1/2 stop bits. Pulse the line the equivalent of two data bits, and you have two stop bits.

Start and stop bits are a crucial key to successful asynchronous data transfer. Without the timing signals they provide, a receiving system would be unable to determine when it has received a NUL character (eight zeroes or no pulses). But if the receiving system senses a start bit, then a time span equivalent to eight bit pulses passes without a pulse, followed by a stop bit, the receiving system knows it has received a NUL.

Understanding Parity

You have probably guessed that without some type of error detection, serial communications would be nearly impossible to accomplish. While start and stop bits are an important mechanism for ensuring that both systems can follow one another, *parity* bits ensure that the data between the start and stop bits is transferred and interpreted correctly. Parity checking takes on one of four forms: odd, even, mark, and space.

With odd parity (see fig. 3.3), the sending device adjusts the value of the parity bit, turning it on or off to make the total number of on bits in the word add up to an odd number. If the word contains an even number of on bits, the parity bit is turned on to make the total number of on bits odd. If the total number of on bits in the word are odd, the parity bit is turned off so the total remains odd. The receiving system checks the number of odd bits it receives in a word, and if the number is odd, it assumes that the word was transmitted correctly. If it reads an even number of bits, however, it generates an error and depending on the transfer protocol being used, requests that the word be resent.

Even parity uses a similar method, but the total number of bits in the word is always even. The sending system adjusts the value of the parity bit according to the total number of bits in the data word, making the total come out even.

In mark parity, the parity bit is always turned on, regardless of whether the number of on bits in the data word is even or odd. Mark parity enables the receiving system to check for a pattern that marks the bounds of the data. With space parity, the parity bit is always turned off. With *no parity*, a parity bit is not included in the data at all.

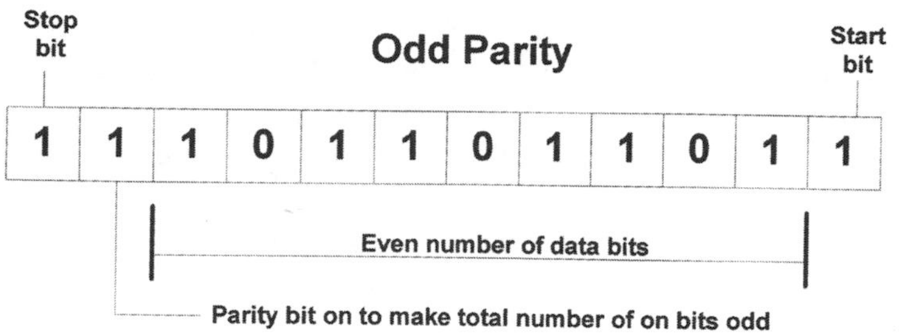

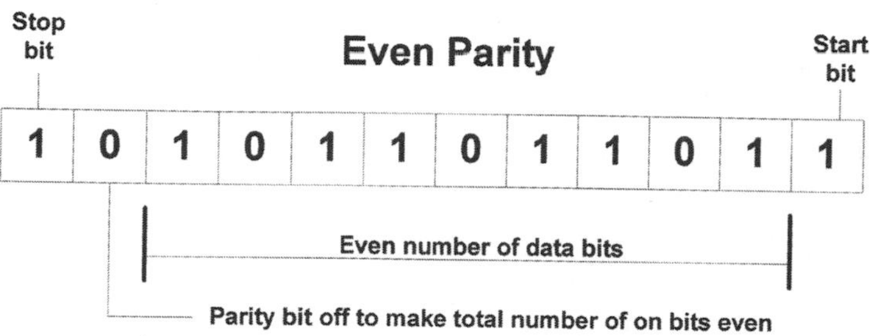

Fig. 3.3
Odd and even parity checking are two common error detection methods.

Eight, None, and One

If you've ever connected to a BBS or online service, you probably saw a reference in the instructions to set your modem to something like 8-N-1, or 7-E-1. These numbers and letters define the number of data bits, stop bits, and parity method required by the remote system. 8-N-1, for example, means eight data bits, no (N) parity, and one stop bit. 7-E-1 means seven data bits, even (E) parity, and one stop bit.

Flow Control

Devices communicating over a serial connection need some method of controlling the flow of data between devices. *Flow control* enables the receiving device to "tell" the sending device to halt transmission until it is ready to process some more data. Flow control also enables the receiving device to signal the sender when it is ready to receive more data. Flow control, therefore, helps eliminate *data overrun*, in which a receiving device is overrun with data faster than it can process that data.

The three common methods of flow control include none, Xon/Xoff, and hardware (RTS/CTS). Xon/Xoff is a software-based method of flow control, in which the Xon (11 hex, DC3, or Ctrl+Q) and Xoff (13 hex, DC1, or Ctrl+S) characters are used to tell the sending device when to start and stop transmission. Hardware flow control uses a wire in the cable (or line on the bus for an internal device) to signal the sending device when to start and stop transmission. Hardware flow control typically offers better speed and less software overhead, so it is the preferred method. Some devices don't support hardware flow control, however, and these devices require software (Xon/Xoff) flow control. The important point is that you configure your devices for whichever flow control method the device at the other end of the connection needs.

Modulation

The term *modulation* refers to the method the modem uses to convert digital signals—from the CPU to analog signals that can be transmitted over the phone line and incoming analog signals back to digital. A variety of *modulation protocols* exist that define the data transfer speed and encoding method used by the modem. Windows 95 supports the most common protocols that are generally recognized as industry standards.

UARTs and FIFO Buffers

Each serial port includes a device called a Universal Asynchronous Receiver/Transmitter, or UART for short. Remember that the parallel byte coming from the CPU has to be converted to a series of bits to be transmitted and that incoming serial bits must be translated back into bytes? The UART performs that function. The UART also is responsible for other aspects of the serial data communication.

Many older serial ports and modems contain model 8250 or 16450 UARTs, which buffer only a single byte of data at a time. As each byte is received, the serial port must signal the CPU that the byte needs to be processed. Because Windows 95 is a multitasking operating system, it's a good bet that the CPU is busy with another task and can't service the serial port right away. In the meantime, another byte comes in, overwriting the waiting byte and causing data overrun. The overwritten byte must be transferred again, slowing down performance.

▶ See "Configuring the FIFO Trigger Values," p. 60

Later systems use an improved model 16550 UART, which contains a 16-byte FIFO (First In/First Out) buffer that helps improve performance by providing a much larger buffer. Instead of the CPU servicing the port for each byte, it can service the port after 16 bytes have been received. This means that data transfer can continue even when the CPU is busy with another task. The 16550 includes a level-sensitive trigger that specifies when the 16550 requests service from the CPU. With Windows 95, you can easily set these trigger values to fine-tune performance.

Changing Your UART

You can tell what type of UART your system contains by using MSD, which is a DOS-based diagnostic utility included with Windows 95. Choose Start, Run, type **MSD**, and click OK. Click the COM Ports item in MSD, and look at the bottom of the list of properties for the port. The last item lists the type of UART used by the port.

If your PC's serial ports or modem use an 8250 or 16450 UART that is installed in a socket, you can replace the UART(s) with a 16550 and improve serial port performance. The 16550 is pin-compatible with these two earlier UARTs. To determine the type of UART your serial ports use, look on the serial port adapter or motherboard for a chip marked with the 8250 or 16450 designation. If they're socketed, buy 16550 UART chips (usually $10 or less) from a computer dealer, remove the old ones, and install the new ones.

If your serial ports use soldered UARTs or the UART is integrated into a VLSI (Very Large Scale Integration) chip, you only have one option—replace the I/O adapter. If the serial ports are built into the motherboard, consider disabling the on-board serial ports and installing an I/O adapter that contains 16550 UARTs.

If you have a high-speed modem (14.4kbps or higher), it is unlikely that you'll be able to use the modem at its highest connection speeds without a 16650 UART.

Configuring COM Ports

Now that you have some background knowledge about serial ports, you're ready to begin configuring your system's ports. Armed with the knowledge you gained in the previous sections of this chapter, you should have no problems setting up your COM ports. First, however, you should learn how to view and print your PC's hardware settings so you'll be able to identify the correct IRQ and base address settings for your COM ports.

Viewing and Printing Hardware Settings

The Device Manager property page, which is contained in the System object in Control Panel, lets you view and modify the resources used by each item of hardware in your computer. Another very nice feature of the Device Manager is its ability to print a hardware summary of one or more devices, which gives you a log of your PC's hardware settings. You can use this log to identify available resources (such as IRQ and I/O ranges) for the new hardware you install in your PC.

To view a particular hardware item's resources (in this example, the settings for your existing COM ports), follow these steps:

1. Open the Control Panel and double-click the System icon.
2. From the System Properties sheet, click the Device Manager tab to display the Device Manager property page (see fig. 3.4).

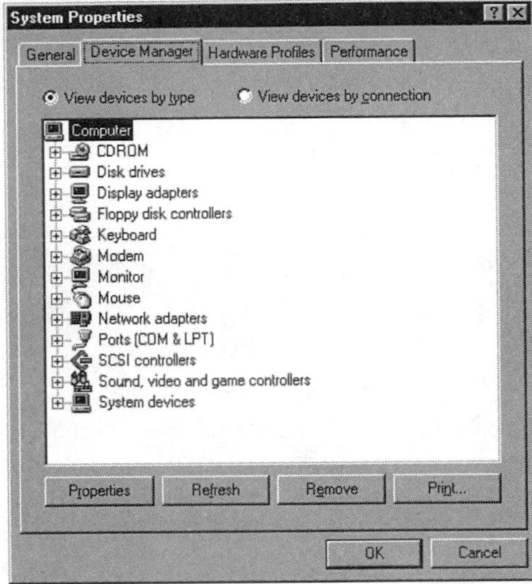

Fig. 3.4
The Device Manager page lets you view and change hardware settings.

3. Double-click the Ports item to expand its branch.
4. Double-click the COM1 entry to display its property sheet, or select the item and click the Properties button.
5. From the Communications Port (COM1) Properties sheet, click the Resources tab to display the Resources page. The Resources page shows the IRQ and I/O range used by the port (see fig. 3.5).

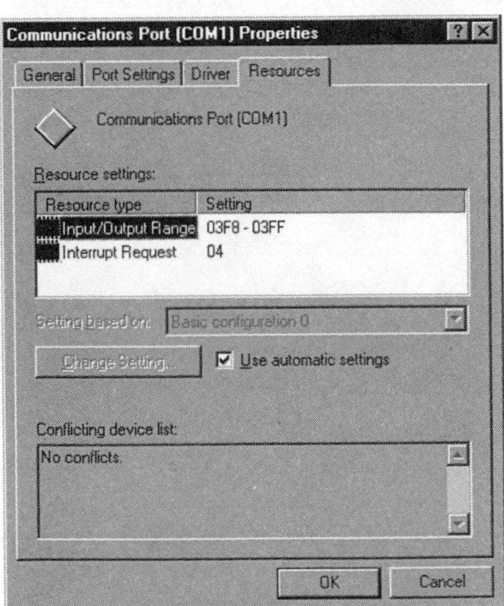

Fig. 3.5
The Resources page shows the IRQ and I/O range properties for the port.

The process for viewing any other device's resource properties is the same. Instead of selecting the Ports branch, just select the branch that contains the hardware item whose resources you want to view.

To print a list of a particular item's resources and other properties (such as the drivers the item uses), use the following procedure:

1. Open the Control Panel and select the System icon.
2. From the hardware tree, locate the item for which you want to print a settings and properties log.
3. Click the Print button to display the Print dialog box (see fig. 3.6).

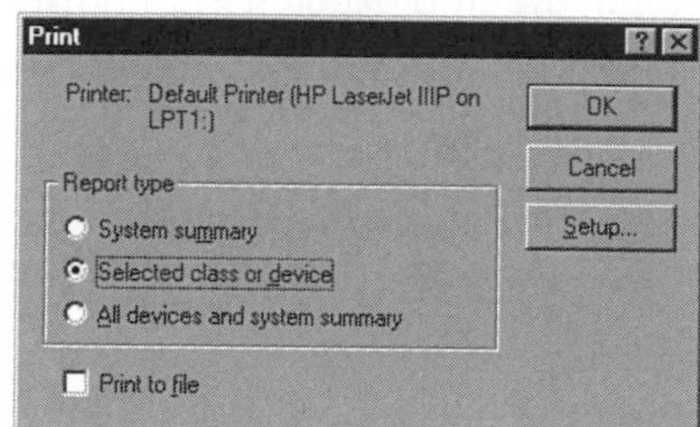

Fig. 3.6
You can print a report for a single device or multiple devices using the Print dialog box.

4. To print a report for only the selected device, choose the Selected Class or Device option button, then choose OK. Or, to print a summary of all your PC's hardware, choose the System Summary option button, then choose OK. If you want to print a summary as well as a report for each device, choose the option button labeled All Devices and System Summary, then choose OK.

Tip

If you prefer to have a copy on file of your device report or system summary, place a check in the Print to File check box. The report will be directed to a file instead of the printer. If you want a text-only file, first run the Add Printer wizard in the Printers folder and install the Generic/Text Only printer. Then, choose the Generic/Text Only printer as the target for your printed report.

Armed with a printout of your system's resources, you're ready to install and configure your COM ports.

Adding a New I/O Adapter

When you install Windows 95, Setup detects your system's hardware and sets properties for most of that hardware. Therefore, your COM ports probably are already properly configured. Even if you are installing an internal modem or new I/O adapter, you still should have little trouble installing the new device, thanks to Windows 95's support for Plug-and-Play.

Plug-and-Play enables Windows 95 to automatically detect and install support for new devices, even on legacy systems (systems that don't have a Plug-and-Play BIOS, which includes most of the PCs in use today). All you have to do to install most devices is turn off the computer, install the device, then turn on the computer. When Windows 95 starts, it automatically detects the new hardware, installs any necessary drivers, and if necessary, prompts you to reboot the system so you can begin using the device.

If your system already contains an I/O adapter or built-in I/O ports, and you want to install an additional I/O adapter, follow these steps:

1. Use the Device Manager as described previously in "Viewing and Printing Hardware Settings" to determine available IRQ and I/O range addresses for the COM port(s). Also use tables 3.1 and 3.2 to determine the correct settings.
2. Shut down Windows 95 and turn off the PC.
3. Read the new I/O adapter's manual to determine how to set the IRQ and I/O range (base address) for the adapter, and set these two values on the adapter or modem according to the information you find in step 1.
4. Open the PC and install the adapter or modem, then replace the cover on the PC.
5. Turn on the PC and let Windows 95 boot. Windows 95 should automatically recognize the new hardware and install support for it.

If for some reason Windows 95 does not properly recognize or configure your new COM port(s), see "Configuring a COM Port," for help.

Tip

If you're not sure what settings to use for your COM ports, read the section "Avoiding COM Port Conflicts" later in this chapter for tips on choosing the correct settings.

Troubleshooting

I've installed a new serial port adapter, but Windows 95 doesn't automatically recognize it.

You can install the port manually. Open the Control Panel and choose the Add New Hardware icon to start the Add New Hardware wizard. Choose No when the wizard prompts you to specify whether you want it to detect the new hardware. Follow the prompts provided by the wizard to manually select the serial port.

Configuring a COM Port

You can configure COM ports in a few different ways in Windows 95, but one of the most direct methods is to use the Control Panel. As you begin working with various communications programs, you'll find that you can change COM port settings from within most of the programs, as well.

To configure the speed, data bits, stop bits, parity, and flow control for a COM port, follow these steps:

1. Open the Control Panel and double-click the System icon.
2. From the System Properties sheet, click the Device Manager tab to display the Device Manager property page.
3. Open the Ports tree, select the COM port whose settings you want to modify, then choose Properties to display the port's property sheet.
4. Click the Port Settings tab to display the Port Settings page.
5. From the Bits per Second drop-down list, choose the speed for the port based on the speed of the device you are connecting to the port.
6. From the Data Bits drop-down list, choose the number of data bits for the port.
7. From the Parity drop-down list, choose the parity method you want to assign to the port.
8. From the Stop Bits drop-down list, choose the number of stop bits the port should use.
9. From the Flow Control drop-down list, choose the type of flow control required by the port.

If you're not sure which settings you need to use, don't worry. Almost all communications programs will override the settings according to their needs. Use the default settings if you're unsure which settings your programs require.

Configuring the FIFO Trigger Values

If your COM ports or internal modem uses 16550 UARTs, you can control the trigger values the 16550 uses to determine when to generate an interrupt to request service by the CPU. Windows 95 supports two trigger values for the 16550: a transmit trigger and a receive trigger. The transmit trigger specifies how many bytes the FIFO buffer will contain before the bytes are sent, and the port generates an interrupt for the CPU to provide more bytes. The receive trigger specifies the number of bytes that must be received and stored in the buffer before the port signals the CPU to process the bytes.

The default value for the transmit trigger is 16 bytes, which means the FIFO buffer is completely filled before the port flushes the buffer and generates an interrupt to signal the CPU to provide more data. The default value for the receive trigger is 14 bytes, which means the buffer will receive 14 bytes before the port generates an interrupt to signal the CPU to process the waiting bytes. Note that additional bytes can still come into the buffer while the port is waiting to be serviced.

If you want to optimize transfer performance, you generally can leave the settings at their defaults. If you believe you're experiencing data overruns because of high CPU usage, you can try changing the trigger values to overcome the problem. Symptoms of data overrun include excessive errors during file transfer, poor overall performance, and jerky multitasking during data transfer.

To set the FIFO buffer trigger levels, use these steps:

1. Open the Control Panel, choose the System object, then open the Device Manager.
2. Open the Ports tree and select the port whose trigger values you want to set, then choose Properties to display the port's property sheet.
3. Click the Port Settings tab, then click the Advanced button to display the Advanced Port Settings dialog box shown in figure 3.7.
4. Enable FIFO support by placing a check in the Use FIFO Buffers check box.
5. Use the Receive Buffer slider control to set the desired receive trigger value (valid values are 1, 4, 8, and 14).
6. Use the Transmit Buffer slider control to set the desired transmit trigger value (valid settings are 1, 6, 11, and 16).

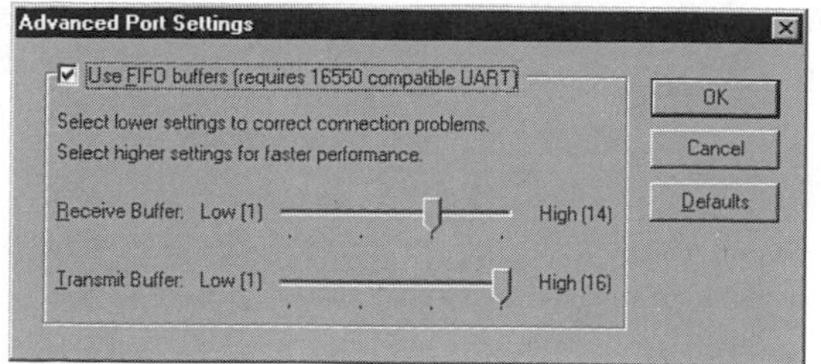

Fig. 3.7
Use the Advanced Port Settings dialog box to set the FIFO trigger values.

> **Note**
>
> By default, Windows 95 enables FIFO support for all applications, including Win32, Win16, and DOS applications.

Avoiding COM Port Conflicts

The majority of PCs in use today don't support IRQ sharing by devices. Instead, each device must use a unique IRQ line. The exceptions are systems that use the EISA and MCA buses. If you take another look at Table 3.2, however, you'll notice that most PCs use the same IRQ for COM1 and COM3, and that COM2 and COM4 share an IRQ line. The convention is that COM1 and COM3 share IRQ4, and COM2 and COM4 share IRQ3.

Does assigning the same IRQ line to two different COM ports cause a problem on ISA-bus systems, even though they're not designed to share interrupts? Generally, the answer is no, but only if you don't try to use the two ports at the same time. If you're using a mouse on COM1, for example, and try to use anything else on COM3, the device on COM3 probably will not work, and your mouse might stop responding properly.

But, assume that you want to use a mouse on COM1 and also connect a modem and a serial printer to the PC. Unless you intend to use the printer at the same time you are using the modem, you can set up the modem on COM2 and attach the printer to COM4. You don't have to do anything special to use either one—just don't use them at the same time.

You should keep in mind, however, that some video adapters conflict with COM4. These include the 8514A, ATI Mach8, and some S3-based adapters. If your system contains one of these adapters, consider connecting your mouse to COM2 and using COM1 and COM3 for the other devices.

Troubleshooting

I installed a new PC Card modem, and Windows 95 automatically configured it as COM5. Some of my older applications can't access COM 5.

If all of your COM ports are already assigned and you install a PC Card (PCMCIA) modem, Windows 95 might configure the PC Card modem as COM5. Unfortunately, some programs can't access the modem on COM5. So, you might have to adjust the base addresses of the other COM ports or disable one of the ports to make a base address available for the modem. This will enable Windows 95 to configure the modem with a lower COM port number. Use the Device Manager to change the base address of a port. You can use Table 3.2 as a guide to selecting a base address.

Configuring PC Card (PCMCIA) Slots

When you install Windows 95 on a system that contains PC Card (PCMCIA) slots, Setup usually can detect and install support for the PC Card slots. If Windows 95 detects that your PC contains PC Card slots, the PCMCIA object appears in the Control Panel and a PCMCIA object appears in the hardware tree in the Device Manager. Windows 95 supports Intel-compatible and Databook-compatible PCMCIA sockets for Plug-and-Play performance. Windows 95 also supports the use of real-mode drivers for other types of PCMCIA controllers.

Note

If Setup is unable to detect your PC Card slots, you can use the PCMCIA wizard to install support for the slots. To run the wizard, double-click the PCMCIA icon in the Control Panel.

When Setup installs support for your PC Card slots, it doesn't enable 32-bit support for the slots. Before your PC Cards will support Plug-and-Play configuration of PC Card devices, you must enable 32-bit PCMCIA support. To enable 32-bit support, run the PCMCIA wizard. The PCMCIA wizard will comment any drivers in your PC's Config.sys and Autoexec.bat files, then enable the 32-bit drivers included with Windows 95.

PC Card Secrets

The secret to getting your PC Card slots to work is making sure you have the latest BIOS revision for your PC, because most current BIOS updates include support for PC Card sockets and services. Most newer PCs contain a flash-ROM BIOS, which can be updated using a special program that comes with the PC. If you're having problems getting your PC Card modem to be recognized by Windows 95, a BIOS update might help.

Call your computer manufacturer's technical support staff to explain the problem and ask if your PC contains a flash-ROM BIOS that can be updated through software. If it can, get instructions on receiving and installing the BIOS update.

If your PC Card controller isn't supported by Windows 95's 32-bit drivers, you'll have to use the real-mode card and socket services drivers provided by your PC's manufacturer. Again, the secret to successful installation is to use the latest drivers. Check with the company's technical support staff to verify that you have the latest drivers.

Installing and Configuring Modems

After your COM ports are properly configured, you're ready to begin installing and configuring your modem. The easiest type of modem to install is an external modem.

Installing an External Modem

There are no switches or jumpers to set on an external modem—it simply plugs into an available COM port in the back of your PC. Installing an external modem is therefore very simple:

1. Connect the modem cable to the back of the PC, then connect the other end of the cable to the appropriate COM port on the back of your PC.
2. Connect the power cord to the modem; make sure the modem is turned off, and then plug in the power adapter to an outlet.
3. Connect a phone line to the Line jack on the modem. If you're installing a fax modem and are using a fax switch to route fax calls to the modem, connect the Line jack on the modem to the Fax port on the switch.
4. If you are connecting the modem in conjunction with a phone, connect the phone to the Phone port on the modem. Or, if you're using a fax switch, connect the phone to the Phone port on the switch.

Next, turn to the section "Installing the Modem Driver" later in this chapter to learn how to add support for the modem in Windows 95.

Installing an Internal Modem

Installing an internal modem is almost identical to adding an I/O adapter. To install an internal modem, follow these steps:

1. Use the Device Manager and tables 3.1 and 3.2 to determine the necessary IRQ and I/O range settings for your new modem.
2. Turn off the PC.
3. If your system already contains two COM ports and you want to keep the existing COM1 and COM2 ports, configure the modem as COM3 (refer to the modem's manual to learn how to set its COM port assignment). You'll have to attach your mouse to COM2.
4. If you don't need three COM ports, disable your existing COM2 and configure the modem as COM2. You can attach your mouse to COM1.
5. Install the modem in the PC.
6. Boot the system and allow Windows 95 to boot. Windows 95 should automatically recognize the modem and install support for it.

If Windows 95 can't detect your modem, you can install the drivers for it manually. See "Installing a Modem Driver" later in this chapter to learn how.

Installing a PC Card Modem (PCMCIA)

If your PC Card slots support Windows 95's 32-bit PCMCIA drivers, installing a PC Card modem should be easy. First, make sure you have enabled the 32-bit PCMCIA drivers on your PC (see "Configuring PC Card Slots" earlier in this chapter for tips on doing so). After the PC Card slots are enabled, you should be able to simply insert the modem in the appropriate slot, and Windows 95 will install support for it.

If your PC's PC Card slots don't support the 32-bit PCMCIA drivers and you are relying on real-mode drivers to support the slots, you will have to use the modem manufacturer's installation procedure and drivers to support the modem under Windows 95.

Installing the Modem Driver

If your modem is not yet installed or Windows 95 did not recognize the modem, you still can install the modem driver. Windows 95 provides a wizard to automate the process. To run the wizard and install the driver, follow these steps:

1. Open the Control Panel and double-click the Modems icon to display the Modems Properties sheet shown in figure 3.8.

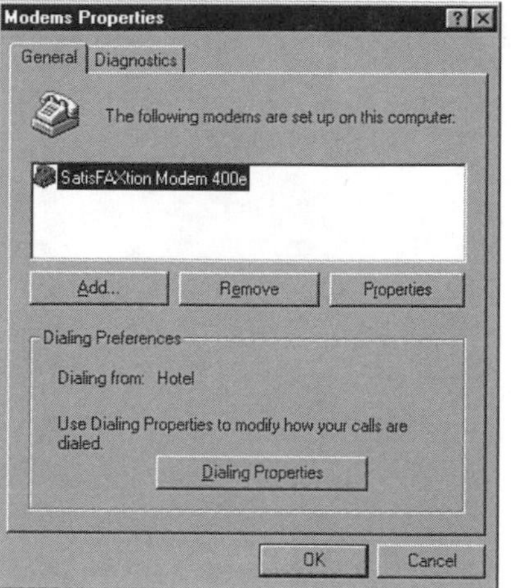

Fig. 3.8
You can add, configure, and remove modems with the Modems Properties sheet.

2. Click the Add button to start the Install New Modem wizard (see fig. 3.9).

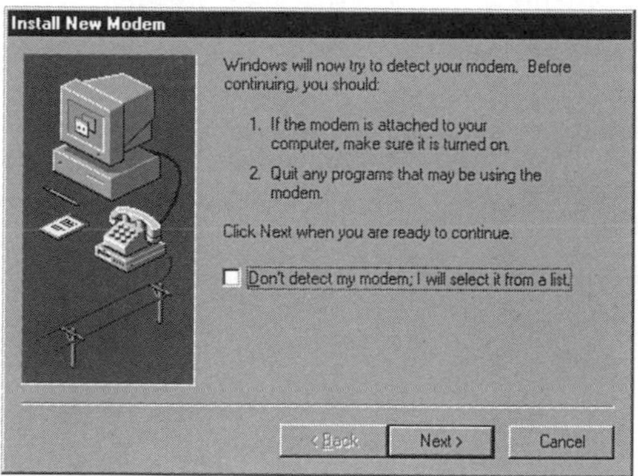

Fig. 3.9
The Install New Modem wizard automates the modem installation and setup process.

3. If you have already installed the modem, click the Next button. If you have not yet installed the modem, place a check in the check box labeled Don't Detect my Modem, then choose Next.

   The wizard displays the modem type for your approval if the wizard is able to detect a new modem. If the wizard is unable to detect a new modem, it informs you of that fact. Choose Next to display the dialog box shown in figure 3.10. This is the same dialog box you'll see if you direct the wizard not to detect your modem.

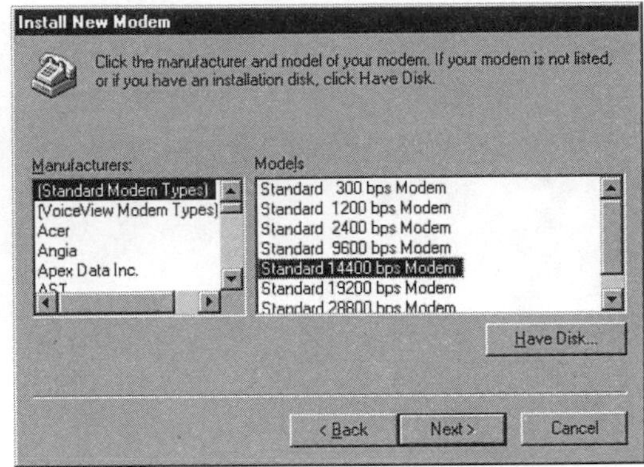

Fig. 3.10
You can specify the make and model of your modem if the wizard does not detect a new modem in your PC.

4. If the wizard prompts you to select your modem manually, choose the modem's manufacturer from the Manufacturer's list, then choose the modem's model from the Models list. If your make and model are not listed and your modem is Hayes-compatible, select Standard Modem Types from the Manufacturer's list, then choose an appropriate speed from the Models list.
5. The wizard then prompts you to specify the port assigned to the modem (see fig. 3.11). Select the appropriate port, then choose Next. The wizard will install the required files, prompting you for the Windows 95 CD or diskettes, if needed.

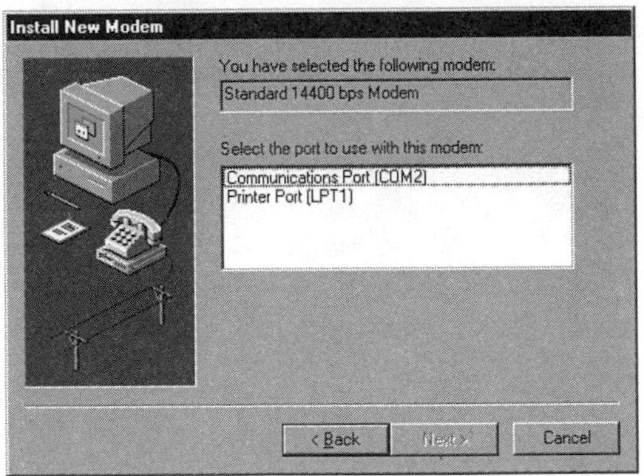

Fig. 3.11
The wizard prompts you to select the port to which the modem is connected.

6. Click the Finish button to complete the installation process.

Multiple Modem Drivers

Windows 95 allows you to install multiple modems for a single COM port, just as you can assign more than one printer to the same LPT port. Although you can't use both modems at the same time, you can install two or more instances of the same modem driver, enabling you to use different sets of settings for various applications.

You might configure one modem driver to use compression, for example, but configure another to disable compression. In each Windows 95 application, you can select the modem configuration you want it to use. This enables you to use different modem configurations in each application without having to reconfigure the modem each time you want to use it with a different application.

Most of the modem settings can be unique from one instance to another, as can various port settings. Some settings, however, are global to all modem instances. The FIFO trigger values are an example of settings that are global.

Troubleshooting

I have a fax modem that doesn't show up in Windows 95's list of supported modems. What should I do to install it?

First, you should let Windows 95 attempt to detect the modem. It's probable that Windows 95 will choose a compatible modem if it is able to detect the modem. If Windows 95 doesn't detect the modem, check the modem's manual to determine if it is compatible with another brand or model. If so, select the compatible modem when Windows 95 prompts you to select the type of modem you're installing. If all else fails, contact the modem manufacturer to determine which modem driver you should use.

Setting Modem Properties

Unlike with Windows 3.x applications that require you to configure modem settings in each application, Windows 95 provides for single-source modem configuration. Instead of sending their own initialization strings, for example, Windows 95 applications simply make a call to TAPI to initialize the modem. Centralizing modem configuration simplifies setup, because usually you only have to configure the modem once.

> **Note**
>
> Even though Windows 95 applications rely on centralized modem configuration and control, Windows 3.x and DOS applications do not. You still have to configure each Windows 3.x or DOS communication application's modem settings separately.

Although Windows 95 configures the modem when you run the Install New Modem wizard, you might want to change settings. For example, you might want to decrease the modem's volume, COM port assignment, maximum connect speed, or other properties.

To configure a modem, use the Modems object in the Control Panel. From the General page of the Modems Properties sheet (see fig. 3.12), select the modem you want to configure, then choose Properties to display the General property page for the modem.

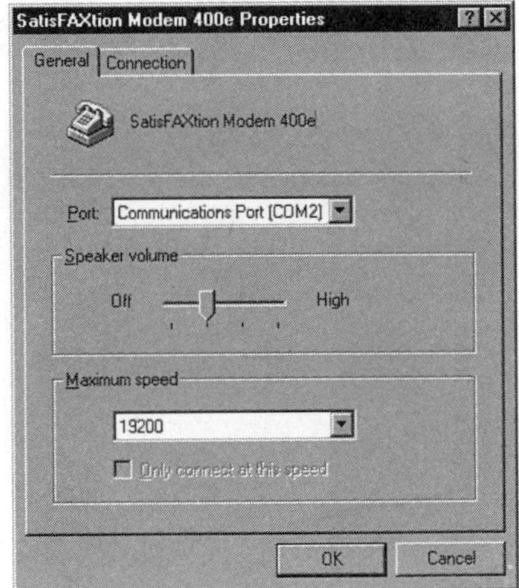

Fig. 3.12 A typical modem General property pages lets you set port ID, speaker volume, and maximum connect speed

From the modem's General property page, select the appropriate port from the Port drop-down list. To set the modem's speaker volume, move the Speaker Volume slider control. Using the Maximum Speed drop-down list, choose the maximum connect speed you want the modem to use. When deciding which option to choose, you should not choose a value that is higher than what your modem can accommodate. If you're not sure of your modem's top speed, see "Testing Your Modem" later in this chapter to learn how to determine its top speed.

If you want the modem to only connect at the maximum speed you specify and not renegotiate the connection to a slower speed, place a check in the check box labeled Only Connect at This Speed. Choosing this option prevents the modem from establishing a connection at a lower speed due to line noise. If you're dialing an on-line service's 14.4kbps access line, for example, and you don't want the connection to fall back to 4800bps because of a bad connection, use this option. If you're not sure of the other modem's speed, you can use trial and error, raising the minimum speed until the modem no longer connects.

Setting Connection Properties

The Connection property page (see fig. 3.13) enables you to set some general properties for the modem that include word structure and call preferences. The three settings in the Connection preferences control group let you set the number of data bits, parity method, and number of stop bits for the modem.

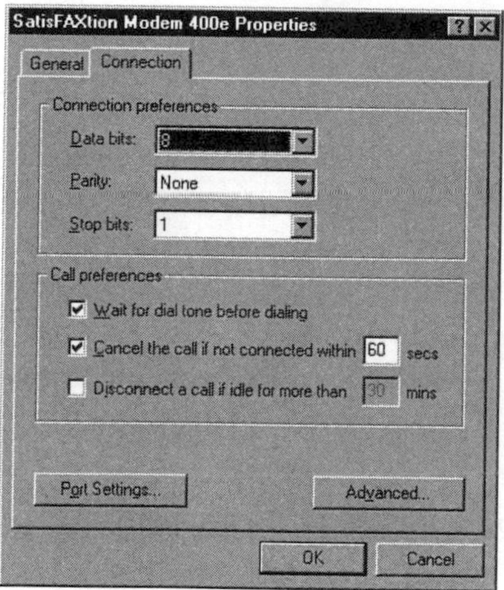

Fig. 3.13
Use the Connection property page to set general port and call properties for the modem.

The Call preferences control group lets you specify how calls are established through the modem. The three options in the Call preferences group are:

- *Wait for Dial Tone before Dialing.* Place a check in this check box if you want the modem to wait and detect a dial tone before it attempts to dial the call. If the modem isn't recognizing the dial tone or you are dialing the call manually, clear this check box.
- *Cancel the Call if not Connected within nn Secs.* Enable this check box if you want the call to be canceled if a connection isn't established in the specified number of seconds. Clear the check box if you want the modem to continue to try to connect until you cancel the call.

- *Disconnect a Call if Idle for more than nn Mins.* Enable this check box if you want the call disconnected when the connection has been idle for the specified amount of time. This ensures that the modem doesn't stay connected if you forget to terminate the connection.

Tip

Click the Port Settings button on the Connection property page if you want to set the FIFO buffer transmit and receive trigger values. Note that these values are global, so changing them for one modem driver instance changes the values for all modems.

Setting Advanced Properties

You can set a number of additional properties for a modem by clicking the Advanced button on the Connection property page. Choosing the Advanced button displays the Advanced Connection Settings dialog box shown in figure 3.14.

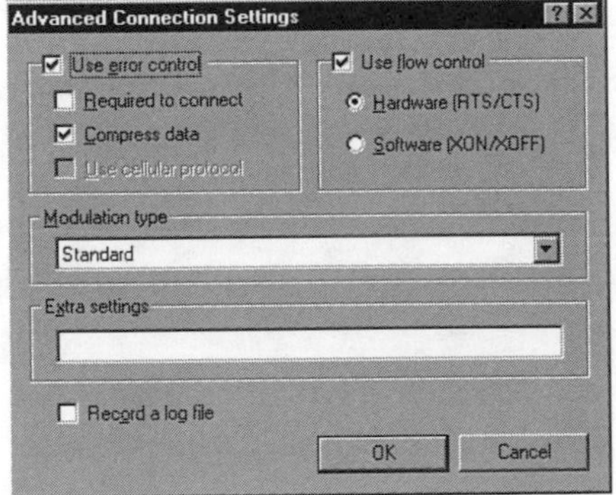

Fig. 3.14 You can set error correction, flow control, modulation, and special setup strings with the Advanced Connection Settings dialog box.

The following settings appear on the Advanced Connection Options dialog box:

- *Use Error Control.* Place a check in this check box if you want the connection to use the modem's error-correction protocol (such as V.42 or MNP-4). With few exceptions, you'll always benefit from using error correction.
- *Required to Connect.* Enable this option if you want the modem to always use error correction. If you clear this check box and the modem can't establish a reliable connection, the connection is refused.

- *Compress Data*. Enable this option to cause the modem to use compression. Generally, you'll see a performance improvement when transferring text and uncompressed binary files. Disable compression if you are transferring files that are already compressed.
- *Use Cellular Protocol*. This option, if enabled, causes the connection to use the modem's cellular error-correction protocol. Many of the faster PC Card modems support cellular protocol, enabling you to establish reliable data connections with your cellular phone. If your modem doesn't support cellular protocol, this option is dimmed.
- *Use Flow Control*. If this option is enabled, the connection uses the flow control method specified by the accompanying two options, Hardware or Software.
- *Modulation Type*. This setting specifies the modulation method the modem uses to establish the connection. The options most often available are Standard and Non-Standard. The Standard setting uses the ITU-TSS standards such as V.32bis, V.32, and so on. The Non-Standard option uses the Bell and HST protocols. The Standard option should work for most modems.
- *Extra Settings*. Use this text box to enter an additional AT command string for the modem. For example, you might enter a string to change the dialing speed, disable call waiting, change the type of response codes generated by the modem, and so on.
- *Record a Log File*. Enable this check box to cause Windows 95 to create a log file named Modemlog.txt and store in the file status information each time the modem is used.

Testing Your Modem

In addition to configuring the modem with the Modems object in the Control Panel, you also can perform a limited amount of diagnostic testing on the modem. To test your modem, use the following procedure:

1. Open the Control Panel and double-click the Modems icon.
2. Make sure your modem is turned on (in the case of an external modem) and that no Windows 95 applications are currently monitoring the port (such as Microsoft Fax or Dial-Up Networking waiting for calls).
3. Select the modem you want to test, then click the More Info button. Windows 95 will communicate with the modem and generate a dialog box similar to the one shown in figure 3.15.

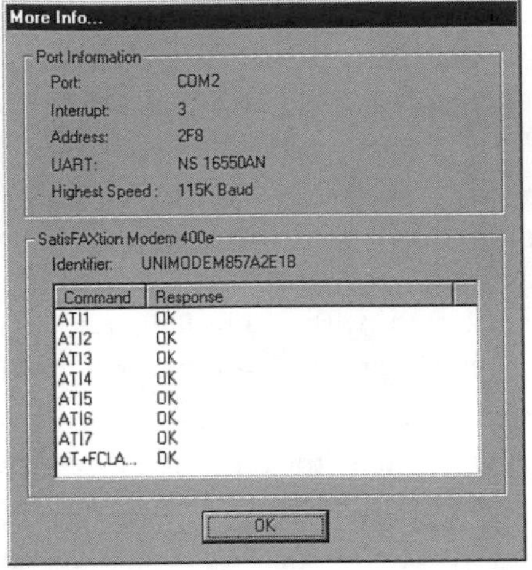

Fig. 3.15
With the Modems object you can test and diagnose your modem.

▶ See "Setting Up a Dial-Up Networking Server," p. 514

In addition to providing general information about the modem such as port number, resources, and UART type, the diagnostics dialog box also shows the responses from the modem to specific commands. An ERROR condition for some of these commands might not indicate an error—instead, the modem might not support that specific command. Multiple ERROR states, however, can indicate a modem configuration or communication problem.

Tip

Oddly, the modem diagnostic utility is a 16-bit application. For that reason, the diagnostics can't gain access to the port if another application is using or monitoring the port. If Microsoft Fax is listening for incoming faxes, turn off auto-answer before running the diagnostics. If Dial-Up Networking server software is running, disable dial-in temporarily to enable the diagnostics to run.

Configuring Telephony Settings

Although most of the TAPI control of the modem and COM ports occurs transparently and is handled by Windows 95 and your applications, you can control a few TAPI properties. TAPI enables you to easily use your credit card to pay for calls, for example. TAPI also simplifies using a modem from different locations by letting you designate dialing locations that define the steps the modem needs to take to make the call (such as accessing an outside line). The following sections explain the TAPI settings you can configure in Windows 95.

Setting Dialing Properties

Each modem driver instance in Windows 95 has various dialing properties. These properties control the way the modem dials a call. Dialing properties are associated with a dialing location, which enables you to create different sets of dialing properties for the different locations from which you use your modem.

If you are dialing from a hotel, for example, you probably need to dial an 8 to access an outside line and might need to use a credit card to pay for the call. If you're dialing from work, you might need to dial a 9 to access an outside line. Windows 95 lets you create dialing locations that take these special dialing requirements into account. Instead of resetting your dialing properties each time you need to dial from a particular location, you simply specify the location from which you're dialing. Windows 95 then automatically uses the correct properties.

> **Note**
>
> Dialing properties apply only to Windows 95 applications (Win32) that use TAPI to access the port and handle calls. Windows 3.x and DOS programs do not (and cannot) make use of dialing locations and their properties. Each Windows 3.x or DOS program must handle its own special dialing requirements.

Typically, you can set dialing properties from within a Windows 95 application, and the Phone Dialer is a good example. To run the Phone Dialer, choose Start, Programs, Accessories, and Phone Dialer. To set dialing properties in the Phone Dialer, choose Tools, Dialing Properties. You also can use the Modems object in the Control Panel to specify dialing properties. To do so, choose the Modems icon in the Control Panel; select the modem whose dialing properties you want to change, and then choose Dialing Properties. Windows 95 displays the Dialing Properties sheet shown in figure 3.16. If you have never set dialing properties before, Windows 95 will first prompt you for your area code before displaying the Dialing Properties sheet.

▶ See "Using the Phone Dialer," p. 78

Windows 95 creates a default location called Default Location and stores in it a set of general dialing properties (see fig. 3.17). To create a new dialing location, choose the New button. Windows 95 will display a simple dialog box to prompt you for a name for the new dialing location. Enter a name and choose OK. Windows 95 will return to the Dialing Properties sheet so you can specify properties for the new location. The following list explains these properties:

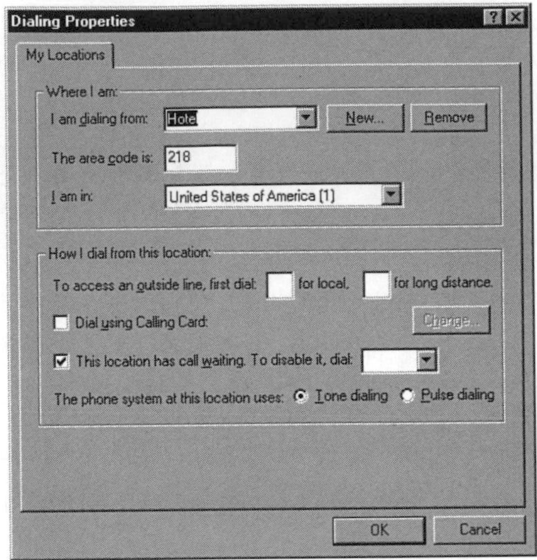

Fig. 3.16
You can configure dialing locations using the Dialing Properties sheet.

- *I Am Dialing from.* The property specifies the name of the location.
- *The Area Code Is.* Enter the area code of the location from which you're dialing. Windows 95 uses the area code to differentiate between local and long distance calls.
- *I Am in.* Choose the country from which you're calling. Windows 95 uses the country code to determine if special international calling codes are required for a call.
- *For Local.* Specify the number required to access a local outside line (if any).
- *For Long Distance.* Specify the number required to access a local long distance line (if any).
- *Dial Using Calling Card.* Enable this check box if you want TAPI to dial the call using a credit card. Read the section that follows, "Configuring Calling Card Options," to learn how to set up and use a calling card.
- *This Location Has Call Waiting.* Enable this check box if the location uses call waiting. Then, choose the method for disabling call waiting that applies to your location. The standard selections are *70, 70#, and 1170. Click in the combo box and enter your own prefix for disabling call waiting if it is different from the three standard options.
- *Tone Dialing and Pulse Dialing.* Choose the type of dialing method supported by your location.

When you have finished setting the dialing properties, you can click New to create another location or choose OK to close the dialog box and save the changes.

Setting Calling Card Options

Unlike Windows 3.x and DOS programs, Windows 95 makes it simple to charge a modem call to your calling card. In Windows 3.x and DOS, you often have to enter complicated dialing strings in a program every time you need to charge a call. With Windows 95 programs and TAPI, it's simple.

Each dialing location can use a different calling card. To define the calling card properties for a dialing location, display the Dialing Properties sheet for the location, then place a check in the Dial using Calling Card check box. Windows 95 then displays the Change Calling Card dialog box shown in figure 3.17.

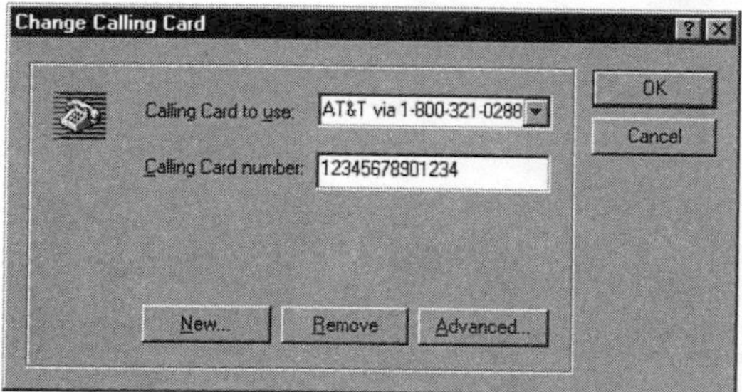

Fig. 3.17
You can easily set up a location to use a phone credit card (calling card) to bill calls.

Calling Card Properties

Charging a call to a credit card isn't the only use for the Calling Card properties in a dialing location. The Change Calling Card properties dialog box includes selections that store the dialing strings necessary to access specific long distance carriers without using a credit card. To access an AT&T carrier, for example, you usually dial 10ATT1 (102881), followed by the number you want to dial. The initial dialing string connects you to the carrier, and the call is billed to the number from which you're calling. When you choose one of these direct-dial options, Windows 95 dims the Calling Card number text box, since no credit card number is required.

To set up a calling card, select from the Calling card to Use drop-down list the carrier and dialing method you want to use. Windows 95 enables the Calling Card number text box so you can enter your calling card number. To view the dialing string Windows 95 will use, click the Advanced button to display the Dialing Rules dialog box shown in figure 3.18.

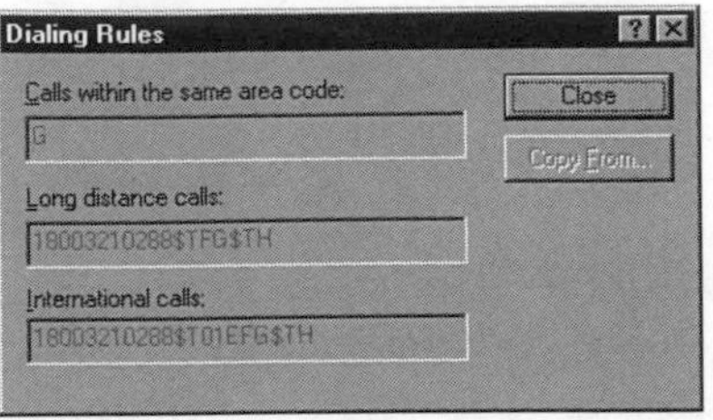

Fig. 3.18
The Dialing Rules dialog box shows the dialing string TAPI uses to dial the call.

> **Tip**
>
> The controls in the Dialing Rules dialog box are dimmed if you select one of the predefined calling card options. This safety feature prevents you from corrupting the standard entries. If you want to change dialing rules, you must first create a new calling card definition (see "Creating a New Calling Card" below).

At this point, you can't change the dialing rules, so just choose OK to close the dialog box. After you specify the calling card properties, close the Dialing Properties and Modem Properties pages. You'll be able to select your new dialing location from your Windows 95 communications programs.

Creating a New Calling Card

You can't change Windows 95's predefined calling card entries, but you can create new ones based on them. These new calling cards can be changed.

To create a new calling card, use the following procedure:

1. Open the Modems object in Control Panel, select the appropriate modem, then click the Dialing Properties button.
2. Place a check in the Dial Using Calling Card check box, or if the check box is already enabled, click the Change button to display the Change Calling Card dialog box.
3. Click the New button.
4. Provide a name for the new calling card when prompted to do so by Windows 95, then choose OK.
5. Click the Advanced button to display the Dialing Rules dialog box. Enter the dialing rules to use or click the Copy From button to copy from an existing calling card definition. Use table 3.3 as a guide to understanding dialing rules.

Table 3.3 Dialing Rule Codes

Code	Description
E	Country code
F	Area code
G	Destination local number
H	Calling card number
P	Pulse dial
T	Tone dial
W	Wait for a second dial tone
@	Wait for a ringing tone followed by 5 seconds of silence
,	Pause for two seconds
$	Wait for a carrier prompt tone if your modem supports it (such as AT&T's chime tone)
?	Display an on-screen prompt to the user to continue dialing manually

Editing the Toll Prefix List

Unless you're in a very large metropolitan area, most calls in your area that use a different call prefix probably are toll calls. In most areas of the US today, you must enter the area code for calls inside your own area code. Through TAPI, Windows 95 keeps track of which calls are toll calls.

There is not a direct method in Control Panel to edit the toll prefix list, but you can edit the list using Phone Dialer or Microsoft Fax. To edit the toll prefix list from Microsoft Fax, open Exchange and choose Tools, Microsoft Fax Tools, and Services. Select the Microsoft Fax item and choose Properties. When the Microsoft Fax property sheet appears, click the Dialing tab to display the Dialing property page. Click the Toll Prefixes button to display the Toll Prefixes dialog box shown in figure 3.19.

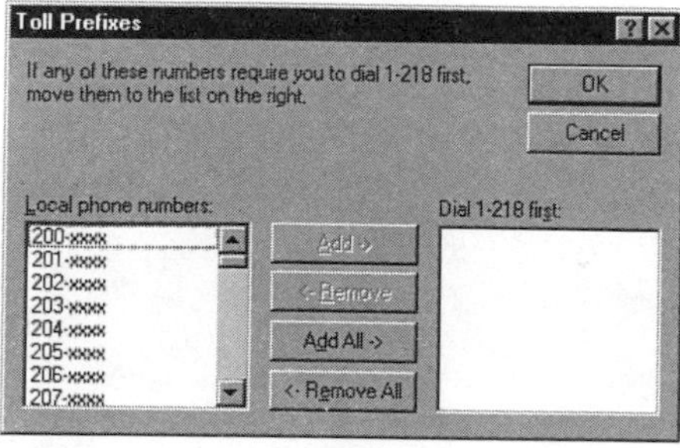

Fig. 3.19 Through Microsoft Fax you can easily edit the toll prefix list.

The Toll Prefixes dialog box lists all phone prefixes from 200 through 999. To specify a prefix as a toll call, select the prefix from the Local Phone Numbers list, then choose Add.

To modify the toll prefix list from the Phone Dialer, open the Phone Dialer (choose Start, Programs, Accessories, and Phone Dialer). Choose Tools, Dialing Properties to open the Dialing Properties page. Enable the check box labeled Dial as a Long Distance Call to add the prefix to the toll list, or clear the check box to remove the prefix from the toll list.

Tip

You can easily add a prefix to the toll list when dialing the number. The application you're using probably lets you set the dialing properties for a connection. Just display the connection's dialing properties page, then place a check in the check box labeled Dial as a Long Distance Call.

Using the Phone Dialer

Windows 95 includes a simple TAPI program called Phone Dialer that you might find useful for speed-dialing your phone or setting various dialing properties. To start Phone Dialer, choose Start, Programs, Accessories, and Phone Dialer. Figure 3.20 shows the Phone Dialer program window.

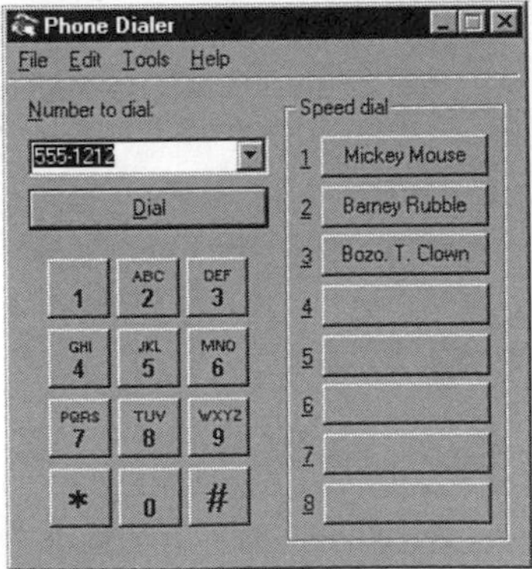

Fig. 3.20
You can use the Phone Dialer to speed-dial calls with your modem.

To store speed-dial numbers in the Phone Dialer, choose Edit, Speed Dial. Phone Dialer displays the Edit Speed Dial dialog box shown in figure 3.22. Click one of the numbered buttons to select it, then enter a name in the Name text box. Enter Number to Dial text box the phone number to associate with the name. When you're satisfied with the speed-dial list, choose Save. The new names will appear on the buttons in the Phone Dialer main window. Just click a button to dial the number.

To dial a number that isn't stored in the speed dial list, type the number in the Number to Dial combo box and click Dial. Phone Dialer keeps track of the numbers you dial this way, so you can just select a number from the Number to Dial combo box if you've dialed the number previously using Phone Dialer. ❖

CHAPTER 4

Configuring Parallel Ports

by Jim Boyce

Until recently, only serial-port communications devices were available for PCs. High-performance parallel ports have been standard on new PCs for a few years now, but their usefulness was limited primarily to printing and the recent range of new parallel port devices such as CD-ROM drives and sound adapters. With the introduction of Windows 95, it's now possible to use parallel port modems to provide a performance boost for data communications.

This chapter explains your PC's parallel ports and offers tips on configuring those ports for devices such as parallel port modems. In this chapter, you learn how to

- Understand the workings of parallel ports
- Enable and configure parallel ports

Understanding Parallel Ports

Although you've probably had your share of problems with printers, your PC's parallel ports have probably worked flawlessly. At least connecting your printer to the PC was easy, even if getting the printer to format the page properly proved to be a challenge.

Parallel ports have long been synonymous with *printer ports*, because by far the most common use for a parallel port has been to connect a printer to the PC. Today, however, an increasing number of other types of peripherals are taking advantage of the parallel port's faster speed. A new crop of portable CD-ROM drives, sound adapters, network adapters, and even modems connect through the PC's parallel port. To understand the advantage that the parallel port offers over a serial port, you need to understand the way in which data is transferred across a parallel port connection.

Parallel Port Data Transfer

In Chapter 3, "Configuring Modems and Ports," you learned that a serial port breaks a byte of data into individual bits, then transfers those bits one at a time. The receiving system must then translate the bits back into bytes before they can be processed. It's like eight cars all going the same way on a one-lane bridge—only one car can cross the bridge at a time, so all eight have to cross in single file.

Parallel ports derive their name from the fact that data travels through the port *in parallel lines*. Eight of the lines in a parallel port are designated as data lines. When a byte is transferred through the port, each bit in the byte travels over its own data line in parallel with the other bits. Now, you have an eight-lane bridge, and all eight of those imaginary cars can travel across at the same time.

Note

In addition to the eight data lines, a parallel port uses other lines to handle flow control and other aspects of the data transfer.

Unidirectional versus Bidirectional

The original parallel port design was intended to only accommodate printers. None of the printers available at the time were capable of sending data to the PC other than general signals such as paper out, and these signals were handled by dedicated lines in the cable. So, communication with the printer was unidirectional—the data flowed only from the PC to the printer, and not vice versa.

With the introduction of the PS/2 line, IBM formally adopted a bidirectional parallel port. Today, most PCs contain bidirectional parallel ports, which make it possible not only for advanced printers to communicate with the PC, but also for devices such as CD-ROM drives, sound adapters, network adapters, and modems to connect to the PC's parallel port. These types of devices cannot work with a unidirectional port.

Therefore, before you buy a parallel port modem or any other device that connects to your PC's parallel ports, you should make sure that the ports support bidirectional communication. You also should verify that your BIOS supports Enhanced Capabilities Ports (ECP) (see the next section for information on BIOS upgrades to support ECP).

ECP and EPP

The parallel ports in most of today's PCs support two additional operating modes: Enhanced Capabilities Port (ECP) and Enhanced Parallel Port (EPP). Both are extensions of the PS/2 bidirectional port that provide increased performance and new capabilities for the PC's parallel port. EPP provides for asynchronous parallel data transfer, and ECP provides for synchronous parallel data transfer. The ECP port, which is supported in Windows 95 for such devices as parallel port modems, offers a data transfer rate of 2 to 4 MB per second. Data transfer through a parallel port modem will not reach those speeds, but can be faster than a serial modem.

Enabling and Configuring Parallel Ports

When you install Windows 95, Setup should detect your PC's parallel ports without any difficulty, and should install support for them automatically. However, your ports might not be configured properly in your PC's BIOS, which will prevent Windows 95 from taking full advantage of the ports. Therefore, your first step should be to configure the ports in the BIOS.

Enabling ECP Ports

ECP is a BIOS-enabled function, which means that ECP support is primarily a function of your system's BIOS, rather than the actual parallel port circuitry. If your PC is fairly old, its BIOS probably doesn't support ECP. Even so, it's likely that you can replace or update your BIOS to support ECP. If yours is an older system without a flash-ROM BIOS, you'll have to replace the BIOS chips. To locate a source of chips, contact your PC's manufacturer.

Tip

If your system contains a Phoenix Ltd. BIOS, you can contact MicroFirmware at 800-767-5465 or 405-321-8333 for information on BIOS upgrades. Before calling, make sure you have your current BIOS revision number available. You can determine your PC's BIOS type and revision number by watching the text that appears on the display when the PC is booting.

If your PC contains a flash-ROM BIOS, the BIOS can be upgraded through a software program provided by your computer manufacturer or the BIOS manufacturer. Check with the PC's manufacturer first to determine if they have available an update for your BIOS. If not, the manufacturer should be able to direct you to a source that will have it.

How you enable ECP in your PC's BIOS depends on the BIOS itself. You'll need to run the BIOS Setup program, which varies from one BIOS to another. How you start the BIOS Setup program also varies from one to another. Check your system's manual to determine how to run the BIOS Setup program, then use the program to enable ECP support for your parallel port(s).

Tip

How you start your system's BIOS Setup program varies with the type of BIOS your system contains. On some systems, you press the Delete key while the system is booting to activate BIOS Setup. On other systems, you press Ctrl+Alt+S or Ctrl+Alt+F1. Because the method varies, you must check your system manual to determine how to start the BIOS Setup program on your PC.

Configuring ECP in Windows 95

Even after you enable ECP in the BIOS, Windows 95 will not recognize automatically that you have an ECP in the system. So, you must manually configure the port.

First, you must remove the existing parallel port entry from the Registry. Then, add the ECP using the same resource settings as the printer port entry. Use the following procedure to remove the existing parallel port entry in preparation for adding an ECP entry to the Registry:

1. Open the Control Panel and double-click the System icon.
2. Choose the Device Manager tab, then expand the Ports branch.
3. Select the printer port you have configured in the BIOS as an ECP, then click Properties.
4. Click the Resources tab to display the Resources property page, then write down the port's I/O range setting. You'll use this same setting for the ECP.
5. Choose Cancel to return to the Device Manager page.
6. Select the printer port you have configured in the BIOS as an ECP, then click Remove. Windows 95 will prompt you to verify the removal, and you should click OK.
7. Choose Close to close the System Properties sheet.

At this point, the parallel port entry is removed. If you restart Windows 95, it will not automatically redetect the port. Therefore, you must manually add the port using the following procedure:

1. Open the Control Panel and double-click the Add New Hardware icon to start the Add New Hardware wizard.
2. Click Next to move to the second wizard page, which prompts you to specify if you want the wizard to search for new hardware.
3. Choose the No option button, then choose Next.
4. From the Hardware types list (see fig. 4.1), choose Ports (COM and LPT), then choose Next.

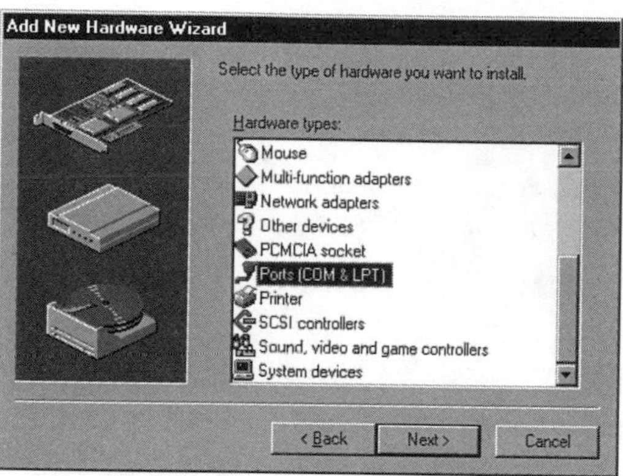

Fig. 4.1
The wizard enables you to select the type of device you are installing.

5. From the Manufacturer's list (see fig. 4.2), choose (Standard Port Types).

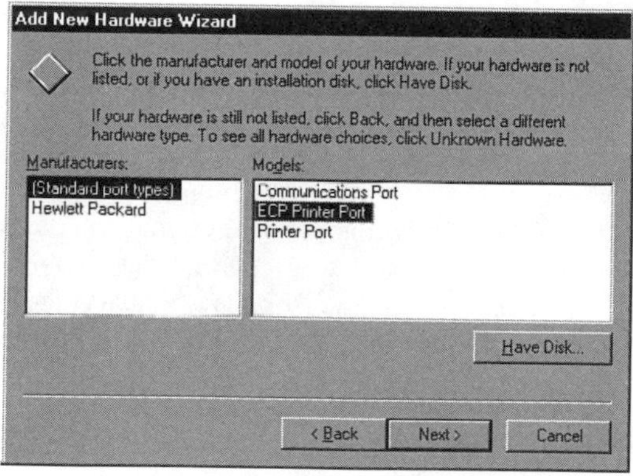

Fig. 4.2
You can manually select hardware to install, rather than letting Windows 95 detect it.

6. From the Models list, choose ECP Printer Port, then choose Next.
7. The wizard displays the resources it is assigning to the ECP. You'll have an opportunity to change resource properties later if necessary. Click Next to continue.

8. Click Finish to complete the process. Windows 95 will prompt you to restart the system. Close all applications, then click the Yes button to allow Windows 95 to restart.
9. After Windows 95 restarts, open the Device Manager again, expand the Ports branch, then select the ECP Printer Port and choose Properties.
10. Click the Resources tab and verify that the settings are correct for the port. If the settings are not correct, choose the correct settings, then choose OK to close the Resources page.
11. Close the System Properties sheet.

Troubleshooting

I'm having difficulty getting my Microcom parallel port modem to work under Windows 95. Are there any special setup requirements for it?

At present, only Microcom manufactures a parallel port modem for PCs.

Parallel port modems have yet to take off in popularity, and it's difficult to predict their future. Here are a few tips you might find helpful in setting up and using your modem in Windows 95:

- The built-in parallel detection and configuration support included with Windows 95 doesn't work properly. Download PPM401.EXE from the Microcom BBS, expand it to diskette, then run SETUP.EXE from that diskette.
- An older model of the modem will not reset/clear its own 300-baud parallel rate. Open a HyperTerminal session direct to the port, and enter the modem command **AT1532** to factory-set the modem. You should then have no problems switching between serial and parallel modes.
- If you're using 16-bit communication software that doesn't recognize the LPT port as a valid communications port, open the Parallel Modem object in the Control Panel (which is installed by Microcom software) to configure the port to emulate a COM port, then configure the software to use the specified COM port. Emulating a COM port should not affect your modem's performance, however.
- The Microcom DeskPorte FAST Reference manual states the modem automatically senses which port is connected and disables the other port. This is incorrect. The modem can be physically connected to both COM1 and LPT1, and will operate via whichever port is currently configured to the modem.

- If your modem doesn't include the V.34 chip update, check with Microcom about an upgrade. You can determine if the modem supports V.34 by checking the product package and manuals.

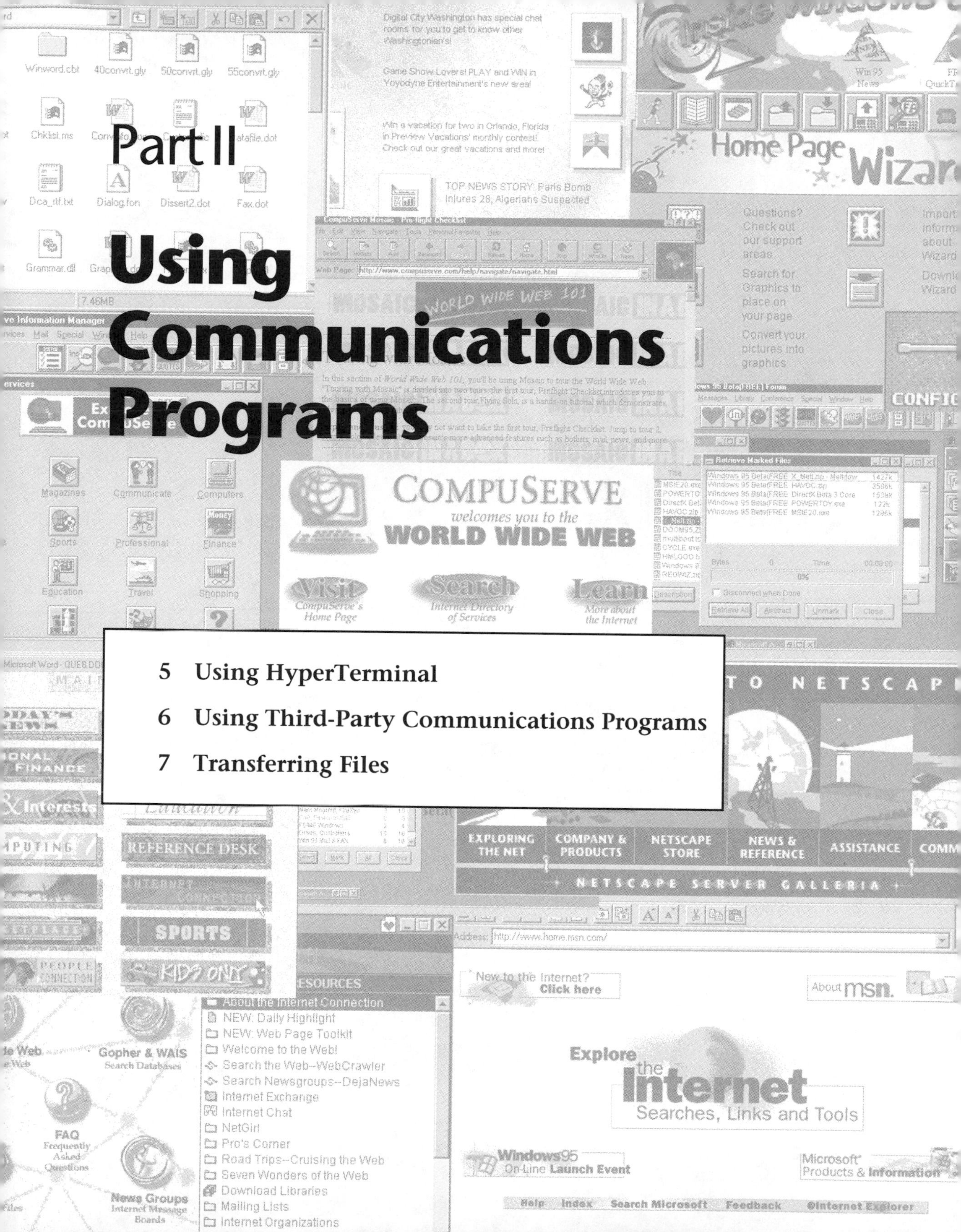

Part II

Using Communications Programs

View Help
Winword.cbt
40convrt.gly
50convrt.gly
55convrt.gly
Chklist.ms
Convinfo.doc
Custom.dic
Datafile.dot
Dca_rtf.txt
Dialog.fon
Dissert2.dot
Fax.dot
Grammar.dll
Graphics.doc
Hy_am.lex
Hyph.dll
7.46MB
Digital City Washington has special chat rooms for you to get to know other Washingtonian's!
Game Show Lovers! PLAY and WIN in Yoyodyne Entertainment's new area!
Win a vacation for two in Orlando, Florida in Preview Vacations' monthly contest! Check out our great vacations and more!
TOP NEWS STORY: Paris Bomb Injures 28, Algerians Suspected
Win 95 News
Home Page Wizard
Questions? Check out our support areas
Search for Graphics to place on your page
Convert your pictures into graphics
CompuServe Mosaic - Pre-flight Checklist
Web Page: http://www.compuserve.com/help/navigate/navigate.html
WORLD WIDE WEB 101
Touring with Mosaic
In this section of World Wide Web 101, you'll be using Mosaic to tour the World Wide Web. "Touring with Mosaic" is divided into two tours: the first tour, Preflight Checklist, introduces you to the basics of using Mosaic. The second tour, Flying Solo, is a hands-on tutorial which demonstrates advanced Mosaic features.
Experienced users: you may not want to take the first tour, Preflight Checklist. Jump to tour 2, Flying Solo, to learn about Mosaic's more advanced features such as hotlists, mail, news, and more
Windows 95 Beta(FREE) Forum
Retrieve Marked Files
Windows 95 Beta(FREE X_Melt.zip - Meltdow 1427k
Windows 95 Beta(FREE HAVOC.zip 3596K
Windows 95 Beta(FREE DirectX Beta 3 Core 1638k
Windows 95 Beta(FREE POWERTOY.exe 122k
Windows 95 Beta(FREE MSIE20.exe 1285k
Disconnect when Done
Retrieve All
Abstract
Unmark
Close
CompuServe Information Manager
Services Mail Special Window Help
Services
Explore CompuServe
Magazines
Communicate
Computers
Sports
Professional
Finance
Education
Travel
Shopping
COMPUSERVE
welcomes you to the
WORLD WIDE WEB
Visit
CompuServe's Home Page
Search
Internet Directory of Services
Learn
More about the Internet
To return to the WinCIM desktop, click on the
Microsoft Word - QUE8.DOC
CompuServe Informat...
MAIN MENU
TODAY'S NEWS
NEWSSTAND
PERSONAL FINANCE
Entertainment
Interests
Education
COMPUTING
REFERENCE DESK
INTERNET CONNECTION
SPORTS
KIDS ONLY
PEOPLE CONNECTION
WELCOME TO NETSCAPE
GENERAL STORE
EXPLORING THE NET
COMPANY & PRODUCTS
NETSCAPE STORE
NEWS & REFERENCE
ASSISTANCE
NETSCAPE SERVER GALLERIA
RESOURCES
About the Internet Connection
NEW: Daily Highlight
NEW: Web Page Toolkit
Welcome to the Web!
Search the Web--WebCrawler
Search Newsgroups--DejaNews
Internet Exchange
Internet Chat
NetGirl
Pro's Corner
Road Trips--Cruising the Web
Seven Wonders of the Web
Download Libraries
Mailing Lists
Internet Organizations
World Wide Web
Browse the Web
Gopher & WAIS
Search Databases
FAQ
Frequently Asked Questions
FTP
Download Files
News Groups
Internet Message Boards
Address: http://www.home.msn.com/
New to the Internet? Click here
About msn.
Explore the Internet
Searches, Links and Tools
Windows95 On-Line Launch Event
Microsoft Products & Information
Help Index Search Microsoft Feedback Internet Explorer

CHAPTER 5

Using HyperTerminal

by Jim Boyce

Previous chapters have explained basic communications concepts in Windows 95 and helped you configure your ports and modem(s). In this chapter, you begin putting to work what you've learned so far about ports and modems. You'll start using a communications program to connect to online services, transfer files, and accomplish other communications tasks.

This chapter explores HyperTerminal—the communications program included with Windows 95. HyperTerminal enables you to dial into a BBS, online service, or other computer to access information and transfer files. Although HyperTerminal is by no means a full-featured communications program, it is an improvement over the Terminal program in Windows 3.x. You'll find HyperTerminal useful if you don't do a lot of file transfers or seldom need to connect to other systems. If you do connect or transfer files often, however, you'll probably want to buy one of the many third-party communications programs available for Windows 95.

This chapter provides an overview of HyperTerminal's features and functions, covering the following:

- Installing HyperTerminal
- Creating a connection
- Setting general properties
- Making and breaking a connection
- Capturing a session
- Using manual dialing

Installing HyperTerminal

▶ See "Using Third-Party Communications Programs," p. 109

If you selected the Communications option when you installed Windows 95, Setup installed HyperTerminal for you by default, and you don't need to add it to your PC. If you opted not to install HyperTerminal during Windows 95 installation or did not install the Communications options, you can easily add HypterTerminal.

To install HyperTerminal, follow these steps:

1. Open the Control Panel and double-click the Add/Remove Programs icon.
2. Click the Windows Setup tab to display the Windows Setup property page (see fig. 5.1).

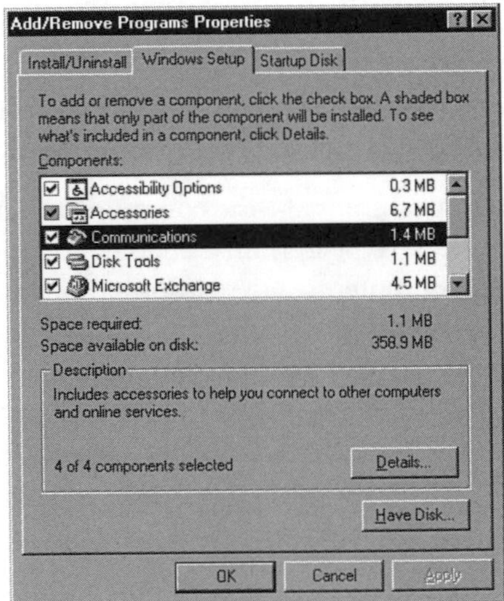

Fig. 5.1
You can easily add Windows 95 components with the Add/Remove Programs Properties sheet.

3. Select the Communications item from the Components list, and then click the Details button.
4. In the Communications dialog box (see fig. 5.2), place a check in the HyperTerminal check box, and then choose OK.
5. Choose OK again and follow Windows 95's prompts to complete the installation process. Windows 95 might prompt you to insert the Windows 95 CD or one of the Windows 95 disks.

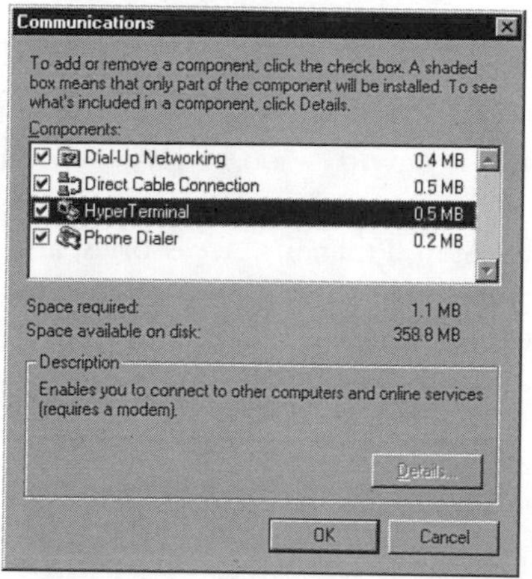

Fig. 5.2
HyperTerminal is one of the options you can install through the Communications item.

After you install HypterTerminal, you'll find a new item in the Accessories menu. Choose Start, Programs, Accessories, and HyperTerminal to open the HyperTerminal folder (see fig. 5.3). The HyperTerminal folder contains the HyperTerminal program. Any new connections you create also show up here. The next section explains how to create those new connections.

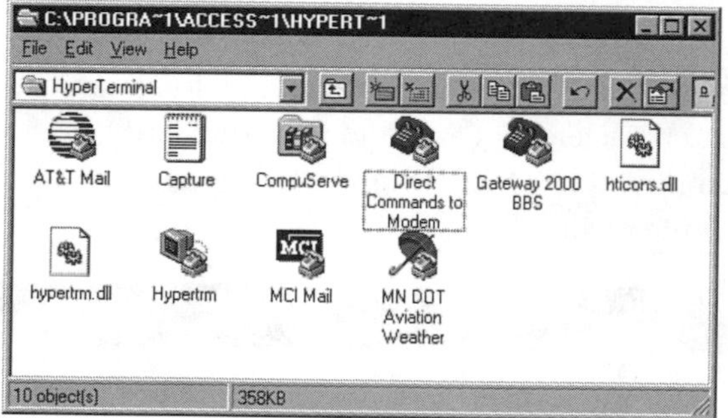

Fig. 5.3
The Hyper-Terminal folder contains any new connections you create.

Working with HyperTerminal

A selection of properties that define how HyperTerminal connects to a remote computer or service is called a *connection*. Each connection includes a phone number, terminal emulation type, and other properties that HyperTerminal uses to connect to the service. Creating a new connection is easy. The next section explains how.

Creating New Connections

All you have to do to create a new connection in HyperTerminal is start the program. HyperTerminal "knows" that it needs a phone number and other information before it can do its job, so HyperTerminal automatically prompts you for that information when you start the program. To start HypterTerminal, choose Start, Programs, Accessories, and HyperTerminal. When the HyperTerminal folder appears, double-click the Hypertrm icon. The HyperTerminal program window opens, and HyperTerminal prompts you to specify a name for the connection and choose an icon to represent it (see fig. 5.4).

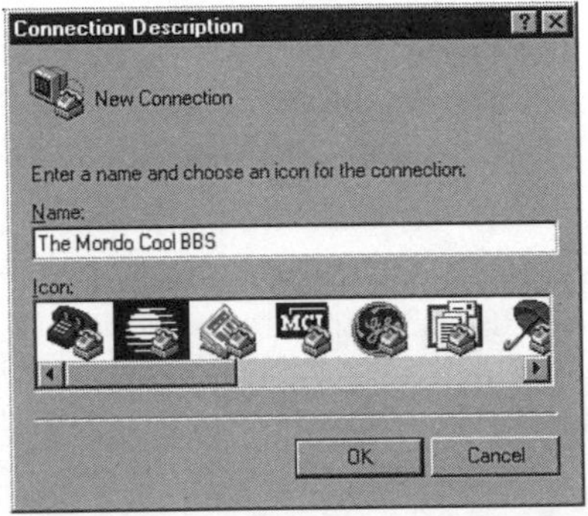

Fig. 5.4
HyperTerminal prompts you to specify a name and icon for a new connection in the Connection Description dialog box.

Type a name in the Name text box. You can use a long name that includes spaces and other characters that are valid for a standard Windows 95 long file name. HyperTerminal stores the settings in the HyperTerminal folder using this name as the file name.

> **Tip**
>
> In addition to letters and numbers, you can use the following characters in a Windows 95 long file name:
>
> $ % ' - _ @ ~ ' ! ( ) ^ # & + , ; = [ ] and space

Next, if you don't want to use the default icon for the connection (the first icon in the Icon box), click one of the 16 icons HyperTerminal displays in the Icon box. After you have selected an icon, click OK. HyperTerminal then displays the Phone Number dialog box that prompts you to enter a phone number and other properties for the connection (see fig. 5.5).

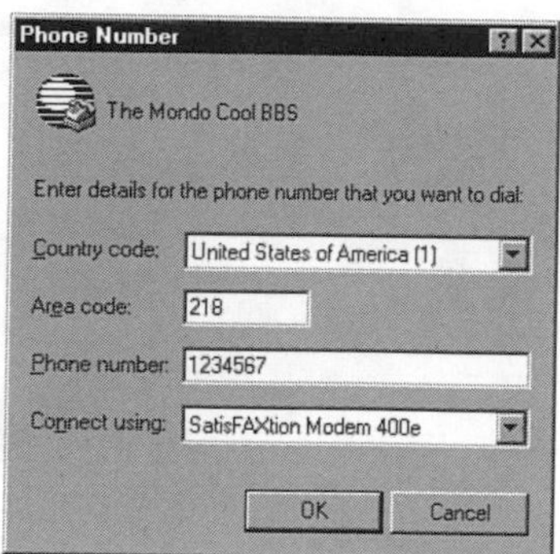

Fig. 5.5 HyperTerminal prompts you for the phone number and other connection properties.

From the Country Code drop-down list, choose the country in which the computer you're calling is located. This property enables HyperTerminal to determine if a country code must be included in the dialing string, and which code to use.

◀ See "Installing and Configuring Modems," p. 63

In the Area Code and Phone Number text boxes, type the area code and phone number of the computer to which you want to connect. Then, from the Connect Using drop-down List, choose the modem you want to use for the connection.

> **Note**
>
> The Connect Using drop-down List displays all of the modems currently installed. If you haven't installed any modems yet, you must do so before you can use HyperTerminal.

◀ See "Setting Dialing Properties," p. 73

◀ See "Installing and Configuring Modems," p. 63

After you specify the phone number and select a modem, choose OK. HyperTerminal then displays the Connect dialog box (see fig. 5.6), which you can use to either begin connecting to the remote computer or specify dialing properties. If you're ready to connect to the service, click the Dial button. To change dialing properties, click the Dialing Properties button. Depending on the computer to which you're connecting, however, you might need to set some additional properties before connecting. To do so, click the Cancel button. The following sections explain these additional properties.

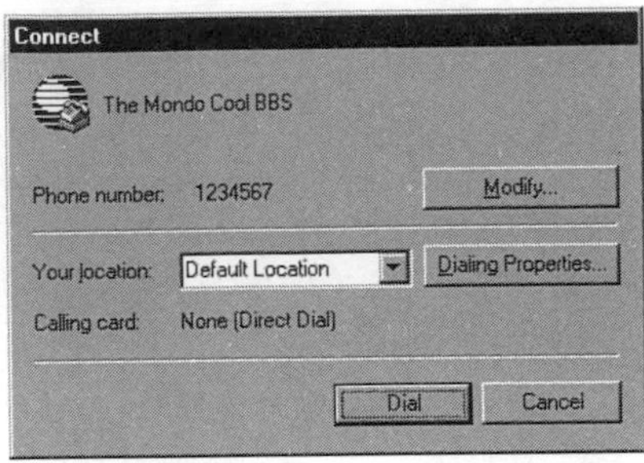

Fig. 5.6 Click the Dial button in the Connect dialog box to start the session.

Setting General Properties

Most online services provide custom front-end applications that provide settings which are tailor-made for the service. If you're dialing into a BBS, mainframe, or other type of system, however, you need to specify *terminal preferences* that define how the remote computer handles information coming and going through the connection. Before personal computers became so prevalent, most connections to mainframes and other multi-user systems were accomplished through *dumb terminals*. These text-only terminals provided the basic function of displaying information to the user and enabling him or her to send information to the computer. The terminal was not capable of running programs; all programs ran on the remote computer.

Therefore, mainframes had to support a variety of different terminal types. Naturally, standards emerged over the years, and these standards were based on various manufacturers' terminals. Today, these standards enable a PC to connect to these types of servers by emulating a dumb terminal. This means that the PC sends information to the system in the same format as the specified terminal type, and the receiving system interprets it accordingly.

HyperTerminal supports six different terminal types that ensure compatibility with almost any computer system. To choose a terminal type for a connection, first determine what terminal type the remote system supports. Then, in HyperTerminal, choose File, Properties. When the connection's property sheet appears, click the Settings tab to display the Settings property page (see fig. 5.7).

The following list explains the properties you can set in the Settings page:

- *Terminal Keys* and *Windows Keys*. These two options control how cursor keys, function keys, and Ctrl keys are interpreted. Choose Terminal Keys if you want these characters to be treated as terminal keystrokes and be transmitted to the remote computer. Choose Windows Keys if you want the Keys to apply to the Windows 95 environment and not be transmitted to the remote computer.

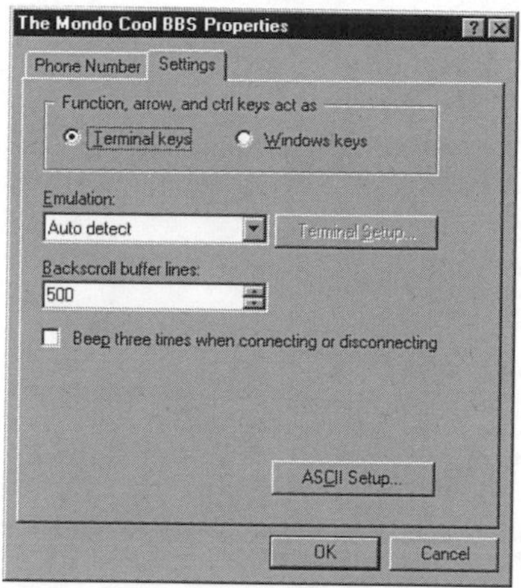

Fig. 5.7
The Settings page enables you to choose a terminal type for Hyper-Terminal to emulate.

- *Emulation*. Select from this drop-down list the type of terminal emulation you want HyperTerminal to perform. The section "Setting Terminal Options" later in this chapter explains this in more detail.
- *Backscroll Buffer Lines*. This spin control specifies the number of lines of incoming data that HyperTerminal will retain in a buffer. If you want to view a screen of information you received from the remote computer, you can scroll up in the terminal window to view it. The maximum is 500 lines. If you want to conserve a little memory (a minimal amount), you can reduce the buffer size.
- *Beep Three Times when Connecting or Disconnecting*. Enable this check box if you want HyperTerminal to beep three times when it connects or disconnects from a remote computer.

Tip

If you're unsure which terminal emulation to use, select the Auto detect setting. Using this setting, HyperTerminal will attempt to detect the proper emulation for you. If this setting fails to work correctly, try the TTY type, which will give you text-only support and should enable you to work connect. If you want to use special graphics characters (such as line-drawing characters), try the VT100 terminal type.

Setting Terminal Options

The settings you can specify for terminal emulation vary from one type of terminal to another. After you select a terminal type from the Emulation drop-down list, you therefore can set a few options for that type. To do so, first select a terminal type, then click the Terminal Setup button. The dialog box that appears depends on the type of emulation you've selected. The VT100 type, however, covers most of the possible options (see fig. 5.8).

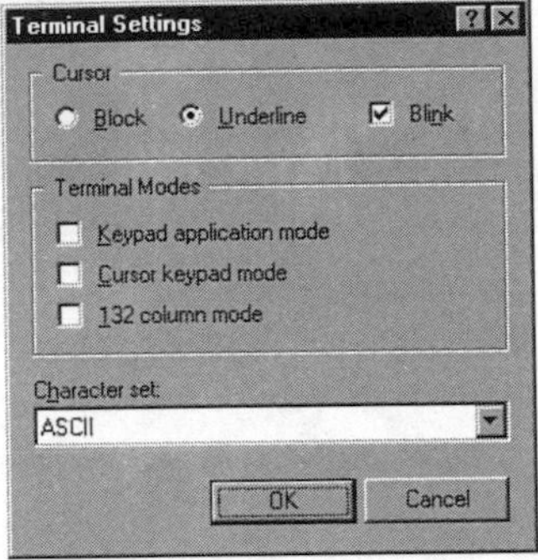

Fig. 5.8
The Settings page enables you to choose a terminal type for Hyper-Terminal to emulate.

The following list explains the most common terminal emulation settings:

- *Cursor*. The three option buttons in this group let you define the appearance of the cursor. You can choose from a block cursor, underline cursor, or blinking cursor.
- *Keypad Application Mode*. Enable this check box if you want numeric keypad entries to be interpreted as special program control codes to control a program running on the remote computer. You can disable this check box for almost all online services and BBSs.
- *Cursor Keypad Mode*. Enable this check box if you want cursor keys to be treated as special application keys. Leave the check box disabled if you want the cursor keys treated as cursor keys.
- *132 Column Mode*. Enable this check box if you want to use 132 columns instead of 80 columns, fitting more characters on a line.
- *Character Set*. Select from this drop-down list the character set you want to use.

Setting ASCII Options

A number of additional settings control the way text is transferred across the connection in both directions. To define these settings, click the ASCII Setup button on the Settings property page. Doing so displays the ASCII Setup dialog box shown in figure 5.9.

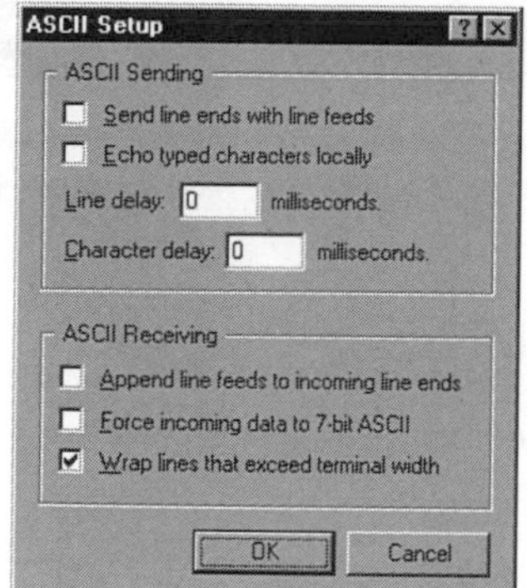

Fig. 5.9
The ASCII Setup dialog box controls how text is handled.

The options in the ASCII Setup dialog box are explained in the following list:

- *Send Line Ends with Line Feeds*. Enable this check box if you want HyperTerminal to append a carriage return character with each line feed character.
- *Echo Typed Characters Locally*. Enable this check box if you want HyperTerminal to echo to the display the characters that you type. If you don't see characters on the display when you type, enable this option.
- *Line Delay*. This option specifies a delay in milliseconds that HyperTerminal waits before transmitting each line. Generally, you can leave this option set to zero. Increase the setting only if you feel characters are being lost by the receiving system.
- *Character Delay*. This option specifies a delay in milliseconds that HyperTerminal waits before transmitting individual characters. As with Line delay, you can usually leave this setting at zero.
- *Append Line Feeds to Incoming Line Ends*. Enable this check box if you want HyperTerminal to append a line feed character to each incoming line (usually required only if the sending system does not append a line feed character on its own).
- *Force Incoming Data to 7-Bit ASCII*. Enable this setting if you need HyperTerminal to convert incoming 8-bit characters into 7-bit ASCII characters (when performing 7-bit ASCII text transfer, for example).
- *Wrap Lines that Exceed Terminal Width*. Enable this check box if you want HyperTerminal to automatically wrap lines longer than your specified column width. Clear the check box if you want the text to scroll past the edge of the terminal window.

Troubleshooting

When I type characters during a communications session, they don't appear in the terminal window, but the remote computer seems to be recognizing them. Why can't I see the characters?

You need to configure the connection to echo characters locally. With echoing turned on, each character is displayed in the terminal window and also sent to the remote computer. To turn on local echo, enable the Echo Typed Characters Locally check box in the ASCII Setup dialog box.

I can see the characters that I type, but they're "stuck" on the same line with incoming text.

To make text that you type start on a new line, enable the Send Line Ends with Line Feeds check box on the ASCII Setup dialog box. To cause incoming text to start on a new line, enable the Append Line Feeds to Incoming Line Ends check box on the ASCII Setup dialog box.

Making and Breaking Connections

After you configure the connection, you're ready to connect to the remote system. To establish the connection, just choose Call, Connect. HyperTerminal displays the Connect dialog box shown in figure 5.6. If the phone number and other settings are correct, click the Dial button. HyperTerminal dials the remote computer.

If you need to change the phone number, country code, modem, icon, or port properties for the connection, click the Modify button instead of the Dial button. The connection's property sheet opens so you can change its properties. After you set the necessary properties and close the property sheet, the new settings appear in the Connect dialog box, and you can choose Dial to start the session based on the new settings.

After HyperTerminal dials and connects to the remote system, you might not see any indication of a connection. Many systems require that you press Enter or Ctrl+C to get the remote system's attention and generate a logon prompt.

To disconnect a connection, first log off of the remote system, if necessary. How you log off depends on the remote system. Most BBSs use either the BYE or EXIT command. Others offer a logoff option in their menus. In most cases, the connection will terminate automatically when HyperTerminal senses that the remote system has hung up the connection. You can manually disconnect the session by choosing Call, Disconnect.

Transferring Files

One common use for communications programs such as HyperTerminal is to transfer files. For example, you might want to transfer a game, driver, or other file from a BBS to your computer. Chapter 7, "Transferring Files," explains file transfer protocols and other topics related to file transfer. To get you started, here is a brief explanation of how to download a file to your computer using HyperTerminal:

1. Connect to the service and determine the name of the file you want to download.
2. Determine which file transfer protocol(s) the service supports. HyperTerminal supports 1K Xmodem, Xmodem, Ymodem, Ymodem-G, Zmodem, and Kermit. Of these, Zmodem is your best choice because of its faster speed and ability to recover from interrupted transfers (see Chapter 7 for a more in-depth explanation.)

▶ See "Choosing a Protocol," p. 134

3. Locate the remote file and choose the remote system's download option (varies from one system to another).
4. Specify to the remote system the protocol you want to use (the system should prompt you to select a protocol after you select the download option).
5. The remote system indicates it is starting the download. In HyperTerminal, choose Transfer, Receive File. The Receive File dialog box appears (see fig. 5.10).

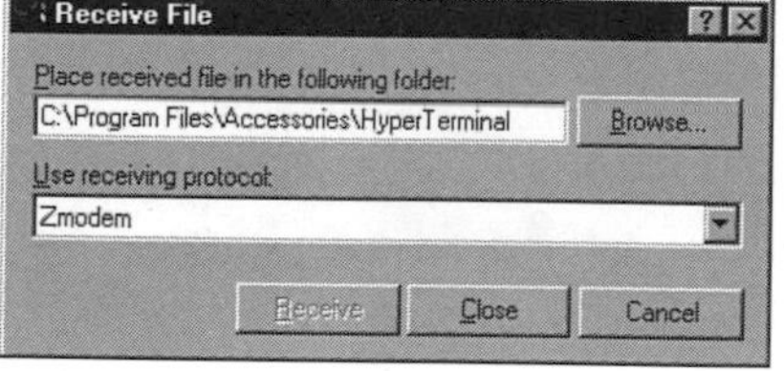

Fig. 5.10
You must specify a file name and protocol when downloading a file.

6. In the text box labeled Place Received File in the Following Folder, enter the path to the folder where you want the file stored. Or, click on the Browse button and browse for a destination folder.
7. From the Use Receiving Protocol drop-down list, choose the protocol you specified to the remote system in step 4.
8. Choose Receive to begin the transfer.

> **Note**
>
> When you request to download a file using the Zmodem protocol, it will start the download automatically using the file name from the BBS. So it is important to tell HyperTerminal the correct Place Received File in the Following Folder before you start your download.

Uploading a file to a remote computer involves much the same procedure, except in reverse. Use these steps when uploading a file:

1. Connect to the service and, if necessary, change to the directory or file area on the remote system in which you want your file placed (varies from system to system).
2. Determine which file transport the remote system supports.
3. Choose the remote system's file upload option.
4. The system should prompt you for a transfer protocol, so choose a protocol supported by HyperTerminal.
5. The remote system might prompt you for a file name. If so, specify a file name by which you want the file stored on the remote system. The remote system displays a message that it is starting the upload.
6. Choose Transfer, Send File.
7. In the Send File dialog box (similar to the Receive File dialog box in figure 5.10), specify the path to the file you are uploading, as well as the protocol you specified in step 4.
8. Choose Send to begin the transfer.

In addition to sending files with the previously explained procedures, you also can send a text file to the remote system. In essence, this capability enables you to "type" a large amount of text to the remote system. For example, you might create an e-mail message with Notepad, then log onto the remote system to upload it. Instead of typing the message after you log on, you can start the e-mail compose function on the remote system, and then upload the text file. The result is the same as if you had typed the entire message line by line.

To send a text file, follow these steps:

1. Create the text file using Notepad or any other ASCII text editor and save it.
2. Connect to the remote system.
3. On the remote system, proceed through the process of composing the message, but don't type the body of the message.

4. Choose Transfer, Send Text File.
5. HyperTerminal displays a common file dialog box. Use the dialog box to locate the text file you want to send to the remote system; then choose Open to begin the transfer.

Tip

In addition to sending a text file in this way, you also can upload a text file. To upload a text file, use the same procedure described earlier for uploading a binary file. When prompted for the file to upload, specify the path to the text file.

Troubleshooting

Occasionally, a file transfer fails, particularly when I'm using Zmodem. Is there a way to avoid those transfer problems?

Because it doesn't acknowledge every packet, Zmodem is more sensitive to errors than other protocols. Often, the packet errors are the result of a noisy phone line. You might be able to limit the problem by making sure the hardware error connect is turned on or by connecting at a lower baud rate. To set the baud rate, choose File, Properties. Click on the Configure button, then choose a baud rate from the Maximum Speed drop-down list. Choose OK, then OK again.

Capturing a Session

If you're reading text files on the remote system, you might want to copy the file to your system as you read it, or simply let the file scroll by on the screen and be stored on your system for reading later. Or, you might want to keep a log of your entire session, complete with all of the text going to and from the remote system. HyperTerminal enables you to capture a session to disk, which writes all incoming and outgoing text to a file, giving you a transcript of your online session. You can start and stop capturing text at any point, and you also can temporarily pause the capture, then resume it when you want.

Tip

Using a capture file is a great way to save a few dollars. Instead of reading a text file online, turn on capture and quickly scroll through the file. After the entire file has scrolled, log off and read the captured text file using Notepad or WordPad.

To begin capturing text, simply choose Transfer, Capture Text. HyperTerminal displays the Capture Text dialog box shown in figure 5.11. Enter the path and file name of a text file in which you want to store the session, or click the Browse button to select a path and file. After you've specified the path and file name, click the Start button in the Capture Text dialog box. All text going to and from the remote system also will be written to the specified file.

Fig. 5.11 Specify the name of the file in which you want to store your online session.

To temporarily pause the session capture, choose Transfer, Capture Text, and Pause. To resume capturing the session, choose Transfer, Capture Text, and Resume. When you're ready to stop capturing the session, choose Transfer, Capture Text, and Stop.

Manual Modem Initialization, Testing, and Dialing

Occasionally, you might need to send commands directly to your modem to test the modem, initiate a connection when normal dialing methods don't apply, or send special setup commands to the modem. HyperTerminal offers an easy means of controlling your modem directly. You can send commands to the modem before it dials, after it dials, or specify that you want to dial the number manually rather than let the modem dial the number. The following sections offer tips on how to accomplish these tasks.

Sending Commands to the Modem

Although you will most often let your communications program initialize the modem through the configuration properties (set through the Modems icon in Control Panel), occasionally you might need to send commands manually to the modem. For example, you can use this method to troubleshoot a connection problem. If one of your communications programs is unable to access or dial the modem, you can open HyperTerminal and use it to send commands to the modem to test it.

Although you don't have to do so, you might want to create a connection specifically for manual modem testing and initialization. To do so, follow these steps:

1. Open the HyperTerminal folder and choose the Hypertrm icon to start HyperTerminal.
2. Specify an appropriate name such as **Direct Commands to Modem**, then select an icon for the connection and choose OK.
3. When prompted for an area code and phone number for the connection, select Direct to Com *n* from the Connect Using drop-down list, where *n* is the port to which your modem is connected. For example, select Direct to Com 2 if your modem is connected to COM 2. The other text boxes will become disabled, indicating you don't have to provide a phone number or any other settings.
4. Choose OK.
5. HyperTerminal displays the property page for the port (fig. 5.12). Set the properties as desired, then choose OK.

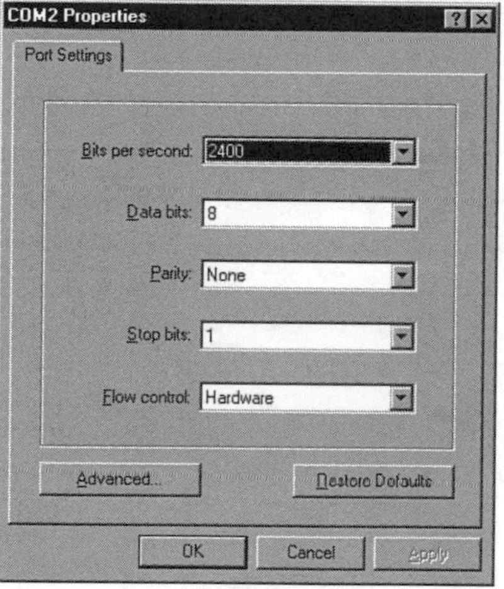

Fig. 5.12
Specify settings for the port.

6. Choose File, Save to save the connection settings.

At this point, you have a connection you can use whenever you want to send commands directly to the modem for testing or initialization. To use the connection, open the HyperTerminal folder and double-click the connection's icon. When the Connect dialog box appears, click the Dial button, or simply begin typing modem commands. If your modem is working properly, you should receive response codes from the modem after each command (see fig. 5.13). To verify that the connection is open, for example, enter the command **AT**. For other modem commands, consult your modem's manual.

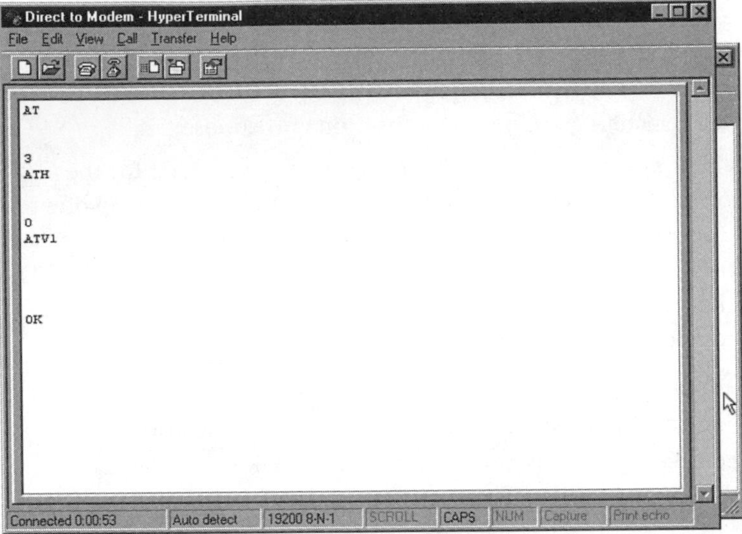

Fig. 5.13
You can send commands to the modem and receive responses to those commands.

Tip

If you need to send commands to the modem after dialing, or you want to monitor the modem's status after dialing, enable the check box labeled Bring up Terminal Window After Dialing on the modem's property sheet. After dialing, Windows 95 displays a terminal window in which you can enter modem commands or simply monitor the status messages coming from the modem. You also can send commands to the modem before dialing by enabling the check box Bring Up Terminal Window Before Dialing.

Troubleshooting

I have a 16-bit Windows communications program that can't seem to see the modem. I don't have any Windows 95 communications programs running. When I try to enter commands to the modem, I receive a numeric response from the modem instead of character response such as OK. Does this indicate a problem?

First, make sure you don't have a program such as Microsoft Fax monitoring the modem port. If not, the problem is probably that the 16-bit program is expecting character response codes and isn't properly interpreting the numeric codes. Some other communications program might be resetting the modem when you use it, and the modem isn't being reset when the program exits. Check your modem manual to determine what command to send to the modem to enable character response codes (typically, ATV1 on Hayes-compatible modems). Send the command to the modem, then exit HyperTerminal and retry. If it works, add the same modem command to the 16-bit application's modem initialization string.

Using Manual Dialing

Occasionally, you might need to dial a number manually, rather than letting the modem do it for you. For example, if you're dialing from a hotel, you might need to connect with an operator first to get an outside line or provide special dialing information. Then, you can dial the number manually. When the connection is established, you can hang up the handset and begin using the connection.

To use manual dialing, follow these steps:

1. Open the connection's property sheet by choosing File, Properties.
2. Click the Configure button.
3. Click the Options tab to display the Options page.
4. Enable the check box labeled Operator Assisted or Manual Dial.
5. If you have configured the dialing properties to use a calling card, use the spin control labeled Wait for Credit Card Tone to specify the number of seconds you want HyperTerminal to wait for a credit card tone before continuing to dial. HyperTerminal doesn't actually wait for the tone, but instead waits the specified number of seconds.

> **Tip**
>
> You can include commas in a dialing string to cause the program to briefly pause dialing.

6. Choose OK to close the modem property sheet, then OK again to close the connection property sheet.
7. When you're ready to make the call, choose Call, Dial.
8. In the Connect dialog box, click the Dial button. HyperTerminal displays the Manual Dial dialog box shown in figure 5.14.

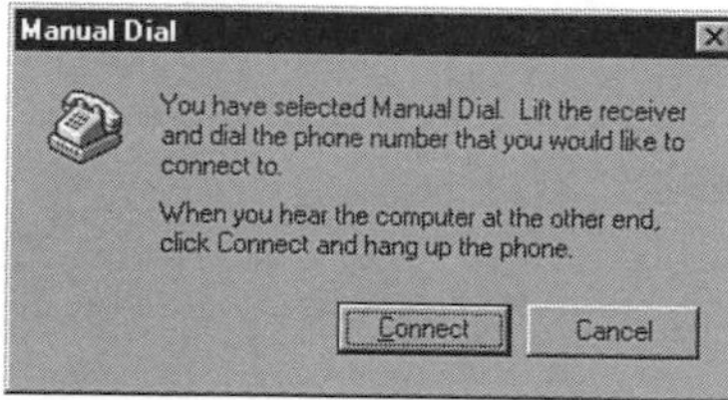

Fig. 5.14
After manually dialing the number, click Connect, then hang up the handset.

9. Lift the handset and dial manually.
10. When you hear the modem connect to the remote system, click the Connect button and hang up the handset. ❖

CHAPTER 6

Using Third-Party Communications Programs

by Robin Schreier Hohman

BBSs were once the only way for computer users to communicate by modem to exchange e-mail and transfer files. Although online services and the Internet are now more popular, thousands of viable BBSs still exist throughout the world.

Unlike commercial services such as CompuServe or America Online, rare is the BBS that provides you with software specifically designed for accessing it. However, nearly all BBSs can be accessed using some type of *communications program* that serves as the interface between you and the BBS. Using these "generic interface" communications programs, you can connect to other computers, send and receive files, send messages back and forth, and, of course, access BBSs.

As you learned in Chapter 5, "Using HyperTerminal," Windows 95 comes with a built-in communications program called HyperTerminal. Although it's a vast improvement over the Terminal program that came with Windows 3.*x*, HyperTerminal still is just a basic, no-frills utility. This is fine for occasional use, but if you want more power and automation, you'll have to look elsewhere.

That's where third-party communications programs come in. Typically, they offer more features than HyperTerminal and a glitzier interface. This chapter introduces you to some of the most popular third-party programs available today, including Mustang Software's Qmo demPro, Delrina's WinCommPRO, and PROCOMM PLUS from Datastorm Technologies, Inc.

In this chapter, you learn to

- Choose the program that's right for you
- Use file transfer protocols
- Work with terminal emulation

- Work in Host mode
- Use scripting languages

Choosing a Program

Which program you choose depends on your needs and your budget. Before you buy, you should give some thought to the specific tasks for which you might use the program. For example:

- Some programs, like Mustang Software's QmodemPro, have powerful Telnet features. Telnet lets you connect to a remote computer as a dumb terminal. This way you can use an Internet connection to connect to BBSs around the world, saving costly phone charges.
- If you're planning to use the software on a network server, find out if the communications program offers network support. Most do, but you'll want to make sure before investing time and money.

Know What You Need

In addition to the preceding examples, there are several other things to consider when determining which third-party communications program you will buy. By answering the following questions and noting which programs support these needs, you should be able to determine which program is right for you.

What Kind of User Are You?

If you are new to online communications, you don't want to be burdened with a high learning curve. Delrina's WinCommPRO offers many of the same features as QmodemPro, but has an easier-to-use interface (see "Earmarks of a Good Interface," later in the chapter).

For power users, Datastorm's PROCOMM PLUS, on the other hand, is not as intuitively designed, but is jam-packed with tools for accessing BBSs and the Internet—and you can customize almost any option.

You'll also have to consider site user license fees if you're going to use the software across a network.

What Kind of Modem Do You Have?

Communications programs generally offer drivers for dozens of popular modems; chances are your modem will be included. However, if you have a brand new, high-speed modem, you'll want to make sure there's an available driver. You can find out by calling the company's technical support or sales staff.

Where Do You Want to Use It?

Some programs allow you to set up sessions so that you can dial in from a remote location, transfer files, and exchange e-mail. QmodemPro, PROCOMM PLUS, and WinComm all support this *Host mode*. PROCOMM PLUS and WinComm take it one step farther and add security features to control who can get in. With PROCOMM PLUS, for example, the Host feature lets you set it up so that the remote user calls in and hangs up. The server or mainframe then calls the PC back, from a list of users and phone numbers. That way, you control who can get into your files.

What Kind of Terminal Emulation Do You Need?

Terminal emulation is another important feature for communications programs. Terminal emulation lets your PC operate as a dumb terminal of the host computer. This is especially important for connection to mini and mainframe systems. Most programs sport more than 30 terminal emulations, but you'll want to make sure that the one you need is supported.

For example, the IBM 3270 terminal emulation is used to connect with IBM mainframe computers. Both PROCOMM PLUS and QmodemPro have this option; WinCommPRO does not. Most BBSs support a range of terminal types that have become de facto standards. These terminal types, which are discussed in Chapter 5, "Using HyperTerminal," include VT100, VT52, and TTY. Most other types of servers, including UNIX servers, also support these terminal types.

Does the Program Include a Scripting Language?

Scripting languages are a powerful tool for communications programs. Scripts let you automate tasks such as logging in and downloading e-mail, accessing online services, or transferring files. All three programs discussed here offer scripting languages and ample documentation for using them. They also offer several sample scripts (see "Scripting Languages" later in the chapter).

QmodemPro uses the SLIQ language; PROCOMM PLUS uses ASPECT; and WinComm uses Delrina Basic, which is based on the same command set as Microsoft's Visual Basic for Applications (VBA) used in Microsoft Office 95. They're all powerful enough for most users. In addition, they all allow you to record a series of keystrokes so that you don't need to use the scripting languages for simple tasks.

Will You Need Chat Features?

When you're online, you'll sometimes want to talk to someone on the other end to ask questions. Chat utilities let you communicate in realtime using the PC's keyboard. Typically, you would invoke the chat utility, and you'll get a split screen to differentiate between the text you're sending and the text you're receiving.

Both PROCOMM PLUS and QmodemPro have chat utilities that are simple to use. The beta version of WinCommPRO used for this chapter didn't have a chat utility.

What About Virus Checking?

Another feature to keep in mind is virus scanning. Of the three programs featured here, WinCommPRO is the only one that scans for viruses while you're downloading.

This feature is intended to give you added security, but, remember, no program can guarantee it will scan for all viruses. There are also many third-party virus scanners that you can run on files after you've downloaded them.

Do You Need Graphics Viewing Capabilities?

The capability to view graphics files while downloading is a new feature for communications programs. QmodemPro, PROCOMM PLUS, and WinCommPRO let you view image files while downloading.

How Well Does the Program Communicate with Other Windows Programs?

DDE (Dynamic Data Exchange) and OLE (Object Linking and Embedding) let you exchange data with other Windows applications. DDE lets you link one application with another so that information updated in one application is automatically updated in the other. OLE essentially provides for an automated framework for expanded DDE capabilities, enabling you to embed objects from one program into another and work on those objects using the parent application's commands, even if the parent application isn't open. WinCommPRO supports DDE; QmodemPro and PROCOMM PLUS don't. QmodemPro, WinCommPRO, and PROCOMM PLUS support OLE 2.0; PROCOMM PLUS does not.

How Easy is the Installation?

Gone are the days when you nearly had to be a rocket scientist to install complicated communications programs. For the CD-ROM versions of PROCOMM PLUS and WinCommPRO, all you have to do is launch the setup program and follow the leader. The QmodemPro, which comes on three floppy disks, is just as easy.

The program defaults are useful to most people, and you can get up and running as soon as you know who to call.

Is the Program 16-Bit or 32-Bit?

All communications programs written specifically for Windows 95 take advantage of the new 32-bit system architecture. Instead of sending 8-bit or 16-bit packets of information, Windows 95 allows 32 bits at a time. That means the information gets where it's going faster, which means your tasks get accomplished faster. This is especially important for communications programs, because you may be paying phone charges or hourly fees for connect time.

Windows 95 also employs *preemptive multitasking*, which means the CPU delegates resources to programs. Under Windows 3.*x*, programs used *cooperative multitasking*. Programs relinquished control of the CPU to let other programs work, which sometimes created traffic jams that caused programs to crash. That should happen much less frequently with preemptive multitasking. Even if one program crashes, others will probably still run.

Notice that Windows 95 is backward-compatible, meaning that it will run applications written for Windows 3.*x*. When it runs 16-bit applications, it uses cooperative multitasking.

Caution

Don't assume that a program is 32-bit unless it specifically says so on the package. Microsoft is handing out "Designed for Microsoft Windows 95" labels for products that meet rigorous design standards for the new operating system.

Does the Program Support TAPI?

An exciting new feature of Windows 95 is its support for 32-bit communications using the Telephony API (TAPI). TAPI lets you run multiple communications programs simultaneously by delegating the basic functions of each program (see Chapter 2, "Getting Started"). For example, you can wait for a fax at the same time you connect to a BBS or online service. You are still, of course, limited by the number of phone lines you have, but you don't have to terminate one communications program to use another.

At least that's what they advertise. Strangely, PROCOMM PLUS lets you launch CompuServe while open, but not connect to the Internet. The beta versions of QmodemPro and WinCommPRO used for this chapter had no conflicts.

Earmarks of a Good Interface

The best computer software interface is one that makes its features and functions apparent, so that you don't have to read paper or online documentation to get up and running. This rarely happens, of course, because programmers aren't always tuned into users' needs, and users aren't always familiar with the tasks a program can perform.

Nevertheless, a program's success often rides on its interface design, regardless of its operating power or features. If people can't figure out how to do things, or if it takes a lot of time to operate the program, the program will soon be relegated to the junk pile.

Software companies are well aware of this problem, and that's why most strive for the easiest yet most inviting interface they can design. Some succeed; most fail.

One of the keys in designing an intuitive interface is creating icons and buttons whose functions are easily understood. This isn't easy; an icon is typically smaller than a half-inch square, and you have to come up with a picture that millions of people will interpret the same way. With programs like PROCOMM PLUS, which is packed with dozens of useful features, there just isn't enough room on a screen to include all the options.

So it isn't enough to make the functions apparent; you also have to organize them logically, so that they follow an intelligent pattern as the user goes through the program.

The three communications programs examined in this chapter vary widely in interface design. By far the most intuitively designed is WinComm; the most feature-rich is PROCOMM PLUS; and the simplest is QmodemPro. We'll take a look at all three interfaces and compare the same functions in each in the rest of this chapter.

Understanding File Transfer Protocols

One of the most important features of a communications program is its capability to transfer files. When you receive a file from a host computer you are *downloading*; when you send a file to another computer you are *uploading*. Thus, it is important that you understand the significance of the various issues surrounding file transfers.

Computers transmit and receive data in blocks. For two computers to transfer files, they must speak the same language. *File transfer protocols* tell the computer how and how fast data will be sent, how error correction is handled, and how the transfer will be monitored. In general, the bigger the block, the faster the transfer rate.

Examining Common Protocols

Because your software program must use the same protocol as the computer you're attempting to communicate with, a variety of protocols are usually included with all communications packages. Among the most common are the following:

- Xmodem
- Ymodem
- Zmodem
- Kermit
- CompuServe B+
- ASCII

Xmodem and Ymodem were once the industry standards, and while they're still in use, Zmodem is fast becoming the hottest protocol. Zmodem is the default protocol for Windows 95, and most of the communications packages written for the new OS. Xmodem, Ymodem, and Zmodem all send blocks of 1,204 bytes. However, Zmodem is faster than any other protocol and is better at detecting and correcting errors in transmission. Zmodem uses 32-bit CRC (Cyclical Redundancy Check), which is a way to detect errors. Xmodem and Ymodem can only use 16-bit CRC.

Note

Some protocols, like KERMIT, Ymodem (Batch), Ymodem G (Batch), and Zmodem will send or receive multiple files.

ASCII can be used only for sending and receiving ASCII-only (text-only) files. ASCII files are text only. You can't transmit binary files (all other files, such as programs and compressed files) with the ASCII protocol. In general, ASCII isn't a good protocol to choose, because it doesn't provide error-checking. It's also very sensitive to line noise, which can easily interfere with the transfer.

If your connection isn't direct—that is, if it's over a public data network or a packet-switching network (such as Tymnet)—your transfer traffic will be slowed considerably as the computers wait for data. The Zmodem and KERMIT protocols can speed up things somewhat, because they are capable of sending data blocks and waiting for data blocks simultaneously.

Which Programs Support Which Protocols?

Although the protocols you're most likely to use are probably supported, it's a good idea to double-check before you buy if you know you need a specific type for a BBS or computer to which you frequently connect.

- HyperTerminal, the communications program that ships with Windows 95, offers more protocols than Terminal did with Windows 3.*x*. HyperTerminal offers 1K Xmodem, Xmodem, Ymodem, Ymodem-g, Zmodem, and Kermit. There is no ASCII protocol.
- PROCOMM PLUS offers Zmodem, Kermit, Xmodem, 1K-Xmodem, 1K-Xmodem-g, Ymodem, Ymodem-g, CIS-B+, ASCII, Raw ASCII, and Ind$file. There's also extensive online help for each of the protocols to help you determine which one to use.
- QmodemPro only includes the ASCII, Kermit, and Zmodem protocols. For general BBS and file transfers, these may be all you need.
- WinCommPRO includes 1K Xmodem, CompuServe B+, HyperProtocol, Xmodem, Ymodem, Ymodem-g, Kermit, and Zmodem.

All four applications let you customize certain options for all the protocols.

Comparing BBS Connections

The best way to see the difference among the three communications programs reviewed here is to access the same BBS with all three. That way, you can get a feel for each interface and decide for yourself which you like best. Actually installing all three programs might not be practical, however, but the following section should at least help you determine which one you're leaning toward.

For the example BBS, I'm going to connect to the CONNect BBS because it's a local phone call for me.

Tip

QmodemPro and PROCOMM PLUS have a list of popular BBSs, so you can find one local to you. You can also find listings of BBSs in magazines and online. See *Que's BBS Directory* for a good collection of BBSs all over the United States.

Using PROCOMM PLUS

PROCOMM PLUS is a very powerful, feature-rich program (see fig. 6.1), but its operations aren't always obvious.

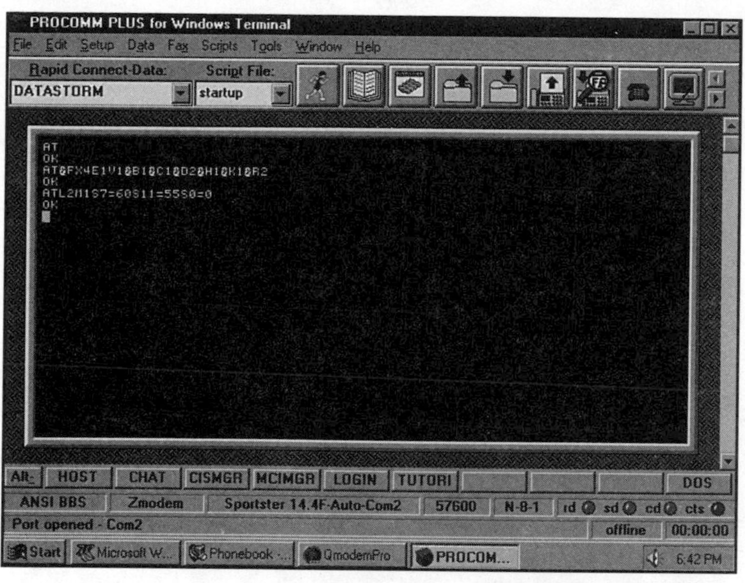

Fig. 6.1
You have a choice of displaying a frame with PROCOMM PLUS.

For example, you have to wade through a series of cascading menus to create a connection entry, and the process isn't readily apparent. To create a connection, you have to choose File, Connection Directory, Edit, New Entry before you can enter the connection information.

Despite that, once you've entered the information, you simply click an entry in a drop-down screen to connect.

One really nice thing about PROCOMM PLUS is that it lets you set a phone number as long distance, even if it's in-state. If you designate a connection that way, PROCOMM PLUS automatically adds a "1" if you specified that prefix and the area code.

PROCOMM PLUS also has a range of options, including disabling call waiting, dialing 9 for an outside number, dialing 1 for long distance, and even letting you block your caller ID for an outgoing call.

After you enter a phone number and direct the software to dial, PROCOMM PLUS displays a dialog box indicating the status of your call, shown in fig. 6.2.

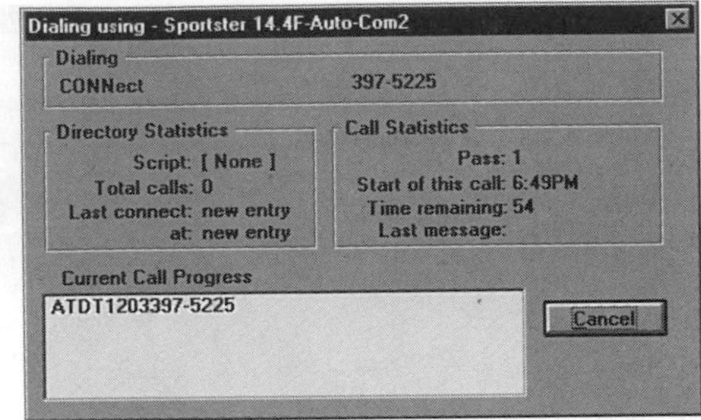

Fig. 6.2
PROCOMM PLUS dials a connection.

After you've made the connection, you're prompted for personal information (see fig. 6.3).

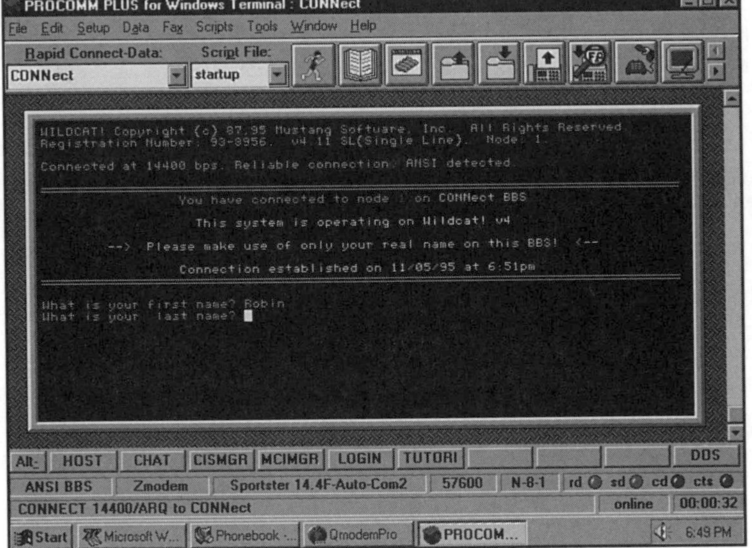

Fig. 6.3
The look of Connecticut's CONNect BBS, using PROCOMM PLUS.

Using QmodemPro

QmodemPro has a simpler interface than PROCOMM PLUS. The main screen is shown in figure 6.4.

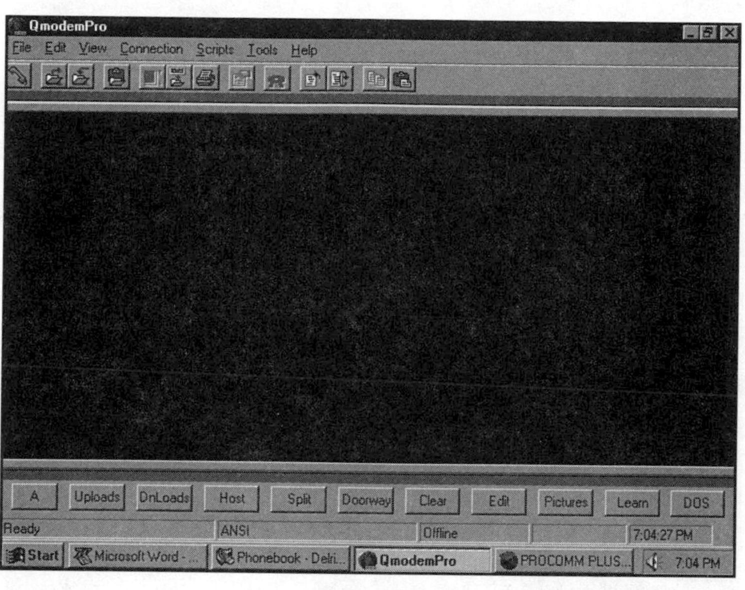

Fig. 6.4
QmodemPro's main screen is relatively free of clutter.

Creating a connection entry in QmodemPro is a little more apparent than in PROCOMM PLUS. To create an entry, click the telephone icon, which brings up the Dialing Directory. Then you choose Edit, New and enter the connection information. That creates an icon in the Dialing Directory, and from there you can double-click the icon to establish the connection. When a connection is initiated, you're shown the status of the call, as in figure 6.5.

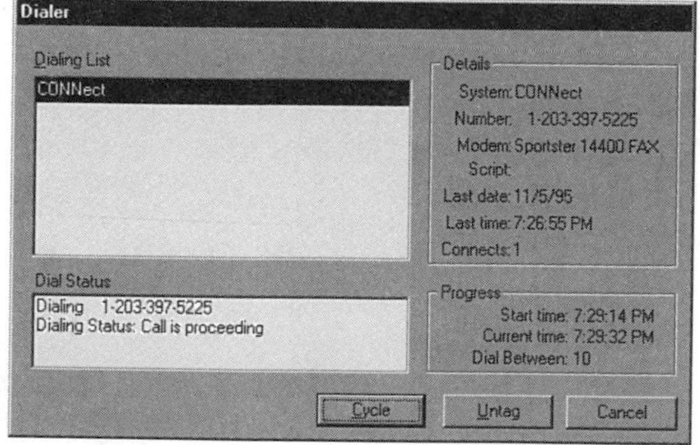

Fig. 6.5
QmodemPro keeps you informed of the status of your call.

Unlike PROCOMM PLUS, one thing you can't do with QmodemPro is set the connection to automatically dial a "1" and the area code for an in-state long distance phone call. This isn't necessary for all states, but it is in Connecticut and many others. Therefore, I have to remember to add the "1" and "203" directly before the phone number, or it won't make the connection.

But you can set up the program so that it dials 9 for an outside line and 1 for a long distance call (out-of-state only).

When you are finally connected to the BBS (see fig. 6.6), there doesn't seem to be much difference between PROCOMM PLUS and QmodemPro.

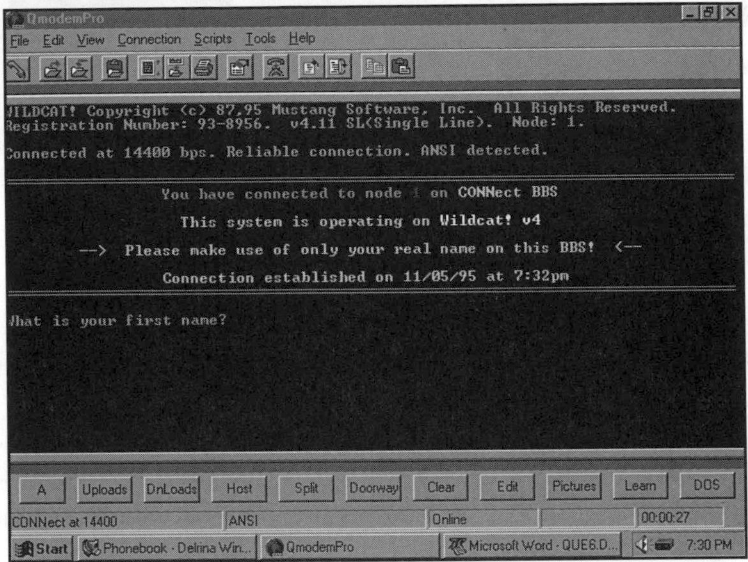

Fig. 6.6
The look of Connecticut's CONNect BBS, using QmodemPro.

WinComm

No one can fault Delrina for the interface on WinCommPRO. It's uncluttered, apparent, and simple to use. WinCommPRO's main screen is shown in figure 6.7.

To create a new connection, choose File, New. What could be easier?

Unfortunately, like QmodemPro, WinCommPRO doesn't allow you to specify a long distance in-state phone number; so if you have to dial the area code in-state, as I do in Connecticut, you have to add the "1" and the area code directly before the phone number.

WinCommPRO does have settings to dial 9 for an outside line and 1 for a long distance call (out-of-state only).

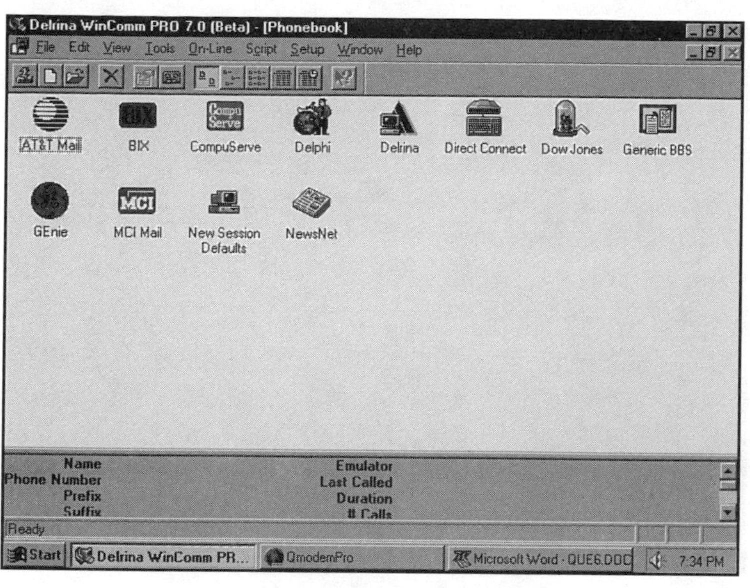

Fig. 6.7 WinCommPRO's main screen defaults to the Phonebook.

After you enter the information, just double-click the icon to make the connection. You get the screen shown in figure 6.8.

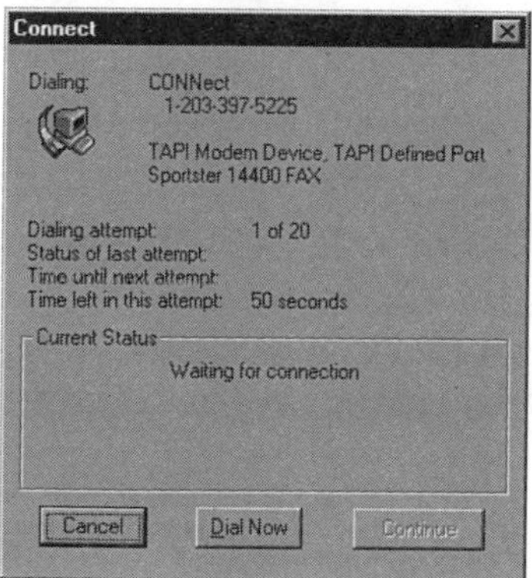

Fig. 6.8 WinCommPRO's connection screen.

As you're probably beginning to realize, after your program is connected to the BBS, the differences in the interface are fairly insignificant because the primary area of concern is on the BBS interface. WinCommPRO's screen is shown in figure 6.9.

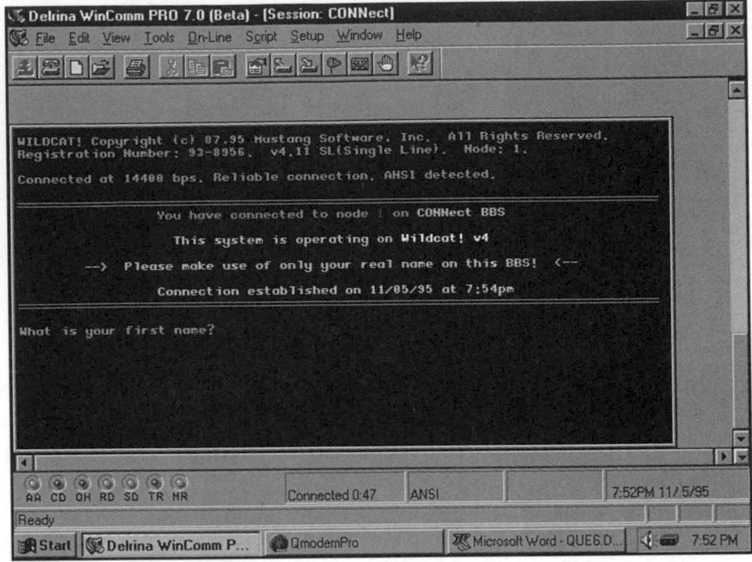

Fig. 6.9
WinCommPRO's terminal screen is similar to those of QmodemPro and PROCOMM PLUS.

Features Are Where the Differences Count

The differences among communications programs lie in the features and in the details. Once you connect to a BBS, you see essentially the same screen with all three programs. Where they differ is how you get to that screen.

All three packages are adequate for calling BBSs and transferring files. And even if some are harder to learn than others, once you learn the process you'll know how to do it.

PROCOMM PLUS comes with a full array of programs to access the Internet. To connect to the Internet with CinCommPRO you need an add-on called CyberJack. You can't connect to the Internet with QmodemPro—but you may not need to.

Scripting Languages

The people who really take advantage of these feature-rich communication programs are Information Systems managers in large corporations. One such feature is scripting. *Scripting* enables you to set up automated sessions to dial in and out of mini and mainframe computers as well as PCs. PROCOMM PLUS, WinCommPRO, and QmodemPro all sport powerful scripting languages. With them you can develop scripts to dial into networked computers as well as mini and mainframe computers and transfer files and exchange e-mail.

Note

Scripts are similar to macros, which are popular among word processing and spreadsheet users. Scripts save you time by automatically entering long strings of keystrokes (in this case, phone numbers, login and system information, and other details necessary when connecting) that you would otherwise have to enter yourself each time you connect.

On the down side, the more powerful the language, the steeper the learning curve. That's why all three programs have ways of recording keystrokes into macros, so that you don't need to learn the scripting language for simple tasks. WinCommPRO and QmodemPRO offer script wizards to walk you through the creation of a few simple scripts.

For example, you can use your communications software to access a commercial online service. You might want to do this to save space on a laptop, or to save time and money on connect and phone charges. Because the connection uses terminal emulation, and not a graphical user interface, the connection is very, very fast. GEnie and Delphi are also accessible via terminal, and both QmodemPro and WinCommPRO have script wizards to connect to these services. You can't connect to Prodigy, America Online, or The Microsoft Network this way; you need their proprietary software to connect.

Scripting in QmodemPro

Connecting to CompuServe using QmodemPro's Script dialog box couldn't be easier. You're presented with the dialog box shown in figure 6.10.

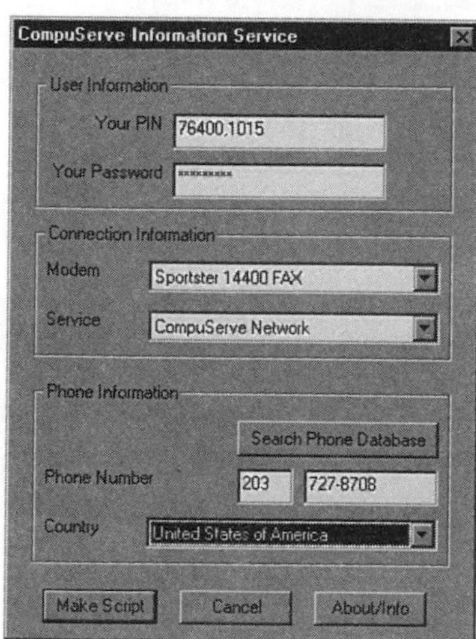

Fig. 6.10
QmodemPro turns your CompuServe connect information into a simple logon script.

There's even a searchable database of CompuServe access numbers. After you fill in the information (the PIN is just your CompuServe ID), you click Make Script, and QmodemPro churns out a simple script that logs you on to the service. Just click the CompuServe icon, and you're in. The interface isn't fancy; in fact, it's just a terminal emulation screen, shown in figure 6.11.

> **Tip**
>
> The next time you want to connect to CompuServe, all you have to do is click the icon created when you make the script.

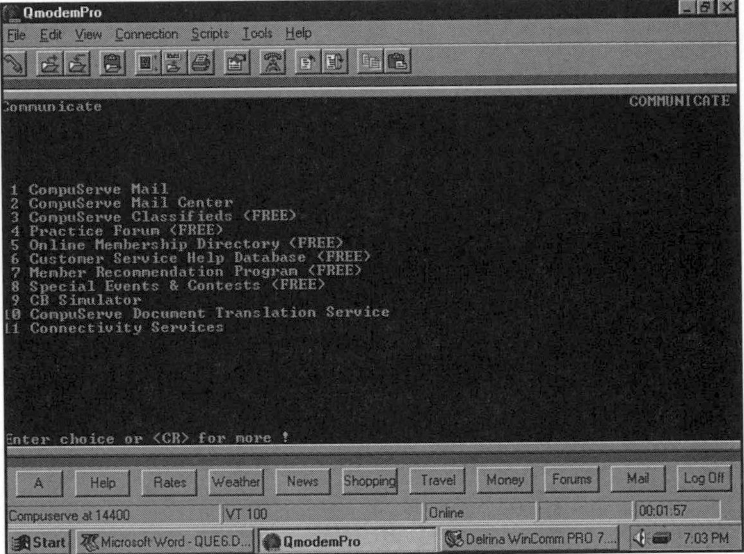

Fig. 6.11
QmodemPro's interface to CompuServe is nothing to write home about, but it makes up for it with speed.

But the connection is fast, and there's a toolbar for certain tasks, like retrieving e-mail.

> **Note**
>
> QmodemPro also ships with script dialog boxes for MCI Mail, Delphi, and GEnie.

Scripting in PROCOMM PLUS

PROCOMM PLUS also offers easy-to-use dialog boxes to create scripts for MCI Mail and CompuServe, shown in figure 6.12.

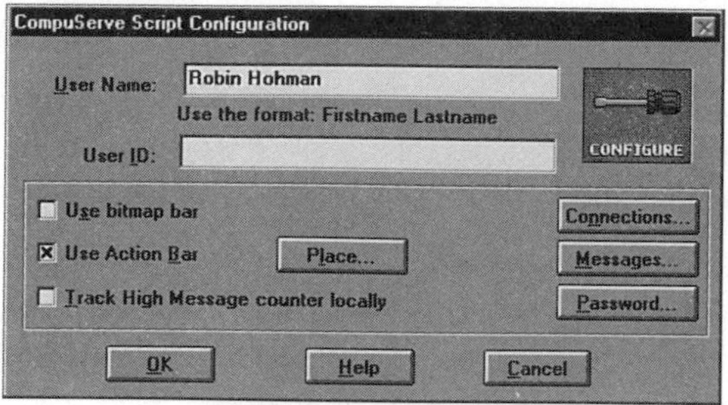

Fig. 6.12
PROCOMM PLUS lets you create an offline mail and browsing utility for CompuServe.

You can also create logon scripts for a host of other online services, including GEnie, Dow Jones, Lexis/Nexis, BIX, and AT&T Mail. Figure 6.13 shows the screen for choosing an online service.

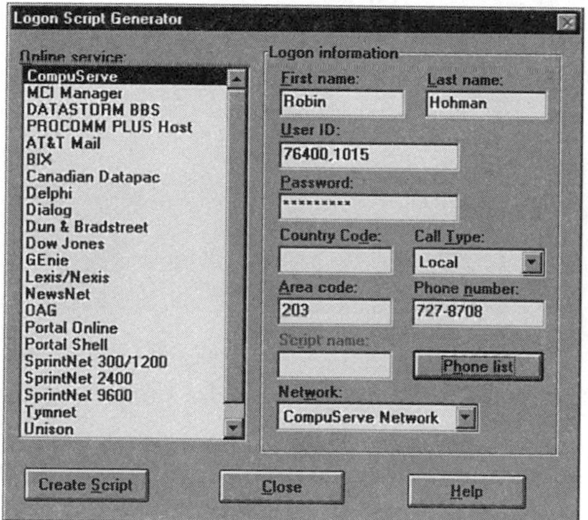

Fig. 6.13
PROCOMM PLUS lets you create automatic logon scripts for a wide variety of commercial online services.

After you've entered all your connect information (like QmodemPro, there's also a searchable database of access numbers), you click Create Script, and the rest is done for you. Figure 6.14 shows the CompuServe front-end.

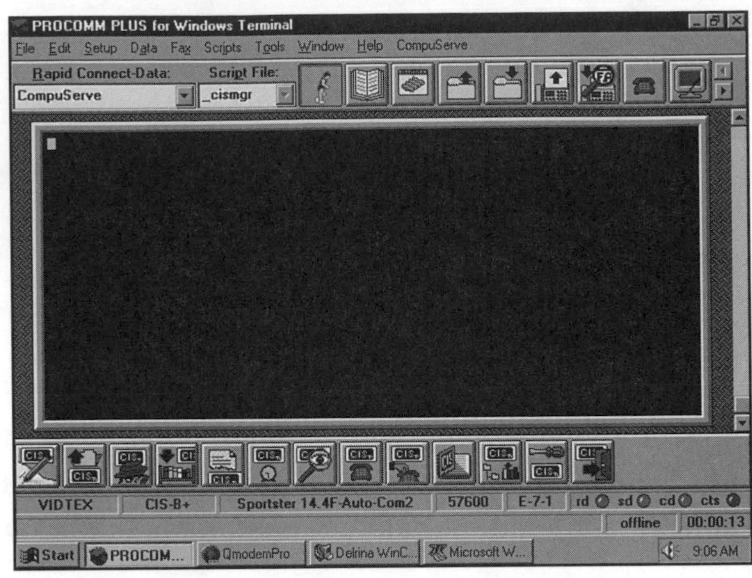

Fig. 6.14
The PROCOMM PLUS front-end for CompuServe combines terminal emulation with some icons. They let you schedule activities like accessing forums or sending e-mail and transferring files.

Scripting in WinCommPRO

Setting up WinCommPRO's interface for CompuServe couldn't be easier; all you have to do is enter the local telephone number and click Dial, as shown in figure 6.15.

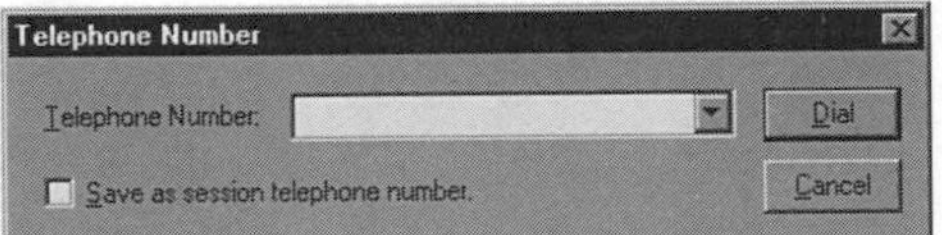

Fig. 6.15
The only thing you have to do with WinCommPRO's CompuServe setup tool is enter your ID, a password, and a phone number.

The WinCommPRO interface is strictly terminal emulation, shown in figure 6.16.

WinCommPRO also ships with script setups for MCI Mail, AT&T Mail, GEnie, Delphi, Dow Jones, and BIX.

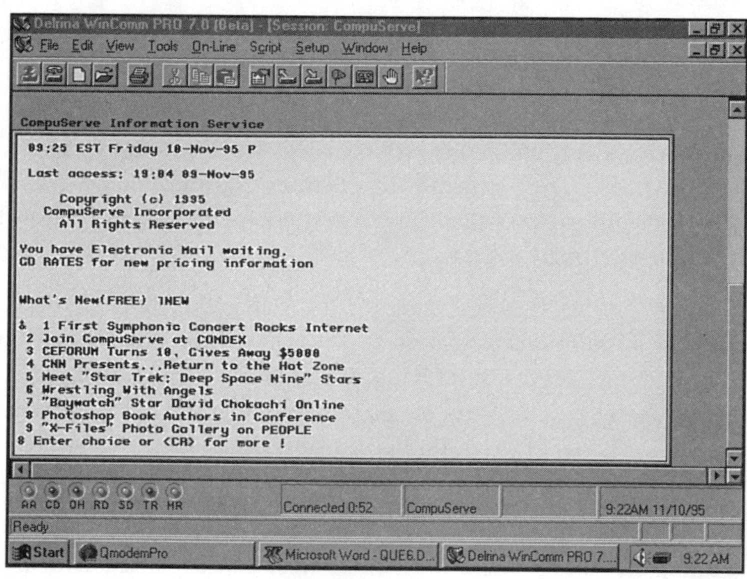

Fig. 6.16
You're prompted to choose an activity with WinCommPRO's front-end for CompuServe.

Recording Your Own Scripts

All three programs let you record keystrokes into a macro, which you can then execute to log on to any service you want.

QmodemPro uses the QuickLearn Script Recorder, which follows the prompts and your responses as you log on to a BBS or online service and writes a script to match. PROCOMM PLUS has a similar feature called Script Recorder, and WinCommPRO doesn't have a name for it, but there is a record script feature.

For more complicated tasks, like unattended automated logins and file transfers, you'll want to use the scripting languages.

If you're not a programmer, but you're determined to write a script, you'll be able to do it with any of these three applications. QmodemPro uses the SLIQ (Script Language Interface for Qmodem) language, which is similar to BASIC. QmodemPro devotes a user's guide nearly as thick as the main documentation to the scripting language alone, and there's also ample online help.

The user's guide wasn't available for the PROCOMM PLUS beta used to write this chapter, so I can't comment on the documentation. PROCOMM PLUS uses ASPECT, which is a full-blown text programming language with a compiler.

WinCommPRO uses BASIC, and it also supports the old Delrina C-style scripts. There's a script reference section in the online help.

Putting It All Together

The key to buying the right communications software for you is realistically assessing your needs and buying the program that fills those needs. Sounds simple, but you may be tempted to buy the most feature-rich program, when a simpler one will do. The problem with the more complicated programs is that they're typically more difficult to learn, there are more features to wade through, and more things to do wrong.

PROCOMM PLUS offers the most bang for your buck, but there are many settings to choose and options to customize. It's also the priciest. If you don't need it, why bother? On the other hand, if you don't mind playing with settings and you really get a kick out of customizing, you can't do any better than PROCOMM PLUS. PROCOMM PLUS is also the only package featured here that ships with integrated fax capabilities. WinCommPRO is available in a suite with Delrina's slick WinFax Pro.

QmodemPro is the simplest (and least expensive) package discussed here. If basic access to BBSs and simple file transfers are all you need, QmodemPro can fit the bill nicely, and it doesn't take much time to learn.

WinCommPRO falls somewhere in between, in features and in price, and will be a big seller to users of WinFax Pro, one of the easiest to use commercial fax programs, because its interface is similar. ❖

CHAPTER 7

Transferring Files

by Jim Boyce

By far one of the most common uses for communications programs is file transfer—sending or receiving files to or from another computer. New Windows-based communications programs have simplified the process of sending and receiving files, but it still isn't always a point-and-click procedure.

In this chapter, you learn to

- Understand file transfer
- Choose a protocol
- Use compression
- Work with batch transfers

First, you need a basic understanding of the methods you can use to transfer files. The next section provides an overview to help you understand those methods.

An Overview of File Transfer

If you have ever used an online service or BBS, you probably are familiar with file transfer. If not, file transfer might seem like an alien concept. In reality, it's simple—you send a file from your computer to another, or receive a file from the other computer to your own. The computer at the other end of the connection might be a large mainframe managed by an online service, or it might be a PC or other microcomputer acting as a BBS or communications host.

The process of sending a file from your PC to another computer (including a BBS or online service) is called *uploading*. Receiving a file to your computer is called *downloading*. Figure 7.1 illustrates the concept.

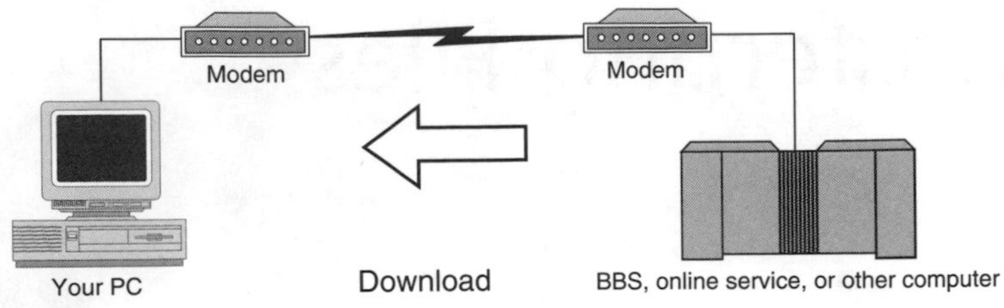

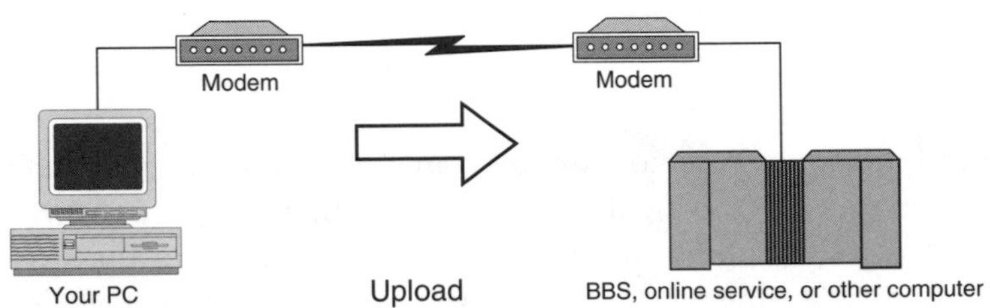

Fig. 7.1
File transfer is also referred to as "uploading" and "downloading."

Why would you upload or download a file? Many possibilities exist. Here are just a few examples:

- *Drivers and updates*. Almost all hardware manufacturers and software publishers maintain either a BBS or a forum on one or more online services such as CompuServe. The BBS or forum provides a means for the company to offer support for their hardware or software. You will often find updated drivers, utility programs, program updates, and support files in these online areas. If you bought a particular peripheral before Windows 95 first became available, you might find new, updated Windows 95 drivers for some of your PC's hardware in these online areas.
- *Games and shareware*. Almost every BBS and online service contains a large selection of games and other programs that are distributed as either freeware or shareware. Freeware is programs that are distributed free of charge as long as you don't profit from the program yourself (such as selling it). *Shareware* is a "try before you buy" type of software. You download the shareware, try it, and if you like it, pay a nominal license fee to the shareware program's developer to use the software.
- *Graphics*. Many BBS and online services offer large collections of images to suit a variety of tastes and interests. These online areas also contain programs you can use to view the images. If the images are stored in

BMP (bitmap) or RLE (Run-Length Encoded) formats, you can use them for Windows 95 wallpaper.

- *Sharing and distributing documents.* File transfer enables you to share documents and other files with other users. You might upload a file as e-mail (explained next) or upload the file to an area on the online service, such as a forum library, so other users can access the file.
- *E-mail.* If you have a long e-mail (electronic mail) message or want to send a *binary file* (program, image, etc.), you often can upload the file as part of the e-mail process. Most commercial online services enable you to attach a file to a message and the file is uploaded automatically when you send the message. Many BBS and other systems require you to use manual methods to upload the file.

One of the most important advantages to using some form of file transfer to send and receive documents is the small amount of time involved. You can transmit a file in a matter of minutes, but sending the file on disk through the mail or by courier could take a day, a week, or even longer. And, file transfer enables you to send a file that won't fit on a disk—you don't have to worry about the fact that your floppy disk holds only 1.44M (using a 3.5-inch disk as an example).

▶ See "Using Exchange for CompuServe Mail," p. 355

Note

It's important to understand that when you transfer a file, the original file remains intact and a copy of the file is transferred. You're not actually sending a file when you upload; you're copying the file.

▶ See "Choosing a Protocol," p. 134

The process you use to upload or download a file varies from one system to another, but there are many common issues and procedures. Regardless of the types of computers or files involved, the general process is the same:

1. You establish a connection between the two computers.
2. If necessary, you log on to the remote computer and initiate either an upload or download.
3. The sending computer, through its communications software, reads the contents of the file being transmitted and begins sending the file one byte at a time through the communications port to the modem.
4. The port and modem convert the data into analog bits for transfer through the phone line. (The data remains in digital form for ISDN and other digital connections.)

5. The receiving modem converts the data back into digital bits (analog modems only), and the receiving port converts the bits back into bytes, then sends the bytes to the CPU for processing.
6. The communications software stores the bytes on the receiving system, building the file byte-by-byte as it comes in.

Throughout the process described in the previous steps, the two computers might also perform error detection and correction on the data as it is transferred, depending on whether an error-correcting transfer protocol is used.

▶ See "Choosing a Protocol," p. 134

Tip

Many communications and transfer protocols support *batch transfers*, which enables you to select a group of files and transfer them with one command, rather than sending each one individually. For an explanation of batch transfer, refer to the section "Using Batch Transfers" later in this chapter. For information on using FTP in batch mode, refer to Chapter 22, "Using FTP, Ping, and Other Internet Tools."

ASCII versus Binary File Transfer

Most computers and communications programs support ASCII file transfer, which is the direct transfer of text files, one 7-bit character at a time. (ASCII files contain only 7-bit alphanumeric characters and symbols, without special formatting or non-printing characters; they essentially are text-only files.) ASCII file transfer is the simplest form of file transfer. The sending computer reads the file and sends its contents character-by-character through the modem and to the other system, just as if you were typing the characters yourself using the keyboard. The only real difference is speed—the computer can read a file and transmit its characters to the other system much faster than you can type (unless, of course, you type at about 20,000 words per minute).

The receiving system can accept the incoming characters as if they were sent from your keyboard. For example, you might create an e-mail message as a text file and store it on your computer. You then log on to the remote computer and start composing a mail message. Instead of typing the message, however, you perform an ASCII upload, which sends the characters from the file on your computer to the input storage area (buffer) on the remote computer. The receiving system has no indication that you are uploading a file. It just treats the incoming characters as if you had typed them.

The receiving system also can accept the characters and store them to a file. Generally, this means you use the remote system's ASCII file upload feature, then begin sending the file from your system.

You also can use ASCII transfers to receive a file. On many BBS and online services, you can view text files that are stored on the remote service. The remote system sends the characters one at a time to your system, where they appear on the display. If you turn on your communication program's capture-to-disk function, however, the characters also are echoed to a disk file as they come in. The result is an ASCII file download—you've transferred an ASCII text file to your computer.

ASCII file transfers are easy to accomplish, but they do suffer from a few drawbacks. It's relatively easy for data to be lost during transfer due to noisy phone lines or data overrun because of the lack of error-correction protocols in ASCII transfers. It's also possible only in a few circumstances to transfer a binary file using ASCII transfer, and then only if the file has been encoded as a text file. Therefore, binary file transfers are more useful.

A binary transfer is similar in some ways to an ASCII transfer, except that the file is transferred as a series of bytes and an error-correction protocol is generally used. By using an error-correcting protocol, you ensure that the file is transferred intact and without errors. Any bytes that are transmitted incorrectly or lost can be retransmitted.

Binary transfer offers the major benefit of enabling you to send any kind of file—an image, program, document, or other file—to someone else without having to convert the file to ASCII format. Most online services provide interface programs that greatly simplify the process of sending a binary file. Windows 95's Exchange e-mail client supports the same ease of transfer, enabling you to simply attach binary files to regular text e-mail messages. The file is then transferred along with the message, and appears as an embedded icon in the message.

Note

Microsoft Exchange is a messaging system included with Windows 95. You can use Exchange to send and receive e-mail and faxes directly to other users or through a variety of mail systems and online services.

▶ See "Using Exchange with Microsoft Mail," p. 307

Binary transfers will be by far the most common type of transfer you perform. The following sections help you choose the protocol for transferring those files.

Choosing a Protocol

When two computers exchange a file, they must agree on the transfer method—or *tranfer protocol*—they use to ensure that the file arrives at its destination intact and error-free. The transfer protocol defines a number of issues, which are explained in the following section.

How Common Transfer Protocols Work

When a communications program transfers a file using an error-correcting transfer protocol, the data is transmitted in *blocks*. A block is a group of bytes, usually of a fixed size, such as 1024 bytes (a 1K block). Different protocols use different size blocks, although 1024 bytes and 512 bytes are common block sizes.

Here's how the process works: the two computers first agree on the protocol to be used (either you specify the protocol as part of the process of initiating the file transfer, or the programs do it automatically). Then, the sending computer reads a block of data from the file to be transferred. Depending on the protocol, the sending computer might add information to the block for error-correction or other purposes to facilitate the transfer. The computer then transmits the block. The receiving computer accepts the block and strips out any information added by the sending system, acting on that information if necessary.

Throughout the transfer, the two computers communicate on whether or not the blocks are received correctly. Typically, the receiver sends an acknowledgment (ACK) if the block is received properly, and sends a negative acknowledgment (NAK) if the block is received incorrectly. If the sender receives a NAK, the bad blocks are retransmitted. Depending on the protocol, this retransmission occurs either right after the bad block is acknowledged or at the end of the transfer. This ensures that the file contains no errors when it is re-created on the receiving system. The protocol does define a limit to the number of times the two systems will try to send the bad block, however, and the transfer aborts if that retry limit is exceeded. This prevents the two systems from continuing to retry the transfer indefinitely.

The protocol also defines the amount of time allowed to transfer a block. After the block is transmitted, the sender waits a specified amount of time, called a *timeout,* for an acknowledgment from the receiver that the block was received correctly. The receiver, after acknowledging a received block, waits a specified amount of time for the next block to begin arriving. If the timeout period is exceeded, the transfer aborts. This prevents one system from waiting indefinitely for the other to respond. Generally, you can specify in a communications program the timeout value your selected protocol will use.

Common Protocols

A handful of transfer protocols are widely supported by BBSs, online services, and communications programs. Some online services, such as CompuServe, support proprietary protocols. Transferring files to and from these services using a proprietary protocol naturally requires that your communications program support the protocol. This typically is not a problem, however, because the online service's interface program (such as CIM in the case of CompuServe) provides that support. Support for proprietary protocols is one important reason for using an online service's front-end program.

Xmodem, 1K Xmodem, and Xmodem/G

Xmodem was developed by Ward Christensen in 1978, and has since become one of the most widely used protocols. Essentially, all online services support Xmodem, as do most communications programs. Xmodem uses a block size of 128 bytes, although there are variations of Xmodem. 1K Xmodem, for example, uses a block size of 1024 bytes.

In an Xmodem transfer, each block is acknowledged by the receiver. If a block is not received correctly, the receiver requests a retransmission. The file is transferred one block after the other until the entire file is successfully transferred, or until a timeout occurs.

Standard Xmodem adds one bit, called a *checksum*, to each block. The receiving system uses the checksum to calculate whether the block was received correctly. With Xmodem CRC (Cyclical Redundancy Check), a second checksum bit is added to the block to increase accuracy.

One other variation of Xmodem is WXmodem, which stands for Windowed Xmodem. Unlike Xmodem, WXmodem doesn't wait for an acknowledgment after each block. Instead, WXmodem assumes that each block is sent correctly and continues sending blocks. The receiver does send acknowledgments, and if it generates a NAK, WXmodem retransmits the bad block. The receiver is always a few blocks behind the sender in transmitting ACKs and NAKs, and this "window" of time is where Windows Xmodem gets its name.

Xmodem/G relies on the MNP hardware-based error correction supported by many modems to eliminate the block-by-block error detection and verification. Relying on hardware to ensure accuracy improves transfer speed significantly over Xmodem.

Ymodem and Ymodem-G

Ymodem, which was developed by Chuck Forsberg, is similar to Xmodem, except that Ymodem supports a variable block size. As with 1K Xmodem, by transferring more bytes with each block, Ymodem increases transfer speed because both systems spend more time transferring the file and less time sending ACKs and NAKs. Ymodem-G relies on MNP hardware-based error correction to speed the transfer process.

Zmodem

Of the non-proprietary protocols, Zmodem is one of the fastest. Zmodem uses 512-byte blocks, but does not monitor ACKs. Instead, Zmodem only monitors for NAKs, assuming that all blocks are transmitted correctly unless otherwise indicated by a NAK. Zmodem also offers the advantage of being able to restart an aborted transfer. If you're half way through a 10M file and the transfer aborts, you can restart the transfer and the protocol picks up in the middle of the file where the error occurred. If you're not using a proprietary protocol, Zmodem is probably your best choice.

Kermit

The Kermit protocol, which originated in the UNIX environment and is named for Jim Henson's Kermit the Frog, is similar in many ways to Xmodem. Kermit offers advantages over Xmodem, however. Kermit can transmit 7-bit characters, can use varying packet (block) sizes, and can resynchronize a transfer if it is interrupted. Kermit also can use wild card transfers to transfer multiple files, use its own compression mechanism to reduce transfer time, and support a server mode in which your computer takes over the transfer process and issues all necessary commands, enabling the computer to automate a batch transfer. However, Kermit is not a particularly fast protocol.

CompuServe B, B+, and QB

CompuServe provides support for all the protocols listed previously, but also supports its own proprietary protocols. These protocols are CompuServe B, CompuServe B+, and CompuServe QB. These protocols offer various advantages, including large block size (2K), transmission restart, and others. Of the three, B+ offers the best solution in terms of speed and reliability. If you are transferring files to or from CompuServe, the CompuServe B+ protocol is your best choice.

Which Protocol?

When you're trying to decide which protocol to use, you naturally have to pick a protocol that is supported not only by your communications software, but also by the remote computer. If you're using a commercial service that provides a proprietary protocol (such as CompuServe), the proprietary protocol often will give you the best performance because it is tailor-made for the service.

If you have to use a non-proprietary protocol, your best bet probably will be Zmodem because of its speed and resynchronization capability. Next in order of preference are Ymodem/G, Xmodem/G, Xmodem, and Kermit.

Note

HyperTerminal supports all of the transfer protocols described here except the proprietary CompuServe protocols.

Using Batch Transfers

In many cases, you might only need to transfer one or two files. But the time will come when you want to transfer a selection of files. Maybe there are a dozen images you want to download from an online service. Or, you might want to download a set of driver files. Whatever the reason, you'll be happy to know that many protocols support *batch transfers*.

The term batch transfer simply means transferring a selection of files with one operation. Rather than go through the process for each file of selecting the file, specifying a protocol, and initiating a download or upload, you mark a selection of files, then initiate the transfer. The computer and transfer protocol take care of transferring the files without any further action by you.

To perform a batch transfer, you must use a protocol that supports batch mode. Ymodem, Ymodem/G, and Zmodem are common protocols that support batch transfers. Online services such as CompuServe and America Online provide the ability to perform batch downloads without requiring you to select a specific protocol. These services accomplish this by building the capability into their interface programs. You simply locate and mark the files you want to transfer, then direct the service to begin downloading the files. Figure 7.2 shows CompuServe's WinCIM program with a selection of files marked for retrieval.

Unfortunately, neither America Online nor CompuServe support batch uploads through their interface programs. Whether you will be able to perform batch uploads with other communications programs to a BBS or other service depends almost entirely on the program you use to access the service. If it does, you'll still have to select a batch-capable transfer protocol as explained previously.

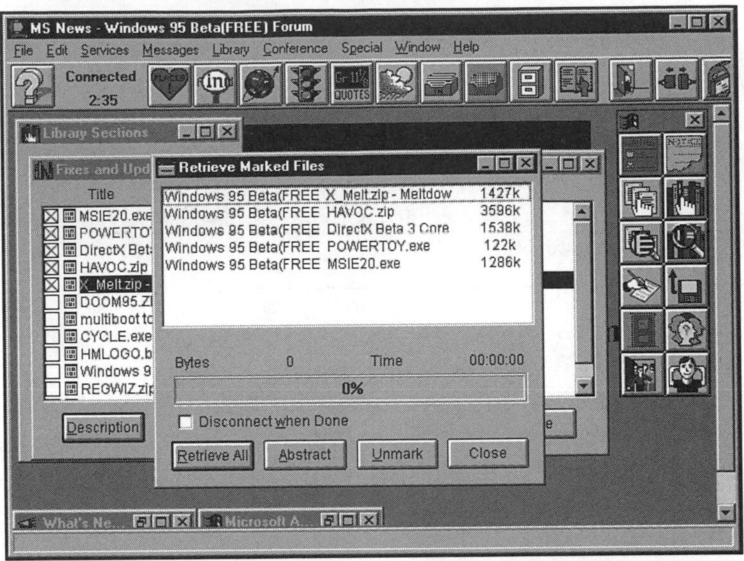

Fig. 7.2
WinCIM makes it easy to perform a batch download.

Troubleshooting

I have a selection of files I need to upload to CompuServe, but I don't want to take the time to upload them individually. Isn't there any way to automate the transfer?

Actually, there is. CompuServe's front-end program, CIM, doesn't support batch uploads, but CompuServe Navigator, which is a program that automates CompuServe sessions, does support batch uploads. CompuServe Navigator is developed and supported by CompuServe, and you can download a copy of Navigator from the CISNAV forum on CompuServe. For help using CompuServe Navigator, check Navigator's Help file or contact CompuServe technical support.

Using Compression

If you consider that a typical file transfer happens byte-by-byte, you can understand that cutting down the number of bytes that have to be transferred can speed up the transfer. The only way to reduce the amount of data that has to be sent is to compress the data, effectively making the data fit in fewer bytes.

You have two options for compressing the data: compress the file before you send it, or allow the modem to use its hardware-based compression to compress the data as it is sent.

Using File Compression

To compress the file before you send it, you can use any of the file compression/archive utilities that are available for the PC. These utilities enable you to compress one or more files into an *archive* file, enabling you to not only use fewer bytes to store a file, but also store (and send) multiple files in a single "container" file.

Most compression utilities work by searching a file for repeating patterns. The utility then replaces these patterns with tokens. Here's an example: assume you create a document that contains 12 instances of the word "compression." When you run the file through a compression utility, the utility replaces each of these words with a small token that takes fewer bytes to store. Also stored with the file is a token table that the utility uses to "remember" what each token represents. When you decompress the file, the decompression program reads the token table and replaces the tokens with their original words, expanding the file once again.

The amount by which a file can be compressed depends on the type of file. Text files can be compressed to a small fraction of their original sizes. Binary files can be compressed as well, although the amount of compression is usually less than with text files. Even so, you often can compress binary files to at least one-half of their original size.

Tip

Although you can compress a file that has already been compressed, the resulting archive will use almost as much space, if not more, as the original compressed file.

One of the most popular file compression utilities is PKZIP, from PKWare. PKZIP is available on practically all BBSs and commercial online services, as well as Internet FTP sites. The utilities that come with PKWare include PKZIP to compress files, PKUNZIP to uncompress files, PKZIPFIX to repair a damaged ZIP archive, and ZIP2EXE, which enables you to create a self-extracting archive. These self-extracting archives essentially are the original ZIP archive combined with a small amount of program code. When you run the self-extracting archive, the program code extracts the files from the archive and expands them to their original forms. This enables someone who doesn't have PKUNZIP to extract the files from the archive.

As a Windows 95 user, however, you're probably looking for a Windows 95 graphical utility that lets you compress and decompress files. By far the most popular is WinZip 6.0, from Niko Mak Computing. WinZip is shareware, so you can try the program, then pay your registration fee if you decide you like it. Figure 7.3 shows the WinZip interface.

> **Tip**
>
> You can find WinZip in the WINZIP forum on CompuServe, at www.winzip.com, or order by phone at either 1-800-242-4775 or 1-713-524-6394.

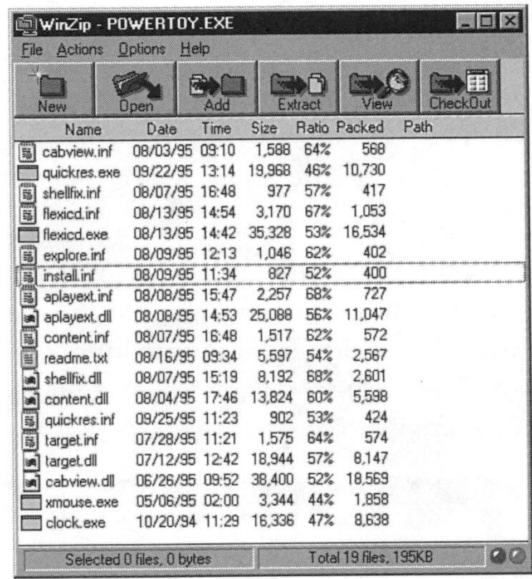

Fig. 7.3
WinZip is a Windows 95-based compression and archive utility.

WinZip doesn't require PKWare's utilities to create and extract from ZIP files. If you want to create ZIP files that span multiple disks, work with password-protected archives, or create self-extracting archives, you need the PKWare command-line utilities. WinZip can make use of the utilities automatically, however, if you have the PKWare utilities on your system. Therefore, WinZip and PKWare make a good combination.

Using Hardware Compression

You also can rely on your modem's hardware compression to compress data as you send it, providing the same general result as compressing a file before you send it. However, you should use one or the other, but not both. If you turn on your modem's compression feature and try to send a compressed file, the transfer actually can take longer than using only one method. The file won't compress any further, and the added overhead of the modem trying to compress the file slows down the transfer.

Therefore, if you are sending compressed files, you should disable your modem's hardware compression. If you are sending uncompressed files, however, you'll experience better performance by turning on hardware compression.

To control hardware compression for your modem, follow these steps:

1. Open the Control Panel and double-click on the Modems icon.
2. Select the modem for which you want to enable or disable compression, then click on the Properties button to display the modem's property sheet (see fig. 7.4).

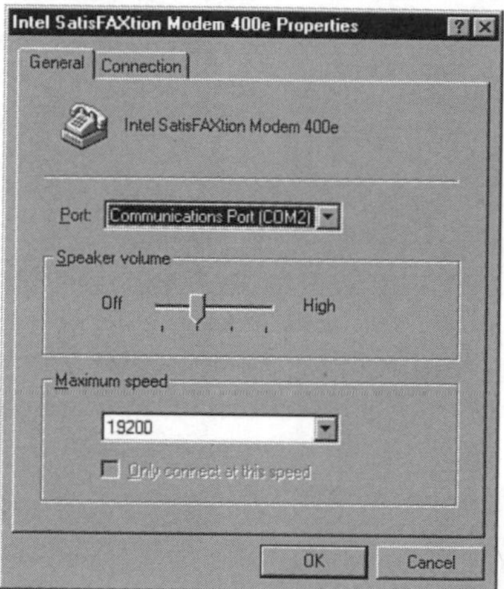

Fig. 7.4
You can control almost all communications options from a modem's property sheet.

3. Click on the Connection tab to display the Connection property page, then click on the Advanced button to display the Advanced Connection Settings dialog box (see fig. 7.5).

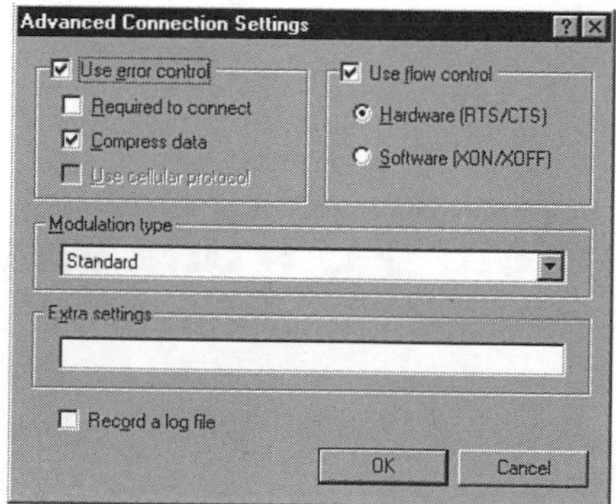

Fig. 7.5
Control compression and other settings from the Advanced Connection Settings dialog box.

4. Place a check in the Compress data check box if you want to use the modem's hardware compression. Clear the check box if you are sending a compressed file.
5. Choose OK to close the Advanced Connection Settings dialog box, choose OK to close the Connection property page, and Close to close the modem property sheet.

Tip

To simplify the process of turning on or off compression, you can add a second instance of your modem as explained in Chapter 3. Then, configure one instance with compression and the other without. When you want to switch between compression and no compression, select the appropriate modem instance from your communications program before you start the connection.

Compression and Incoming Files

If you download files very often, you'll be happy to know you can use compression to cut down transfer time. The same issues that affect compressed file uploads also affect downloads. If you're downloading a file that's already compressed, for example, you should turn off modem compression. Trying to download a compressed file using modem compression typically slows down the transfer, rather than speeding it up.

When you're downloading uncompressed files, however, turning on modem compression can cut down transfer time, but only if the other system is using compression. To turn on compression, use the same process explained in the previous section "Using Hardware Compression."

Tip

Generally, compressed files have an EXE, ZIP, file ARC file extension, making it easy to tell if a file is compressed.

Protecting Your PC from Viruses

If you're new to communications, you might not know that such things as *computer viruses* exist, but they do. Most computer viruses are programs that replicate themselves, copying from one computer to another through an infected file or disk. The infection isn't biological—the file or disk simply contains a copy of the virus program's code. When you open the contaminated file or boot from a contaminated disk, the virus is copied to your system. What happens next depends on the virus.

Some viruses are relatively harmless, doing nothing more than displaying obnoxious messages on your display. Others are much more destructive and can even wipe out your entire hard disk. Others fall in the middle of the "damage spectrum" and merely slow down your system by hogging the computer's processor time and other resources.

If you never connect your PC to another PC, BBS, or online service, and never boot from a floppy disk, your likelihood of infecting your system with a virus is low. But you're reading a communications book, so it's a sure bet that you *are* interested in connecting to online services, and sooner or later you're going to run into an infected file. What can you do?

Protecting Your PC

My best piece of advice is this: Practice safe computing. Here are some tips to help you do just that:

- *If at all possible, never boot your PC from a disk.* Many viruses replicate by infecting the boot sector of a floppy disk, and when you boot from the disk, your system becomes infected. If you do have to boot from a disk, make sure it's one you created yourself when your PC wasn't infected with a virus.
- *Always check disks you receive from others.* You should use a virus scanning program (explained a little later in this chapter) to check any disk you receive from another user. You should also consider checking the distribution disks of commercial software you buy for your PC. Although it isn't common, viruses have infected commercial software.
- *Always check downloaded files.* When you download a file or receive a file in an e-mail message, you should use a virus scanner to check the file for viruses.
- *Use prevention.* Many good virus scanning programs provide protection against virus infection by running in the background and constantly monitoring your system for viruses. When a virus tries to infect the system, the monitoring program can usually prevent the infection and let you know about the attempt so you can delete or disinfect the infected file.

Unfortunately, a virus can still infect your system even if you're careful. Fortunately, you have access to some tools that will help you get rid of the virus and prevent infection. The next section describes a couple of these options.

Getting Rid of Viruses

Many virus scanning and protection programs exist, but you should make sure you use a program specifically designed for Windows 95. This ensures that the virus scanner will be able to detect viruses and protect your system without damaging your long file names, and that the program will be able to take advantage of Windows 95 features, such as the ability to run at a specific time.

It would take a couple of chapters to adequately cover all of the Windows 95 virus products that are available, so this chapter highlights just two: Norton AntiVirus for Windows 95, and McAffee's VirusScan95.

Norton AntiVirus

Norton AntiVirus is a commercial virus-protection program from Symantec. Norton AntiVirus provides a wide range of protection features, including the ability to check your PC during boot, run continuously to monitor for viruses, and actively scan your system at your direction. The program also includes a scheduler that lets you schedule scans to take place at regular intervals (such as when you're not using the PC). Figure 7.6 shows the Norton AntiVirus main program window.

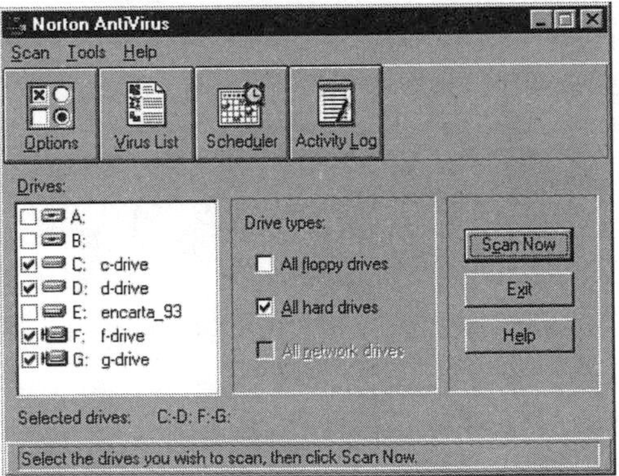

Fig. 7.6 Norton AntiVirus is one of several virus protection programs.

McAffee VirusScan95

If you prefer a shareware virus protection program, you might consider McAffee's VirusScan95. Like Norton AntiVirus, VirusScan95 can scan your system for viruses during boot, and you can run a scan manually at your convenience. VirusScan95 does a nice job of integrating into the Windows 95 interface. The main VirusScan95 program window, for example, looks and works very much like the Windows 95 Find window (see fig. 7.7). Another nice feature about VirusScan95 is its support for context menus. You can right-click on a file or set of folders and choose Scan for Viruses, and VirusScan95 will begin scanning the selected objects for viruses.

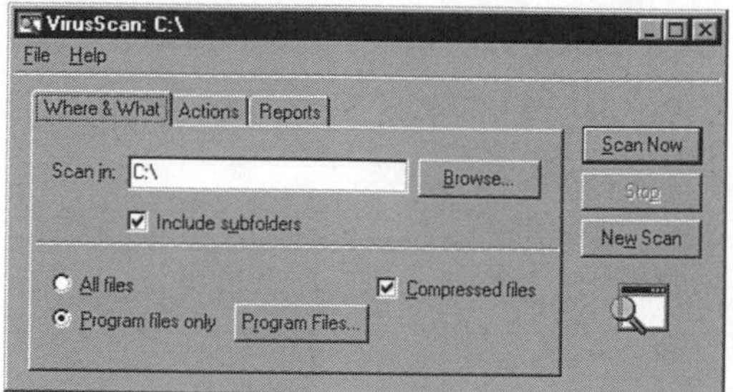

Fig. 7.7
McAffee's VirusScan95 is a good shareware virus protection program.

You can reach McAffee at (408) 988-3832 or by fax at (408) 970-9727, or download VirusScan95 from the MCAFFEE forum on CompuServe.

Other Virus Protection Programs

Norton AntiVirus for Windows 95 and McAffee VirusScan95 are just two of the virus scanning and protection programs available for Windows 95. For other virus utilities and information about viruses, check your favorite online service or a local computer user's group. Your local computer store should also be able to recommend virus protection products. ❖

Part III

Using Online Services

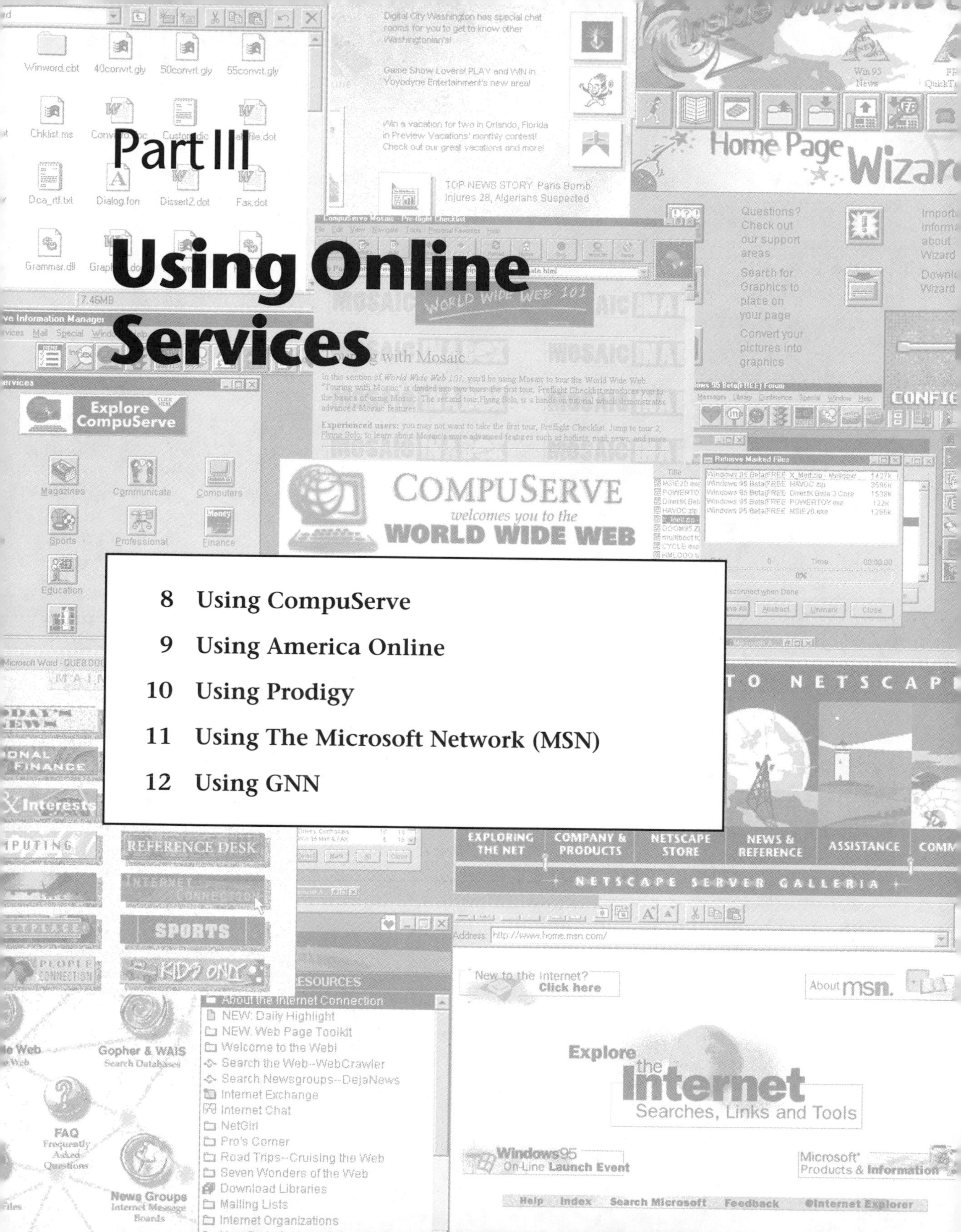

Winword.cbt
40convrt.gly
50convrt.gly
55convrt.gly
Chklist.ms
Convinfo.doc
Custom.dic
Datafile.dot
Dca_rtf.txt
Dialog.fon
Dissert2.dot
Fax.dot
Grammar.dll
Graphics.doc
Hy_am.lex
Hyph.dll
7.46MB
Digital City Washington has special chat rooms for you to get to know other Washingtonian's!
Game Show Lovers! PLAY and WIN in Yoyodyne Entertainment's new area!
Win a vacation for two in Orlando, Florida in Preview Vacations' monthly contest! Check out our great vacations and more!
TOP NEWS STORY: Paris Bomb Injures 28; Algerians Suspected
Home Page Wizar
Questions? Check out our support areas
Search for Graphics to place on your page
Convert your pictures into graphics
CompuServe Mosaic - Preflight Checklist
Web Page: http://www.compuserve.com/help/navigate/navigate.html
WORLD WIDE WEB 101
Touring with Mosaic
In this section of World Wide Web 101, you'll be using Mosaic to tour the World Wide Web "Touring with Mosaic" is divided into two tours: the first tour, Preflight Checklist, introduces you to the basics of using Mosaic. The second tour, Flying Solo, is a hands-on tutorial which demonstrates advanced Mosaic features.
Experienced users: you may not want to take the first tour, Preflight Checklist. Jump to tour 2, Flying Solo, to learn about Mosaic's more advanced features such as hotlists, mail, news, and more
Services
Explore CompuServe
Magazines
Communicate
Computers
Sports
Professional
Finance
Education
Travel
Shopping
Retrieve Marked Files
Windows 95 Beta(FREE X_Meltzip - Meltdow 1427k
Windows 95 Beta(FREE HAVOC.zip 3595k
Windows 95 Beta(FREE DirectX Beta 3 Core 1638k
Windows 95 Beta(FREE POWERTOY.exe 122k
Windows 95 Beta(FREE MSIE20.exe 1288k
Disconnect when Done
Retrieve All
Abstract
Unmark
Close
COMPUSERVE
welcomes you to the
WORLD WIDE WEB
Visit
CompuServe's Home Page
Search
Internet Directory of Services
Learn
More about the Internet
To return to the WinCIM desktop, click on the
Microsoft Word - QUE8.DOC
CompuServe Informat...
MAIN MENU
TODAY'S NEWS
NEWSSTAND
PERSONAL FINANCE
Entertainment
Interests
Education
COMPUTING
REFERENCE DESK
INTERNET CONNECTION
SPORTS
PEOPLE CONNECTION
KIDS ONLY
WELCOME TO NETSCAP
EXPLORING THE NET
COMPANY & PRODUCTS
NETSCAPE STORE
NEWS & REFERENCE
ASSISTANCE
NETSCAPE SERVER GALLERIA
Address: http://www.home.msn.com/
New to the Internet? Click here
About msn.
Explore the Internet
Searches, Links and Tools
Windows95 On-Line Launch Event
Microsoft Products & Informatio
Help
Index
Search Microsoft
Feedback
Internet Explorer
RESOURCES
About the Internet Connection
NEW: Daily Highlight
NEW: Web Page Toolkit
Welcome to the Web!
Search the Web--WebCrawler
Search Newsgroups--DejaNews
Internet Exchange
Internet Chat
NetGirl
Pro's Corner
Road Trips--Cruising the Web
Seven Wonders of the Web
Download Libraries
Mailing Lists
Internet Organizations
Gopher & WAIS
Search Databases
FAQ
Frequently Asked Questions
News Groups
Internet Message Boards

CHAPTER 8

Using CompuServe

by Robin Schreier Hohman

8

CompuServe is one of the oldest commercial online services and has always been one of the best. From its easy-to-use graphical user interface to its wealth of forums and reference information, users have access to the best an online service has to offer.

CompuServe was among the first online services to introduce a Windows interface, called *WinCIM* (for Windows CompuServe Information Manager). This made navigating online easy. The new Windows 95 version is jazzed up a bit, but longtime users will still feel comfortable.

The biggest addition to CompuServe in recent years is access to the Internet through the World Wide Web. With the click of a mouse, users can see all the Web has to offer.

In this chapter, you learn

- CompuServe's new pricing structure
- How to use WinCIM 2.0.1
- How to connect to the Internet
- How to use online Forums

CompuServe's New Pricing Structure

Until recently, CompuServe was one of the priciest commercial online services. Facing stiff competition from America Online, Prodigy, and the new Microsoft Network, which all offer a limited number of free hours with the monthly charge, CompuServe drastically changed its pricing structure in September 1995. Now subscribers get five free hours included with the monthly charge, which is comparable to most other online services.

For most users, the biggest savings comes from the *forums*, which allow a free exchange of e-mail and programs, centered on one topic. In 1994, the forums cost $9.60 an hour; then they dropped to $4.80 an hour. Now they're priced like any other feature on the service.

Although most areas are included in the standard pricing, some features, called Premium Services, still cost extra. For example, Knowledge Index, a database of newspaper and magazine articles and citations, still costs 40¢ a minute or $24 an hour. Magazine Database Plus, a collection of articles from hundreds of magazines, costs $1.50 to view each article.

On the plus side, CompuServe is conscientious about telling you up front what costs more. Each service that carries an extra charge has a $ to the right of the name, whether you go to it directly or look it up using the Find command. In addition, there's always a pricing category so you can see what surcharge each service carries.

On the down side, many services that used to be free aren't. Each minute you access the Associated Press news, weather, and stock prices and receive or send e-mail is now clocked. That's why you might want to use CompuServe Navigator, discussed later in this chapter.

Some areas, such as customer support, are still free. Free areas display the word "Free" on the menu bar while you're in that area.

Tip

To find out current rates when you're online, click the Go icon or press Ctrl+G and enter **rates**. Then choose Rates for Premium Services. From there, choose the service you're interested in, and you'll get a complete listing of the current rates.

Using WinCIM 2.0.1

WinCIM 2.0.1 is the graphical front-end built especially for Windows 95 (see fig. 8.1). Users of previous versions of WinCIM won't see a huge difference in the interface, however, and they may think the new version a little slower than WinCIM v1.4.

The most dramatic difference comes in the gateway to the Internet, which offers a more robust interface and much improved access from CIM. In earlier versions, you used a separate dialer to access the Internet via CompuServe, and there was no bridge to CIM once you were on.

Fig. 8.1
CompuServe's new interface is a little jazzier, but the way you navigate the service has remained the same.

That's all changed. Now you can get to CIM from the Internet browser, and vice versa. You have to use the Mosaic browser, which comes with WinCIM, and it's slower than a PPP/SLIP connection to thc Internet from an access provider. Heavy-duty Internet users may not be happy with the CompuServe gateway, and for them, it might be necessary to foot the bill for uncensored access.

For dabblers and moderate users of the Internet, though, the CompuServe gateway may be all that's needed. Travelers who want to access the Internet on the road will find CompuServe's many nodes mean you can hook up throughout the continental U.S., without paying extra phone fees. You can't do that with a PPP/SLIP connection.

Connecting through CompuServe Access

There are several ways you can obtain WinCIM v. 2.0.1. You can download it or order it online, or use a disk that comes with many computer magazines.

> **Note**
>
> It takes approximately 21 minutes to download the files with a 14,400 connection. The time is not counted against your online time, however, so it's free of charge.

Current CompuServe members can download the updated software online by doing the following:

1. Press Ctrl+G (Go) and enter WinCIM.
2. Double-click English.
3. Click Proceed.
4. Double-click Download WinCIM - Complete Program.
5. Double-click Download Complete WinCIM.
6. Click Proceed.
7. Enter **Y** to download.

   The downloaded file is a self-extracting executable file, which means all you have to do is click Setup and you will be guided through the installation.

Note

If you're already a member, it's safe to install the new version over an older version. Your preferences, access number, address book, and filing cabinet will be retained.

To order disks of WinCIM 2.0.1 online, do the following:

1. Click the traffic light icon or press Ctrl+G (Go) and type **store**.
2. Click Proceed.
3. Click Proceed.
4. Double-click Order from CompuServe Store.
5. Press Enter (twice if necessary).
6. Enter the number of the WinCIM 2.0.1 Upgrade and press Enter.
7. Enter the number corresponding to the size disk you want and press Enter.
8. Press Enter (note there is no charge for the upgrade).
9. Type **2** and press Enter to order the item.
10. Type the quantity and press Enter.
11. Type **Yes** and press Enter.
12. Type **3** and press Enter to exit the ordering system.
13. Type **Yes** and press Enter.
14. Press Enter and write down the order number.
15. Press Enter to exit the store.

    The disks will be shipped to your home address.

To load the WinCIM v. 2.0.1. from a disk, do the following:

1. Insert the first disk into your floppy drive.
2. Click Start, Run.
3. Type **a:\setup**.
4. Click OK.

Follow the prompts to insert subsequent diskettes and specify the file locations.

After you install the software, you can save time by installing a shortcut to WinCIM on your desktop. To create a shortcut, open the Windows Explorer and navigate to the WinCIM subfolder under the Cserve folder. Click the WinCIM application file (it says Application under type) and select File, Create Shortcut. Drag and drop the shortcut to your desktop. From now on, all you have to do is double-click the shortcut to launch WinCIM.

First-time users need an agreement number and a serial number from CompuServe before setting up WinCIM. The numbers come with free copies of WinCIM distributed through magazines and other sources. If you are using a friend's software to sign on from your machine (it's all legal—CompuServe is interested in getting you to sign up), you have to call CompuServe to find the numbers. Call 1-800-848-8990 and ask for an Intro Pak.

If this is your first time on the service, you'll need to follow the on-screen instructions for finding a local access number and setting up your COM ports, phone number, and modem.

Many people in the United States will find a local access number so that they can use the service without racking up heavy phone charges. Some people, however, especially those in remote areas and those outside the U.S., will have to go a different route. You can choose to use the closest number to you, but remember to figure those charges in with your CompuServe budget.

You also can use an alternative network, such as TYMNET, which bills per hour, based on a prime and non-prime rate. Even then, you may have to use a long-distance phone number, which piles on another charge.

You may have a way around all this, if you have an Internet connection on a LAN. You can use TCP/IP to connect to CompuServe.

Connecting through TCP/IP

Connecting to CompuServe through TCP/IP allows you to use a LAN connection to the Internet as a gateway to CompuServe. You still have to be a CompuServe member, but you won't have to pay long-distance phone charges.

To configure WinCIM to use a TCP/IP connection through a LAN, do the following:

1. Launch WinCIM.
2. Select Special.
3. Select Session Settings.
4. Select Connector.
5. Scroll down to INT14 and select it. The LAN button becomes enabled.
6. Select Configure. Make sure the Host Name is **gateway.compuserve.com**. Leave the Host IP Address blank.
7. Click OK. You should have the screen shown in figure 8.2.
8. Click OK.

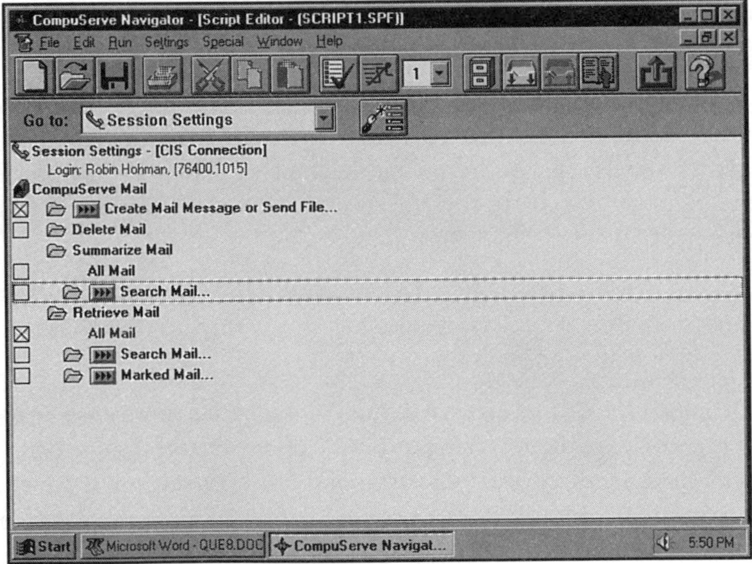

Fig. 8.2
You can use WinCIM's Session Settings to set up a TCP/IP connection to CompuServe.

Establish whatever connection your LAN has to the Internet. Launch WinCIM. Go to or find any service on CompuServe, and WinCIM makes the connection through the TCP/IP software. Remember, when you exit from CompuServe, your LAN will still be connected to the Internet.

Making the Connection

After you've set up your session settings and obtained a local access number, you can connect to CompuServe.

To connect to CompuServe, launch the software by double-clicking the CompuServe shortcut icon on the Windows 95 desktop; then click the large Explore CompuServe button, which signs you onto the service and takes you to the Explore window.

Alternatively, you can tell WinCIM in advance that you want to go to a particular place when you sign on. For example, if you want to get your mail immediately when you sign on, you would double-click the Mail icon on the button bar. After you sign on, your new mail is displayed.

Exploring Forums

The best service CompuServe offers are the many, many forums, each dedicated to a single topic or group of related topics. The forums provide a place where people exchange e-mail to ask for help, offer advice, list complaints, and even post job openings. There are also library files where people post jobs, upload files, and do anything else that relates to the forum topic.

One popular forum is the Computer Consultant's Forum, which covers a wide range of computer-related issues especially geared to the freelance programmer, analyst, and sometimes, technical writer.

To access the Computer Consultant's Forum (or any other forum), you have to find it first. The best way to find anything on CompuServe is by using the Find command, which you can get by clicking the Index icon on the main toolbar.

Tip

If you know the name of the forum, click the Go icon (or press Ctrl+G) and enter the name.

When you click the Index icon, you get the screen shown in figure 8.3.

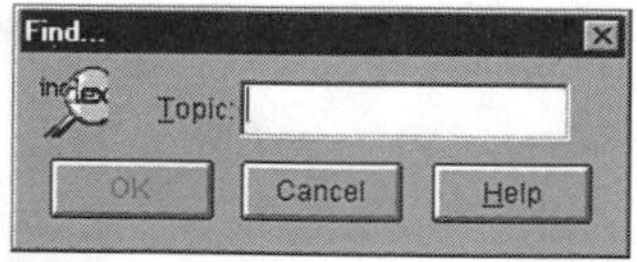

Fig. 8.3
You can find anything on CompuServe by using the Index icon.

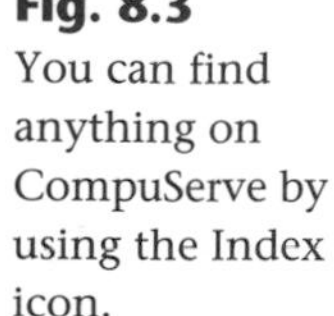

Type in the word(s) you're interested in finding. When you type in **computer consultant**, you'll get the screen shown in figure 8.4.

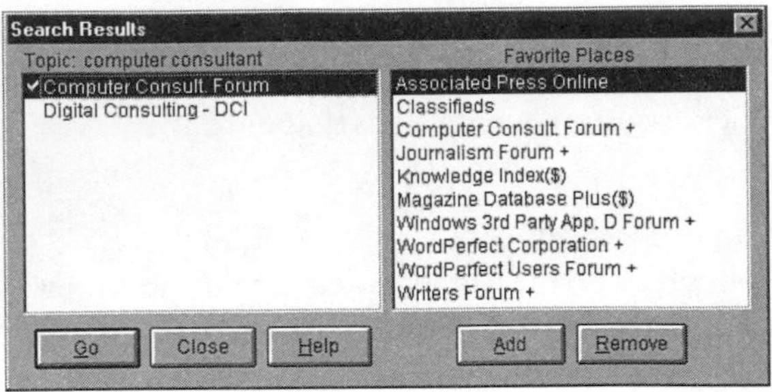

Fig. 8.4
Two items match the search for "computer consultant."

To go to a place, highlight the appropriate entry, and click Go. If you think you'll visit the area frequently, you can add it to your list of Favorite Places, shown to the right of the search results, by clicking Add. To remove a listing from your Favorite Places, highlight the listing and click Remove.

The first time you enter a forum, you have to join it. If you don't join, you can't participate in any of the discussions. It doesn't cost anything to join, and it doesn't obligate you for anything. You may get a cheerful note from the forum administrator (SysOp) welcoming you to the forum, but that's about it. After you're in a forum, you get a screen similar to the one in figure 8.5.

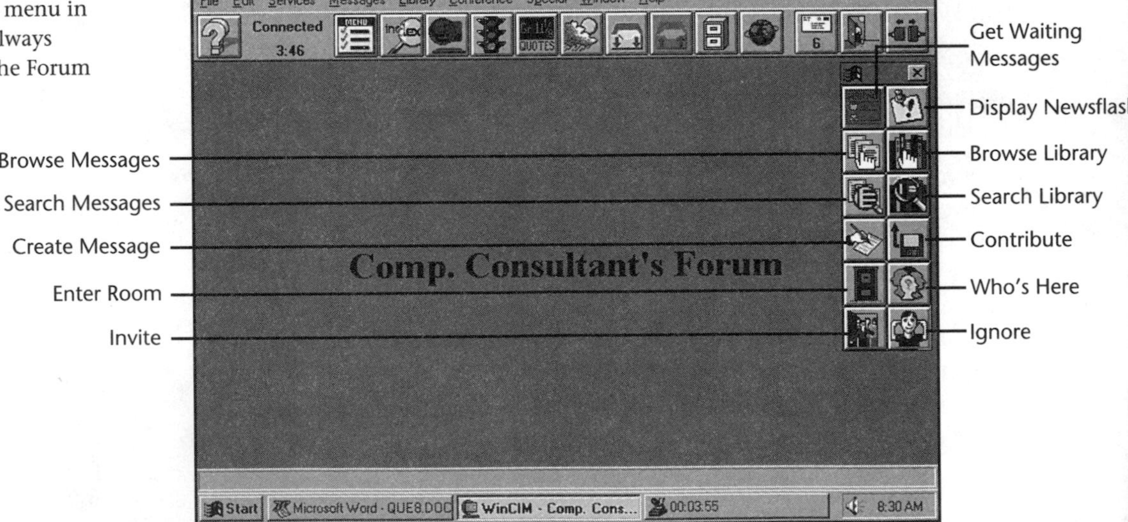

Fig. 8.5
The main menu in a forum always displays the Forum toolbar.

Tip

To bring up the menu of Favorite Places later, click the Favorite Places icon on the button bar.

Working with Messages and Threads

Messages are often the heart of a forum. If you're interested in knowing what the forum members are doing or talking about, you'll want to scroll through current messages.

To look through forum messages, double-click the Browse Messages button on the toolbar. Clicking the Browse Messages icon brings up the messages menu, shown in figure 8.6.

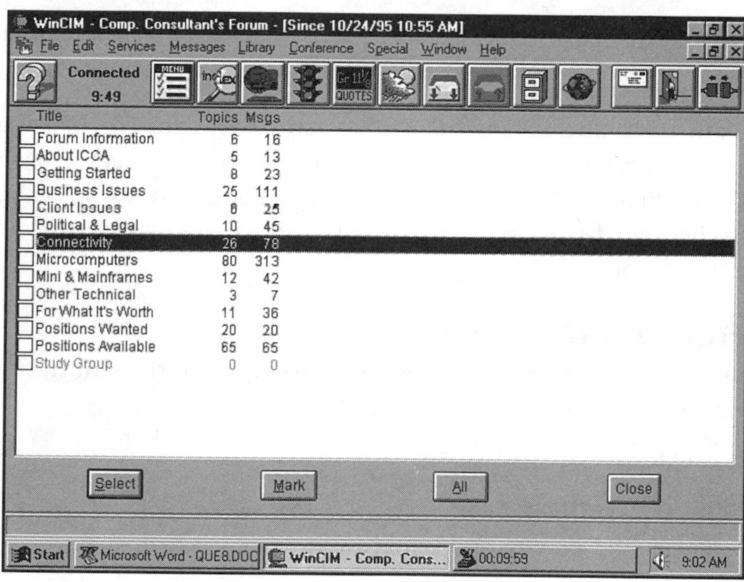

Fig. 8.6
At this writing, there are 14 different message sections in the Computer Consultant's forum.

To read currently posted messages, double-click the topic. You'll get a listing of *threads*, which refers to the string of messages centered on one topic, as shown in figure 8.7.

The message sections are set and rarely change. The messages, however, change all the time. When you enter a forum, the date you last accessed that forum is shown on the bottom left side of the main forum screen. Every time you enter the forum, you see only the messages added since the last time you visited that forum.

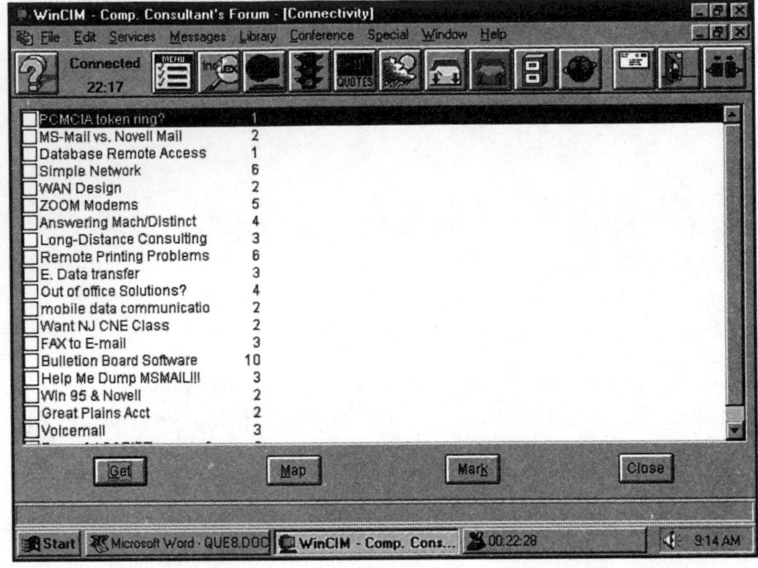

Fig. 8.7
The number of messages within an individual thread listed under a forum message topic is displayed to the right of the thread name.

That can be frustrating, because sometimes you get only the end of a message thread. If a message has scrolled off the thread, you're out of luck. However, you can sometimes see the top of the thread by clicking the up arrow. You can also click the Map button to see who has written messages and in what order in the thread.

Searching for Messages

You can search for messages by subject, message number, the sender, or the recipient. To do so, do the following:

1. Select Messages.
2. Select Search Messages.
3. Make sure the sections you want to search are selected.
4. Select Subject, Message Number, From or To.
5. Enter the appropriate information in the dialog box (for example, a user's id).
6. Indicate a date to start searching from.
7. Select Search.

You can read older messages by setting a date for messages to read. To change the date, select Messages, Set Date and enter a date.

Replying to a Message

To reply to a message, click the Reply button. Then all you have to do is enter the content of your reply. The message will be added to the message thread. Remember, anyone can read this message because it becomes part of the thread. If you want to respond privately to someone, you have to click the Private button.

> **Note**
>
> Don't expect your reply to appear instantly. Forums are administered by *SysOps*, who monitor forums to make sure that messages and library uploads conform to CompuServe and forum standards. Your reply (or message) won't be posted until a SysOp has had a chance to approve it. If it's not approved, it will be sent back to you with the reason.

Posting a New Message

To post a new message, select Messages, Create Message. Choose a message section by scrolling down the Section box, as shown in figure 8.8.

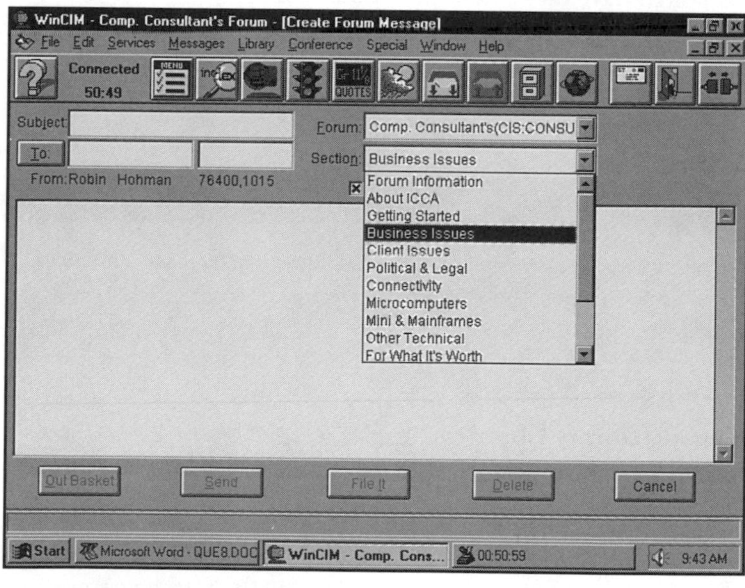

Fig. 8.8 You can only post a new message to an existing message section.

Messages are commonly addressed to "all," or to "sysop." You can post a message to an individual; but remember, any message posted in the forum can be read by everybody, unless you enable the Private option by clicking it. If you choose Private, it will be sent through the forum, but not listed in the general message threads. The recipient will only be able to read the message the next time he or she accesses the forum. If you send it Via mail, the recipient will be able to read it the next time he or she gets new mail. (See "Using CompuServe Mail" later in this chapter.)

Saving Messages in the Filing Cabinet

You can save messages by using CompuServe's Filing Cabinet feature. The Filing Cabinet lets you organize your saved messages in different groups or folders.

File It

To use the Filing Cabinet feature, open the message you want to save. Click the File It button.

Create a new folder by clicking New and entering a name for the new folder. Click Store to save the message. Messages are saved to your hard drive, so they're available when you're offline.

Working with Libraries

The library sections of a CompuServe forum are similar to the message sections, and often have the same section names. Library postings, however, differ in content. People usually post files, including software, information files, press releases, and text files containing archived materials from the forum, to the library sections. Unlike messages, library files don't scroll off after time—they stay there until a SysOp takes them off.

Tip

Library sections are often referred to by number instead of by name. To turn on the library section numbers, select Special, Preferences, Forums. Click Show Library Section Numbers.

Downloading Library Files

All library files can be downloaded to your hard drive. Some smaller files can be viewed online as well.

Click Description to see a short description of the file's contents and any special instructions, such as the file's format or how to extract a compressed file, as in figure 8.9.

To download library files, click in the box to the left of the file's name. Enter the desired file name and path; then click OK. The file will be marked.

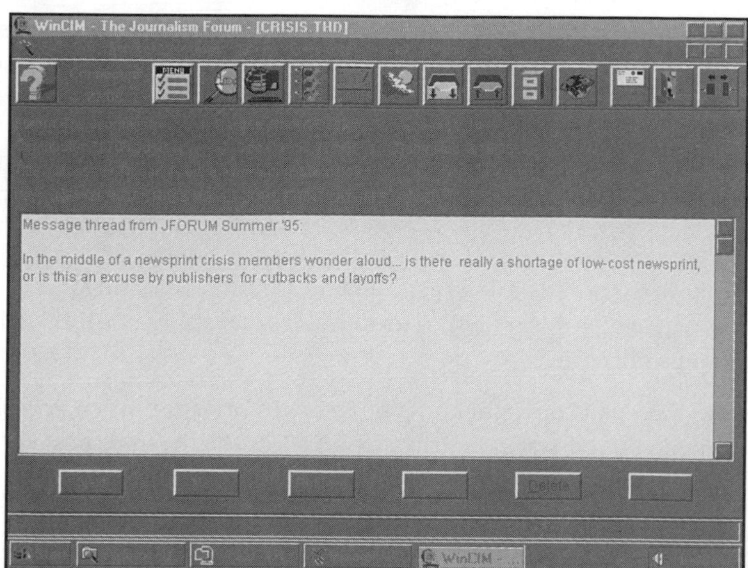

Fig. 8.9
All library files contain a short description of the contents of the file.

> **Tip**
>
> You can mark any number of files during the same session, just remember that the more files you select, the longer the download takes (and the more connect time you rack up).

When you've marked all the files you want to download, select Library, Retrieve Marked. You'll be shown a list of the files marked for retrieval, and given the options to Unmark a file, Retrieve All, or Abstract (which will just give you the short description).

One nice feature is the Disconnect When Done option. If you select it, you can go off and do something else while the files are downloaded, and you don't have to worry about wasted online time.

Uploading Files to a Library

You can upload files to the library by clicking the Upload icon. You'll be presented with a dialog box asking you to provide a File Name (the path and name of the file on your hard drive), a Destination Name (the name it will be listed under in the forum), a Title (a few words that convey the essence of the file), Keys (keywords people would most likely use to search for the file), and Description.

Try to make the file name as meaningful as possible, with standard abbreviations. The DOS-based 8.3 convention sometimes makes that difficult, and people often use the three-letter extension as a continuation of the name. That causes a problem when people try to open up the file. For example, if I named my resume resume.rsh, Windows 95 would ask you what program to use to open an .rsh file. The user would have to rename the file to a standard .doc or .txt before he or she could read it.

You also have to choose a File Type, which just means indicating if it's binary (good for text and program files) or text (good for text only); or JPEG, GIP, or PNG (graphic file formats).

Be sure to respect all copyright and proprietary information when you upload files. If you don't, the SysOp probably won't allow the file to be posted.

Also, it's common courtesy to run an anti-virus program on the file before you upload it. CompuServe is pretty good about screening for viruses, but you wouldn't want to upload one.

Files that take more than a half-minute or so to upload should be compressed using a standard compression program, usually PKZIP or WINZIP. If you must use a different compression program, indicate the type within the short description of the file.

Leaving a Forum

To leave a forum without exiting CompuServe, click File, Leave. If you have files to download but haven't retrieved them yet, you are prompted to do so.

Using CompuServe Mail

The most-used feature of CompuServe has to be e-mail. You can send messages and files to anyone on CompuServe. You also can send messages (but not files) to anyone on another online service or the Internet. There's also an address book that lets you keep track of people's addresses on CompuServe or any other online service, including the Internet.

You used to get a $9 e-mail allowance, but now the service is priced like any other. The time you spend composing, sending, and reading e-mail is charged to your account by the minute.

Tip

To save money, compose your e-mail offline and store it in the Out-Basket. Then the next time you sign on, select Mail, Out-Basket, Send.

Retrieving Incoming Mail

If you have new messages waiting when you log on, or old messages you didn't delete after retrieving, the New Mail icon gives you a count of the messages. An improvement over earlier versions of WinCIM is that the new interface shows you how many messages you have waiting, instead of just showing you a mailbox with a flag up.

To get the new messages, either double-click the Mail icon or select Mail, Get New Mail. You can read and respond to these messages one at a time, but you're better off downloading them to your In-Basket and working with them offline. See "Working Offline" later in this chapter to learn more about this subject.

Composing New Mail

To compose a mail message, do the following:

1. Select Mail, Create/Send Mail. You get the dialog box shown in figure 8.10.

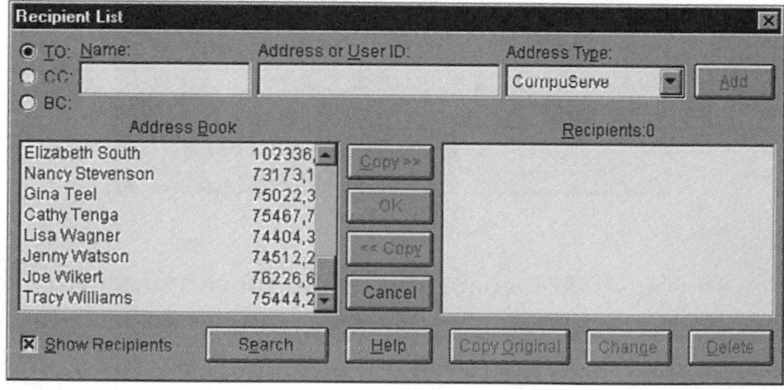

Fig. 8.10
When you create a new message, you start by choosing who you want to send the message to or by typing in a new address.

2. Type the recipient's name under Name.
3. Type his or her address under Address or User ID.
4. To send mail to the Internet or another online service, scroll down to the appropriate entry under Address Type. (To find out how to send mail to other commercial online services, Go mail while online.)
5. To add the recipient to your address book, choose Add, Copy. The name will be entered in your address book, and you just have to type in enough letters of the name so that it's unique, and the address will be entered.
6. Click OK.

7. If you don't want to add the recipient to your address book, press Enter.
8. Click OK.
9. Enter a Subject (this is not optional).
10. Enter the text of the message.
11. To send immediately, select Send Now.

    Or

    To send later, select Out-Basket.

Message Options

Whenever you send e-mail, you usually won't know when (and if) the recipient gets it or ever opens it. If you specify a receipt, you'll be notified by e-mail of the time and date the recipient opens it.

To specify a receipt, choose the Options button after you create a message. You get the screen shown in figure 8.11.

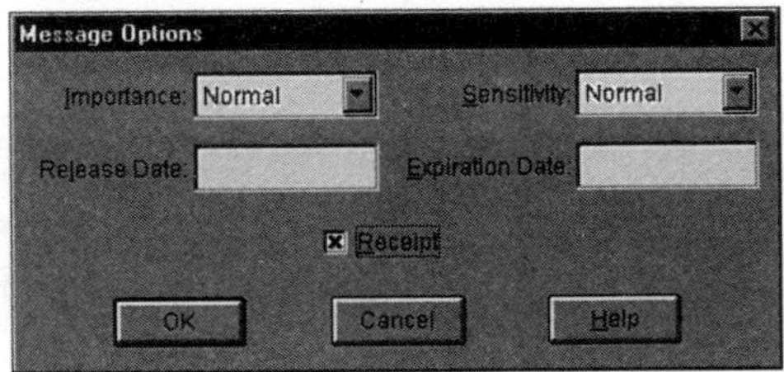

Fig. 8.11
If you check the Receipt box, you'll be sent an e-mail message indicating when the recipient opens the message.

From this screen you can also change the Importance and Sensitivity settings. Both settings are indicated in the recipient's mailbox. These Sensitivity settings are really intended for people who use CompuServe in an office, where you might not want to open a personal or private message in public.

The Release Date option is used to specify when a message should be mailed. To use this feature, compose a message and send it to the Out-Basket. It will be mailed on the appropriate day.

The Expiration Date option is used to delete a message when that day is reached.

Attaching Files

You can attach files of text, binary, video, audio, graphics, or virtually any kind of file, to an e-mail message. Remember the recipient can only read it if he or she has the proper viewers. You may have trouble sending non-ASCII files to recipients on the Internet or other online services.

Tip

It's a good idea to compress anything but the shortest files with a compression program such as WinZip, because you are charged for the time it takes to send the files.

◄ See "Using Compression," p. 138

To send an attachment, create a message as usual; then select the Attach button. In the box next to the File button, type the path and file name of the file you want to send (for example, d:/cserve/download/attach.doc). Then choose a File Type. You can specify text, JPEG, GIF, or PNG files. If you're not sending one of those file types, try binary. For most files, binary will cover it.

After you've named the path and file name, click OK.

You can also send files by themselves, without an accompanying message. It works much the same way as sending a message, and there's even a spot to include a short note. To send files by themselves, click Mail, Send File, and proceed as you would with a regular message.

Working Offline

One way to save money is to compose messages offline, place them in your Out-Basket, and then send them all at once when you're online. You also can download incoming mail to your In-Basket, then read it after you've signed off.

Composing Messages Offline

To compose a message offline, double-click the CompuServe shortcut on the Windows 95 desktop to launch the program. Create as many messages as you want, but instead of clicking on Send Now, click the Out-Basket button. The messages are placed in the Out-Basket, where they remain until you are ready to connect with CompuServe and send them.

You can make changes to or delete any message in the Out-Basket before you send it by selecting Mail, Out-Basket or clicking the Out-Basket button on the toolbar. From there Open the message you want to change, make the desired changes, and click the Out-Basket button in the dialog box again.

When you finish creating and changing your messages, you can click Send to send a single message, or Send All to send all of them. If you do so offline, CIM connects you to the service and sends the message(s).

Reading Incoming Messages Offline

Rather than read all your incoming mail while you're connected to CompuServe, you can save time and money by downloading the messages to your In-Basket. To use this option, click Mail, Send/Receive All Mail. Choose the option to Disconnect when done unless you want to do some other things online after you've received your mail.

Your new mail will be filed in your In-Basket. To read your new messages, select Mail, In-Basket or click the In-Basket button on the toolbar.

Setting Up Your In-Basket

You can use the In-Basket feature to save copies of all outgoing messages. This is a better idea than you think. After you become fluent in using e-mail and begin using it every day, you probably won't remember what you sent to whom. You can also choose to save or delete retrieved messages.

To change the mail options, select Special, Preferences, Mail. You get the screen shown in figure 8.12.

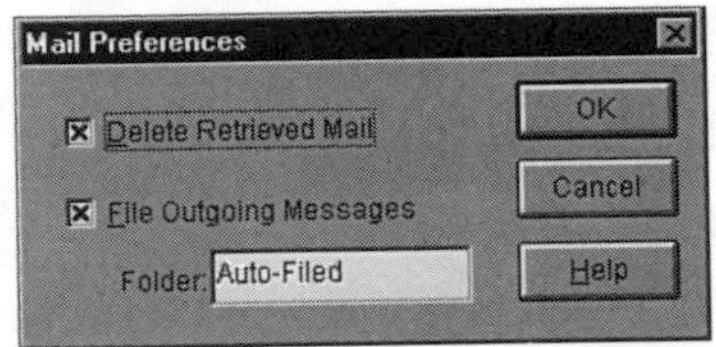

Fig. 8.12
You can save copies of all outgoing messages for future reference.

Click Delete Retrieved Mail so that once you select the Get button on a message, the message is deleted from your new mail folder. If you don't click this, the messages will stay interminably, until you manually delete them.

Click File Outgoing Messages to save a copy of every message you send. Then click the name of the folder in your Filing Cabinet where you want to store the messages. The default is Auto-filed, which is automatically created when you install WinCIM.

Using the Filing Cabinet

Spend any time on CompuServe and the Filing Cabinet will soon become your best friend. The Filing Cabinet is used to store messages. You can create as many drawers as you like so that you can keep all your messages neatly filed and organized.

To create a new drawer in your Filing Cabinet, do the following:

1. Select Mail, Filing Cabinet.
2. Click New.
3. Enter a Folder Name.
4. Click OK.

When you want to save a message to a specific folder, do the following:

1. Double-click the message to open it.
2. Select File It. The Filing Cabinet dialog box appears.
3. Click the drawer you want to save the message in.
4. Click Save.

Automating Your Sessions

As you already learned, you can save time and money by doing certain things offline with WinCIM, such as creating messages. Although that saves money, in the long run, the bulk of your online time will still be spent finding the information you need and downloading it.

That's where CompuServe Navigator comes in. CompuServe Navigator allows you to automate sending and receiving not just e-mail, but files and forum messages as well. You can write a script to log on, go into a forum, look for all new messages, and log off. Then you can read the message headings offline and write another script specifying the messages you want to download.

You can order CompuServe Navigator from the CompuServe Store while online by pressing Ctrl+G and entering **store**. From there, follow the instructions to the store, and click CompuServe Software to order Navigator. You can also download the software only (it's cheaper, but you don't get a manual). To download the program, enter **Navigator** in the Find menu. Click CompuServe Software; then click CompuServe Navigator Software. Follow the instructions for downloading the Windows version.

Creating Scripts

The main Navigator screen is shown in figure 8.13. The services you can automate are listed on the left side of your screen, in the Services Window. The Script Editor is shown on the right.

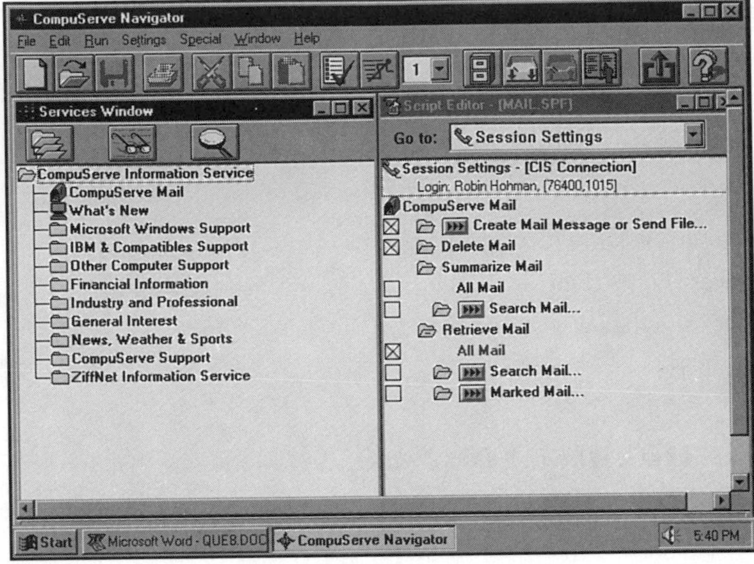

Fig. 8.13
You can use CompuServe Navigator to automate your sessions.

Creating a New Script

To create a new script, do the following:

1. Select File.
2. Select New.
3. Select File, Save As and give the script a name. Make sure that it has a .spf file extension.

Under the Services Window, select a task you want to automate. For example, if you want to automatically retrieve and send mail messages, click the line that says CompuServe Mail. Double-click the item and click Add to Script Editor Window. Select the script to use and click OK. You get the screen shown in figure 8.14.

You're not done yet. To enable a task, you have to click the check box so that it's marked with an x.

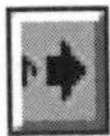

Any service that has an arrow button next to it means that you have to specify required information, such as a time period of mail to retrieve. Click the appropriate arrow button to provide further information.

When you click a check box to enable a task, the task is displayed in green letters. That tells you the task is enabled, and this script will run when you sign on. If you want to save the instructions to perform a task but you don't want to run the script this time around, click on the box to temporarily disable it.

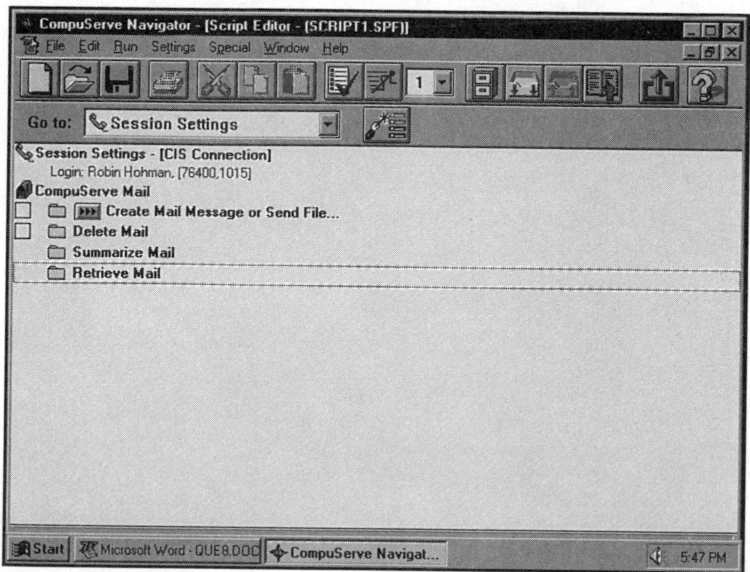

Fig. 8.14
The Mail Service has been added to the Script Editor Window.

All the CompuServe services accessible through the Navigator are listed in the Services Window. If you regularly visit a forum, you might want to use Navigator to download the topics of the latest messages so you can decide offline which ones you want to read.

To write a script to read messages in a forum, double-click the category you want to read. For example, if you want to download the latest messages in the Journalism Forum, you would double-click the folder next to Industry and Professional. All the forums in that category are listed in alphabetical order.

Adding a Forum to a Script

To add a forum to a script, do the following:

1. Double-click the forum name.
2. Click Add to Script Editor Window.
3. Select the script you want to add it to.
4. Click OK.

The forum name is added to the script window, and three services are listed under it: Message Commands, Library Commands, and Options.

To retrieve message summaries, click the Message Commands folder. You get the screen shown in figure 8.15.

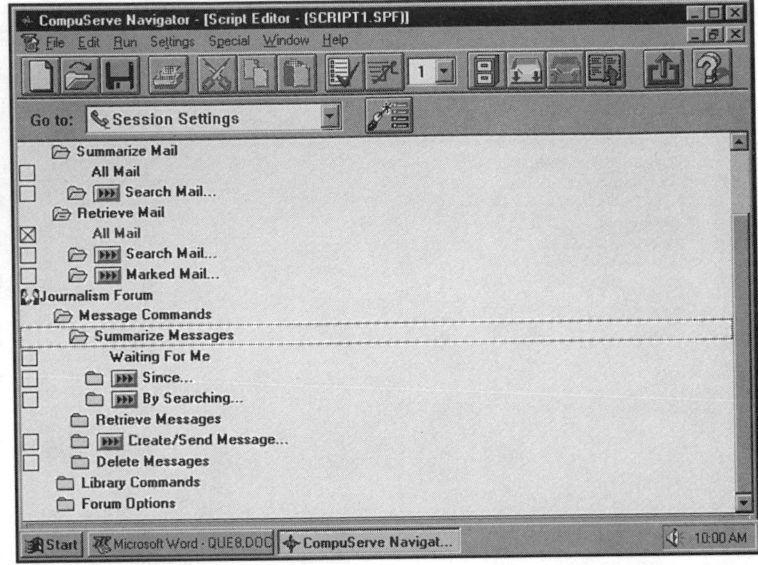

Fig. 8.15
You have to specify which messages you want CompuServe Navigator to pick up.

If you want all messages since you last signed on, click the icon next to Since. You get the screen shown in figure 8.16.

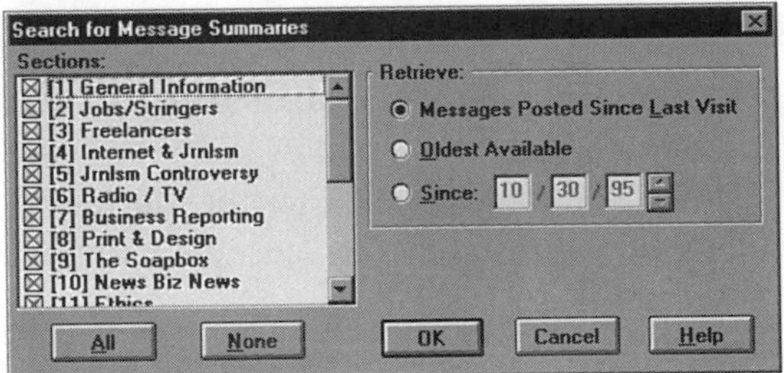

Fig. 8.16
You can choose only those categories you want to search for new messages.

Check Messages Posted Since Last Visit. All the message categories default to an enabled position. To disable the categories you're not interested in, click the check boxes so that they're not checked. If you only want the messages in a few categories, click None to disable all of them and then click the ones you want.

Click OK. Now the Since line displays in green letters, which means it's enabled.

To read a summary of what your script will do, select Run, Preview Script. You get a screen showing you, in plain English, what your script will do.

When you're ready to sign on and run CompuServe Navigator, click Run, 1 - Run Pass 1.

Reviewing Your Session

After you've run a script, you get a screen similar to the one in figure 8.17.

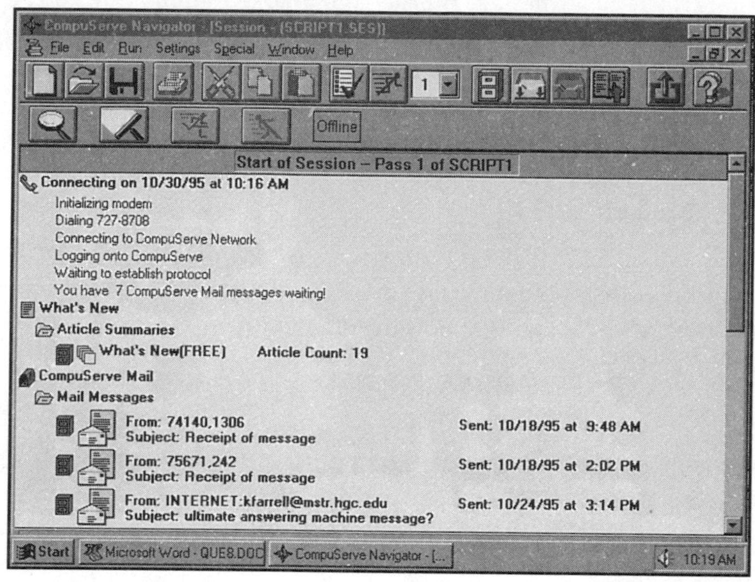

Fig. 8.17
The results of a CompuServe Navigator script session show a summary of mail messages retrieved.

To read an e-mail message, click the green filing cabinet next to it.

To review forum message summaries, click the green filing cabinet under Message Summaries. You get the screen shown in figure 8.18. If you want to retrieve any of these forum messages, click a message entry and click New, Single, or All. Mark each message this way.

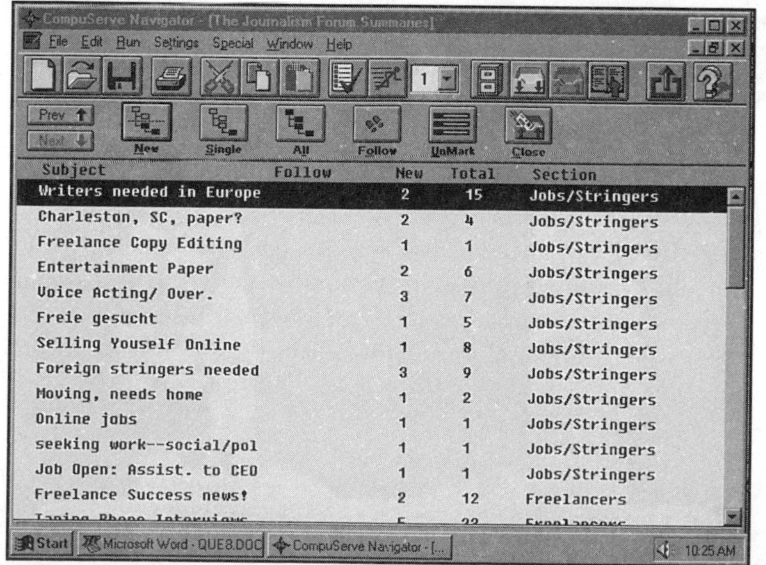

Fig. 8.18
The listing of messages from the Journalism Forum.

When you finish marking the messages you want to retrieve, click Close. If you look at a preview of the script, a line will have been added that indicates Navigator will Retrieve message threads from marked summaries. Next time you run the script, those messages will be downloaded automatically, and you can read them offline.

Accessing the Internet through CompuServe

The Internet browser, which on CompuServe is NCSA Mosaic, is now fully integrated with WinCIM. That means you can jump from CompuServe to the Internet and back again without logging off and on.

If you use CompuServe Navigator, you have to change your Winsock setting before you can access the Internet.

Troubleshooting

I can't connect to the Internet.

You may have to change your Winsock settings. To change your Winsock settings, select Special, Session Settings. Make sure that Use Winsock is enabled. Under Configure, make sure that the Host Name is set to compuserve.com.

I don't want to use the Internet connection, and it makes logging on take forever.

You can disable the Winsock connection by selecting Special, Session Settings. Select Use Winsock so that it's disabled (Configure becomes grayed out).

Accessing the Internet

To access the Internet from CompuServe, log on to CompuServe and click the Globe icon.

That launches the NCSA Mosaic World Wide Web browser. It opens to the default site, shown in figure 8.19. The default site provides links to CompuServe's home page, a Web search tool, and a CompuServe World Wide Web tutorial. Notice that on the bottom of the screen, the regular CompuServe icon is minimized. You can jump from CompuServe to the Internet whenever you want, because the Internet is now integrated into WinCIM.

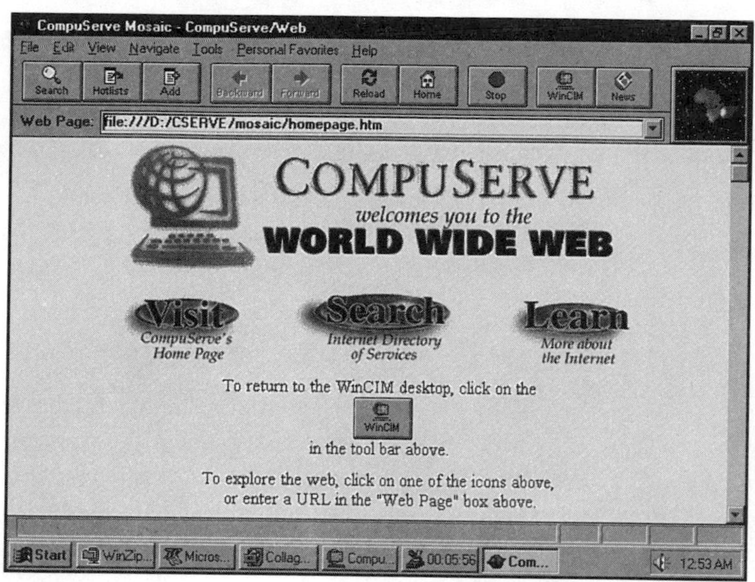

Fig. 8.19
You can connect to the Web with CompuServe's Web browser.

Click Search Internet Directory of Services, which takes you to Yahoo, a search engine for the Web. You can enter a keyword and click the Search button to find sites.

Adding Sites to a Hotlist

After you've found a site, you can add it to your *hotlist* of sites, and then you don't have to remember the URL (Uniform Resource Locator, the address system on the Web). To add a site to your hotlist, select Navigate, Add Web Page to Hotlist.

To access a site on your hotlist, select Personal Favorites and the site.

Click the Backward button to go to the previous page.

Click the Forward button to go to the next page (this is only available if you have already gone backward).

Hotlinks are the best part of the Web, the much ballyhooed hypertext. Hypertext links are displayed in blue underlined letters. Click on the text to jump to another site.

When you start jumping around on the Web, you sometimes lose your place. History is a neat feature that charts your jumps for your entire session. To see your history, select Navigate, History. Click the location you want to jump to and click Load.

If you get hung up on a page that's taking too long to load or won't load at all, click the Stop icon. That stops the incoming data and allows you to jump somewhere else.

To get back to WinCIM, click the regular CompuServe icon on the toolbar.

To actually leave the Web, select File, Exit. You'll still be connected to WinCIM. To exit WinCIM, select File, Exit. Then click the Telephone icon at the bottom of your screen and click on Hangup.

Creating Your Own Home Page

You can create your own home page on the Internet, using CompuServe's Home Page Wizard. Once you've created your own home page, you can place it on CompuServe's Web server free of charge. It's also free to download the wizard. To access the wizard, enter **home page** in the Find menu in WinCIM.

Downloading and Installing the Home Page Wizard

Highlight the CompuServe Home Page Wizard entry and select Go. You'll get the wizard screen shown in figure 8.20.

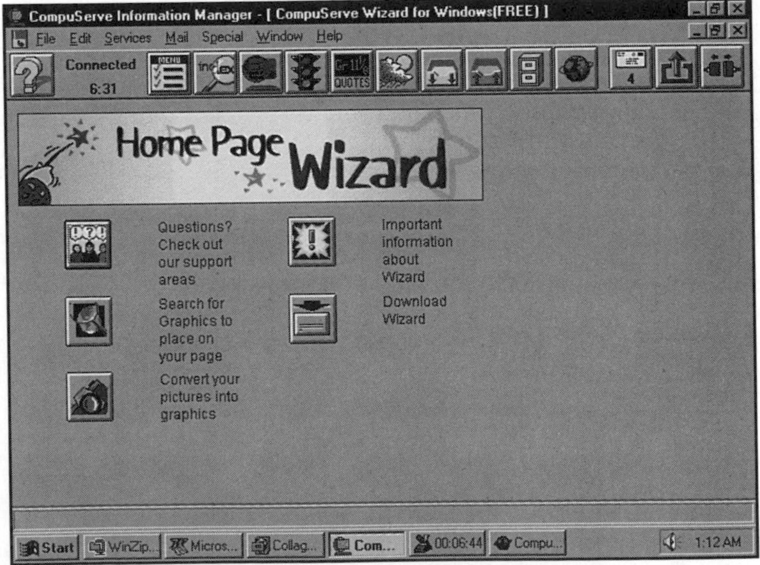

Fig. 8.20
CompuServe's new Home Page Wizard makes a home page possible even for the technically impaired.

You have to download the Wizard by clicking on Download Wizard. Also download the installation instructions, available in the same dialog box. (See, "Using the Filing Cabinet," earlier in this chapter.)

The Wizard is a self-extracting executable file, so all you have to do is run it by doing the following:

1. Execute the program by double-clicking it in Windows Explorer or using the Run command on the Start toolbar.
2. Click OK.
3. Specify a file name and path for the unzipped files.
4. Click OK. The Install Shield Wizard will launch.
5. Click Next.
6. Click Typical.
7. Browse to the proper destination directory.
8. Click Next.
9. Choose a Program Folder.
10. Click Next.
11. Click Yes I Want to View the ReadMe File Now.
12. Click Finish.

To launch the Wizard, double-click the icon.

You get the screen shown in figure 8.21.

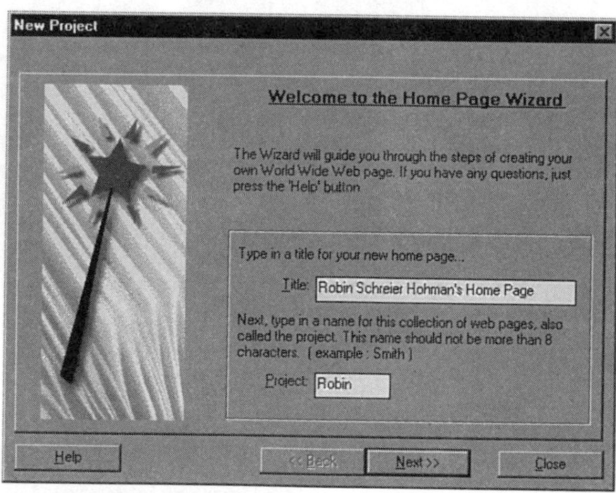

Fig. 8.21
You have to specify a title for your home page.

To create a home page, do the following:

1. Enter a Title for your home page (it should be descriptive).
2. Enter a Project name.
3. Click Next.

4. Enter your personal information.
5. Click Use Personal Information in Home Page if you want.
6. Click Next.
7. Select a Template from which to build your home page. (I'll choose Career.)
8. Click Finish.
9. Click Close when you're shown the Tip of the Day.

When you finish, you are presented with your own home page, as shown in figure 8.22.

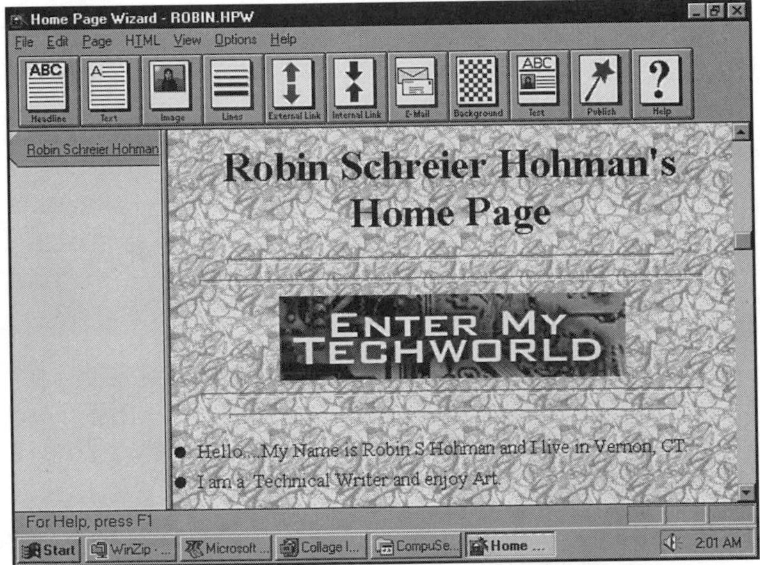

Fig. 8.22
In just a few minutes, you have your own home page.

To add text to the home page, do the following:

1. Click the Text icon or select HTML, Text.
2. Enter the text you want to add in the Text tab.
3. Click the Styles tab.
4. Choose Center on page to center the text; Pre-Formatted Text to keep the text exactly as you type it; or Bulleted to create a bulleted list.
5. Click OK. The text appears on the home page.

Headline styles are a good way to present information on the Web. Web browsers support six different headline styles that vary in size. Heading 1 is the largest; heading 6 is the smallest. To add a headline, do the following:

1. Click the Headline icon or select HTML, Headline.
2. Enter the text you want to add in the Text tab.
3. Click the Styles tab.
4. Choose a headline size (don't be afraid to experiment—Ctrl+Z can undo anything).
5. Click OK.

The procedures for adding hypertext links to other pages or to text within your home page are similar to the preceding procedures. An online help file should answer any questions you have.

Tip

The first thing you should put on your Web page is a notice that it's still under construction so that people don't think you're presenting a finished product when you're not.

Testing Your Home Page

The Web uses HTML (HyperText Markup Language) to display information. This way, any browser can read the information. However, not all browsers read the information in the same way.

Therefore, it's wise to view your home page in several different browsers to see how it will look in each. Be aware, however, this means you must keep a copy of each browser on your hard drive.

To view your home page through an external browser, do the following:

1. Click the Test button on the toolbar.
2. Click Browse and click on the browser's executable file.
3. Click OK.
4. Click OK.
5. Select Proceed.
6. To exit the browser, click File, Exit.

Sending Your Page Out to the Web

As good-looking as your page may be, it's not going to be seen by anyone unless you actually upload it to CompuServe's Web server.

To upload your home page to the server, do the following:

1. With the home page open, choose File, Save Project.
2. Double-click the Publishing Wizard icon in the CompuServe folder.
3. Click Next.
4. Click Upload Files.
5. Click Next.
6. Enter your personal information.
7. Click Next.
8. Enter Directory Information.
9. Click Next.
10. Click Next.
11. Double-click project under Directory.
12. Double-click your project name under Directory.
13. Press the Control key and click the three files listed under Files.
14. Click Add.
15. Click Next.
16. Click the homepage.htm file.
17. Click Next.
18. Enter your user ID and password.
19. Click Next.
20. Click Next.
21. Go online through WinCIM.
22. Click Proceed.
23. Write down your URL!!! This can't be emphasized strongly enough. If you don't, you may never find your page again.
24. Click Finish.

That's it. Now you're swimming with the big boys and girls. To access your home page from the CompuServe Web browser, select File, Open and type in your URL. ❖

CHAPTER 9

Using America Online

by Kate Chase

Just a few years ago, America Online was a fledgling, mostly Macintosh online service with a limited membership and perhaps an even more limited technical support base. Today, AOL is nearing the 4 million member mark, most of its members access with Windows, and it has greatly expanded its computer support forums to accommodate the needs of veteran users as well as novices. Until the release of The Microsoft Network in August 1995, America Online's Computing Department online technical help base was arguably surpassed only by that of CompuServe.

One key factor in America Online's success is its friendly graphical user interface, offering point-and-click access to popular features like live conferencing, the Internet, large file libraries containing perhaps a quarter of a million files, interactive games, and online versions of popular periodicals such as *The New York Times*, *Scientific American*, *Windows* Magazine, and *PC World*.

In this chapter, you learn how to

- Use different methods to access America Online
- Install America Online
- Get help using America Online
- Do e-mail both online and off
- Find Windows 95 resources on America Online
- Use message boards and use files from America Online

Getting America Online Software

First, you need the software, because AOL uses its own proprietary front-end. Currently, no Windows 95 version of its software is offered, but America Online for Windows V2.5 works just fine under Windows 95.

If you have an earlier version of America Online, you definitely want to upgrade to take advantage of enhancements to some features, in particular the World Wide Web browser. The latest version also makes using other means of access, like AOLnet and TCP/IP, easier to implement (see "Accessing America Online," later in this chapter).

If you do, indeed, have AOL software, there are two ways to check the version:

- If you have the installation disk, the version number will be printed under the logo.
- If you have AOL already installed on your computer, your Sign-On screen will report the version number on most versions. If you find none there, click Help from the AOL menu bar, then click About America Online. The version number is always provided there.

If you've bought a PC magazine in the last six months, you likely have some free AOL installation disks, because they've flooded the publishing world with free pack-ins.

However, if you don't have one, or your version is outdated, you can call 1-800-827-6364 to request a new disk.

Installing America Online

Once you have the software, installing it and getting online to establish your new AOL account should take about five minutes.

To install America Online:

1. Place your AOL install disk in your A: or B: floppy drive.
2. Open the Start menu.
3. Select Run.
4. For a path, type **A:SETUP.EXE**.
5. As Setup prepares to install the software, it will search for a previously installed version, and then prompt you to choose Install, Review, or Cancel.

   Install enables you to continue along with the express installation, while Review allows you to change the directory into which the AOL software will install itself.

   Click Install or Review.

6. An install meter measures the progress of the software's transfer to your hard disk, and then announces when the installation is complete.

   It will then search for your modem, and once the modem is identified, the software reports, `You're ready to use America Online!`.

   Click OK to exit Setup.

7. Click the AOL icon on your desktop.

   or

   Click Start, point to Applications, point to the AOL folder, then click the name "America Online."

8. A screen appears stating it will now help you establish a regular phone number for AOL connections, and provides a brief profile.

   If you fit the profile—which "believes" you're likely to be logging in from home and using a high-speed modem—then click Yes.

   If you don't, click No and answer a few quick questions about your computer setup.

   You're then warned to have your payment method information as well as certificate number and certificate password ready (the two latter items are packed with your AOL software; you need them to get online). See "Getting Help with America Online," later in this chapter.

   Press OK.

9. The software then dials up a special 800 number from which you'll choose (hopefully) local access numbers. What this means is that you'll try to find numbers within your free calling area that your modem will call when you sign on to AOL. The node answering your call will, in turn, dial AOL's host system in Virginia and establish a connection between both of you.

   When you're prompted to do so, enter your area code and the three-digit prefix of your phone number.

   Click OK.

10. As seen in figure 9.1, you're then presented with a list of access numbers in your calling area. You need to choose a primary number from the first screen, and a secondary (backup) number from the second.

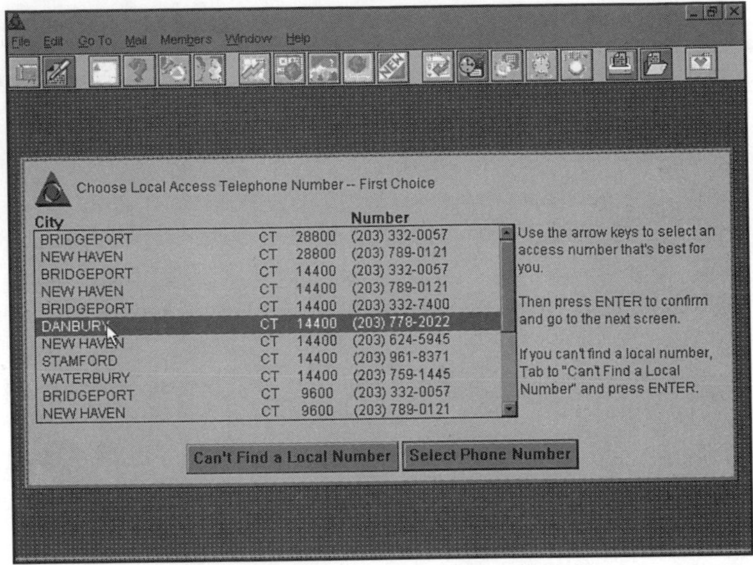

Fig. 9.1
For more information on the differences between Sprintnet and AOLnet, for example, see "Accessing America Online," later in this chapter.

Look for the highest speed access your modem will allow within your local calling range. Highlight your choice and press Enter or click OK to confirm your selection.

If you cannot find an access number within your local calling range, or your local access is at a much slower baud rate than your modem's capacity, see "AOLnet," later in this chapter.

The AOL software will then review your selections and, if you are satisfied, press OK.

11. Once the software disconnects from the 800 number, checks for your newly selected local access number, and dials AOL as a "New User," you will be prompted for your certificate number and password, as seen in figure 9.2.

    Double-check the spelling of your certificate registration number and password, then click OK.

12. AOL will then ask for your billing information and prompt you to select an online screen name and permanent password to replace the temporary ID sent to you with the installation disk.

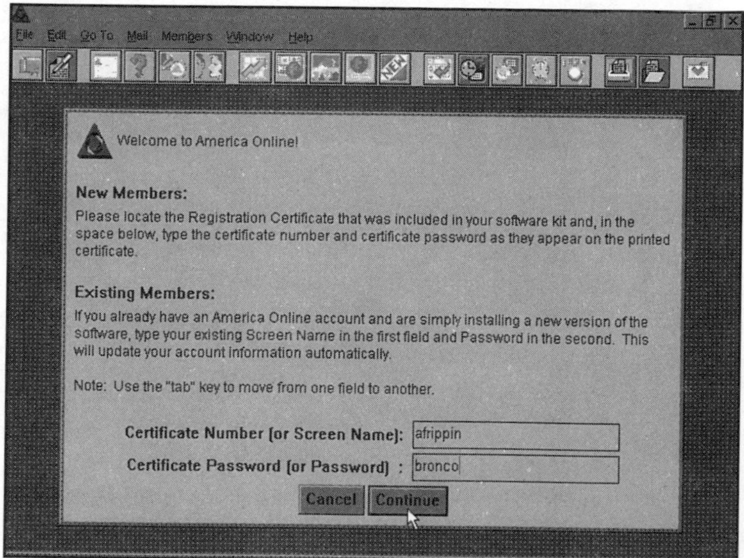

Fig. 9.2
If you already have access to an AOL account, you can substitute your existing AOL screen name and system password here.

Tip

Choose your first AOL screen name wisely, because this screen name will stay with you for the entire time you have an account there.

You can add up to four additional screen names onto your AOL account, and can delete these and create new ones at will, but the first name created, called the Master name, remains fixed. Use keyword: NAMES. See "Getting Around on America Online," later in this chapter, to add new names.

Click OK when you're satisfied. You should now be AOL's newest member.

Troubleshooting

When installing my AOL software, I noticed it checked for modems up to 57.6K bps speed? Why, then, can I only log on at 14.4K bps?

While AOL's software can recognize higher speed modems, it doesn't have a method for them to connect at this speed—yet.

Accessing America Online

There are several ways in which you can access America Online, depending on your needs and location. Check out all the options, and choose the one that best meets your needs.

Regular Local Node Access

Traditionally, most users access America Online through carriers such as Sprintnet and Tymnet (and Datapac in Canada). This means you can usually call a local carrier node, connect to it, and then the node establishes the connection between you and America Online's main host in Vienna, Virginia at no additional charge. All of this is set up for you when you first install America Online, making it very easy. However, there are some limitations. For example, not all communities have a carrier node within their local calling range, meaning you may encounter long distance charges to get online. Also, the traffic on these local carriers can be heavy at times of peak usage, such as evenings, weekends, and holidays, because these carriers provide connections for many different telecommunications services, and only have a set number of direct connections into America Online.

Higher-speed access can be limited in different communities as well, which means you may only be able to access at 9600 or 14.4K bps even if you have a faster modem. This, coupled with peak-hour volume, can leave you feeling as if you're on a slow node to China. For these reasons, you may want to explore AOLnet or TCP/IP and dial-up connections to access America Online.

AOLnet

AOLnet was first introduced in *beta*—a working test phase for programs in development—about two years ago to relieve some of the modem traffic jams users experienced trying to get online, and it seems to do the job. Before AOL V2.5, you could only use AOLnet by downloading and installing a whole separate AOLnet version of the software, but AOLnet is now accessible through the V2.5 software in regular release.

Basically, AOLnet is America Online's own data carrier network that allows you to access at speeds up to 28.8K bps. Like Sprintnet and Tymnet, there is no additional cost to access beyond your connect time with America Online. Not only does AOLnet provide for faster modems, the speed often seems faster still because you're not fighting all the traffic going elsewhere on Sprintnet or Tymnet. Many find the connections through AOLnet more reliable, too, since they don't have to go through an intermediary.

The disadvantage is that AOLnet is still new and not all communities are served by local numbers, which translates into long distance charges if you are like me and live in the sticks. To address this, AOL established an 800 toll-free number to reach AOLnet, but the convenience will cost you eight cents a minute or $4.80 per hour applied to your AOL bill above and beyond normal monthly charges (refer to "America Online Pricing," later in this chapter). If you don't have an AOLnet local number, you need to check your long distance carrier's rates to determine if it's cheaper to use the 800 number or to call long distance to get the speed advantage.

Tip

Once you're online, you can check for AOLnet access numbers at keyword: AOLnet. You'll need the number before you can sign on using AOLnet.

To use AOLnet, it is recommended that you have a UART 16550 chip installed on your modem. If you don't know if you have it, you can run any system checking software like Microsoft's MSD (Microsoft System Diagnostics), which will report if it finds this chip. You may still be able to use AOLnet even if you don't, but this chip provides some advantages, so you may want to look for the UART 16550 listed as a feature next time you shop for a modem.

To use AOLnet follow these steps:

1. Click Start from your Windows 95 desktop.
2. Select Programs
3. Click America Online
4. From your America Online Sign On screen, click Setup.
5. Choose Edit Location. The Network Setup dialog box appears.
6. Type your AOLnet local access number in the phone number field. To access using the toll-free number, type **1-800-716-0023**.
7. Select the correct baud rate for your modem from the Baud Rate drop-down box.
8. Select AOLnet from the Network drop-down box as shown in figure 9.3.
9. Choose Save.
10. Choose Setup Modem.

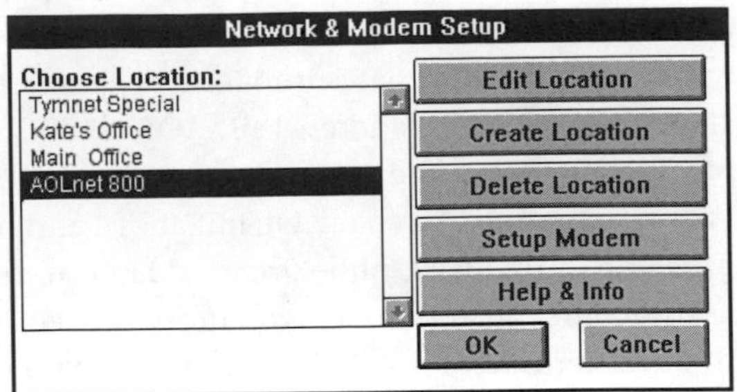

Fig. 9.3
You can have several different setups with different access numbers, depending on your needs.

11. Select the correct profile (ending in 2.5) for your modem from the list in the Choose Modem Box. Specifically, look for profiles ending in "2.5" because these are designed for use with this version of AOL.

    If yours is not listed, you may need a custom modem string. Consult your modem's manual.
12. Choose OK to save your changes.
13. Choose OK to return to the Sign On screen.
14. Sign on to America Online using AOLnet by clicking Sign On.

TCP/IP and Dial-Up Network Access

TCP/IP is a communications/data transfer protocol for networks. If you have TCP/IP available on your computer as part of a network, you can use this instead of your modem to connect to America Online. One major advantage to this is that a TCP/IP connection is usually appreciably faster than modem-based connections. Another is that by entering AOL through TCP/IP enables you to use favorite TCP/IP-based tools such as Netscape or Mosaic while on AOL, just as if you were anywhere else on the Internet.

▶ See "Using Dial-Up Networking," p. 495

If you are one of many nodes off a network, your best bet is to contact your system administrator to see if you have local TCP/IP capabilities to reach America Online.

It's also possible to use a modem-based version of TCP/IP, referred to as SLIP or PPP, to connect to AOL through a local Internet service provider. Again, this is usually a bit faster than accessing the service through Sprintnet or Tymnet, and comes in handy if you do not have a local access number for AOL. For more information on keywords, see "Getting around on America Online." For more information on FILESEARCH, see "How to Get and Use Files Found on America Online," later in this chapter.

Tip

Lists of public Internet service providers are published frequently, and you can locate one online by using keyword: FILESEARCH or pressing the red arrow icon on your top toolbar, and searching on LIST INTERNET PROVIDER.

Once you have TCP/IP capabilities, follow these steps to connect to America Online:

1. Establish your SLIP or PPP connection. Because how you do this is dependent on your particular setup and what Internet service provider (ISP) you use to access the Net, you will need to consult your ISP's documentation or your network or system administrator.
2. Click Start from your Windows 95 desktop.
3. Point to Programs, point to your America Online folder, and click America Online.

   This will bring you to the AOL Sign On screen.
4. Click Setup on the America Online Sign On screen.
5. Select Edit Location.
6. Select TCP/IP in the Network drop-down box.
7. Choose OK to save this setting.
8. Choose OK to return to the Sign On screen.
9. Choose Sign On button to sign on to America Online using TCP/IP.

Getting Help with America Online

If you experience problems connecting with America Online or using any aspect of the service, America Online provides several different ways for you to reach its Customer Relations division.

- Call 1-800-827-6364.
- From online, type keyword **SERVICE**. There are options for leaving messages or you can select Tech Support Live which is open around-the-clock. Customer Services areas are free, meaning the connect-time counter is paused while you're within a free area. You'll know because a window will pop up asking if you want to enter the free area, and alerting you that all windows will be closed until you return from the free area. There is also no additional fee for using TechLive or Customer Service.

Troubleshooting

Help! Whenever I enter a free area on AOL, like Customer Service, I lose my e-mail and other windows. What's going on?

Sorry, this is typical. Free areas on AOL are limited to very specific purposes, like helping members with online difficulties. Normal services like e-mail, instant messages, chat, and file transfers are suspended until you exit a free area.

- To use America Online's free FAX Link Service, call 1-800-827-5551 from a touch-tone phone. An automated voice menu will guide you through a request for a list of available informational faxes, and prompts you for your fax number. If your fax line is open, the list will be faxed to you quickly. However, this isn't an immediate reply service so response time may vary between a few minutes and a few hours. Call tFAX Link's 800 number again to request up to five of the topics available, and these will be faxed to you. You can always call again if you want additional topics.

◀ See "Using Third-Party Communications Programs," p. 109

- Using your modem and communications software (not America Online's software), you can reach the America Online Technical Support BBS toll-free at 1-800-827-5808. Have your communications settings at 8 (data bits), N (no stop bits), 1 (stop bit). You can download America Online software here if you connect at 9600 or higher.

Tip

Interested in a fast way to get from an application in Win95 to a specific forum or site on America Online? Try AOLINK, a small freeware utility from Bill Pytlovany, a Windows/online developer, which provides a shortcut to get you online and to your desired destination faster than an express train. You can get a copy by pointing your Web browser at **HTTP: //users.aol.com/tartan**, where you can also find other America Online add-on utilities, like Whale Express (a scripting program to automate tasks online) and CROOM (a utility to enhance chat room capabilities such as sound, color, and organizing the participant list).

America Online Pricing

America Online's pricing tends to be fairly competitive with other online services, and includes almost all functions you can perform online covered under the same connect rate. This translates into no surcharge for Internet access, downloading, searching and reading most databases and news services, playing games, or participating in live conferences.

For $9.95 per month, you get five free hours of online time with additional hours billed at the rate of $2.95 per hour. If you're opening a new account, you get 10 free trial hours to preview the service before your regular billing kicks in.

Major credit cards are accepted for account billing, as is direct debit from checking accounts. Have your account information available when you log on for the first time, because you can't get online until you've made payment arrangements.

Getting around on America Online

The first screen you will seen on AOL is the Main Menu, seen in figure 9.4, which gives you a feel for the service's simple but snazzy interface.

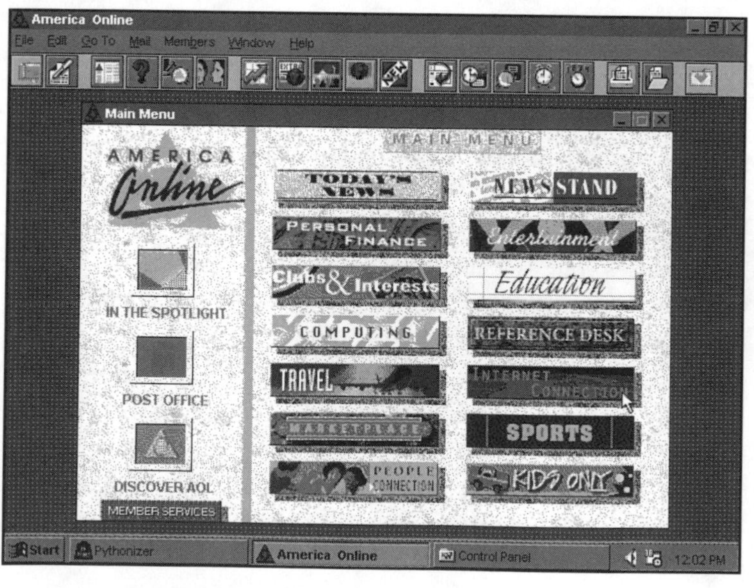

Fig. 9.4
AOL's Main Menu gives you instant, easy-to-read access to major departments online, like Computing, Reference Desk, and the Internet Connection.

Many options, like mail, member information and services, and file searching are directly accessible from the top menubar and toolbars, as shown in figure 9.5. Just point your mouse at any option and up pops a title, taking the guesswork out of the icons.

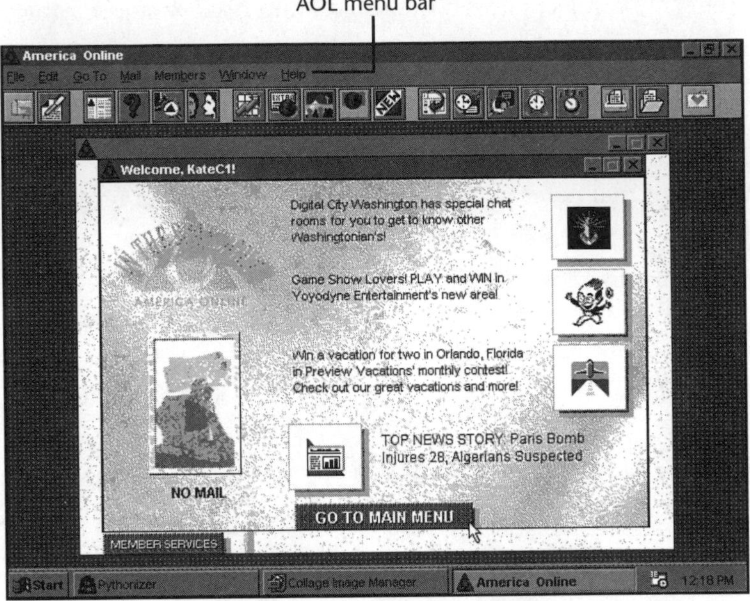

Fig. 9.5
AOL's menu bar gives you pull-down menus to perform many important online functions, like reading mail.

- *File* lets you open, save, print, log sessions, and exit AOL.
- *Edit* enables you to cut/paste/copy, and resize images you view online.
- *Goto* permits you to set up a personalized GoTo menu for two-keystroke access to your favorite online areas. You can also search the news or file database, enter the People Connection lobby, and more.
- *Mail* accesses your AOL mailbox options, like Read, Check Mail Sent, or Compose Mail (Ctrl+M). See "Doing Mail on America Online," later in this chapter for more information on this subject.
- *Members* can link you to Member Services, let you search the Member Directory, look for another member online or call up their member profile, and edit your own profile.
- *Window* not only lets you Cascade or Tile your AOL windows, it provides a listing of all AOL windows open. You'll welcome this when you're 25 windows-deep into reading.
- *Help* is just that, a quick and helpful reference tool for using AOL for Windows.

Table 9.1 describes the default icons seen in the main AOL screen.

Table 9.1 America Online Icons

Icon	Description
	AOL's mailbox: flag up means you have mail and flagdown means no mail
	Compose Mail, same as Ctrl+M
	Main Menu
	Question Mark links you to AOL's Help services
	Directory of Services—where you find what AOL has to offer
	People Connection links you to a public lobby general discussion room
	Quotes and Portfolios for managing investments
	Today's News
	Center Stage hosts major events, like movie star or book author online appearances
	Internet Services—Web, UseNet, FTP, Gopher, WAIS, e-mail
	NEW features and services
	GoTo Keyword brings up the keyword dialog screen, mentioned later in this section.
	Download Manager (Ctrl+T) organizes the files you download from AOL
	FILESEARCH
	Clock tells you current time, and your time online this session

(continues)

Table 9.1 Continued

Icon	Description
	Personal Choices lets you customize AOL names, password, profile, and tool preferences
	Print
	Save to disk
	Favorite Places maps you like to visit

The fastest means to move around online is through the use of keywords. These are titles that provide a direct link to a specific site online. There are three ways to get to the keyword screen. One is the red-arrow icon on the top toolbar. A second way is by clicking Go To on the top menu bar and selecting Keyword. But the way I use most is typing Ctrl+K.

When the keyword dialog box pops up, simply provide the name of the keyword you wish to access. For example, keyword: windows takes you to Windows Services. A list of keywords frequented by new AOL and Win95 users is provided in table 9.2. To find keywords used online, click Go To on AOL's top menu bar, and select Search Directory of Services, or click on the red question mark icon.

Table 9.2 America Online Keyword Quick Reference

Keyword	Forum/Department
ACCESS	Access Numbers
COMPUTING	Computing Department: computer support areas
FILESEARCH	Searchable database of all files in Computing
INDUSTRY CONNECTION	Computing firms with support sites online
INTERNET	Internet Services: WWW, newsgroups, WAIS/Gopher, Telnet, FTP
NEWSBYTES	Computing Industry news service
PAP	PC Applications
PHW	PC Hardware

Keyword	Forum/Department
SERVICE	Account Information/Member Services/Technical Help
SOFTWARE CENTER	Software Center
TITF	Tonight in The Forums (listing of night's events)
VENDORS	Searchable database of computer product vendors
WIN95	Windows 95 Resource Center
WINDOWS	Windows Services: choice of Windows Forum or *Windows* Magazine
WINDOWS FORUM	Windows Forum
WINMAG	*Windows* Magazine
WIN NEWS	Web site offering Windows news

Doing Mail on America Online

You can send and receive mail on AOL from other AOL members as well as friends and colleagues on other online services and the Internet. Just about everything you'll want to do is accessible under the Mail menu

Relatively new to the Windows version of AOL is the addition of FlashMail, an offline mail reader that will dial AOL for you, and grab your e-mail and download it into an index on your hard disk. You can then read and respond to it offline, at your leisure and without the billing clock running. I'll talk more about this in a moment, as we look at how to perform basic mail functions on AOL.

Composing Mail while Online

1. Press Ctrl+M to open the Compose Mail screen.
2. At the To: prompt, type the screen name or Internet address of the person to whom you're addressing this mail (for example, PC Robin, as shown in fig. 9.6).
3. Tab to the CC: prompt if you wish to copy someone else on this e-mail. Placing parentheses around the screen name in the CC: field makes this a blind carbon copy, with the CC: recipient's name invisible to the primary addressee.
4. Tab to the Subject: prompt and type the subject of your message.

5. Tab to the blank message space and type the body of your message.
6. Select from Send to send your message now or later, and click the appropriate icon.

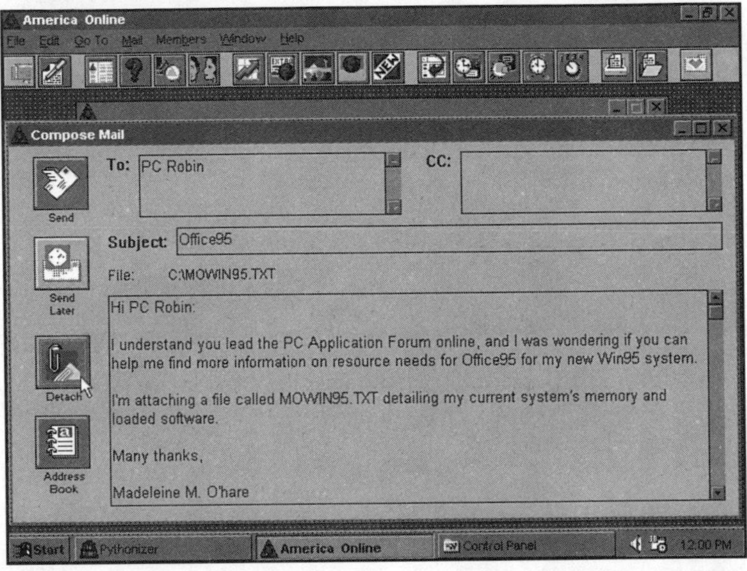

Fig. 9.6
You can keep the name of AOL help experts in your Addressbook, and then consult them using e-mail.

> **Tip**
>
> You can send a file along with e-mail by using the Attach icon. A window pops up enabling you to specify the name and location of the file to send.
>
> Just remember you can only send one file (or multiple files in a single file archive) per e-mail message. You can attach files to Internet mail, as well, but the file will be encoded during transit and will require a decoding program on the recipient's end.

Composing Mail while Offline

1. Press Ctrl+M from the AOL Sign On screen.
2. Create your mail as detailed in the preceding steps.
3. When done composing, click Send Later.
4. When you're ready to send the mail, click Sign On.
5. Click Mail from AOL's menu bar and select Read Outgoing Mail.
6. When the Outgoing Mail list appears, click Send All.

   Your mail will automatically be transferred to AOL and sent.

Reading E-Mail while Online

1. Press Ctrl+R to Read Mail.
2. A list box appears which lists the date, sender, and subject of your unread e-mail.

   Highlight a piece of e-mail and then click to open the e-mail for reading.

   Radio buttons at the bottom of this window also give you the ability to Read, Ignore, Keep as New (keeps read mail in your inbound mail list), and Delete.

Reading Mail while Offline:

Now to discuss FlashMail and FlashSessionsin a bit more detail. In order to use the offline reader to move some of your mail work off AOL to be handled at your convenience, you will need to set up your AOL software to run FlashSessions.

1. While online, press Alt+M to pull down your Mail menu, and click FlashSessions.
2. From the FlashSessions menu, you can schedule FlashSessions, activate one immediately, select which screen names you wish to have use FlashSessions (your password is required for each name).

   You'll also see a checklist of functions FlashSessions can perform, including retrieving all unread mail with or without file attachments, sending outgoing mail, downloading any files you have queued, as well as sending and retrieving UseNet newsgroup postings.

   Because you're likely new to FlashSessions, click the Walk Me Through icon.
3. You're led step-by-step through each of the functions just mentioned so you can make choices for how much and how often you want FlashSessions to work.

   When complete, you'll have your FlashSessions established so your software can automatically log on to do mail on a schedule you've set, whenever the AOL software is open on your desktop.

   If you need to do a FlashSession immediately, just press Alt+M, and select Activate FlashSession Now.
4. Once the FlashSession is complete, press Alt+M to pull down the Mail menu once more.

   Select Read Incoming Messages and follow the same basic directions as for Reading Mail while online, see "Reading E-Mail while Online," earlier in this chapter.

Caution

Even an already-read e-mail message will remain on your hard disk, as well as on your list of Incoming Messages, until you use the Delete radio button on the Read Incoming Mail list screen to purge it.

The capacity of the offline reader to store messages is only limited by the size of your hard disk.

Replying to E-Mail while Online

1. With the e-mail you wish to respond to still open on your screen, click the Reply icon.

   If more than you and the Sender have been copied on the e-mail sent, you may use the Reply to All icon to copy the reply to everyone on the original mail.

   Tip

   Before clicking Reply when reading e-mail, move your cursor down to the body of the e-mail you are reading, either to a paragraph you wish to quote, or at the beginning of the e-mail to copy it in its entirety.

   Click the right mouse button, hold it, and drag the cursor down the screen to highlight text you wish to quote.

   Press Ctrl+Ins to copy it to buffer.

   Click Reply; the text you highlighted from the previous e-mail screen will be automatically added to your Reply message space with brackets to indicate it's a quote.

2. Type your message.
3. Click the Send icon to send the message.

Replying to Mail while Offline

1. Press Alt+M to pull down AOL's Mail menu.
2. Select Read Incoming Messages.
3. Once you highlight and click a message, then read it, click Reply.
4. When you're done typing the reply, click Send Later. Your mail will be saved until the next FlashSession for sending.

   or

   Click Sign On.

5. When you're logged on, press Alt+M to open the Mail menu.
6. Select Read Outgoing Messages.
7. Select Send All.

   Your outgoing e-mail replies will be delivered automatically.

Finding Windows 95 Resources on America Online

Because America Online is made up of many different departments and dozens if not hundreds of sites or forums located within each department, there are several places online to find Windows 95 information, and dozens more you can access through America Online's Internet gateway.

Win95 Center

The first place you'll want to stop is the Win95 Center at keyword: Win95 (see fig. 9.7). On the downside, Microsoft isn't here providing direct support for its operating system. But on the plus side, many others—including America Online forum personnel, visiting industry customer support representatives, and publishers—do, offering up a cornucopia of suggestions, programs, tips, tricks, solutions, and configuration tuning.

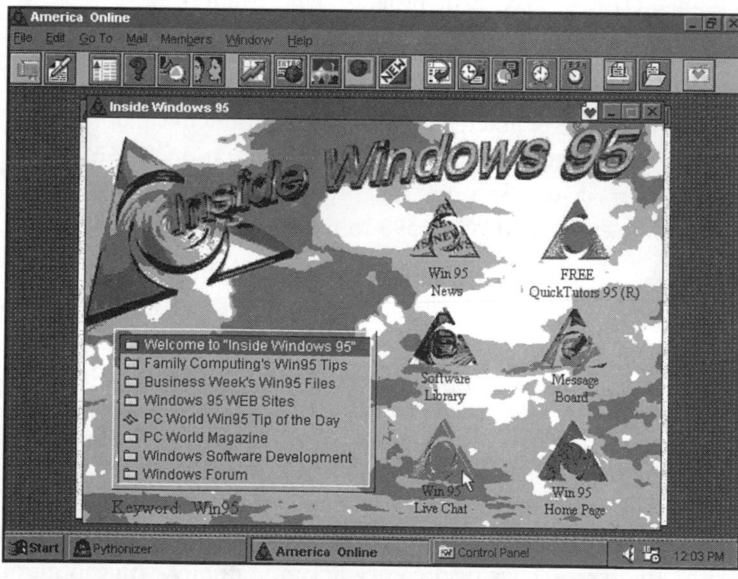

Fig. 9.7
The Win95 Center offers the most extensive collection of Windows 95 resources online, with free tutorials and Web hyperlinks.

From the left-hand list box pictured, you can learn more about the Center, browse *Family Computing*'s Win95 tips and *Business Weekly*'s Windows 95 files, visit select Web sites specializing in Windows 95 news and software, visit *PC World* Magazine, or join America Online's Windows or Windows Software Development Forums.

Icons then direct you to some of the Center's other features, which include a Windows 95 tutor, software libraries, message boards, conference rooms and schedules for live Win95 discussions, as well as a direct link to Microsoft's Win95 Home Page (**http://www.microsoft.com/windows**).

One warning though: Web browsing can get painfully slow at times, even accessing at 14.4K bps. If you plan to navigate the Web here with any frequency, upgrade to a 28.8K modem if you don't have one, and try AOLnet. Getting the files you want, if available, via America Online's gateway to FTP (file transfer protocol) might work better. Use keyword: FTP to check it out. And yes, you can reach Microsoft from there at **ftp.microsoft.com**.

The tutor here, E-Soft's QuickTutors95, offers 40 mini-tutorials covering everything from installing new hardware to using new features and resides on your desktop for quick reference. It is offered free except for the usual connect charges; the transfer takes about twenty minutes at 14.4K bps. Once you download it, just select Run from Windows 95's Start menu and double-click the file named QT95AVI.EXE. The program will install itself.

In the Software Libraries, don't miss browsing through HOT!, a listing of top-ranked Windows 95 files. McAfee Associates' Scan 95 is here, and is considered by some to be the premiere virus scanning product available currently for Windows 95, particularly with its Explorer integration. The Windows 95 Resource Kit Help File can be found here, too, as well as a nice Win Tutor from Usability Sciences, and WinZip95 to handle your ZIP archived files.

Other libraries you can browse house applications, utilities, games, and there's also another gateway to selected Web sites specializing in Win95 software. Even without venturing out onto the Web, the Win95 Center offers at least a few hundred program and help choices in its libraries, and new uploads arrive daily.

Live conferences touching on all aspects of Windows use are held several nights each week. A complete current schedule of these conferences can be found by clicking the Win95 Live Chat icon. If a chat is in session when you visit, just highlight and click Conference Room. Actually, you can monitor the schedule for all live computing forum conferences by going to keyword: TITF (Tonight in The Forums), where you can read the schedule and click Check for Active Rooms. A room list pops up. Just highlight one and click it to enter.

To get the most help out of your session, let's take a look at how to use America Online's message boards and file libraries for finding help.

Using Message Boards to Get Help

The Win95 Center offers a good jumping-off platform to introduce new America Online members to how its message boards function. This is important because message boards are open 24 hours a day, and provide an avenue for you to post questions and get feedback on your problems. The message boards are monitored daily by forum personnel, and other users offer their advice, too.

To get to the Win95 message boards, type keyword: **WIN95** which brings you, as before, to the Win95 Center. Click Message Boards, and select the document entitled "Navigating the Message Area." This Help file gives some detail on how to get the most out of posting and reading the message boards here.

Briefly, each message board center is divided into different message areas covering a major topic like "Networking," "Desktop," and "Configuration." These major topics are then broken down into subtopics, and organized into folders containing messages oriented around different aspects of the subtopic. Some messages pose questions, while others offer solutions or tips. It's a good idea to scan through the messages on topics that interest you, because you may find the answer to a problem even before you ask.

From here, click again on Message Boards to reach the actual major topics listings (see fig. 9.8). Icons located at the bottom of the screen allow you to List Topics or folders in each message board, Find New allows you to look at messages new since the last time you visited, and Find Since pulls up messages new within the number of days you specify. When you visit a message board for the first time, all messages will be new, but America Online's software keeps track of what you visit and when, so that on subsequent visits, you can choose to read only messages new since the last time you were there. However, you can still Read All to catch previous messages you may have missed.

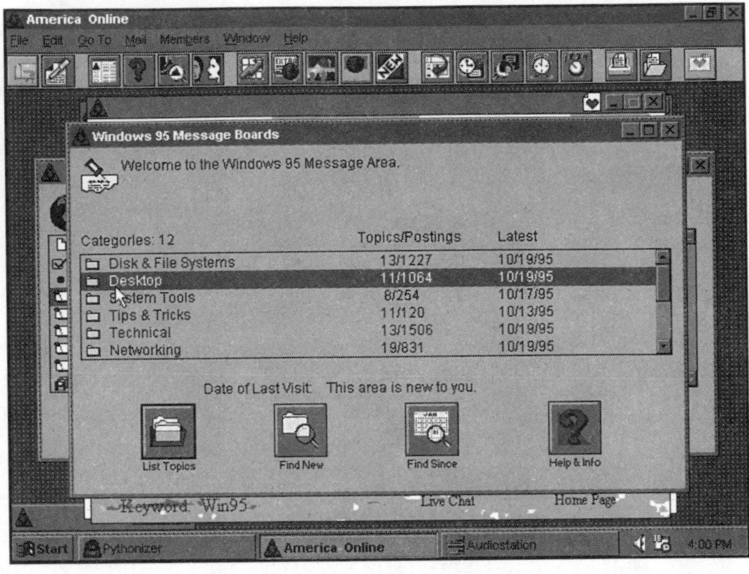

Fig. 9.8
Windows 95 Message Center: Seasoned AOL veterans say these can be a gold mine of useful information.

Choose a message board category such as "Desktop" by placing your cursor on the line to highlight it, then click. A list of all folder subjects will be displayed (see fig. 9.9), along with information about how many messages are contained within, when the folder was created, and when the last message was posted to it.

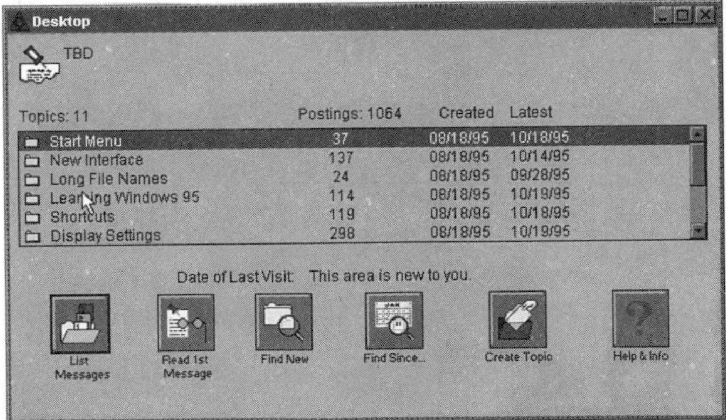

Fig. 9.9
Deeper in Win95 Message Center: Read only the folders you wish, or use Create Topic to open a new one.

Of more interest are the buttons below that allow you to List Messages, Read the First Message in a folder, Find New, Find Since, and Create Topic, which lets you open a new folder to begin a fresh discussion. Once you choose Create Topic and fill in the subject, you'll be asked if you would like to post a message to the folder. Say yes and a message field will pop up. State your question or comment and relevant information as briefly as you can while giving necessary details, then click Post. The message will automatically be added to the new folder, and made available to other forum visitors.

Highlight a folder to read, click, and see a list of all messages. Then highlight and click a message of interest (see fig. 9.10), and it will be displayed, providing options to page back one message, page forward one message, or Add a Message.

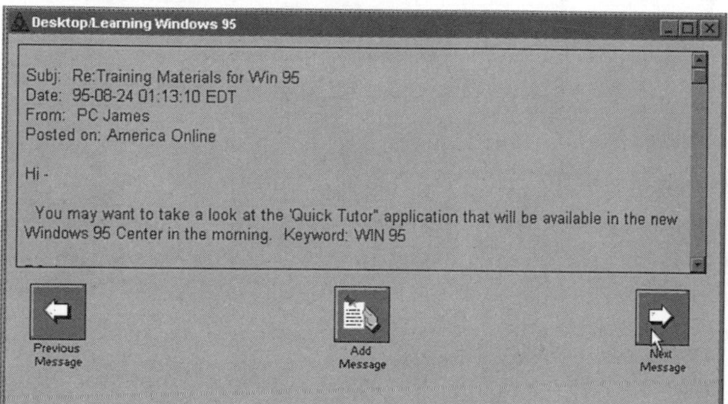

Fig. 9.10
A message from one of the Windows Forum personnel in the Win95 Center.

Tip

Need help identifying computing forum personnel? All have a PCx prefix before their names indicating their rank. For example, PC James tells you James is a forum leader or the person who supervises a computing forum online. The prefixes PCA and PCC are used as well to designate forum assistants and consultants. You can get a roster of forum personnel whenever you visit a computing forum online, like the one at keyword: Windows Forum. This is useful if you need to send e-mail to a forum staff member requesting assistance.

How to Get and Use Files Found on America Online

There are two fast avenues for locating files from wherever you are online. As mentioned before, the top toolbar of the America Online software features a magnifying-glass-over-a-diskette icon which brings you directly to a search screen, as does keyword: FILESEARCH (see fig. 9.11).

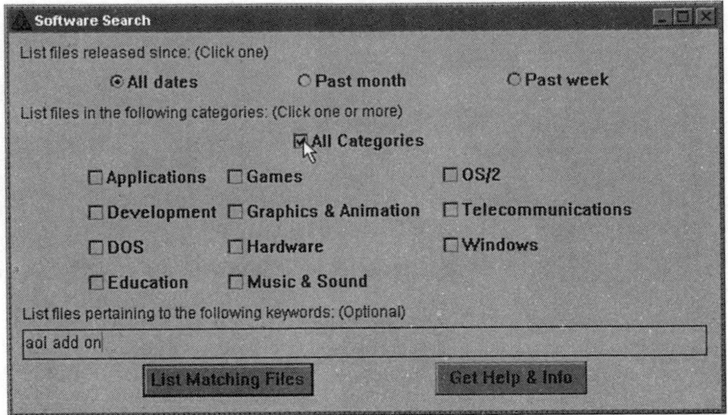

Fig. 9.11
FILESEARCH enables you to search throughout the hundreds of libraries available online.

At the top of the search form, you can pick whether to search through all files regardless of date, by files released online within the past month, or for the past week. Next, you can select from a list of forums you think might have files of interest to you. Finally, in the wide dialog box near the bottom of the screen, you can add any search criteria you think might aid the database in identifying a file you want.

In the example just given, I was looking for America Online for Windows add-on utilities. Since I didn't care about the release date and wasn't certain which forum might have them, I let it search ALL dates and ALL categories listed. However, in the dialog box, I needed to narrow down the focus of my search, so I typed "AOL ADD ON". You can use clauses like AND, OR, and NOT to further narrow or expand your search focus. Also, FILESEARCH is not case-sensitive, so you can type in all lowercase or all uppercase. For example, you can highlight Windows in the forum options, then search on SCREEN AND SAVER, or GAMES NOT TETRIS.

The search produces a list of files that meets that criteria. Highlight a file that interests you from the list. Buttons at the bottom of your screen give you the option to:

- Read Description: Every forum file on America Online offers a complete description of what the program is, who publishes it, and what you need to know to use it (see fig. 9.12). Descriptions usually note, too, any special hardware or software needed to run a program. Additionally, all files in forum libraries are checked for computer viruses and functionality before they are released to the public to help reduce the chance of user problems. From the description screen, you can choose again whether to Download Now or Later, or double-click the left-upper edge of the open window to close it without downloading.

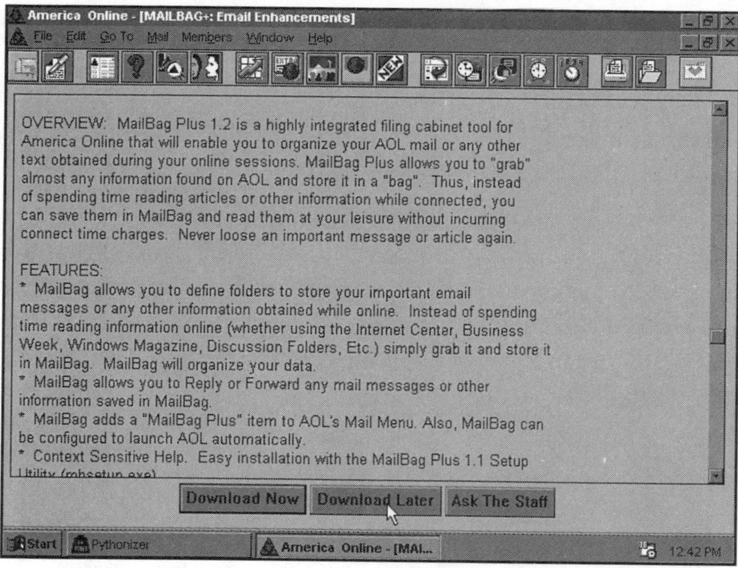

Fig. 9.12
America Online's Windows Forum libraries label each program with a description telling you how to use it.

- Download Now prompts you for the path or location in which to place the downloaded file. As a default, it will download to your America Online download directory, which with V2.5 is C:\AOL25\DOWNLOAD.

> **Note**
>
> AOL software is automatically configured to expand file archives, as in those ending with the file extension .ZIP and .ARC, into a file-specific subfolder of your AOL25 Download folder. For example, if you download a file called WIDGET.ZIP, you can find it unzipped in the subfolder marked AOL25 DOWNLOAD WIDGET. You can run your expanded downloads right from this subfolder or move them to a more appropriate location.
>
> The original .ZIP file, however, will remain intact in your AOL25 Download Directory until you delete it.

- Download Later allows you to queue the program to download at another time. The request to download the program is stored in your Download Manager, available at anytime by pressing Ctrl+T or by clicking File from the top menu bar and selecting Download Manager. It's also available as the clock-over-disk icon on the top toolbar. If you haven't initiated the download before you sign off that session, the software will prompt you by asking if you want to download the file automatically before your connection is severed. You can click Yes to proceed, or No if you want to perform the download at a later session. You can set up one or several files to download this way.

- List More Files does just that, if more files are available.

This same method of reading descriptions and downloading applies when you browse through libraries on America Online as well. Just click the Software Libraries icon from the Win95 Center or elsewhere, and scan through the list of available libraries until you select one by highlighting it. Then click, and that library's roster of files is displayed (see fig. 9.13). You can proceed from there.

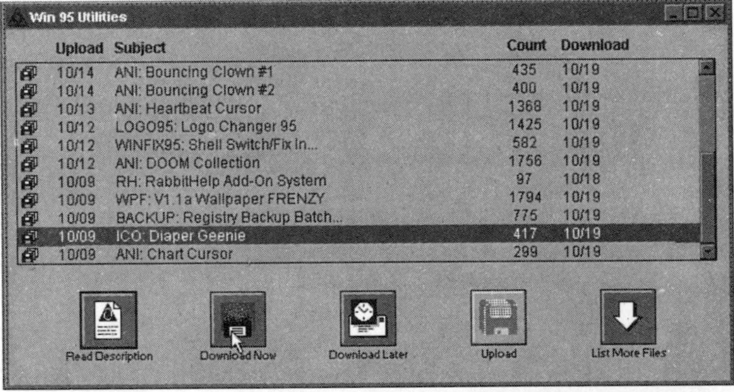

Fig. 9.13
The Win95 Center offers libraries of shareware and public domain software for download, including the Windows 95 Utilities collection pictured here.

Tip

Offline and don't want to sign on to America Online just to check to see if they offer a particular file? Check out AOLDBF, a database system that tracks the files available online. Once you download AOLDBF, you can get weekly updates covering all the new uploads for the previous week, so you'll always be current. Type keyword: **FILESEARCH** and search on AOLDBF.

Additional Windows 95 Resources Online

The Win95 Center actually is part of the Windows Forum on America Online, and this forum features support and files for the many versions of Microsoft Windows still in use, predominantly Windows 3.1 (see fig. 9.14).

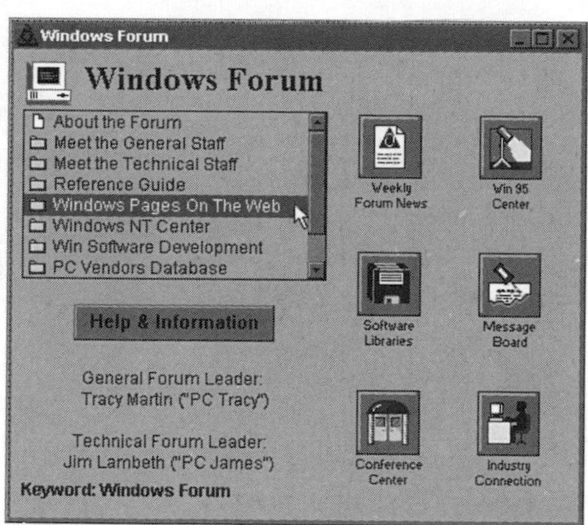

Fig. 9.14
The Windows Forum (keyword: Windows Forum of America Online) provides support for just about any version of Microsoft Windows.

As with the Win95 Center and other computing forums online, this main menu offers you entry to software libraries and message boards, weekly forum news updates, a conference center for live discussions and a link to other sites of interest. These include the WinNT (WindowsNT) Center, Windows software development, a computing vendors database, and more.

Elsewhere, you can get assistance with Windows 95 applications like Excel95 by visiting the PC Applications Forum (keyword: PC Applications or PAP), which covers spreadsheets, word processors, databases, and desktop publishing packages, to name a few. Within the PC Graphics and Sound Forum (keyword: PC GRAPHICS or PGR), Corel offers support for its Windows 95-compatible version of CorelDRAW!. Hardware problems are tackled within the PC Hardware Forum (keyword: PC HARDWARE or PHW) and America Online's Software Center (keyword: Software Center) offers a rotating roster of popular downloads which often include Windows programs.

Elsewhere, you may want to check out Kim Komando's Komputer Klinic (keyword: KOMANDO), a general computer help clinic that fields its share of Windows 95 "911" calls. Ms. Komando also produces a line of computer tutoring products that are featured there for sale.

Windows Magazine (keyword: Windows Magazine or WINMAG), a popular CMP Publication, offers an online version of its magazine, plus libraries of utilities and demo programs, and access to archives of past issues (see fig. 9.15). So, too, does *PC World* (keyword: PC World), and both have covered Windows 95 extensively. Additional computing magazines online can be found at keyword: COMPUTING under the Print and Broadcast icon.

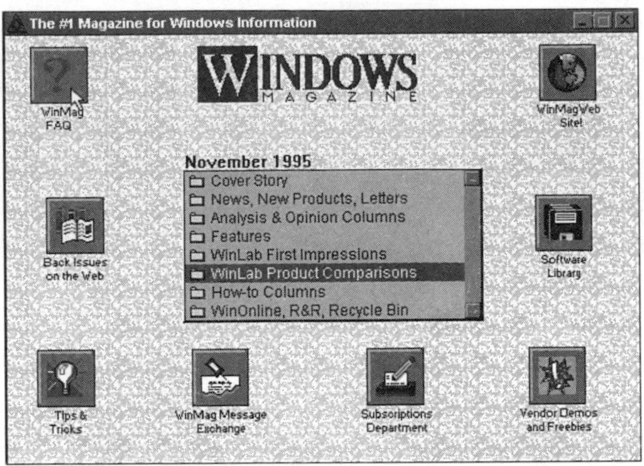

Fig. 9.15
CMP's *Windows* Magazine is just one of several computing periodicals offering online versions of their magazines, plus libraries and message boards.

Beyond this, you can always use keyword: INTERNET to access America Online's gateway on to the Net. Currently, most of the major features on the Net are available here, including FTP, World Wide Web (via America Online's browser), UseNet newsgroups, Gopher/WAIS, and limited Telnet. If you don't have access to the Internet through a private provider, consult the Internet resources found elsewhere in this book, and use America Online's Net gateway to surf to them. The advantage here is convenience and the many resource guides provided within the Internet resource center to help newcomers navigate, while disadvantages here include sometimes slow performance and a tendency for the gateway to go down.

You may also want to investigate KnowledgeBase, a Microsoft technical database that resides within the Microsoft Resource Center (keyword: Microsoft). It's a compendium of information relating to Microsoft products and how they interact with hardware and other software. However, America Online's version of this great information utility tends to be less-than-very-current, or has been many times in the past. If you also have access to a CompuServe account, you might have better luck with its KnowledgeBase site to find the latest Windows 95 technical reference material.

Add-Ons for America Online for Windows (WAOL)

Dozens of third-party shareware and freeware utilities to add-on to America Online's Windows software have appeared in the last two years. Some, like Tartan Software's CROOM, which helps you colorize and organize chat room participation, offer a solid step up from the stand-alone software while other less ambitious utilities do simple tasks like clearing a stuck hourglass or turning off instant messages (a quick private message you can create by typing Ctrl+I).

Partly in response to the popularity of its product and perhaps partly also due to the fact that it weathered a few add-ons that "hacked" or improperly used the service, AOL is currently developing its own software developer's kit, available in limited release now.

To reach the add-on library online, use keyword: Windows or keyword: PC Development (which covers, among other things, Windows software creation). Click Software Libraries, and browse the list until you see WAOL (for Windows America Online) Add-ons. Click again, and you have a listing of available files. You can also use keyword: FILESEARCH (see "How to Get and Use Files Found on America Online," earlier in this chapter), or the magnifying-glass-over-disk icon on the top toolbar.

Here are a few recommended shareware ones to try:

- Power Tools v1.9 by BPS Software; incorporates a macro "phrase" manager with online answering machine, and enhances chat room and address book functions. It takes about eleven minutes to download at 14.4K bps.
- Way-to-Go V2.6 by Prism Elite; offers floating toolbar, menus and keyboard shortcuts, manages lists of people and forums, enhances chat room functions, and offers an offline reader and retriever for e-mail, message boards, and UseNet newsgroups on the Internet. About eight minutes.
- MailBag Plus by Next Generation (which also publishes WCSpell, an online spell checker, compatible with CompuServe's WinCIM, Delrina's WinFax, and PC Eudora); allows you to store any mail or text online into user-defined mailbags. About two minutes.
- VOICEAOL by BONZI Software; a Windows 95-compatible utility to add speech, sound, and music to your America Online e-mail. Under 30 minutes. ❖

CHAPTER 10

Using Prodigy

by Kate Chase

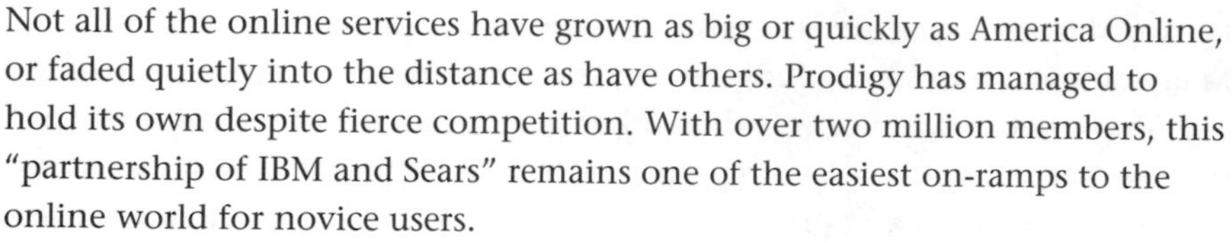

Not all of the online services have grown as big or quickly as America Online, or faded quietly into the distance as have others. Prodigy has managed to hold its own despite fierce competition. With over two million members, this "partnership of IBM and Sears" remains one of the easiest on-ramps to the online world for novice users.

When Prodigy introduced the Windows version of its software in 1995, it also beefed up its features. Now, most venues on the Internet like the World Wide Web and newsgroups are offered alongside expanded options like chat, download libraries, and electronic versions of well-known consumer magazines such as *Newsweek*. In other words, if you haven't tried Prodigy recently, you may be pleased with the facelift. Its screens are easy-to-read, it offers point-and-click access to many features, and it's probably the least stressful introduction to cyberspace for brand-spanking new computer users, including children and older adults.

Prodigy's reputation has been made in ease-of-use, and not as a vast technical resource. But it's made progress, too, in offering more of a support base for users troubled by their hardware and software. Until recently, Prodigy had no live conferences and very little software to download. Now there is ZD Net, a searchable online collection of computer information provided by Ziff-Davis (publisher of popular user magazines like *PC Magazine* and *Computer Shopper*), as well as several other software collections, and live conference and bulletin board discussion sites to discuss computers.

In this chapter, you learn to

- Install and Access Prodigy
- Get Help using Prodigy
- Use Prodigy Mailbox

- Find Windows 95 resources on Prodigy
- Use Prodigy's bulletin boards and files
- Use add-on utilities to enhance Prodigy

Accessing Prodigy

Plans for a Windows 95 version of Prodigy to take better advantage of some of the new operating system's enhanced options are currently under development, but it's not available yet. However, Prodigy's V1.2 for Windows software will run under Windows 95. If you have an earlier version of the Prodigy software, order an upgrade because it updates certain parts of the service, such as the Web browser.

Having the most current version can help save you time as well as money. Many online services, including Prodigy, offer on-demand software updates. Put simply, what this means is that rather than Prodigy putting out frequent full upgrades that you would then have to install, Prodigy chooses to send you short updates of artwork and files as needed, or when you enter a new area online or reenter an area that has been redesigned since your last visit. Even having the most current version, I spent a considerable amount of online time watching my software get updated for e-mail and the Web via my 486/DX2 66 connecting at 14.4 Kbps.

Once you are connected, Prodigy offers a user-friendly interface that virtually guides you anywhere you want to go (see fig. 10.1).

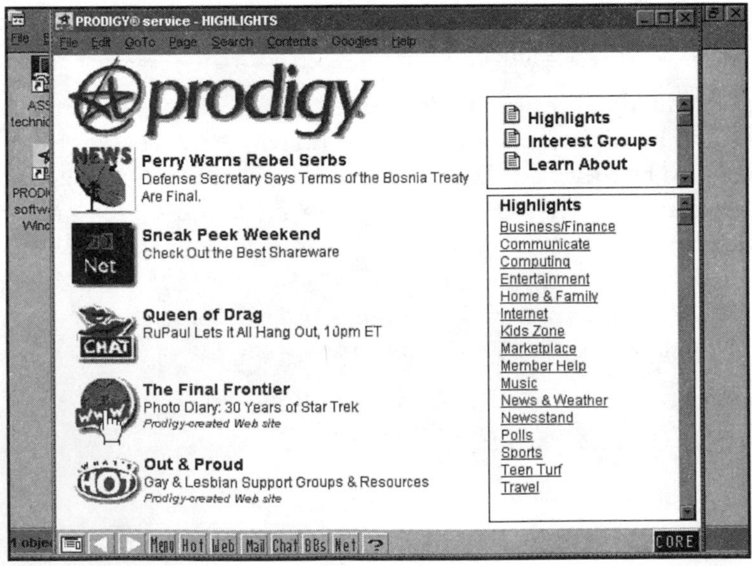

Fig. 10.1
HIGHLIGHTS is Prodigy's default opening screen and offers a cornucopia of entryways into special events, areas, and items online. It's updated at least once daily.

Note

Because Prodigy has its own proprietary software, you can't access it by using terminal communications software as you can with CompuServe or Genie.

Tip

Prodigy's AUTOLOGON option permits you to store your user ID and password, as well as a desired first location to log in to. This makes sign-on faster since you won't have to type everything in once you load the software. The downside is that the AUTOLOGON feature is less secure because you can access Prodigy so quickly. To begin using this feature, press Ctrl+J to bring up the jumpword window and type: **AUTOLOGON**, complete the enrollment form, then use AUTOLOGON next time you log on. See "Getting Around on Prodigy" later in this chapter for more information on this subject.

Prodigy Pricing

Prodigy's pricing is competitive, with a base membership fee of $9.95 per month that includes five hours of core access as part of its Value Plan. Additional hours are billed at $2.95 each, with extra fees charged for some Plus areas. They also offer a 30/30 plan, giving you the option of paying $30 for 30 hours. New members receive 10 free hours to try out the service, with the first month's membership waived.

You need a major credit card or a checking account to pay for your Prodigy account, and have that information ready before you sign on.

Extra fees are applied to certain special areas on Prodigy, where premium information or services are located. One example of this is Homework Helper, a kids resource for aiding children with schoolwork where $7.95 per month gives you access and two "free" hours each month, with each additional hour billed at $2.95. Mutual Fund Analyst is another, offering financial guidance for $5.95 per day.

You can check your account and change your billing method at any time by selecting the Member Services button from any Prodigy screen. Use Ctrl+T to bring up Tools to access info.

Getting Prodigy Software

Prodigy occasionally packs free disks of its software in with popular magazines, so you might want to check through any piles of "freebies" you've been storing away for a boring afternoon.

If you don't have the software, you can order it by calling 1-800-PRODIGY.

Installing Prodigy

Once you have the disk, installing Prodigy and getting online for the first time takes just five or ten minutes, depending on the speed of your computer.

To install:

1. Place Prodigy Installation Disk #1 in your floppy drive.
2. Click Windows 95's Start button.
3. Click Run.
4. When prompted for path of program to run, type **A:INSTALL.EXE** (see fig. 10.2).

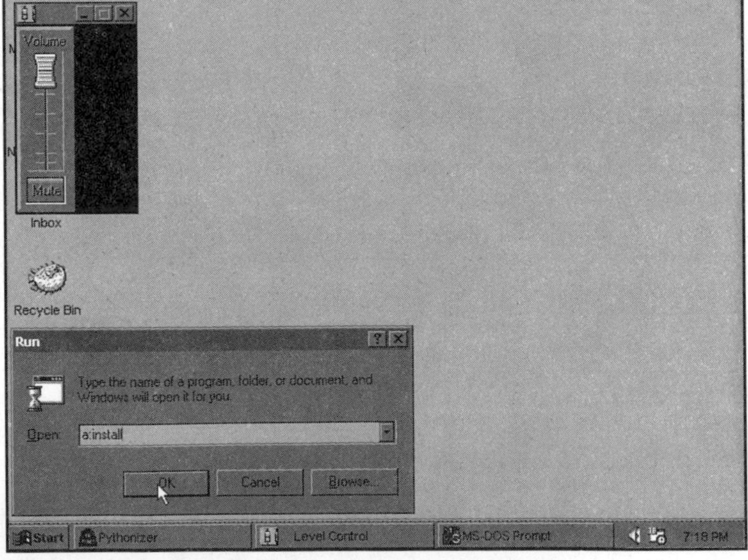

Fig. 10.2
Once you set up Prodigy to install, don't disappear. You need to change to Disk #2 soon.

5. You will be prompted for a path, or location on your hard disk, in which to install the Prodigy software. By default, this is C:\PRODIGY, but you may change it as desired. Verify the path, and then click OK (see fig. 10.3).

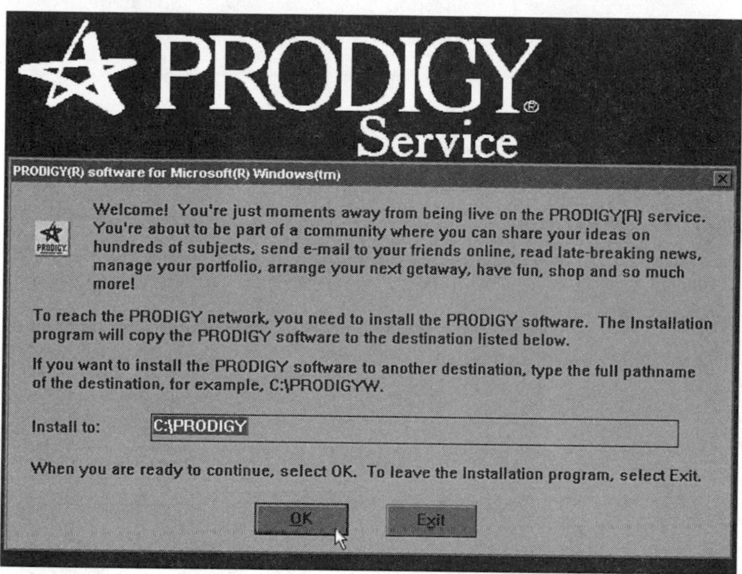

Fig. 10.3
Prodigy's Install will create a Prodigy directory for you.

6. The install meter monitors the installation's progress and, when completed with the first disk, prompts you for Prodigy Installation Disk #2.

   A message will alert you when the installation is complete.

7. To establish your Prodigy account, you may click the Prodigy icon on your Windows 95 desktop.

   Or

   Choose Start, Applications, and then Prodigy. This loads the Prodigy software.

8. The Prodigy Sign-On screen appears. Type in your service ID and temporary password as provided within your Prodigy installation package, as seen in figure 10.4.

   Click a location listed below the ID box. Highlights or Members Services is highly recommended as a first stop.

   Click Connect.

Troubleshooting

I have the Prodigy Installation Disks, but I don't have an ID or password so I can't log on.

You're right: You can't log on without them. However, you can get a temporary ID and password to establish your account by calling 1-800-PRODIGY.

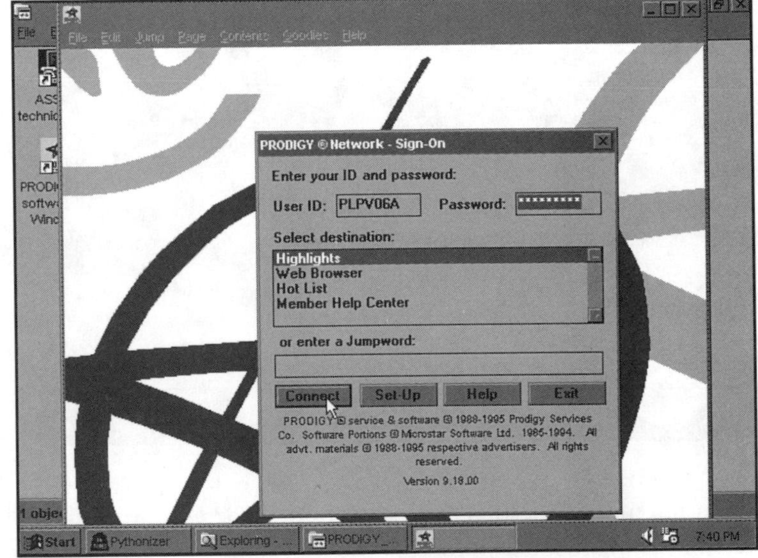

Fig. 10.4
Remember to keep your password secure. Don't write it down in an obvious place, or choose a password someone could guess.

9. Once you are connected to Prodigy, the software prompts you for a billing method as well as to choose a service plan (refer to "Prodigy Pricing," earlier in this chapter).

You will also be directed to the Prodigy Phone Directory to choose your local access numbers.

If you find you do not have an access number within a local calling area for you, Prodigy has 800-number access available, but there is a 10 cent per minute surcharge to use it, applied to your Prodigy bill. Check your long distance rates to see if those rates are higher than this surcharge, and decide which is best for you. Prodigy only provides the actual 800 number for access once you register for the service. Just click a Member Services button wherever you see it on your current Prodigy screen to find out more.

Prodigy supports up to 14.4kbps modems, but 1200-9600 baud may only be available in some areas. Access for higher speed modems is being tested, yet 28.8kbps modems and above aren't supported yet. The only thing left, then, is to welcome yourself as Prodigy's newest account holder.

Getting Help with Prodigy

Prodigy gives its users several different ways to get help with running their proprietary software and resolving problems. Some are located online—if the trouble doesn't prevent you from getting there—as well as offline. Here is a quick rundown of the ways you can seek help.

ASSIST Technical Help Icon

Located within the Prodigy group, ASSIST should be your first stop in troubleshooting a problem that keeps you from connecting to Prodigy. ASSIST is basically a collection of diagnostic tools that help identify and fix a range of hardware and software issues such as an incorrect modem setting or troublesome communications (com) port. It checks for the last error code received while using Prodigy, tells you what the code means, and tries to help you get it fixed. This can be very useful, though not every error code seems to be addressed. For example, I kept receiving an Error 403 while using Prodigy's web browser and had no luck finding it in ASSIST.

Click ASSIST to bring it up. You have two options:

- CONTINUE allows ASSIST to work to resolve the problem for you.
- EXPERT MODE lets ASSIST run to offer suggestions, but you maintain ultimate control to delete or modify settings at your discretion. If you're in doubt, it's probably wise to select CONTINUE.

Also, if you happen to be using an older version of Windows, you can run ASSIST from DOS for maximum control by typing **ASSIST** at the DOS command line.

Customer Service by Phone

If ASSIST doesn't do the trick in resolving your connection dilemma, you can use your telephone to call Prodigy directly at 1-800-PRODIGY. A voice menu will step you through the process to get assistance. Depending on the time of day and volume of calls, you may need to wait several minutes for a representative to help you.

Online at JUMP: HELP

If you can connect to Prodigy but have other problems in using the service, probably the fastest help route is through JUMP: HELP. This is a free area, meaning that you won't be charged for the time you are there.

At JUMP: HELP, you can get real-time assistance from 10 a.m. to 2 a.m. Eastern Time, order Prodigy software, read notes from help staff and other members on the Help Bulletin Board, and check for access phone numbers and high speed modem set-ups.

Tip

You also can reach the help area by clicking the blue underlined Member Help option anywhere you see it online.

Getting Around on Prodigy

As mentioned before, Prodigy's easy Windows interface makes it simple to move around. The top Hot Keys menu provides pull-down windows covering many features and tools available online, including File, GoTo, and Search (see fig. 10.5).

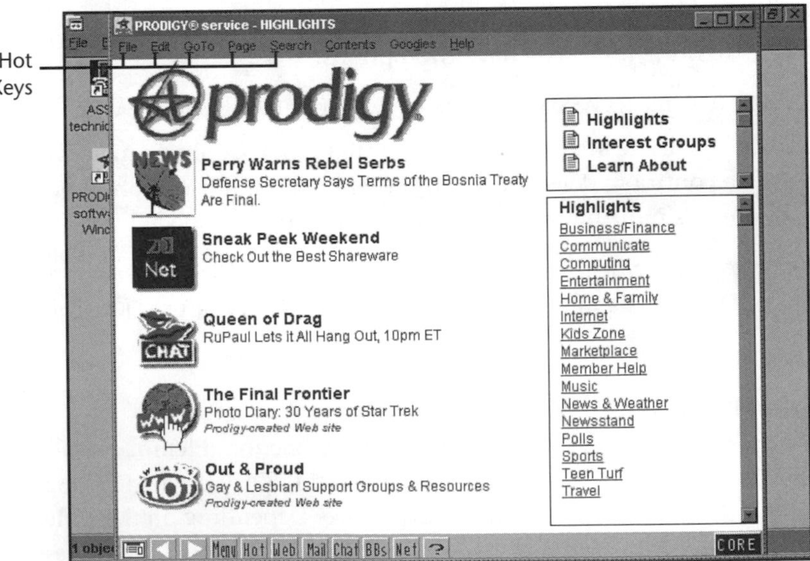

Fig. 10.5 Hot Keys give you drop-down menus offering up access to many tools and resources on Prodigy, everything from printing to assigning sounds to online events.

- *File* lets you open and close files, print, and exit Prodigy.
- *Edit* enables you to cut/paste/copy, delete, take a screen "snapshot," or work with Scratchpad or Clipboard Viewer.
- *GoTo* aids you in navigating Prodigy by accessing JUMP, the Hot List, read mail or send an instant message. Tools, located under GoTo, can also be accessed by pressing Ctrl+T, and assists you in areas like changing your password and reviewing your account information.
- *Page* helps you move forward, back, and between menus.
- *Search* gives you the opportunity to perform Quick or Power Searches through Prodigy's news and information resources such as AP wire stories.
- *Contents* list different departments on Prodigy like Kids' Zone and Computers.
- *Goodies* offers up the little extras, like recording a macro to automate some regular process you perform online, or assign sounds to an online event like connecting or receiving an instant message. Toolbar setup is also found here, so that you can configure your bottom toolbar for your needs.
- *Help* is just that.

The bottom toolbar gives you button-style immediate access to major options which you can alter as you wish. Table 10.1 takes a closer look at the Prodigy toolbar.

Table 10.1 The Prodigy Toolbar

Icon	Description
	HIGHLIGHTS is like a virtual message hall, telling you who's on and what's hot, with direct links to advertised areas
	The left arrow takes you to the previous screen
	The right arrow takes you to the next screen
Menu	Menu takes you to the last Prodigy menu you visited. This helps when you get several layers deep in reading

(continues)

Table 10.1 Continued

Icon	Description
Hot	Hot brings up the Hot List of favorite Prodigy places you're likely to drop by—Great for keeping track of sites
Web	Web expresses you to Prodigy's World Wide Web browser info screen
Mail	Mail loads Prodigy Mailbox. Internet mail is here, too.
Chat	Chat brings you to the anteroom of Prodigy's live chat rooms—choose a room
BBs	BBs links you to Prodigy's Bulletin Boards
Net	Net leads you to Prodigy's gateway to the Internet

Tip

Many Prodigy tools and options are available from one quick menu, by pressing Ctrl+T. From here, you can change your password and path, get print options, modify your display or personal information, get account information, add a member, initiate AUTOLOGON, and look at your latest Prodigy usage.

Jumpwords—the keywords used to JUMP from place to place—provide the shortcuts for moving around online, and can be accessed two ways:

- Ctrl+J
- Click GoTo from the underlined Hot Key menu at the top of the screen and select JUMP

A Jump dialog box appears (see fig. 10.6). You can type in the jumpword, if you know it, and select whether the site you want is on Prodigy, the Web, in a UseNet newsgroup, FTP, or Gopher. If you don't know the jumpword, type your best guess. If Prodigy doesn't recognize it, you will be prompted if you'd like to see the closest matches it can find.

You can also select View Hot List, located just beneath the jumpword entry line, which presents a listing of popular spots online Prodigy recommends to visit, such as ZD Net and Newsweek. The Hot List can be customized to meet your particular needs as you move about and get to know what places you wish to visit regularly.

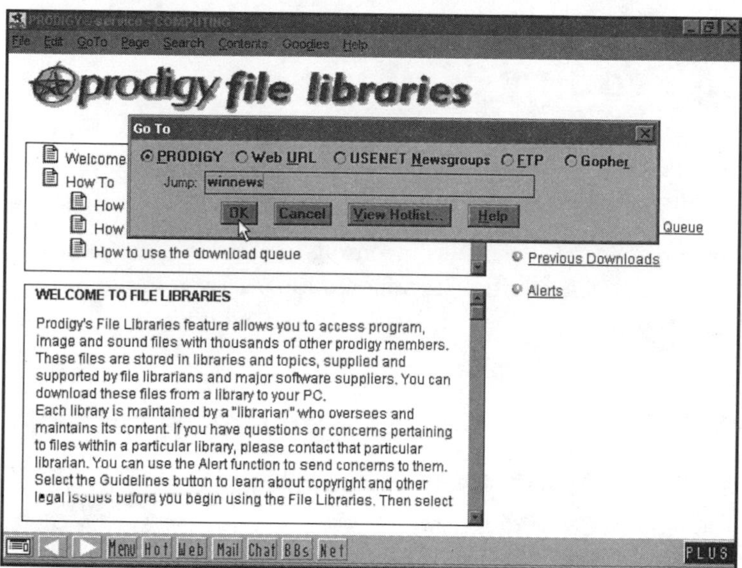

Fig. 10.6
The Jump dialog window (also referred to as a GoTo window), displayed when you press Ctrl+J, will try to match an unrecognized jumpword you may type to its list of known sites.

Table 10.2 lists some of the most commonly used jumpwords for new users looking for computer support and Prodigy help.

Table 10.2 Prodigy's Jumpword Quick Reference

Jumpword	Location Online
BOARDSA-Z	Prodigy's Main Bulletin Boards Menu
CALL OPTION	Access Menu
COMPUTER BB	Computer Bulletin Board
COMPUTERS	Computers Main Menu
COMPUTING	Computing Main Menu
HELP	Help Area (free)
WINNEWS	Microsoft Windows 95 News
ZDNET	Ziff-Davis Net (plus)

> **Tip**
>
> You will see blue, underlined text on many Prodigy menus. These are *hyperlinks,* which can take you to whatever feature or site they mention. Just click the hyperlink to access it.

Using Prodigy Mailbox

Using Prodigy Mailbox may seem a little intimidating at first to the novice e-mail user. Prodigy loads Mailbox as a separate utility when you request it, and the result proved to be very slow on a 386/33 I logged in with one day.

When Mailbox loads, you can view incoming mail (new pieces as well as items read but not deleted from previous sessions) as seen in figure 10.7. Mail is sorted by its read status, time and date received, who wrote it, and what it's about.

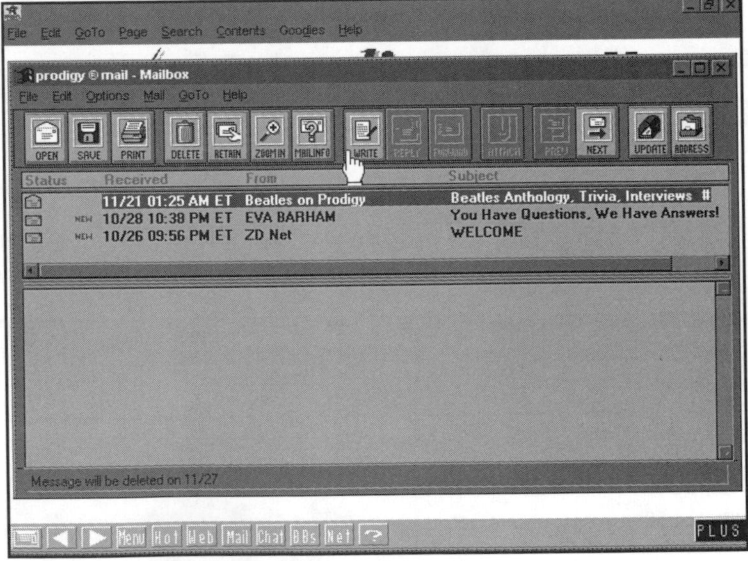

Fig. 10.7
Incoming mail is displayed each time you open Mailbox.

Options (represented by radio buttons on the upper screen) require a little orientation. You can import files from another source, save or print, clear the mail screen, retain in the box or delete, write a new message, or reply to or forward received mail.

Troubleshooting

Help! When I load Prodigy Mailbox, I lose the ability to use my Prodigy toolbar.

This is normal. Prodigy Mailbox is more of a task-swapping utility, so you can use Mailbox or the toolbar. You can press Ctrl+Esc to move between the two, however, once Mailbox is loaded.

Let's do a quick overview of how to perform the three most common functions in Mailbox:

Read Mail

To read your mail, do the following:

1. Click the Mail from toolbar or JUMP: MAIL.
2. Once Prodigy Mailbox loads, you can see any mail in the listbox. Never-seen mail is indicated with a red "NEW." Click the mail entry you wish to read. This piece of mail will display in the scroll box below the mail list. You can always resize the window to give yourself more reading room.

Reply to Mail

Prodigy has an extra feature built into its Write and Reply mail functions—a spellchecker! To reply to e-mail you have received:

1. If you're not already there, click Mail from the toolbar or JUMP: MAIL.
2. When Mailbox loads, point to the mail entry you wish to reply to, and then click the Reply radio button.
3. An empty scroll box appears above the e-mail you're responding to in which you can type your reply. The reply will automatically be addressed to the original mail sender, with the subject repeated.

   Type in your reply.
4. You can then choose to Spellcheck, or

   send up to 3 files with your e-mail by clicking ATTACH and then click SEND, or

   SEND to post the e-mail by itself, or

   CLEAR to clear what you've written.

Write New Mail

Instructions for writing new mail follow, but remember—if you want to practice, you can always experiment by sending e-mail to yourself.

1. If you're not already there, click Mail from the toolbar or JUMP: MAIL.
2. Once the Mailbox loads, click Write to open a new mail message.
3. In the To field, type the name of the Prodigy member to whom you wish to send mail. The Address radio button lets you keep a list of people to whom you regularly send mail, so you won't have to type in their IDs each time you wish to send them mail.

   You can send Internet e-mail this way, too, but you'll need the complete Internet address before you start (see fig. 10.8).

   Press the Tab key to move to the Subject field.

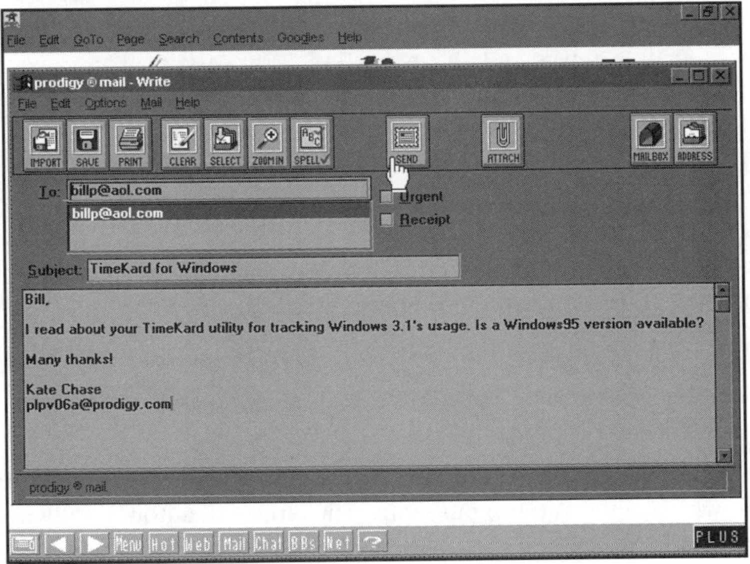

Fig. 10.8
Use Prodigy e-mail to ask questions of program developers and industry experts over the Internet.

4. In the Subject field, type the name of the subject of your mail.

   Press the Tab key to move down to the body of the message, and begin typing your note.

   Radio buttons give you several options, including to Import a file from your disk, Print, Clear (message), Save, Attach, and Send.

   When you're satisfied with your message, click Send.

   If you need to Attach a file, click Attach and specify the file(s) as directed, then click Send.

You can mark Prodigy mail as urgent or needing receipt by clicking the entries for each to the right of the address.

Finding Windows 95 Resources on Prodigy

As previously mentioned, Prodigy's reputation is more as a user-friendly "first" online service than as a support powerhouse. Still, its expanded support truly does give new onliners a chance to cut their teeth on cyberspace.

The libraries online—even when you enroll in the optional ZD Net—are not exhaustive collections, but offer some good basic resources. Let's be honest, when we're new, 30 choices can be easier to sift through than 3,000. Point-and-click menus pace you through the process to find major software libraries with more specific topics. However, if your needs are specialized or technical, you may outgrow Prodigy's offerings quickly.

One big plus though is that Windows 95 is covered in several different locations online. Even a first-time user can pretty swiftly jump around to view the shareware and freeware offered for download, participate in the Bulletin Boards, and even a live Windows 95 chat room (see fig 10.9).

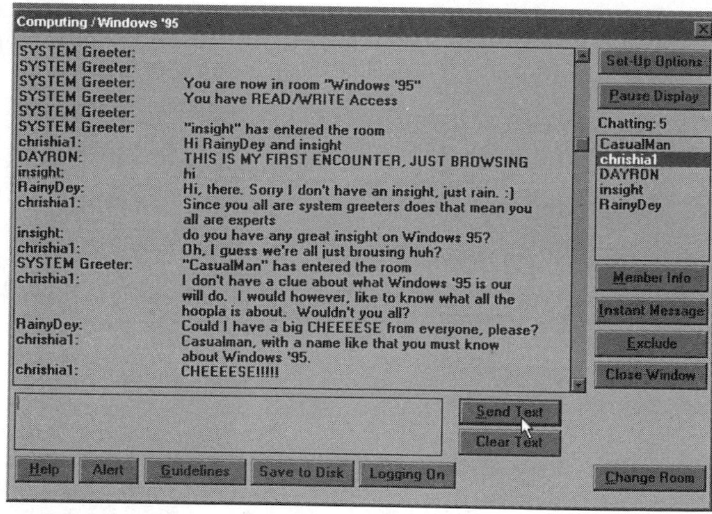

Fig. 10.9
The Windows 95 chat room offers live interactive conferencing with other Win95 users.

JUMP: COMPUTER BB

The Computer Bulletin Board or BB on Prodigy acts as a launch pad to several discussions on issues facing you as a computer user (see fig. 10.10). These discussions, organized into topics to which notes are posted by subject, range from specific computer brands to hardware to software and operating systems.

The left side of the screen has information about the Bulletin Board's function and who serves as board leader.

On the right, you can choose from several options to enter into different topical discussions posted to the board. By default, Prodigy will look for notes (their term for posted messages) written within the last five days. But you can adjust the time and date to read from by clicking the appropriate black dialog boxes present.

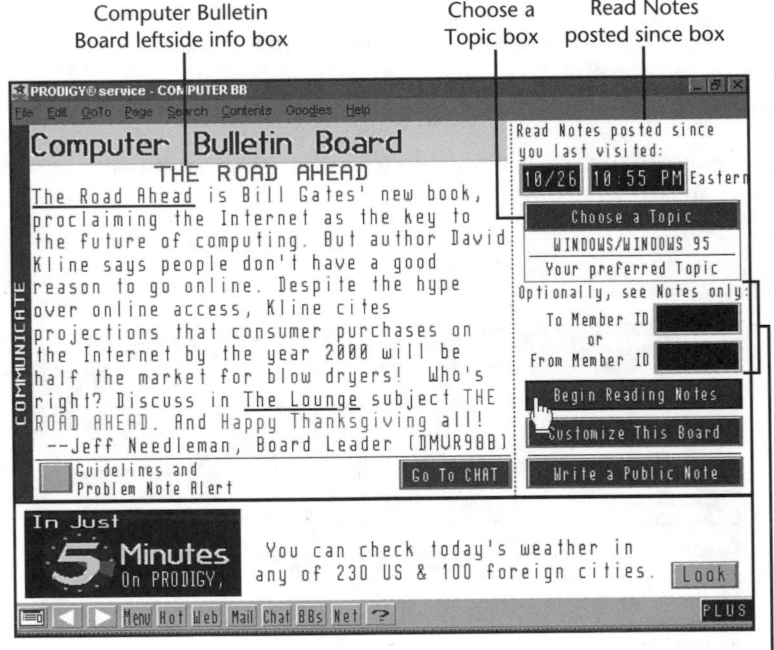

Fig. 10.10 JUMP: COMPUTER BB takes you to Prodigy's Computer Bulletin Board. Use JUMP: BOARDS A-Z to get to a listing of all Bulletin Boards.

Other options available by point-and-click include:

- *Choose a Topic.* A topic list appears.
- *Choose to see Notes only to/from a specific member ID.* Black dialog boxes provided to type the ID. Only use this if you know the Prodigy ID of the person you want to ignore or read.
- *Begin Reading Notes.* Select and click this after you Choose a Topic.

- *Customize This Board.* Enables you to set note reading options depending on your preferences and needs.
- *Write a Public Note.* Lets you post a note to the topic you choose.
- *Go To CHAT* (lower center). Takes you to the chat room menu. Highlight a room of interest and click to enter it.

If you want Windows 95 information, choose a topic, and select Windows/ Windows 95. You can then select from a number of different discussions in a subject list or use the top black dialog box to type in a keyword that describes your desired subject. Recent subjects for bulletin board discussions include uninstalling Windows 95, using its new disk cache, and resolving MS-DOS problems with Windows 95.

Once you select a subject, a list of notes within that discussion group appears, as in figure 10.11. This list provides lots of information, organized by the note's subject, to whom the note is addressed, the number of replies available to it, as well as who posted the note and when. Bottom buttons allow you to Read Choices, Read All, Clear Choices, and Return to Main Menu. Just click or type an X in the check-box to the left of the note list to choose notes to read, then click the appropriate button below when you're done.

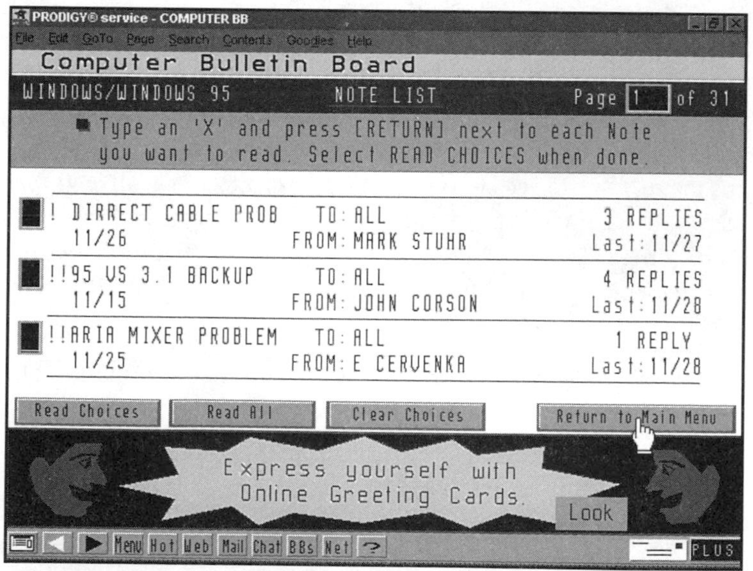

Fig. 10.11
Putting your cursor on a checkbox puts an "x" in it to select it for reading.

For more information on reading and posting notes to Prodigy Bulletin Boards, see "Reading and Posting Notes on Bulletin Boards to Get Help," later in this chapter.

JUMP: WINNEWS

JUMP: WINNEWS takes you to a small but specialized Microsoft Windows 95 news area. While what you see here is "local" to Prodigy, it's actually a smaller version of a Web-based service offering more files and news.

Click on Downloadable Files to see a short but select listing of files providing comprehensive background information on Windows 95 (see fig. 10.12).

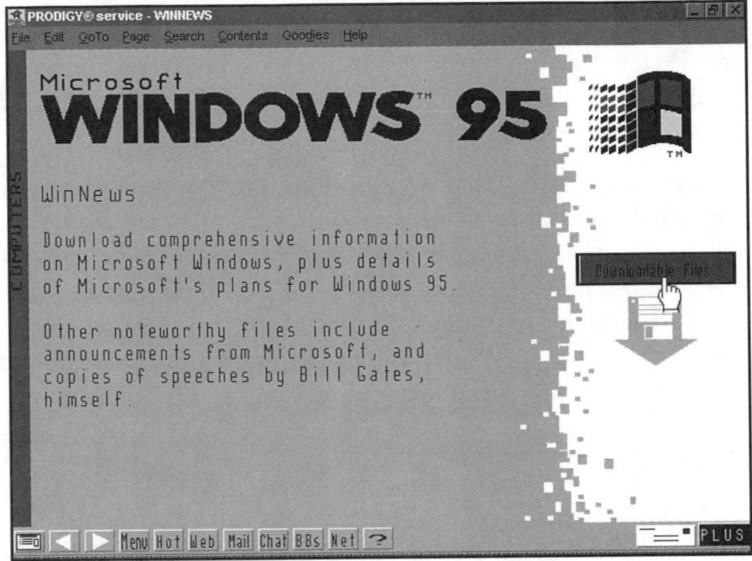

Fig. 10.12 Microsoft information files, as well as a collection of speeches by Bill Gates, are available at JUMP: WINNEWS.

From this menu you can select Top Menu to return to the WinNews main screen, Download Files, or Must Read. If you select Download Files, a listing of files is presented. These include information files for TCP/IP networking, OLE 2.0, network support including Client Service Netware, multimedia development, and more.

Click the left-hand check-box to select a file. Additional information about it is displayed, which includes the file's size and the number of files within the .ZIP archive.

JUMP: COMPUTING

JUMP: COMPUTING takes you to a center that offers links to Web sites on the Internet, as well as links to special areas, events, and offers available right within Prodigy, related to Computing (see fig. 10.13). The features highlighted change at least daily, but certain core features like File Libraries and Member Help are always accessible here.

Specific instructions for using the File Libraries option to find Windows 95 files are included later in this chapter, in the section "How to Get and Use

Files Found on Prodigy." Some of the recommended Windows 95 programs to locate here include MEMSTAT1.ZIP, a current memory status tool, and WINIMA22.EXE, a disk DMF disk imager.

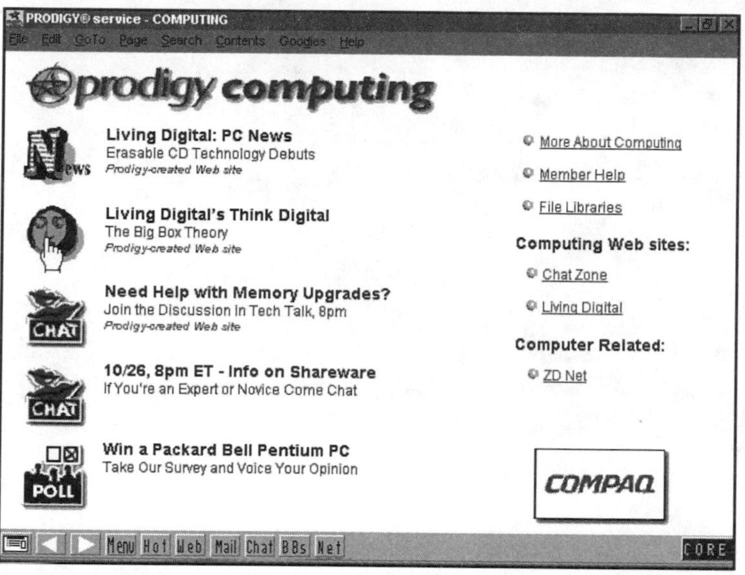

Fig. 10.13
JUMP: COMPUTING highlights special features and events available online and through links to the Internet. Just click on an item that interests you to get there.

> **Tip**
>
> Located in the bottom right corner of your Prodigy screen is a blue billing indicator. FREE indicates you're in an area which doesn't count against your online time. CORE means you're in a basic access area which counts against your time online. PLUS indicates you're in a special service like ZD Net that may charge a premium or additional monthly access fee for use. Until you're familiar with what is FREE, and what is PLUS, pay attention to this blue billing indicator.

Click on More About Computing to access live chats, computing-related Web sites and UseNet newsgroups, and other online resources.

JUMP: COMPUTERS

JUMP: COMPUTERS takes you to a centralized offering of PC software and hardware manufacturers giving support online. It also provides links to special support groups like the IBM Club, shopping information or outlets like PC Catalog (see fig. 10.14), OfficeMax, and Computer Express. Special features are available, too, such as a link to the Jones Computer Network, a media network that focuses on computers and the industry.

The Microsoft Win News area also is located off this menu.

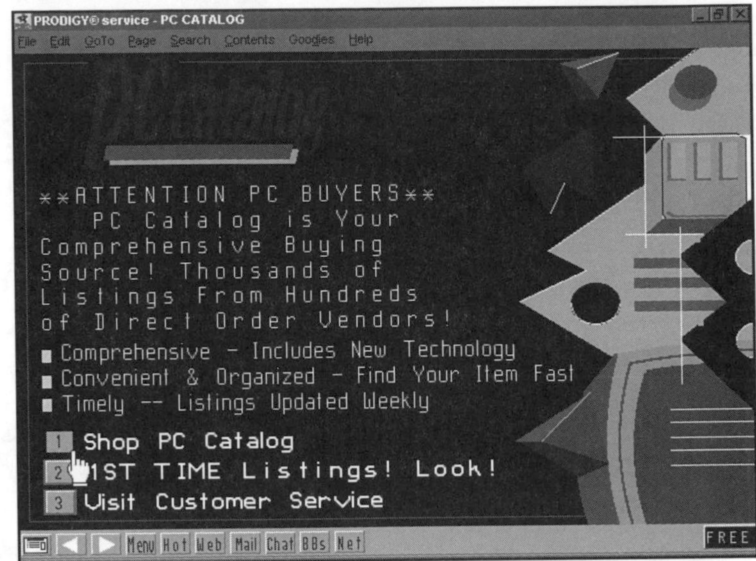

Fig. 10.14
PC Catalog, one of the options at JUMP: COMPUTERS, offers computer comparison shopping information to help take the pricing mystery out of cybershopping.

JUMP: ZD NET

ZD Net, as described earlier, is a premium feature on Prodigy offered by Ziff-Davis Publishing. The cost is an additional $3.50 membership fee above your usual Prodigy monthly membership (refer to "Prodigy Pricing," earlier in this chapter) and requires you to enroll before you can access it.

Within ZD Net, you can use ZD Select to locate downloadable files or click on ZD Magazines to access Web-based electronic versions of their computer periodicals like *PC Magazine* and *Windows Sources*.

ZD Select gives you the ability to search for files using specific criteria like software category or title. It also lists favorite downloads to help you make an educated guess about what software to try, and also offers the ZD Shareware Club, a program to save money on the shareware files here.

Unlike files available in most of Prodigy's direct file libraries, ZD Net adds a price for each file downloaded. That price, usually ranging between $1.50 and $5, is listed on each file description. If you download a file here, the listed price is added onto your Prodigy bill.

ZD Net predominantly offers selections for earlier versions of Microsoft Windows. However, this is likely to change as Windows 95 expands its user base. Windows file categories here include business, business and finance, communications (where third-party Prodigy add-ons can be found), databases, graphics, references and utilities, to name just a few.

Additional Windows 95 Resources Online

Most of the Windows 95 resources found on Prodigy have already been described, and ones added since press time will likely be available from the areas already noted here.

However, additional Windows 95 information can be located at other sites of interest, like C/Net, a computer information network which also produces the syndicated television program, c/net Central (JUMP: CNET). Its area features a link to its own Virtual Software Library.

You also can explore around COMPUTING and COMPUTERS for new areas providing the latest Windows 95 files and information.

Beyond that, if you want to examine Windows 95 resources on the Internet covered elsewhere in this book, do give Prodigy's Web Browser a try. Prodigy's browser, in my speed tests, appears to function significantly faster than the Web browsers offered on America Online and CompuServe's Dial-up Internet service. Part of that speed is accounted for because Prodigy locally stores popular home pages. Thus, you don't have to sit and wait for the gateway to connect to begin seeing a Web site's home page.

Yet, even when accessing less popular Web locales, the browser operates faster at 14.4kbps access than I've come to expect when navigating the Web through commercial online services.

Reading and Posting Notes on Bulletin Boards to Get Help

Now that you know how to get into a Prodigy Bulletin Board to look for Windows 95 topical discussions, let's take a step deeper to discuss how to read and post notes online.

To do this, Go to the Windows/Windows 95 Topic board found at COMPUTER BB.

1. Press Ctrl+J or JUMP from the bottom toolbar, then type **COMPUTER BB** and press Enter.
2. Select Choose a Topic
3. Select Windows/Windows 95 from the Topic List
4. Click Begin Reading Notes
5. A Read Post menu appears offering the post with several options. Click Topic and you can switch to another topic on the list. You can do the same by clicking Subject. The usual information is provided about who wrote it, to whom it's addressed, and the date and time it was posted to the bulletin board.

6. You can Read Replies, see Next Note, see Next Subject, Reply to the post, send an e-mail Reply, or select Options. The latter lets you select a new subject or topic, return to the main menu, reply publicly to the note, create a new note on this subject, or Reply by private message.
7. If you select Reply, you also have the option to import a .txt or .doc file on disk into the note as well as review the original note. Click OK when you want to post it, Clear if you want to wipe the Note of text, or Cancel Note to escape this form (see fig. 10.15).

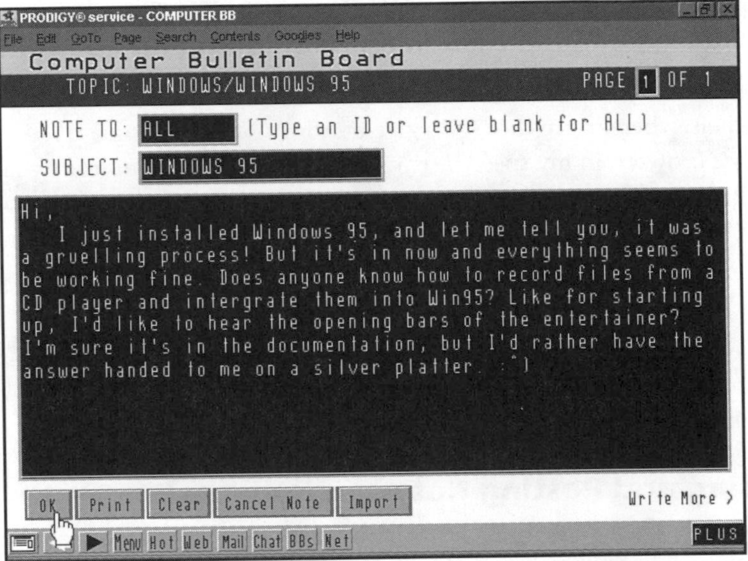

Fig. 10.15 Prodigy's Post Note and Reply screens make it easy to create a new post to add to a public Bulletin Board requesting help or offering some.

When reading notes on Prodigy, you can use other tools listed as options on the screens, such as Note Preview that lets you view the first line of up to eight notes to better select which to read, and Export, which allows you to save notes or whole subjects to disk for off-line perusal.

How to Get and Use Files Found on Prodigy

To learn how to get and use files found online with Prodigy, let's take a look at the Computing File Libraries, where three primary Windows 95 collections are located.

1. JUMP: COMPUTING
2. Click on blue underlined File Libraries option, which takes you to a main File Libraries information screen. Here, you can spend a little time reading documents covering how to download, how to use the Download Queue, and How to Search.
3. Click on File Libraries.
4. What you see now is a list of libraries available on the left, and a list of topics or file categories under each on the right (see fig. 10.16).

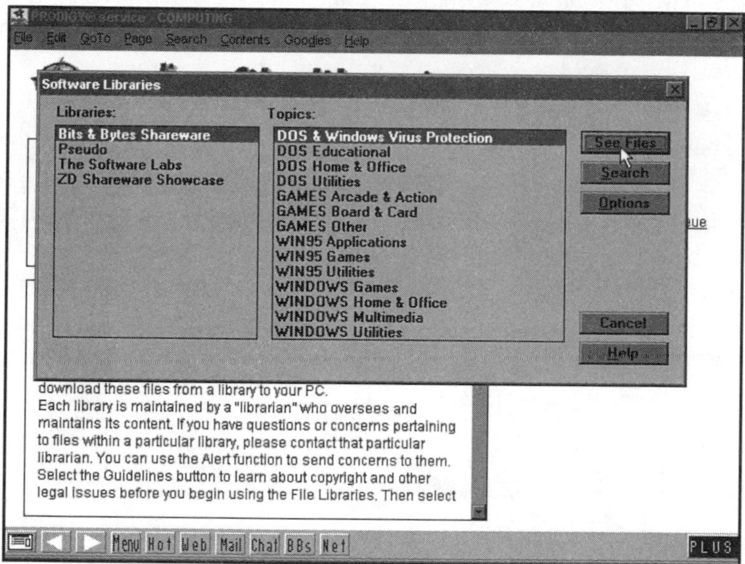

Fig. 10.16
Prodigy's Bits and Bytes collection offers several categories of files available for download. Click on a topic to bring up the file roster.

5. Select Bits and Bytes, and then click Windows 95 Utilities as a topic. Buttons on the right give you the option to See Files, Search, and Options such as specifying to log off when a download is finished.
6. Click on Search. A search screen appears, as seen in figure 10.17, from which you can search a specific library or all libraries. Key words are used to narrow the search, with commas used to separate multiple keywords. When looking for a Windows-based program, use "windows" as a keyword to search on.

   You can use the resulting file listing from the search or click on Cancel to return to the previous menu, then click on See Files.

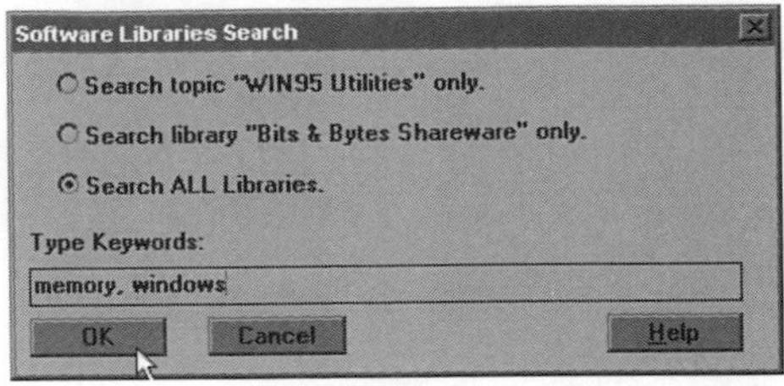

Fig. 10.17
Prodigy's File Libraries Search option gives you quick access to locate a file within one specific library, or throughout all.

The library's list of files is organized with information on each file's title, when the file was last downloaded, and its size in bytes. Buttons located on the right of the screen allow you to view File Info, Download Now, Download Later, access Download Queue, or Cancel and return to the previous listing. Using the Ctrl key will let you highlight multiple selections for download.

7. Click on Download Queue. Download Queue keeps track of files you designate to Download Later. From this menu, you can see a listing of files you have set up to download and initiate the transfer of the file(s) to your hard disk. You can change its path destination, start downloading everything, or just selected files. You can also Remove a file you no longer want to transfer.
8. Click Close when you're done.

Add-Ons for Prodigy for Windows

Prodigy spotlights several add-on utilities to help you get the most out of your Prodigy for Windows software. Among them are:

- Bulletin Board Note Manager (JUMP: BB NOTE MGR): Prodigy Bulletin Board discussion manager. Priced at $19.95, which is added to your Prodigy bill after download.
- E-Mail Connection (JUMP: E-MAIL CONNECTION): An offline e-mail handler.
- Journalist (JUMP: JOURNALIST): A customized newspaper for Prodigy you fill with selected content following your design. The cost is about $30 when ordered through Prodigy, but it also is available through select software retail outlets.

Prodigy also maintains a collection of third-party free- and shareware Prodigy add-on programs at JUMP: UTILITIES FOR PRODIGY. Some also are located within ZD Net's Windows Communications library. ❖

CHAPTER 11

Using The Microsoft Network (MSN)

by Robin Schreier Hohman

The Microsoft Network comes built-in to Windows 95, and that makes it a natural for people who don't want to bother with choosing a service. At least that's what Microsoft is betting on. Other online services tried to stop Microsoft from including it with the new operating system, but they weren't successful. The competitors needn't have kicked up such a fuss. So far, they don't have too much to worry about.

In this chapter, you learn to

- Sign on to The Microsoft Network
- Navigate the network
- Send and receive e-mail
- Access the World Wide Web through the network

Compared to CompuServe, Prodigy, and America Online (AOL), The Microsoft Network is a lightweight. And it's slow. It takes longer to sign up, sign on, and get going than any of the other commercial online services. And that's including not having to load additional software. But it does have the inside track on Microsoft products. On any given day, you're likely to get free goodies unavailable elsewhere. For a while, you could download a beta version of Microsoft Bookshelf.

It also uses the most sophisticated mail program online, Microsoft Exchange, which lets you use all of your computer's capabilities for sending, receiving, filing, and sorting mail.

While Windows 95 was in beta testing, The Microsoft Network was free. Now that it's announced its pricing structure, it's clear it's competitive with the other major online services. Like AOL, CompuServe, and Prodigy, you pay a monthly fee for a set number of hours, with additional time billed at an hourly rate.

One thing that The Microsoft Network doesn't offer that Prodigy, AOL, and CompuServe do is the option to debit your checking account for payment. That means you have to have a major credit card to use The Microsoft Network, something not everyone has and even those who do might be reluctant to have the number exist online.

Trying MSN

Microsoft has become aggressive about its Internet presence. Not only is Microsoft making its Internet Explorer software available for free, but it also is making part of The Microsoft Network (MSN) available for free on the Internet. This free access to MSN will give you a taste of the full service, which will help you decide if you want to join MSN to gain full access. To browse the public-access portion of MSN, connect with your web browser to www.home.msn.com for more pointers and directions.

You also can still sign up to MSN through Windows 95 and receive full service to the network. This chapter explains that full connection.

Signing On to The Microsoft Network

Windows 95 installs and creates a desktop shortcut for The Microsoft Network when you install the program.

To sign up to the Network for the first time, do the following:

1. Double-click The Microsoft Network icon. You'll get the screen shown in figure 11.1.

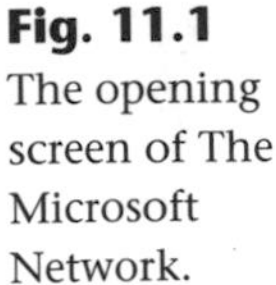

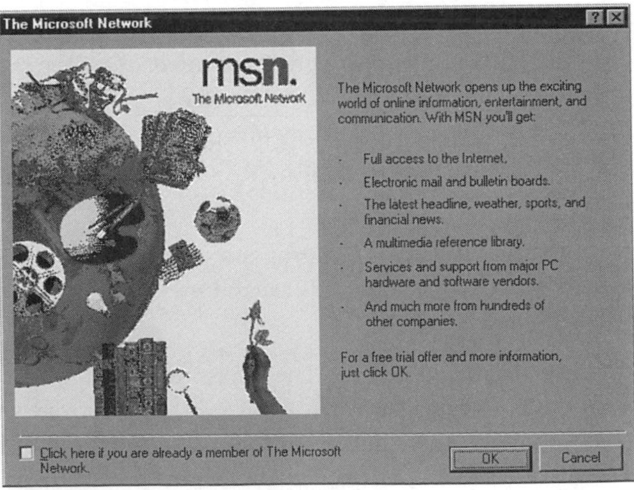

Fig. 11.1
The opening screen of The Microsoft Network.

Caution

Don't delete The Microsoft Network desktop icon. If you do, you won't be able to connect and will have to reinstall the Network software. To reinstall the software, insert the Windows 95 CD-ROM and select Start, Settings, Control Panel, Add/Remove Programs. Click the Windows Setup tab and click The Microsoft Network. Click OK. The Microsoft Network will be reinstalled.

2. If you already have an account and are just setting it up on a different computer, click in the lower left-hand box that says Click here if you are already a member of The Microsoft Network. If you're not a member, you can get a free trial period.
3. Click OK to continue the signup process.
4. To find a local access number, enter your area code and the first three digits of your phone number.
5. Click OK to proceed. You'll get a screen telling you the local access number that will be used to call The Microsoft Network.
6. Click Connect to call the Network to get the latest access phone numbers and information on the free trial period. It will take a few minutes to download the information. The Network will then hang up and you're presented with the screen in figure 11.2.

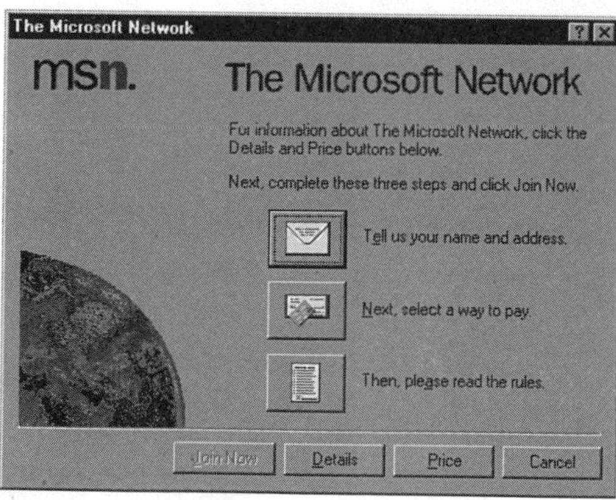

Fig. 11.2 Your first encounter with The Microsoft Network gives you information on pricing.

7. Click Tell us Your Name and Address.
8. Fill in the information. If you don't want to be put on a mailing list, click the cleverly worded paragraph in the lower left corner.
9. Click OK.
10. Click on Price and Details to find out the latest information.

11. Click Next, Select a Way to Pay.
12. When you click Choose a Payment Method, a form comes up for your credit card information. Remember, you can only pay with a major credit card. You can't debit your checking account as you can with some other online services.
13. Fill in the credit information and click OK.
14. Click Then, Please Read the Rules. If you don't go through this step, you won't be able to proceed.
15. Click I Agree, or you won't be able to join.
16. Click Join Now.

Tip

If you don't think the first three digits of the chosen access number is a local call for you, click Settings, Access Numbers, Change to choose a different one.

17. Click Connect. If you hang on Dialing, you may have to alter your access number to take out the 1 and the area code. To alter your access number, click Settings, Access Numbers, Change, and make your change.

Setting Up an Account

To set up an account, do the following:

1. Enter a name for your Member ID and a Password.
2. Click OK. Since MSN members typically use a first name for an ID, you may get a notice saying the ID is already in use. If you do, you'll have to keep trying until you hit upon a unique one.
3. If you want full Internet access (including the World Wide Web), click Yes. If you click No, you'll only have access to Internet e-mail and newsgroups. To find out more information, click on About the Internet.
4. Click OK. If there's no local phone number for you for Internet access, you'll get an error message advising you to pick a new number or a new access type. If you can't find a local number, you may have to pay a toll charge to access the Internet.
5. If MSN detects another Internet access, it may display the screen shown in figure 11.3. Click No to preserve your settings. However, if you do this, you won't be able to access the Internet through MSN. Click Yes to change your Internet access to MSN. You have to restart your computer for the changes to take effect.

6. Click OK.

> **Caution**
>
> If you have Internet access another way, make sure to click No. Otherwise you might have trouble with your other Internet access.

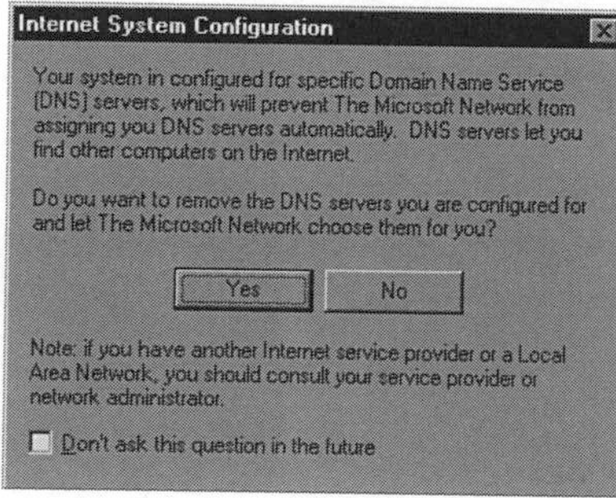

Fig. 11.3
If MSN detects another Internet connection on your computer, you will be asked if you want to replace that connection. Make absolutely sure you want to do that before choosing Yes.

7. Click Finish.

Changing Phone Numbers

After you've signed on, you can change your primary and backup phone numbers. You might want to do that if you move, or if you're taking your laptop on the road.

To change the primary or backup phone numbers, do the following:

1. Double-click The Microsoft Network icon.
2. Click Settings.
3. Double-click Access Numbers.
4. Click Change to change the Primary number, or Change to change the Backup number.
5. If you're on the road and need to change to a different state, click and hold the scrollable arrow in the State/Region dialog box.
6. Click a phone number and click OK.
7. Click OK to return to the Session Settings dialog box.

Changing Dialing Properties

You may have to change the dialing properties with a different access number. Also, people sometimes make the mistake of including the area code in the phone number to call when it's a local call. To change your dialing properties, do the following:

1. Click Settings.
2. Click Dialing Properties.

   Change your dialing properties as appropriate. There are settings for dialing an outside line and for long distance. You can also disable call waiting or enter a credit card number.
3. Click OK.

Connecting to The Microsoft Network

Once you've signed on and set all your dialing properties and access numbers, you can begin a session by doing the following:

1. Double-click The Microsoft Network icon on your desktop. You'll get the screen shown in figure 11.4.

Fig. 11.4
To sign on to The Microsoft Network you have to supply your member ID and password.

2. Enter your Member ID and Password.

> **Tip**
>
> If security's not an issue, click Remember My Password so that you don't have to keep typing it in.

3. Click Connect. MSN will log you in. This will take several minutes.

> **Tip**
>
> If you click Connect but the connection hangs, make sure that you haven't included extraneous digits, such as a 1 or an area code, in the dialing properties. For more information, see "Changing Dialing Properties" earlier in this chapter.

When you're logged on, you'll first see the MSN Central screen, which lets you jump to MSN Today, E-Mail, Favorite Places, Member Assistance, and Categories, as shown in figure 11.5.

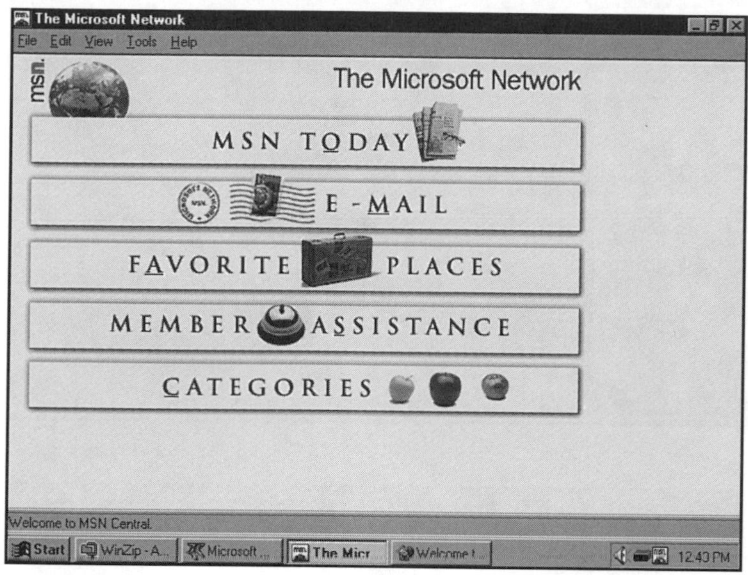

Fig. 11.5
When you first log on to The Microsoft Network you're given several destination choices from the MSN Central screen

You'll also get a welcome screen, complete with a mugshot of Bill Gates.

The first place you'll probably want to go is to the MSN Today screen, which is a large image map that will take you almost anywhere on MSN, shown in figure 11.6. To go there, click on MSN Today from the MSN Central screen. Depending on your computer and modem, the MSN Today screen could take a minute or more to load.

> **Tip**
>
> If you don't want MSN Today to load automatically when you log on, you can change that option from the MSN Central screen. Select View, Options, and deselect Show MSN Today title on startup.

An *image map* is a graphic actually made up of more than one hot spot. That is, when you click different areas of the graphic, you jump to different locations.

To go to a specific area, click on that area. If you click any of the graphic boxes, you'll get a secondary box that gives you the opportunity to go to that area. For example, if I click the Windows 95 Chat box in the image map, I get the pop-up screen shown in figure 11.7.

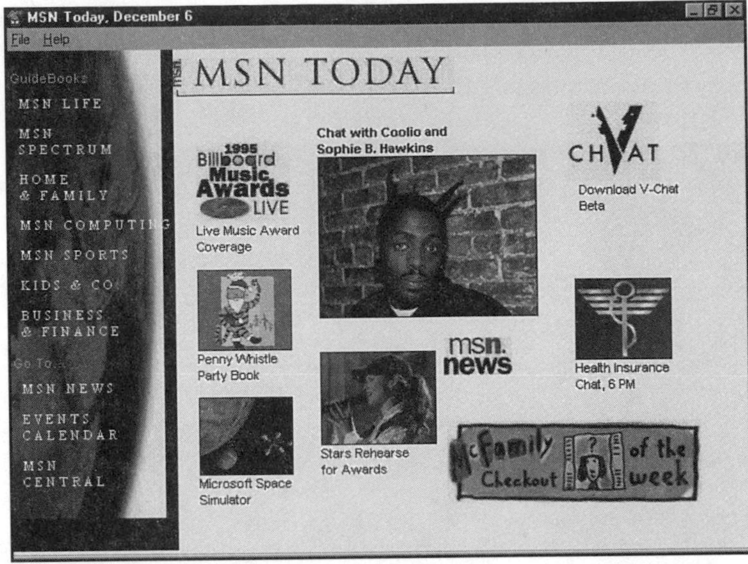

Fig. 11.6
The MSN Today screen is an image map that enables you to click anywhere on it to go to that area.

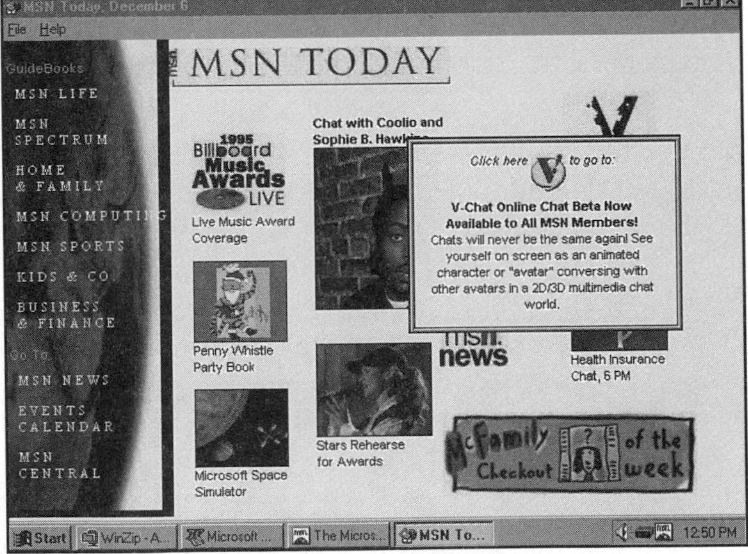

Fig. 11.7
You have to click the icon to go to the selected area on the image map.

To get rid of the pop-up, click anywhere on it (except on the chat icon).

The listing of subjects on the left-hand side of the image map takes you to other image maps that give you options of places to go.

Troubleshooting

I lost my connection to MSN, and when I tried to sign on again a message popped up telling me that I was already signed on, even though I'm not. What can I do?

You'll have to restart your computer and then launch MSN again.

I forgot my password. Can I get another one?

You'll have to call Customer Service at 1-800-386-5550 in the U.S.; 1-800-840-9890 for TDD.

Is there a place to find help online?

From the MSN Central screen, click on Member Assistance. You can also click on the Help pull-down menu from any screen on the network.

Navigating the Network

After you're logged on, you can navigate from the MSN Today screen or the MSN Central screen.

As with all Windows 95 applications, you can click the button bar at the bottom of the screen to switch between MSN Central and MSN Today.

Another way to switch easily between the two is to press the Alt+Tab keys to bring up the screen shown in figure 11.8. While holding down the Alt key, press and release the Tab key to move among the open applications. When you get to the desired application, release the Alt key. The application appears on-screen.

Fig. 11.8 Pressing Alt+Tab lets you choose among open applications.

The MSN Today screen is a compilation of the latest news and events. The MSN Central screen lets you perform administrative tasks, retrieve or send e-mail, and go to favorite places.

If you accidentally close the MSN Central screen, you can get it back in one of two ways. From the MSN Today screen, click MSN Central in the lower portion of the image map. Make sure that your mouse pointer has changed to a hand before you click, or it won't work (that indicates you're on the linked area of the image map).

You can also click The Microsoft Network icon on your desktop, but this usually takes much longer.

Joining Chats

The Microsoft Network makes heavy use of real-time conferences, called *chats*, where people discuss predetermined issues. To participate in a chat, you have to find out when it will be held and then show up at the appropriate time.

You can find out when chats are scheduled from the MSN Today screen or the Calendar of Events, which is accessed from the top left of the MSN Today screen.

To open the Calendar of Events, move yourmouse pointer to the words Events Calendar. When the mouse pointer changes to a hand, click on that area of the image map. You get the screen shown in figure 11.9.

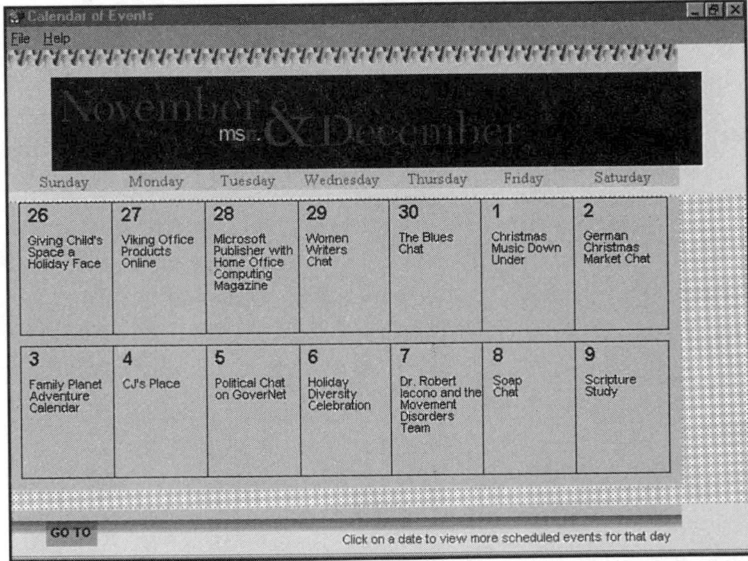

Fig. 11.9
The Events Calendar lists upcoming chats.

> **Tip**
>
> The times listed are Pacific Time, presumably because Microsoft's headquarters is in Redmond, Washington. Be sure to adjust for your local time. You can find other local times by clicking once on the up arrow to the right of the time.

To attend a chat, click on the folder at (or soon after) the appropriate time.

Getting the Latest News

You can get the latest news from United Press International by clicking on the MSN News area of The MSN Today image map. That brings up the folder shown in figure 11.10, which gives you several options.

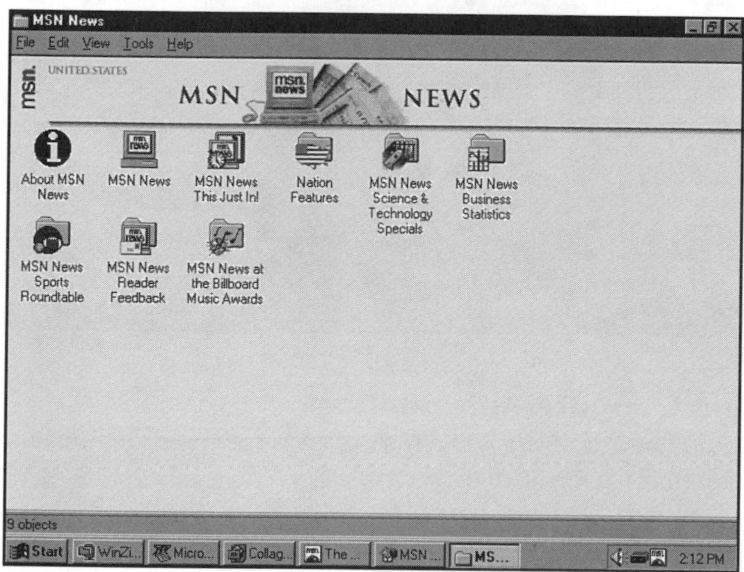

Fig. 11.10 You have several options for viewing the day's news.

You can choose MSN News This Just In! for a short summary of the news. Or you can choose MSN News, for a glitzy image map made up like a newspaper page. The first time you choose this option, MSN will automatically download some software to your computer. Of course, the second option takes longer.

If you choose the image map, you'll be able to navigate to different categories, shown in figure 11.11.

Fig. 11.11
You can browse the latest news in several categories from the MSN News page.

Finding Computer Information

One nice feature The Microsoft Network offers is computing information that's broken down for different levels of users.

To go to the computing area from the MSN Today screen, move your mouse pointer over the words MSN Computing (on the left side of the screen) until the arrow changes to a hand; then click once.

Once you're in MSN Computing, press the forward arrow icon to go to a menu of Computing forums.

There are software and hardware vendor forums, which provide news, tips and discussion, and sometimes patches and other software to download. Several computer magazines and book publishers also have forums on MSN.

To access a forum, double-click the name of the forum. For example, the magazine Computer Shopper forum is shown in figure 11.12.

As with many other forums, there's an icon you can click to get to a subject's Web site. In the Computer Shopper forum, there are also icons for files and utilities and a BBS, where you'll find discussions of subject-related issues, shown in figure 11.13.

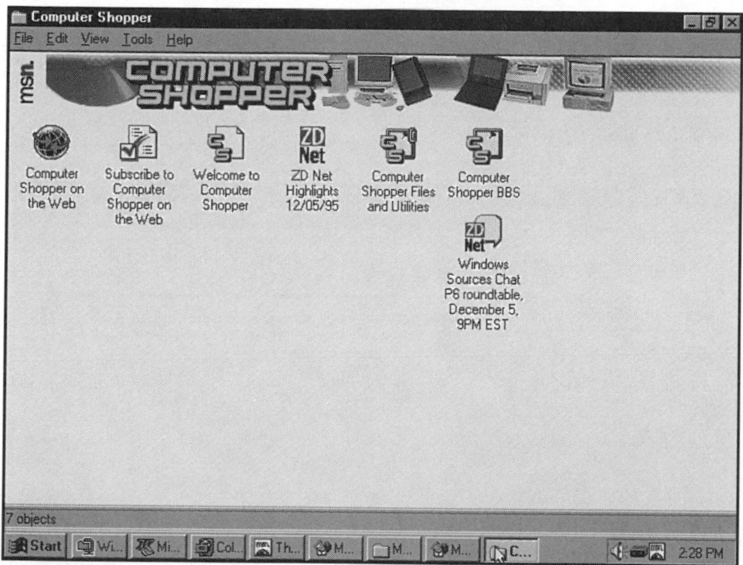

Fig. 11.12
The magazine *Computer Shopper* has a forum on MSN.

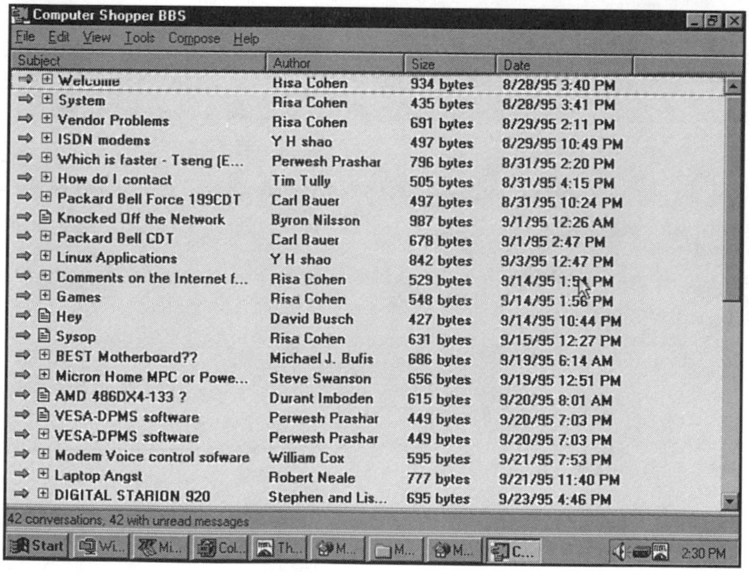

Computer Shopper BBS

File Edit View Tools Compose Help

Subject	Author	Size	Date
Welcome	Risa Cohen	934 bytes	8/28/95 3:40 PM
System	Risa Cohen	435 bytes	8/28/95 3:41 PM
Vendor Problems	Risa Cohen	691 bytes	8/29/95 2:11 PM
ISDN modems	Y H shao	497 bytes	8/29/95 10:49 PM
Which is faster - Tseng (E...	Perwesh Prashar	796 bytes	8/31/95 2:20 PM
How do I contact	Tim Tully	505 bytes	8/31/95 4:15 PM
Packard Bell Force 199CDT	Carl Bauer	497 bytes	8/31/95 10:24 PM
Knocked Off the Network	Byron Nilsson	987 bytes	9/1/95 12:26 AM
Packard Bell CDT	Carl Bauer	678 bytes	9/1/95 2:47 PM
Linux Applications	Y H shao	842 bytes	9/3/95 12:47 PM
Comments on the Internet f...	Risa Cohen	529 bytes	9/14/95 1:54 PM
Games	Risa Cohen	548 bytes	9/14/95 1:56 PM
Hey	David Busch	427 bytes	9/14/95 10:44 PM
Sysop	Risa Cohen	631 bytes	9/15/95 12:27 PM
BEST Motherboard??	Michael J. Bufis	686 bytes	9/19/95 6:14 AM
Micron Home MPC or Powe...	Steve Swanson	656 bytes	9/19/95 12:51 PM
AMD 486DX4-133 ?	Durant Imboden	615 bytes	9/20/95 8:01 AM
VESA-DPMS software	Perwesh Prashar	449 bytes	9/20/95 7:03 PM
VESA-DPMS software	Perwesh Prashar	449 bytes	9/20/95 7:03 PM
Modem Voice control sofware	William Cox	595 bytes	9/21/95 7:53 PM
Laptop Angst	Robert Neale	777 bytes	9/21/95 11:40 PM
DIGITAL STARION 920	Stephen and Lis...	695 bytes	9/23/95 4:46 PM

42 conversations, 42 with unread messages

Start 2:30 PM

Fig. 11.13
The Computer Shopper BBS listing of posted messages is organized by date.

A plus to the left of the subject indicates a thread; that is, two or more messages on the same topic. To read a message, double-click the subject line.

To respond to a message, click the Reply to BBS icon.

Using the Categories Option

Perhaps the best way to begin exploring The Microsoft Network is to use the categories option of the MSN Central page. That will take you to a wide variety of places, as shown in figure 11.14.

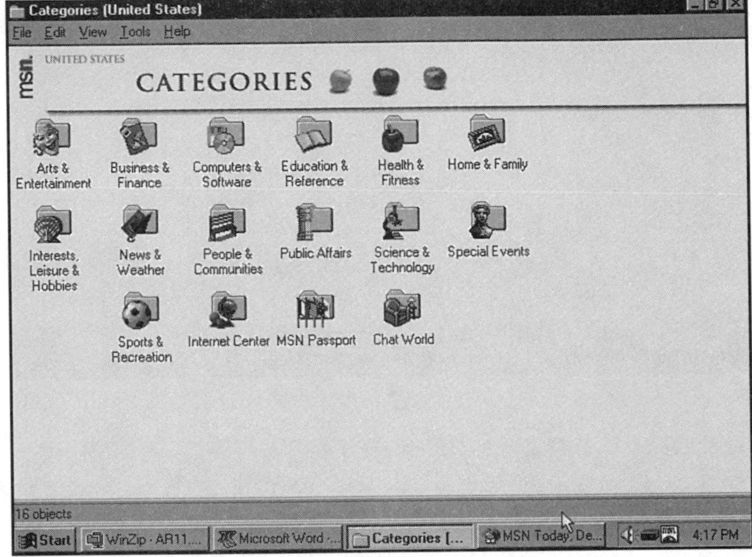

Fig. 11.14
The Categories option in the MSN Central page introduces the whole network to you.

From the categories folder, double-click a folder to go to Education & Reference, Computers & Software, Science & Technology, or any other area.

For example, if you double-click the Education & Reference folder, you'll get the screen shown in figure 11.15.

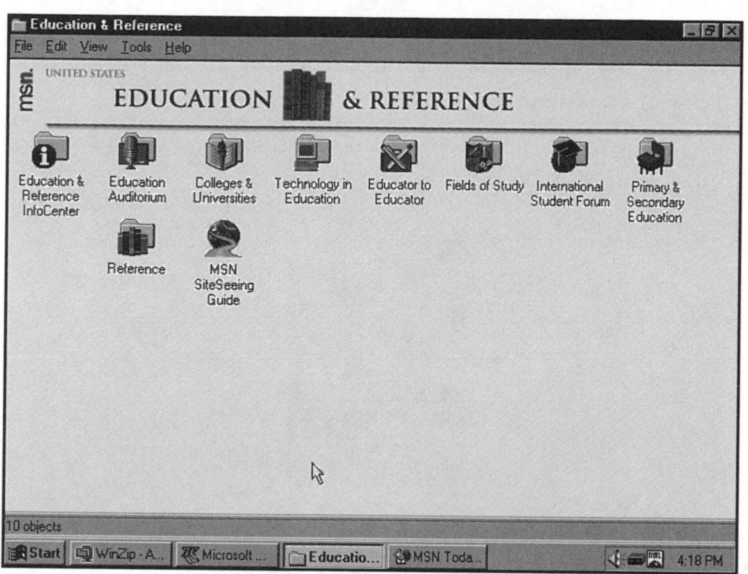

Fig. 11.15 You can choose from among ten folders in the Education & Reference screen.

Double-clicking the Reference folder brings up the screen shown in figure 11.16.

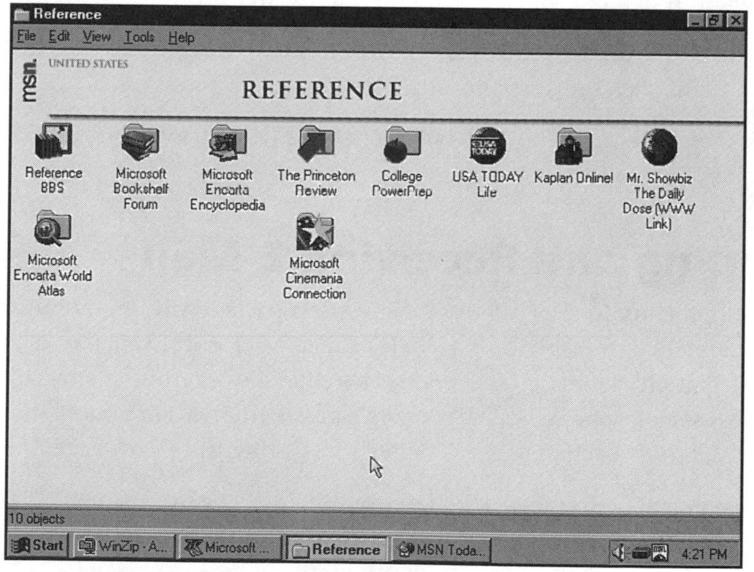

Fig. 11.16 The Microsoft Bookshelf Forum, the Microsoft Encarta Encyclopedia, and the Princeton Review are some of the reference tools available on MSN.

To go into the Microsoft Bookshelf Forum, double-click the folder. You'll be able to access a BBS with messages about the forum, and download an introductory copy of Bookshelf.

To get back to the previous level (in this case the Education & Reference screen), click File, Up One Level, shown in figure 11.17.

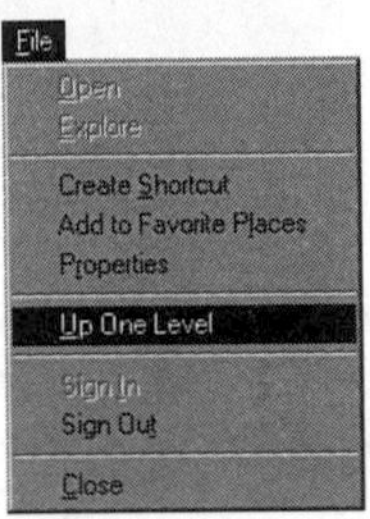

Fig. 11.17
Use File, Up One Level to get back to the previous screen.

Logging Off the Network

You can't simply exit from a screen to log off the network. You have to sign out from the MSN Central screen.

To sign out, click File, Sign Out. You will be prompted to make sure that you really want to sign out. Click Yes to sign out; No to cancel.

You can also log off anytime by using the MSN icon next to the time on the taskbar. Right-click the icon and click Sign Out.

There's one more way to log off, but it's not available in every screen. Click File, Sign Out.

Sending and Receiving E-Mail

The mail program for The Microsoft Network is packed with many features, more than you'll probably ever need. It's called Microsoft Exchange, a complex integration of e-mail, fax services, as well as a workgroup manager. We'll just cover some of the basics here so you can get around. For a more in-depth look at Microsoft Exchange, see Chapter 13, "Configuring Exchange."

To access e-mail, you can click E-Mail from the MSN Central screen. That launches Microsoft Exchange, Windows 95's built-in e-mail program, and brings you to the Inbox, shown in figure 11.18.

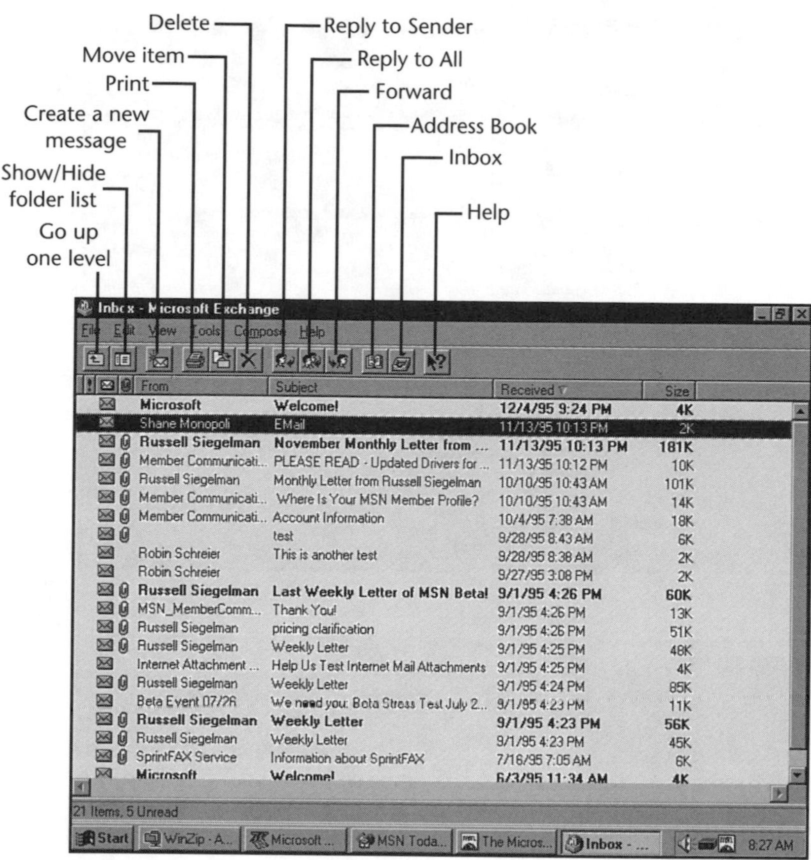

Fig. 11.18
Your inbox maintains all received mail until you purge it.

You can also double-click the Inbox icon on the desktop to launch Microsoft Exchange. You don't have to be online.

There are two ways to view e-mail folders. You can hide the folder list, as in figure 11.20; or you can show the folder list, as in figure 11.19. To switch between the two views, click the Show/Hide Folder List icon on the toolbar.

To read a message, double-click the message. After you've opened a message, you can save it as text, print it, forward it, copy it, or delete it.

To create a new message, click the New Message icon, or click Compose, New Message. You get the screen shown in figure 11.20.

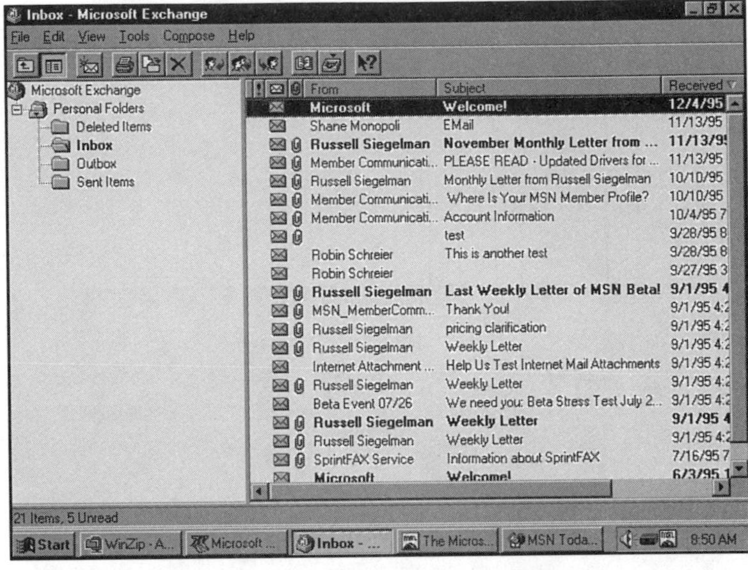

Fig. 11.19
If you display the folder list, you can easily move among your e-mail folders.

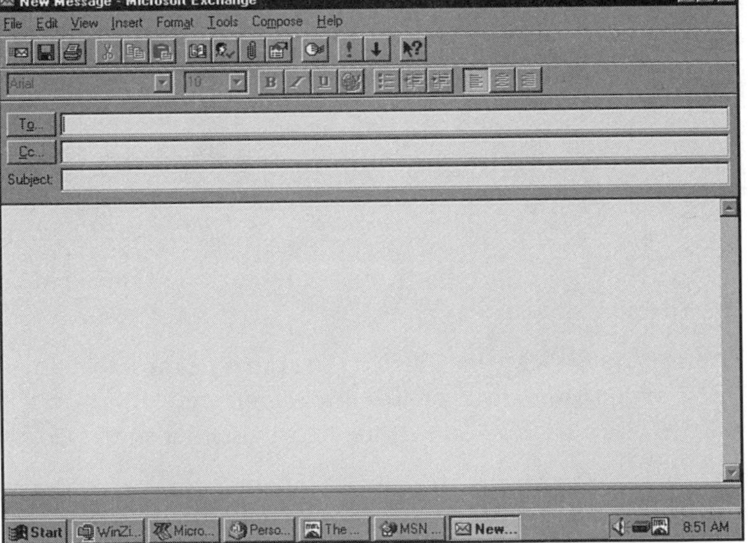

Fig. 11.20
You have many options when composing new messages.

Addressing E-Mail

The Microsoft Exchange interface is very similar to MS Mail, but if you know any mail program you can probably figure out the basics.

An address on The Microsoft Network consists of a user ID typed immediately before **@msn.com**. For example, my address is **RobinSH@msn.com**. Remember, your user ID is the name you chose when you signed on.

To send e-mail to someone else on The Microsoft Network, type the user ID followed by **@msn.com**. Unlike some other online services, you can't just use the user ID. You have to include @msn.com.

If you want to send a copy of the message to someone else, enter the address in the CC: box.

The subject line and, in fact, the text itself, is optional.

Microsoft Exchange enables you to format the message with different fonts and point sizes, and even to include colored type.

You can also attach files. To attach files, click the paper clip icon on the toolbar.

If you know the name and location of the file you want to attach, type it in File Name box. You can also maneuver through the folder hierarchy to find the file.

Once you've selected the file, click OK. You are returned to the message and the name of the file appears within the text as an icon.

To check the attachment to make sure that you chose the correct file, double-click the file icon to open the file. Click File, Exit to close the file again.

To send the file, select File, Send or click the Send icon on the toolbar. If you're online, the message is sent immediately. If you're offline, it goes to the outbox. You won't be prompted to send mail in the outbox the next time you log on; you'll have to remember to send it.

Sending Mail from the Outbox

To send mail from the outbox, log on to the network. From the MSN Central screen, click E-mail. If necessary, click the Show/Hide Folder List icon. Click the Outbox and double-click the message you want to send. When the message opens, click File, Send.

Receiving E-Mail

When you log on to the network, you are notified if you've received any new mail with the screen shown in figure 11.21.

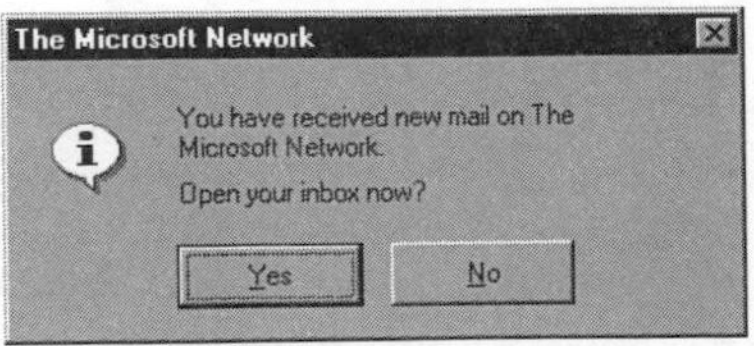

Fig. 11.21
When you sign on, you are notified of new mail.

To open the inbox, click Yes. To ignore the new mail, click No.

> **Tip**
>
> You can specify the way mail is sorted by choosing View, Sort at the top of the screen.

If you click Yes, the inbox opens. You can then double-click the new mail to open it. If there is an attachment, double-click the attachment file icon to open it.

You can save the attachment as an independent file by clicking File, Save As and specifying a location and name.

The mail message is automatically saved until you delete it. To delete the mail message, click the closed message and select File, Delete. To delete an open message, you also click File, Delete. The deleted messages are sent to the Deleted Items folder. From there, you can permanently delete the messages by selecting them and clicking on File, Delete. You are prompted to make sure that you really want to remove them permanently. Click Yes to remove them; No to cancel the action.

> **Tip**
>
> To delete more than one message at a time, hold down the Shift or Ctrl key while clicking the messages.

> **Caution**
>
> Unlike other delete actions under Windows 95, clicking File, Delete really deletes the messages. You won't have the chance to retrieve them from the Recycle Bin.

Sending E-Mail to and from the Internet

It couldn't be easier to exchange e-mail with the Internet. Simply type the Internet address in the To: box in the new message screen.

To send e-mail from the Internet to The Microsoft Network, just type in the user ID followed by **@msn.com**.

Accessing the Internet

The Microsoft Network doesn't really offer full Internet access because you can't access FTP (file transfer protocol) or use Archie, WAIS, and other search tools (see Chapter 21, "Using Internet Resources"). However, you can read and post messages to newsgroups and access the World Wide Web. For many people, that will be enough.

To get to the Internet through MSN, go to the MSN Central screen. Click Categories. Double-click the Internet Center folder. You'll get the screen shown in figure 11.22.

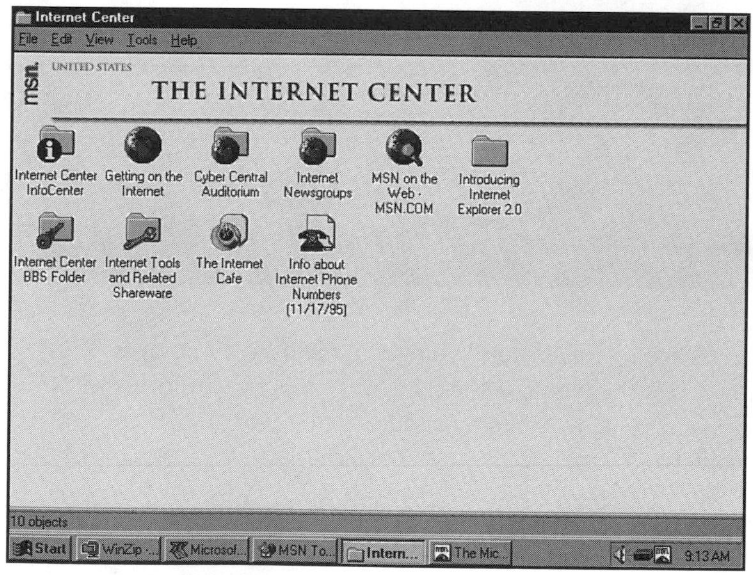

Fig. 11.22
The Internet Center is your gateway to the Internet.

Internet Newsgroups

You can exchange e-mail with the Internet and read and post messages to Internet newsgroups without adding any software.

Internet newsgroups are like CompuServe forums or BBSs. There are hundreds of newsgroups available, each one devoted to a separate topic.

To find newsgroups you might be interested in, do the following:

1. From the Internet Center screen, double-click Internet Newsgroups.
2. Double-click NetNews. This gives you an alphabetical listing of all available categories of newsgroups.
3. Double-click a category to get a complete listing of the folders available in each category. For example, figure 11.23 shows the folders available in the comp category.

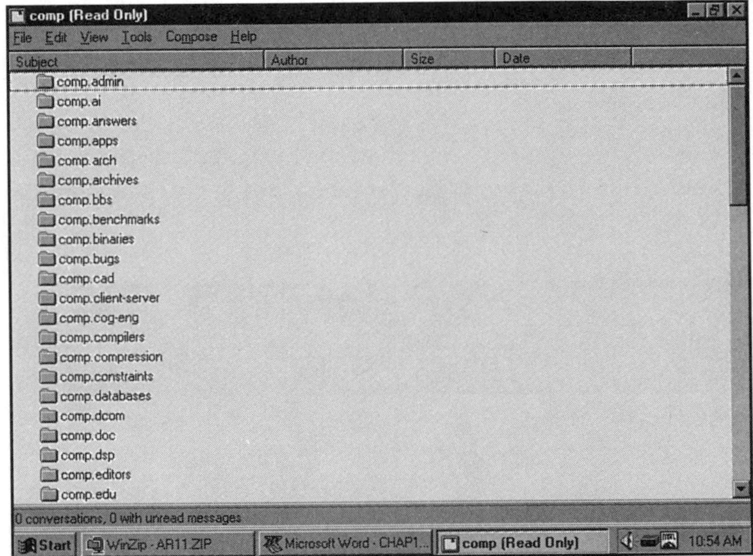

Fig. 11.23
You can see a listing of the folders in the comp newsgroup.

4. Keep clicking folders until you get to the lists of messages. You can access the messages the same way you can with other MSN messages (refer to "Sending and Receiving E-Mail" earlier in this chapter).

You can save shortcuts to various newsgroups by adding them to your Favorite Places listing by doing the following:

1. Find the list of newsgroups as detailed in the preceding section.
2. Place your mouse pointer over the desired newsgroup.
3. Select File, Add to Favorite Places.
4. To go to the newsgroup, click Edit, Go to, Favorite Places. You get a screen showing your favorite places.
5. Double-click the desired folder to go there.

From the MSN Central screen, click the Favorite Places button to go directly to the Favorite Places folder.

Accessing the World Wide Web

To read the instructions from Microsoft, you would think anyone who signed up to Internet and MSN access is all set to go to browse the World Wide Web.

Not so. If you don't have the MSN Internet icon on your desktop, you have to download additional software, and the online instructions are unclear.

To download the software necessary to access the World Wide Web, do the following:

1. Click The Internet Center in the Categories option of MSN Central.
2. Click the Getting on the Internet icon. You get the screen shown in figure 11.24.

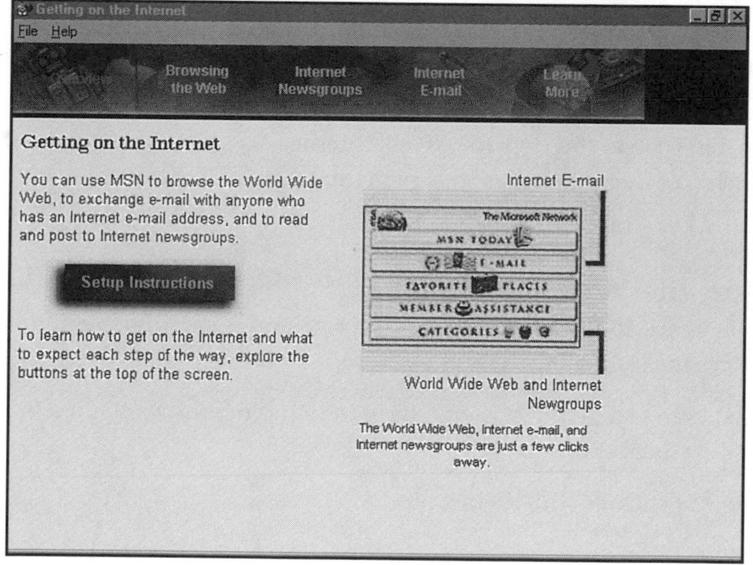

Fig. 11.24
Connecting to the Internet is easy when you use The Internet Center.

3. You need to download additional software to access the World Wide Web.
4. Click the Setup Instructions button. The instructions are confusing; you're not specifically told that you must download software to access the World Wide Web.

5. Click Troubleshooting: How to reinstall MSN 1.05.
6. Click the star to download the software. You'll get the screen shown in figure 11.25.

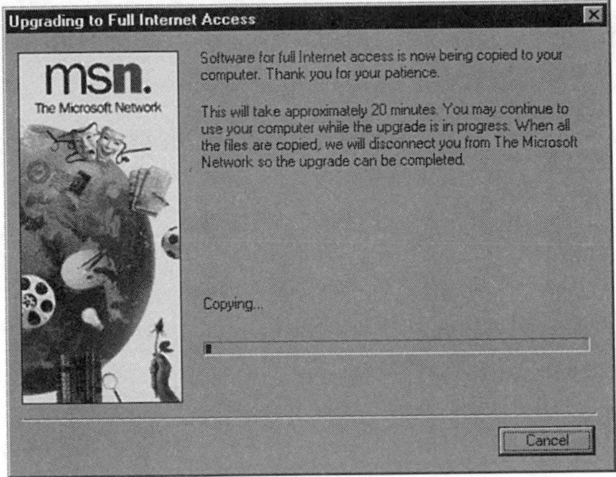

Fig. 11.25
You have to download additional software to access the World Wide Web.

7. After the files are downloaded, you will be disconnected from MSN. Click Yes to continue the procedure.
8. When you get the Upgrade to Full Internet Access pop-up, follow the instructions to close all applications and return to the dialog box.
9. Click OK. Your computer will be restarted.

Surfing the Web

After you've downloaded the Internet software and restarted the computer, you'll have the Internet icon on the desktop.

Before you can access the Web, you have to set up the software. To set up the software, do the following:

1. Double-click the Internet icon.
2. Click Next.
3. Click Connect Using my Phone Line (unless you're connected to a LAN, then click that).
4. Click Next.
5. Click Use The Microsoft Network.
6. Click Next.
7. Click Yes.

8. Click Next.
9. Click OK.

The software's still a little buggy on this. When I tried to do it, I was forced to go through some of the procedures for signing up again.

Double-click the Internet icon to launch The Microsoft Network Internet application. If you are logged on, you go directly to The Microsoft Network's home page on the Web. If you're not logged on, the home page appears behind the Connect screen. Click Connect to log on to the network.

> **Note**
>
> If you can't connect, see "Changing Dialing Properties" earlier in this chapter for troubleshooting tips. You may be dialing an extraneous digit, usually an extra 1.

After you've connected, you see The Microsoft Network home page (see fig. 11.26).

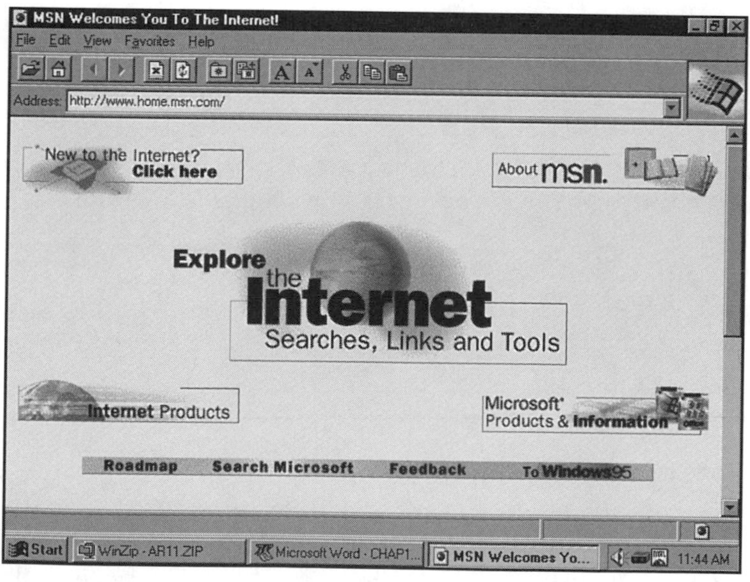

Fig. 11.26 The top of the MSN home page on the World Wide Web.

The Microsoft Network Internet browser is very similar to the Mosaic browser. We'll just cover the basics of getting around the Web here. For more detailed information on the World Wide Web, see Que's *Special Edition Using the World Wide Web*.

To find a World Wide Web page, you need to know its location, which is given as a URL (Uniform Resource Locator). All URLs on the Web begin with http:// followed by the location of the page.

To open a URL, do the following:

1. Click File, Open. You get the screen shown in figure 11.27.

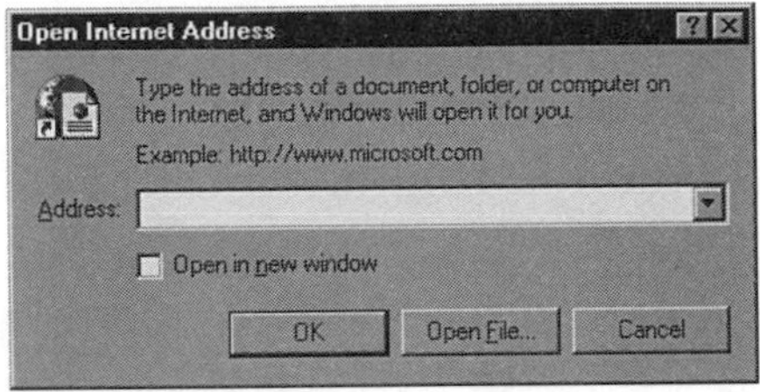

Fig. 11.27
Enter a World Wide Web address to jump to a home page.

2. In the Address text box, enter the URL (try **http://www.yahoo.com** for a nifty search tool).
3. Click OK.
4. The Yahoo home page appears on the screen. From there, you can enter words to search the entire Web.

Changing the Start Page

By default, the page you open up to, or the Start Page, is The Microsoft Network's home page. You can change that by doing the following:

1. Open the URL of the page you want to be your Start Page.
2. Click View, Options.
3. Click the Start Page tab.
4. Click Use Current.
5. Click Apply.
6. Click OK.

Creating a Shortcut to a Home Page

You can create a shortcut to a home page by selecting File, Create Shortcut, when you're on any Web page. This creates an icon to that page on your desktop.

Saving a List of Favorites

You can save any number of pages to a list of favorites, which are then easily available for you to access without having to remember complicated URLs.

To save a page as a favorite, do the following:

1. Open the URL of the page you want to save.
2. Click Favorites, Add to Favorites.
3. Click Add.

Now the next time you want to go to this page, all you have to do is click Favorites.

Logging Off

To hang up at any place on the Web, click File, Exit, then click Yes. You'll be disconnected from MSN. If you click No you'll stay connected to MSN, but be disconnected from the Web. To go back on the Web, double-click the Internet icon from your desktop.

From the Web, you can get back to MSN by right-clicking the MSN icon on the taskbar. From there, you can go to MSN Central, Favorite Places, Send Mail, or Sign Out. ❖

CHAPTER 12
Using GNN

by Gene Steinberg

Global Network Navigator (GNN) is a complete Internet-based online service run by the folks who brought you America Online. Unlike many Internet providers, GNN doesn't just plug you into the Internet without a safety net. The service offers its own software and a wide range of features that you can tap directly from its own site on the World Wide Web. In the next few pages, I'll describe those features and give you some hints and tips on joining and accessing its unique software components.

In this chapter, you discover

- America Online's new Internet-based online service
- GNN's exclusive program features
- GNN's World Wide Web page
- A wide range of Internet-based services from UseNet newsgroups to Internet chatting

A Brief Overview of GNN Features

Global Network Navigator standard installation consists of four programs and a registration program, and you can easily switch from one to the other simply by clicking on a toolbar icon or by using your Windows 95 multitasking capabilities. Here's the list of the programs and what they do:

- *GNNconnect.* This is a telecommunications program used to select access numbers to the GNN network, adjust your modem settings, and actually make your GNN connection.
- *GNNworks.* This is a speedy, multitasking World Wide Web browser that is the centerpiece of GNN's software. You can use it to visit sites on the World Wide Web and to download files from WWW and FTP (file transfer protocol) sites.

- *GNNmessenger*. This is the communications component of GNN's service. You can use this program to exchange e-mail with other members of the service and anyone with Internet access. The program also includes a newsgroup reader that you can use to read and post articles in your favorite newsgroups.
- *GNNchat*. This program lets you participate in live, one-to-one conversations with other Net surfers. It may be the most exciting experience of all of GNN's services, because of all the friends you're likely to meet from around the world.

The GNN programs also have a number of features that speed up your Internet access and let you work in other Windows 95 programs. Here are some of them:

- *Direct V.34 (28,800 bps) access*. Provides access from hundreds of cities throughout the U.S. and in major population centers around the world.
- *Multitasking and multithreading*. GNN's Web browser lets you open several viewing windows and open a different World Wide Web page on each one. In addition, you can work in another Windows program while downloading files during your GNN session.
- *OLE 2.0 support*. You can make a link to run GNNworks from any programs that support OLE 2.0, such as the various Microsoft Office applications.
- *Intelligent document caching*. When a document (such as a WWW page) is sent to your computer, it's cached on your disk by the GNN software. So when you return to that document, you can access it almost instantaneously. GNN will transfer new artwork only if the WWW page has been updated.
- *Offline mail reading*. You can read and write your messages offline, which keeps your online bill as low as possible.
- *Card catalogs*. You can create a customized collection of your favorite sites, which you can use to help speed up your online sessions.
- *Winsock-compliant*. This feature gives you the option to use any Winsock-compatible program to run GNN sessions, including a different e-mail or newsgroup reader or even another WWW browser, such as Netscape.

How to Get Your GNN Software

You'll find ads for GNN in many of the major computing magazines. In case you haven't seen the offer, just phone GNN at (800) 819-6112 and request a software disk. If you can't wait, and you have FTP access through another service, you can download the latest version of GNN software from **ftp.megaweb.com**. Once you download the software, though, you'll have to ring up GNN and request a certificate number and password. This information is needed in order for you to set up your new account.

Fast Windows 95 Installation

Your GNN software comes on a single floppy disk (or as mentioned earlier, as a file you can download directly from GNN's FTP site), and installation is easy (you don't even have to use your Windows 95 Add/Remove Programs utility). If you've installed the Window's version of America Online's software on your PC, you'll find the entire process of installing the software and setting up an account is very similar.

First, make a backup of your original software disk. But before you actually install the new software, you'll want to get ready to set up your account. For that you'll need the registration certificate you got from GNN, which has the certificate name and password you must enter to activate your account.

You'll also want to keep your credit card or checking account information at hand so that you can provide the right information when you see the appropriate information prompts.

Now you're ready to get the software up and running. Just follow these steps:

1. Insert the floppy disk into your PC's floppy drive.
2. Click the Windows 95 Start button.
3. Choose Run.
4. Type **A:\SETUP.EXE**. (If you've simply downloaded the installer program to your PC, substitute "A:" with the correct drive label.)

The installation process takes a few minutes to complete, and you see an ongoing progress bar that shows the files being installed on your computer. Unless you choose to customize settings at the start of the installation to recognize a custom modem setup, you don't have to do anything during the installation but observe the march of the progress bar.

After the software has been installed, you see an open folder window on your Windows 95 desktop with two programs, GNNconnect and GNNregistration. The second program is used to help you create your new account. Once you've set up your account, you can use either GNNconnect (or one of the other GNN programs) to initiate your connection to the service.

In case you're wondering about those other programs referred to at the start of this chapter, we'll get to those after I describe the signup process.

How to Set Up Your GNN Account

The first time you run your GNN software, it offers to dial up the service to find an access number in your city. All you need to do is enter your area code in the information screen (see fig. 12.1), and the program takes over from there to call up GNN's host computers, using an 800 phone number stored in the program to look up those local numbers. You are offered the option of choosing two phone numbers, so if one is busy, the other can be contacted.

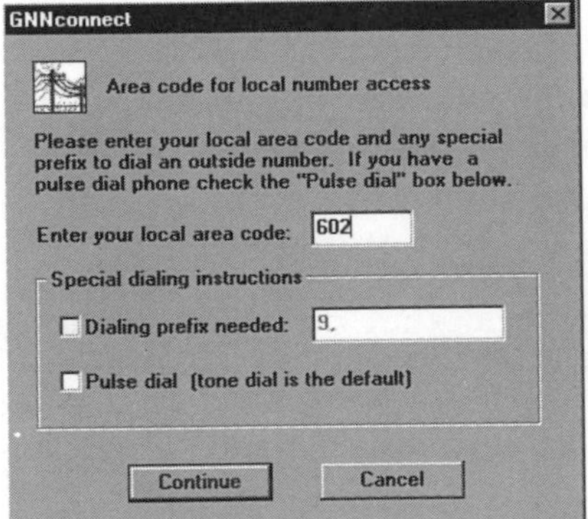

Fig. 12.1
First enter your area code so that GNN's servers can help you find a convenient local dialup number.

After your numbers are selected, you are first logged off GNN's servers and then logged on again, using your first selected local access number. Now's the time to have your registration certificate and billing information handy, as you need to use them now.

The first screen when you connect to your local access number is a request for your certificate number and password information (see fig. 12.2).

After you enter that information, you see a number of information prompts that ask for your name and address and other billing information. After you fill in the blanks, the final selection is the one where you can exert your creativity. You can select your own network name (also called a *screen name*), which will be used as your Internet mailing address.

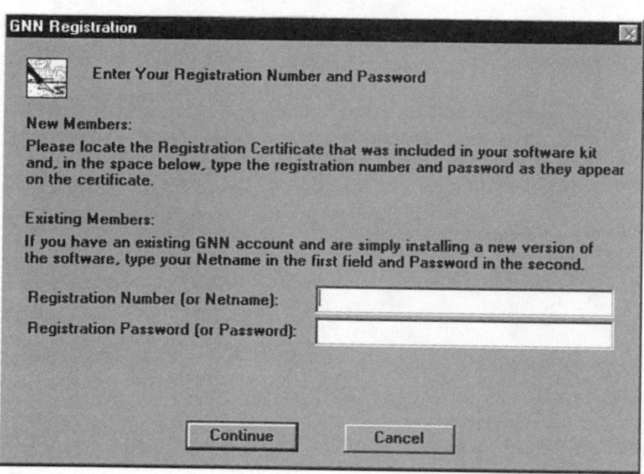

Fig. 12.2
Enter your certificate information in this screen to begin the process of setting up your GNN account.

The most common choices in a network name are of course your own name, or your first name and last initial (I use GeneS for my GNN visits). Your Internet mailing address will thus be: *<networkname>*@megaweb.com. The information after the "@" or "at" symbol represents GNN's Internet domain or address.

> **Caution**
>
> Even if you are already a member of America Online, you are not automatically enrolled in GNN. You have to join GNN separately, set up a separate account for it, and create a separate network name for yourself. Assuming that someone else isn't using the name, it's convenient to try to have the same network name for both services. You do not need to use AOL's software to run GNN, but you can access GNN's World Wide Web site from AOL's browser or any other browser program.

How to Configure Your Modem for Top Performance

During the software installation, GNN's software takes a peek at your modem and makes a basic profile of its capabilities. But the results are usually generic, such as "Hayes Extended" for a high-speed modem, no matter who makes it. To get the best possible performance, click the Modem menu of your GNNconnect software (or type Ctrl+M) to bring up a list of modem drivers. Unless you have a very new or obscure make and model modem, you're likely to find one that matches the one you have. When you choose that modem driver and then click OK, it's stored in the program's settings. From then on, GNN's software will use that information to provide optimum connections to its network servers.

Troubleshooting

Help! My modem keeps disconnecting each time I try to run a GNN session. What's wrong?

Maybe you just need to set up GNN's software to work better with your modem. Follow the steps just outlined to configure the program for the make and model of the modem you have. You may also want to check your Windows 95 modem settings to make sure they are also adjusted to recognize your modem properly.

How to Choose Access Numbers

When you first sign up with GNN, you have the option to choose a pair of local phone access numbers. If you move, or are traveling, or want to see if you can get a better connection with another number, click the Local icon from the GNNconnect program to get a list of available numbers. You are logged on to GNN's servers through an 800 phone number, and you are presented with a listing of available numbers in the area code you select. From that list, you can make a new Network profile to offer you more access options.

Tip

If you plan to access GNN from different locations (say your home or office or various places to which you travel regularly), you can create a separate Network file for each to help speed up your connections.

Using GNN's World Wide Web Browser

Your GNNworks software is the central program you use to run your GNN sessions. But as you no doubt recall from the signup process I've just described, something is missing. When you first joined GNN, you only had two software components in your program folder, and GNNworks wasn't one of them.

There's yet one more step before your initial connection process is finished, but it occurs *only* if you've installed your GNN software from a floppy disk. Since the software consumes too much space to fit on a single disk, you'll have to download the remaining software modules directly from GNN's servers. When you first create your new account, and log on to the service, you see an information prompt that you select to begin the final file transfer process. Once that's done, all the GNN software is transferred to your computer and placed in the GNN program folder. The process will usually take from ten to twenty minutes—but, of course, you won't need to go through this download if you downloaded the installer program directly from GNN.

To use that software, you need to end your session once again, repeat the log on process, and select the program module you want to use for your initial connection. We'll start with GNNworks.

GNNworks offers you speedy access to your favorite WWW sites. Through its handy toolbar (see fig. 12.3) you're able to quickly access other GNN features without having to launch any of the other programs (they'll be opened when necessary).

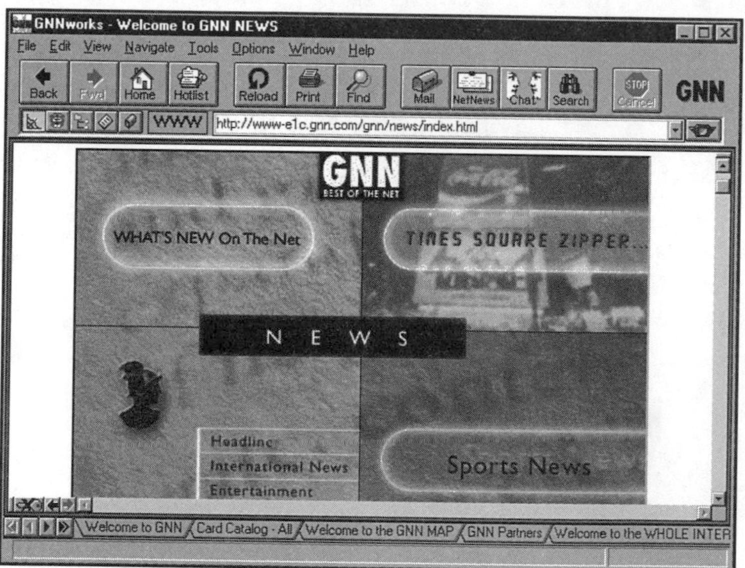

Fig. 12.3
GNN's clearly labeled toolbar lets you quickly navigate from one WWW site to another and access other GNN features.

> **Tip**
>
> If you don't have this book handy during your GNN session and you need to know what a particular button in the toolbar does, just place the mouse pointer over the button to see its label. To see a full description of the function in the status bar, press and hold down the left mouse button.

A Quick Tour of GNN Services

Whether you're new to the Internet or an experienced Net surfer, you'll want to spend your first online visits touring the service to get an idea of what features are available.

I'm just going to list some of the most popular GNN services right now. I'll cover some more throughout the chapter, and you'll want to take your time during your initial visit to explore each feature further and try them out for size. As with any of the major access services, GNN will be signing up many new information providers as the service grows, so you can be assured that what you see here is just the beginning.

Your visit to GNN begins with the opening screen (see fig. 12.4). From there, you can access a set of informative features that are exclusive to GNN's own Web site. Each of these services can be selected from GNN's Home page:

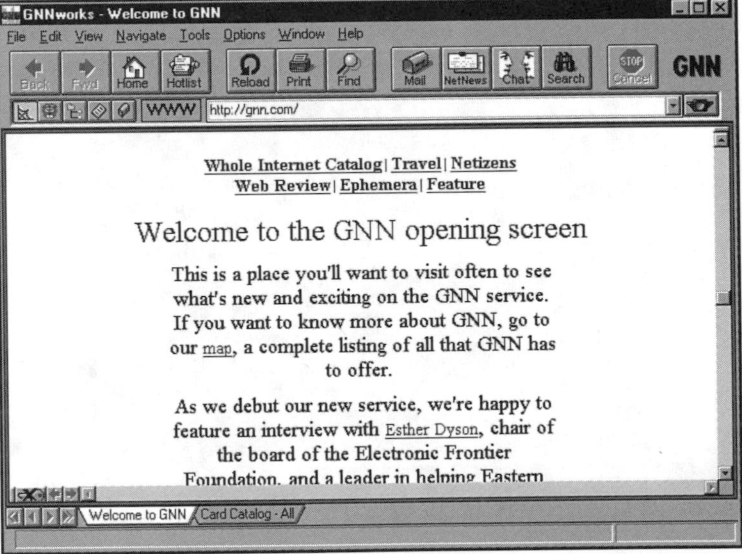

Fig. 12.4 The day's highlights are shown when you access GNN's Home Page.

> **Tip**
>
> Get there faster with a keyboard shortcut. To access a WWW site, simply press Ctrl+U and then enter the URL you want to access, press the Enter key, and you'll see it display on your computer's screen in seconds.

- *GNN Voices*. This is one of the service's exclusive programming features. It provides information from a number of authors on such subjects as Education, Personal Finance (see fig. 12.5), Sports, a Story Cafe, Travel, and a Web Review.

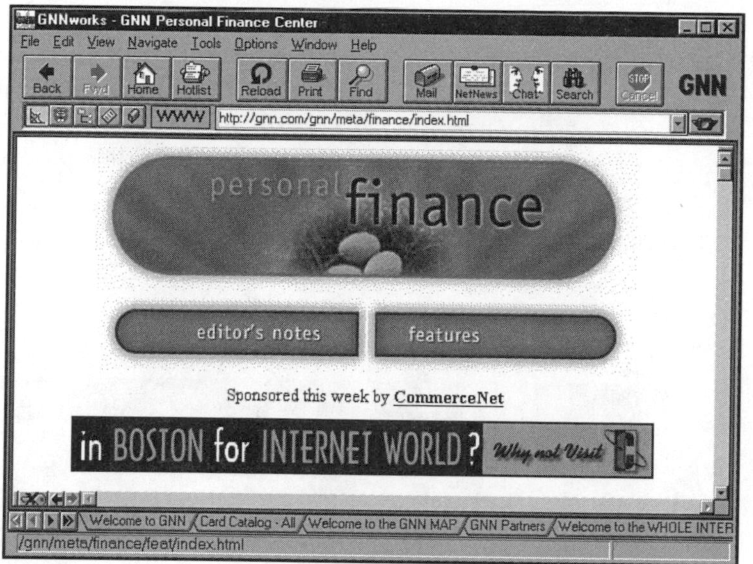

Fig. 12.5
One of GNN's Voices is devoted to up-to-date personal finance information.

- *GNN Partners*. The GNN service has teamed with major firms to provide additional services (see fig. 12.6). They include such companies as American Airlines and Compaq Computers. You also get the latest hourly news summaries from Reuters.

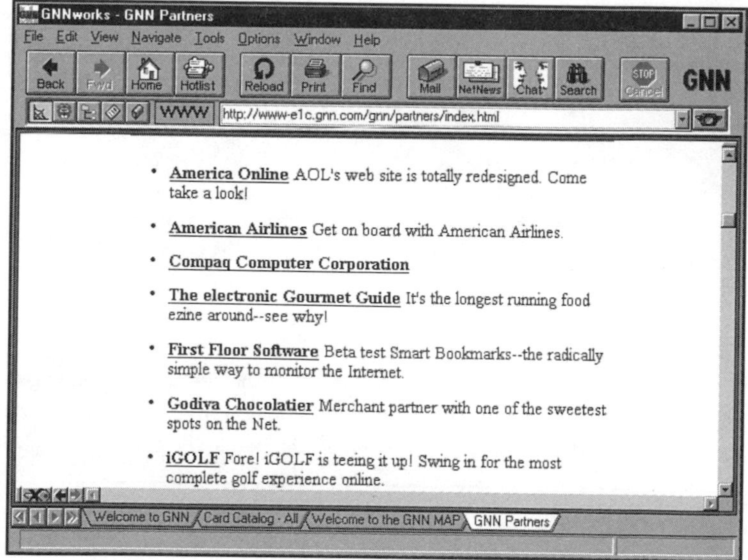

Fig. 12.6
A huge roster of GNN partners is on hand to provide expanded services, such as online shopping and computing advice.

- *Online shopping*. One of the fastest growing features of the World Wide Web is the ability to shop for popular merchandise. GNN offers both online catalogs and the ability to place your order online from such companies as Fossil Watches, Godiva Chocolatier, and Hammacher Schlemmer. In addition, hundreds of other firms offer their products on their own WWW sites.
- *Online news and views*. GNN offers you hourly updates on the latest national and world news from Reuters New Media, The Sports Network, Web Review, and other major information services. Accessing the latest news is just a point and click process.

Tip

Here's more keyboard power to make your GNN session go faster: Use Ctrl+left arrow to return to a previously opened WWW page, and Ctrl+right arrow to go forward to the next page you've accessed.

- *Fast access to the entire worldwide Internet*. In addition to its locally originated content, you'll be able to access all the standard Internet-based services simply by clicking the appropriately labeled program icon.

Tip

If you want to print text you see in a GNN document window for later reference, simply click the Print icon in your GNN software. The active document window will be printed. If you haven't set up your printer yet, you'll first see a dialog box prompting you to set up your printer before printing can proceed.

Troubleshooting

When I connect to GNN, I notice the images on its WWW site don't match the ones in this book. Why?

The World Wide Web is a fluid place, and service providers are always changing their look and feel to attract more people to their sites. This is normal, and you shouldn't be alarmed if things don't look quite the same as pictured in this book.

Internet E-Mail

Sending e-mail to your friends and business associates around the world is one of the joys of Internet service, and GNN's e-mail reader is an extremely flexible tool that makes the task truly simple.

If you want to get right down to the business of writing e-mail, just launch the GNNmessenger program directly by double-clicking on the program icon. Or if you are already working in another GNN program, click the Mail button from the toolbar to bring the program to the front. The first thing you see is your GNNmessenger In Box, which displays a list of the e-mail you've received since your last visit. During your session, your software frequently checks GNN's mail servers for new mail, and you see your display update as new e-mail arrives.

If you have a color monitor, you'll see a little red box next to your unread mail. Just double-click the appropriate directory listing to open your e-mail. After you've read your message, you can respond to it simply by clicking on the Reply window, which brings up a document window showing the text of the message you've just read, with standard Internet quote marks (see fig. 12.7).

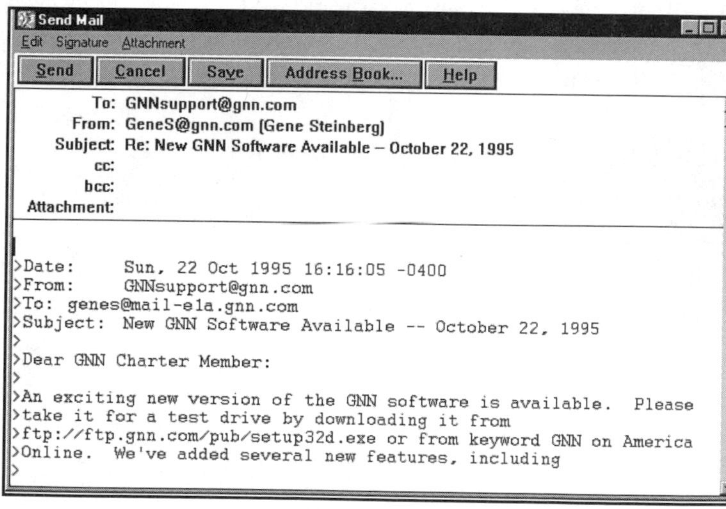

Fig. 12.7
You can enter the text of your e-mail message above or below the quoted text (the proper method is below it).

Your other e-mail option is activated by the Forward button. That function lets you send the original e-mail, along with any comments you care to make, to another recipient or group of recipients.

Another handy feature of GNN's e-mail reader is the Address Book function, which allows you to keep a handy Rolodex of your regular contacts. Once you've written your e-mail message, click the Address Book button to bring up the list (see fig. 12.8).

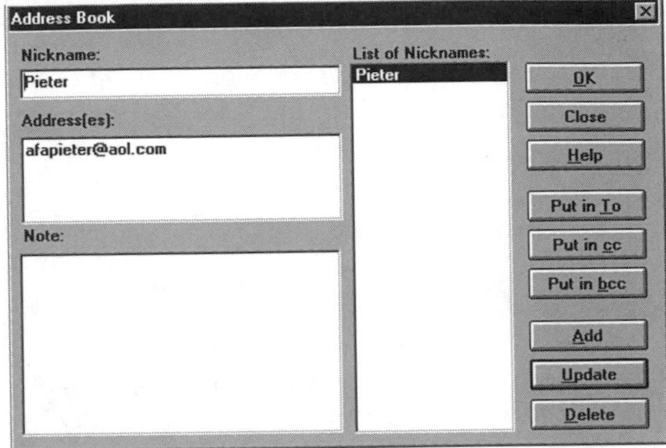

Fig. 12.8
Store a list of your regular friends and business contacts here.

Here's the rundown of some more GNN e-mail features:

- As with other e-mail services, your standard GNN e-mail message includes a To: line for the recipient, the From: line where your GNN e-mail address is shown, and a subject line.
- If you're responding to an existing message, the subject of that message will be listed in the subject line, preceded by "Re:".
- You can send a carbon copy of your message to another recipient or group of recipients by entering their e-mail addresses next in the cc: field.
- You may opt to use the blind carbon copy (bcc) feature, which hides the names of anyone other than the actual recipient in the message.
- You can also attach a file to your GNN e-mail. If the recipient of the message is on another service, you may want to contact them in case they need a special translator program to be able to use the file you send.
- If you want to keep your e-mail on hand, you can Save it, which will store the messages in a File Box for later retrieval.

GNN's UseNet Newsgroups Reader

Your GNNmessenger software also has another feature you'll use often. It's the capability to search and access UseNet newsgroup messages, those freewheeling message boards where you can discuss most any topic that interests you or just read exciting discussions that can often get hot and heavy.

To access GNN's newsgroup feature, just click the NetNews button that you find on the GNNmessenger or GNNworks software. It brings up the News Box, which allows you to access any newsgroup available from GNN's host computer.

When you first install your software, you'll already have a small list of newsgroups available to you, shown in the Subscribed directory at the left of your GNNmessenger News Box (see fig. 12.9).

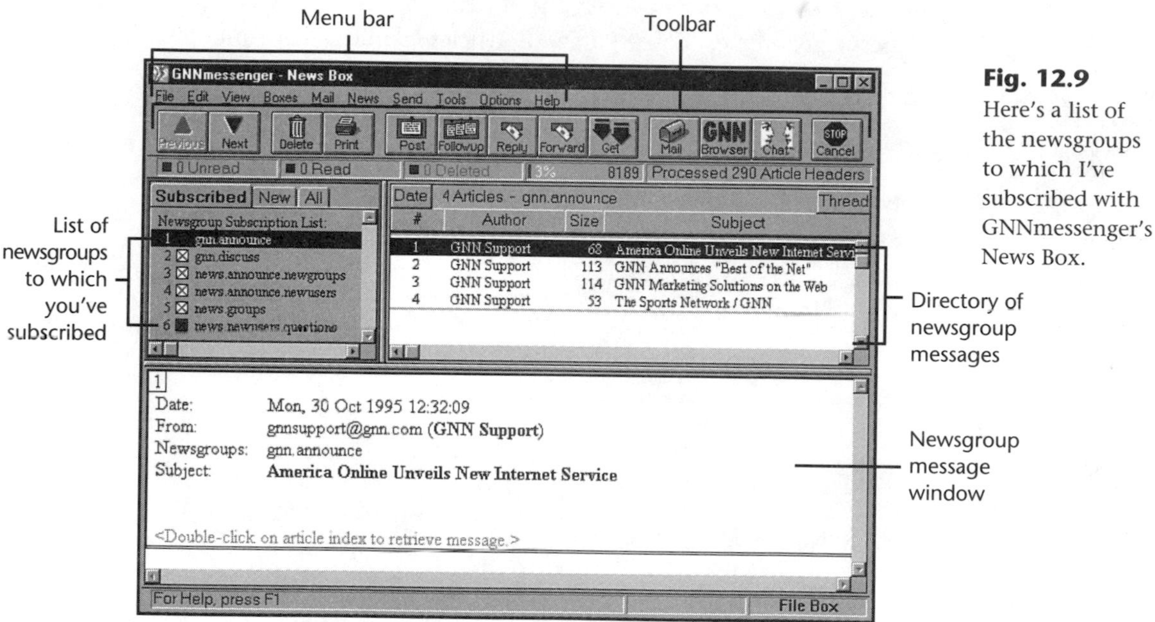

Fig. 12.9 Here's a list of the newsgroups to which I've subscribed with GNNmessenger's News Box.

When you click on the name of your newsgroup, you see the listing of the unread articles on the right. After the list has displayed on your computer, just double-click on the article index to bring up the message on your screen.

Your newsgroup messages are grouped by *threads* (topics), so that you can quickly scroll to the ones that interest you.

If you decide you want to subscribe to another newsgroup, you can click the All tab at the left side of your News Box, which brings up a list of the available newsgroups. But the list is quite long, and it'll take a while for it to display fully. As you scroll through the list, just click the check box adjacent to a newsgroup's title to subscribe to that newsgroup (or uncheck the ones you no longer want).

The New tab brings up a list of newsgroups added since your last visit to GNN.

Tip

You can jump quickly from one GNN document to another simply by clicking the appropriately labeled tab at the bottom of the document window.

After you've read a message, you have the option to reply to the sender, post a response in the newsgroup itself (see fig. 12.10), or just move on to the next message. Messages can be deleted one at a time, or as a group. To get rid of all the messages at once, choose Purge All Articles from the News menu.

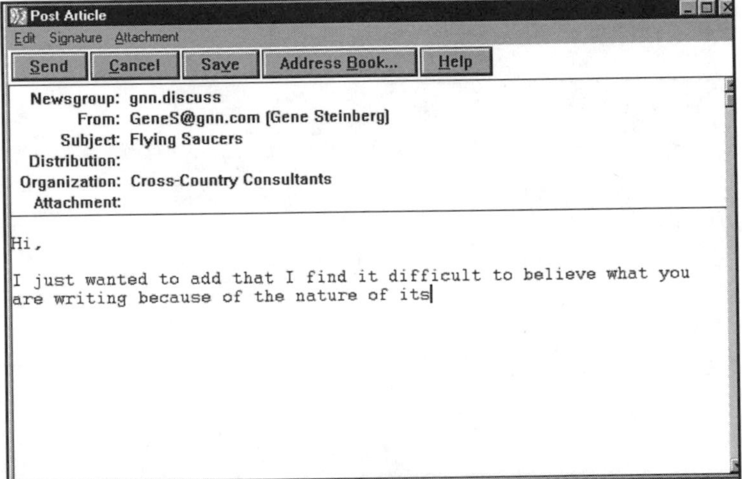

Fig. 12.10
The message window to post a message in a newsgroup is similar to the one you use to send an e-mail message.

Tip

You can also use the GNNworks browser window to access a newsgroup. Just click the News button, enter the name of the newsgroup in the exact Internet format, and the contents of the unread messages are then transferred to your computer.

Although most newsgroup messages are all text, some are in binary form. You'll know that because the message itself displays a blue triangle next to the title in the message index. If the files are in binary form, your GNNmessenger software can decode it automatically; you don't have to reconfigure the software (unless you want to turn off the feature to automatically translate such files).

Internet Database Searching and File Transfers

Many of your favorite WWW sites offer seamless access to FTP sites or to a Gopher database search. So you normally need not do anything special to access these features, other than to click the appropriate underlined title or button on a particular WWW page. When you do that, you access the FTP or Gopher sites automatically.

If you want to access a particular site directly, just press Ctrl+U, and enter the correct URL (using a "gopher" or "ftp" prefix as needed). Then press Enter to quickly bring up the service (assuming it's active, of course).

Tip

If you decide that you don't want to download a file being transferred during your GNN session, simply click the Cancel button in the toolbar while the file transfer is taking place. In just seconds, the file transfer will stop.

Internet Relay Chats (IRC)

One of the most exciting features of GNN's Internet services is the capability to have a one-to-one conversation in real time with millions of other Internet surfers. Access to the Internet Relay Chats (IRCs) is done through your GNN chat software.

Caution

Although the Internet can sometimes be a free-for-all, you should always be on your best behavior. Show respect to others, refrain from using vulgar language, and resist the temptation to get involved in a "flamefest," which is the Internet equivalent of having a shouting match.

When you first access GNN's IRC server, you are given a nickname, which is based on the first nine characters of your network name. If that name is already taken, you are asked to choose a different name.

Each chat group is listed as a channel in the Channels dialog box (see fig. 12.11). The listing is grouped into titles that roughly describe the topics under discussion.

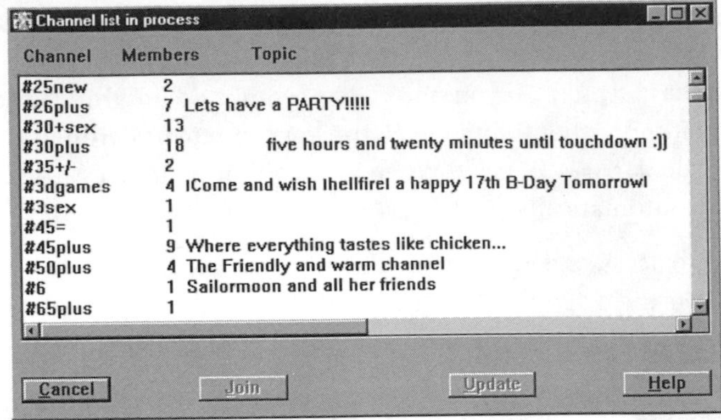

Fig. 12.11
Here's a short list of some of the IRC chats in progress when I wrote this chapter.

To join a specific chat, simply select a Channel by clicking once on its name; then click the Join button, and you're off into a world of exciting conversation and the subjects in which you're interested.

As you see an IRC chat in progress, you'll want to jump in and make some comments yourself. To do that, simply type your message in the Outgoing Messages field, and then press Enter to send it on its way.

In seconds, you'll see your nickname appear in the chat window and your comments to the right of it. From time to time, you'll also see comments from members whose network name has an "@" before it. That member is the Channel operator or host (very much like the sysop of a regular bulletin board).

Your GNNchat software also lets you chat and exchange files with another person without having to use the IRC network feature. To send a private message to another user, simply click the Private button on the GNNchat program's toolbar. You then see a message window similar to an e-mail window where you can enter the nickname of the person you want to contact and then the body of the message.

To send files, you need to set up what's called a *Direct Client Connection*. To start that process, choose Options, DCC Send and enter the name of the file you want to transfer in the Send File field. The recipient's nickname should be entered in the To field. If you're not sure of the name and path of the file, use the Browse feature to locate it on your computer's drive.

To send the file on its way, click OK.

Caution

Internet Relay Chats are not governed by the rules of conduct that you find on a regular online service, such as America Online. Discussions can be freewheeling, and even over the top in terms of the use of language and discussions about erotica. Expect the unexpected, and be careful about allowing your children to access these features of your GNN software.

A Look at the Whole Internet Catalog

One of the most valuable sources of information about the Internet is GNN's Whole Internet Catalog. It's a comprehensive online catalog listing some of the most popular Internet sites (see fig. 12.12).

You'll find hundreds of Internet resources conveniently grouped by topic. Simply click on any underlined reference to access a site directly. If you don't find an entry for a topic that interests you, just click the Yahoo! or WebCrawler buttons on the opening Whole Internet Catalog screen. Either choice brings up a comprehensive Internet search tool that quickly guides you to the source of information you want, whether it's a spot for online shopping, a software update, or a resource for reference material. If one of these tools doesn't bring the results you want, you will often find the other will seek out the information you are looking for.

Tip

Want to save information for later review? Just choose File, Save and the text in the active document window is quickly saved to your PC's hard drive.

One popular catalog feature is the Best of the Net, which is a list of the favorite Internet hot spots, specifically selected by GNN's own editorial staff. Some of these sites are funny and offbeat, such as one devoted to Useless WWW Pages. Others are educational, such as a site that covers the Complete Works of William Shakespeare. You can spend many happy hours here simply exploring the choices available to you.

Another Handy GNN Feature

Over time, you'll begin to build up a list of your favorite sites, ones you want to visit over and over again. Your GNNworks software offers a convenient way to create your own, customized Hotlist of your favorite sites that you can easily access during your online sessions (see fig. 12.13).

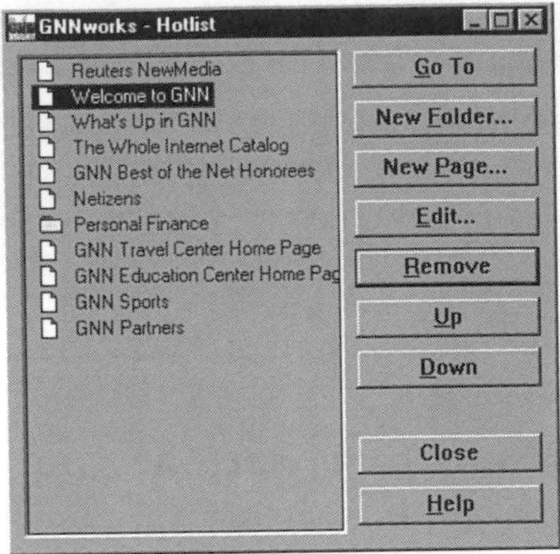

Fig. 12.13 Use a Hotlist to give you fast access to your favorite Internet-based areas, whether on GNN's own site or elsewhere.

Here's how to make your own Hotlist:

1. Be sure the document representing the site you want to add is active by clicking anywhere in that document window.
2. Click the Navigate menu and choose Add to Hotlist.
3. Then choose File, Close.

From now on, whenever you want to access that site, simply click the Hotlist button on the toolbar of your GNNworks program, and you'll see a handy list of your favorite places. You'll also see some other documents listed there, representing areas specially selected by GNN's own staff for you to check out further.

Tip

Need assistance in using your GNN software? Simply press the F1 key to bring up a comprehensive Help menu that offers answers to most of the questions you may have.

Troubleshooting

How come some of my favorite WWW sites are no longer available? What am I doing wrong?

Sometimes the inability to communicate with a WWW site just indicates a network problem with GNN's host computer network, or a problem with the site's own server computers. But it's a sure thing that many Web sites will disappear or change their URL addresses over time. If you find you cannot locate a particular site you've accessed previously, you can use GNN's search tools (such as Yahoo and WebCrawler) to find the current site address.

A Look at Some GNN Power User Settings

After you are familiar with the service and software, you'll want to find ways to make your visits faster and more productive and to fine-tune the software to work best for you. The following are a few of the settings you can make with your GNN software choosing Options, Preferences:

- *User Change*. Here's where you can change your connection information for both the GNNworks and GNNmessenger software components. You can enter such things as your business or personal affiliations as part of this description. You can also specify a directory on your computer's drive in which to store files transferred to your computer from the service.
- *External Viewers*. You can use this feature to associate other programs with files you download during your visits to GNN. For example, you can use a painting program to handle bitmap (.BMP) files.
- *Cache Manage*. As explained earlier in this chapter, the WWW pages and other items you download from GNN are saved on your computer. You can use this setting to control the amount of hard drive space you specify as a cache for these documents. When that space is filled, the oldest pages are automatically deleted.
- *Misc. Choose*. You can use this setting to select a different home page to access when you first connect to GNN (perhaps one representing a favorite site or a business you're connected with). You can also use these settings to set up the appearance and size of the document windows that display on your computer.
- *Screen Fonts*. You can use these settings to change the fonts in which documents and card catalogs are displayed on your screen. Only the fonts that appear on your screen are changed and not the fonts that appear in your printed documents. For that you need printer fonts (see the next item).
- *Printer Fonts*. You can use this feature to change the fonts used in the documents you print. And remember, the changes you make to your printed documents are not reflected in the screen display unless you make the same choices in the Screen Fonts option.
- *Load Images*. WWW connections work best with 14,400 bps hookups or better. If you don't have a speedy connection to GNN or a fast modem, you can turn off the option to load images and see image placeholders instead. This speeds up GNN's performance, at the expense of the loss of those attractive graphic displays.

In addition to the changes you make in the GNNworks program, you can adjust the settings in your GNNmessenger and GNNchat software to make them run the way you want.

Getting Help

Your visits to GNN should be fairly trouble free. The software comes with easy access toolbars, clearly labeled menu bar commands, and a complete help menu. If you run into trouble, you'll find many helpful hints available via the help menu. The information ranges from basic instructions on using the software to advice for power users.

If the information there doesn't answer your question or solve your problem, you can try one of the following:

- Click the Help listing you'll see near the top of GNN's Home Page to bring up a list of frequently asked questions and answers.
- Send an e-mail message to **gnnsupport@gnn.com**. Please be sure to provide as much information as you can about your problem, and also describe your PC setup, including the kind of modem you have, and some basic details about your computer, memory, and hard drive capacity.
- If the problem needs a quick solution (perhaps you cannot get connected or the software is crashing), you may reach GNN's technical support department at (800) 819-6112. Before you dial your phone, you may want to write down a brief outline of your PC setup, so you'll have the information ready when the technical support person answers. ❖

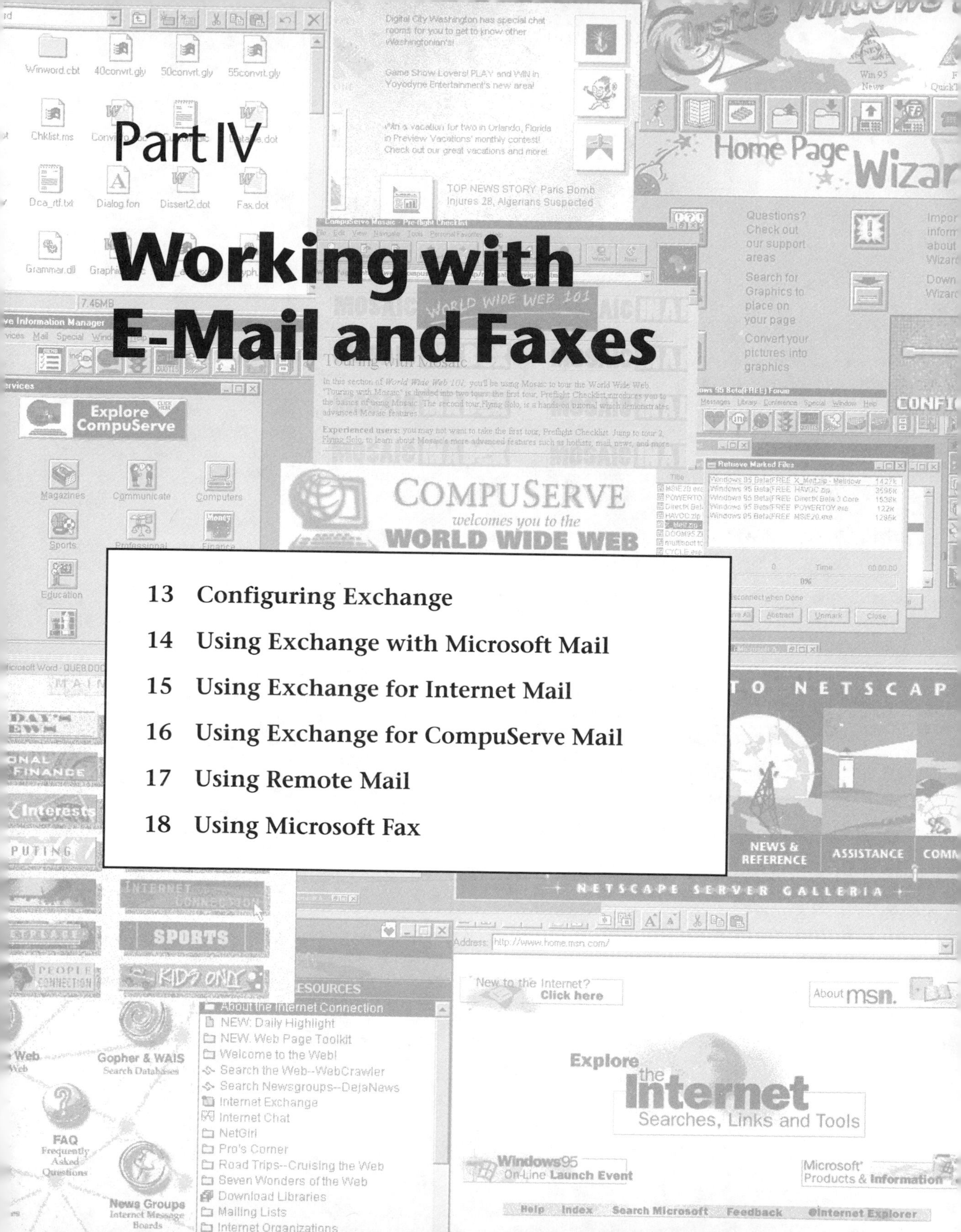

Part IV

Working with E-Mail and Faxes

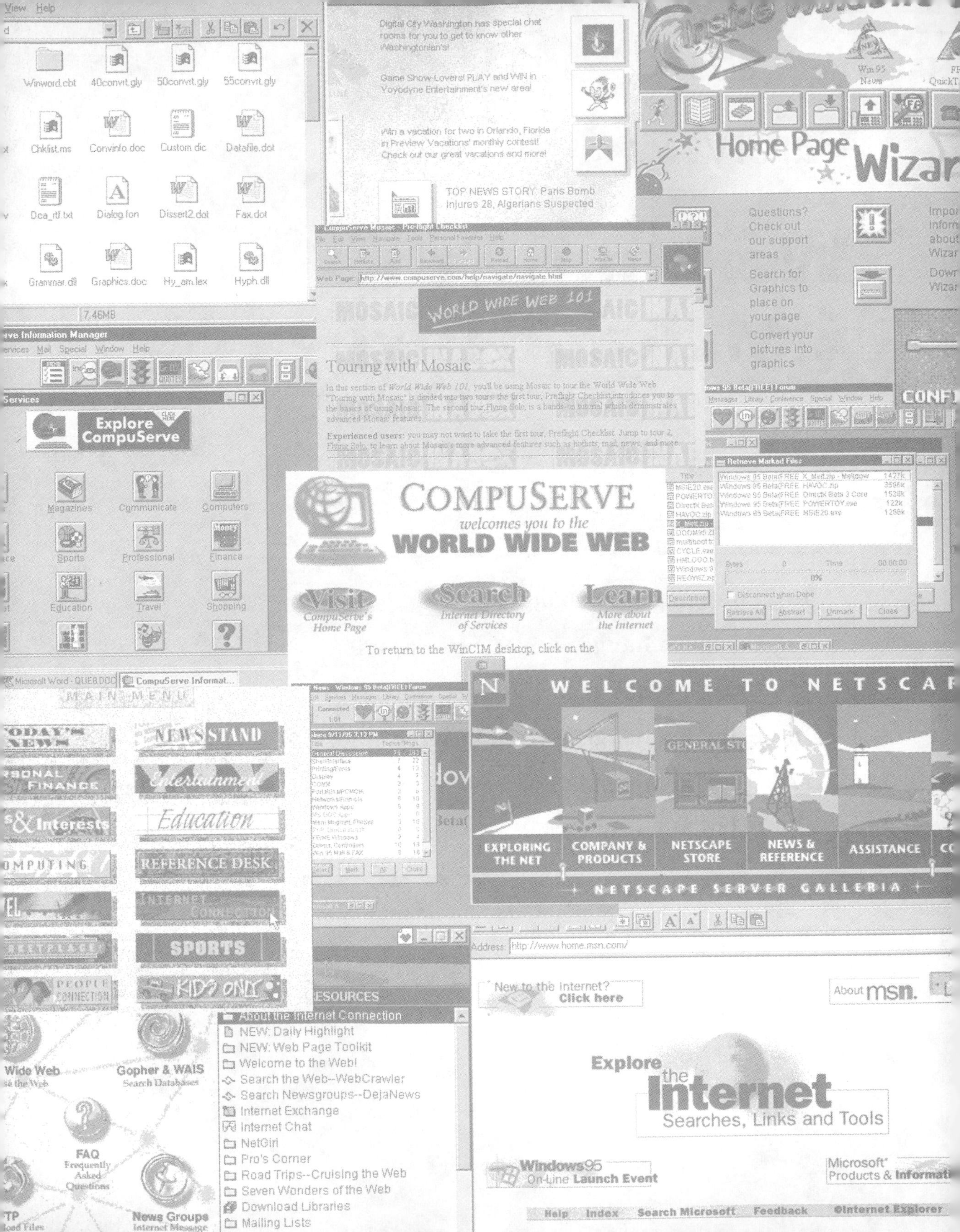
Winword.cbt
40convrt.gly
50convrt.gly
55convrt.gly
Chklist.ms
Convinfo.doc
Custom.dic
Datafile.dot
Dca_rtf.txt
Dialog.fon
Dissert2.dot
Fax.dot
Grammar.dll
Graphics.doc
Hy_am.lex
Hyph.dll
7.46MB
Digital City Washington has special chat rooms for you to get to know other Washingtonian's!
Game Show Lovers! PLAY and WIN in Yoyodyne Entertainment's new area!
Win a vacation for two in Orlando, Florida in Preview Vacations' monthly contest! Check out our great vacations and more!
TOP NEWS STORY: Paris Bomb Injures 28, Algerians Suspected
Home Page Wizard
Questions? Check out our support areas
Search for Graphics to place on your page
Convert your pictures into graphics
CompuServe Mosaic - Pre-flight Checklist
http://www.compuserve.com/help/navigate/navigate.html
WORLD WIDE WEB 101
Touring with Mosaic
Explore CompuServe
Magazines
Communicate
Computers
Sports
Professional
Finance
Education
Travel
Shopping
COMPUSERVE
welcomes you to the
WORLD WIDE WEB
Visit
CompuServe's Home Page
Search
Internet Directory of Services
Learn
More about the Internet
To return to the WinCIM desktop, click on the
Retrieve Marked Files
MAIN MENU
NEWSSTAND
Entertainment
Education
REFERENCE DESK
SPORTS
KIDS ONLY
WELCOME TO NETSCAPE
EXPLORING THE NET
COMPANY & PRODUCTS
NETSCAPE STORE
NEWS & REFERENCE
ASSISTANCE
NETSCAPE SERVER GALLERIA
Address: http://www.home.msn.com/
New to the Internet? Click here
About msn.
Explore the Internet
Searches, Links and Tools
Windows95 On-Line Launch Event
Help
Index
Search Microsoft
Feedback
RESOURCES
About the Internet Connection
NEW: Daily Highlight
NEW: Web Page Toolkit
Welcome to the Web!
Search the Web--WebCrawler
Search Newsgroups--DejaNews
Internet Exchange
Internet Chat
NetGirl
Pro's Corner
Road Trips--Cruising the Web
Seven Wonders of the Web
Download Libraries
Mailing Lists
Gopher & WAIS
Search Databases
FAQ
Frequently Asked Questions
News Groups

CHAPTER 13

Configuring Exchange

by Jim Boyce

Windows 95 includes an e-mail application named Exchange that enables you to combine much, if not all, of your e-mail and faxes into a single inbox. With Exchange, you can send and receive e-mail to a Microsoft Mail post office, the Internet, The Microsoft Network, and CompuServe. Exchange's support for Internet and CompuServe e-mail gives you a gateway to send and receive messages to almost anyone in the world who has an e-mail account on the Internet or on an online service such as CompuServe, America Online, Prodigy, or others.

This chapter helps you install and configure Exchange to enable you to send and receive e-mail and faxes, both locally on your network and through your modem to remote sites and services. In this chapter, you learn how to

- Install Microsoft Exchange
- Configure Exchange and service providers
- Create and edit an Exchange profile
- Set up your personal message store and address books
- Add other e-mail and fax services to Exchange
- Set up Exchange for remote mail access
- Customize Exchange

Installing the Exchange Client

Microsoft Exchange is a typical Windows 95 application (see fig. 13.1) that works in conjunction with various *service providers* to enable you to send and receive e-mail and faxes to others. You can think of a service provider as an add-on module that enables the Exchange client to work with specific types of mail and online services. For example, Windows 95 includes service providers that enable it to work with Microsoft Mail, Microsoft Fax, and the Microsoft Network. The Windows 95 CD contains a service provider that enables Exchange to send and receive e-mail to and from CompuServe. Microsoft Plus! for Windows 95 includes a service provider that lets you send and receive mail on the Internet through a network or dial-up connection to the Internet.

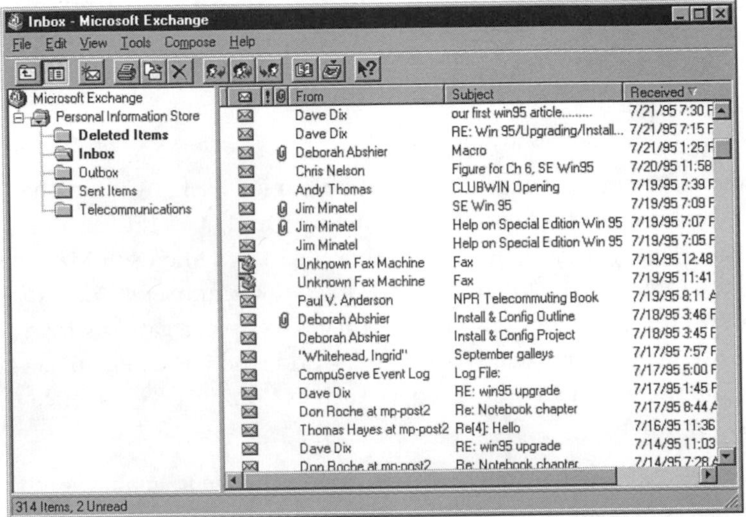

Fig. 13.1
Exchange provides a unified inbox for all of your e-mail and faxes.

Tip

You can expect other e-mail vendors to offer service providers for Microsoft Exchange that support their e-mail applications. Also look for online services such as America Online and Prodigy to provide Exchange service providers that work with their online services.

Installing and configuring Exchange consists of four phases, which are described in the following list:

- *Install Exchange.* You can install Exchange when you install Windows 95, or you can easily add Exchange to your PC at any time after you install Windows 95.
- *Create at least one profile.* Your Exchange settings and service providers are stored in an Exchange *profile*. Each profile can contain one or more service providers to support different e-mail and fax systems. A profile is a collection of settings you can use to specify which service providers and settings you want to use with Exchange.

- *Add a personal information store and address book.* You need somewhere to store your messages, so the third phase in configuring Exchange is to add a personal information store to your profile, along with an address book to store e-mail and fax addresses.
- *Add service providers.* The final phase of installing Exchange is to add to your profile the service providers you want to use. These could include Microsoft Mail, CompuServe Mail, The Microsoft Network, and Internet Mail.

Setup doesn't automatically install Exchange when you install Windows 95. Instead, you must specifically select Exchange as an option to install when you run Setup. Or you can add Exchange after installing Windows 95. The following sections explain how to install the Microsoft Exchange client software. Later sections in this chapter explain how to create and modify Exchange profiles, add service providers, and set other Exchange options.

Installing Exchange During Windows 95 Installation

If you have not yet installed Windows 95, you can install Exchange at the same time you install Windows 95. To install Exchange, use the following steps:

1. Run Setup from the Windows 95 floppy disk 1 or the \Win95 folder on the Windows 95 CD.
2. Proceed through the installation until the Setup Options dialog box appears (see fig. 13.2) and prompts you to select the type of installation you want. Choose Custom; then choose Next. (The Typical, Portable, and Compact selections will not install Exchange.)

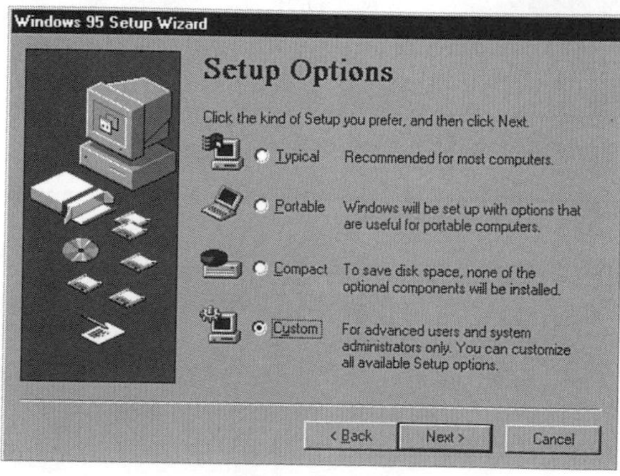

Fig. 13.2
Select the Custom option to install Exchange with the rest of the Windows 95 components.

3. Follow the prompts and dialog boxes to enable Setup to detect your PC's hardware.

4. When the Get Connected dialog box shown in figure 13.3 appears, select the service provider(s) you want to use with Exchange. The listed providers include Microsoft Mail, The Microsoft Network, and Microsoft Fax. You can select one, or more than one. If you want to use only the Internet or CompuServe mail providers that are included with Plus! and the Windows 95 CD, respectively, and not use any of the three service providers in the Get Connected dialog box, leave all the check boxes cleared—you'll have an option to install only Exchange in step 5. When you've made your selections, choose Next.

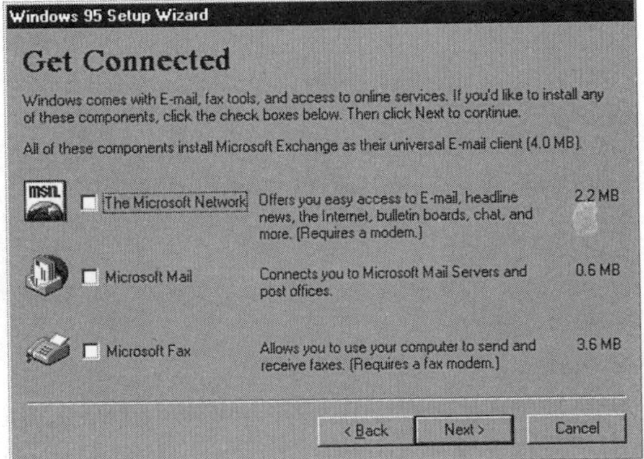

Fig. 13.3
Choose one or more service providers from the Get Connected dialog box.

> **Note**
>
> If you forget to add a service provider when you install Windows 95 or add Exchange to your system, you can add the service provider later. See "Creating and Editing User Profiles" later in this chapter to learn how to add a service provider.

5. In the Select Components dialog box (see fig. 13.4), click Microsoft Exchange; then choose Details to display the Microsoft Exchange dialog box. If the Microsoft Exchange check box does not contain a check mark, enable the check box. If you also want to install the Microsoft Mail provider, enable the Microsoft Mail Services check box. Then choose OK.

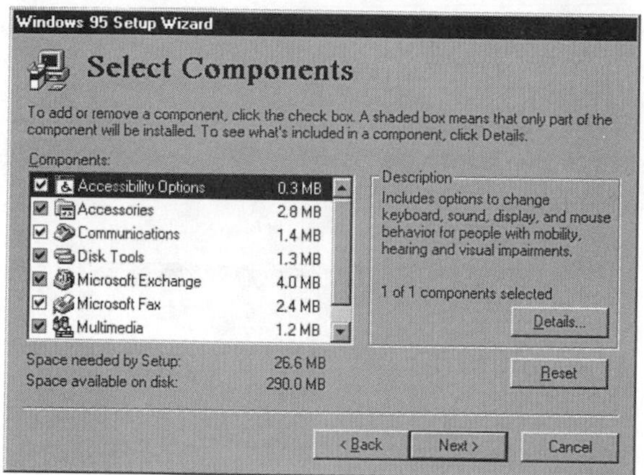

Fig. 13.4
Double-click the Microsoft Exchange item to install Exchange.

6. Choose Next; then follow Setup's remaining prompts to complete the installation process.

After Setup completes the installation process and you start Windows 95, you see an Inbox icon on the desktop. This is the object you later will use to start Exchange. Before using Exchange, however, you need to complete the configuration process. Skip to the section "Creating and Editing User Profiles" later in this chapter to learn how to complete the configuration process for Exchange.

Troubleshooting

When Exchange starts, I receive error messages that my Internet Mail server is not available. I don't have an Internet Mail server and don't use Internet Mail. What's wrong?

You probably have installed Plus! for Windows 95 and ran the Internet Wizard, which installed the Internet Mail service provider. Open Control Panel and choose the Mail and Fax icon. From the list of installed services, choose Internet Mail; then choose Remove. Windows 95 prompts you to verify that you want to remove the Internet Mail service provider from your profile. Choose Yes to remove the service from your profile.

Adding Exchange After Installing Windows 95

If you didn't install Exchange when you installed Windows 95, don't worry—it's easy to add. Use the following steps to add Exchange after installing Windows 95:

1. Choose Start, Settings, Control Panel to open the Control Panel.
2. Double-click the Add/Remove Programs icon to open the Add/Remove Programs Properties sheet.
3. Click the Windows Setup tab, and the Windows Setup page shown in figure 13.5 appears.

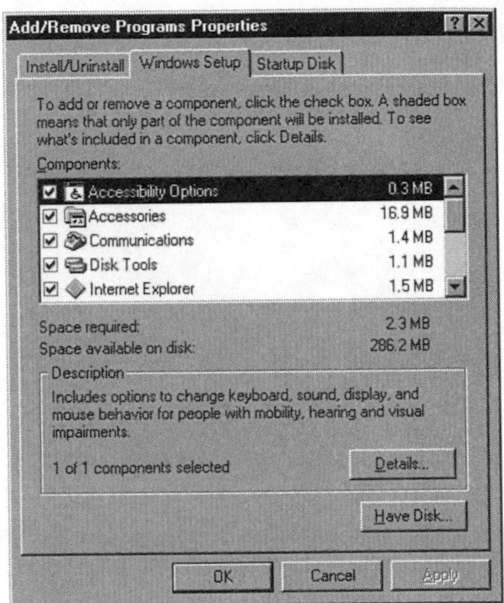

Fig. 13.5
Use the Windows Setup page anytime you need to add a Windows 95 component.

4. Scroll through the Components list to locate and select Microsoft Exchange; then choose Details.
5. In the Microsoft Exchange dialog box, place a check mark beside Microsoft Exchange. If you want to use Exchange to connect to a Microsoft Mail post office, place a check mark beside the Microsoft Mail Services item. Then choose OK.
6. If you want to use Microsoft Fax, place a check mark in the Components list beside the Microsoft Fax item.
7. Choose OK. Windows 95 adds the necessary software to your system, prompting you if necessary to supply one or more of the Windows 95 diskettes or the Windows 95 CD, if needed.

Tip

If you want to use Microsoft Exchange to send and receive messages on The Microsoft Network, you must first install The Microsoft Network on your system. In the Components dialog box, place a check mark beside The Microsoft Network item. You can add The Microsoft Network to your system at the same time you add Exchange, or you can add it separately.

Creating and Editing User Profiles

Besides installing Exchange, you need to configure at least one user profile. The following section explains user profiles to help you understand how to create and edit them.

▶ See "Setting Up a Workgroup Postoffice," p. 333

Understanding Profiles

A collection of information stores, address books, and service providers is called a *user profile*. For example, you might use a profile that contains your personal information store, one address book, a Microsoft Mail service provider, and a CompuServe service provider. In addition to giving you a means of grouping the service providers and information you use most often into a named group, Exchange profiles also store the settings for each item in the profile. Figure 13.6 shows items in an Exchange profile.

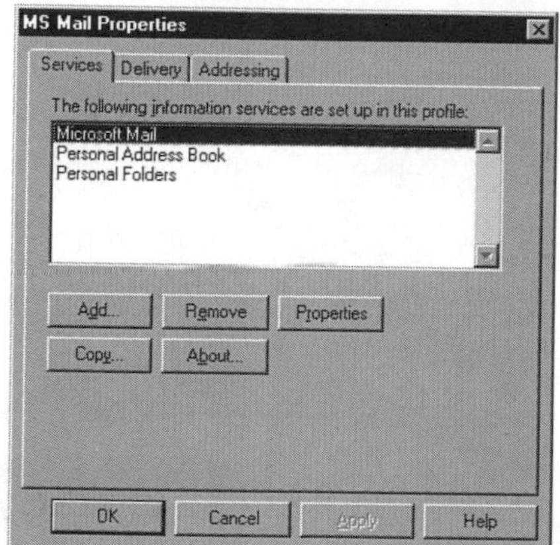

Fig. 13.6
An Exchange profile stores your Exchange settings by name.

Tip

The Microsoft Fax service provider isn't compatible with the Internet Mail and Microsoft Network service providers. The Microsoft Fax provider attempts to initialize the modem as soon as Exchange starts, preventing any other providers from also accessing the modem. The Microsoft Fax provider does, however, work with the CompuServe Mail provider.

▶ See "Adding Microsoft Fax to a Profile," p. 378

If you're like most people, you will use a single profile. But you can use multiple profiles. For example, if you use Microsoft Fax very seldom but use Microsoft Mail all the time, you might want to place the Microsoft Fax provider in a separate profile. When you have to use Microsoft Fax, you can make the Microsoft Fax profile active (explained in the next section); then start Exchange to use it.

> **Tip**
>
> Information stores and address books are service providers, just like Microsoft Mail, CompuServe, and other service providers. All these service providers are often referred to as just *services*. A personal information store is really just a set of special Exchange folders in which you store your messages, and is something you must add to your default profile—Exchange doesn't create an information store for you automatically.

Configuring Profiles

As with most configuration tasks in Windows 95, you create and edit user profiles from the Control Panel. When you install Exchange, Windows 95 creates a default profile for you named MS Exchange Settings. To view or edit your default profile, open the Control Panel; then double-click the Mail and Fax icon to display the MS Exchange Settings Properties sheet shown in figure 13.7.

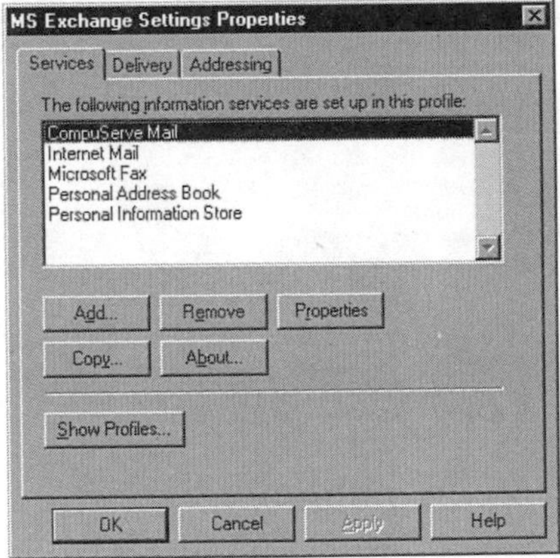

Fig. 13.7
Windows 95 creates a default profile for you named MS Exchange Settings.

From the MS Exchange Settings Properties sheet, you can add services to a profile, delete services, set properties for services, and create and view other profiles. You also can set the properties of services in a profile. If you are using the CompuServe Mail provider, for example, you can specify your CompuServe user ID, password, and other properties that control how and when the CompuServe provider logs on to CompuServe to send and receive your CompuServe mail.

Each service is different from another, so the properties that you can set for each service vary from one service to another. Later sections, "Setting Up Personal Information Stores," "Setting Up Address Books," and "Adding Other Information Stores," explain how to add services and set their properties. The following section explains how to create and delete profiles.

Creating and Deleting Exchange Profiles

As explained earlier, you might want to use more than one Exchange profile to store different sets of properties and services. You can create a profile in one of two ways—create a completely new profile or copy an existing profile. Regardless of which method you use, you can edit the profile to add, remove, or edit services after you create the profile.

To copy your existing profile, follow these steps:

1. Open the Control Panel and double-click the Mail and Fax icon to display the MS Exchange Settings Properties sheet.
2. Click the Show Profiles button to display the Microsoft Exchange Profiles dialog box shown in figure 13.8.

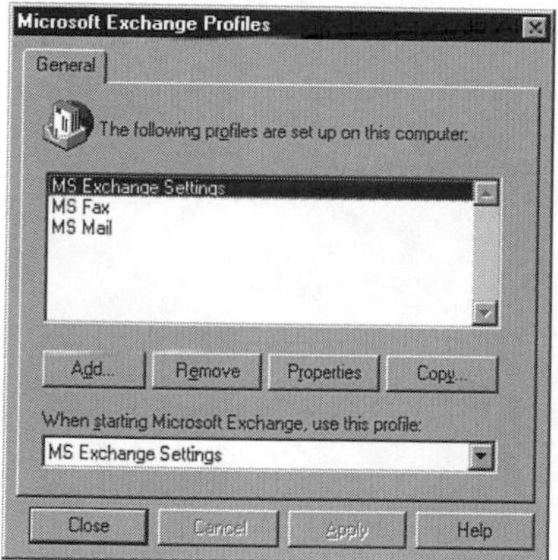

Fig. 13.8
With the Microsoft Exchange Profiles dialog box, you can create a new profile or copy an existing profile.

3. Select the profile you want to copy; then click Copy. A dialog box prompting you to enter a name for your new profile appears (see fig. 13.9).
4. In the New Profile Name text box, enter a unique name for your new Exchange profile; then choose OK. Windows 95 then copies all the services and settings in the selected profile to your new profile.

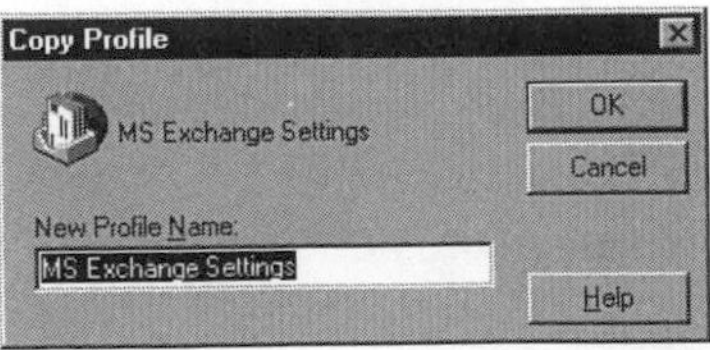

Fig. 13.9
Enter a unique name for your new profile.

5. Use the steps explained in the following sections of this chapter to configure the services in your new profile.

Tip

After you create a profile, you need to specify it as your default profile before you can use it with Exchange. See the section "Setting Your Default Profile" later in the chapter to learn how to begin using your new profile.

In addition to copying an existing profile, you also can create an Exchange profile from scratch. Windows 95 provides a wizard to step you through the process. Use the following steps to create a new Exchange profile:

1. Open the Control Panel and double-click the Mail and Fax icon.
2. Click the Show Profiles button to display the Microsoft Exchange Profiles property sheet.
3. Click the Add button, and the Inbox Setup Wizard shown in figure 13.10 appears.

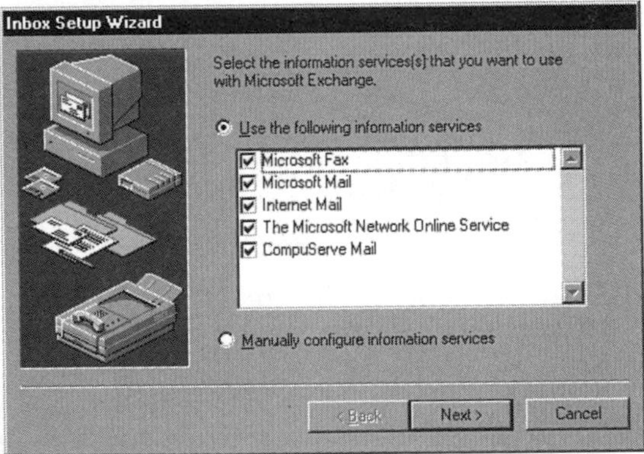

Fig. 13.10
Exchange provides a wizard to help you set up a profile.

4. Click the Use the Following Information Services option button.

5. Place a check mark beside each of the services you want to include in your profile. Deselect any services you don't want included in the profile; then choose Next. The wizard displays a new dialog box prompting you for a name for your new profile (see fig. 13.11).

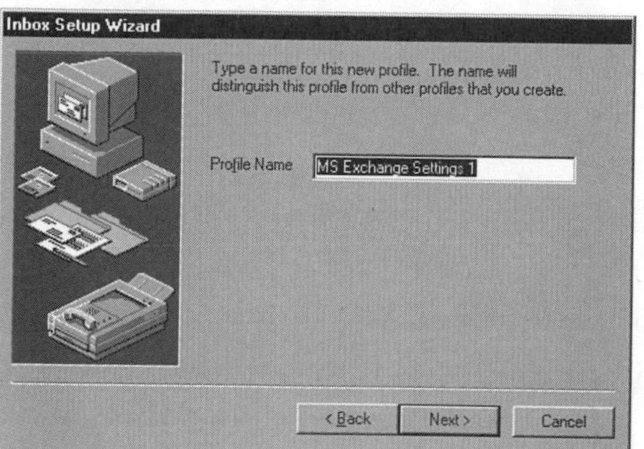

Fig. 13.11
Enter a unique name for your new profile.

6. Enter a unique name for your profile; then choose Next.
7. Depending on which services you selected, the wizard prompts you for information to configure the services. Refer to the sections later in this chapter that describe setup options for services to help you configure the services.

Tip

If you use the preceding steps to create a profile and add services to the profile, Windows 95 uses a wizard to step you through the process of configuring the services. If you add services manually as explained later in this chapter, Windows 95 doesn't use a wizard, but instead displays a set of property sheets for the service. Use these sheets to set its properties. If you read through the following sections on configuring services manually, you'll have no trouble at all configuring the services using the wizard.

Setting Your Default Profile

Although you can create as many Exchange profiles as you want, you can only use one profile at a time. You have two options for specifying which profile Exchange uses. Each time you want to use a different profile, you must exit Exchange, use the Control Panel to specify which profile to use, and then restart Exchange. Or you can configure Exchange to prompt you to specify which profile to use each time Exchange starts.

To specify a default profile, follow these steps:

1. Open the Control Panel and double-click the Mail and Fax icon.
2. Click the Show Profiles button.
3. From the drop-down list labeled When Starting Microsoft Exchange, Use This Profile, choose the profile you want Exchange to use as a default.
4. Choose Close; then start Exchange to verify that it is using the correct profile.

To have Exchange prompt you to select a profile each time Exchange starts, follow these steps:

1. Start Exchange (double-click the Inbox icon on the desktop).
2. Choose Tools, Options to display the Options property sheet.
3. From the control group named When Starting Microsoft Exchange, choose the option labeled Prompt for a Profile to be Used. Then choose OK. The next time you start Exchange, you'll be prompted to select which profile you want to use.

To learn about other general Exchange options you can specify, see the section "Setting General Exchange Options" later in this chapter.

Setting Up Personal Information Stores

Without a place to store all your messages, Exchange wouldn't be much use to you. So each profile should include at least one *information store*. An information store is a special type of file that Exchange uses to store your messages. Whether the message is a fax, an e-mail message from your network mail post office, or other service, incoming messages are placed in the Inbox folder of your default information store. A typical information store contains the following folders:

- *Deleted Items*. This folder contains all the messages you have deleted from other folders. By default, Exchange does not delete items from your information store unless you select them in the Deleted Items folder and delete them. As explained later in the section "Setting General Exchange Options," you can configure Exchange to immediately delete a message instead of moving it to the Deleted Items folder.

- *Inbox.* Exchange places all your incoming messages—including error and status messages generated by the various service providers, e-mail, and faxes—in the Inbox.
- *Outbox.* Items that you compose are placed in the Outbox until the appropriate service delivers the message automatically or you manually direct Exchange to deliver the message(s).
- *Sent Items.* By default, Exchange places in the Sent Items folder a copy of all messages you send. You can configure Exchange not to keep a copy of sent messages (see the section "Setting General Exchange Options" later in this chapter).

In addition to the folders listed previously, you can add your own folders to an information store. And you're not limited to a single information store—you can add as many information stores to a profile as you like. The folders in each information store show up under a separate tree in the Exchange window. Figure 13.12 shows Exchange with two information stores being used, which are named Personal Folders and Personal Information Store.

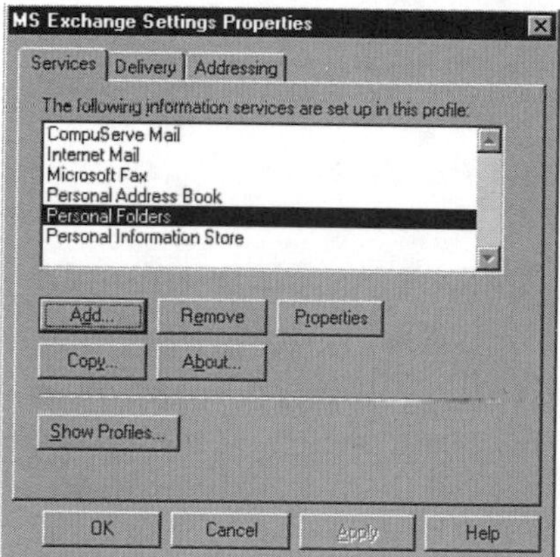

Fig. 13.12
You can use as many information stores in a profile as you like.

Adding multiple message stores to a profile is useful mainly for copying messages between message files. If you are using the latest version of the Microsoft Mail service provider that supports shared folders, however, you can add a shared folder message store to your profile. The shared folder enables you to share messages with other users.

There is one other reason to add a set of personal folders to your profile: you can't use encryption on the Personal Information Store, but you can use encryption on a personal folder. The two are identical in function, so if you want to use encryption for your message file for extra security, add a Personal

Folders item to your profile, copy your messages from the Personal Information Store to the personal folders, and then remove the Personal Information Store from your profile. Make sure that you configure Exchange to use the personal folders to store incoming messages, as explained in the next section.

Troubleshooting

I want to add a second Personal Information Store to my profile, but Exchange tells me I can only have one in a profile. Is it possible to add another?

You can only have one Personal Information Store in a profile, but you can add as many Personal Folders to a profile as you like. Personal Folders are essentially identical to the Personal Information Store. The only difference is that your incoming mail is directed into the Personal Information Store.

If you simply want more places to segregate your incoming mail, create new folders in your Personal Information Store instead of adding Personal Folders to your profile. You can create as many additional folders as you like. To create a new folder, open the folder in which you want the new folder created. Then choose File, New Folder. Exchange displays a simple dialog box in which you can enter the name for the new folder. Then you can drag messages to the new folder as you desire.

Configuring Your Personal Information Store

You can change a handful of settings for a Personal Information Store. To change properties for a Personal Information Store, use the following steps:

1. Open the Control Panel and double-click the Mail and Fax icon.
2. If you want to set properties for a Personal Information Store in a profile other than the default profile, choose the Show Profiles button, select the profile you want to change, and then choose Properties.
3. Select Personal Information Store from the list of services in the profile; then choose Properties. The Personal Folders property sheet shown in figure 13.13 appears.
4. Set the properties for the Personal Information Store according to the following descriptions and your needs:
    - *Name.* If you like, enter a new name for the Personal Information Store. This name will appear in the profile instead of "Personal Information Store."
    - *Change Password.* Click this button to change the password for your Personal Information Store. The dialog box shown later in figure 13.14 appears. The four properties you can set in the password dialog box are described in table 13.1.

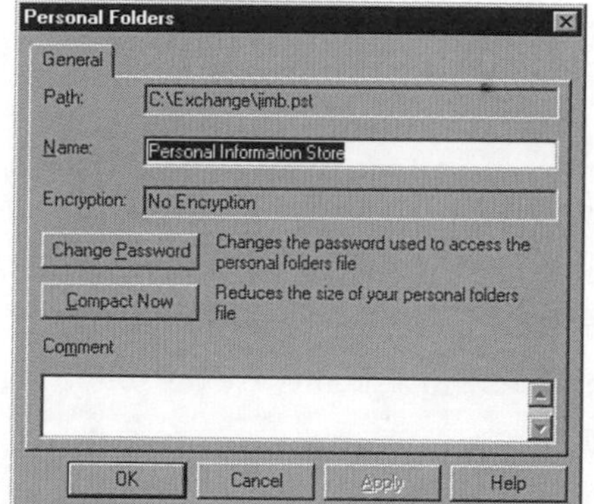

Fig. 13.13
Use the Personal Folders property sheet to set properties for the information store.

Table 13.1 Password Properties for an Information Store

Property	Purpose
Old Password	Enter in this text box the current password, if any, for the Personal Information Store.
New Password	Enter in this text box the new password you want to assign to the Personal Information Store.
Verify Password	Enter in this text box the new password you want to assign to the Personal Information Store to enable Windows 95 to verify that you have entered the password correctly.
Save this Password in Your Password List	If you want the password stored in your password cache so you don't have to enter the password each time you open Exchange, place a check mark in this checkbox.

- *Compact Now.* Choose this button to compress (compact) your Personal Information Store. Windows 95 compresses the file, reducing its size. Compressing a Personal Information Store has no effect on your ability to use the file to store messages.
- *Comment.* If you want to add a short comment about the Personal Information Store, enter it in this text box.

After you have specified all the necessary properties, choose OK; then choose OK again to save the changes.

Adding Other Information Stores

As explained earlier, you can add as many information stores to a profile as you like. These additional stores are called Personal Folders, but they have essentially the same structure and function as your Personal Information Store. You can add a new Personal Folders file to a profile or add an existing file. Adding an existing file enables you to easily import messages from other information stores that you or others have created separately.

To add an information store to a profile, use the following steps:

1. Open the Control Panel and double-click the Mail and Fax icon.
2. If you want to add Personal Folders to a profile other than the default profile, choose the Show Profiles button, select the profile you want to change, and then choose Properties.
3. Choose Add; then from the Add Service to Profile dialog box, select Personal Folders and choose OK.
4. The Create/Open Personal Folders File dialog box appears. If you are adding an existing file, locate and select the file in the dialog box; then choose Open. If you want to create a new file, enter a name for the file in the File name text box, and then choose Open.
5. If you are adding an existing Personal Folders file, skip to step 6. If you are creating a new file, Windows 95 displays a dialog box similar to the one shown in figure 13.14. The Name and Password properties are the same as those explained in the preceding section. From the Encryption Setting group, choose one of the following options:
   - *No Encryption.* Choose this option if you don't want the file to be encrypted. If the file is not encrypted, other users can open the file and read its contents with another program, such as a word processor.
   - *Compressible Encryption.* Choose this option if you want the file to be encrypted for security, but you also want to be able to compress (compact) the file to save disk space.
   - *Best Encryption.* Choose this option if you want the most secure encryption. You will not be able to compress the file if you choose this option.
6. If you are adding an existing Personal Folders file, the dialog box shown in figure 13.13 appears. Adjust settings as explained previously.

7. Choose OK; then choose OK again to close the MS Exchange Settings Properties sheet.

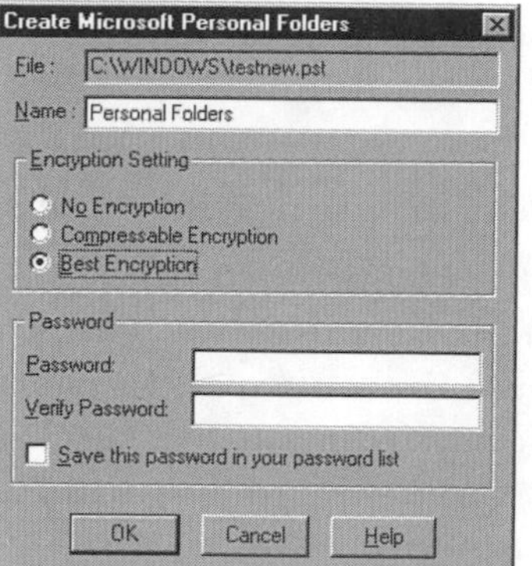

Fig. 13.14
The Create Microsoft Personal Folders dialog box enables you to set various properties for your information store.

Setting Delivery Options

Even though you can add multiple information stores to a profile, only one can be assigned to receive incoming messages. You can, however, assign an alternate information store to be used to store incoming messages if the primary store is unavailable for some reason.

To set these delivery options, follow these steps:

1. Open the Control Panel and double-click the Mail and Fax icon.
2. Click the Delivery tab to display the Delivery property page (see fig. 13.15).

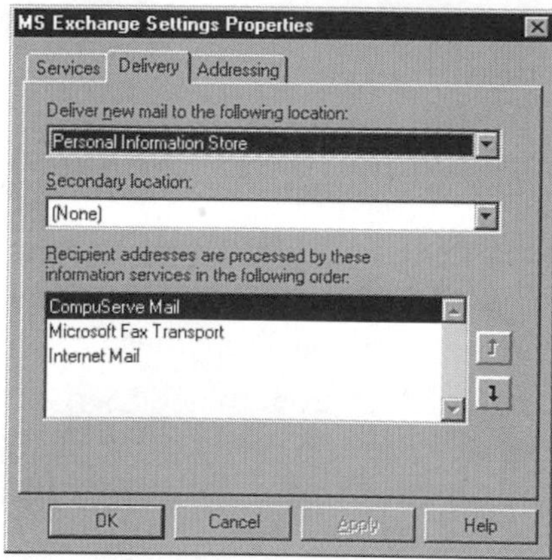

Fig. 13.15
Specify which store will receive incoming messages.

3. Specify settings in the Delivery property page based on the following descriptions:

   - *Deliver New Mail to the Following Location.* Select from the drop-down list the information store in which you want incoming mail to be placed.
   - *Secondary Location.* Select from the drop-down list the information store in which incoming mail should be placed if the primary message store is unavailable.
   - *Recipient Addresses are Processed by these Information Services in the Following Order.* This control lists the order in which mail providers distribute mail when you direct Exchange to deliver mail using all services. To move an item in the list, select it; then click either the up or the down arrow.

4. After specifying the desired settings, choose OK to save the changes.

Setting Up Address Books

Although you can send and receive mail without an address book, adding an address book to your profile makes it possible for you to store addresses and quickly select an address for a message. You can add addresses to the address book yourself, or let Exchange add originating addresses of received mail.

A profile can contain only one Personal Address Book. When you install Exchange, Windows 95 automatically adds a Personal Address Book to your default profile. You can add a new, blank address book, or add an existing address book that already contains address entries.

If you want to add a Personal Address Book to a new profile or you have accidentally deleted your Personal Address Book from your default profile, follow these steps to add the address book:

1. Open the Control Panel and double-click the Mail and Fax icon.
2. If you want to add a Personal Address Book to a profile other than the default profile, choose the Show Profiles button, select the profile you want to change, and then choose Properties.
3. Choose the Add button; then from the Add Service to Profile dialog box, choose Personal Address Book and click OK. The Personal Address Book property sheet shown in figure 13.16 appears.

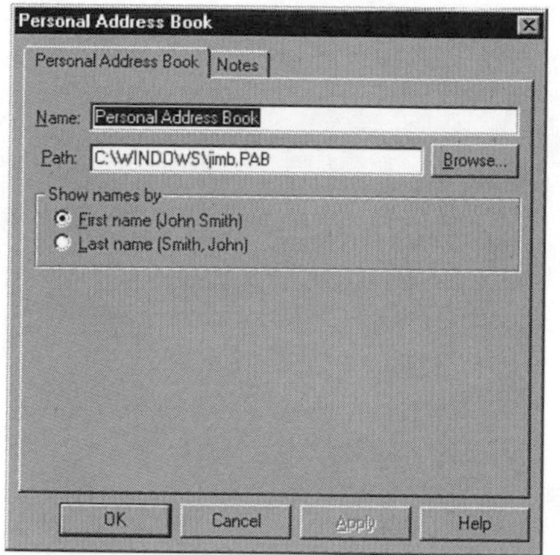

Fig. 13.16
Set properties for your Personal Address Book.

4. In the Name text box, enter a name for the address book (or leave the name as-is, if you prefer).
5. In the Path text box, enter the path and file name for the new address book file, or in the case of an existing address book, enter the path and file name of the existing file. If you prefer, you can choose the Browse button to browse for the file.
6. From the control group Show Names By, choose how you want names to appear in the address book (sorted by first name or last name).
7. Choose OK; then choose OK again to save the changes.

Setting Addressing Options

Although you can have only one Personal Address Book in a profile, you can add other types of address books. For example, a CompuServe Address Book is included in the CompuServe Mail provider. Other service providers that you add might also include their own address books. For this reason, you need a way to specify which address book Exchange displays by default and other addressing options.

To set addressing options, open the Control Panel and double-click the Mail and Fax icon. Then click the Addressing tab to display the Addressing property page shown in figure 13.17.

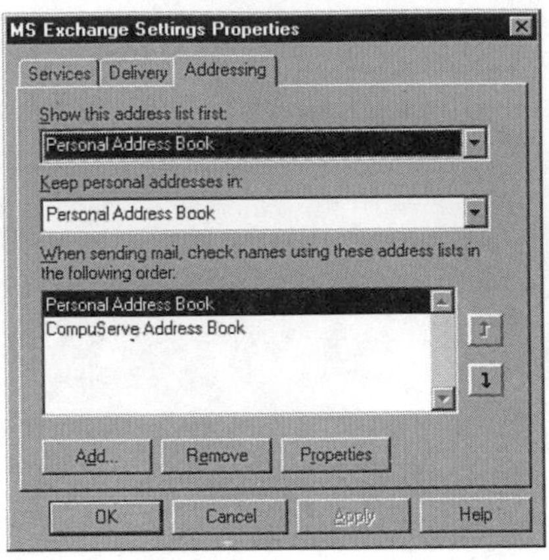

Fig. 13.17
Use the Addressing page to specify your default address book.

The properties you can specify on the Addressing page are described in the following list:

- *Show this Address List First.* Select from this drop-down list the address book you want Exchange to display when you click the To button in the compose window, or choose Tools, Address Book. You'll have the option in Exchange of selecting a different address book if more than one is installed.
- *Keep Personal Addresses In.* Select from this drop-down list the address book in which you want a new address to be added unless you specifically choose a different address book.
- *When Sending Mail, Check Names Using these Address Lists in the Following Order.* Use this list to set the order in which Exchange checks addresses for validity when you send a message or click the Check Names button in the compose window toolbar.

After you specify the Addressing properties you want to use, choose OK to save the changes.

Tip

For help adding and modifying addresses, see Chapter 14, "Using Exchange with Microsoft Mail."

Setting General Exchange Options

It might sometimes seem like Exchange offers an overwhelming number of properties and options that you can set. This section helps you understand and set those properties and options. If you've read through the earlier parts of this chapter, you've already set some general Exchange options, including delivery and addressing options. The following sections explain the other options you can set. To reach the property pages referenced in the following sections, open Exchange; then choose Tools, Options.

Setting General Options

The General property page specifies a handful of properties that control how Exchange alerts you to new incoming messages and other common actions, such as deleting messages (see fig. 13.18).

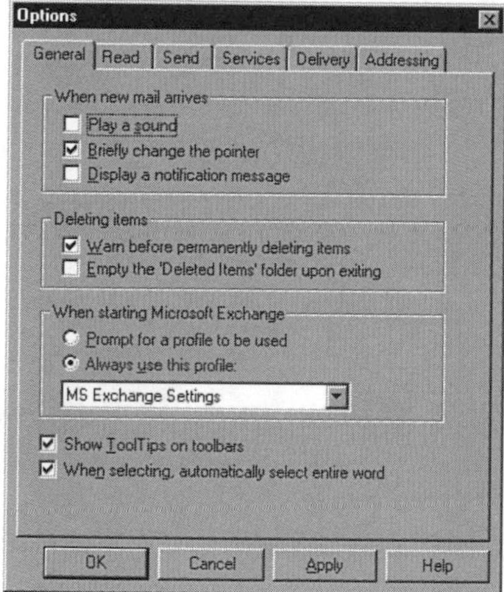

Fig. 13.18
Use the General property page to set general Exchange options.

The following list explains the properties you can set on the General property page:

- *When New Mail Arrives.* This group contains three options you can enable to control how Exchange notifies you of incoming messages.
- *Deleting Items.* Enable the option Warn Before Permanently Deleting Items if you want Exchange to warn you before you permanently delete a message (rather than deleting it to the Deleted Items folder). Enable the option named Empty the 'Deleted Items' Folder Upon Exiting, if you want Exchange to permanently delete messages from the Deleted Items folder when you exit Exchange.

- *When Starting Microsoft Exchange.* Use the options in this group to either specify a default Exchange profile or cause Exchange to prompt you to select a profile each time Exchange starts.
- *Show ToolTips on Toolbars.* Enable this option if you want Exchange to display a ToolTip for a toolbar button when you rest the pointer on the button for a second.
- *When Selecting, Automatically Select Entire Word.* Enable this option if you want Exchange to automatically select entire words when you drag over the words with the pointer.

Setting Read Options

The properties on the Read property page control the way Exchange handles messages when you read, reply to, or forward the messages (see fig. 13.19).

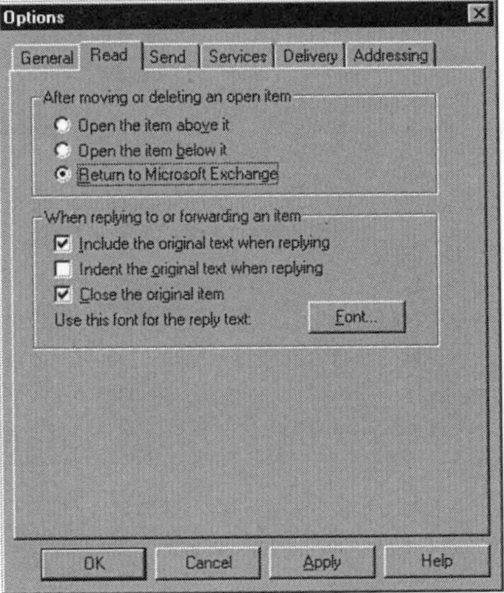

Fig. 13.19
Set options for reading messages using the Read property page.

The properties you can set with the Read property page are explained in the following list:

- *After Moving or Deleting an Open Item.* The three options in this group control Exchange's actions when you read, move, or delete a message. The options are self-explanatory—select whichever option suits your preferences.
- *When Replying to or Forwarding an Item.* These properties control how Exchange handles messages when you reply to or forward a message. Enable the option labeled Include the Original Text when Replying if

you want Exchange to include the text of the original message in your reply. If you want the original message text to be indented in the message, with your new text at the left margin, enable the Indent the Original Text When Replying check box. Enable the option labeled Close the Original Item if you want Exchange to automatically close the original e-mail message window after you start your reply. Choose the Font button to specify the font used for your reply text.

Tip

If you indent original message text or use a special font in a reply or a forwarded message, the recipient sees those message characteristics only if he or she is using Microsoft Exchange and a service provider capable of sending and receiving messages in RTF (Rich Text Format). Examples of such providers are the Microsoft Mail and the Microsoft Network services.

Setting Send Options

You also can specify a few properties that control the way Exchange handles items you are sending. Click the Send tab to display the Send property page shown in figure 13.20.

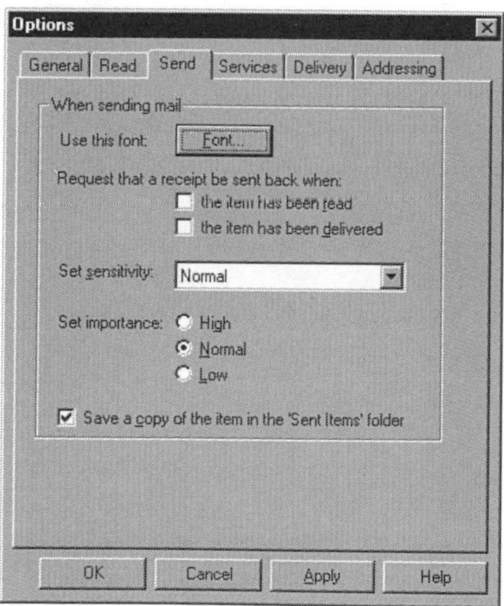

Fig. 13.20
Control outgoing message options with the Send property page.

You can click the Font button to choose the font Exchange will use by default for your outgoing messages. As with indented text, the recipient must also be using Exchange and a service provider that supports message transfer in RTF.

The two options in the group labeled Request That a Receipt Be Sent Back When control whether you will receive a return receipt from the recipient's mail system. The available options are as follows:

- *The Item Has Been Read.* If you choose this option, you receive a return receipt only after the recipient reads the message, which could happen well after he receives the message.
- *The Item Has Been Delivered.* Choose this option to receive a return receipt as soon as the message is delivered, regardless of whether the message has been read.

The Set Sensitivity and Set Importance options are self-explanatory. Choose the options you want to use by default. Note that you can override either of these settings when you create a message.

If you enable the option labeled Save a Copy of the Item in the Sent Items Folder, Exchange automatically places a copy of your outgoing message in the Sent Items folder. This is helpful if you need to review a message you previously sent. Just remember to periodically clean out the Sent Items folder to avoid having a huge message file filled with old messages. ❖

CHAPTER 14

Using Exchange with Microsoft Mail

by Jim Boyce

Chapter 13, "Configuring Microsoft Exchange," introduced you to Microsoft's new universal communications tool, Microsoft Exchange. In that chapter, you discovered that you can use Exchange to collect e-mail from various sources such as Microsoft Mail, CompuServe, and the Internet.

Now that you understand the basics of Exchange, this chapter explains how to use Exchange to read, compose, and sort your e-mail.

Note

This chapter assumes that you're using the Microsoft Mail service provider to connect to a Microsoft Mail post office, but you can use the information in this chapter to manage your messages for other service providers (such as CompuServe Mail and Internet Mail).

You must install Exchange before reading this chapter. In this chapter, you learn to

- Receive and compose messages in Exchange
- View and print messages in Exchange
- Use the Personal Address Book
- Use distribution lists

Working with Microsoft Exchange

When you first start Exchange, you'll find that the Exchange interface is simple and easy to use. If you are familiar with e-mail applications, such as Microsoft Mail, cc:Mail, and others, you shouldn't have any problem becoming comfortable using Exchange.

To start Exchange, double-click on the Inbox icon on the desktop. Or, choose Start, Programs, Microsoft Exchange to open the Inbox. When Exchange starts, you should see a window similar to the one shown in figure 14.1.

> **Note**
>
> Figure 14.1 shows the Exchange window with only the Inbox pane displayed. You also can configure Exchange to display a folder pane that lists all of the folders in your message store(s). Figure 14.2 shows Exchange with the folder pane visible.

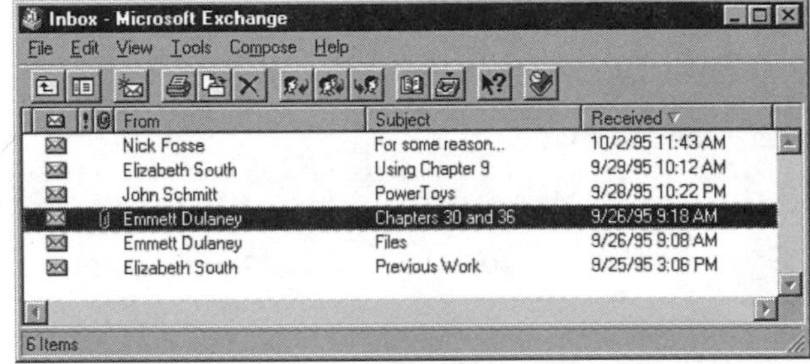

Fig. 14.1
Microsoft Exchange offers a simple, easy-to-use interface.

> **Tip**
>
> When Exchange is running and you have new e-mail or fax messages waiting in your Inbox, an envelope icon appears on the tray (the area at the right edge of the taskbar when the taskbar is in the horizontal position, or at the bottom when the taskbar is in the vertical position). Double-click on the envelope icon to open the Inbox window so you can read the message. After you have read the message, the envelope icon will disappear from the tray.

Examining the Exchange Window

▶ See "Using Exchange for Internet Mail," p. 343

▶ See "Using Exchange for CompuServe Mail," p. 355

You should take a few minutes to familiarize yourself with each component of the Exchange interface. When you first activate Exchange, you should see two panes. The left pane is the Exchange folder pane (see fig. 14.2), which shows the common folders in your message store and any other personal folders you have created. Folders can contain e-mail messages, files created in other applications, fax messages, and messages from other information services, such as online services.

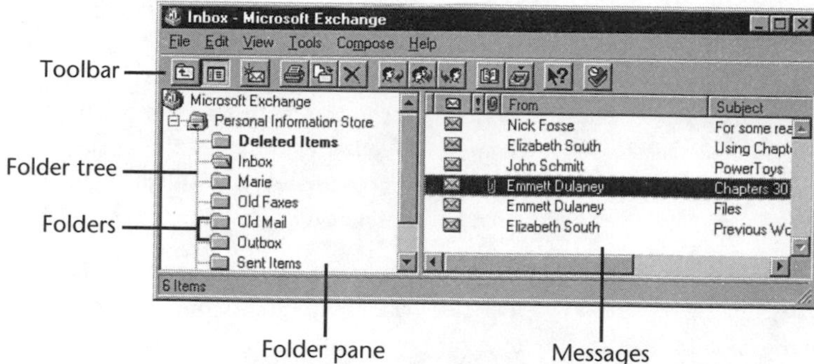

Fig. 14.2
The left side of the Exchange Viewer includes your mailbox personal folders.

Tip

You can use the personal folder area to store related documents. You can, for instance, store spreadsheets, word processing documents, and e-mail all in the same place. This enables you to easily keep track of these files and view them quickly when you need to.

To turn on or off the folder pane, choose View, Folders. Or, if the toolbar is displayed, click the Show/Hide Folder List button. To turn on or off the toolbar, choose View, Toolbar.

To view a folder's contents, double-click the folder. The contents appear in the Contents pane, sorted under specific default fields (you can add others). The From field shows you the sender's name, the Subject field shows the subject of the message, and the Received field shows the date and time you received the message.

▶ See "Customizing the Exchange Window," p. 311

Other fields in the Contents pane include the following:

- *Importance.* Each message or item you send or receive can have a priority attached to it. The Importance field, denoted by an exclamation point (!), shows you the type of priority the message has. A red exclamation point icon tells you the message has the highest importance. No icon indicates normal priority. A blue down-arrow indicates that the message has low priority.

Prioritize Your Messages

If you belong to a workgroup environment that tends to send a large amount of e-mail or faxes, you might want to devise a system that denotes high-,

(continues)

(continued)

normal-, and low-priority messages. You might, for instance, attach a high-importance flag to messages that contain information pertaining to meeting scheduling or events that require immediate feedback. Messages of normal importance tend to indicate general information gathering or dissemination. Low-priority messages can be ignored for several days or altogether.

You might find it difficult to think of your messages as anything less than urgent (why would you send them if they weren't important), but you should get in the habit of attaching priorities to your messages to help increase the productivity of your workforce. Also, consider before you send a message whether the message really needs to be sent at all, and avoid replying to everyone on a message's distribution list unless you know all of the recipients are interested in receiving your reply.

- *Type of message.* Because Exchange was designed to handle a number of different types of messages and documents, you need to know the type of message that awaits you in your Inbox. You can determine this by looking in the field denoted by the Envelope icon. If your document is an e-mail message, an envelope appears on this line. A red arrow next to your message name indicates a returned mail notification. A fax machine icon indicates a fax message.
- *Attachment.* One of the most useful parts of Exchange is its capability to handle rich-text messages, which enables you to embed OLE 2 objects, use RTF (Rich Text Format) document elements, and add special characters to your messages. The attachment field, denoted by a paper clip, shows whether the message contains an attachment such as a file.
- *Size.* This column, to the right of the Received column, indicates the message's file size.
- *Conversation topic.* If the message belongs to a specific thread, such as to one on The Microsoft Network, you see the thread name in this column. This column does not show up if no messages are part of a thread.

Other parts of the Exchange window include the menu bar and toolbar. The menu bar stores commands and options associated with Exchange. The toolbar, which you can customize or turn on or off, includes tools that help you quickly select actions you want to perform.

ToolTips pop up for each toolbar button over which you stop the mouse pointer. ToolTips look like the one shown in figure 14.3 and give you a hint of the action associated with each button. When you stop your mouse pointer over the button that displays an X, for instance, a ToolTip pops up that reads "Delete," which tells you that you can delete the selected message or folder by simply clicking on this button.

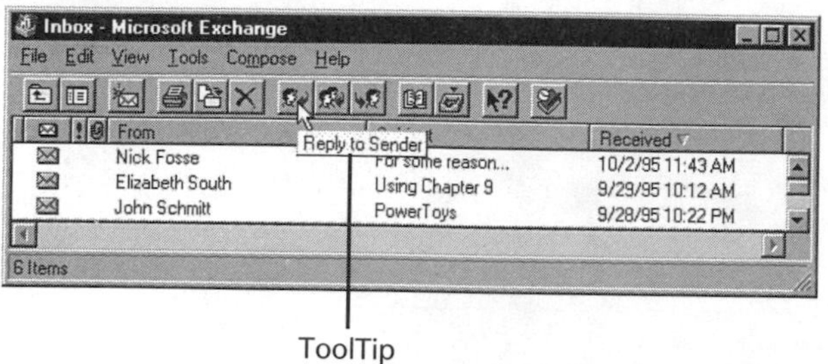

Fig. 14.3
ToolTips remind you of the action associated with the toolbar button.

Customizing the Exchange Window

You have quite a bit of control over the appearance of the Exchange window. The following sections offer tips on customizing the Exchange window to suit your preferences.

Changing Pane Size

You can resize the viewing area in the Exchange Viewer the same way you resize columns in Microsoft Windows 3.*x*'s File Manager. Drag the thick bar that runs vertically between the folder area and message area to the left or right to increase or decrease the viewing area. This enables you to see more of the fields in the message area or view long folder names. Sometimes you might not be able to see the last two or three fields to the right of your Subject field without resizing the columns.

Changing and Resizing Fields

You can easily resize each field in the Contents pane. Simply place the pointer on the vertical bar at the edge of the column's description, then drag the bar to the left or right to resize the field. If you can't see all of the characters in the Subject field, for example, drag its right edge to the right to enlarge the field.

Tip

The Move Up and Move Down buttons in the Columns dialog box enable you to move a field up or down in the list, which changes the order in which the fields appear in Exchange. Use the Width text box to specify in pixels the width of a selected column (or just drag the column to resize it).

In addition to resizing the fields, you also can specify which fields Exchange displays in the Contents pane. To do so, choose View, Columns. The Columns dialog box appears (see fig. 14.4).

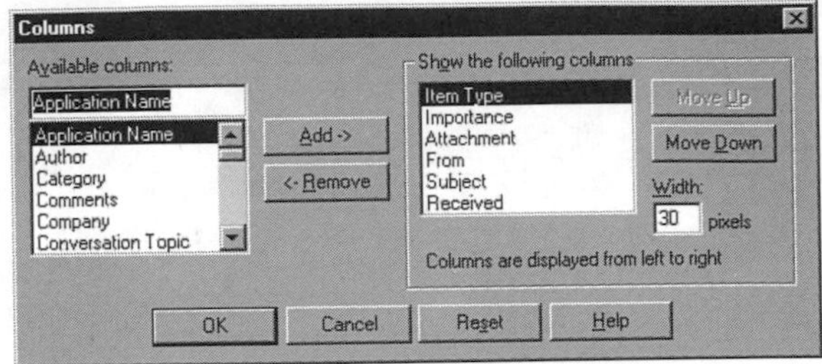

Fig. 14.4 With the Columns dialog box you can specify which fields (columns) to view in the Contents pane.

Exchange provides 44 different field types. To add a field to the Contents pane, select the desired field from the Available columns list, then click Add. To remove a field, select from the Show the Following Columns list the field you want to remove, then click on Remove. To change the order of the fields as they are displayed from left to right, select a field and click the Move Up or Move Down buttons. The order in which the fields are listed from top to bottom in the Show list matches the order in which they are displayed from left to right in the Contents pane.

Tip

If you want to return Exchange to its default set of columns, click the Reset button in the Columns dialog box.

Sorting Your Messages

You can configure Exchange to sort and display your messages based on any of the displayed fields. For example, you might sort the messages in descending order with the most recent message at the top. This way, all of your new and recent messages will be at the top of the list, and the oldest messages will be at the bottom. The easiest way to sort your messages is to click the column heading of the field by which you want to sort the messages. Exchange automatically sorts the messages using the selected field as the sort key.

Whether or not the messages sort in ascending or descending order depends on the type of column you select. Generally, text fields sort in ascending order, placing the messages in alphabetical order based on the sort key. Numeric/date fields sort in descending order, placing the messages in order with most recent at the top. If you want to specify either ascending or descending, right-click on the column header. A context menu containing the commands Sort Ascending and Sort Descending appears, and you can select the appropriate choice.

To choose a sort option using Exchange's menu, choose View, Sort to display the Sort dialog box (see fig. 14.5). From the Sort Items by drop-down list, select the column you want to use as the sort key. Then choose either the Ascending or Descending option buttons as desired. Click on OK when you're ready to sort the messages.

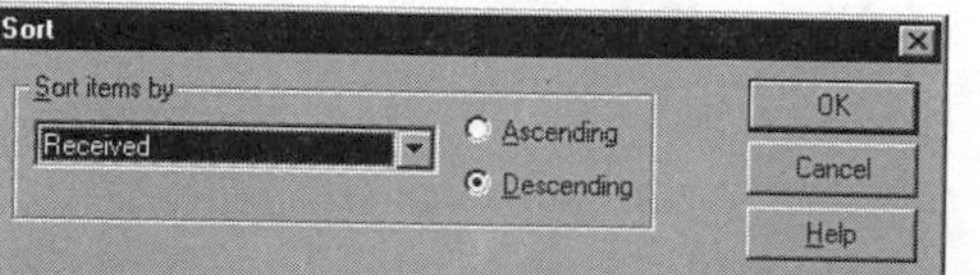

Fig. 14.5
You can sort your messages using the mouse or the Sort dialog box.

> **Tip**
>
> If you look closely at the column descriptions, you'll notice that one contains an arrow. The presence of the arrow in a column indicates that the column is being used as the current sort key. If the arrow points up, ascending order is in use. An arrow pointing down indicates descending order.

Customizing the Toolbar

You can customize the toolbar by selecting Tools, Customize Toolbar. The Customize Toolbar dialog box appears (see fig. 14.6), from which you can select toolbar buttons from the Available Buttons list and add them to the Toolbar buttons list. Conversely, you can select items from the Toolbar buttons list and remove them from the toolbar. If you make a mistake or change your mind about these changes and want to return to the original toolbar, choose the Reset button.

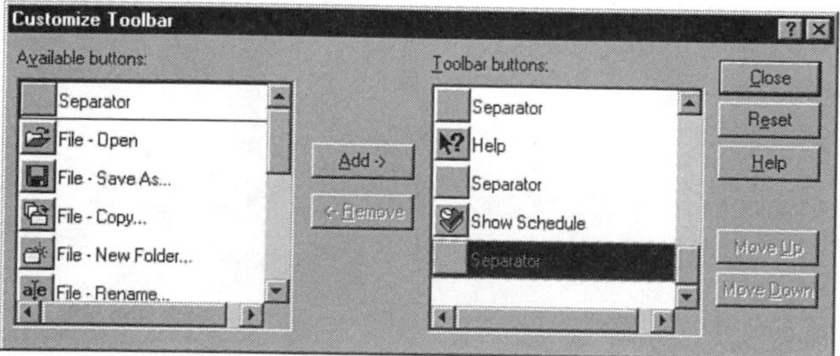

Fig. 14.6
You can customize the toolbar in Exchange using the Customize Toolbar dialog box.

Reading Messages in Exchange

After you gain familiarity with the Exchange interface, you should become more comfortable using it. New messages or those you have not yet read are indicated by boldface in the Inbox folder in the message area. To read a message, double-click it or click it and choose File, Open. The message opens in a new window, such as the one in figure 14.7, in which you can read the message and perform other related tasks, such as printing, storing, or deleting the message.

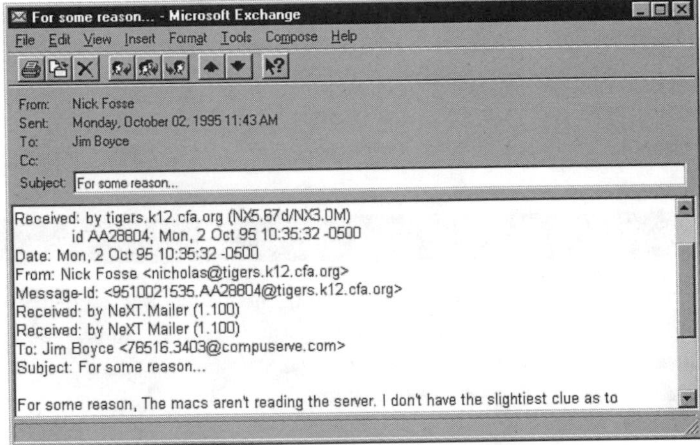

Fig. 14.7
Reading a message in Exchange.

After you read your message, you can perform several tasks. The most common action is to reply. If you want to reply to the sender of the e-mail, click the Reply to Sender toolbar button, or choose Compose, Reply to Sender, to open a new window in which you can write a response to the message (see fig. 14.8). Type your message and then choose File, Send, or click the Send button on the toolbar.

Another option you might want to use when you reply to a message is the Reply to All option in the Compose menu or toolbar. This option enables you to send a reply to all the people listed on the recipient list of the message to which you reply.

Tip

You don't have to open a message to reply to it. Click the message to which you want to reply, choose Compose, and then select the option you want. An area appears in which you can write your new message. The only problem that might occur when you use this method is if you pick the wrong message to which to send a reply. Before you send the message, you might want to double-check that the message was sent to you or the recipient's name to ensure that you aren't going to embarrass yourself.

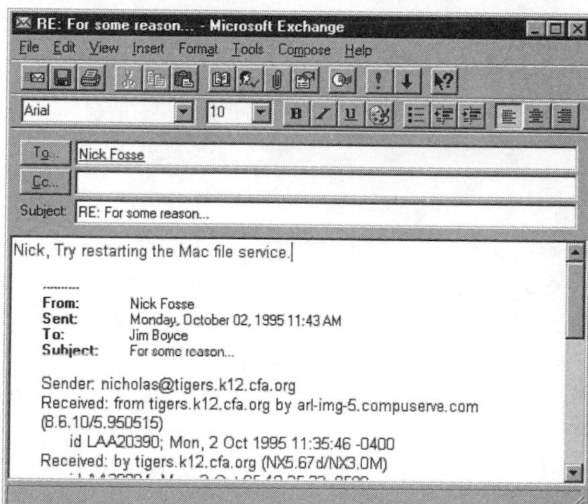

Fig. 14.8
Replying to a message in Exchange.

When you reply to a message, or others reply to your messages, Exchange copies the content of the message to the bottom of the reply. If the message bounces back and forth more than a few times, the message can become rather lengthy. Instead of simply replying to messages and retaining the original message every time, you should consider not including the original message text with your reply message. This reduces the file size of the message and, if you send the message over a commercial service provider, saves you online time and charges. To turn off the Include Original Message Text In Reply option, choose Tools, Options, and click on the Read tab (see fig. 14.9). In the Read page, click in the Include the original text when replying check box to clear it.

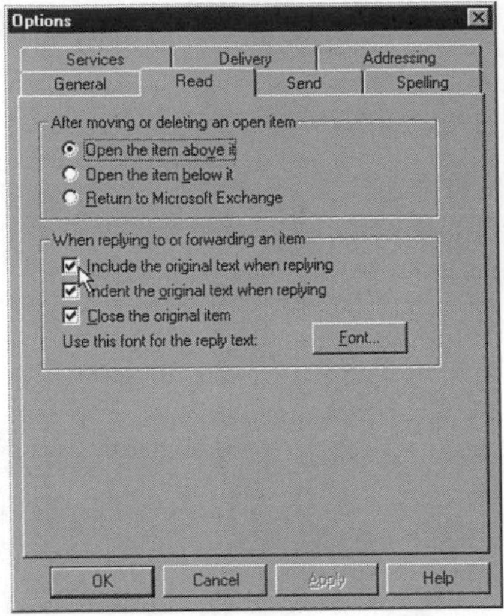

Fig. 14.9
You can turn off the option to send the original message text with your reply.

Saving Messages in Exchange

Similar to other e-mail applications, such as Lotus cc:Mail or Microsoft Mail, Exchange enables you to store your messages after you create or read them. Exchange saves these files with the name, location, and file format you specify. Exchange also enables you to save messages or other files that might be attached with your message. To save a message or file in the default directory on your hard disk or network disk, click the Disk button on the toolbar, or choose File, Save. Either method displays a Save As dialog box (see fig. 14.10).

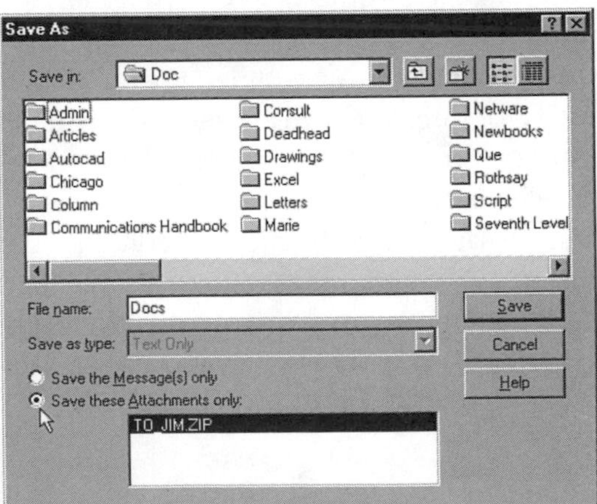

Fig. 14.10
Saving a file or attachment in Exchange.

Other ways to save your messages or attachments are to change the folder in which you store them, save the items in a specific format, or change the file name. Exchange offers the following options when you choose File, Save As:

- *Save In.* This control enables you to select a location in which to save your file. You might want to create a new folder in which to store all your read messages.
- *File Name.* This text box displays the subject of the selected message, which will be used by default as the file name unless you change it. You can highlight this name and modify it as you choose.
- *Save as Type.* This drop-down list enables you to select one of three formats for the file: text only, rich text, or message.

Saving Messages

You're not sure what these three formats are? Text Only (*.txt) saves your message without extra formatting. As you see later, in the section "Creating a New Message," you can use RTF formatting characters in your Exchange messages. The Text Only option strips out these special characters. You should select the Text Only format only if the destination application cannot read rich text format.

The Rich Text Format (*.rtf) option enables you to save the message with all its formatting intact. During the save operation, Exchange automatically converts your message to instructions that other applications, including Microsoft-compatible applications, can read and interpret. This is handy when you want to apply special fonts, character enhancements, or other special features to your messages.

When you have to keep a message intact exactly as it arrives, including saving the To, From, and Subject properties, select the Message Format (*.msg) option. This saves the message as a message file.

- *Save the Message(s) Only.* This option enables you to save an open message or one (or several) selected in the Contents pane. If you select more than one message, this option saves the messages in one text file, which comes in handy if you have a thread of messages you want to store together. You can append a message to an existing file by selecting the file and choosing Save. When the Save As message box appears, choose Append to. Choose Overwrite if you instead want to replace the existing file.

- *Save these Attachments only*. This option saves selected attachments. Attachments previously selected in a message are selected in the list. You can select or clear attachments in the list before you save.

Printing Messages in Exchange

Electronic documents are ideal for many of the business and personal communications needs you have. Sometimes, however, you need to file or distribute hard copies of messages or documents. Microsoft Exchange enables you to quickly and easily print one or many of your messages. With the Exchange window open, select the item or items you want to print, and then choose File, Print. In the Print dialog box (see fig. 14.11), select the desired printer from the Name drop-down list, select the number of copies you want to print and any other properties, and choose OK.

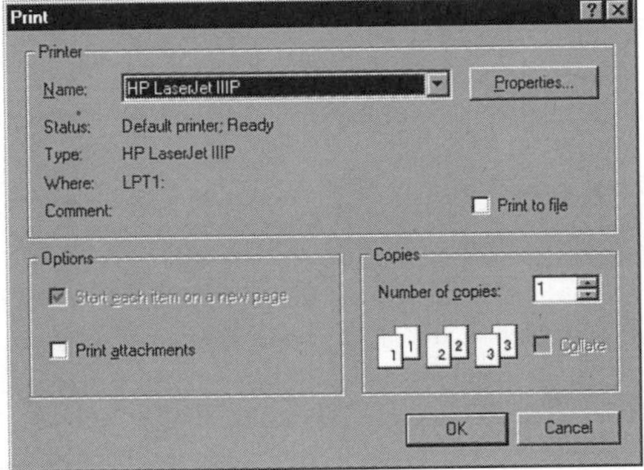

Fig. 14.11
You can print one or more messages from Exchange.

Additional options in the Print dialog box include Start Each Item on a New Page and Print Attachments. The Start Each Item option enables you to select several messages and print each of them on a new page. If you don't enable this option, your messages print one after another without page breaks. Use the Print Attachments option when you want to print attachments to your message. You might want to check the size of the attachments before you select this option, in case the attachment is a large document that could tie up your printer for a long time. Someone might send you an attachment that is several hundred pages long, not intending for you to print it all out.

Tip

Another option you can choose from the Print dialog box is the Print to File option. You use this feature to print the document to a file rather than a printer. When you select this option, Windows 95 prompts you to provide a file name and file location. Windows 95 uses the currently selected printer driver to create the file, so the content of the file varies depending on the type of printer you've selected.

Composing and Delivering Messages in Exchange

When you're ready to create your own message in Exchange, you'll find that Exchange presents a friendly yet powerful interface (see fig. 14.12). In many ways, this interface looks like a word processor, such as Microsoft WordPad. Many users create memos and general correspondence primarily through an e-mail application. Unfortunately, the appearance of standard e-mail messages often is difficult to read. When Microsoft designed Exchange, it included features that enable you to apply formatting and special character properties to your messages, making them easier to read and more visually appealing.

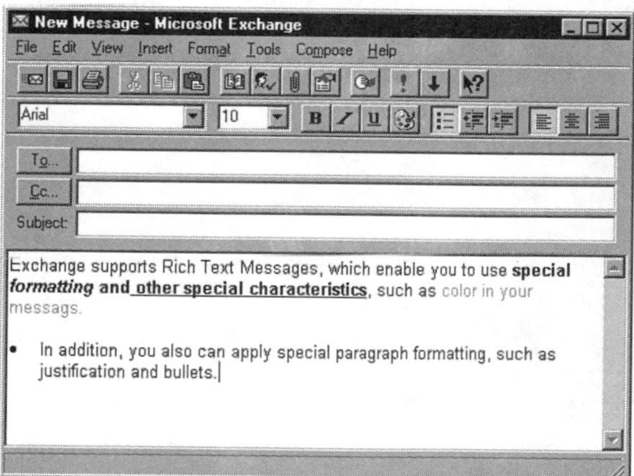

Fig. 14.12
You can create rich-text messages in Exchange.

> **Note**
>
> Not only are standard e-mail messages formatted in ASCII text, they also sometimes come across in weird configurations. How many times have you received e-mail messages that seem to have been written in some unknown or lost language? Sporadic line breaks and unreadable character conversions (such as when you try to use something from an enhanced character set) make reading some messages difficult, if not impossible. You can eliminate many of these problems by using features that Exchange provides along with the RTF formatting feature.

Exchange addresses many of the problems associated with difficult-to-decipher e-mail messages by enabling messages to include specific fonts (including resizable TrueType fonts), colors, shortcuts, and objects. Because Exchange is an OLE-compliant application, you also can embed several types of objects into your messages, which enables you to create messages that include spreadsheet objects, graphics objects, and similar items.

Creating a New Message

To create a new message, choose Compose, New Message from the Exchange window to open the New Message window (refer to fig. 14.12). To help you get an idea of the type of message you can create, you can follow this set of steps, which leads you through creating a message that includes special formatting and an Excel spreadsheet object:

1. In the To: field, enter the recipient or recipients for your message. To access the universal address book, choose the To: button, which opens the Address Book dialog box (see fig. 14.13). (See "Understanding Address Books," later in this chapter.)

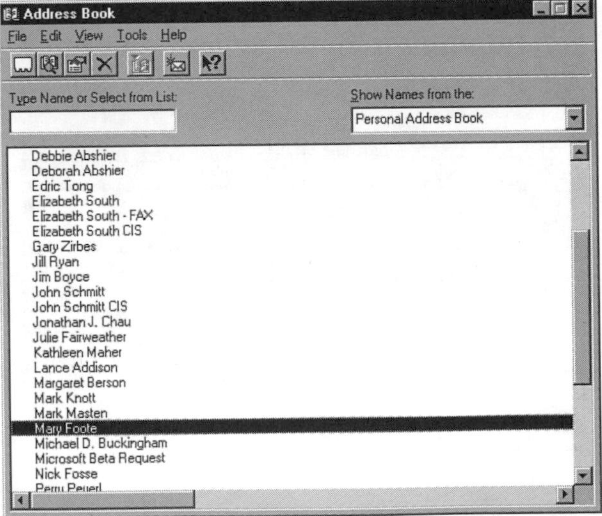

Fig. 14.13
Select a user or set of users in the Address Book dialog box.

> **Note**
>
> As Chapters 15 through 18 explain, you also can use this address book when you create new fax messages, Microsoft Online Network messages, CompuServe mail, and Internet e-mail messages. Microsoft Exchange controls all these actions, enabling you to create one source with your contact information and use it for several different information sources.

2. In the Address Book dialog box, select the name and address of the recipient of your message. To choose a different address list, select the desired list from the Show names drop-down list.
3. In the Type Name or Select from List area, double-click the name of the person to whom you want to send your message, or type the person's name in the field. This places the name in the To: section in the Message recipients box. If you want to send your message to the selected person as a Cc: recipient ("carbon copy"), click the name in the Type Name or Select from List area and choose the Cc: button. Choose OK to return to the New Message window.

> **Note**
>
> Exchange only displays a Bcc (Blind Carbon Copy) field if the service provider supports Bcc. The Microsoft Mail provider, for example, does support Bcc.

4. Move your cursor to the Subject line and type a message subject. This subject name also becomes the default name of the message file if you decide to save the message. With Windows 95's long file name feature, your subject can contain as many as 255 characters—about the size of this paragraph.
5. Type your message in the message section, such as **Boss, the Fiscal '95 Sales Report is shown below. Tell me what you think.** You can use the various toolbar buttons, such as bold, italic, and underline, to format this text. You also can choose the Format menu and use the Font or Paragraph options. For the most part, if you know how to use a Windows word processor or Windows 95's new WordPad application, you should understand the various formatting features of the New Message window.
6. To illustrate Exchange's power and OLE capabilities, insert a new Excel worksheet. To do this, choose Insert, Object from the New Message window menu bar to open the Insert Object dialog box (see fig. 14.14), where you can choose the type of object you want to insert in your message. Scroll down the Object Type list and click the Microsoft Excel Worksheet item.

> **Note**
>
> Does this dialog box look familiar? It should. It's the same dialog box that appears when you use OLE 2-compliant Windows applications, such as Word 6
>
> (continues)

(continued)

or Excel 5, and insert embedded or linked objects into a document. Because of Microsoft's commitment to make using compound documents in your messages easier, regardless of the application that originally created the document or object, Exchange has been built from the ground up with OLE 2 functionality, which makes inserting a worksheet or graphics file into your message very easy.

One final note: For this example, you need to have Microsoft Excel 5 for Windows. If you have another OLE 2.0-compliant application, such as Word 6 for Windows, CorelDRAW! 5, Office 95, or Visio 3 (or later versions), you can substitute that application for the following Excel example.

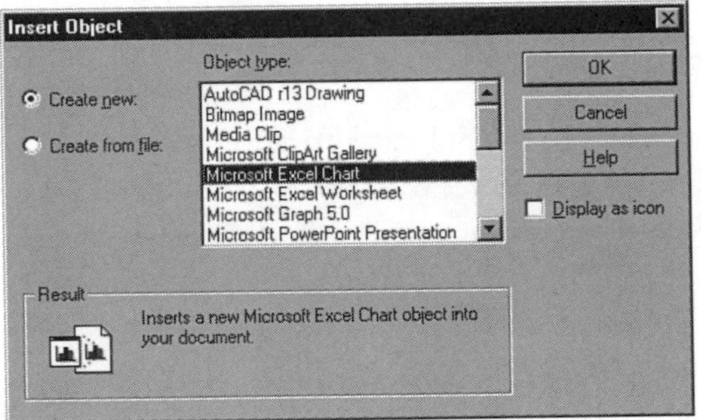

Fig. 14.14
The Insert Object dialog box enables you to insert specific OLE objects into your Exchange messages.

7. Choose OK to return to your new message, but notice the new look of the interface, including the toolbars and menus. If you are familiar at all with OLE 2 in Windows 3.1*x*, you recognize what happened. The container application interface—in this case, the Exchange New Message interface—adopted the Microsoft Excel 5 interface to enable you to create and edit your new Excel object inside your new message.

   In figure 14.15, for instance, notice how the interface now has many more tools on the toolbars. Also, look at the new menu choice, the Data menu. It has replaced the Compose menu, which you don't need for Excel. Although you can't see it in the illustration, the contents of the menus have changed to reflect Excel's. The Tools menu, for example, has changed from Spelling, Address Book, and so on, to Spelling, Auditing, AutoCorrect, and so on.

   If you have never experienced this type of behavior (that is, inserting OLE objects in a document), don't worry. The New Message interface returns to normal after you create your new Excel worksheet and click outside the worksheet.

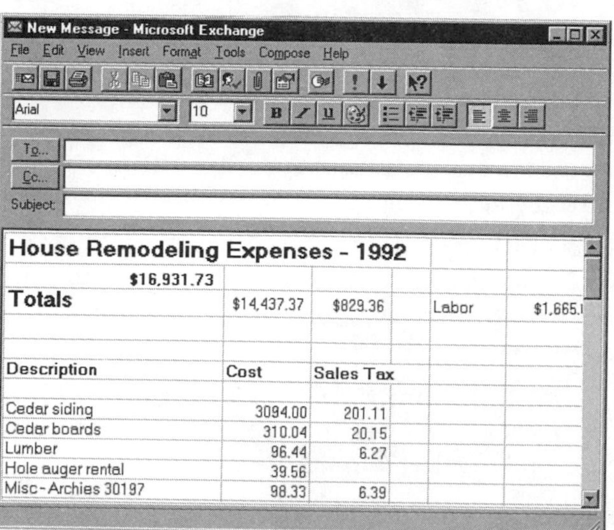

Fig. 14.15 When you insert an OLE object, such as an Excel worksheet, your container application changes.

8. Fill in some data in the worksheet and format it or add formulas as needed. You can create a worksheet that is as sophisticated as you want. Exchange allows you to do this. Why? Because it's an OLE-compliant application. You might, for instance, want to add one of Excel's custom table formats to the worksheet. Choose Format, AutoFormat and then select the type of format you want from the Table Format list.

Inserting Existing Objects

You also can insert a worksheet that has already been created. To do this, in step 7 before you choose OK in the Insert Object dialog box, choose the Create from File button on the left side of the dialog box, which enables you to open a file from your hard disk or server. Type the full path and file name of the document, or use the Browse feature to locate it.

To save file space when you choose this option, you should choose the Link button in the Insert Object dialog box, which inserts a "picture" of the file into your message and links the picture to the file. When you want to edit the document, simply double-click the picture, which activates the host application so that you can edit the file. Unlike embedding the object in the container application, when you link an object the New Message interface does not change when you double-click the picture. The host application starts up and displays the file. After you edit the file, choose File, Save to automatically update the picture in your message. To close the container application, choose File, Exit.

To shift the focus away from the worksheet or any other object you have inserted in your message, click anywhere outside the object. This returns the New Message interface to its original state. If you need to edit the object again, double-click anywhere inside the object. This changes the toolbars and menus to the Excel ones, enabling you once again to edit your worksheet.

If you want to delete this object you have embedded in your new application, click on the object and press Del or click on the Cut toolbar button. You also can choose Edit, Cut after you select the object you want to cut.

9. After you create your message, choose File, Send from the New Message window, or click the Send button on the toolbar. Exchange sends the file to the Outbox folder in your Personal Folder.

In the next section, you learn how to deliver your new message.

Delivering New Messages

When you send a new message in Exchange, Exchange stores the message in the Outbox folder until you use one or several of the services you have configured to deliver it. These services can be Microsoft Mail, The Microsoft Network, Microsoft Fax, the Internet, CompuServe, and other supported systems.

> **Note**
>
> As of this writing, Microsoft had not announced all the services available to which Exchange could send messages. To get a complete list of these services, see the Windows 95 documentation that comes with your software. You also should be able to find discussions of this topic on The Microsoft Network and Microsoft-related CompuServe forums. Understand, however, that Microsoft will not be developing Exchange service providers for information services such as America Online or Prodigy. These services might, however, create their own service providers for Exchange.

To deliver a message or several messages, click the Outbox folder in Exchange Viewer to display the messages awaiting delivery. In figure 14.16, for instance, two messages are queued up for delivery. Click the message you want to deliver, or hold down the Ctrl key and click other messages you want to select. (To select the entire list of messages, choose Edit, Select All.)

Next, choose Tools, Deliver Now Using to display the flyout menu that contains the services you have configured. To send your message(s) to all the services, select All Services. Exchange then will deliver all messages pending for each service provider. If only one service provider has messages pending, only those messages are acted upon.

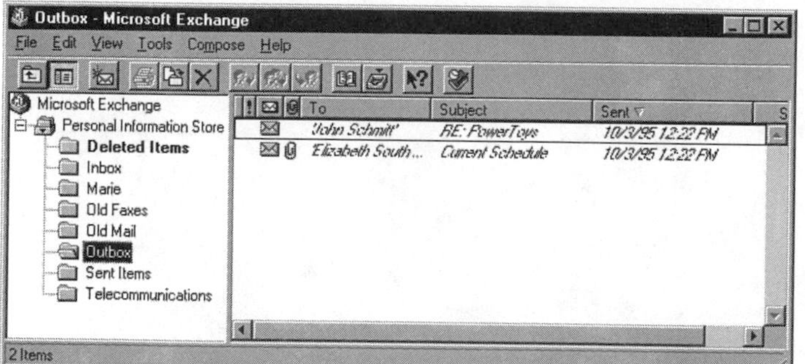

Fig. 14.16
Queuing messages for delivery in MS Exchange.

Understanding Address Books

Microsoft Exchange uses address books, including a Personal Address Book (PAB), that you can fill with contact information, e-mail addresses, and other interesting tidbits about a person. This contact information, in keeping with the Windows 95 theme, is collectively called the address *properties*.

Deciding which Address Book to Use

When you create your first profile (as shown in Chapter 13), Exchange creates two address books. You maintain the Personal Address Book, and the post office administrator maintains the Post Office Address List, which you can download periodically from the post office to update your copy of the POA. Other address books you might create can include a Microsoft Network (MSN) address book and a CompuServe address book.

If you have a Microsoft Mail post office set up, you can use the Post Office Address List across the network, enabling you to access the entire list of contacts your company maintains and ensuring that you have the most current address of a contact. If you want to work out of your Personal Address Book but use the Post Office Address List for names and updates, you can quickly and easily copy addresses and properties into your PAB.

To specify the address book you want to use, choose Tools, Address Book in Exchange. (When you create a new message, you also can select the address book from the Compose menu.) In the Address Book dialog box (see fig. 14.17), select the address book from the Show Names from the: drop-down list. Depending on the type of services you configured in Chapter 13, such as Microsoft Mail, Microsoft Network, or others, you see a list of address books from which to choose.

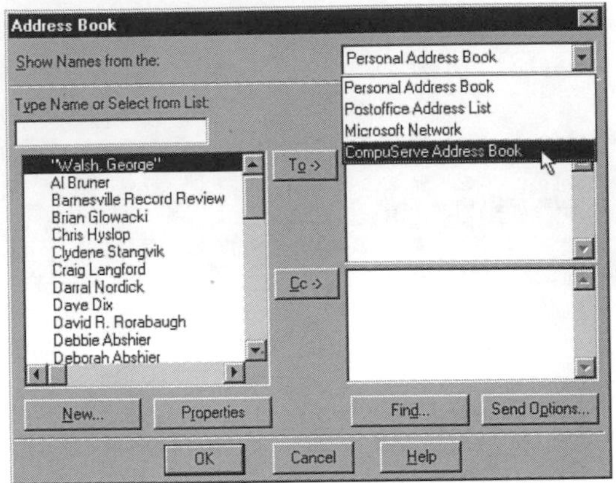

Fig. 14.17
Select the address book to use.

Click the address book you want to use. The names in the address book you select appear in the resulting list box.

Finding a Name in the Address Book

To find a name in the address list, type the name in the Type Name or Select from List text box. As you type the name, Exchange starts searching for this name and, as you continue to type the name, highlights a name that matches your search criteria. As you provide more information, Exchange continues to jump from name to name until the correct one is found. As nerve-racking as this might sound, in practice it's not that bad. In fact, Exchange usually doesn't start searching for a match until you pause for a moment as you type or when you place a space between names.

Tip

You can type the first or last name, or both names, of the person for whom you search. This is convenient if you don't remember the exact spelling of someone's last name, or if you commonly refer to someone by his or her first name. This feature is also nice when you have several Daves or Jims or Tracys stored in your address books. You can key in their first name and just the initial of their last name.

After you find a name, you can store it in your Personal Address Book (if you haven't already) by choosing File, Add to Personal Address Book. The convenience of adding names from other address books to your PAB is a welcome feature when you are locating names in a large list, such as on The Microsoft Network or the networked Post Office Address Book.

Viewing Properties of Address Listings

Each name has properties associated with it. These properties include e-mail addresses, business addresses, phone numbers, and other items. You can even include notes on the contact. The following sections detail the pages you can fill in for each contact person.

> **Tip**
>
> Another way to see the properties of a person in your address book is to select the person's name and right-click. This displays a context-sensitive menu from which you can choose Properties. Or, in the New Message window, double-click on an address name in the To or Cc fields.

Address

The *Service* - Address page (see fig. 14.18) shows two common fields: Display Name and E-mail Address. Other fields and controls also appear on the page depending on the type of address selected. The Display Name field lists the name of the contact person. This field can include any name or word, so you also can use aliases or nicknames in this field. The E-mail Address field contains the full e-mail address.

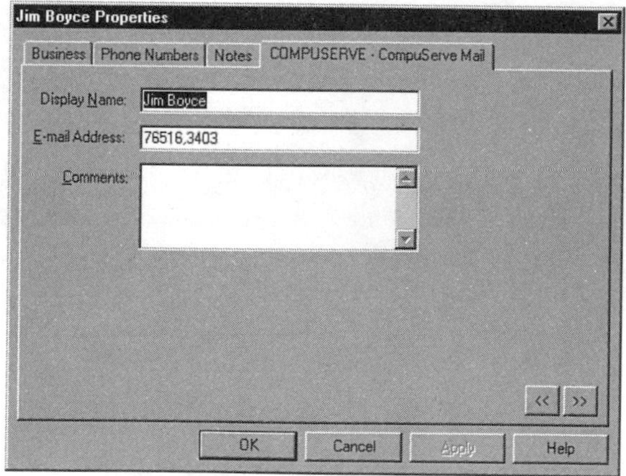

Fig. 14.18
The *Service*-Address page in the Address Book area of Exchange defines the e-mail address.

The E-mail type field lists the type of service that carries the e-mail, such as MSN, the Internet, CompuServe, or others. Exchange uses the name you place in this field as the title of the tab, such as MSN - Address.

The *Service* - Address page also contains a check box you can use to specify whether or not a message will always be sent using RTF format, or instead will be stripped of formatting when it is sent.

Business

The Business page (see fig. 14.19) shows the mailing address, phone numbers, title, company names, and other address criteria. These fields are basically self-explanatory. The Phone Number drop-down list at the bottom right of the page is handy when your contact has numerous phone numbers, including Business, Business 2, Fax, Assistant, Home, Home 2, Mobile, and Page.

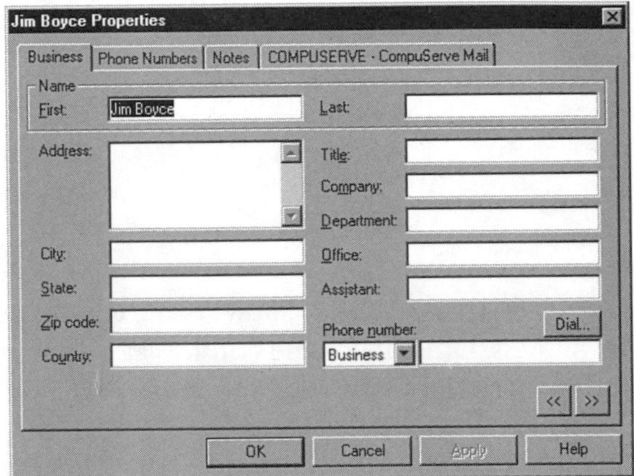

Fig. 14.19
The Business page.

Tip

Here's a cool option on the Business page (and the next one—Phone Numbers) that uses Windows 95's TAPI support. You can dial a phone by choosing the Dial button, lifting up your hand set, and talking. To be able to do this, you need to have your phone connected to your modem device directly. By having your computer make the connection, you can avoid keying in the number by hand or constantly changing your autodial numbers on your phone.

Phone Numbers

The Phone Numbers page (see fig. 14.20) simply lists all the phone numbers associated with the Phone number drop-down list in the Business properties tab. Use this page when you want to quickly change the number of one of these fields.

Notes

The Notes page (see fig. 14.21) is useful for jotting down simple notes about a contact. Unfortunately, you can't automatically add a date or time header to your notes, but you can use this tab to help remind you of conversations, actions, or other items specific to a contact.

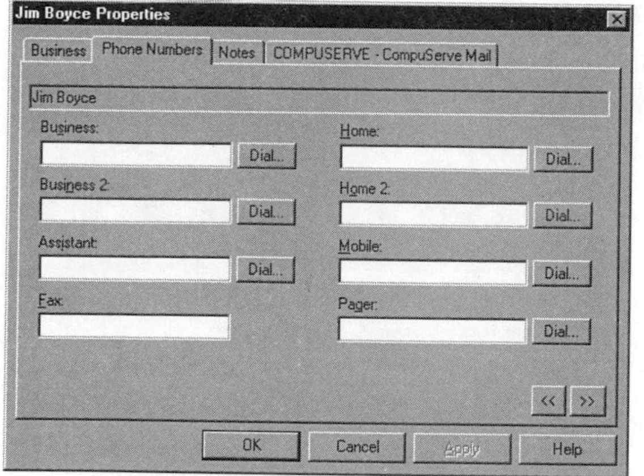

Fig. 14.20
The Phone Numbers properties page.

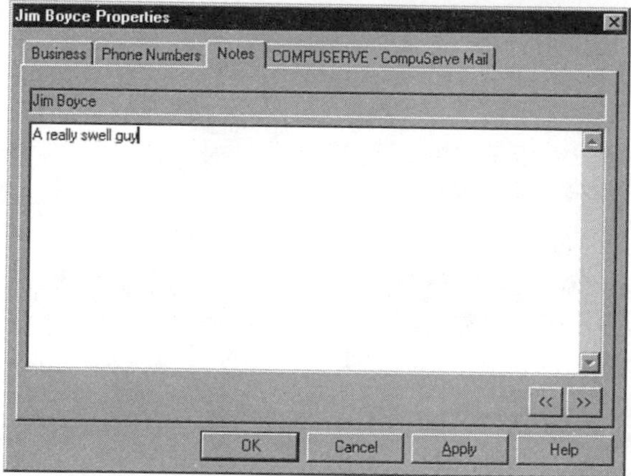

Fig. 14.21
You can keep notes on someone in the Notes page.

Creating New Entries in a Personal Address Book

One of these days you're going to need to create a listing in your Personal Address Book. To do this, open the Personal Address Book and click on the New Entry icon (which looks like an index card) on the toolbar, or choose File, New Entry to open the New Entry dialog box (see fig. 14.22), in which you select the type of entry you want to create. You can, for example, create entries for Microsoft Fax, CompuServe, the Internet, and MSN (but only if those providers are installed). If you can't find an address type that suits your contact's e-mail address syntax, select the Other Address option.

Before you choose OK in this dialog box, look at the Put This Entry area. This area gives you two main options. The In the drop-down list box lists the various address books in which you can place your new entry. For the most part, you want to make sure that you have the Personal Address Book option selected here. The other option in this area is the In This Message Only option, handy if you create a new message and need to create a one-time address listing for your message. When you select this option, Exchange does not store the information as a permanent record.

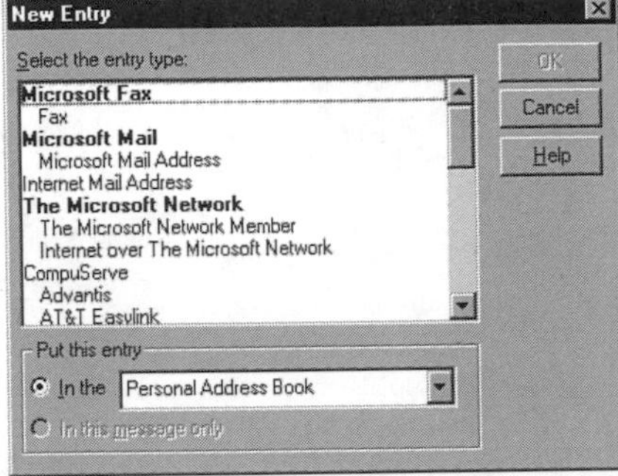

Fig. 14.22
The New Entry dialog box.

After you select your options, choose OK to display the New Address Properties pages. Simply fill in these boxes for the contact information. For specific information on any of these pages, see the previous sections that describe each field and option.

> **Caution**
>
> Clear the Always Send to This Recipient in Microsoft Exchange Rich-Text Format check box on the New-Address page if your contact person is not using an MS Mail or Microsoft Network address. Otherwise, you might create a message that has embedded objects or enhanced characters that you can't send over most e-mail systems.

Storing an Incoming Address

Many times your incoming messages will be from people whose addresses are already stored in your PAB. It's a pretty sure bet, however, that sooner or later you'll receive a message or fax from someone whose address is not stored in your PAB. Although you can reply to the message without storing the address in the PAB, you might want the address in the future so you can originate messages to the person. Exchange makes it fairly easy to store a person's address.

To store the address of an e-mail message, first display the message. Then, double-click on the sender's address in the From field. Exchange then opens a property sheet for the address similar to the one shown in figure 14.23. Make any changes necessary, then click on the Personal Address Book button to add the address to your PAB.

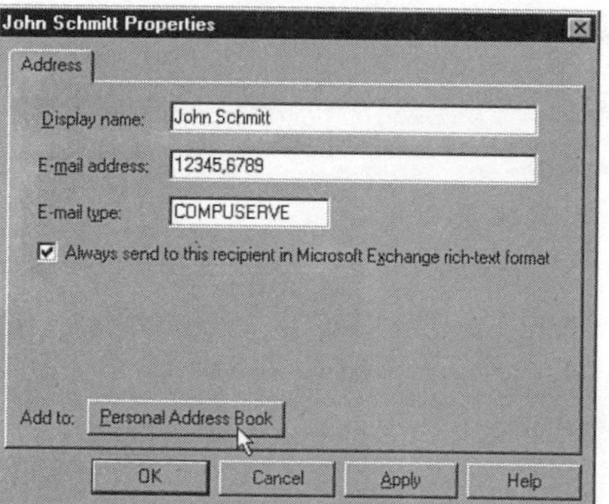

Fig. 14.23
You can easily add a sender's address to your PAB for future use.

The process for adding a sender's fax address is slightly different. From the Contents pane in Exchange, select the fax for which you want to store the sender's address. Then, click on the Reply to Sender button in the toolbar or choose Compose, Reply to Sender. Exchange opens a composing window in which you can create a reply. Double-click on the sender's fax address in the To field to display a property sheet for the address similar to the one shown in figure 14.23. Click on the Personal Address Book button to add the address to your PAB. You then can complete the reply, or simply cancel the reply if all you wanted to do was store the address.

Using Personal Distribution Lists (PDLs)

Most businesses rely heavily on e-mail for daily communications. In fact, many businesses seem to shut down when the e-mail system crashes. Gone are the rapid updates, concise conversations, and information exchange associated with e-mail. As a business person, you probably send several e-mail messages to different people during the day or course of a week. You rely on this system because it is efficient. So why, when you create a new message, do you still select recipient names one at a time when you have a message that goes out to several people at the same time?

To make Exchange more efficient and work for workgroup or team environments, Microsoft added a handy feature that enables you to build distribution lists. In the Distribution List page of the New Personal Distribution List property sheet (see fig. 14.24), you can create groups of recipients that you can quickly attach to a new message. Best of all, the addresses in the distribution list can be for different address types. For example, you can include

CompuServe, Microsoft Mail, and Internet addresses in the same distribution list.

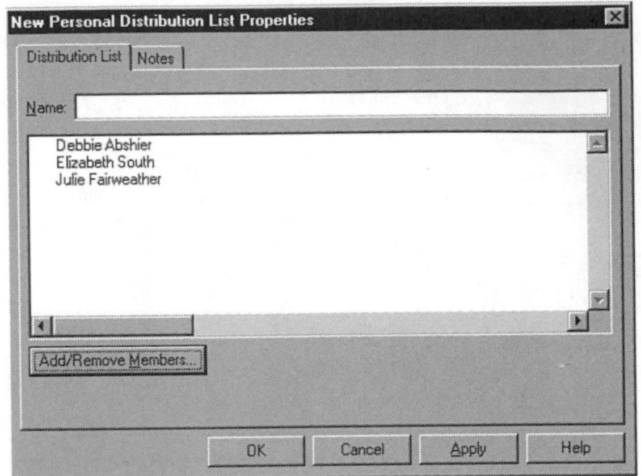

Fig. 14.24
The Personal Distribution List enables you to set up logical groups of recipients.

You can create a new PDL by selecting the Personal Distribution List option in the New Entry dialog box. The New Personal Distribution List property sheet appears, with the Distribution List tab displayed (refer to fig. 14.24). In the Name field, type a logical name of the group, such as **Windows 95 Consultants** or **Senior Management**. This name appears in the address book.

After you enter the name, choose the Add/Remove Members button to open an Edit dialog box in which you can select all the names you want to add to your new distribution list. To add a name, select the name from the address list at the left of the dialog box and click on the Members button. To remove a member from the distribution list, select the person's name from the Personal Distribution List box and press Del.

After you modify the list to your liking, choose OK twice. You return to the Address Book dialog box, which displays the new distribution list in bold letters with an icon to the left of the name to denote that it is a distribution list.

Now, when you create a new message and add recipients to the message, you can select the Personal Distribution List item and Exchange adds it to the recipient list. You can add more than one PDL to your address book and use as many as you want in your recipient list.

Tip

Forget who belongs in which PDL? Don't worry. You can easily find out the identities of the members of your PDL by checking out its properties. Just right-click on the PDL and select Properties on the context menu to reveal the names of the PDL's members.

Working with Microsoft Mail

If you are using Windows 95 on a Microsoft-based network (Windows NT, Windows for Workgroups, or Windows 95), it's a good bet that you want to use the Microsoft Mail service provider—all of these Microsoft operating environments include a workgroup version of Microsoft Mail. Or, you might want to connect through Dial-Up Networking to a remote site, such as your district office, that uses Microsoft Mail. In either case, you need to create and configure a workgroup post office (WGPO) if your network does not yet include one. The following sections will help you do just that.

Tip

A *workgroup postoffice* is a special set of directories that Microsoft Mail clients and Microsoft Mail Exchange clients can use to send and receive e-mail. Before you can begin sending and receiving mail on your LAN using the Microsoft Mail provider, you must have a WGPO on your LAN. Fortunately, Windows 95 makes it easy to create and manage a WGPO, as you will learn in the next section.

Setting Up a Workgroup Postoffice

The Control Panel contains an object specifically for creating and managing a workgroup postoffice. Open the Control Panel and double-click the Microsoft Mail Postoffice icon. Windows 95 starts a wizard as shown in figure 14.25. This wizard lets you either create a new WGPO or administer an existing WGPO.

Note

When you create a WGPO, you also create an administrator's account. The administrator is responsible for creating and managing user mail accounts. Before you begin creating the WGPO, decide who will be administering the postoffice. In the following steps, you'll create an administrator account and should be ready to provide the name of the person who will be administering the postoffice.

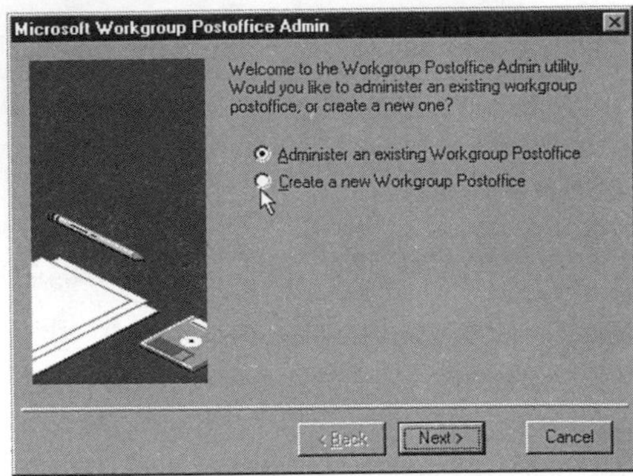

Fig. 14.25
You can create a new WGPO or administer an existing one.

To set up a new WGPO, follow these steps:

1. Start the Microsoft Workgroup Postoffice Admin wizard by opening the Control Panel and double-clicking the Microsoft Mail Postoffice icon.
2. Choose the Create a new Workgroup Postoffice option, then choose Next. Windows 95 then prompts you for the name and location for your new postoffice (see fig. 14.26). Enter the name or choose Browse to browse for a folder for the WGPO.

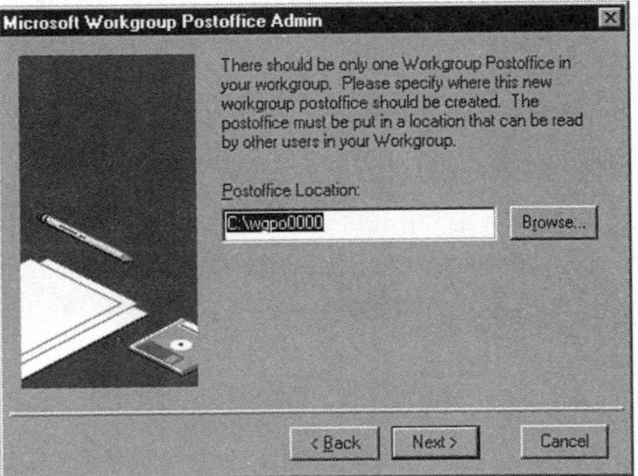

Fig. 14.26
Enter the path and file name for your new postoffice.

> **Note**
>
> You must choose an existing folder in which to create the WGPO. The wizard will not create a folder for you, but instead creates the WGPO folder structure in the existing folder that you choose.

3. After you click Next, the wizard prompts you to verify the path and file name you entered. Choose Next if the path and file name are correct, or choose Back to change the path or file name. After you click Next, the wizard displays the Enter Your Administrator Account Details dialog box shown in figure 14.27.

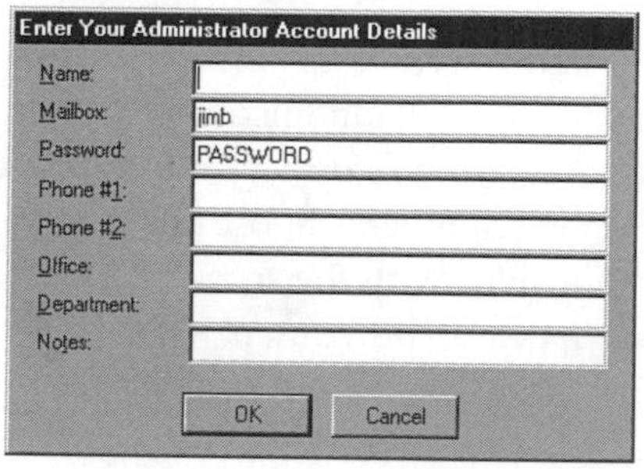

Enter Your Administrator Account Details

Name:	
Mailbox:	jimb
Password:	PASSWORD
Phone #1:	
Phone #2:	
Office:	
Department:	
Notes:	

OK Cancel

Fig. 14.27
You must specify details for an administrator account for your WGPO.

4. Fill out the fields in the account dialog box. You must provide entries for the following three items:

- *Name.* In this field, enter the first and last name of the person who will be administering the postoffice.

Tip

If you don't want to specify a particular user's name, use *Postmaster* as the Name and Mailbox entries for the account. When you or anyone else needs to log in to the postoffice to administer it, simply log in using the Postmaster account.

- *Mailbox.* Enter in this field the name of the mailbox for the administrator's account. Windows 95 suggests your Windows 95 network name, but you should consider creating a general Postmaster account.

- *Password.* Although you can leave the password blank, it's a bad idea to leave your WGPO administrator's account unprotected. Windows 95 uses PASSWORD as the default account password. You should enter a different password that others won't be able to guess.

> **Caution**
>
> Make sure you don't forget your account password. If you do, you won't be able to administer the WGPO without re-creating the entire WGPO (and losing all messages contained in it).

The remaining options in the account dialog box are optional and are self-explanatory. They enable a system administrator to fine-tune individual user accounts and provide background information to others of your office information, such as your phone number. Choose OK after you have specified the information you want included with the account. The general information (not the password) will appear to other users when they browse the postoffice list of accounts.

Administering a Postoffice

After you create the administrator account, you can begin adding, removing, and modifying mail accounts for users. To administer mail accounts, follow these steps:

1. Open the Control Panel and double-click the Microsoft Mail Postoffice icon.
2. Choose Administer an Existing Workgroup Postoffice, then choose Next.
3. Enter the path to your WGPO (or choose Browse to browse for the WGPO), then choose next.
4. Windows 95 prompts you for the account name and password of the administrator's account. Enter the mailbox name and password, then choose Next. A Postoffice Manager dialog box similar to the one shown in figure 14.28 appears.

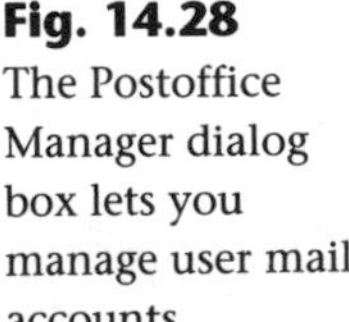

Fig. 14.28
The Postoffice Manager dialog box lets you manage user mail accounts.

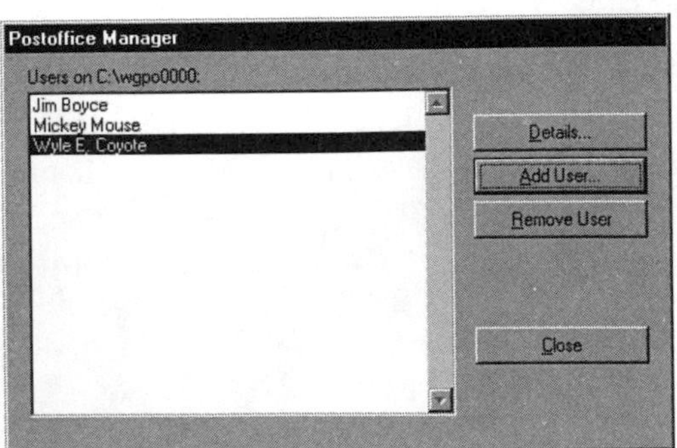

5. To view the account details for a user's account, select the account and choose the Details button. A dialog box similar to the one shown in figure 14.29 appears. Modify any of the properties for the user, then choose OK.

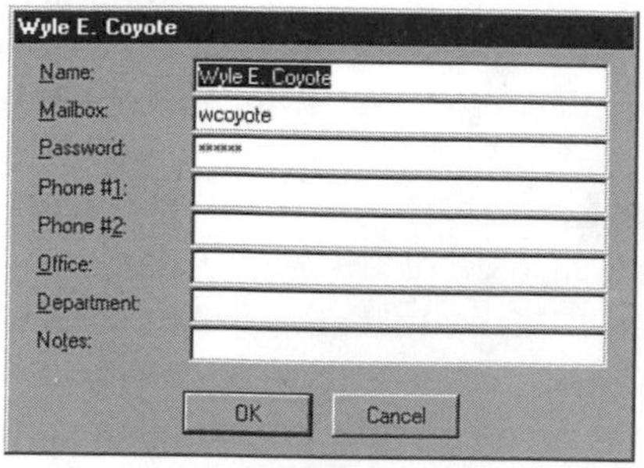

Fig. 14.29
You can modify any mail account property, including the password.

6. To add a user, click the Add User button. Windows 95 displays a dialog box nearly identical to the Details dialog box shown in figure 14.27. Enter the account details for the mail account, then choose OK.
7. To remove a user, select the user and choose Remove User. Windows 95 will prompt you to verify that you want to remove the account. Choose Yes to delete the account, or choose No to cancel the deletion.
8. When you are finished administering the WGPO, choose Close.

Changing Your Password

Your account in your Microsoft Mail WGPO is protected by a password to ensure that your messages are safe from snooping by others. To improve security, you should periodically change your mail account password. To do so, in Exchange choose Tools, Microsoft Mail Tools, and Change Mailbox Password. Exchange displays a simple dialog box in which you enter your current password, then enter your new password in two separate boxes to confirm the new password. When you're satisfied with your new password, choose OK.

Using the Postoffice Address List

You probably will most often use a Personal Address Book (PAB) to store addresses. When you're working with Microsoft Mail, however, you have an additional address source available—the postoffice address list, which stores the addresses of all accounts in the WGPO. As new accounts are added and as accounts change, those changes are reflected in the postoffice address list. To make sure you have available the most current copy of the postoffice address list, you should periodically download the postoffice address list to your PC. To do so, choose Tools, Microsoft Mail Tools, and Download Address Lists.

Exchange will connect to your WGPO and download the postoffice address list.

To work with addresses in the postoffice address list, begin composing a message. Click on the To button to display the Address dialog box. Choose Postoffice Address List from the Show Names drop-down list. Exchange will display the postoffice address list, and you can choose addresses from it just as you would with other address sources, such as the PAB.

Using a Session Log

For the most part, Exchange should have no problems connecting to your e-mail account in the WGPO and sending and receiving your messages. If you run into problems, however, the Microsoft Mail provider offers a means for you to troubleshoot the problem—you can direct the Microsoft Mail provider to maintain a log of its connection sessions. You can view the log to identify connection or other problems.

To turn on logging, follow these steps:

1. In Exchange, choose Tools, Services. Or, open the Control Panel and double-click on the Mail and Fax icon. Either of these two actions displays the property sheet for your message service(s).
2. Choose Microsoft Mail from the list of installed services, then click on Properties.
3. When the Microsoft Mail property sheet appears, click on the Log tab to display the Log property page (see fig. 14.30).

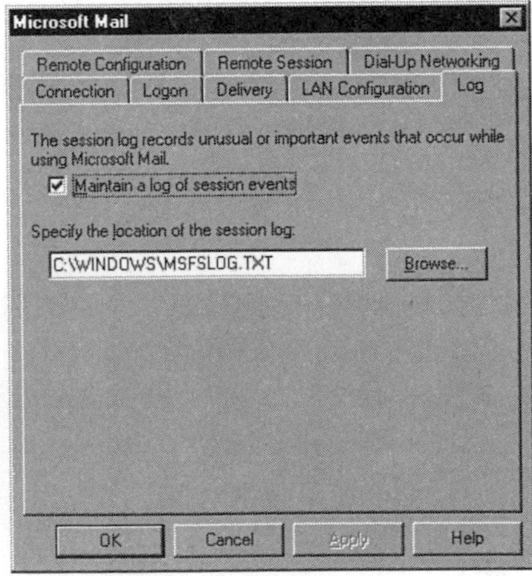

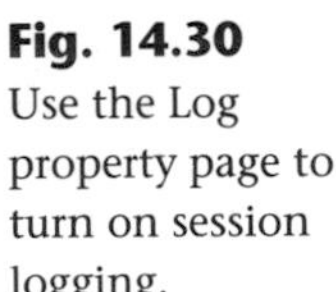

Fig. 14.30
Use the Log property page to turn on session logging.

4. Place a check in the check box labeled Maintain a log of session events.
5. If you want to specify a file other than the default (MSFSLOG.TXT) in which to store the file, enter the file name in the text box or click the Browse button to specify the file.
6. Choose OK to apply the change, then OK again to close the property sheet.

To view the log, simply locate it and double-click on it. Windows 95 will open Notepad (or WordPad if the file is too large for Notepad) and display the file.

Setting Microsoft Mail Options

Like each Exchange service provider, the Microsoft Mail provider offers many options that control how the provider sends and receives mail to and from your WGPO. To set these options, use one of the following two methods:

- From the Exchange window, choose Tools, Services.
- Open the Control Panel and double-click on the Mail and Fax icon.

Either of these two methods displays the Services property page, although using the second method (through the Control Panel) displays the Delivery and Addressing pages.

After the Services page appears, select Microsoft Mail from the information services list, then click on Properties to display the Microsoft Mail property sheet shown in figure 14.31.

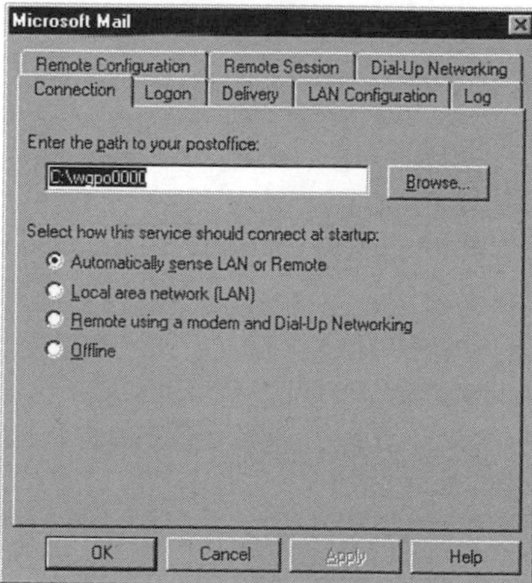

Fig. 14.31
The Microsoft Mail provider's property pages are similar to those of other service providers.

The following sections describe the settings found in each property page. Note that only some of the pages are discussed because the remaining pages are described in Chapter 17.

Connection

- *Enter the Path to Your Postoffice*. In this text box, enter the path to the shared directory containing your workgroup postoffice (WGPO). Or, click on the Browse button to browse for the WGPO. If you are connecting to a WGPO on a remote system, you might map a local drive ID to the remote shared WGPO directory and specify the drive ID in this text box. Or, you can specify a UNC pathname to the postoffice.

▶ See "Configuring Exchange for Remote Mail," p. 363

- *Automatically Sense LAN or Remote*. Choose this option button if you want Exchange to automatically determine whether you are connecting to the WGPO through a LAN or through a remote connection. If Microsoft Mail is unable to determine the type, it will prompt you to specify the connection.
- *Local Area Network (LAN)*. Choose this option if you are connecting to the WGPO on your LAN.
- *Remote Using a Modem and Dial-Up Networking*. Choose this option if you are connecting to the WGPO through a Dial-Up Networking connection.
- *Offline*. Choose this option if you are not connecting to your WGPO, but instead want to work offline to compose and reply to messages. Incoming and outgoing mail will not be delivered until you reconnect to the WGPO. Outgoing mail will be stored in your Outbox, and incoming mail will remain in your WGPO mail box.

Logon

- *Enter the Name of Your Mailbox*. Enter the name of your WGPO mail account (mailbox) in this text box.
- *Enter Your Mailbox Password*. Enter your mailbox password in this text box. The password will appear as asterisks for security. If you prefer to enter your password each time you log on and not store your password on your system, leave this text box blank.
- *When Logging On, Automatically Enter Password*. Enable this check box if you want Microsoft Mail to automatically enter your password for logon when you start Exchange. Clear this check box if you want Microsoft Mail to prompt you for the password before logging on.

- *Change Mailbox Password*. Click on this button to display a simple dialog box you can use to change your password. You must supply your old password in order to specify a new one. You should change your password periodically to ensure security.

Delivery

- *Enable Incoming Mail Delivery*. Enable this check box to allow messages to be delivered from your WGPO mailbox to your Exchange Inbox.
- *Enable Outgoing Mail Delivery*. Enable this check box to allow messages in your Inbox to be delivered to the WGPO.
- *Enable Deliver to...Address Types*. Click on the Address Types button to specify address types to which you don't want messages delivered. A simple dialog box will appear that you can use to select the types of addresses to which you want messages to be delivered.
- *Check for New Mail Every nn Minutes*. Specify the frequency at which you want Microsoft Mail to check for new messages and send pending messages.
- *Immediate Notification*. Enable this check box if you want recipients of your messages to be notified when you send them messages. This option, when enabled, also causes you to receive notifications when others send you messages (if these other users have enabled this feature, also). This feature requires the use of a network protocol supporting NetBIOS.
- *Display Global Address List Only*. Enable this check box if you only want to work with the Global Address List (postoffice address list) and not your PAB.

LAN Configuration

- *Use Remote Mail*. Enable this check box if you want Microsoft Mail to retrieve message headers instead of messages, allowing you to preview your mail before retrieving it. For information on using remote mail, refer to Chapter 17.
- *Use Local Copy*. Enable this check box to cause Microsoft Mail to use a local copy (stored on your computer) of the postoffice address list. To download the address list, choose Tools, Microsoft Mail Tools, and Download Address Lists.
- *Use External Delivery Agent*. Enable this check box if you want the EXTERNAL.EXE delivery agent to deliver your mail. EXTERNAL.EXE must be running on the server for you to make use of it. ❖

CHAPTER 15

Using Exchange for Internet Mail

by Jim Boyce

Microsoft Plus! for Windows 95 is an add-on product from Microsoft that includes a selection of useful tools and interface enhancements for Windows 95. Among these additional features is an Internet Mail service provider for Exchange that enables you to use Exchange to send and receive mail through an Internet mail server. This chapter explains how to install and configure the Internet Mail provider and use it to send and receive e-mail through your Internet connection.

In this chapter, you learn how to

- Install the Internet Mail provider
- Configure your Internet Mail connection
- Send and receive Internet mail
- Set Internet Mail provider options

Naturally, your first step is to install the Internet Mail provider as explained in the next section.

Note

Unless you specifically want the Internet Mail provider for Exchange, you don't need to purchase Plus! to access the Internet in Windows 95. You can use any web browser. Other e-mail programs exist that enable you to send and receive Internet Mail. You can retrieve a copy of the Internet Explorer from Microsoft at **www.microsoft.com**.

Installing the Internet Mail Provider

To install the Internet Mail service for Exchange, you must use the Plus! Setup program, which takes you through the process of installing the Plus! options. Unfortunately, Plus! Setup does not let you choose which of the Internet components you want to install; instead, Setup installs all of the Internet components, which includes Internet Explorer and the Internet Mail provider for Exchange. If you are using a Web browser other than Internet Explorer and don't want to switch to Internet Explorer, you should jump to the section "Installing Only Internet Mail" later in this chapter.

If you want to install all of the Internet tools included with Plus!, use the following steps as a guide to help you install the Internet Mail service:

1. Start Windows 95 and insert the Plus! CD in your CD-ROM drive. The Plus! CD will autoplay, opening a window on the desktop.
2. Choose the Install Plus! button, which starts the Plus! Setup program.
3. When Setup prompts you to select what Plus! components to install, make sure you select the Internet Jumpstart Kit (see fig. 15.1), and then choose Next.

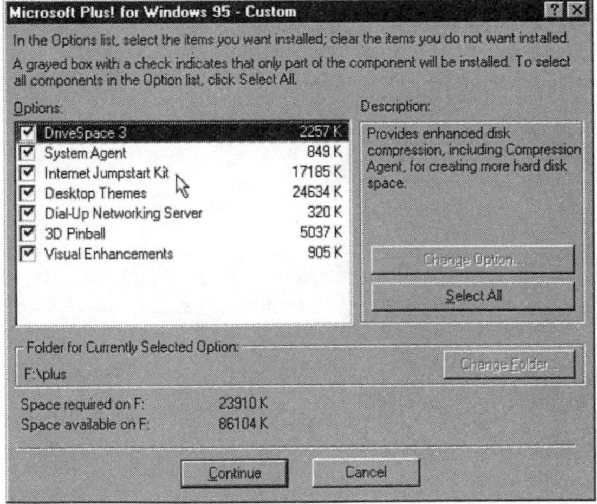

Fig. 15.1
To install the Internet Mail provider, select the Internet Jumpstart Kit.

▶ See "Installing and Configuring TCP/IP in Windows 95," p. 420

4. Follow the prompts to continue the installation process. Eventually, Setup starts an Internet Setup Wizard. When this wizard appears, choose Next.
5. Through the next few dialog boxes, the wizard prompts you to specify information about how you connect to the Internet, the DNS (Domain

Name Service) servers to use, and the default gateway. Provide the settings that apply to your connection.

6. The wizard then displays the dialog box shown in figure 15.2, prompting you to specify your e-mail address and mail server. Place a check mark in the Use Internet Mail check box.

▶ See "Installing and Configuring TCP/IP in Windows 95," p. 420

7. In the text box labeled Your Email Address, type your e-mail address in the form *user@domain*, such as **jimb@tigers.k12.cfa.org**.

8. In the Internet Mail Server text box, type the domain name of your Internet e-mail server. If you're not sure what to type for these properties, check with your system administrator or Internet service provider for help. After you type the necessary information, choose Next.

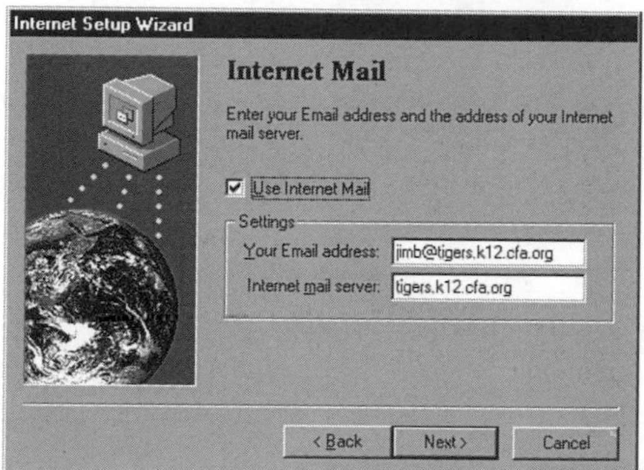

Fig. 15.2
Type your e-mail address and mail server names.

9. The Internet wizard then displays the dialog box shown in figure 15.3, prompting you to specify which Exchange profile you want to place the Internet Mail service provider in. Select an existing profile from the drop-down list, or choose the New button to create a new profile.

Fig. 15.3
Select or create a profile to contain your Internet Mail service.

10. After you create or specify a profile to contain your Internet Mail provider, choose Next, then follow the prompts and dialog boxes to complete the installation process.

Troubleshooting

I've installed the Internet Mail provider, but it can't seem to access the modem when Exchange starts. I think it's trying to dial the server to check my mail, but never succeeds. What should I do?

If you have the Microsoft Fax provider installed in the same profile as the Internet Mail provider, Internet Mail will be unable to access the modem to connect to the Internet. If you are connecting to the Internet through your LAN, this isn't a problem. If you must use Dial-Up Networking to connect to the Internet and also want to use Microsoft Fax, your only solution is to separate the two services into different profiles. To have Exchange prompt you to select a profile when Exchange starts, open Exchange and choose Tools, Options to display the property sheet for Exchange. In the General property page, choose the Prompt for a Profile to be Used button, and then choose OK.

Installing Only Internet Mail

If you currently are using Netscape or another Internet Web browser, or you only want to install the Internet Mail service provider and not Microsoft's Internet Explorer, you can easily do so. To install the Internet Mail files and configure the service provider, follow these steps:

1. Hold down the Shift key and insert the Plus! CD-ROM in the CD drive. (Holding down the Shift key prevents the CD from autoplaying.)
2. Choose Start, Programs, and MS-DOS Prompt to open a DOS session.
3. At the DOS command line, enter the command **EXTRACT E:\PLUS_7.CAB MINET32.DLL C:\WINDOWS\SYSTEM**. This extracts the file Minet32.dll from the Plus_7 cabinet file on the CD to your Windows System folder. (Replace the E drive specification with the correct letter of your CD-ROM drive.)
4. At the DOS command line, enter the command **EXTRACT E:\PLUS_7.CAB INETAB32.DLL C:\WINDOWS\SYSTEM**.
5. At the DOS command line, enter the command **EXTRACT E:\PLUS_7.CAB INT-MAIL.* C:\WINDOWS\HELP**.
6. Close the MS-DOS Prompt window.
7. Open the Control Panel and double-click the Mail and Fax icon.

8. From the Services property page, click the Add button.
9. From the Add Service to Profile dialog box, select Internet Mail, and then choose OK. Windows 95 displays the Internet Mail property sheet shown in figure 15.4.

Note

See the following section "Configuring the Internet Mail Provider" to configure the Internet Mail provider and complete the installation process.

Configuring the Internet Mail Provider

If you add the Internet Mail provider through the Control Panel, Windows 95 automatically opens the property sheet shown in figure 15.4 as soon as you add the Internet Mail provider to a profile. You also can use this property sheet to configure the Internet Mail provider after you install it.

Setting Mail Properties

To set your Internet Mail properties, open the Control Panel and double-click the Mail and Fax icon. Select the Internet Mail provider, and then choose Properties to display the General property page shown in figure 15.4.

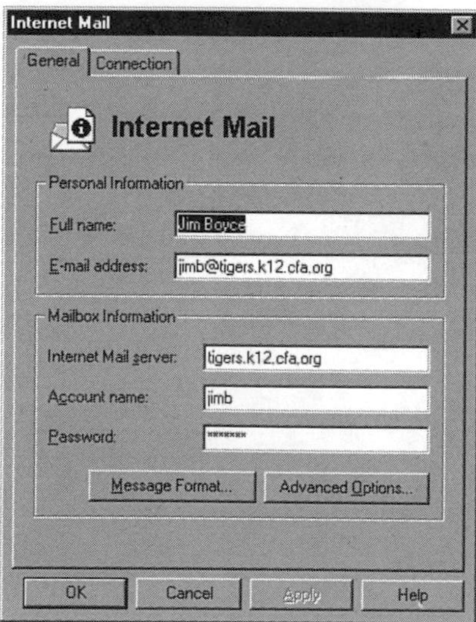

Fig. 15.4
Use the General property page to set general Internet Mail properties.

The following list explains the settings on the General property page:

- *Full Name.* Type your first and last names as you want them to appear in the message headers.
- *E-mail Address.* Type your e-mail address in the form *user@domain*, where *user* is your e-mail account name and *domain* is the domain name of your Internet Mail server. Example: **jimb@nowhere.com**.
- *Internet Mail Server.* Type the domain name of your Internet mail server. Example: **nowhere.com**.
- *Account Name.* Type your e-mail account name (generally, the account you use to log on to the Internet server). Example: **jimb**.
- *Password.* Type the password for your Internet e-mail account.
- *Message Format.* Click this button to specify whether the Internet Mail service uses MIME encoding to send your e-mail messages and attachments.
- *Advanced Options.* Click this button to specify the name of a server to which you want all of your outbound mail forwarded. This is necessary if your default Internet Mail server doesn't process outbound mail.

Configuring the Connection

In addition to specifying mail properties, you also can specify how Internet Mail connects to the Internet. To do so, click the Connection tab of the Internet Mail property sheet to display the Connection page shown in figure 15.5.

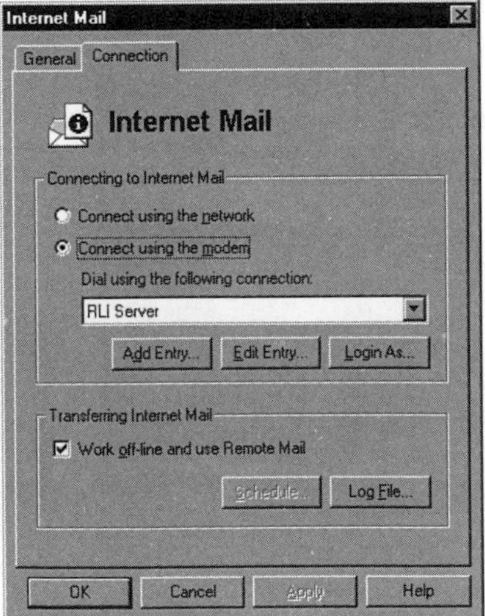

Fig. 15.5
The Connection page determines how Internet Mail connects to the Internet.

The following list describes the properties on the Connection page:

- *Connect Using the Network.* Choose this button if you connect to the Internet through your local area network.
- *Connect Using the Modem.* Choose this button if you connect to the Internet using Dial-Up Networking.
- *Dial Using the Following Connection.* If you selected the Connect Using the Modem option, choose the correct Dial-Up Networking connection from this drop-down list. If you have not set up a Dial-Up Networking entry, click Add Entry.
- *Add Entry.* Click this button to create a Dial-Up Networking connection to your Internet service provider. See Chapter 20, "Connecting to the Internet," and Chapter 23, "Using Dial-Up Networking," for help creating the connection.
- *Edit Entry.* Click this button to edit the selected Dial-Up Networking connection properties.
- *Login As.* Click this button to display the dialog box shown in figure 15.6. Specify the user name and password required to log on to the remote Internet server.

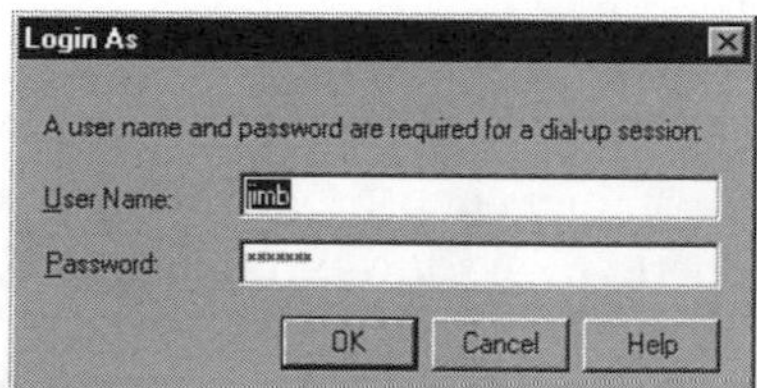

Fig. 15.6
Specify the login name and password required by your Internet server.

- *Work Off-line and Use Remote Mail.* Enable this check box if you want to use remote mail and not send and receive Internet mail automatically.
- *Schedule.* Click this button to display the dialog box shown in figure 15.7, which enables you to specify how often Exchange should check for new messages.
- *Log File.* Click this button if you want the Internet Mail provider to maintain a log of your Internet connection sessions. The Log File dialog box appears, enabling you to select the logging method and location of the log file.

▶ See "Working with Remote Mail," p. 370

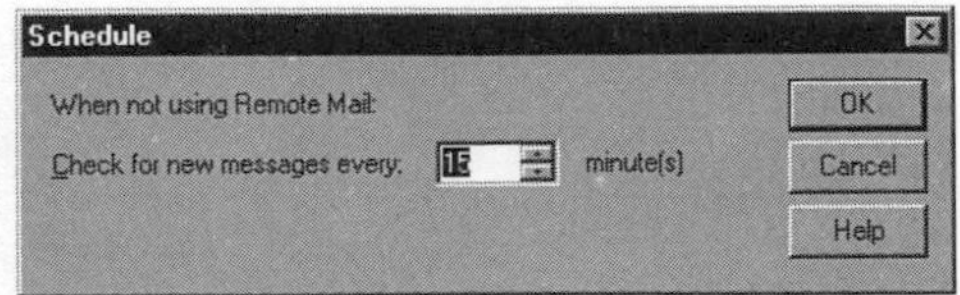

Fig. 15.7
Specify how often Exchange should check for new mail and send waiting mail.

Using the Internet Mail Provider

◀ See "Working with Microsoft Exchange," p. 307

In most respects, you send and receive messages through the Internet Mail provider in the same way you use other providers. This section provides tips on sending and receiving messages on the Internet.

Addressing Internet Messages

To address a message to an Internet recipient, follow these steps:

1. Begin a new message.
2. In the Compose window, click the To button to display the Address Book.
3. If the PAB (Personal Address Book) is not displayed, choose Personal Address Book from the Show Names drop-down list.
4. If the address you want to use is not in the Address Book, click the New button to display the New Entry button.
5. Scroll to the bottom of the Select the Entry Type list and choose Internet Mail Address; then choose OK. Exchange displays the SMTP-Internet property page shown in figure 15.8.

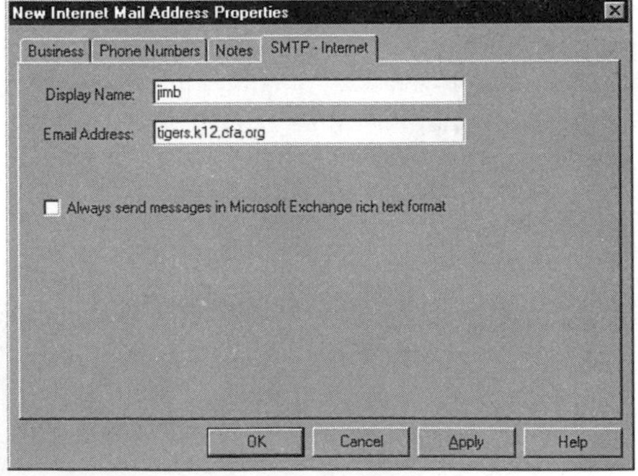

Fig. 15.8
You can create an Internet address with the SMTP-Internet page.

6. In the Display Name text box, type the address name as you want it to appear in the Address Book.
7. In the Email Address text box, type the Internet address of the recipient in the form *account@domain*, where *account* is the user's mail account name and *domain* is the name of the user's Internet mail server. Example: **jimb@nowhere.com**.
8. Fill in other properties for the address as desired using the other property pages.
9. Choose OK.

Sending and Receiving Messages

You can configure Internet Mail to use one of two methods to deal with your incoming and outgoing messages. First, you can configure Internet Mail to connect to your Internet server automatically at specific time intervals to deliver mail from your outbox to the server and retrieve messages waiting for you on the server. Second, you can configure Internet Mail to work offline and connect to your mail server using Remote Mail. This second option enables you to preview message headers and download only those messages you want to retrieve. This makes it possible for you to postpone retrieving large or unimportant messages.

To configure automatic send/receive, follow these steps:

1. Close Exchange, open the Control Panel, and double-click the Mail and Fax icon.
2. Select the Internet Mail service and click Properties.
3. Click the Connection tab, and on the Connection page, clear the Work Off-line and use Remote Mail check box.
4. Click the Schedule button to display the Schedule dialog box.
5. Use the spin control on the Schedule dialog box to specify the amount of time between automatic connections.
6. Choose OK to close the Schedule dialog box, and then choose OK to close the Internet Mail property sheet.
7. Restart Exchange.

If you prefer that Internet Mail transfer messages only when you direct it to do so, place a check in the Work Off-line and use Remote Mail check box. When you next start Exchange, you can choose Tools, Remote Mail to retrieve your waiting message headers.

▶ See "Working with Remote Mail," p. 370

Using Binary Attachments

Unlike other message transport mechanisms, the Internet doesn't support direct transfer of binary files through e-mail messages. With Microsoft Mail, for example, you can attach a binary file to a message and send the message to another user. The file is transferred as a binary file without any translation or conversion. To send that same binary file through the Internet, however, requires that the binary file be converted to text characters and transferred as a text message. The recipient then has to convert the message from its text format into its original binary format.

Fortunately, the Internet Mail provider and Exchange can perform that conversion for you automatically. This is because the Internet Mail provider acts as an encoder/decoder for the binary attachment. Internet Mail supports coding methods for MIME and UUENCODE. MIME stands for Multipurpose Internet Mail Extensions. UUENCODE comes from a UNIX program of the same name that provides the same function on UNIX systems.

When you send an attached binary file using Internet Mail, the file is converted to 7-bit text and sent with the rest of your message as text. At the other end, the recipient's system converts the text back into a binary file. This conversion occurs automatically if the recipient's e-mail program supports decoding. Otherwise, the recipient must run the message through a decoding program to convert the text back into a file.

When you receive a message that contains an embedded binary file (embedded as text), Internet Mail detects the embedded file and converts it back into a binary attachment. When you read the message, you'll see the file's icon embedded in the message (see fig. 15.9). You can choose File, Save As to save the attachment to a separate file, or you can double-click the icon to open the file.

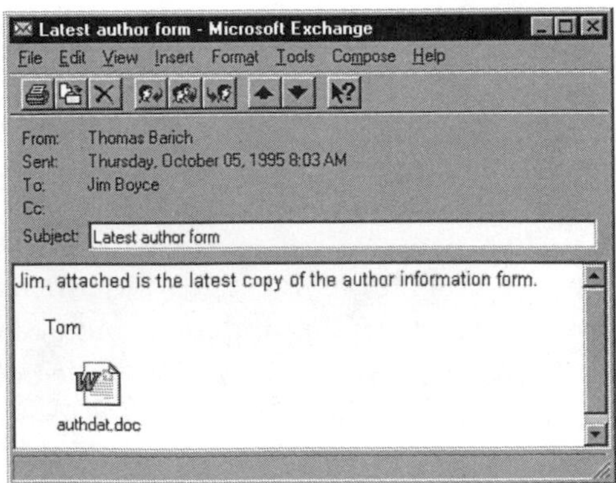

Fig. 15.9
Binary attachments appear as icons in a message.

To set Internet Mail's coding options, follow these steps:

1. Open the Control Panel and double-click the Mail and Fax icon; or in Exchange choose Tools, Services.
2. Select the Internet Mail provider from the list of installed services, and choose Properties to display the Internet Mail property sheet.
3. From the General property page, choose Message Format to display the Message Format dialog box (see fig. 15.10).

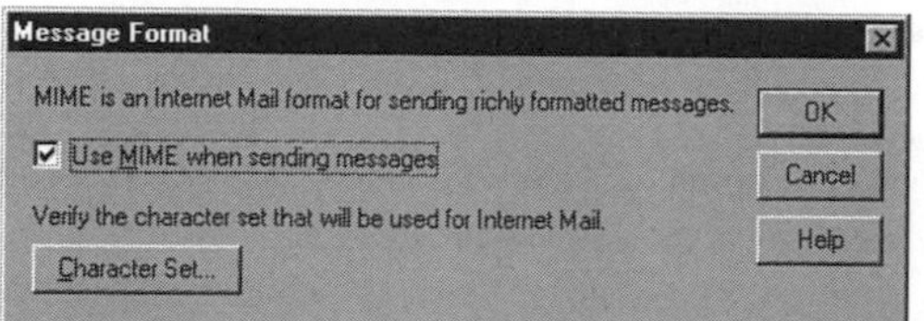

Fig. 15.10
The Message Format dialog box lets you select the coding method to use for binary attachments.

4. To use MIME (recommended), enable the check box labeled Use MIME When Sending Messages. To use UUENCODE, clear this check box.
5. Click the Character Set button to display the Character Set dialog box (fig. 15.11).

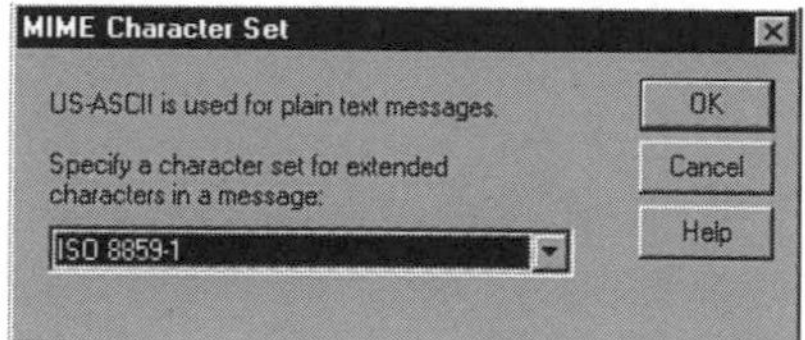

Fig. 15.11
Use the Character Set dialog box to specify the character set that will be used for extended characters in the message.

6. Choose the character set required by your Internet mail server. Generally, you can use the default ISO 8859-1. Notice that if you enable the Use MIME When Sending Messages check box, this character set is used for MIME coding. If you cleared the Use MIME check box, this character set is used for UUENCODE coding.
7. Choose OK three times to close all dialog boxes and the property sheet.
8. To test Internet Mail for attachments, compose a short message to your own Internet address and attach a binary file to the message. Send the message, wait a few minutes, then retrieve your mail. If the binary attachment does not come through correctly, try changing to coding method and/or character set.

Troubleshooting

Occasionally, a message comes through Internet Mail that I can't decode properly and I end up with a lot of gibberish in the message. Did I do something wrong?

It's really not gibberish—that's what a coded file looks like. In these situations you often can save the message and use an external coding program to convert the message to a binary file. To acquire a MIME encoder/decoder, connect via ftp to ftp.andrew.cmu.edu:pub/mpack/. You'll find versions of a MIME coder to suit most operating environments, including DOS. If you need more advanced MIME capability, check the site ftp.thumper.bellcore.com:pub/nsb for a program called MetaMail that provides advanced MIME coding.

You also might need a program capable of uuencoding and uudecoding messages. One particularly good one is WinCode, which you can find in the WUGNET forum on CompuServe in Library 3. You also can find WinCode on the Internet at http://www.ccn.cs.dal.ca/Services/PDA/WindowsMisc.html.

CHAPTER 16

Using Exchange for CompuServe Mail

by Jim Boyce

If you are a CompuServe member, you'll be happy to know that Windows 95 includes a service provider that allows you to use Exchange to send and receive mail through CompuServe. Because CompuServe acts as a mail gateway to the Internet, the CompuServe Mail provider lets you exchange e-mail with anyone who has an Internet mail account. This chapter explores the CompuServe Mail provider, covering the following topics:

- Installing the CompuServe Mail provider
- Configuring Microsoft Mail options
- Using CompuServe Mail

Installing and Configuring CompuServe Mail

You probably use a front-end application such as WinCIM, CompuServe Navigator, or GoCIS to send and receive mail on CompuServe. These programs all work well, but you might prefer to use Exchange for your CompuServe mail, bringing all your messages into Exchange's common Inbox.

The CompuServe Mail provider for Exchange enables you to do just that. With the CompuServe Mail provider, you can connect to CompuServe to send and receive messages through CompuServe's mail system. Although you can't send and retrieve forum messages through Exchange, at least you can handle your CompuServe mail. You can enjoy the advantages of remote mail preview, a common Inbox, automatic scheduled send/receive, and the other features supported by Exchange.

The CompuServe Mail provider is contained on the Windows 95 CD in the folder \Drivers\Other\Exchange\Compusrv. You also can download the CompuServe Mail provider from the CSMAIL and CISSOFT forums on CompuServe.

Installing CompuServe Mail

The CompuServe Mail provider includes its own Setup program to automate the installation process. To install the CompuServe Mail provider, follow these steps:

> **Note**
>
> This installation procedure assumes you are installing the CompuServe Mail provider from the Windows 95 CD. If you have downloaded the CompuServe Mail provider from CompuServe, first create a folder to contain the CompuServe Mail files. Open a DOS session and change to that directory. Extract the CompuServe Mail files to the directory by running the compressed file. If you downloaded the file to \Wincim\Download, for example, enter **\Wincim\Download\Csmail.exe**. If you renamed the file during the download, substitute the appropriate name in place of Csmail.exe. After extracting the files, proceed with step 3 (run the Setup program).

1. Hold down the Shift key while you insert the Windows 95 CD (this prevents the CD from autoplaying).
2. Open My Computer, right-click the CD icon, and then choose Open from the context menu.
3. Open the folder \DRIVERS\OTHER\EXCHANGE\COMPUSRV (or other folder containing the CompuServe Mail files if you have downloaded the files from CompuServe) and double-click the Setup icon. Setup starts and copies the necessary files to your system.
4. Setup asks you if you want to add CompuServe Mail to your default Exchange profile. Choose Yes to add the service to your default profile, or choose No if you want to later add the service to the default profile or a different profile.

Configuring the CompuServe Mail Service

After you add the CompuServe Mail service to your Exchange profile, you need to configure various settings that define how Exchange connects to CompuServe and sends and receives your CompuServe mail. To configure your user account information in the CompuServe Mail service, follow these steps:

1. Open the Control Panel and double-click the Mail and Fax icon.
2. Select CompuServe Mail from the list of installed services, and then choose Properties.
3. In the Name text box on the General property page (see fig. 16.1), enter the name you want to appear in mail message address headers (not your CompuServe account name).

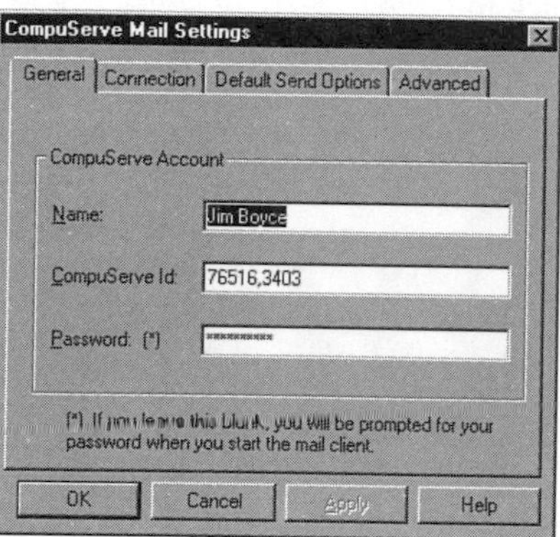

Fig. 16.1
Use the General page to specify your CompuServe account information.

4. In the CompuServe Id text box, enter your CompuServe account ID.
5. In the Password text box, enter your CompuServe account password.

In addition to configuring your account information, you also need to specify how the service will connect to CompuServe. To do so, use the Connection page and the following steps:

1. Click the Connection tab to display the Connection page (see fig. 16.2).

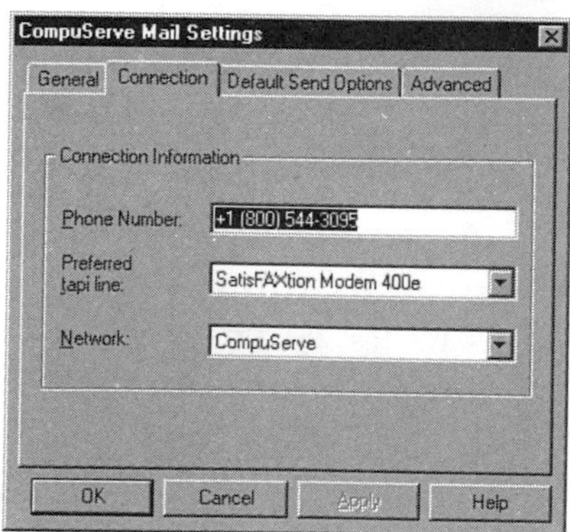

Fig. 16.2
Use the Connection page to specify how the connection to CompuServe is made.

2. In the Phone Number text box, enter your CompuServe access number.
3. From the Preferred Tapi Line drop-down list, choose the modem you'll be using to connect to CompuServe.
4. From the Network drop-down list, choose the type of network connection provided by your CompuServe access number.

◀ See "Installing and Configuring Modems," p. 63

At this point, you can choose OK, then OK again to begin using your CompuServe Mail service in Exchange. (Choosing the Apply button saves your current settings without exiting the property sheet.) You might, however, want to set a few advanced options. The Default Send Options page contains a selection of properties that define how messages are sent (see fig. 16.3).

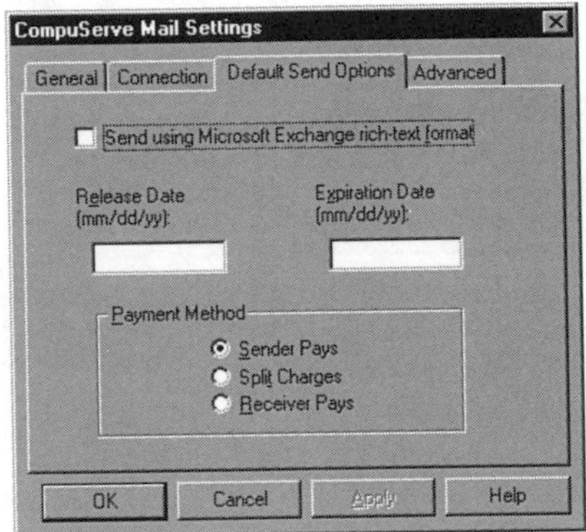

Fig. 16.3
The Default Send Options page controls how messages are sent.

The following list explains the properties on the Default Send Options page:

- *Send Using Microsoft Exchange Rich-Text Format.* Enable this check box if you want Exchange to include character (color, font, and so on) and paragraph formatting in your message. Only recipients who are using Microsoft Exchange will see the special formatting—other recipients will receive plain text.
- *Release Date.* If you enter a date in this field, messages will be held in your Inbox until the date specified, then forwarded on that date to the intended recipients. Leave this field blank if you want the messages to be sent as soon as the service connects to CompuServe.
- *Expiration Date.* If you enter a date in this field, the message will be deleted from the recipient's mail box when the date is reached.
- *Payment Method.* Select one of the three option buttons in this group to specify who pays for surcharged messages.

You can use the Advanced property page to schedule automatic connection to CompuServe and other advanced connection options (see fig. 16.4).

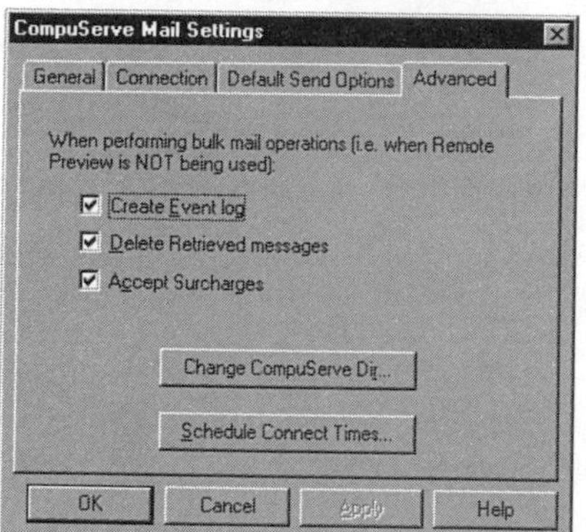

Fig. 16.4
Use the Advanced page to control advanced service options.

The following list describes the controls on the Advanced page:

- *Create Event Log.* Enable this check box if you want the CompuServe Mail provider to place log messages describing the results of each connection attempt in your Inbox. These log messages are helpful for troubleshooting connection problems.
- *Delete Retrieved Messages.* Enable this check box if you want the CompuServe Mail provider to delete mail from your CompuServe mailbox after the mail is retrieved and stored in your Exchange Inbox.
- *Accept Surcharges.* Enable this check box if you are willing to pay for messages that carry a surcharge. Messages such as those from the Internet generally carry a nominal postage-due fee.
- *Change CompuServe Dir.* Click this button to change the folder in which the CompuServe Mail provider stores configuration and address book settings. If you are using another CompuServe product such as WinCIM, the CompuServe Mail provider can use the same address book and connection settings as your other CompuServe product.
- *Schedule Connect Times.* Click this button to display the Connection Times dialog box (see fig. 16.5) and schedule automatic connections to CompuServe. If you want, you can use a selection of different scheduled connection times.

After you have specified all the settings and properties you want to change for the CompuServe Mail provider, choose OK, then OK again to save the changes. Restart Exchange to begin using the new settings.

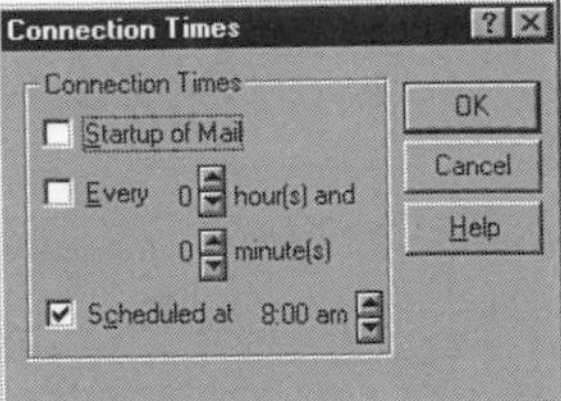

Fig. 16.5
You can schedule the CompuServe Mail provider to connect automatically to CompuServe.

Connecting On Time

Assume you configured the CompuServe Mail provider to check for messages at 8:00 a.m. and also every four hours, including times when you're away from your computer (like overnight). But, Exchange doesn't check at 8, 12, 4, and so on. It checks for mail at 8 a.m., but the four-hour interval falls at odd times. You might be wondering why this happens.

The CompuServe Mail provider doesn't base its interval connection times on the explicit 8 a.m. setting you've specified. Instead, the provider checks at four hour intervals based on the last time it automatically checked for mail. Open Control Panel and choose the Mail and Fax icon. Select the CompuServe Mail provider and choose Properties. Choose the Advanced tab, then choose the Schedule Connect Times option to display the Connection Times dialog box. Clear the Every check box and close the dialog box, then close the Profile property sheets. Shortly before the time when you want one of your interval connections to be made, open the Control Panel, choose the Mail and Fax icon, then enable the Every check box in the Connection Times dialog box and specify the interval you want to use. Close the property sheets. Exchange should then connect close to the time you want.

Using CompuServe Mail

There are few differences between using CompuServe Mail and using the Microsoft Mail provider. Most tasks are the same regardless of the service provider you're using, which is one of the advantages to using Exchange. For example, the Remote Mail feature works much the same whether you use the CompuServe Mail provider or Internet Mail provider.

▶ See "Using Remote Mail," p. 363

To create a CompuServe address for a message, open the compose window and click the To button, or choose Tools, Address Book to open the Address Book dialog box. If you click the Show Names drop-down list, you'll notice that CompuServe Mail has added a CompuServe Address Book. You can store CompuServe addresses in the CompuServe Address Book, or you can store them in your PAB (Personal Address Book) along with your other addresses.

To create a new CompuServe address, choose File, New Entry from the Address Book dialog box, or click the New Entry button on the toolbar. When the New Entry dialog box appears, you'll notice many new CompuServe address types from which to choose (see fig. 16.6).

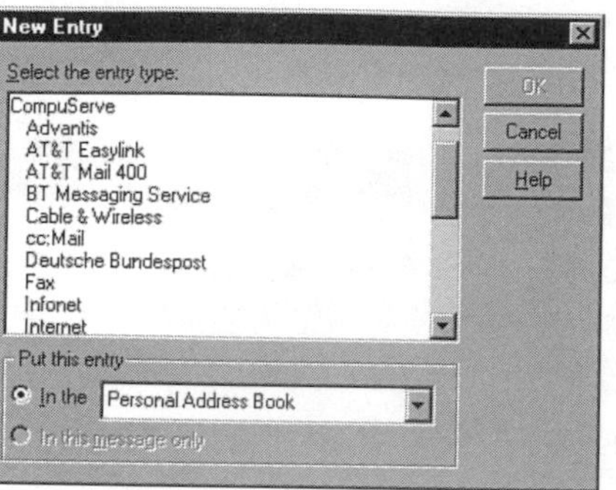

Fig. 16.6
CompuServe Mail supports a wide variety of different e-mail address formats.

The address types listed under CompuServe in the New Entry dialog box are those supported by CompuServe's mail system. To create an address for another CompuServe user, just click CompuServe, and then choose OK. If you need to send e-mail to a different type of address (such as the Internet) through CompuServe, choose the address type from the list. Then, choose OK. CompuServe Mail then displays the address property sheet shown in figure 16.7.

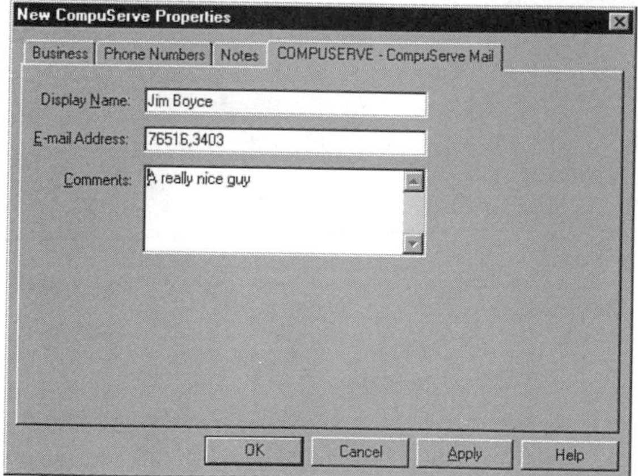

Fig. 16.7
The property sheet for a CompuServe address is very similar to those for other address types.

In the Display Name text box, type the name you want to appear in the address book for this address. In the E-mail Address text box, enter the user's CompuServe ID. Choose OK to add the new address to the address book.

Note

If you choose one of the address subtypes (such as Advantis, cc:Mail, and so on), the property sheet CompuServe Mail displays will be different from the one shown in figure 16.7. The property sheet is tailored to the address type, prompting you for the information required for the selected address type.

Troubleshooting

Occasionally, the CompuServe Mail provider is unable to connect to CompuServe to check my mail, but I don't receive any kind of notification about what went wrong. How can I determine the problem?

You can turn on logging. When logging is on, the CompuServe Mail provider places a log message in your Inbox each time it attempts to connect to CompuServe. You can read the log message like any other e-mail message—just double-click the message in the Inbox. Although the log messages don't contain detailed troubleshooting information, they at least provide a limited indication of what problem occurred.

To turn on logging, open the Control Panel and double-click the Mail and Fax icon. Select the CompuServe Mail provider and choose Properties. Click on the Advanced tab to display the Advanced property page. Enable Create Event log check box, then choose OK to close the CompuServe Mail Settings property page. Choose OK again to close the Exchange property sheet.

CHAPTER 17

Using Remote Mail

by Jim Boyce

Exchange's Remote Mail feature enables you to dial into your mail server to exchange e-mail when you are working from home or out of town. It also enables you to preview your messages, downloading only those messages you feel are important. You can use Remote Mail with the Microsoft Mail, Internet Mail, MSN, and CompuServe Mail service providers. All of these service providers support Remote Mail through a dial-up connection, and the Internet Mail and Microsoft Mail providers also support Remote Mail through a LAN connection.

In this chapter, you learn to

- Configure Exchange for Remote Mail
- Use Remote Mail

Except for the Internet Mail provider, all of the other service providers rely on Windows 95's Dial-Up Networking to provide a connection to a remote mail server. If you have not yet configured Dial-Up Networking on your computer, see Chapter 23, "Using Dial-Up Networking," to set up remote access on your system.

Configuring Exchange for Remote Mail

After you have installed the service provider as explained in the three previous chapters, you need to configure each service for Remote Mail.

Setting Up Microsoft Mail for Remote Mail

After you install the Microsoft Mail service provider (explained in Chapters 13 and 14), you can configure it for either LAN access or remote access.

Microsoft Mail supports Remote Mail for message preview for both types of connections. In most cases, however, it isn't necessary to preview messages when connecting to the post office over a LAN because the connection is much faster than a remote connection. Nevertheless, the option is still available to you.

To configure Microsoft Mail for a remote connection, follow these steps:

▶ See "Using a Dial-Up Networking Session," p. 501

1. First use the Make New Connection wizard in the Dial-Up Networking folder to create a Dial-Up Networking connection to your LAN's dial-in server (see Chapter 23, "Using Dial-Up Networking" for an explanation of how to set up a Dial-Up Networking connection).
2. Open the Control Panel and double-click the Mail and Fax icon.
3. Select the Microsoft Mail service, then choose Properties to display the Connection property page shown in figure 17.1.

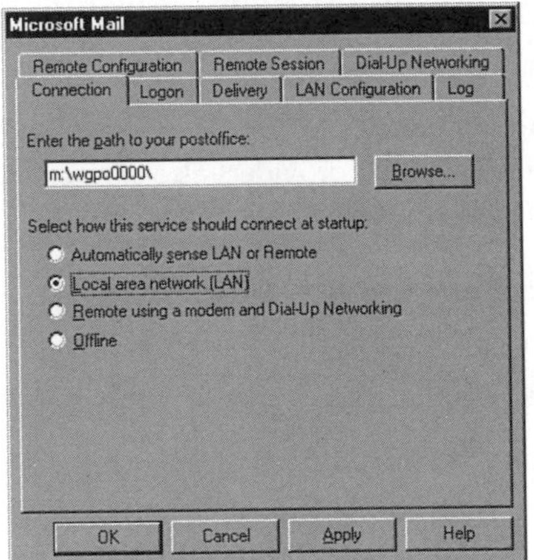

Fig. 17.1
Use the Connection page to configure Micro-soft Mail for a remote connection.

4. Choose the option labeled Remote Using a Modem and Dial-Up Networking.
5. Click the Dial-Up Networking tab to display the Dial-Up Networking property page (see fig. 17.2).
6. From the drop-down list, choose the Dial-Up Networking connection you want to use for the remote mail connection (the one that points to your Microsoft Mail server). You'll only see connections you have previously created.
7. In the Retry text box, enter the number of times you want the connection to be attempted if the initial attempt fails, then use the Times at text box to specify the frequency of connection attempts.

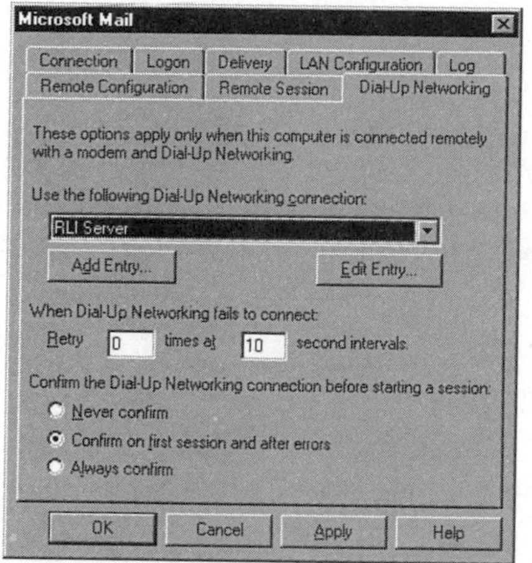

Fig. 17.2
Use the Dial-Up Networking page to specify which connection to use for remote mail.

8. Choose one of the three confirmation option buttons to specify whether Windows 95 will confirm that the Dial-Up Networking connection is working before starting the remote Microsoft Mail session. Configuring Remote Mail not to confirm the connection can save a little connection time. The Confirm on first session and after errors option is the default.

9. Click the Remote Session tab to display the Remote Session page (see fig. 17.3).

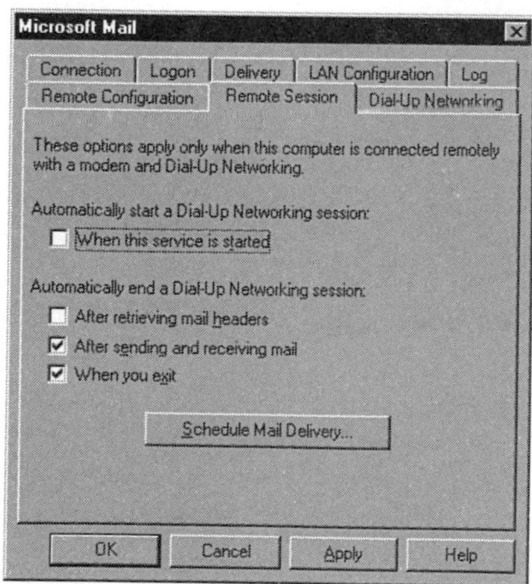

Fig. 17.3
Use the Remote Session page to control when the Dial-Up Networking session is started.

10. If you want the Dial-Up Networking session to start as soon as you start Exchange, enable the check box labeled When this Service is Started.

If you don't want the Dial-Up Networking session to start until you direct Exchange to send and retrieve your mail, leave this check box cleared.

11. Specify when you want the Dial-Up Networking session to be terminated using any combination of the following check boxes (if you leave all check boxes blank, the Dial-Up Networking connection won't terminate automatically):
    - *After Retrieving Mail Headers.* Enable this check box if you want the Dial-Up Networking session to disconnect after Microsoft Mail retrieves your message headers.
    - *After Sending and Receiving Mail.* Enable this check box if you want the Dial-Up Networking session to disconnect after Microsoft Mail sends and receives pending mail.
    - *When You Exit.* Enable this check box if you want the Dial-Up Networking connection to disconnect when you exit Microsoft Exchange.
12. Choose OK, then OK again to save your configuration changes. Or, choose Apply to apply the changes without closing the property sheet.

If you want to use Remote Mail to preview messages when connecting to a WGPO (Workgroup Post Office) on your LAN, follow these steps:

1. Open the Control Panel and double-click the Mail and Fax icon.
2. Select the Microsoft Mail service, then choose Properties to display the Connection page of the Microsoft Mail property sheet.
3. Select the Local Area Network (LAN) option button or the Automatically Sense LAN or remote option button.
4. Click the LAN Configuration tab to display the LAN Configuration page shown in figure 17.4.
5. Place a check in the check box labeled Use Remote Mail to enable Remote Mail.

Tip

Place a check in the Use Local Copy check box if you want to use a local copy of the post office address instead of checking addresses on the WGPO. When you're using Remote Mail through a Dial-Up Networking connection, you generally should check this box to enable Microsoft Mail to check addresses without connecting to the mail server. The Use external delivery agent check box controls whether or not Microsoft Mail uses the EXTERNAL.EXE program running on the server to expedite delivery. This check box does not apply specifically to Remote Mail.

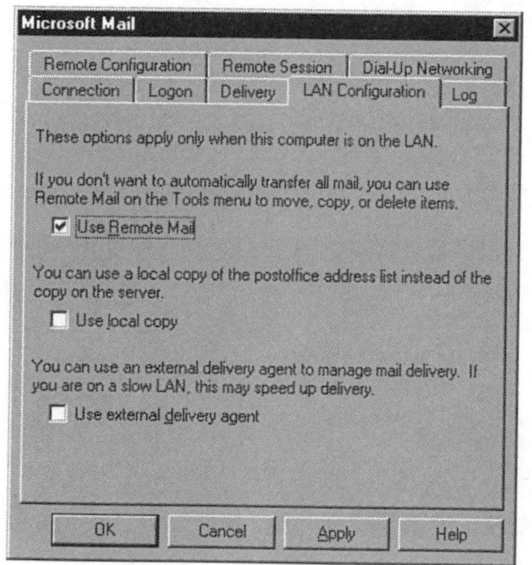

Fig. 17.4
Enable Remote Mail for a LAN connection through the LAN Configuration page.

6. Choose OK, then OK again to close the property sheets.

In the section "Working with Remote Mail" you learn how to preview messages, upload mail, and use other Remote Mail features. First, though, you need to decide how often Remote Mail will connect to your WGPO.

Setting Schedules

Although you can use Microsoft Mail interactively to check your mail, you also can configure the Microsoft Mail service to automatically connect at scheduled times to send and receive pending mail. This feature works with Remote Mail only if you're connecting to your WGPO over a Dial-Up Networking connection.

Tip

If your WGPO is located on the LAN, you can use Remote Mail to preview messages and control other message transfer options. But, you can't have Remote Mail automatically connect to the WGPO to update headers and perform other Remote Mail actions. Microsoft Mail's Remote Session property page, which enables you to specify a connection schedule (using the Schedule Mail Delivery button), only applies if you are connecting to the WGPO through a Dial-Up Networking connection. The Check for New Mail Every xx Minutes control on the Delivery page controls how often Microsoft Mail checks your WGPO for mail, but is ignored by Remote Mail.

To configure scheduled connection times for a Dial-Up Networking connection to your WGPO, follow these steps:

1. Open the Control Panel and double-click the Mail and Fax icon.

2. Select the Microsoft Mail item; then choose Properties.
3. Click the Remote Session tab, and then choose the Schedule Mail Delivery button to display the Remote Scheduled Sessions dialog box shown in figure 17.5.

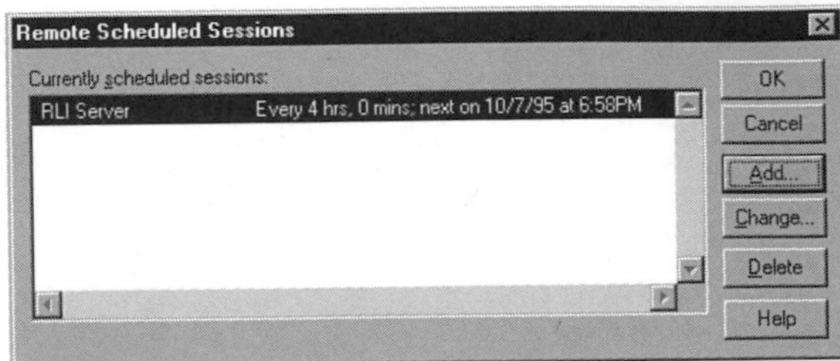

Fig. 17.5
You can schedule Microsoft Mail to connect automatically to check your mail.

4. Click Add, and then use the Add Scheduled Session dialog box to specify the time at which you want Microsoft Mail to connect automatically. You can schedule connections at periodic intervals, weekly on the same day and time, or once only at a specific date and time. Choose OK after you specify the desired connect time.

> **Note**
>
> Fixed-interval connections (such as every four hours) are not executed based on a specific time such as 8 a.m., 12 p.m., 4 p.m., etc. The connection times are based on the last connection's completion time plus the specified fixed time interval.

5. Repeat step 4 to add as many other connect times as you like. Then, continue to choose OK until you have closed the Exchange property sheet and saved your new settings.

Setting Up CompuServe Mail for Remote Mail

▶ See "Working with Remote Mail," p. 370

If you prefer to preview your CompuServe mail before downloading it, you can use Remote Mail. This is particularly useful if you routinely receive numerous messages or mail containing large binary attachments. When you install the CompuServe Mail provider, Remote Mail is enabled automatically. There are no additional configuration tasks to perform.

Setting Up Internet Mail for Remote Mail

Whether you connect to your Internet mail provider through a LAN or Dial-Up Networking connection, you can use Remote Mail to preview your messages and control message transfer. To configure Internet Mail for Remote Mail, follow these steps:

1. Install the Internet Mail provider as explained in Chapter 15, "Using Exchange for Internet Mail."
2. Open the Control Panel and double-click on the Mail and Fax icon.
3. Select Internet Mail from the list of installed services, and then click Properties to display the Internet Mail property sheet.
4. Click the Connection tab to display the Connection page (see fig. 17.6).

◀ See "Installing the Internet Mail Provider," p. 344

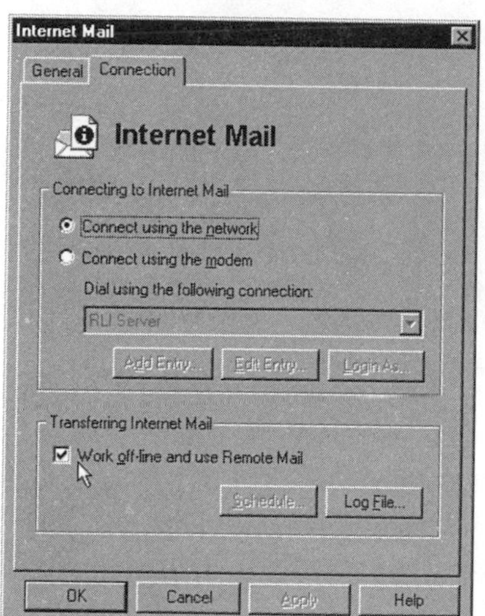

Fig. 17.6
Enable Remote Mail for Internet Mail through the Connection property page.

5. Place a check in the check box labeled Work Off-line and use Remote Mail.
6. Choose OK, then OK again to close the property sheets.

Setting Up MSN Mail for Remote Mail

The Microsoft Network (MSN) Mail provider also supports Remote Mail, enabling you to preview your MSN mail and reduce the amount of time you spend online. When you install the MSN provider, Remote Mail is automatically enabled. There are no additional setup or configuration steps to perform.

Working with Remote Mail

The primary advantage that Remote Mail offers is the ability to preview messages waiting for you in your mail server, which lets you review the messages' headers and download only those messages you feel are most interesting or important.

> **Tip**
>
> Previewing your messages will save you money by reducing the amount of time you are connected to your online service.

Remote Mail is simple to use, and works much the same way regardless of which Exchange mail provider you're using. The following sections explain Remote Mail's features.

Starting Remote Mail

After you start Exchange, choose Tools, Remote Mail. If only one service provider is installed that supports Remote Mail, selecting the Remote Mail command opens the Remote Mail window. If more than one installed provider supports Remote Mail, the Remote Mail menu acts as a cascading menu that contains the names of the services supported by Remote Mail (see fig. 17.7). Select from the Remote Mail menu the service for which you want to use Remote Mail.

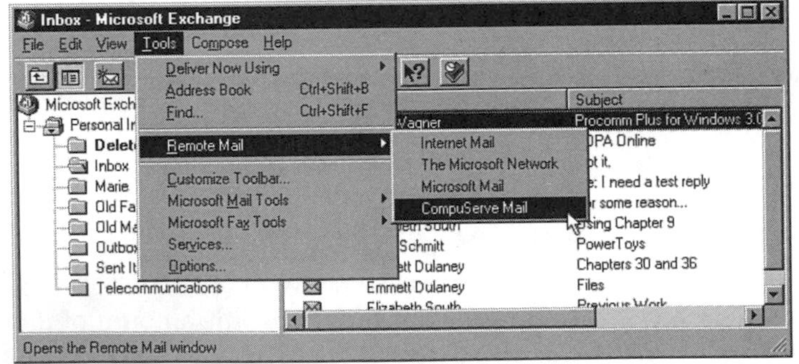

Fig. 17.7
The Remote Mail menu cascades when more than one installed service supports Remote Mail.

The Remote Mail window is a typical Windows 95 application window that includes a menu and toolbar. The main area of the window is a Header pane similar to the Contents pane in Exchange. The Header pane lists the message headers of messages waiting for you on your mail server (see fig. 17.8). Message headers remain in the Header pane until you mark the messages for retrieval and allow Remote Mail to retrieve them (or mark them for deletion and let Remote Mail delete the messages).

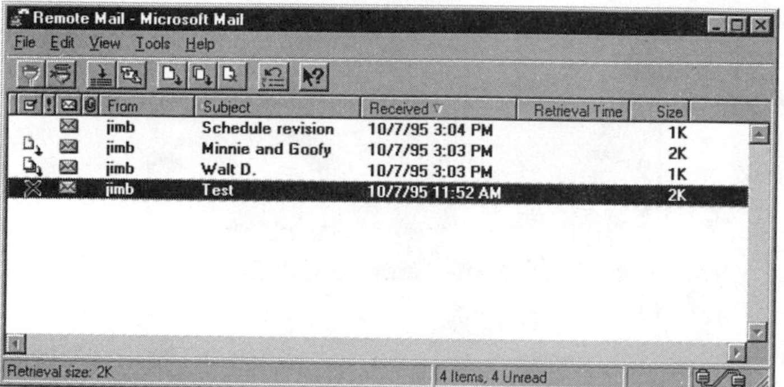

Fig. 17.8
The Remote Mail window containing a list of waiting messages.

Think of the Header pane as a cache of waiting messages. If the Header pane is empty, you have processed all of the messages that Remote Mail detected on your mail server. However, there might be new messages in your mail server that have arrived since you last used Remote Mail. Therefore, you need to let Remote Mail connect to your mail server to check for new messages. The next section explains how.

Previewing, Retrieving, and Sending Messages

Message headers in the Header pane appear in one of four ways as described in the following list and shown in figure 17.9:

- *Unmarked.* No icon beside a message indicates you have not marked it for retrieval or preview, and the message will be ignored during processing, with no action being taken on it. The message remains in the mail server. To unmark a message, double-click it until there is no icon beside it.
- *Marked to Retrieve.* An icon of a single document page and down arrow indicates the message is marked for retrieval. When you direct Remote Mail to transfer mail, the message downloads to your Inbox and the copy in the mail server is deleted. To mark a message for retrieval, just double-click the header in the list.
- *Marked to Retrieve a Copy.* An icon of a double document page and down arrow indicates the message is marked for copying to your Inbox. When you direct Remote Mail to transfer mail, the message downloads to your Inbox, but the original copy of the message remains in your mail server.

- *Marked to Delete.* An X icon indicates the message is marked for deletion. When you direct Remote Mail to transfer mail, the message will be deleted whether or not it has been read. To mark a message for deletion, select the message and click the Delete button in the toolbar.

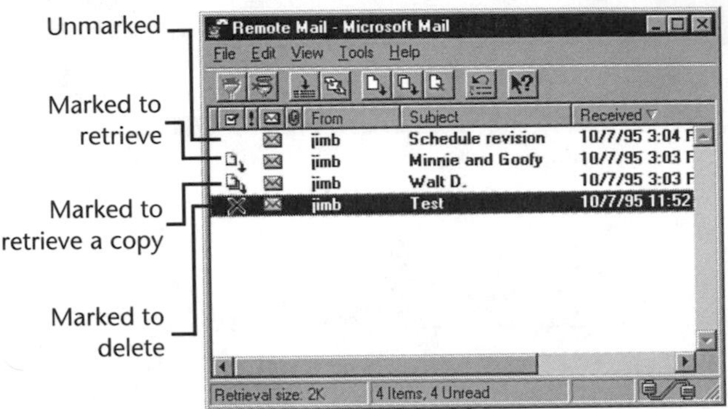

Fig. 17.9
Messages are represented in one of four ways in the Header pane.

To mark one or more messages using the menu, first select the messages (hold down the Ctrl or Shift key while clicking the headers to select multiple messages); then, choose Edit, Mark to Retrieve, Mark to Retrieve a Copy, or Mark to Delete. To unmark a message, double-click the header until there is no icon beside the header.

After you have marked all of the messages you want to process, you direct Remote Mail to connect to the mail server and process the messages. How you do so depends on whether you are connecting to the mail server across your LAN or through a Dial-Up Networking connection. If you are connecting through the LAN, the Tools menu includes two commands to process messages:

- *Update Headers.* Choose this option to have Remote Mail connect to the mail server and add to the Header pane any additional messages that have arrived in your mail account.
- *Transfer Mail.* Choose this option to process messages, including downloading marked messages, deleting messages, and uploading mail from the Outbox.

When you choose the Update Headers or Transfer Mail commands with the Microsoft Mail provider, Microsoft Mail displays the dialog box shown in figure 17.10. Select the options you want to use for the session, and then choose OK.

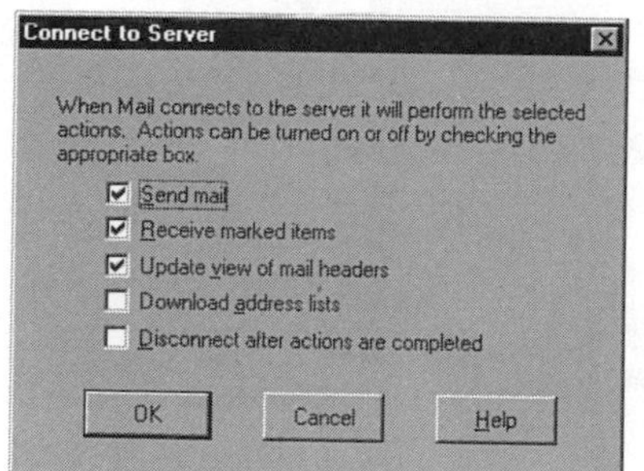

Fig. 17.10
Microsoft Mail offers a selection of options when transferring mail.

When you are connecting to the mail server through a Dial-Up Networking connection, the commands in the Tools menu are different:

- *Connect.* Choose this command to have Remote Mail connect to the mail server without processing any messages. After connecting, you can selectively update and process messages.
- *Connect and Update Headers.* Choose this command to have Remote Mail connect to the mail server and add to your Header pane any new messages waiting in your mail account.
- *Connect and Transfer Mail.* Choose this command to have Remote Mail connect to the mail server and process messages.

Remote Mail might or might not disconnect automatically from the mail server after processing is complete, depending on which service you are using. For example, the CompuServe Mail provider doesn't disconnect automatically. After processing is complete, choose Tools, Disconnect to disconnect from the service if the service provider doesn't automatically disconnect.

Setting Filter and Other Options

Remote Mail enables you to control the way information appears in the Header pane, as well as filtering and sorting messages to "weed out" messages you don't want to process. The following sections explain these options.

Setting Column Display

You can control which columns of information appear in the Header pane. To do so, choose View, Columns. Remote Mail displays the dialog box shown in figure 17.11. To add columns to the display, select from the Available columns list the columns you want to add, then choose Add. To remove columns from the display, select from the Show the following columns list the columns you want to remove, then click Remove. When you're satisfied with your selections, choose OK.

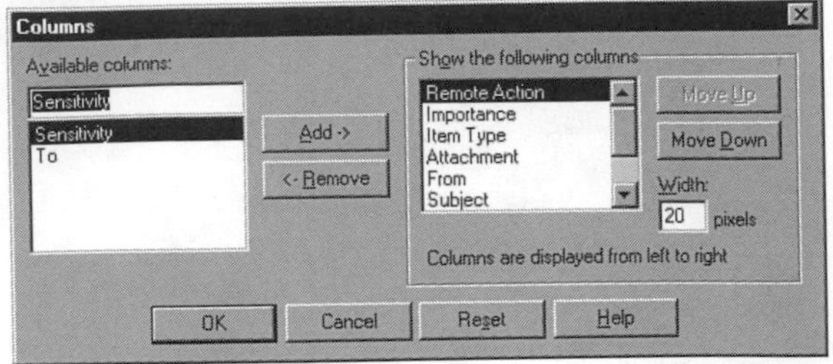

Fig. 17.11
Use the Columns dialog box to specify which columns appear in the Header pane.

Tip

As in the Exchange Inbox window, you can change the width of columns simply by dragging the column's heading border with the mouse. However, you must use the Columns dialog box to control which columns appear in the Remote Mail window. The two lists in the Columns dialog box list all of the columns you can view.

Filtering Messages

Remote Mail enables you to use filters to control which message headers are displayed in the Header pane. This feature makes it possible for you to view and process only the headers that meet your filter specifications. To set the filter options, choose View, Filter. Remote Mail displays the Filter dialog box shown in figure 17.12.

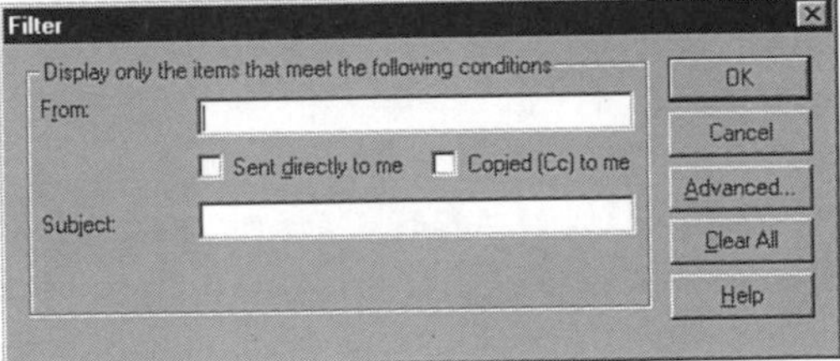

Fig. 17.12
Use the Filter dialog box to selectively display headers.

The following list explains the options in the Filter dialog box:

- *From.* In this text box, enter the names of the senders whose messages you want included in the Header pane. Separate multiple names by semicolons (;).
- *Subject.* In this text box, enter a message subject. All messages that have a matching subject will be included in the Header pane.
- *Sent Directly to Me.* Enable this check box to include messages for which you are included in the To field, rather than the Cc field.

- *Copied (Cc) to Me.* Enable this check box to include messages for which you are included in the Cc field. This includes messages for which you are included in the Bcc (Blind carbon copy) field.

Remote Mail also provides advanced options that enable a finer degree of control over which message headers are displayed. To set these advanced options, click Advanced on the Filter dialog box. Remote Mail displays the Advanced dialog box shown in figure 17.13.

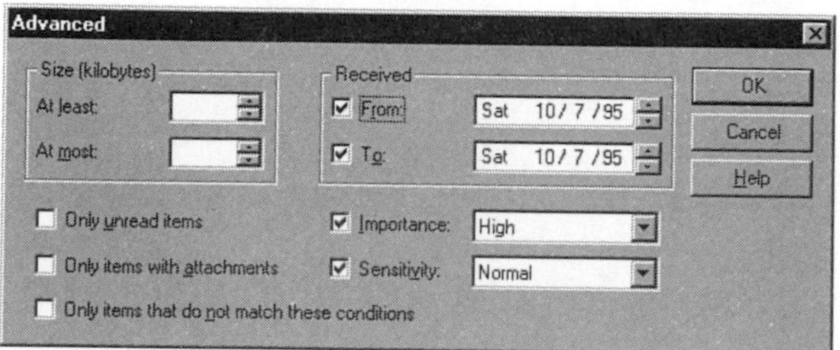

Fig. 17.13
Remote Mail provides advanced options for filtering messages.

The options in the Advanced dialog box are self-explanatory.

Sorting Messages

Remote Mail enables you to control how message headers are sorted and displayed in the Header pane. As in Exchange, you can choose which column to use as the sort key simply by clicking the column's header. As in the Exchange window, clicking a text field uses ascending order. Clicking a numeric or date field uses descending order. To explicitly specify either ascending or descending, right-click the column heading and select the appropriate option from the context menu.

If you prefer to use the menu to set the sort options, choose View, Sort. Remote Mail displays the Sort dialog box shown in figure 17.14. Select the desired sort field from the Sort items by drop-down list. Choose the Ascending or Descending option button as desired, then choose OK.

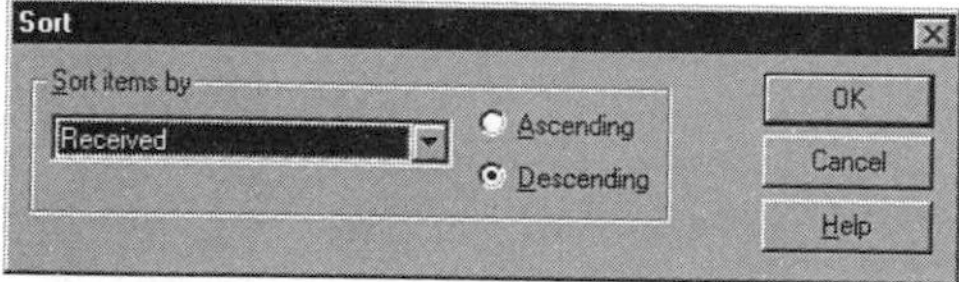

Fig. 17.14
You can choose sort options through the Sort dialog box.

CHAPTER 18

Using Microsoft Fax

by Jim Boyce

Windows 95 includes a fax application that enables you to send and receive faxes through a fax modem. This fax capability is accomplished through an Exchange service provider called Microsoft Fax. Because it works with Exchange, Microsoft Fax processes fax messages like your e-mail messages—incoming faxes are placed in the Exchange Inbox, and outgoing faxes are processed through the Outbox. Microsoft Fax makes use of other Exchange features such as the Personal Address Book, enabling you to store fax addresses along with e-mail addresses.

In this chapter, you learn how to

- Install and configure Microsoft Fax
- Send and receive faxes
- Share a fax modem
- Work with cover pages

As you use Microsoft Fax, you'll realize that it is not a full-featured fax program. For example, Microsoft Fax doesn't include the capability to annotate or modify faxes that you have received, nor does it include OCR (Optical Character Recognition) that would enable you to convert faxes to text-based documents.

Installing and Configuring Microsoft Fax

It's possible that you installed Microsoft Fax when you installed Windows 95, because Microsoft Fax is one of the options you can choose during setup. To determine if Microsoft Fax is installed, open the Control Panel and double-click the Add/Remove Programs icon. Click the Windows Setup tab to display the Windows Setup page. Scroll through the Components list to locate the Microsoft Fax item. If the item contains a check, Microsoft Fax is already installed on your PC. If you didn't install Microsoft Fax during setup, you can easily add it to your system. The next section explains how.

Installing Microsoft Fax

As with other Windows 95 components, you can add Microsoft Fax by using the Add/Remove Programs object in the Control Panel. To add Microsoft Fax, follow these steps:

1. Open the Control Panel and double-click the Add/Remove Programs icon.
2. Click the Windows Setup tab to display the Windows Setup page (see fig. 18.1).

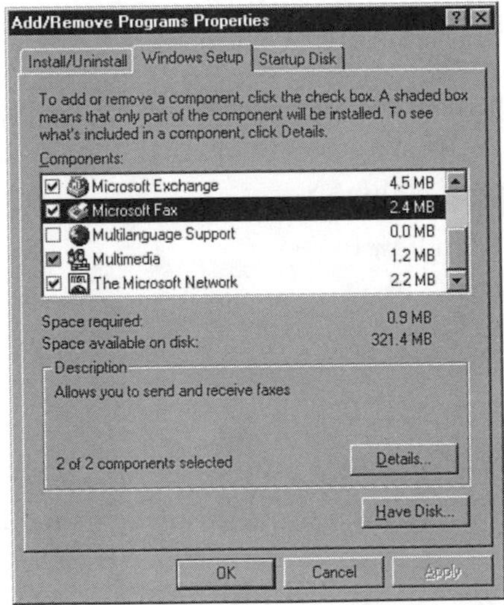

Fig. 18.1
Install Microsoft Fax and other Windows 95 components using the Windows Setup page.

3. Scroll through the Components list, locate Microsoft Fax, and enable its check box.
4. Choose OK. Windows 95 adds the necessary files, prompting you for the Windows 95 CD or disks, if necessary.

Adding Microsoft Fax to a Profile

After you install Microsoft Fax, you need to add it to an Exchange profile. You do so in essentially the same manner that you add other service providers to a profile. The following steps help you add Microsoft Fax to a profile:

1. Open the Control Panel and double-click the Mail and Fax icon.
2. Select the profile in which you want to add Microsoft Fax; then choose Properties.
3. Click the Add button to display the Add Service to Profile dialog box (see fig. 18.2).

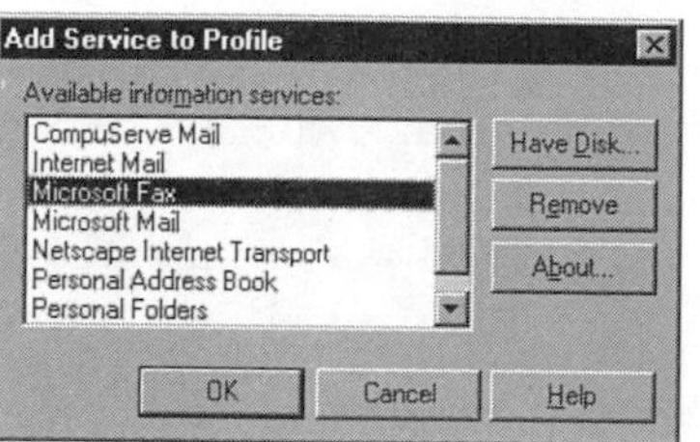

Fig. 18.2 Select Microsoft Fax from the list of providers available to Exchange.

4. Click the Microsoft Fax item in the list of available services; then click OK.
5. Windows 95 prompts you to specify whether you want to enter the Microsoft Fax configuration information. Click Yes. Windows 95 then displays the Microsoft Fax Properties sheet, shown in figure 18.3.

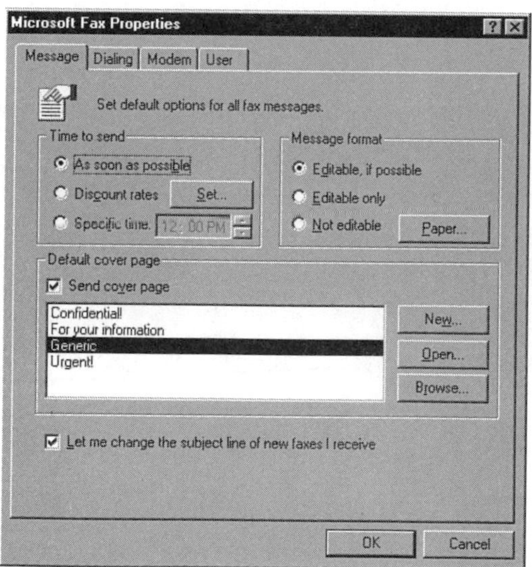

Fig. 18.3 Configure Microsoft Fax using the Microsoft Fax Properties sheet.

6. Set Microsoft Fax properties in each of the four property pages based on the explanations in the following sections.

Setting User Properties

The User property page for Microsoft Fax lets you specify information about yourself and your fax number. Much of this information Microsoft Fax uses to build cover pages for your outgoing faxes. The following list explains the properties you can set on the User page:

- *Your full name.* Enter your name as you want it to appear on your fax cover pages as the sender.
- *Country.* Select from this drop-down list the country from which you are calling. This enables Microsoft Fax to determine when it must add a country code to the dialing string for outgoing faxes.
- *Fax Number.* Enter the number of your fax machine, including the area code. The area code and prefix enable Exchange to determine whether the area code is required in the dialing string for outgoing faxes. This information all appears on the fax cover page, as well as the connection information senders see when they connect to your fax modem.
- *Mailbox.* If your LAN provides fax routing to a mailbox, enter the mailbox name in this text box.
- *Company.* Enter the name of your company as you want it to appear on cover pages.
- *Title.* Enter your job title.
- *Department.* Enter your department, if applicable.
- *Office Location.* Enter some text that describes the location of your office.
- *Home Telephone Number.* Enter your home phone number (if you want it included on fax cover pages).
- *Office telephone number.* Enter your office voice number as you want it to appear on cover pages.
- *Address.* Enter your address as you want it to appear on cover pages.

Note

You must supply your full name, country, and fax number. All other properties are optional.

Setting Modem Properties

After you specify properties on the User page, click on the Modem tab to display the Modem property page (see fig. 18.4). The Modem page enables you to specify the fax modem you want to use with Microsoft Fax, as well as configure and share the fax modem (see "Sharing a Fax Modem" later in this chapter for more information).

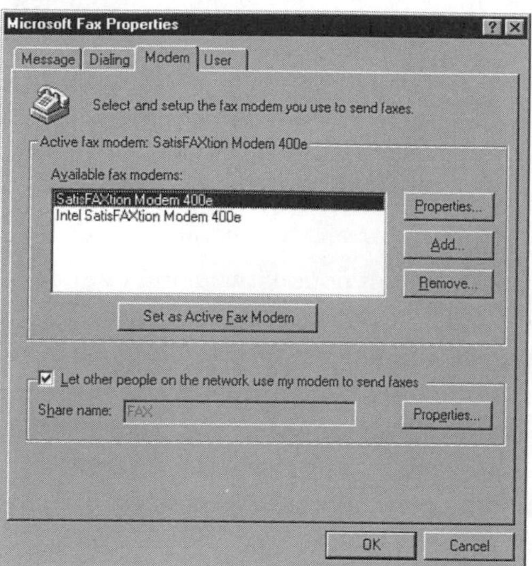

Fig. 18.4
Use the Modem page to specify and configure a modem for Microsoft Fax.

From the Available Fax Modems list, select the modem you want Microsoft Fax to use. If you need to add a new fax modem, click the Add button and follow the procedure explained in Chapter 3, "Configuring Modems and Ports," to add the modem.

To set the modem as the active fax modem, click the Set as Active Fax Modem button. Then click the Properties button to display the Fax Modem Properties sheet, shown in figure 18.5.

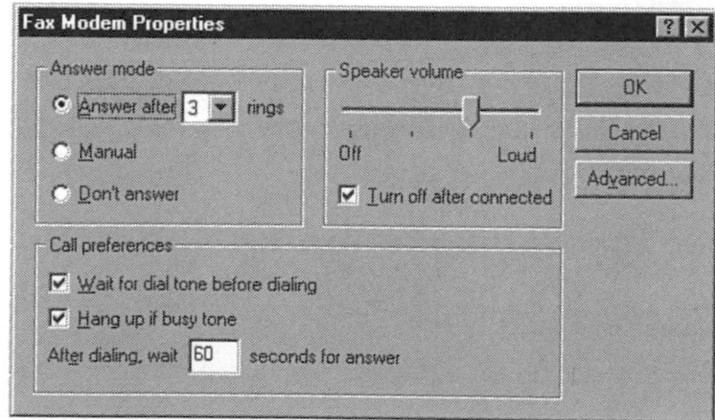

Fig. 18.5
Configure fax modem settings with the Fax Modem Properties sheet.

The following list explains the options on the Fax Modem Properties sheet:

- *Answer after xx Rings*. Choose this option button if you want Microsoft Fax to automatically answer the phone when a call comes in. Use the drop-down list to specify how many times the phone will ring before Microsoft Fax answers the call.
- *Manual*. Choose this option button if you want Microsoft Fax to monitor the fax modem for incoming calls, but not to answer the phone. When the line rings, Microsoft Fax displays a simple dialog box informing you that the line is ringing. Click the Answer button in this dialog box to have Microsoft Fax answer the call.
- *Don't Answer*. Choose this option if you don't want Microsoft Fax to monitor the port for incoming calls. Choose this option if you have other communications programs (such as a 16-bit Windows communications program) and want these programs to be able to access the port when Microsoft Fax is running, or if your fax and phone are on the same line and you're not expecting a fax. Choosing either the Answer or Manual options prevents non-TAPI communications programs from accessing the port.
- *Speaker Volume*. Use this slider to control the modem's speaker volume.
- *Turn Off after Connected*. Enable this check box to have Microsoft Fax turn off the modem's speaker after a connection is established.
- *Wait for Dial Tone before Dialing*. Enable this check box if you want Microsoft Fax to detect a dial tone before it attempts to dial.
- *Hang Up if Busy Tone*. Enable this check box to allow Microsoft Fax to detect a busy signal when attempting to send outgoing faxes.
- *After Dialing, Wait xx Seconds for Answer*. Specify in this text box a timeout value for Microsoft Fax to wait for a connection before terminating the connection attempt.

Tip

If Microsoft Fax is running, a fax machine icon appears on the Tray. To set properties for your current fax session, right-click the fax machine icon and choose Modem Properties. Microsoft Fax then displays the Fax Modem Properties sheet, enabling you to control the modem settings. This is useful when, for example, you want to turn off auto-answer so that a 16-bit Windows application can access the modem.

You also can set various advanced properties for the fax modem. To do so, click the Advanced button to display the Advanced dialog box, shown in figure 18.6.

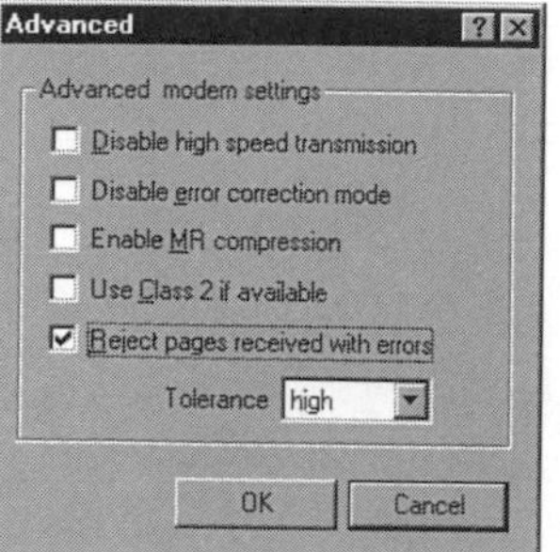

Fig. 18.6
Set additional fax modem properties with the Advanced dialog box.

The following list explains the properties on the Advanced dialog box:

- *Disable High-Speed Transmission.* Enable this check box to prevent Microsoft Fax from connecting at speeds higher than 9600 bps. Enabling this setting can overcome some connection and transmission problems, particularly with noisy phone lines.
- *Disable Error Correction Mode.* Enable this check box to prevent Microsoft Fax from using the modem's error correction protocol. Turning off error correction can overcome transmission problems in some cases.
- *Enable MR Compression.* Enable this check box if you want Microsoft Fax to use the modem's compression capability to compress outgoing faxes. This speeds transmission, but makes the fax quality more susceptible to line noise.
- *Use Class 2 if Available.* Enable this check box if you want Microsoft Fax to operate the modem as a Class 2 device (the modem must support Class 2 operation). In general, only enable this setting if your modem supports both Class 1 and Class 2, and you experience problems when sending or receiving faxes in Class 1 mode. If you enable this setting, you won't be able to send attached files as editable files or use compression.
- *Reject Pages Received with Errors.* Enable this check box if you want incoming pages that contain errors to be rejected. Microsoft Fax will request a retransmission of the page from the sender.
- *Tolerance.* Use this drop-down list to specify the level of tolerance Microsoft Fax uses when determining whether to reject a page that contains errors.

After you specify the Advanced modem settings, click OK; then click OK to close the Fax Modem Properties sheet.

> **Tip**
>
> The check box labeled Let Other People on the Network Use My Modem to Send Faxes enables you to share your fax modem with others. For an explanation of sharing a fax modem, refer to "Sharing a Fax Modem" later in this chapter.

Setting Dialing Properties

The Dialing property page (see fig. 18.7) lets you control how Microsoft Fax dials outgoing calls.

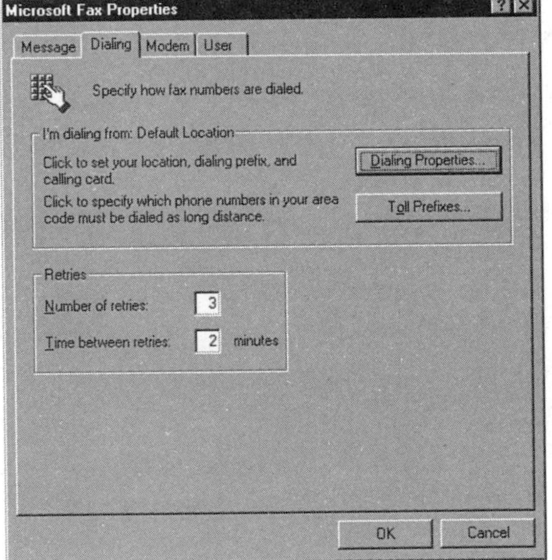

Fig. 18.7
Use the Dialing Properties page to control how Microsoft Fax establishes outgoing calls.

The Dialing Properties button displays a standard Dialing Properties sheet you can use to specify your area code, country, calling card settings, and other properties. For an explanation of setting dialing properties, refer to Chapter 3, "Configuring Modems and Ports," and Chapter 5, "Using HyperTerminal." These two chapters also discuss how to edit the toll prefix list, which you can access by clicking the Toll Prefixes button.

The Number of Retries text box on the Dialing property page lets you specify how many times Microsoft Fax attempts to connect for each outgoing fax. If the number you specify is exceeded, Microsoft Fax aborts the send and places an error message in your Inbox. To specify the number of minutes between each connection attempt, enter a number in the Time between Retries text box.

Setting Message Properties

The Message property page (see fig. 18.8) specifies default settings that control how outgoing faxes are sent. You can override many of these settings when you compose the fax. The Message page also lets you specify whether you can change the description of received faxes.

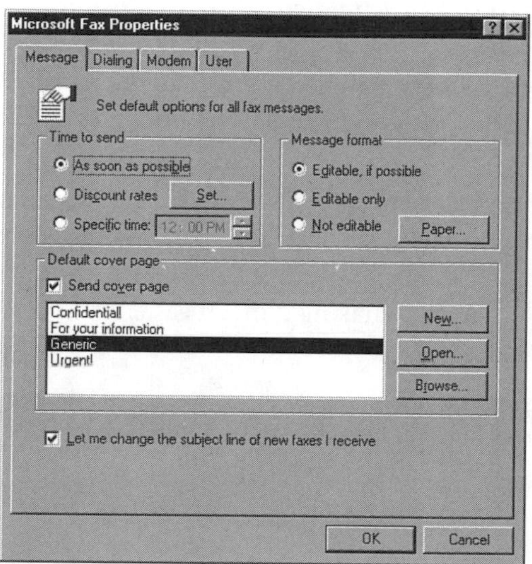

Fig. 18.8
With the Message page, you control how Microsoft Fax sends outgoing faxes.

The following list explains the options you can set in the Message page:

- *As Soon as Possible.* Choose this option button if you want Microsoft Fax to transmit faxes as soon after you compose them as possible. If the modem is available, the fax is usually transmitted within a minute.
- *Discount Rates.* Choose this option if you want Microsoft Fax to hold outgoing faxes until off-peak phone rates take effect. Click on the Set button to specify when off-peak rates are in effect.
- *Specific Time.* Choose this option to cause Microsoft Fax to hold all outgoing faxes until the specified time. Set the trigger time using the accompanying spin control.
- *Message Format.* These options let you specify how Microsoft Fax handles faxes with attached binary files. Choose Editable, if possible to have Microsoft Fax send binary files in e-mail format rather than fax

format if the receiving system supports this type of transfer (such as another Microsoft Fax system). Choose Editable Only to have Microsoft Fax send binary attachments only as files and not in fax format, even if it means the files will not be transferred. Choose Not Editable if you want Microsoft Fax to always send binary attachments in fax format. Click the Paper button to specify properties for paper size, orientation, and resolution.

- *Default Cover Page.* These controls determine whether a cover page is sent with each fax and which cover page is used. Enable the Send Cover Page check box if you want Microsoft Fax to include a cover sheet by default; then choose from the list which cover sheet to use by default. You can override these settings when you compose the fax. There is more information on Cover Pages in "Working with Cover Pages," later in this chapter.
- *Let Me Change the Subject Line of New Faxes I Receive.* Enable this check box if you want to be able to rename a fax you have received. Instead of "Fax from 12345678," for example, you can rename the fax "Request for Sales Information," making it much easier to determine what is contained in a stored fax.

Tip

If you want to customize one of the four standard cover pages included with Microsoft Fax, or create your own cover pages, see "Working with Cover Pages" later in this chapter.

After you've set the Message properties you want to use with Microsoft Fax, choose OK to close the property sheet. Then choose OK to close the profile property sheet.

Troubleshooting

When I add Microsoft Fax to a profile and run Exchange, the Internet Mail provider in the same profile can't access the phone line to connect to my Internet mail server.

The problem is that Microsoft Fax initializes the modem when Exchange starts up, preventing other providers such as Internet Mail from accessing the modem. This happens even if you set Microsoft Fax to not answer the line. The Internet Mail provider can't grab the line to connect to your mail server. Unfortunately, the only thing you can do is use Remote Mail with the Internet Mail provider. For an explanation of how to do that, refer to Chapter 17, "Using Remote Mail."

Sending a Fax

Microsoft Fax makes composing and sending a fax an easy task. The process you use depends on whether you are faxing a document from the application you used to create the document, or are composing a fax from Exchange. The following two sections explain these different methods.

Tip

In addition to the two methods explained in the following sections, you also can use a document's context menu to send it as a fax. To do so, locate the document through My Computer or through Explorer. Right-click the document's icon; then choose Send To, Fax Recipient. Microsoft Fax starts the Compose New Fax wizard to step you through the process of composing the fax. This technique works only with document types supported by OLE-compliant applications.

Faxing from an Application

In many cases, you can fax a document from the application you used to create the document. If you've created a document in Word, for example, you don't have to switch to Exchange to compose the fax. Depending on the application, you'll have one of two options for sending the fax. You can either choose File, Send or File, Print. If you choose File, Send (the better of the two options), a standard Exchange compose window appears with the file embedded in the message body as an icon (see fig. 18.9).

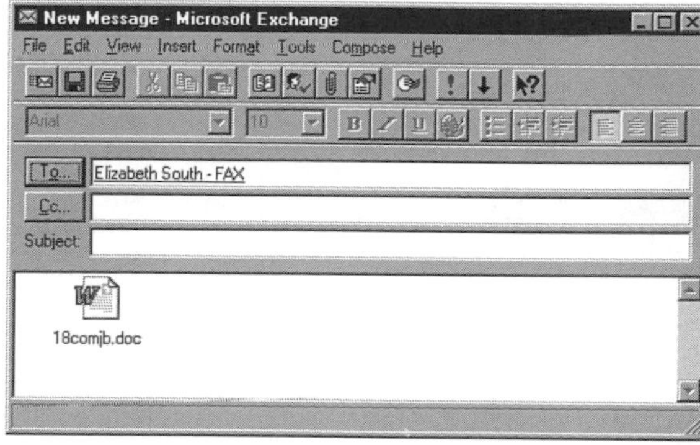

Fig. 18.9 Choose File, Send to embed a document in a new message.

To prepare the fax, click the To button and select a fax address for the message. Then return to the compose window and type a subject in the Subject text box. To set options for the fax, such as the cover sheet to use (if any), choose File, Send Options to display the Send Options dialog box, shown in figure 18.10. The properties on the Send Options dialog box are a combination of the properties on the Microsoft Fax property sheet and options displayed by Microsoft Fax in the fax compose wizard, both of which are discussed earlier in this chapter. After setting the desired options, choose OK to return to the compose window. Set any additional options as desired in the compose window; then click the Send button on the toolbar or choose File, Send to send the fax.

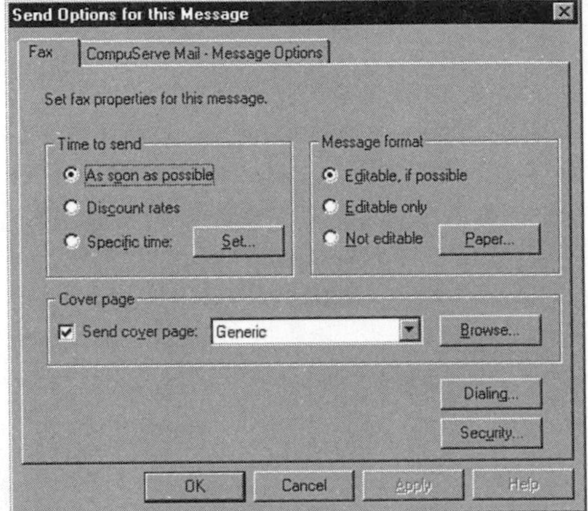

Fig. 18.10
The Send Options dialog box lets you control fax transmission options.

If your application doesn't display a File, Send command, you can either choose File, Print or compose the fax in Exchange. If you choose the Print command, the application displays a standard Print dialog box (or the program's custom Print dialog box in some cases), similar to the one shown in figure 18.11. From the Name drop-down list, choose the Microsoft Fax printer driver. Set any other print options (such as pages to print); then choose OK.

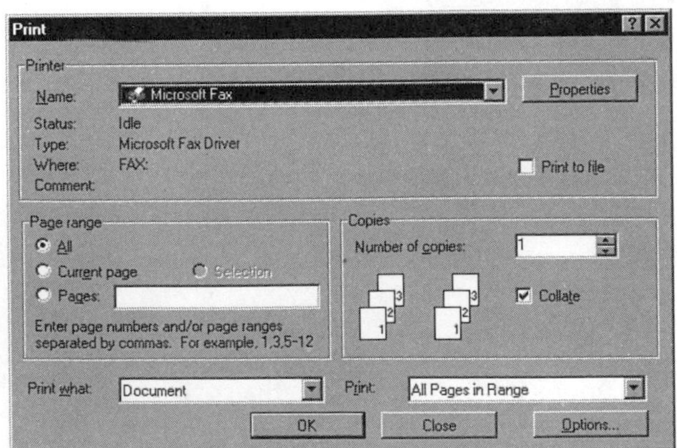

Fig. 18.11
You can print to the Microsoft Fax driver.

Troubleshooting

When I try to print from an application to the Microsoft Fax driver, the application asks me to select a print file name and then prints to a file. But Microsoft Fax never takes over to send the fax.

Although you can print to the Microsoft Fax driver, this is one area in which Microsoft Fax seems to suffer from bugs. In some cases, the application is not able to successfully print to the fax driver. If your application includes a Send command in the File menu, you should use it to fax. If not, save the document; then open Exchange and choose Compose, New Fax to compose the fax as explained in the following section.

Faxing from Exchange

In addition to faxing from an application, you also can compose a fax from within Exchange. To simplify the process, Microsoft Fax provides a wizard that steps you through the process of composing the fax. To use the wizard, follow these steps:

1. In Exchange, choose Compose, New Fax. Microsoft Fax displays a Compose New Fax dialog box that prompts you to specify your dialing location. To choose a different dialing location, click the Dialing Properties button. If the location is correct, click Next.
2. Microsoft Fax then prompts you to specify the phone number for the fax (see fig. 18.12). Enter the information directly in the dialog box or click the Address Book button to select a fax address from your Personal Address Book. After you select the address(es) for the fax, click Next.

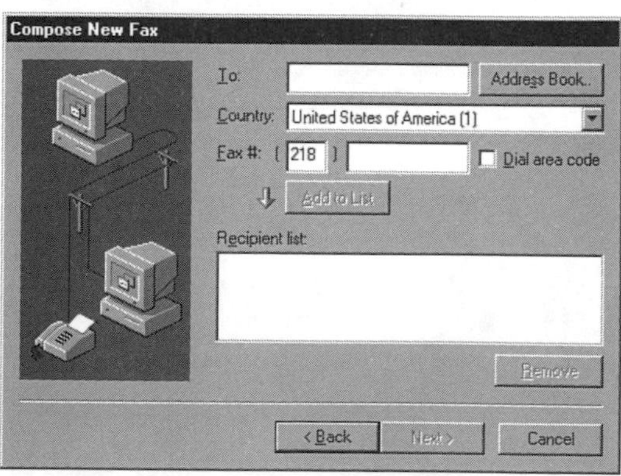

Fig. 18.12
Microsoft Fax prompts you to select or type an address for the fax.

3. Microsoft Fax then prompts you to provide cover sheet information (see fig. 18.13). If you do not want to include a cover page, choose the No option button. To include a cover page, choose the Yes option button; then select a cover sheet from the list.

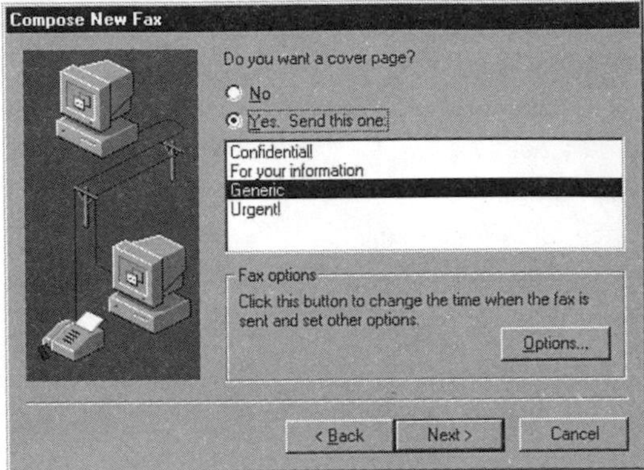

Fig. 18.13 Specify which cover sheet to use and other options for the fax.

4. If you want to set options for the fax such as delivery time, click the Options button. Microsoft Fax displays a property sheet similar to the one previously shown in figure 18.10. After you specify your desired options, choose OK in the Fax property page to return to the wizard; then click Next.
5. The wizard then prompts for a subject and notes for the fax (see fig. 18.14). Type a subject description in the Subject field if you want one included on the cover page. Enter a text message in the Note field to have it included on the cover page. If you want the note sent as a separate page, clear the Start Note on Cover Page check box.

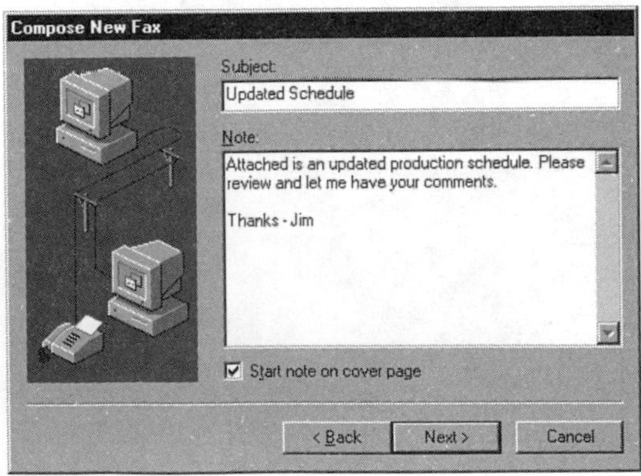

Fig. 18.14 You can include a subject and note for the fax.

Tip

If you don't send a cover page but do include a subject, the subject text appears in the header of the fax. If you include a note but no cover page, the note text is sent as a separate page, essentially like a cover sheet without any graphics.

6. The Compose New Fax wizard then prompts you to select files to include with the fax. Click the Add File button to open a common file dialog box you can use to select files to be included with the fax. Choose Next; then choose Finish after you select all the files you want to include with the fax.

Caution

If you have a document open in its parent application, you might have to close the document before Microsoft Fax will be able to open it for faxing.

After you click Finish, Microsoft Fax begins preparing the fax for transmission. If you have included one or more document files, Microsoft Fax automatically opens the document with the document's parent application and prints the document to the Microsoft Fax driver. The outgoing fax is placed in your Outbox, and is processed according to the options you specified in step 4. If you specified transmission to occur as soon as possible, for example, Microsoft Fax attempts to dial the remote fax recipient as soon as the fax modem becomes available.

Receiving a Fax

In addition to sending faxes, Microsoft Fax enables your PC to receive incoming faxes through your fax modem. You can receive faxes manually or automatically, depending on your needs. The following sections explain these two options.

Receiving Faxes Automatically

It is likely that you will want Microsoft Fax to monitor for incoming faxes and receive those faxes automatically, enabling unattended receipt of faxes. You can leave your PC and Microsoft Fax running all the time, enabling others to send you faxes at any time.

The only real disadvantage to using automatic reception is that Microsoft Fax must monitor the modem port continuously, preventing all 16-bit Windows and DOS communications programs from accessing the fax modem, and also preventing some Windows 95 communications from accessing the port. The Internet Mail provider, for example, can't access the port to check your Internet mail if Microsoft Fax is also running. You can, however, turn off Microsoft Fax's monitoring without shutting down Exchange. This enables you to keep Exchange running while enabling other applications to use the fax modem.

To configure Microsoft Fax to receive faxes automatically, follow these steps:

1. If Exchange and Microsoft Fax are not running, open the Control Panel and double-click the Mail and Fax icon. If Exchange and Microsoft Fax are running, right-click the fax machine icon on the Tray; then choose Properties from the context menu (and skip to step 4).
2. Select Microsoft Fax from the list of installed providers; then click the Properties button.
3. Click the Modem tab to display the Modem property page, select the fax modem, and then click the Properties button to display the Fax Modem Properties sheet, shown in figure 18.15.

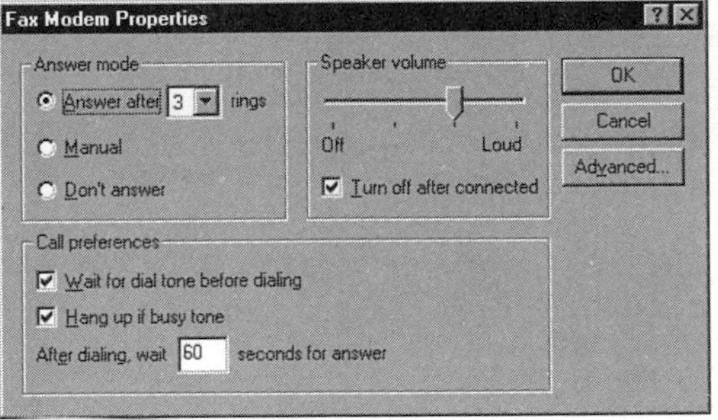

Fig. 18.15
Choose the Answer after *xx* Rings option to enable automatic fax reception.

4. Choose the Answer after *xx* Rings option button; then select from the drop-down list the number of times the line will ring before Microsoft Fax answers the call. Choose OK; then close the remaining property sheets (if displayed) by choosing OK or Close in each one.

When the line rings, Microsoft Fax detects the ring. After the specified number of rings, Microsoft Fax picks up the line and attempts to establish a connection with the calling system. If the connection succeeds, Microsoft Fax begins receiving the fax and places the fax in your Inbox when reception is complete. You then can open the Inbox and double-click on the new fax message. Microsoft Fax opens a Fax Viewer window to display the fax pages (see fig. 18.16).

> **Note**
>
> If Microsoft Fax displays a message window containing an icon instead of the first fax page, double-click the fax icon in the message body to open the Fax Viewer.

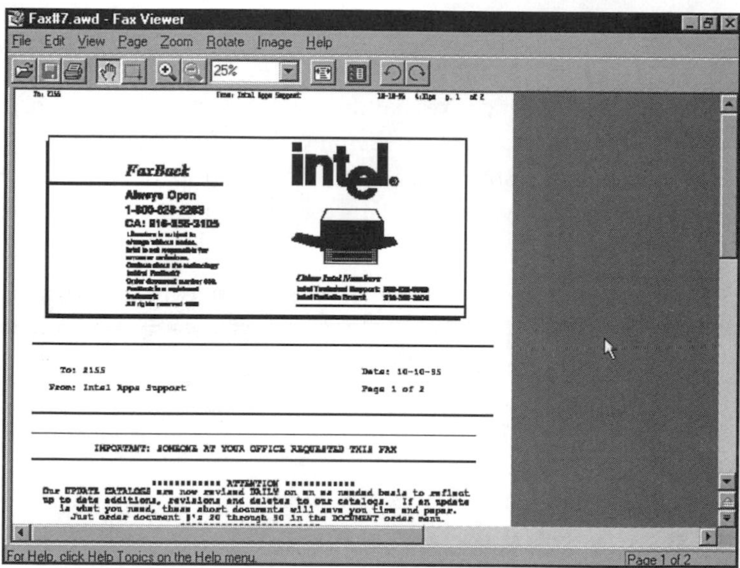

Fig. 18.16 Microsoft Fax provides a limited number of tools to view and manipulate a fax.

The Fax Viewer provides a limited set of tools to enable you to view the fax page-by-page, rotate the pages, zoom in or out, and print the pages. Microsoft Fax, however, doesn't include tools for editing the fax. For that, you need a third-party fax application such as WinFax.

Receiving Faxes Manually

If you seldom receive faxes or want to control when your faxes are received, you can place Microsoft Fax in manual receive mode. When in this mode, Microsoft Fax monitors the port for incoming calls but doesn't answer automatically. Instead, when the line rings, Microsoft Fax displays a dialog box telling you that the fax line is ringing. If you want Microsoft Fax to answer the call, click the Answer Now button in the dialog box. Microsoft Fax then picks up the line and attempts to establish the connection. This technique will also work if you have already picked up the handset.

To place Microsoft Fax in manual receive mode, follow the steps in the previous section for placing Microsoft Fax in automatic receive mode. When the Fax Modem Properties sheet appears, select the Manual option button; then choose OK.

Tip

You also can initiate a fax reception by right-clicking the fax machine icon on the Tray and choosing Answer Now from the context menu.

Turning Off Fax Reception

If you want to be able to send faxes but don't want Microsoft Fax to receive faxes, or you want to make the fax modem available to other applications, you need to turn off Microsoft Fax's fax receive. To do so, open the Fax Modem Properties page as previously explained and choose the Don't Answer option button. Then choose OK.

Tip

The quickest way to open the Fax Modem Properties sheet is to right-click the fax machine icon in the Tray and choose Properties from its context menu.

Sharing a Fax Modem

With Microsoft Fax, other people on your network who also are running Microsoft Fax can send faxes through your fax modem. Microsoft Fax doesn't actually share your fax modem, but instead shares a folder on your PC. When another person on the network sends a fax directed to your fax modem, their Microsoft Fax program renders the fax file and places it in your shared folder. Microsoft Fax on your PC then takes over, sending the fax. So Microsoft Fax acts essentially like a fax spooler—when faxes appear in your shared fax folder, Microsoft Fax processes them in the order received.

Sharing your fax modem is easy:

1. Open the Control Panel and double-click the Mail and Fax icon.
2. Select Microsoft Fax from the list of installed services, and then click the Properties button.
3. Click the Modem tab to display the Modem property page (see fig. 18.17).

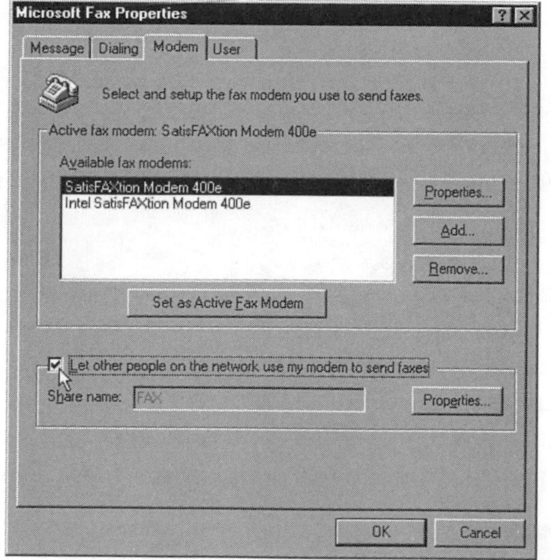

Fig. 18.17
You can share your modem from the Modem property page.

4. Place a check in the check box labeled Let other People on the Network Use My Modem to Send Faxes.
5. Microsoft Fax then displays a simple dialog box prompting you to select the drive on which the shared folder will reside. Select a drive and choose OK. Microsoft Fax creates a folder named NetFax on the selected drive and shares the folder under the name FAX.
6. If you want to view or modify the share properties for the shared NetFax folder, click the Properties button. Microsoft Fax displays a property sheet similar to the one shown in figure 18.18. Modify properties as desired, and then choose OK. Notice that you must leave the Shared As option selected. However, you can change the share name if you want.

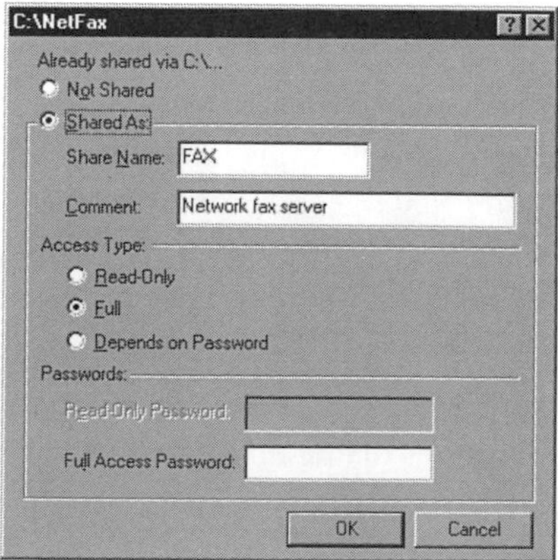

Fig. 18.18
You can view and modify share properties for the shared fax folder.

7. Choose OK to close the Microsoft Fax property sheet; then choose OK to close the profile property sheet.

Now other users can begin sending faxes through your fax modem. Remember, however, that your PC must be running and connected to the network and your fax modem must be turned on for others to fax through your PC.

Sending Secure Faxes

Microsoft Fax provides a set of security features you can use to transmit confidential information. These security features don't work when sending a fax to a fax machine, but they do provide security when faxing to other Microsoft Fax users. You can password protect a fax, encrypt the fax, and add a digital signature to the fax. The following sections explain these features.

Tip

It's important to emphasize that Microsoft Fax's security features don't apply to faxes transmitted to a fax machine. These faxes are rendered on the recipient's fax machine without requiring the recipient to provide a password or encryption key (because most fax machines have no facility for this type of security). Security in Microsoft Fax works only when sending to other Microsoft Fax-compatible systems. In addition, security isn't used if you send a fax as non-editable, even if you send it to another Microsoft Fax system.

Protecting a Fax with a Password

The simplest form of security in Microsoft Fax is password protection. You can scramble an outgoing fax based on a password, and the recipient must supply the password to view the fax. This means you must provide the password to the fax recipient.

To password protect a fax, use the following procedure:

1. If you compose the fax using the Compose New Fax wizard, step through the wizard until it prompts you for a cover page. Then click the Options button to display the Fax property page. If you are faxing from an application, first choose File, Send in the application; then choose File, Send Options from the New Message window to display the Fax property page.
2. From the Fax property page, click the Security button to display the Message Security Options dialog box (see fig. 18.19).

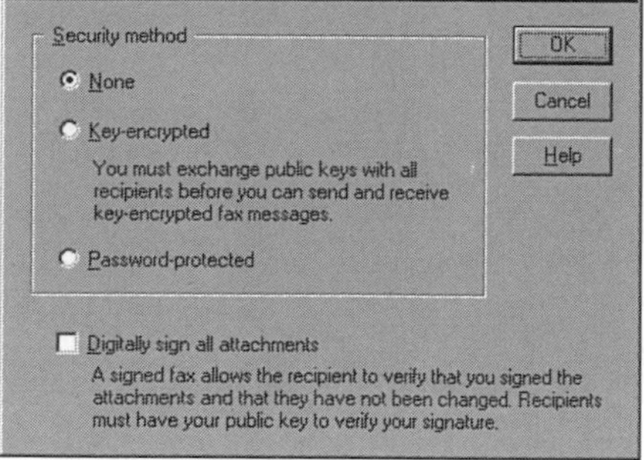

Fig. 18.19
Select one of three security methods from the Message Security Options dialog box.

3. Click the Password-protected option button; then choose OK.
4. Microsoft Fax prompts you to enter the password. Enter the password in the Password and Confirm Password text boxes; then choose OK.
5. Continue with the process of composing the fax as you normally would.
6. Notify the recipient of the password.

Sending Key-Encrypted Faxes

Microsoft Fax provides a higher level of security than simple password protection through the use of encryption keys. When you use encryption keys, Microsoft Fax assigns two keys to you—a public key and a private key. You then share your public key with others with whom you want to exchange secure faxes. When you send a key-encrypted fax, Microsoft Fax uses your private key and the recipient's public key to encrypt the fax. At the receiving end, Microsoft Fax uses the recipient's private key and your public key to decrypt the message.

Tip

Encryption keys are just passwords. You specify your public key, and Exchange assigns your private key automatically.

Creating a Set of Keys

The first step in using key-encryption is to create your keys. To do so, follow these steps:

1. In Exchange, choose Tools, Microsoft Fax Tools, Advanced Security to display the Advanced Fax Security dialog box (see fig. 18.20).

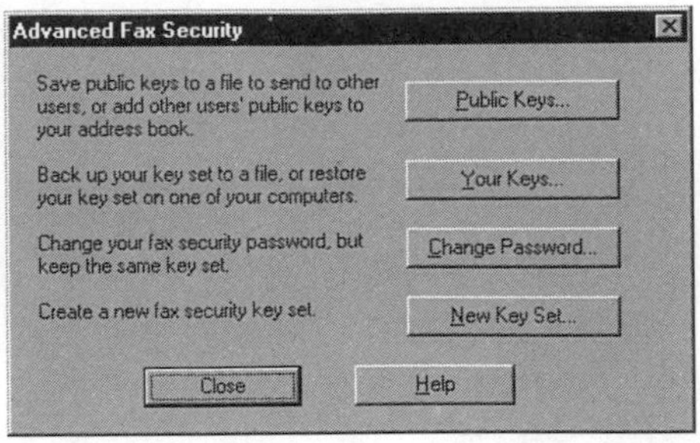

Fig. 18.20
Use the Advanced Fax Security dialog box to manage encryption keys.

2. Click the New Key Set button to display the Fax Security - New Key Set dialog box (see fig. 18.21).

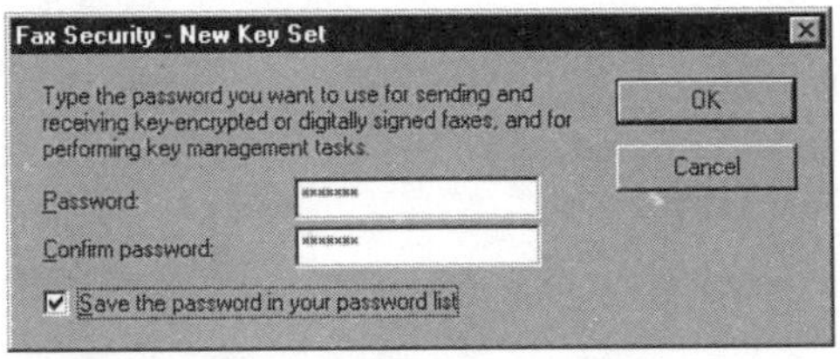

Fig. 18.21
Enter your public key in the Fax Security - New Key Set dialog box.

3. In the Password and Confirm Password text boxes, type the password that you want to use as your public key. If you want the password stored in your password cache, enable the check box labeled Save the Password in Your Password List. Then choose OK. Microsoft Fax creates your private key automatically.
4. Choose Close to close the Advanced Fax Security dialog box.

Publishing Public Keys

After you create your key set, you need to send your public key to others to whom you will be sending encrypted faxes. Follow these steps to distribute your key:

1. In Exchange, choose Tools, Microsoft Fax Tools, Advanced Security.
2. Click the Public Keys button to display the Fax Security - Managing Public Keys dialog box (see fig. 18.22).

Fig. 18.22
Use the Fax Security - Managing Public Keys dialog box to export and import encryption keys.

3. Click the Save button to display the Save Public Keys dialog box (see fig. 18.23).

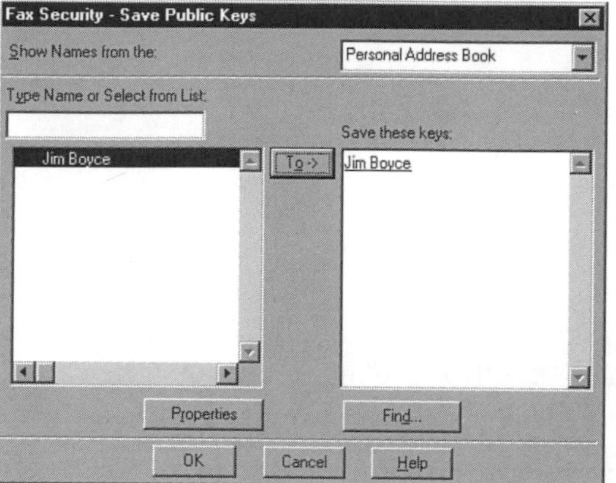

Fig. 18.23
Select the users whose keys you want to export.

4. Select your own public key from the list at the left side of the dialog box, as well as any other users whose keys you want to distribute; then click the To button.
5. When you're satisfied with the list, click OK, and Microsoft Fax displays a standard file save dialog box. Save the file to your hard disk if you'll be transmitting the keys through e-mail, or save it to a floppy if you want to send the recipient(s) a floppy disk containing the key(s).
6. Choose Close, and then Close again to close the security dialog boxes.

Importing Keys

To decrypt incoming faxes, you need to add the sender's public key to your address book. To import keys into your address book, open Exchange and choose Tools, Microsoft Fax Tools, Advanced Security. Click the Public Keys button to display the Fax Security - Managing Public Keys dialog box. Click Add, and Microsoft Fax displays a standard file open dialog box. Select the file containing the key(s) you want to add; then choose Open. Microsoft Fax then displays the Add Public Keys dialog box, shown in figure 18.24.

Tip

Encryption key files have a file extension of AWP.

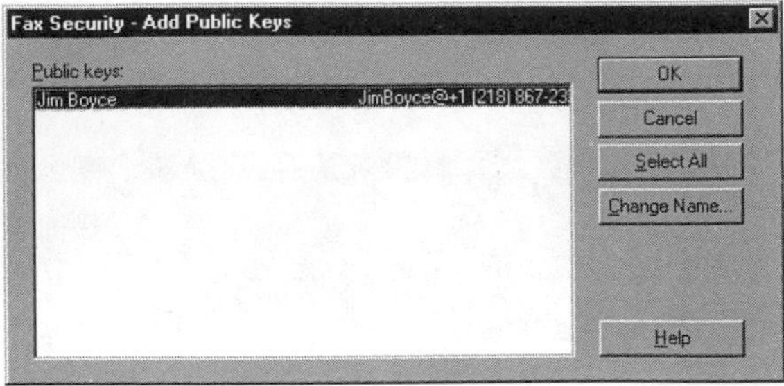

Fig. 18.24 From the list, select the names of the people whose keys you want to add to your address book.

From the list of names in the Add Public Keys dialog box, select the names of the people whose keys you want to add to your address book. To add all the names, click Select All. When you're finished selecting names, click OK. Then close the Managing Public Keys and Advanced Fax Security dialog boxes.

> **Note**
>
> You can remove user keys from your address book with the Managing Public Keys dialog box. You also can change the name for the key entry in your address book from this dialog box.

Sending an Encrypted Fax

After you publish your public key, you're ready to send a key-encrypted fax. To do so, follow these steps:

1. If you compose the fax using the Compose New Fax wizard, step through the wizard until it prompts you for a cover page. Then click the Options button to display the Fax property page. If you are faxing from an application, first choose File, Send in the application; then choose File, Send Options from the New Message window to display the Fax property page.
2. From the Fax property page, click the Security button to display the Message Security Options dialog box.
3. Click the Key-encrypted option button; then choose OK.
4. Choose OK to close the Fax property sheet; then complete the fax as you normally would. Microsoft Fax transmits the fax using key encryption.

Using Digital Signatures

A digital signature serves much like a notarized signature, proving that you are the true sender of the fax. The digital signature also prevents anyone but you from modifying the document while it is being sent.

Using a digital signature is easy. The first step is to create your key set as previously explained. When you compose the fax, open the Fax property page and click the Security button. Place a check in the check box labeled Digitally Sign All Attachments; then choose OK. Complete the fax process as you normally would.

Note

A digital signature is not a scanned copy of your physical signature. It is simply a unique encryption key that identifies the message as having been sent by you.

Requesting a Fax

Microsoft Fax includes a useful feature to help you retrieve documents and files from remote systems. You can retrieve faxes from fax machines, fax-on-demand systems (fax-back systems), and other information services that support Group 3 poll-retrieve, which is a standard that enables fax servers to respond to requests for faxes. Some remote systems enable you to retrieve binary files, enabling you to retrieve drivers, software updates, and other information through Microsoft Fax.

To request a fax or file, open Exchange and choose Tools, Microsoft Fax Tools, Request a Fax. Microsoft Fax starts the Request a Fax wizard, shown in figure 18.25.

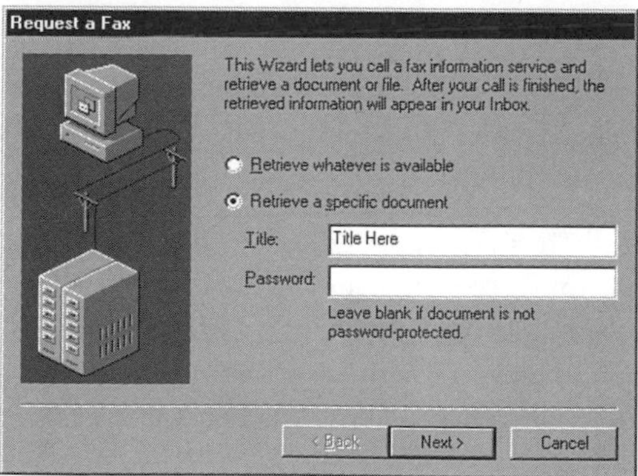

Fig. 18.25
With Microsoft Fax you can request faxes and files from systems that support Group 3 poll-retrieve.

To request the default fax or file from the remote system, choose the option button labeled Retrieve Whatever is Available. Often, this default document provides a directory of the documents that you can retrieve from the service.

If you want to retrieve a specific document, choose the Retrieve a Specific Document option button. Then type the title of the document in the Title text box and a password in the Password text box, if necessary. Then choose OK.

Request a Fax then prompts you to specify the fax number for the remote fax system, just as it does when you send a regular fax. Enter the address or select it from your address book, and then click Next.

Microsoft Fax then prompts you to specify when you want to connect. Specify the connection time and click Next; then click Finish to complete the fax request. At the time you specified, Microsoft Fax will connect to the remote fax system and retrieve the document.

Working with Cover Pages

Microsoft Fax includes four standard cover pages you can send along with your faxes—Confidential, For Your Information, Urgent, and Generic. These cover pages include fields that Microsoft Fax fills in automatically when you send the fax. For example, the cover pages include your name, the recipient's name, address information, and other data you supplied when you configured Microsoft Fax. These standard cover pages also include graphics to spice up the cover pages.

Microsoft Fax includes a utility that lets you modify these standard cover pages or create new ones. To start the Cover Page Editor, choose Start, Programs, Accessories, Fax, Cover Page Editor. The Fax Cover Page Editor program window appears (see fig. 18.26).

The Fax Cover Page Editor is easy to use, so this chapter doesn't explain the editor in detail. Instead, the following tips will help you find and use the features you need in the editor.

- *Inserting fields.* The Cover Page Editor lets you insert a selection of predefined fields on the cover page. The data for these fields comes from your user information, the recipient's address entry, and other data you provide when you compose the fax. Microsoft Fax fills in these fields automatically when you compose the fax. Table 18.1 lists the fields you can use.
- *Drawing graphics and text.* The Cover Page Editor includes a selection of tools for drawing text and graphics on the cover page. These tools are located in the drawing toolbar.

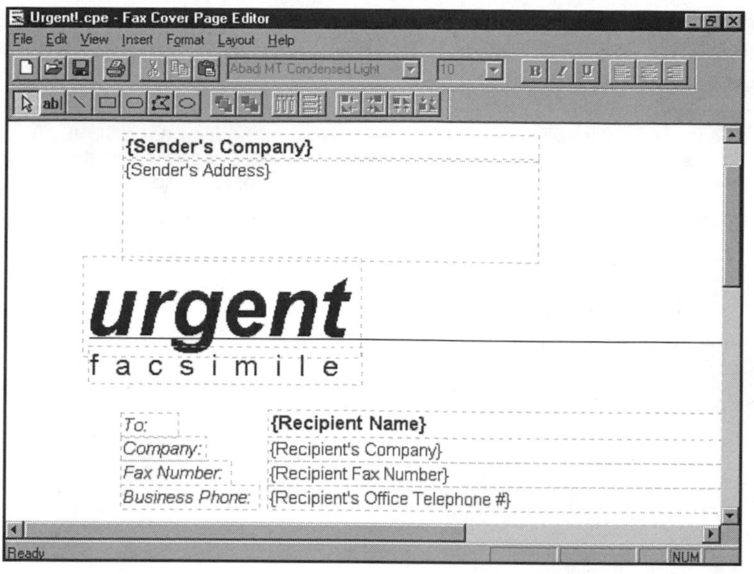

Fig. 18.26
Use the Fax Cover Page Editor to create and modify fax cover pages.

- *Inserting graphics.* You might want to include a company logo or other graphic on the cover page. You can insert a bitmap, Windows metafile, or other graphics types by choosing Insert, Object.
- *Using foreground and background properties.* Graphical and text elements can overlap one another on the cover page. Use the Bring to Front and Send to Back commands on the Layout menu to move objects between the foreground and background. If you want to place some text on a logo image, for example, send the logo to the background and bring the text to the foreground.
- *Using a grid and alignment.* Choose View, Grid Lines to turn on a non-printing grid you can use to align elements on the cover page. Use the Layout menu to align elements on the page.
- *Moving elements.* To move an element, just click it and drag it to its new location.
- *Using formatting.* You can format text with various fonts and styles, but remember to use a font that faxes well. Script and other fancy fonts often are not very legible when transmitted as a fax. Also, use font sizes of 10 points or larger to make sure that the text is legible when faxed.
- *Using the scrap area.* At the right of the page area is a gray scrap area. You can drag elements from the page onto this area as a "holding area" when you are moving elements and creating the cover page. Any elements that you leave in the scrap area will not print or be transmitted with the cover page.

Table 18.1 Fax Cover Page Information Fields

Type	Available Fields
Recipient	Name, Fax Number, Company, Street Address, City, State, Zip Code, Country, Title, Department, Office Location, Home Telephone Number, Office Telephone Number, To: List, and Cc: List
Sender	Name, Fax Number, Company, Address, Title, Department, Office Location, Home Telephone Number, and Office Telephone Number
Message	Note, Subject, Time Sent, Number of Pages, and Number of Attachments

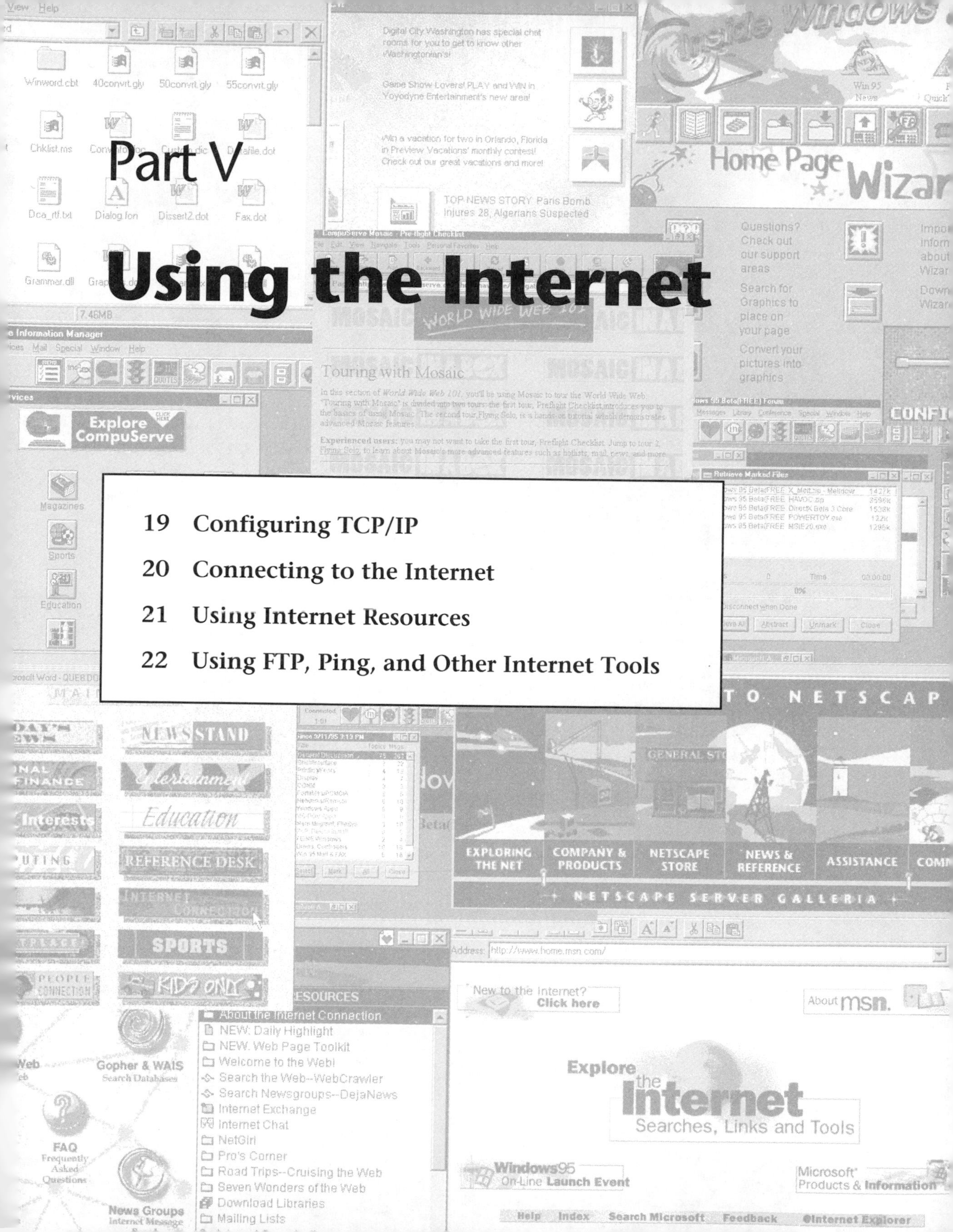

Part V

Using the Internet

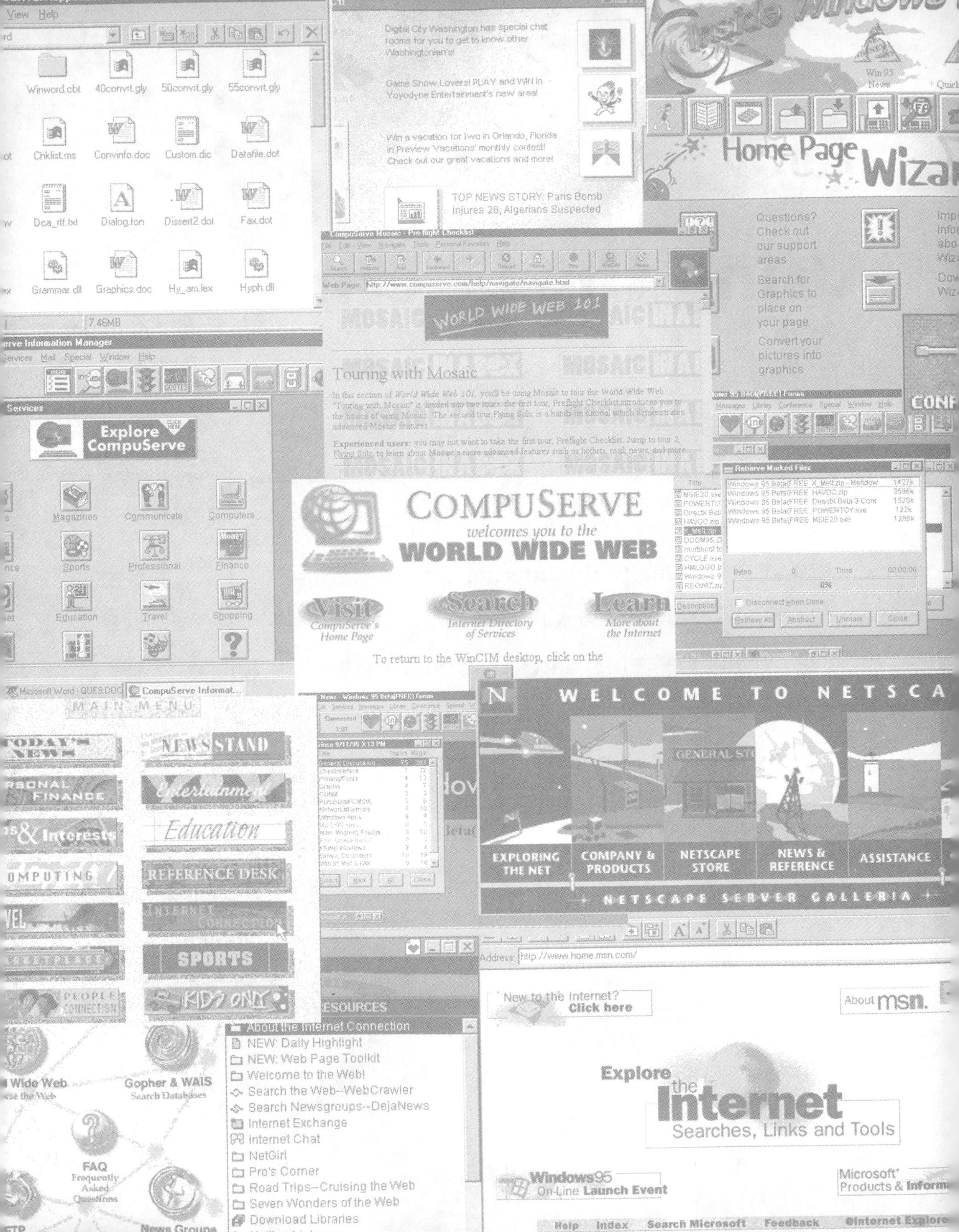

Digital City Washington has special chat rooms for you to get to know other Washingtonian's!
Game Show Lovers! PLAY and WIN in Yoyodyne Entertainment's new area!
Win a vacation for two in Orlando, Florida in Preview Vacations' monthly contest! Check out our great vacations and more!
TOP NEWS STORY: Paris Bomb Injures 28, Algerians Suspected
Home Page Wizar
Questions? Check out our support areas
Search for Graphics to place on your page
Convert your pictures into graphics
WORLD WIDE WEB 101
Touring with Mosaic
Explore CompuServe
Magazines
Communicate
Computers
Sports
Professional
Finance
Education
Travel
Shopping
COMPUSERVE
welcomes you to the
WORLD WIDE WEB
Visit
CompuServe's Home Page
Search
Internet Directory of Services
Learn
More about the Internet
To return to the WinCIM desktop, click on the
Retrieve Marked Files
WELCOME TO NETSCA
EXPLORING THE NET
COMPANY & PRODUCTS
NETSCAPE STORE
NEWS & REFERENCE
ASSISTANCE
NETSCAPE SERVER GALLERIA
MAIN MENU
NEWSSTAND
Entertainment
Education
REFERENCE DESK
INTERNET CONNECTION
SPORTS
KIDS ONLY
PEOPLE CONNECTION
Address: http://www.home.msn.com/
New to the Internet? Click here
About msn.
Explore the Internet
Searches, Links and Tools
Windows95 On-Line Launch Event
Help
Index
Search Microsoft
Feedback
RESOURCES
About the Internet Connection
NEW: Daily Highlight
NEW: Web Page Toolkit
Welcome to the Web!
Search the Web--WebCrawler
Search Newsgroups--DejaNews
Internet Exchange
Internet Chat
NetGirl
Pro's Corner
Road Trips--Cruising the Web
Seven Wonders of the Web
Download Libraries
Mailing Lists
Gopher & WAIS
Search Databases
FAQ
Frequently Asked Questions
News Groups

CHAPTER 19

Configuring TCP/IP

by Jim Boyce

Although the Internet has existed since the 1960s, it has only recently become widely popular outside academic, government, and military circles. The Internet's explosive growth in the year leading up to the release of Windows 95 stimulated a strong demand for support of TCP/IP (Transfer Control Protocol/Internet Protocol) and Internet-related utilities and programs. Windows 95 offers a set of foundational components and general utilities that make it an excellent platform for TCP/IP internetworking.

This chapter helps you understand, configure, and use TCP/IP to provide connectivity between computers on your LAN as well as a connection to the Internet.

In this chapter, you also learn how to

- Install and configure TCP/IP in Windows 95
- Use Hosts and Lmhosts files for name resolution

This chapter helps you configure and use TCP/IP and begin connecting to the Internet. To learn about the TCP/IP and Internet utilities included with Windows 95, refer to Chapters 20, 21, and 22. You also can use TCP/IP in conjunction with Windows 95's Dial-Up Networking.

Note

This chapter provides a general overview of Microsoft TCP/IP to help you understand how to configure and use TCP/IP. If you require a more technical description of how TCP/IP works, consult the *Microsoft Windows NT Resource Kit, Microsoft Windows 95 Resource Kit,* one of the many resources and FAQs (Frequently Asked Question documents) available on the Internet. You might also want to consult Que's *Special Edition Using the Internet* and *Windows 95 Connectivity.*

An Overview of TCP/IP and the Internet

See "Using Dial-Up Networking," p. 495

The two primary topics in this chapter—TCP/IP and the Internet—generally are closely related; you need the TCP/IP protocol to connect to and use the Internet. But even if you don't need to access the Internet, TCP/IP still offers an excellent means of interconnecting disparate operating systems on a single network. This section of the chapter provides a brief overview of TCP/IP and the Internet.

TCP/IP

TCP/IP stands for Transfer Control Protocol/Internet Protocol. TCP/IP is a network transport protocol widely supported by a majority of operating systems, including all versions of UNIX, Windows NT, Windows 95, Windows 3.x, Novell NetWare, Macintosh, Open VMS, and others. TCP/IP originally was developed through the Defense Advanced Research Projects Agency to support defense-related projects. TCP/IP offers a number of advantages that make it an excellent network transport protocol, particularly for connecting dissimilar computers and for enabling wide-area networking.

The TCP/IP protocol included with Windows 95, dubbed Microsoft TCP/IP, operates as a 32-bit, protected-mode transport that you can use as your only network protocol or in conjunction with another protocol. You might use NetBEUI within your LAN, for example, and use TCP/IP to connect to the Internet through a router or dial-up connection. The following list describes some of Microsoft TCP/IP's features and advantages.

- *32-bit protocol.* As a 32-bit, protected-mode network protocol, Microsoft TCP/IP uses no conventional memory. You also can use Microsoft TCP/IP in conjunction with other network protocols, enabling your computer to connect to a variety of systems.
- *Winsock 1.1.* Microsoft TCP/IP supports the Windows Sockets (Winsock) 1.1 specification, which enables you to use Winsock-based TCP/IP programs without requiring an additional Winsock driver. Some older programs, however, still require the use of a separate Winsock driver such as Trumpet Winsock (a shareware implementation of TCP/IP) because they have not been written to support the generic Winsock standard.
- *DHCP.* Microsoft TCP/IP supports Dynamic Host Configuration Protocol (DHCP), which enables a DHCP server, such as a Windows NT server, to automatically assign IP addresses to workstations on the

network, including computers that connect to the network through a dial-up connection. DHCP enables you to more efficiently manage a pool of IP addresses for a given set of workstations.

- *WINS.* Microsoft TCP/IP supports Windows Internet Naming Service (WINS), which provides automatic resolution of IP addresses into logical computer names (such as resolving tigers.k12.cfa.org into 198.87.118.2).
- *Protocol support.* Microsoft TCP/IP supports Point-to-Point (PPP) and Serial Line IP (SLIP), enabling remote access to TCP/IP-based servers through dial-up connections.
- *Core TCP/IP utilities.* Windows 95 includes a number of TCP/IP applications for file transfer, terminal emulation, troubleshooting, and other general tasks.

Although setting up TCP/IP is not difficult per se, it can prove to be a complex task. See "Understanding TCP/IP," later in this chapter to find more information about the technical aspects of TCP/IP. First, however, you should have some additional background about the Internet.

The Internet

The Internet began as a small group of interconnected LANs and has grown into a world-wide network that spans many thousands of networks and millions of computers. Although the Internet began primarily as a defense- and education-related network, it has grown to encompass government and commercial networks and users, as well as individual users. The Internet really is nothing more than a huge wide area network. On that network, however, you can access an amazing variety of services and data. You can send and receive e-mail around the globe, transfer files, query enormous databases, participate in special-interest groups, and more.

Many ways exist to access the Internet. If you have a user account on one of the popular online services, such as CompuServe or America Online, or are a member of The Microsoft Network (MSN), you can gain access to the Internet through those services. Or, your network at work might be connected to the Internet through a dedicated or dial-up connection. You might connect from your computer to an Internet service provider through a dial-up connection. Regardless of the method you use to connect to the Internet, you can't do it without TCP/IP. Understanding TCP/IP is critical to configuring and initiating your Internet connection. The next section provides an examination of some key issues for TCP/IP networking.

Note

There is one exception to the TCP/IP requirement for accessing the Internet. If you're connecting to the Internet through a commercial information service such as America Online or CompuServe, you don't need TCP/IP running on your computer. These online services do, however, use TCP/IP to connect you to the rest of the Internet, but serve as a TCP/IP emulator for your computer.

Understanding TCP/IP

TCP/IP is versatile, but also complex. Before you can set up a TCP/IP network and correctly configure the computers and other devices on the network, you must understand many key issues. The following sections explain these issues, beginning with IP addressing.

Understanding IP Addressing

On a TCP/IP network, a *host* is any device on the network that uses TCP/IP to communicate, including computers, routers, and other devices. Each host must have a unique address, called an *IP address* (IP stands for Internet Protocol). An IP address identifies the host on the network so that IP data packets can be properly routed to the host. IP data packets are simply data encapsulated in IP format for transmission using TCP/IP. Every IP address on the network must be unique; conflicting (identical) IP addresses on two or more computers prevents those computers from correctly accessing and using the network.

An IP address is a 32-bit value usually represented in *dotted-decimal notation,* in which four octets (eight bits each) are separated by decimals, as in 198.87.118.1. The IP address actually contains two items of information: The address of the network and the address of the host on the network. How the network and address are defined within the address depends on the class of the IP address.

IP addresses are grouped into three classes: A, B, and C. These classes are designed to accommodate networks of varying sizes. Table 19.1 describes the IP address classes, where the variables w.x.y.z designate the octets in the address structure.

Table 19.1 IP Address Classes

Class	w	Network ID	Host ID	Available Networks	Available Hosts per Network
A	1–126	w	x.y.z	126	16,777,214
B	128–191	w.x	y.z	16,384	65,534
C	192–223	w.x.y	z	2,097,151	254

Tip

The address 127 is reserved on the local computer for loopback testing and inter-process communication, and therefore is not a valid network address. Addresses 224 and higher are reserved for special protocols, and can't be used as host addresses. Host addresses 0 and 255 are used as broadcast addresses and should not be assigned to computers.

As table 19.1 shows, class A networks are potentially quite large, encompassing as many as 16,777,214 hosts. If you set up your own TCP/IP network, yours most likely falls into the class C network category, which is limited to 254 hosts.

You might wonder what's so important about an IP address. Routing data packets between computers is impossible without an IP address. By referencing the network portion of your IP address, a sending computer can route packets (with the help of intermediate routers and networks) to your network. The host portion of your IP address then routes the packet to your computer when the packet finally reaches the network.

Using Subnet Masks

A *subnet mask* is a 32-bit value expressed as a series of four octets separated by periods, just like an IP address. The subnet mask enables the recipient of an IP data packet to strip *(mask)* the IP address to which the IP packet is being sent into network ID and host ID. Basically, the subnet mask enables the IP address to be broken into its two component parts. Table 19.2 shows the default subnet masks for standard class A, B, and C networks, with each subnet mask shown in binary and dotted-decimal forms.

Table 19.2 Default Subnet Masks

Class	Bit Value	Subnet Mask
A	11111111 00000000 00000000 00000000	255.0.0.0
B	11111111 11111111 00000000 00000000	255.255.0.0
C	11111111 11111111 11111111 00000000	255.255.255.0

In addition to enabling an IP address to be resolved into its network and host components, subnet masks also serve to segment a single network ID into multiple local networks. Assume that your large company has been assigned a class B IP network address of 191.100. The corporate network comprises 10 different local networks with 200 hosts on each. By applying a subnet mask of 255.255.0.0, the network is divided into 254 separate subnetworks, 191.100.1 through 191.100.254. Each of the 254 subnetworks can contain 254 hosts.

Tip

The subnet masks described in table 19.2 are not the only masks you can use. Sometimes you have to mask only some of the bits in an octet. The network address and subnet mask must match, however, for every host on a local network.

Acquiring an IP Address

Although theoretically you could arbitrarily assign your own IP network address for your network, any address you might choose probably would already be assigned to someone else's network. If your network is self-contained and not connected to the Internet, duplicate addressing shouldn't cause any problems. If your network is connected to the Internet or you decide to connect it in the future, however, duplicate addressing causes serious routing problems for both networks.

Note

There is no charge to register an IP address. InterNIC does, however, charge for network domain name registration. Currently, the cost is $100 for the first two years, then $50 annually beginning in the third year.

To assure uniqueness of network addresses, a governing organization known as InterNIC (Internet Network Information Center) is responsible for assigning and maintaining IP addresses. If you set up a TCP/IP network, you should contact InterNIC to obtain a unique network IP address for your network. You can register through the Internet by sending a registration request to **hostmaster@internic.net**. If you want more information about InterNIC and IP addressing, connect through the Internet to **is.internic.net**, log on as anonymous, and browse the directory /INFOSOURCE/FAQ. To contact InterNIC through standard mail, phone, or fax, use the following information:

Network Solutions
InterNIC Registration Services
505 Huntmar Park Drive
Herndon, VA 22070
Voice: 703-742-4777
Fax: 703-742-4811

Understanding Gateways and Routing

To interconnect and provide routing of data packets, TCP/IP subnetworks interconnected with one another or connected to the Internet use gateways (routers). A default gateway generally is a computer or router that maintains IP address information of remote networks (networks outside its own network). Default gateways are required only on interconnected networks—stand-alone TCP/IP subnets do not require default gateways.

Before a host transmits an IP packet, IP inserts the originating and destination IP addresses into the packet. It then checks the destination address to determine whether the packet is destined for the same local network as the originating host. If the network addresses match (based on the subnet mask), the packet is routed directly to the destination host on the same subnet. If the network addresses don't match, the packet is sent to the subnet's default gateway, which then handles routing of the packet. The default gateway maintains a list of other gateways and network addresses, and routes the packet accordingly. Although the packet might pass through many gateways, it eventually reaches its destination.

If yours is a stand-alone subnet, you don't need a default gateway. Otherwise, you need at least one functioning default gateway to communicate outside of your subnet. If for some reason your default gateway becomes inoperative (a router fails, for example), you can't communicate outside your subnet, but you still can work within your subnet. If you need to ensure a connection, you might want to consider using multiple default gateways.

Tip

You can use the route utility from the command prompt to specify a static route and override the default gateway.

Using Dynamic Address Assignment

▶ See "Using FTP, Ping, and Other Internet Tools," p. 471

In TCP/IP, networks that comprise relatively few nodes, or in which the network configuration is static (computers do not access the network remotely and the number of hosts doesn't fluctuate), IP address administration is relatively easy. The network administrator simply assigns specific IP addresses to each host.

On large or dynamic networks, however, administering IP addresses can be difficult and time-consuming. To help overcome this problem, Windows 95 supports Dynamic Host Configuration Protocol, or DHCP, which enables a host to automatically obtain an IP address from a DHCP server when the host logs on to the network. When you move a host from one subnet to another on your network, the host automatically receives a new IP address, and its original IP address is released, making it available for other connecting hosts.

By providing dynamic addressing, DHCP enables you to manage a pool of IP addresses for a group of hosts. Assume that your company has 100 employees who often dial into your subnet from remote locations, but not at the same time. At any one time, 25 to 30 remote users might be connected to the network, but your subnet has only 50 available subnet host addresses. If you assign IP addresses manually, you can accommodate only 50 of the remote users. You can't assign the same IP address to two users, because if they both connect to the network at the same time, routing problems prevent them from using the network.

Through DHCP, you can allocate a pool of 50 IP addresses to be assigned automatically to the dial-in users. When a user dials in and connects, DHCP assigns its host a unique IP address from the pool. As long as no more than 50 users attempt to log on to the network remotely and acquire IP addresses, you can accommodate all 50 with unique addresses. If the number of users who need to connect exceed the number of available addresses, the only solution is to expand your pool of available addresses or modify the subnet mask to accommodate more than 50 addresses. For more information on this subject see "Installing and Configuring TCP/IP in Windows 95," later in this chapter.

DHCP in Windows 95 relies on a Windows NT DHCP server that can assign IP addresses to hosts on the local subnet when the hosts start Windows 95, and can assign IP addresses to hosts that connect to the network remotely. For more information see "Configuring IP Addressing," later in this chapter.

In addition to using DHCP, Windows 95 can request an IP address from a PPP (Point-to-Point Protocol) dial-up router. Whether you use DHCP or connect to a PPP dial-up router, you use the same configuration option to configure dynamic address assignment.

Understanding Domains and Name Resolution

Computers have no problems using IP addresses to locate other networks and hosts. The average user, however, can have trouble remembering those dotted-decimal addresses. Domain names and computer names make specifying the addresses or other networks or hosts much easier.

A *domain name* is a unique named formatted much like an IP address, except that the domain name uses words rather than numbers. The domain name identifies your network and is associated with your network's IP address. If your company is Foo Fang Foods, Inc., for example, your departmental subnet might be known as sales.foofang.com. The first portion, sales, identifies your subnet. The second portion, foofang, identifies your corporate network. The last portion, com, specifics the type of organization, and in this example, indicates a commercial network. Table 19.3 lists common network type identifiers.

Table 19.3 Common Network Type Identifiers

Identifier	Meaning
com	Commercial entity
gov	Government entity
net	Networking organization
org	General organization
edu	Education
mil	Military

Tip

As with your IP address, your domain must be unique. If you connect your network to other networks or to the Internet, contact the InterNIC to apply for a unique domain name.

A *computer name* specifies a host on the subnet. Your host computer name is combined with your domain to derive your Internet address. Your host name doesn't have to match your computer's name that identifies it in its workgroup, but it can. By default, Windows 95 uses as your host name the NetBIOS computer name you specify during setup, but you can specify a different name when you configure TCP/IP. Whatever name you specify as the computer name in the TCP/IP configuration is registered with the network when Windows 95 starts.

Note

The computer name you specify for your computer when you install Windows 95 is its NetBIOS name. A computer's NetBIOS name bears no relationship to its host name under TCP/IP. The two names can be different or the same.

No direct translation or correlation exists between IP addresses and domain names and host names. Some method, therefore, is required to enable computers to look up the correct IP address when a user specifies a name rather than an IP address. Your Windows 95 host can use one of two methods: DNS or WINS.

Note

For a technical discussion of DNS and WINS, you can consult Que's *Windows 95 Connectivity* or volume 2 of the *Microsoft Windows NT Resource Kit*, "Windows NT Networking Guide."

Understanding DNS

DNS stands for Domain Name System. *DNS* is a distributed database system that enables a computer to look up a computer name and resolve the name to an IP address. A DNS name server maintains the database of domain names and their corresponding IP addresses. The DNS name server stores records that describe all hosts in the name server's zone.

If you use DNS for your Windows 95 workstation, you specify the IP address of one or more DNS server in your TCP/IP configuration. When your workstation needs to resolve a name into an IP address, it queries the DNS servers. If the server doesn't have an entry for the your specified name, the name server returns a list of other name servers that might contain the entry you need. The workstation then can query these additional name servers to resolve the name.

Tip

You can define multiple DNS servers in your Windows 95 TCP/IP configuration.

Besides a DNS server, you can use the Hosts file to resolve host.domain-formatted names to IP addresses. For an explanation of the Hosts file, refer to the section "Using Hosts and Lmhosts Files," later in this chapter.

Understanding WINS

WINS stands forWindows Internet Name Service. WINS provides a dynamic database for managing name resolution. WINS relies on a Windows NT server to act as a WINS server. When you install TCP/IP on your workstation, the client software necessary to connect to a WINS server is installed automatically.

One advantage of using WINS is that it's dynamic, rather than static like DNS. If you use DHCP to assign network addresses, WINS automatically updates the name database to incorporate DHCP IP address assignments. As computers move from one place (and address) to another on the network, the WINS server automatically updates and maintains their addresses.

Another advantage of using WINS is that it includes NetBIOS name space, which enables it to resolve NetBIOS names into IP addresses. Assume that your computer's NetBIOS name is joeblow, your computer's TCP/IP host name is JoeB, and your domain name is bozos.are.us. A DNS server could only resolve JoeB.bozos.are.us, but a WINS server could resolve JoeB.bozos.are.us *and* joeblow.bozos.are.us into the correct IP address.

When you configure TCP/IP in Windows 95, you can specify the IP addresses of up to two WINS servers to handle name resolution. If your network uses DHCP, you can configure your workstation to resolve the addresses of WINS servers dynamically using DHCP.

If you don't have a WINS server available to provide name resolution of NetBIOS computer names to IP addresses (such as resolving your computer's name to its IP address), you can use the Lmhosts file to resolve NetBIOS names. For an explanation of how to use Lmhosts, see the section "Using Hosts and Lmhosts Files," later in this chapter.

Issues for NetWare

The NetWare client provided with Windows 95, Client for NetWare Networks, supports the IPX/SPX protocol also included with Windows 95. The IPX/SPX protocol provides full compatibility with NetWare networks and replaces the NetWare IP protocol. The Client for NetWare Networks, however, doesn't support NetWare IP protocol. Also, the Microsoft TCP/IP protocol stack that comes with Windows 95 does not support any NetWare clients owing to differences in the protocol implementations of TCP/IP and NetWare IP. Therefore, you must use the IPX/SPX protocol or a NetWare-supplied protocol for NetWare connectivity.

Even though you can't use Microsoft TCP/IP for NetWare connectivity, you can use Microsoft TCP/IP to provide internetworking for other clients and services. You might use IPX/SPX for connectivity with NetWare servers on the network, for example, and use Microsoft TCP/IP for connectivity and resource sharing with Microsoft- or UNIX-based servers. Or, you might use Microsoft TCP/IP for Internet connectivity through a router or a dial-up networking connection.

If you use only a NetWare client (because you have a homogeneous NetWare environment with no other server types), and want to use Microsoft TCP/IP for connectivity through a router or dial-up connection to the Internet, you don't have to install any other networking clients or services to enable that TCP/IP connection. TCP/IP connectivity to the Internet does not require a network client or service of its own.

Preparing to Install TCP/IP

Now that you have a little background in how TCP/IP works, you're almost ready to install, configure, and begin using TCP/IP on your Windows 95 workstation. Before you begin the installation procedure, however, you need to gather together the information you must provide when you configure TCP/IP. In particular, you need to know the following information:

- *Network address and domain.* If you set up a new TCP/IP network that you intend to eventually connect to the Internet, you must register with InterNIC for a unique domain name and network IP address. Even if you do not plan at this time to connect the network to the Internet, you still should acquire a unique domain name and network address from InterNIC for future compatibility.
- *IP address.* Determine whether your workstation will use static IP addressing or will obtain an IP address from a DHCP server. If you require a static address, contact your system administrator for an address, or if

you are the administrator, assign an available address for the workstation. If you plan to use DHCP to acquire an IP address dynamically, or you dynamically acquire an IP address from a PPP dial-up router, you do not need to know the IP address of the DHCP server or router.

- *Subnet mask*. You must know the appropriate subnet mask for your subnet. If yours is a standard class C network with fewer than 256 hosts, your subnet mask should be 255.255.255.0. If you're not sure what your subnet mask should be, contact your system administrator.
- *WINS*. Determine whether your network provides one or more WINS servers for name resolution. If so, you need to know the IP address of the primary WINS server, as well as the IP address of a secondary WINS server if you choose to use a secondary server. If your workstation uses DHCP, however, you need not know the IP addresses of the WINS servers—DHCP automatically resolves them. If your network uses NetBIOS over TCP/IP, you might need a scope ID. If you're not sure, check with your system administrator.
- *Default gateway(s)*. If your subnet is connected to other networks or to the Internet, you need to know the IP address of the gateway (router) through which IP routing is accomplished. If your network has access to multiple gateways, you can specify multiple gateways to provide fault tolerance and alternative routing.
- *Domain name resolution*. You must know the domain name of your network, as well as the host name you use. The host name defaults to the computer name assigned to the computer at startup, which you specify through the Identification property page for your Network settings. If you use DNS for name resolution, you must know the IP addresses of the DNS servers you use.
- *Bindings*. You must know which clients and services use the TCP/IP protocol. If you dial into a server for TCP/IP access (such as dialing into an Internet service provider or an NT Server) to gain Internet access, you do not need to bind TCP/IP to any clients or services. If you use TCP/IP as your only protocol and want to dial into a server to access files and other shared resources, or you want to share your resources, you must bind TCP/IP to the appropriate client and service, such as Client for Microsoft Networks and the File and Printer Sharing for Microsoft Networks (or corresponding client and service for NetWare networks). If you use TCP/IP over a LAN, and no other protocol provides sharing services, you need to bind TCP/IP to your network client and sharing service.

Installing and Configuring TCP/IP in Windows 95

Before you can begin taking advantage of TCP/IP, you naturally have to install it. Of all network protocols, TCP/IP is the most complex to install and configure owing to its many settings and options. This section explains those settings and options, beginning with the installation process.

> **Note**
>
> If you have not read the previous section of this chapter, you should do so to learn what items of information you need before you install and configure TCP/IP.

Installing Microsoft TCP/IP

Microsoft TCP/IP installs like any other network transport protocol—through the Control Panel. To install TCP/IP, follow these steps:

1. Open the Control Panel and choose the Network object.
2. From the Configuration property page, choose the Add button. Windows 95 displays a Select Network Component Type dialog box from which you can choose the type of network component you want to install.
3. Select Protocol from the supplied list, then choose Add. Windows 95 displays a Select Network Protocol dialog box similar to the one shown in figure 19.1.
4. From the Manufacturers list, select Microsoft. Then, from the Network Protocols list, select TCP/IP.

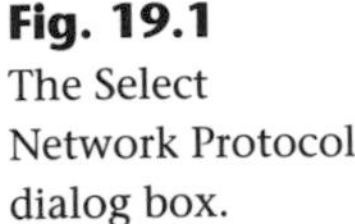

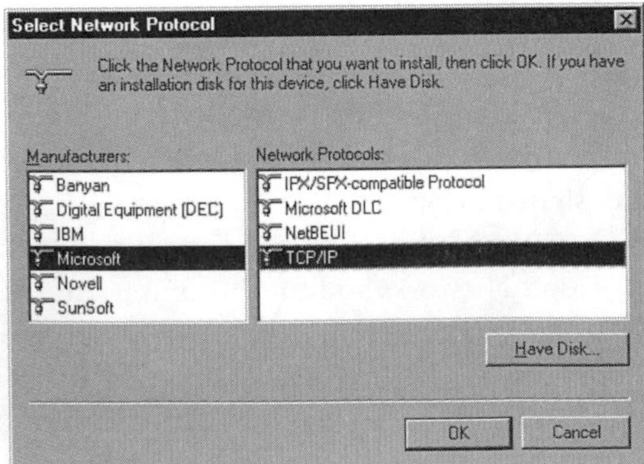

Fig. 19.1
The Select Network Protocol dialog box.

After you choose OK, Windows 95 adds the TCP/IP protocol to your PC, copying files as necessary from the Windows 95 distribution disks or CD. After it copies the files, the TCP/IP protocol appears in the installed components list on the Configuration property page. If you have more than one adapter, Windows 95 adds TCP/IP to each one. If your workstation contains a network adapter, for example, and you also use the Dial-Up Adapter for remote access, Windows 95 binds TCP/IP to both adapters. If you need TCP/IP on only one adapter, select the instance of the TCP/IP protocol that you don't need, then choose Remove.

Next, you need to specify a number of settings to properly configure TCP/IP, beginning with the IP address. To do so, select the TCP/IP protocol from the Configuration property page, then choose Properties to open the TCP/IP property sheet. The following sections explain how to set the values on the property pages for the TCP/IP protocol.

Tip

You can configure and use multiple sets of TCP/IP settings. You can use one configuration for your LAN TCP/IP connection, for example, and specify different settings for each dial-up connection you use. For information on using TCP/IP over a dial-up networking connection, refer to Chapter 23, "Using Dial-Up Networking."

Configuring IP Addressing

When Windows 95 first displays the property sheet for the TCP/IP protocol, the IP Address page appears (see fig. 19.2). If you use a static IP address for your workstation, choose the Specify an IP Address option button, then enter the IP address and subnet mask for your workstation in the IP Address and Subnet Mask fields. If you want to rely on a DHCP server or PPP server to assign an IP address automatically for your workstation, choose the Obtain an IP Address Automatically option button. You do not have to specify the IP address of the DHCP server.

If you specify an explicit IP address, take the time to verify that you have entered the correct address and subnet mask before you continue to the other configuration steps.

Configuring a Gateway

If your subnet is connected to other subnets, to other networks, or to the Internet, you must specify at least one default gateway. To do so, choose the Gateway tab to open the Gateway property page (see fig. 19.3).

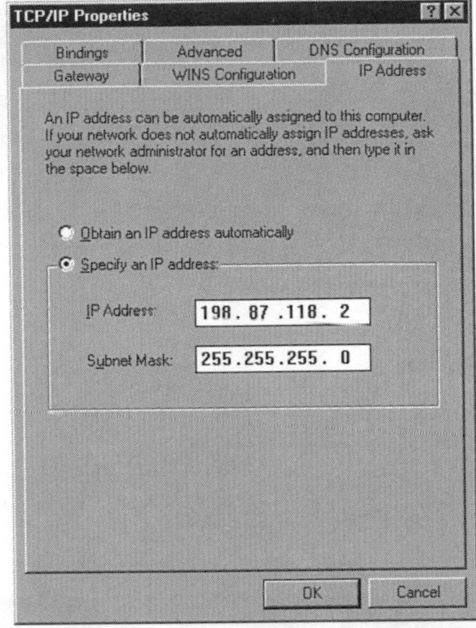

Fig. 19.2
The IP Address property page.

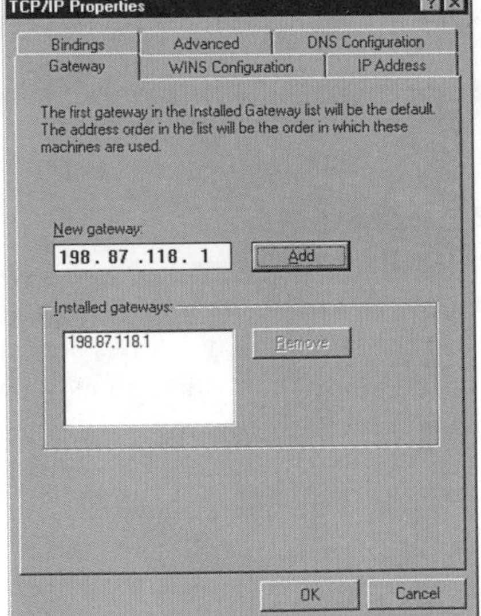

Fig. 19.3
The Gateway property page.

Tip

Your network's router typically is the default gateway.

If your network is connected to multiple gateways, you can specify as many gateways as necessary to allow for fault tolerance if one gateway becomes unavailable. To add a gateway, enter its IP address in the New gateway field, then choose Add. Windows 95 adds the gateway's IP address to the Installed gateways list. If you add multiple gateways to the list, the IP address at the top of the list serves as the default gateway. Other gateways in the list are used only if the default gateway is inaccessible. Unfortunately, you can't simply drag the IP addresses in the Installed gateways list to prioritize them. Instead, the gateway addresses are placed in the list in the order in which you add them. To prioritize a set of gateways, write down the gateway addresses, remove the addresses, and add them back in using your preferred order of priority, adding the default gateway first.

Troubleshooting

I can dial into my Internet service provider, but I can't seem to access any other sites on the Internet. How can I get past the service provider to other computers on the Internet?

Your default gateway setting is probably incorrect. Check with the service provider to determine the IP address you should use as the default gateway, as well as a secondary address, if applicable. Then, use the procedure explained in the previous section to configure the gateway. You'll have to restart your PC after changing the TCP/IP configuration. Then, connect again and try to connect to another computer on the Internet. If that fails, use the ping command to test the connection to the gateway. Refer to Chapter 22, "Using FTP, Ping, and Other Internet Tools," for help using Ping.

Using DNS

If your workstation requires Domain Name System (DNS) services, click the DNS Configuration tab to open the DNS Configuration property page shown in figure 19.4. To enable DNS, choose the Enable DNS option button.

Tip

If your computer needs to use Lmhosts to resolve network names, you must enable DNS.

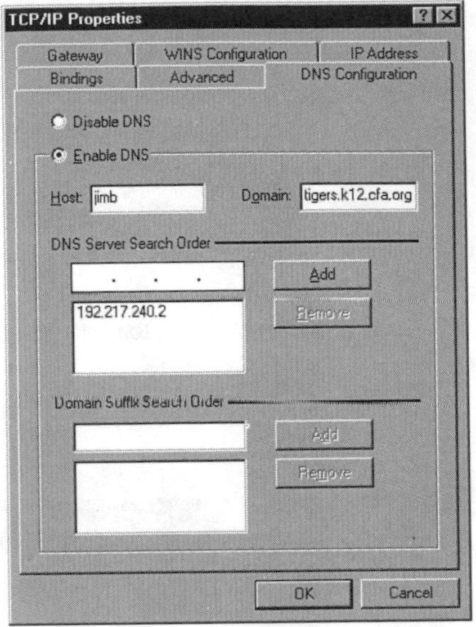

Fig. 19.4
The DNS Configuration property page.

Specifying Host and Domain Names

After you enable DNS, you need to specify some additional items of information. First, you need to specify the host name for your computer in the Host text box. By default, the host name is your computer's name as specified in the Identification property page of the Network property sheet. You can use any host name, however; you might use your name as the host name, for example. You can use any combination of letters and numbers, a dash, or a period, but not a space or underscore character, in the host name.

Next, specify the domain name for your network in the Domain text box. TCP/IP combines the host name you specify with the domain name you specify to derive a Fully Qualified Domain Name (FQDN) for your computer. If your host name is JimB and your domain name is que.mcp.com, the FQDN for your computer is JimB.que.mcp.com.

> **Note**
>
> Some TCP/IP utilities use your host name, domain name, and FQDN to authenticate your computer name. Note that a computer's FQDN is not the same as a user's e-mail address. Although the FQDN might be JimB.que.mcp.com, the e-mail address might be jboyce@que.mcp.com. Also, a DNS domain name and a Windows NT or LAN Manager domain name are in no way related.

Specifying DNS Server IP Addresses

If you do not use DHCP to define IP addresses, you must provide the IP addresses of the DNS servers you use. If you do use DHCP, the DHCP server can automatically provide the IP addresses of the DNS servers.

You can specify up to three DNS server addresses in the DNS Server Search Order group of controls. First, determine the IP address of the DNS server you want to use by default. Then, enter the server's IP address in the IP address text box and choose Add. Enter a second IP address if you want, then choose Add. Enter a third IP address in the same manner if you have a third DNS server.

> **Note**
>
> The DNS server IP addresses are placed in the list in the order in which you add them. Therefore, you should enter the DNS server with the highest priority first, followed by any other servers in descending order of priority. To change priority of DNS servers in the list, you must remove and re-add the IP addresses. Windows 95 uses the secondary and tertiary DNS servers only if the primary DNS server does not respond. If the primary DNS server responds that the requested name is not recognized, Windows 95 does not query the secondary or tertiary DNS servers. If you know the name is correct, you can use the Hosts file to enable proper resolution of the name, as explained later in the section "Using Hosts and Lmhosts Files."

Adding Domain Suffix Entries

Normally, DNS appends the domain name specified in the Domain text box to your host name to resolve the FQDN of your computer. You can specify up to five additional domain suffixes that DNS can use if it can't resolve the FQDN using the default domain name. A DNS server attempts to resolve the FQDN using these additional suffixes in alphabetical order (which is how they appear in the list after you add them).

To add additional domain suffixes, enter a domain name in the Domain Suffix Search Order text box, then choose Add. Repeat the process to add up to five domain names.

> **Troubleshooting**
>
> *I can connect to other computers on the Internet using their IP addresses, but using domain names doesn't work. How can I get the domain names to work?*
>
> (continues)

(continued)

Something is wrong with your DNS configuration. Verify that you've specified a DNS server in your TCP/IP configuration as explained previously. If you have specified a DNS server, try to ping the server (see Chapter 22). If you can ping the server, it might not actually be a DNS server. If you're using a Hosts file, verify that the domain name of the computer you're trying to reach matches the domain name specified in the Hosts file, including case and spelling. See the section "Using Hosts and Lmhosts Files" later in this chapter for more help.

Using WINS

If your network includes one or more Windows NT servers configured as WINS servers, or access to WINS servers, you can configure your Windows 95 TCP/IP stack to use WINS to resolve names. WINS offers numerous advantages over DNS, particularly in conjunction with DHCP. To configure WINS, click the WINS Configuration tab to display the WINS Configuration property page shown in figure 19.5.

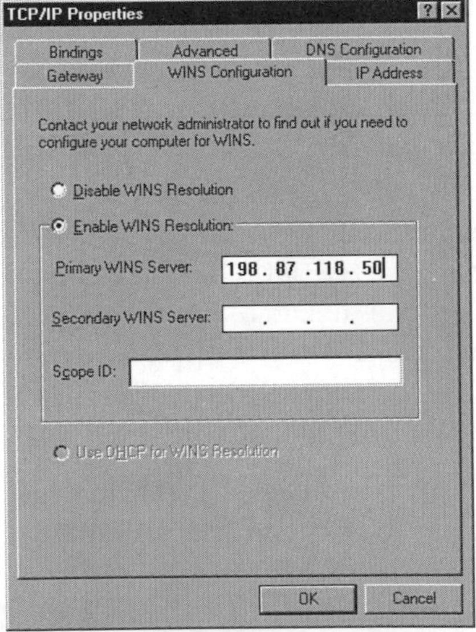

Fig. 19.5
The WINS Configuration property page.

To enable WINS for your computer, choose the Enable WINS Resolution option button. You can specify a primary and a secondary WINS server by entering their IP addresses in the fields provided for that purpose on the property page. If your computer uses DHCP to resolve names, however, you can leave the IP address fields blank and choose the Use DHCP for WINS Resolution option button, and Windows 95 queries the DHCP server for the WINS server addresses.

Binding the TCP/IP Protocol

If you use TCP/IP for resource access and/or resource sharing, you must bind the protocol to the necessary network client and/or resource sharing service. To do so, click the Bindings tab to open the Bindings property page (see fig. 19.6). Enable the checkbox beside the client or service to bind the protocol to the client or service.

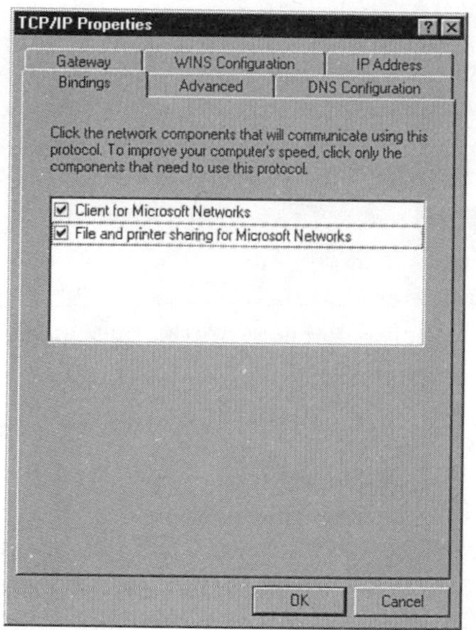

Fig. 19.6
The Bindings property page.

> **Note**
>
> If you use TCP/IP only to provide access to the Internet, and use a different network protocol to provide local resource sharing, you don't have to bind TCP/IP to your clients or services.

Using Hosts and Lmhosts Files

DNS name servers resolve FQDN names provided in the host.domain format to IP addresses. A WINS server can resolve IP host.domain names to IP addresses, and it also can resolve a computer's NetBIOS name into its address name. Sometimes, however, being able to resolve names locally without relying on a DNS or WINS name server comes in handy. You might not have a DNS or WINS name server available to you, for example, or the server might be temporarily unavailable.

Windows 95 provides two methods for resolving names to IP addresses locally, which you can use in conjunction with or in place of DNS and WINS name resolution. Both methods rely on simple ASCII files to store database entries for names and corresponding IP addresses. The first of these files, Hosts, resolves DNS-formatted names, and works with or in place of DNS. The second file, Lmhosts, resolves NetBIOS names into IP addresses, and works with or in place of WINS.

The following section explains the Hosts file. The Lmhosts file is explained in the section after that one.

Using the Hosts File for Name Resolution

If you can't access a DNS server, or you want to supplement a DNS server with your own entries, you can use the Hosts file to maintain a database of host names and their corresponding IP addresses. The Hosts file is called a *host table* because it contains a table of host names and their IP addresses. Windows 95 can look up entries in the Hosts file to resolve names.

When you install Microsoft TCP/IP, Windows 95 creates a sample Hosts file named Hosts.sam in the Windows folder. The Hosts.sam file is an ASCII file that you can edit using Notepad, WordPad, Edit, or any other ASCII editor. You should copy Hosts.sam to Hosts (omitting a file extension) and retain the sample file for future reference in case your Hosts file becomes corrupted or is accidentally deleted. The following lists the contents of the Hosts.sam file:

```
# Copyright (c) 1994 Microsoft Corp.
#
# This is a sample HOSTS file used by Microsoft TCP/IP for Chicago
#
# This file contains the mappings of IP addresses to host names.
# Each entry should be kept on an individual line. The IP address
  ➥should
# be placed in the first column followed by the corresponding host
name.
# The IP address and the host name should be separated by at least
  ➥one space.
#
# Additionally, comments (such as these) may be inserted on
  ➥individual
# lines or following the machine name denoted by a '#' symbol.
#
# For example:
#
```

```
#       102.54.94.97      tools.acme.com          # source server
#        38.25.63.10      x.acme.com              # x client host

127.0.0.1        localhost
```

The Hosts file uses the same format as the hosts file used on 4.3 BSD UNIX, stored in the /etc/hosts file. The Hosts.sam file contains comments identified by a leading # character and a single address entry for localhost. The localhost entry is always 127.0.0.1 and is used for loopback testing. You should not change the IP address for localhost or remove it from the Hosts file.

To add an entry to the Hosts file, enter the IP address, then tab to the second column and enter the host name. You can specify more than one host name for an IP address, but you must use multiple entries for the different domains, each with the same IP address, as in the following example:

```
102.54.94.97      tools.acme.com
102.54.94.97      TOOLS.ACME.COM
102.54.94.97      fooyang.gruel.com
```

Entries in the Hosts file are case-sensitive. The two entries for tools.acme.com and TOOLS.ACME.COM would enable the correct host name resolution if you specified the host name in lowercase or uppercase.

You can include a single host name for each entry or specify multiple host names for a single IP address. The following, for example, are valid entries:

```
198.87.118.72   me                theboss
tower.tigers.k12.cfa.org
198.87.118.50   TheServer         theserver        THESERVER
```

Each of the entries in this example specify three host names for each IP address.

Windows 95 parses the entries in the Hosts file in sequential order until it finds a match. If you have a large Hosts file, you can speed up lookup time by placing the most often-used host name entries at the top of the file.

Using the Lmhosts File for Name Resolution

If you want Windows 95 to be able to resolve NetBIOS computer names to IP addresses, you need to use a WINS or Lmhosts file. NetBIOS names are the computer names assigned to computers on Microsoft-based networks, such as the name you assigned to your computer through the Identification page of the Network property sheet. As explained previously, your computer's NetBIOS name is not equivalent to your TCP/IP host name, although the two can use the same name.

Windows 95 automatically resolves NetBIOS names for computers running TCP/IP on a local network. To resolve IP addresses of computers on other networks to which yours is connected by a gateway (when a WINS server is not available), you need to use Lmhosts.

Note

Like Hosts, Lmhosts is an ASCII file, and the format of an entry is similar to entries in a Hosts file. The Lmhosts file, however, supports special keywords, which are explained later in this section. Windows 95 includes a sample Lmhosts file named Lmhosts.sam, located in the Windows folder. To use Lmhosts, copy Lmhosts.sam to Lmhosts without a file extension, then modify Lmhosts to add entries.

Microsoft TCP/IP reads the Lmhosts file when you start the computer. As it does the Hosts file, Windows 95 parses each line sequentially, which means you should place often-accessed names at the top of the file for best performance. You also need to place entries that contain special keywords at specific locations in the file (these placement rules are explained later in this section). First, here are a few rules for structuring a Lmhosts file:

- Each entry must begin with the IP address in the first column, followed by its computer name in the second column. Any additional keywords appear in subsequent columns. Columns must be separated by at least one space or tab character. Some Lmhosts keywords follow entries, while others appear on their own lines (explained later).
- Place each entry on a separate line.
- Comments must begin with the pound (#) character, but special Lmhosts keywords also begin with the # character. Keeping comments to a minimum improves parsing performance. Place often-accessed entries near the top of the file for best performance.
- The Lmhosts file is static, so you must manually update the file you need to create new entries or modify existing entries.

Tip

Although Microsoft TCP/IP reads the Lmhosts file at system startup, only entries designated as preloaded by the #PRE keyword are read into the name cache at startup. Other entries are read only after broadcast name resolution queries fail.

You can use any or all of six special keywords (described in the following list) in a Lmhosts file:

- *#PRE*. This keyword causes the associated entry to be preloaded into the name cache, rather than loaded only after broadcast resolution queries fail. If you want names stored in a remote Lmhosts file to be added to the name cache at startup, use the #INCLUDE and #PRE statements in combination, such as the following:

```
#INCLUDE      \\server\pub\lmhosts      #PRE
```

- *#DOM:<domain>*. This keyword designates a remote domain controller and enables you to identify Windows NT domain controllers located across one or more routers. Entries that use the #DOM keyword are added to a special internetwork group name cache that causes Microsoft TCP/IP to forward requests for domain controllers to remote domain controllers as well as local domain controllers. The following example identifies a domain controller named appserver in a domain named thedomain, and also causes the entry to be preloaded into the name cache at startup:

```
184.121.214.2  appserver  #PRE  #DOM:thedomain
➥#This is a comment
```

- *#INCLUDE<filename>*. Use this keyword to include entries from a separate Lmhosts file. You can use #INCLUDE to include your own set of entries stored on your own computer, but you most commonly would use #INCLUDE to enable use of a centralized, shared Lmhosts file for multiple users. The following example includes a Lmhosts file from a local drive and directory:

```
#INCLUDE  c:\mystuff\Lmhosts      #Includes local file
```

> **Note**
>
> If you reference a remote Lmhosts file on a server outside of your network in a #INCLUDE statement, you must include an entry for the IP address of the remote server in the Lmhosts file. The server's entry must be inserted in the Lmhosts file before the #INCLUDE statement that references it. You also should not use #INCLUDE to reference a Lmhosts file on a redirected network drive, because your drive mappings might be different from one session to another. Use the UNC path for the file instead. Centralized Lmhosts files should never use drive-referenced entries, because the drive mappings in the file probably will not apply to all users who might use the file.

- *#BEGIN_ALTERNATE*. This statement signals the beginning of a block of multiple #INCLUDE statements (called a *block inclusion*). The statements within the block designate primary and alternate locations for the included file. The alternate locations are checked if the primary file is unavailable. The successful loading of any one entry in the block causes the block to succeed, and any subsequent entries in the block are not parsed. You can include multiple block inclusions within a Lmhosts file. The following is an example of a block inclusion:

```
#BEGIN_ALTERNATE
#INCLUDE        \\server\pub\lmhosts          #Primary source
#INCLUDE        \\othersrvr\pub\lmhosts       #Alternate source
#INCLUDE        \\somewhere\pub\lmhosts       #Alternate source
#END_ALTERNATE
```

- *#END_ALTERNATE*. This statement signals the end of a block of multiple #INCLUDE statements.
- *\0xnn*. This keyword enables you to specify nonprinting characters in NetBIOS names. You must enclose the NetBIOS name in quotation marks and use the \0x*nn* keyword to specify the hexadecimal value of the nonprinting character. The hexadecimal notation applies to only one character in the name. The name must be padded to a total of 16 characters, with the hexadecimal notation as the 16th character. Example:

```
109.88.120.45   "thename   \0x14"      #Uses special character
```

Adding an Entry to Lmhosts

NetBIOS computer names of computers on your LAN are resolved automatically. To resolve remote names when a WINS server is not available, add the NetBIOS names and their corresponding IP addresses to the Lmhosts file. To add an entry, use Notepad, WordPad, Edit, or any other text editor that enables you to edit and save ASCII files.

Each line consists of the IP address and NetBIOS name, and also can contain optional keywords and comments as explained previously. The following are examples of Lmhosts entries:

```
192.214.240.2    me                                  #Alias for my
                                                     ➥computer
198.87.118.72    tower                               #Fred's computer
198.87.118.50    rli-server  #PRE                    #Application
                                                     ➥server
120.89.101.70    server      #PRE    #DOM:tigers     #Some comment
                                                     ➥here
182.212.242.2    sourcesrvr  #PRE                    #Source for
                                                     ➥shared Lmhosts
```

```
182.212.242.3     source2    #PRE          #Source for
                                           ➥shared Lmhosts
182.212.242.4     source3    #PRE          #Source for
                                           ➥shared Lmhosts
187.52.122.188    images                   #Imaging server

#INCLUDE          c:\mystuff\lmhosts       #My private
                                           ➥Lmhosts file

#BEGIN_ALTERNATE
#INCLUDE          \\sourcesrvr\pub\Lmhosts #Primary central
                                           ➥Lmhosts
#INCLUDE          \\source2\pub\Lmhosts    #Alternate
                                           ➥source
#INCLUDE          \\source3\pub\Lmhosts    #Alternate
                                           ➥source
#END_ALTERNATE
```

In the preceding example, only the rli-server, server, sourcesrvr, source2, and source3 entries are preloaded into the name cache at system startup, because only they include the #PRE keyword. Other entries are parsed only after broadcast name resolution requests fail.

Tip

The addresses of servers you specify in a block inclusion must be preloaded through entries earlier in the file. Any entries not preloaded are ignored.

Troubleshooting

I'm using an Lmhosts file, and although it works, it takes a relatively long time to connect to some of the systems I use frequently. How can I speed it up?

If you have a large Lmhosts file, it's likely that the entries you're having trouble with are located near the end of the file. The names are processed sequentially during a resolution search, which means that the entire file has to be parsed before the needed address is reached. Either move to the top of the Lmhosts file the addresses of the systems you connect most often, or preload the entries as explained previously.

CHAPTER 20

Connecting to the Internet

by David Rorabaugh

The Internet is one of the fastest growing phenomena in the world today. Millions of users around the world are connecting in ever-increasing numbers. More than anything else, the depth and breadth of news, information, and entertainment—along with fast, cheap, and global communications—combine to offer limitless possibilities. The Internet has truly reached "Critical Mass." Whether you're looking for information on computers or cars, decoupage or dance, Pantera or Pink Floyd, you'll find just about everything under the sun on the Internet.

In this chapter, you learn what's needed to get on the "Information Superhighway." You also find out how to configure Windows 95 to make your connection as fast and easy as possible.

In this chapter, you learn to

- Use Internet Service Providers
- Set up dial-up connections
- Connect over a network
- Connect through Online Services

If you're already connected to the Internet, and just want to take immediate advantage of what's available, turn to Chapter 21, "Using Internet Resources," to begin browsing, searching, and using information. If you are just starting on the Internet, then this chapter explores the scope and history of the Internet, and teaches you how to get connected.

An Overview of the Internet

From a practical standpoint, the first two questions most people ask about the Internet are "What IS the Internet?" and "What can the Internet do for ME?". We'll try to answer those questions with a brief review of what the Internet is and how it happened, what the common Internet tools are, and what you can do with them.

History

Nuclear war. That's how it all started. Or, more accurately, the threat of nuclear war. In the early 1960s, there was a perceived need for a communications network that could survive a nuclear attack. The military-industrial-complex of the Pentagon, defense contractors, and strategic planners needed a way to maintain communications, command, and control, even in the midst of an atomic war. This communications network would have to be completely decentralized because any central network control center would be an immediate target for destruction.

In 1964, the Rand Corporation made public a proposal for a multi-node, packet-switched network. There were some immediately recognizable features: There would be no set routes, and packets could simply be forwarded around a failure by other machines that remained operational. With no central authority and an almost random routing scheme, the Rand Corporation proposal was at once intentionally inefficient, but also tremendously rugged.

It would be another four years before the first test "node" was built. The National Physical Laboratory in Great Britain was the first to set up a network and test these principles and assumptions. This was followed in 1969 by the Pentagon, whose Advanced Research Projects Agency (ARPA) funded a larger project, linking four "supercomputers" at research facilities across the country. ARPANET, named for the agency which funded it, was an immediate success with scientists and researchers, who initially used it to share scarce computer time.

From its initial four nodes in 1969, the ARPANET grew to 37 nodes by 1972. By the mid 1970s, ARPA had evolved its communications protocols into TCP/IP ("Transmission Control Protocol/Internet Protocol"), and was using TCP/IP to connect other networks to ARPANET. Gradually, as more networks were interconnected, ARPANET became more commonly referred to as the Internet.

In 1983, the military portion of ARPANET split off to become MILNET, still linked but separated by a more secure division than existed between various nodes on ARPANET. In 1984, the National Science Foundation began an aggressive expansion of the Internet, not only in terms of linking new networks, but in funding several dramatic expansions of the Internet infrastructure, providing more and faster links between networks. While ARPANET officially died in 1989, the Internet continued to grow at a furious pace. While current estimates vary wildly, it is safe to say that there are now tens of thousands of networks, in more than 50 countries, and ten million or more "users" connected.

What's Out There?

As you might expect, defining the Internet is difficult. In almost any discussion, you'll start to get confused over the difference between what you can do, and how (technically) you do it. In this sense, many applications have become synonymous with the protocols they use. To make matters worse, the Internet thrives on acronyms—the end-all, be-all of alphabet soup.

In general, though, you can look at several classifications of Internet features:

- E-mail (electronic mail) is a way of sending messages and/or files to other users or groups.
- WWW (World Wide Web) is the current "big thing," a collective set of hypertext and links that makes navigation simple.
- FTP (File Transfer Protocol) is a way of retrieving files from a remote location.
- Telnet is a way of logging into remote computer systems as if you were a local user.
- USENET News is a large collection of "newsgroups," publicly accessible discussion groups. The most recent explosion has been the World Wide Web (WWW), which is a graphic, hypertext network of documents and links.

This list only scratches the surface. There is practically no limit on what you can find on the Internet, but there are several core tools or techniques that open the doors. These facilities are covered in detail in the next chapter, with descriptions of various tools you can use, and examples of the news, information, and data you can access. For now, let's concentrate on getting connected.

Choosing a Connection

As the Internet has expanded, so has the number of access methods. Your options are by no means limited to those discussed here, but these are the most common, easiest to use, and most accessible methods. Probably the most important thing to mention is that you are not limited to any single means of access; you can connect different ways for different purposes, or switch access methods if you find a new one that works better for you. Getting connected is more important than how you get connected, and you can always change later as you learn more, as the market expands, or as your needs change.

Internet Service Providers

The growing popularity of the Internet has spawned a whole new class of business, the *Internet Service Provider*, or ISP. These companies provide access to the Internet, usually for a fee. Different ISPs concentrate on different markets—some target business, some target education, some target consumers, and some provide special services in addition to basic connectivity. For home (personal) use, most ISPs charge somewhere between $20-$30 per month, usually covering a fixed number of hours of connect time. Beyond that, additional time may be billed at an hourly rate. You may find a local ISP that offers an unlimited number of hours at a very attractive price if you shop around.

The more extensive your needs, the more likely it is that you'll want to establish a relationship with an ISP. This is the route that most businesses will take, and it is becoming increasingly popular with end-users as well. Why? Most ISPs can provide you with the basic connection, any hardware and software you might need, as well as various special services—all for one price. One-stop shopping, performance, and reliability are among the reasons why ISPs have become a dominant force in the industry.

One stop shopping can have its price, though. Be sure to understand what is and is not included before you sign an ISP service agreement. You may have to provide your own hardware, or you may be obligated to purchase it from the ISP for an additional fee. You may have different rate structures for different parts of the day, and additional hours may be billed at a much higher rate than the default. Make sure you get all the details and ask any questions before you sign. If you can't get the deal you want, walk away. There are hundreds of other ISPs, and in most areas you've got a choice of several—go with the one that best suits your needs.

Locating ISPs can be somewhat frustrating, since the easiest way of locating them is to search online, which you may not be able to do if you're just starting out. If you are online, check out **http://www.thelist.com/**, which lists almost 2,000 different ISPs, and provides ratings and contact information for each. (That's an URL, or Uniform Resource Locater, and we'll discuss these in detail in Chapter 21, "Using Internet Resources.") If you're not already online, try asking friends, checking out the advertisements in the local paper's business section, or looking in the yellow pages under Computer Services.

Direct Network Connections

Many businesses and organizations have already made the investment in connecting to the Internet, and in many cases, an Internet connection is available from your desktop. This is fine while you're at work, school, or whatever, but it seldom provides any real capability for connecting your personal computers at home.

The normal advantages of direct network connections are speed and simplicity. The frequent disadvantages are organizational restrictions on usage, mandates of specific software products, and the need to work with your system administrator in order to gain access.

Dial-Up Network Connections

The most common method of obtaining a true Internet connection is by a dial-up connection, using your modem or ISDN (Integrated Services Digital Network) adapter. You may be placing a call to an Internet Service Provider (ISP), to a bulletin board system (BBS), a FreeNet, or some other point-of-presence, but the methods are usually similar.

In most cases, this gives you access with a local phone call, usually as fast as your modem is capable of communicating. You are connecting directly to the Internet, and you can usually use any software you want to over that connection.

As we discussed in Chapter 3, "Configuring Modems and Ports," you need to be aware of the speed with which you connect. In most cases, the faster the better, especially with the graphic nature of many current Internet services. A 14.4kbps modem may be adequate, but a 28.8kbps modem may be several times faster. Likewise, you may find the extra cost of an ISDN adapter easily justified if your usage demands the higher speeds (56-128kbps). Whatever your decision, make sure that your ISP supports the type of connection you're trying to make, or you may not realize full value from your investment.

Online Services

If you're already a member of an online service, or if your needs are not overly demanding, you may find that one or more of the commercial online services offer everything you'll need at a low monthly rate. The big four services—America Online, CompuServe, Microsoft Network, and Prodigy—all provide varying degrees of Internet connectivity as part of their basic service plans. While many require that you use their own software (and may not support third-party Internet tools), the cost of membership is usually less than $10 a month. That's roughly half what most Internet Service Providers charge for Internet access.

> **Note**
>
> Each of the information services covered in this chapter is covered in more detail in other chapters. This chapter covers only the Internet-specific connection information, while the other chapters include full coverage of the membership sign-up process, and the different services and features offered. For Internet-specific information, see the sections in this chapter. For general purpose coverage of the information services, see the companion chapters elsewhere within this book.
>
> CompuServe Information Service is covered in detail in Chapter 8.
>
> America Online is covered in detail in Chapter 9.
>
> Prodigy is covered in detail in Chapter 10.
>
> Microsoft Network is covered in detail in Chapter 11.

The online services have their own benefits as well. Unlike the Internet, the service-specific content on most online services is usually quite well organized, and finding things is generally easy. In this regard, you may well find that the online service complements your Internet usage. However, if your needs go beyond the standard package that the information service provides, you may need to look to another method of connecting to the Internet, simply to gain flexibility.

Connecting

Once you've decided how you're going to connect, based on your needs, preferences, and budget, it's time to actually do it. Let's start with the simplest and move on to the more complex methods.

Connecting Over a Local Area Network (LAN)

If you are blessed with a direct network connection where you want to work from, you're home free. You may need some assistance from your system administrator in configuring TCP/IP services as discussed in the previous chapter, and in obtaining the software you will need.

Different networks operate differently, and different companies and organizations provide Internet services to the desktop differently. You may have to request access, and you may have to use specific products, but you're probably on your way to the fastest, simplest, and most reliable connection.

◀ See "An Overview of TCP/IP and the Internet," p. 408

> **Note**
>
> Once you have configured TCP/IP, you are ready to move on to the next chapter, "Using Internet Resources."

Dial-Up Network Connections

If you're working with an Internet Service Provider, or a remote connection to an existing network connection, you'll be using Dial-Up networking in one form or another.

To put it simply, dial-up network connections are made by configuring your modem as a network card. When you attempt an operation that requires the network connection, Windows will dial the phone and attempt to connect to your provider. Most providers are connected to in similar ways, and the configuration is largely the same regardless of which provider you choose.

What may differ is the connection itself, the software (if any) that is provided, and how much you have to do when setting up. Most providers provide dial-up access, and some provide ISDN access. If you have an ISDN adapter, ISDN service is often a much better value, providing 56-128k bps as opposed to the 14.4-28.8k bps access most dial-up providers offer, and usually at the same or at least competitive prices. Even with the same provider, sign-up procedures may vary between dial-up and ISDN. Some providers offer a suite of software, and even an installation utility, and others provide you with a connection, and leave the software and configuration up to you. This section steps through a common type of connection, where most of the configuration is done manually. This will be overkill if your provider provides a Windows 95 installation program, but this is a step that most providers have yet to take.

Step 1—Choosing a Provider and Obtaining Account Information

To get started, you first need to get an account with an Internet Service Provider. This can be any of a wide variety of types, from commercial ISPs to BBSs, FreeNets, or even a communications server at the office. Whatever the source of your service, the steps remain largely the same. The actual sign-up process may vary dramatically from one ISP to another, though. Some give you sign-up software on disk, some give you a phone number to call, some have a BBS, and some make you wait for forms in the mail which you have to mail back. Follow the guidance or instructions from the specific ISP you choose.

When you get your account, you need to get some specific information from your provider. You need your user name, password, and the access number to call. You may also need to get some more technical information, including a host and domain name, an IP address and subnet mask, a gateway address, the address or addresses for a Domain Name Server, and the Domain Name Server search order if you list more than one.

That may seem like a lot, but not every connection requires every piece of information. Another thing that may vary widely between different providers is the procedure you actually use when connecting. With most providers, this involves opening a terminal window when the connection is being made, so you can enter your account number, your password, and the connection type you are requesting. Depending on the type of connection you're using, and your provider's requirement, this may be something you can script.

> **Note**
>
> Like support for SLIP, the scripting tools are only included with the CD-ROM edition of Windows 95, not in the floppy disk release. The scripting tools also are included with the Windows 95 Resource Kit.

Step 2—Configuring Your Communications Adapter

If you haven't set up your modem or ISDN adapter, you need to do this next. For modems, run Control Panel (choose Settings, Control Panel, from the Start button) and double-click Modems. If you have not installed a modem, Windows 95 automatically runs the Install New Modem wizard to step you through the installation. If you are using an ISDN adapter, you probably need an installation disk from your ISDN hardware manufacturer—not that many ISDN adapters are directly supported by Windows 95, but most can easily be installed with an update from your vendor.

Step 3—Installing Dial-Up Networking

The next step is to install Dial-Up Networking and related components. In Control Panel, double-click Add/Remove Programs, and click the Windows Setup tab. Click Communications, then click Details. As shown in figure 20.1, check the box for Dial-Up Networking, then click OK. Once you finish copying the required components, you will be prompted to restart your system.

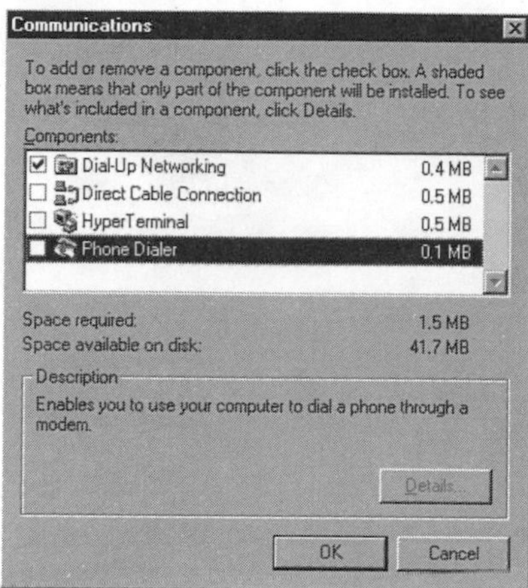

Fig. 20.1 Install Dial-Up Networking in Add/Remove Programs to allow Windows 95 to use your modem or ISDN adapter as a network connection.

Step 4—Installing and Configuring TCP/IP

After you have restarted your system, you will need to add the TCP/IP protocol. In Control Panel, double-click on Network. As shown in figure 20.2, click on Add, double-click on Protocol, click on Microsoft, and click on TCP/IP, then click on OK. Check to make sure that TCP/IP has bound to your dial-up adapter. If not, click on Dial-Up Adapter, then click Properties. Click on the Bindings tab, and check TCP/IP. Again, you may be prompted to restart your computer.

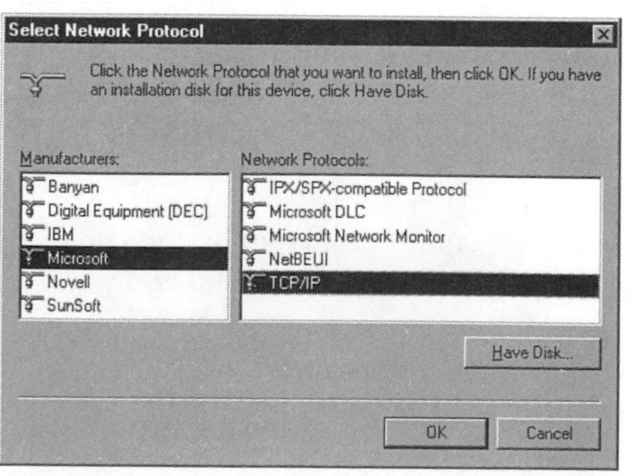

Fig. 20.2 Add the TCP/IP protocol so you can speak the Internet's native tongue.

Next, you need to add some details for your TCP/IP connection. Click on TCP/IP (if there is more than one entry, click on the entry which is bound to the dial-up adapter), and click on Properties. On the IP Address tab, shown in figure 20.3, either enter the IP address you received from your provider (and the subnet mask if provided), or click Obtain An IP Address Automatically.

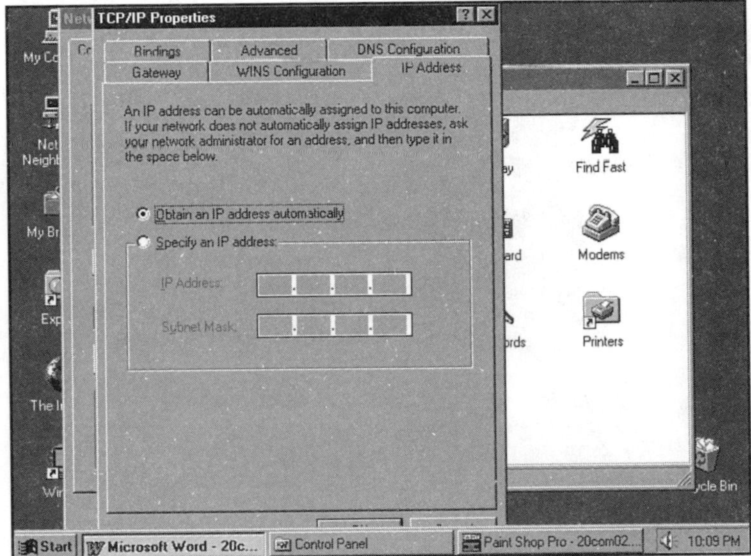

Fig. 20.3 Entering TCP/IP information: The IP Address must be unique; somctimes you get this from your provider, sometimes it is automatically assigned when you connect.

Step 5—Creating a Dial-Up Connection

Now, we need to define the connection to your service provider. From the Start menu, choose Programs, Accessories, Dial-Up Networking. If this is your first connection, the Make New Connection wizard runs automatically. If you are adding an additional connection, double-click on Make New Connection. On the first screen, enter a name for the new connection, and choose the modem or ISDN adapter you wish to use to make the connection. Click on Next, and enter the area code and phone number you received from your provider. Click on Next; then click on Finish. You have now created the connection. A new icon will appear in your Dial-Up Networking folder.

Right-click on the newly created connection, and choose Properties. If your provider supports multiple connection types on the same line, it is possible that your provider will require you to enter your account number and password manually, and specify a connection type when you connect. To allow this, click on Configure, choose the Options tab shown in figure 20.4, and check Bring Up Terminal Window after Dialing, and then click OK. If your provider allows you to automatically enter your account number and password as part of the connection process, skip this step. You will be prompted later for an account number and password when you initiate the dial-up connection.

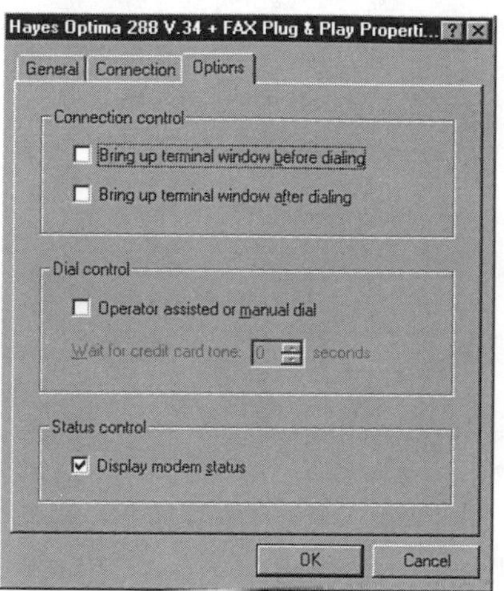

Fig. 20.4
If your provider requires you to interactively choose your session type, you will need to bring up a terminal window when connecting.

Next, click on the Server Type button, and let's set some options. Unless your provider allows you to choose your logon and password, they will be different than your Windows 95 logon and password. If your provider allows you, choose a logon and password that matches your Windows 95 logon and password, and leave the Log On To Network box checked. Otherwise, uncheck this box to speed up your connection. Under Allowed Network Protocols, you will probably want to uncheck NetBEUI and IPX/SPX Compatible if they are checked, unless you have a specific need to use these protocols. Most Internet providers only support TCP/IP, and disabling the additional protocols will improve performance. At the top of the page, make sure you are set for PPP, as shown in figure 20.5.

Note

If you need SLIP support, you must install SLIP support separately from either the Windows 95 CD-ROM or the Windows 95 Resource Kit. PPP is the preferred connection method, and most Internet providers now support PPP. If your provider requires SLIP, install SLIP support, then set the server type to SLIP. Finally, click OK to save your settings.

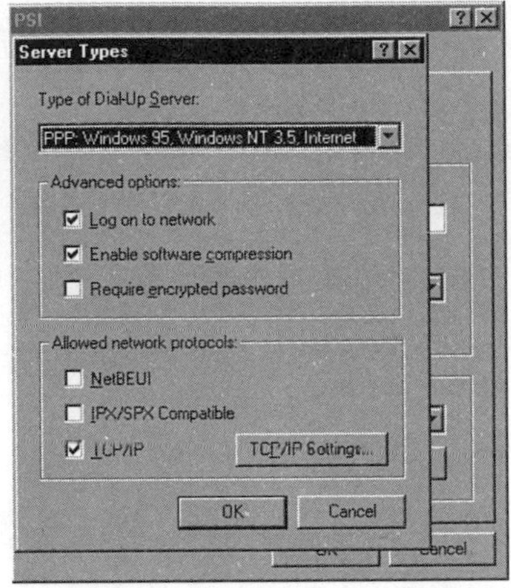

Fig. 20.5 Make sure you are configured for PPP. If you have installed the optional SLIP support, you can also choose SLIP.

Step 6—Making the Connection

You have now configured your dial-up connection. You should now be able to double-click on the icon in your Dial-Up Networking folder to make the connection. Enter your account number and password, as shown in figure 20.6, and click on Connect. If you set that option earlier, you may see a terminal window come up once the connection is established, this will allow you to enter your logon and password, and specify the connection type you want.

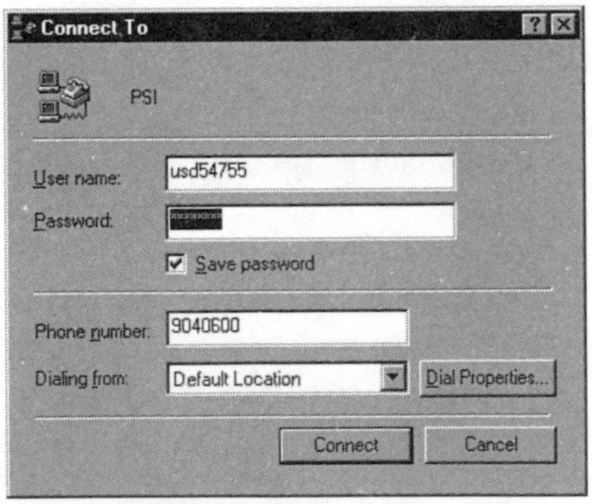

Fig. 20.6 Enter the user name and password you received from your provider.

Choosing SLIP or PPP

There are two protocols in common use for remote Internet connectivity, Serial Line Internet Protocol (SLIP) and Point-to-Point Protocol (PPP). SLIP is the older of the two. While SLIP was never an official standard, it shipped with many UNIX implementations, making its usage widespread. In a perfect world, SLIP is faster than PPP, but not as reliable. PPP, which is an official standard, adds support for error detection and data compression, and allows negotiation of many parameters that must be expressly specified with SLIP. There is a Compressed Serial Line Internet Protocol (CSLIP), which is simply standard SLIP with compression.

A lot depends on your provider, its systems and volume. SLIP is less demanding to implement, and SLIP was available before PPP, so some vendors may still stick with the old ways. Windows 95, with its preference for PPP, has convinced a number of providers to upgrade to PPP, or offer it as an additional option. Most ISPs now offer both SLIP and PPP. If you have a choice, you should choose PPP.

With Windows 95, the preferred method of making dial-up Internet connections is via Point-to-Point Protocol, or PPP. Serial Line Internet Protocol, or SLIP, is supported, but this support is not included on the floppy disk release of Windows 95. You must either purchase the CD-ROM edition or the Windows 95 Resource Kit to get the extra files you need. If you do need a SLIP connection, you will need additional information from your provider to configure some of the details, but the general steps are the same.

Online Services

If you are already a member of one of the major online services, such as America Online, CompuServe, Microsoft Network, or Prodigy, you may find that the service offers all the Internet connectivity you need as part of its standard service, or as an upgrade. Most of the online services offer access to most Internet resources, but most also require that you use their standard software. This has advantages if you want everything to work through a common interface, or have a common look-and-feel, but it may have disadvantages if you want to pick and choose various tools from separate sources.

In some cases, the online services provide the quickest and easiest route to the Internet, especially for existing users. In other cases, you may want more flexibility than a specific online service can provide. As you'll see, different services offer different options, different software, and different levels of flexibility. You should also consider how you want to use the Internet, what connectivity options each service offers, and what other alternatives exist before making a decision. However, if you're already a member of one of these services, you should at least explore the Internet options available before going out and signing up with another provider or service.

The following sections review what is necessary to get Internet access through each of the four leading online services. A few precautionary notes are in order, though.

- Of the four services listed, only one, Microsoft Network, provided Windows 95-specific software at the time of this writing. The remainder were all Windows 3.1 software which functioned under Windows 95, but did not take advantage of any of Windows 95's new features. It is therefore likely that significant updates may follow.
- Of the four services listed, two, America Online and Prodigy, provide Internet access entirely within the bounds of their existing access software and interface, except for companion WWW browser applications. This means you are limited to the software provided by these two services. CompuServe provides its services by means of a proprietary WINSOCK.DLL implementation, which may make the use of much third-party Internet software rather problematic. Microsoft Network provides all Internet services through standard dial-up networking and TCP/IP, which makes it compatible with almost all third-party applications, and is the most open of the four services in this regard.
- America Online and Prodigy provide "parental controls" over content, which allow you to restrict what is available to you or your family. Both services turn these restrictions on by default. America Online tends to allow more flexibility in what content or services are excluded. Prodigy tends to limit access only by access type (such as WWW or News), but provides more options for filtering individual content or messages. MSN and CompuServe allow unrestricted access by default, although you may find some of the more questionable material is only accessible if you ask for it by name. MSN warns you about the uncontrolled nature of the Internet in this regard, CompuServe doesn't. If you're looking for access you can tailor for yourself and your children, parental controls and filters may be a serious concern.

Here, now, is a walk-through for each of the major online services. We'll cover what software you need to start with, what updates you may need along the way, and an overview of what services are offered, how they are implemented, and some of the pros and cons of each service.

America Online

Chapter 9 worked through the process of connecting to America Online, and taught you how to use and navigate the information service. America Online's Internet services are tightly integrated with their regular access software. If you are using version 2.5, you already have most of what you need. If not, you will need to get the 2.5 upgrade before you start using Internet services. As they have become famous for, AOL frequently mails out disks with its software, and many of the newer mailings even include the WWW browser in addition to the current release of their software.

> **Note**
>
> AOL also operates GNN (Global Network Navigator), which is covered in detail in Chapter 12.

AOL makes it straightforward to get on the Internet. After connecting and signing on, click the Internet Connection. If you need a software update, you'll be told. If not, you'll get the Internet Connection window, as shown in figure 20.7. If you want WWW access, it will be another few minutes (free) while you download AOL's WWW browser, if it wasn't included with your initial software installation. Everything is installed and configured for you immediately; you don't have to answer questions, make decisions, or restart your system.

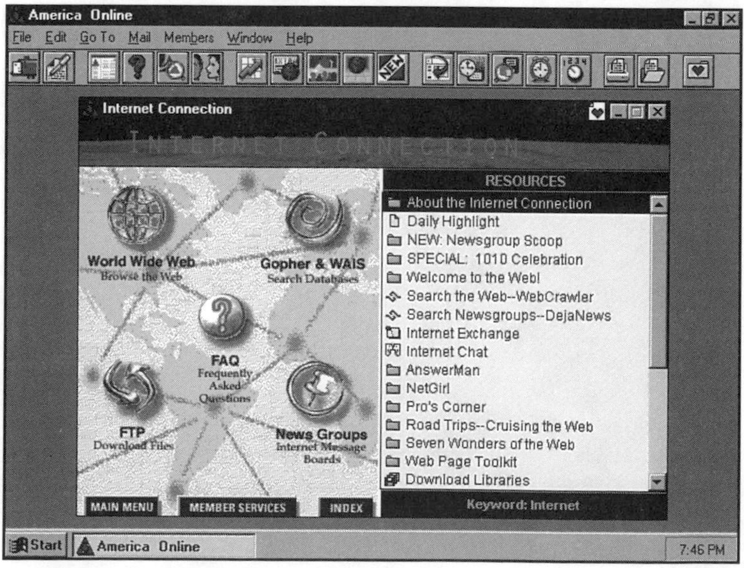

Fig. 20.7
America Online's Internet Center offers centralized Internet access.

There are some interesting idiosyncrasies, related to both the way in which the various Internet components integrate, and to the "parental control" settings you get by default. AOL provides a WWW browser that provides complete WWW access, but other functions, such as news, ftp, etc., call up standard AOL functions. In this way, you will find using AOL's Internet services much like using AOL itself, and somewhat different than using a full TCP/IP connection. The "parental control" features are turned on by default, and this may confuse you initially if you notice large areas missing.

AOL provides Internet access as an extension of its normal client software, not as a separate package. It is tightly integrated with AOL features, and the transition between actual Internet services and AOL areas may be hard to discern. If you're using AOL to access the Internet, you will be using AOL software exclusively. This is probably great for current AOL users, but doesn't give a lot of flexibility to users seeking full and open Internet access.

CompuServe

Chapter 8 looked at the process of connecting to CompuServe, and taught you how to use and navigate the information service. In this chapter, we'll cover adding Internet services to the basic CompuServe connection. CompuServe offers Internet services in two forms. Some services are offered directly from the Information service, as shown in figure 20.8, while others are available only on a direct PPP connection.

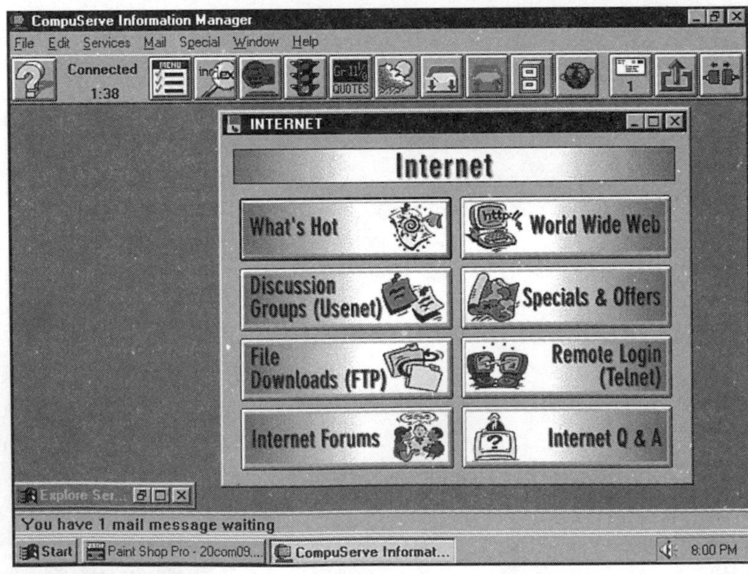

Fig. 20.8
CompuServe Information Services Internet Services menu offers access to several Internet options, while others are available through a PPP connection.

CompuServe has recently released the 2.0 version of its software. While this is still a 16-bit Windows 3.1 application, it has been rewritten to work properly under Windows 95, especially regarding Internet access. If you are running a version of WinCIM below 2.0, you should upgrade to the current version before proceeding. While CompuServe provided utilities to enable WinCIM 1.4 users to add an Internet connection, it is not stable under Windows 95, and its installation program may cause significant problems with your system. For the purposes of this chapter, we will cover version 2.0. A maintenance release, 2.0.1, was scheduled to ship close behind the 2.0 release, and should be available by the time you read this. If you are currently running WinCIM 1.4 or below, order the upgrade disks from CompuServe. At this writing, CompuServe was unclear as to its plans for placing the new version online for downloading. Follow the installation instructions that come with the upgrade disks. The installation process is quick and simple, with only one potential problem area. If you already have an Internet connection through another provider, DO NOT install CompuServe's WINSOCK.DLL file. This is the default behavior for the installation program. However, if you WANT to use CompuServe for your Internet access, you should install CompuServe's WINSOCK.DLL. If you are NOT using another provider, and you accept the default options, you will have to rerun the installation to install CompuServe's WINSOCK.DLL—save yourself a step by anticipating this during the initial installation. Once the installation is complete, you'll find a few new items in your CompuServe folder. These include the CompuServe Internet Dialer (its own dial-up networking component), Spry Mosaic (its WWW browser), and the ImageView application (which provides GIF and JPEG displays). At this point, you're ready to launch Spry Mosaic and "surf the net."

The CompuServe Internet Dialer (CID) uses the default settings for CIM (CIS Connection) and connects to CompuServe when you initiate a session in Spry Mosaic. Because WinCIM now directly supports WinSOCK, you can keep WinCIM and Spry Mosaic open at the same time; they will cooperatively use the same connection.

CompuServe's WINSOCK.DLL file is specific to CompuServe. It is also a 16-bit DLL file. Because of these limitations, you may have difficulty with some third-party applications. Effectively, this may limit you to the Spry Mosaic that CompuServe includes with WinCIM. In the next major release, WinCIM 3.0, CompuServe plans to deliver a fully 32-bit Windows 95 application.

Microsoft Network

Chapter 11 reviewed the process of connecting to The Microsoft Network, and taught you how to use the information service. Now, we're going to take it a step further, and actually use The Microsoft Network as our Internet connection. MSN makes this easy, so you'll be online in no time.

First, you need an update to the MSN software, that provides access to the Internet in addition to MSN. To get this update, start at MSN Central and click on Categories. From the Categories list, double-click on the Internet Center. This is where we get down to business, as shown in figure 20.9.

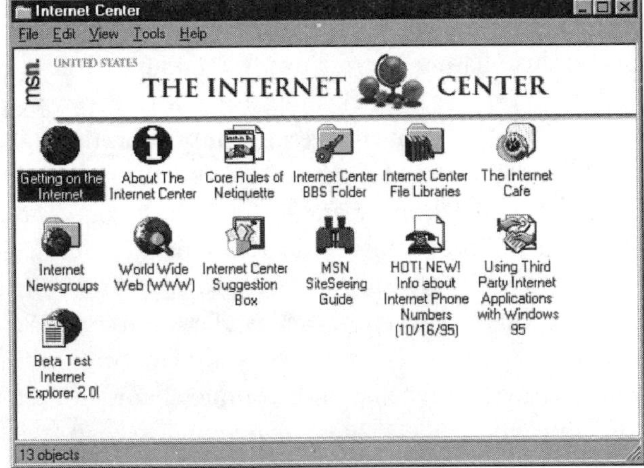

Fig. 20.9 The Microsoft Network's Internet Center contains the access points, the software, and the documentation.

Double-click on "Getting on the Internet," and let's start the process. First, you'll get a bit of documentation. Read it, then continue. Next, you'll get the upgrade information for MSN that includes the Internet connection.

Read carefully for a while here. You have the option of checking for available phone numbers in your area. Don't skip this step unless you already know that there is an MSN Internet access number in your local calling area. There is little point of spending half an hour downloading software, then having to pay long-distance phone charges for your Internet connection. As Microsoft correctly points out, if there is not an access number in your local calling area, you should probably wait until there is one before upgrading.

There is one side benefit. The standard MSN access numbers don't support connections faster than 14.4k bps. However, the Internet access numbers support connections at 28.8k bps. If there is an Internet access number in your local calling area, and you have a 28.8k bps modem, you may want to get this upgrade even if you don't plan to use Internet services.

Once you have verified that there is a local MSN Internet access number, and you've read all the provided information, click on the last icon to upgrade. This will start a process that takes about 30 minutes. First, an update program is downloaded, then the actual upgrade files are transferred. Be ready with your Windows 95 CD-ROM or disks, you'll be prompted for several files along the way. When all of the upgrade files are installed, you'll be prompted to re-start your computer, so that the upgrade process can complete.

As the setup process completes, you'll again be prompted for your Windows 95 CD-ROM or disks so Windows 95 can install the various needed compo-nents. This includes TCP/IP, Dial-Up Networking, and related utilities. You also will connect to MSN to obtain the latest phone number list, and a new access number will be selected. Be warned, in most localities, this will leave you without a backup access number, since there are far fewer Internet access numbers. Once MSN and Windows 95 have completed this second round of setup, you will again be prompted to restart your system.

When you complete the update process, you will have a new icon on your desktop for the Microsoft Internet Explorer, Microsoft's WWW browser, and new networking entries for Dial-Up Networking and TCP/IP. When an Internet application touches WINSOCK.DLL, it will relay the request to TCP/IP, which will initiate a dial-up connection through MSN to the Internet. Compared to other services, this is one of the easier, although time consum-ing, installation procedures. Microsoft and MSN use standard Windows 95 components for your Internet connection, except that MSN serves as your Internet Service Provider, eliminating a couple of steps when connecting. This means that you can use *any* WINSOCK-compliant application, not just those provided by Microsoft.

Prodigy

Chapter 10 worked through the process of connecting to Prodigy, and you learned how to use the information service itself. In this section, you'll take a look at Prodigy's Internet services. Prodigy provides integrated Internet access in much the same way as America Online does. While you may receive vari-ous minor updates along the way, you will find a button labeled "Web" on the main Prodigy toolbar. This takes you to the Internet area, shown in figure 20.10, and download or update the WWW browser as necessary.

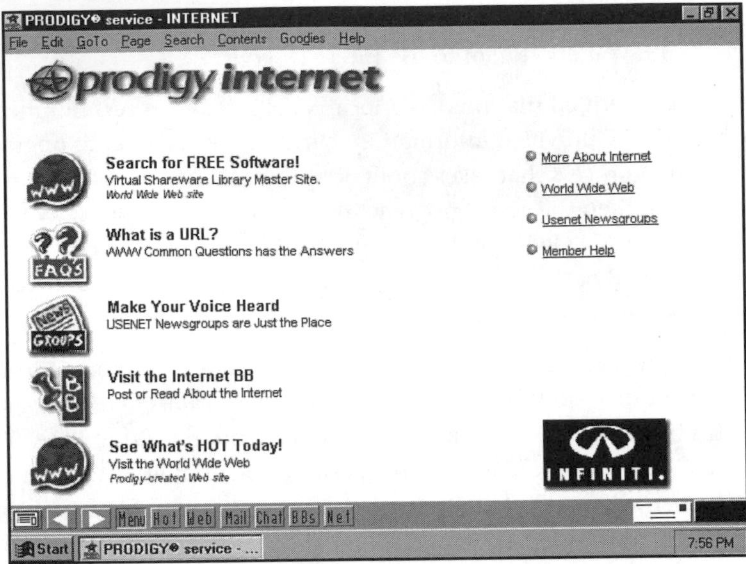

Fig. 20.10
Prodigy's Internet Center.

Prodigy, to an even greater extent than AOL, restricts access to certain areas under "parental control." If you want access to Internet services such as WWW or Newsgroups, you will have to modify your permissions for the account(s) which you wish to be able to access these features.

Prodigy's WWW browser is quick and excellent. FTP and Gopher access also are provided by the WWW browser. The separate newsreader is slower and less reliable. In the newsreader, there is no provision for automatically decoding binary files, you must save them as files and manually decode them later. Except for the WWW browser, the provided tools are relatively basic, although the "ignore" function in the newsreader is the closest any of the major services come to an actual kill file, allowing you to have some control over from whom, and regarding what subjects, you receive news.

Like AOL, Prodigy provides all of its Internet access through its normal communications program and interface, although the WWW browser will spawn in a separate window. You will not have the ability to use third-party tools if you are getting your Internet connection through Prodigy. ❖

CHAPTER 21

Using Internet Resources

by Dave Rorabaugh

Getting connected isn't enough if you don't know where to go or how to get there. Now that you've made the connection, we'll give you some of the rules of the road, take you by a few favorite places, and teach you to use some standard types of tools.

This chapter gives you an overview of the most popular types of Internet software for Windows 95, and how to use it. In addition to explaining the software and how to choose and use it, this chapter also acts as a tour guide, to show you the depth and diversity of the Internet, and give you some starting points for your own explorations.

In this chapter, you learn to

- Browse the World Wide Web
- Work with Newsgroups
- Use Telnet to log in remotely
- Transfer files with FTP
- Search using various tools and techniques

If you're ready to start exploring the Internet to take full advantage of what it has to offer, read on.

The World Wide Web

While the Internet has a long and established history, the World Wide Web (WWW) is a relatively recent development. In search of a user-friendly improvement on several existing technologies such as Gopher, which offered a hierarchical series of links to either documents or folders, the WWW takes it all several steps further.

The WWW is based on the concept of hypertext. *Hypertext* was initially championed and evangelized by Ted Nelson, and refers to an arrangement of documents in which there are several paths available to the reader. In reading a piece of information, for example, the reader would be able to immediately switch to related information, definitions, or illustrations; follow a logical process; or connect to other related information. Hypertext, an idea virtually impossible before the computer age, is the core of the WWW. Unless you're new to Windows, you're probably familiar with hypertext from using the Windows help files.

There are three elements that make up documents on the WWW: text, graphics, and links. A *link* is a connection to another document or function. Links can be attached to either text or graphics within a document. The documents are created in a special format, HyperText Markup Language (HTML). HTML provides the commands for implementing the links, including graphics, and formatting the text in a WWW document.

The WWW has its own protocol, known as HyperText Transfer Protocol (HTTP). Combined with HTTP as a common language, there are two other elements to the WWW: HTTP servers, otherwise known as web servers, and the client software, commonly referred to as Web browsers. Originally developed by the University of Illinois at Champaign's National Center for Supercomputing Applications (NCSA), the first widely popular browser was Mosaic. Several subsequent commercial implementations from companies such as Spyglass, Netscape, and Microsoft, have expanded and refined the definition of "browser." The technology is expanding at a rapid pace, and new features and capabilities are being added all the time.

Mosaic, along with it's variants and derivatives, combines several functions into a single application. Not only do most browsers have the ability to work with WWW or HTML data, but most also support other types of connections, such as Gopher (a precursor to the WWW), news, FTP, and mail. In addition to the inherent popularity of the WWW, this type of integrated client has helped solidify its own popularity. Many browsers are good enough at these other functions that you may find you need but one tool for all but the most complicated tasks.

These new multifunction browsers have helped create a new type of syntax for resources on the Internet, providing a standard way of specifying different types of resources for use within a single application. The *Uniform Resource Locator*, or *URL*, has become the new standard. There are three parts of the

URL: the application or protocol identifier, the actual address and (optionally) document name, and (optionally) the TCP/IP port number if a non-standard port is used. In this schema, most URLs take on a common appearance.

Let's look at a few WWW URLs:

http://www.microsoft.com/

http://www.dsmllp.com/weird.htm

http://www.phoneycorp.com:88

The first example simply specifies that we are using HTTP (HyperText Transfer Protocol) to access a WWW resource, which is located on the system www.microsoft.com. We didn't specify the document name, so we'll get the default document on that server. We didn't specify a port number, so we'll use the standard port. In the second example, we have also specified a specific document to load (weird.htm). In the third example, we have also specified a non-standard port number. Non-standard port numbers are not frequently used, but are occasionally implemented where multiple servers are running on the same host, or where the administrators have taken steps to either hide their server, or at least keep people from tripping over it.

Note the frequent use of www in the host name. It's common for companies to name their Web server www.*corpname*.com. Since many companies are new to the Internet and are still installing or growing their internal capabilities, naming conventions of this sort are important to recognize. The company that starts with a single system and doesn't use this type of naming convention will find it more difficult to split their services onto separate servers later when demand increases.

You can also use URLs that point to non-WWW resources. Take a look at the following examples:

news:rec.music.gdead

mailto:dave@vcs.mhs.compuserve.com

telnet:xyz.phonycorp.com:9000

In the first example, the URL points to a specific newsgroup, which we will cover later in this chapter in "Working with Newsgroups." The second URL creates a mail message to the address specified. The third example starts a Telnet session (covered later in this chapter in "Using Telnet") to xyz.phonycorp.com, using the non-standard TCP/IP port of 9000. Learning to recognize the way in which URLs are constructed, and being able to identify what a URL refers to, will greatly improve your ability to navigate on the WWW.

Let's fire up a browser and take a tour. Netscape Navigator, as shown in figure 21.1, is one of the most widely used browsers. Most browsers exhibit the same default behavior. Your "home page"—the page which your browser loads by default—is initially set to the vendor or developer's home page. This is usually a good way to keep track of recent or upcoming updates, but it may not be the way you want to work. However, all the browsers we've worked with make it simple to change the default page to whatever you want.

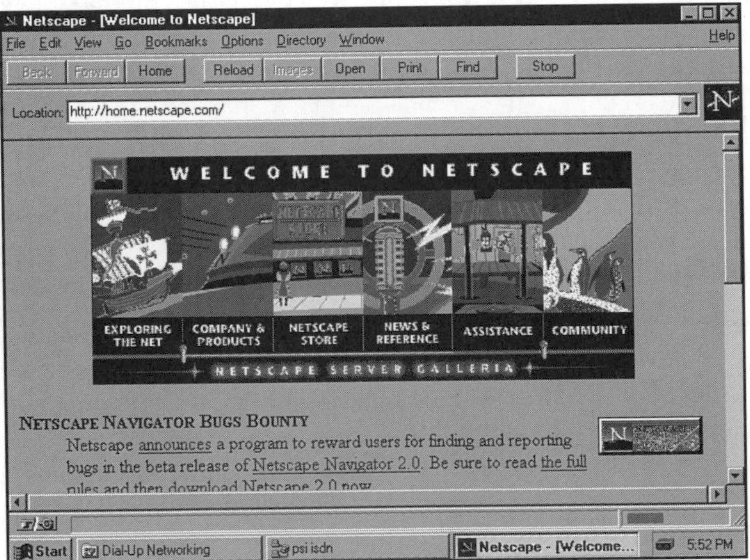

Fig. 21.1
Netscape Navigator is one of the most popular WWW browsers.

You navigate from one place to another by clicking links. A link will be a pointer to another URL, or occasionally a different location within the current URL. Links are usually highlighted in one of several ways. Most commonly used is the text link, where the link is associated with a block of text, which will usually be uniquely colored and/or underlined.

Images can also serve as links, in which case the image will usually have a colored border to indicate that it is a link. Another frequently encountered type of link is the *imagemap*, in which a graphic containing several links is displayed, and the link is chosen by determining the location within the graphic where the reader clicked. For an imagemap, the browser passes the coordinates along when the link is chosen, and a program on the Web server decodes these coordinates to determine which element of the imagemap was chosen. It's also common for the individual elements in an imagemap to be listed later in the document in text form. This allows users who aren't loading the graphics to still use the links. While this redundancy may seem awkward or unnecessary at first, it is simply being provided for the convenience of other users.

Most browsers will change the cursor or indicate the destination of a link in a status bar when you pass your cursor over it. Some links will take you to other HTML documents, and others will take you to other things. You can follow links to graphic files, FTP servers, and even specific files (see "Transferring Files with FTP" later in this chapter), Telnet sessions (see "Using Telnet" later in this chapter), e-mail addresses, newsgroups, gopher servers, and several other types of sites.

For your convenience, most browser programs allow you to use two personal lists. Your *history list* is a list of all the sites you've visited, in the order you've visited them. This can allow you to review or retrace your steps, and get back to places you've visited previously. Your *hotlist* file is a list of your favorite or most frequently visited locations. Most browsers allow quick menu access to the sites on your hotlist. This can make getting to your most frequently used sites a much quicker task. Used together, the history and hotlist files are important WWW navigation aids.

Some types of links may require *helper applications*, which load a different application to provide support for a specific type of data. Sound and video are two common examples of this type of application. When you click a link to a video file, the browser makes the connection and transfers the file itself, then launches the defined helper application for that type of file to actually play the video.

In Windows, the two most common types of video files will be .AVI (Audio/Video Interleave) files, which are playable by the Windows 95 Media Player, and .MOV (Apple's QuickTime) files, which are playable by a separately installed viewer from Apple. For audio files, there are three common formats, .WAV, or standard Windows 95 wave audio, .AU, Sun's standard for audio files, and .MPG, the Motion Picture Experts Group (MPEG) audio format. Windows 95's Media Player can handle the .WAV files, but you'll need a third party application to play .AU or .MPG files. In most cases, the sites offering these types of files contain links to software you can download.

Just like different helper applications, there is a wide variety of browsers available. If you are getting your Internet connection through an online service, you may have few choices. However, if you're connecting through an ISP (Internet Service Provider) or another type of open connection, you have many choices available.

The two most popular browsers are Netscape's Navigator and Microsoft's Internet Explorer. The Microsoft Internet Explorer is available in the Plus! Pack for Windows 95, and also available from MSN or Microsoft's WWW site (**http://www.microsoft.com/** or **http://www.home.msn.com/**). Netscape's Navigator, though a commercial product, is available from Netscape's WWW site (**http://home.netscape.com/**). There are a wide variety of other browsers available, and many are available for the downloading. Your best option is to use one of the search tools described later in this chapter to locate several browsers that sound interesting, download them, and see which you like best.

Once you've chosen a browser (a decision your provider may make for you, especially with an online service), configured any helper applications you may need, and learned to use your history and hotlist files, you're really ready to surf the Net.

Working with Newsgroups

Think of newsgroups as electronic discussion groups. If you're familiar with online services or bulletin boards, you can equate them with forums, conferences, sections, and so on. However, unlike other systems, Internet newsgroups have two unique things going for them: critical mass and almost universal propagation. Internet newsgroups are truly global in scope, with people around the world participating in myriad conversations. Critical mass is the important factor—there are enough people participating that almost any topic can find enough participation to be rewarding.

Newsgroups are arranged in hierarchies, with the top level being the general theme, and the intermediate levels further defining the specific discussion topic. Normally, the description will get more specific from left to right. Wildcard notation is often used to delineate sections of a hierarchy. For example, the rec.* hierarchy would contain several different rec.crafts.* newsgroups, among which would be rec.crafts.brewing.

There are several major classifications of newsgroups. UseNet newsgroups, known as the "Big 8," comprise the most widely used hierarchies. Comp (for computers), hum (for humanities), misc (for miscellaneous), news (for news), rec (for recreation), sci (for science), soc (for social/society), and talk (for talk) are the top-level hierarchies which fall under the administration of UseNet, a sort of spontaneous volunteer bureaucracy which arose to take over management of the Internet newsgroups. UseNet created sets of policies and procedures to govern the creation and management of newsgroups, trying to bring some measure of order to what was often chaos.

In response, users who perceived UseNet as an evil intrusion into the intentional anarchy of the Internet formed a new hierarchy, alt (for alternative) in which the UseNet rules do not apply. Alt, though not available at all sites, has become the most popular hierarchy, at least in terms of volume. There are also a number of hierarchies for regional news, such as ba (for the San Francisco Bay Area), dc (for Washington DC), can (for Canada), and so on. There are also a number of independent hierarchies, some of which charge for access. For example, ClariNet (clari.*) and the Legal Domain Network (law.*) offer high levels of specialization within their fields. ClariNet is a paid service, while the Legal Domain Network is limited to law schools and law firms. Combined, the UseNet, alt, regional, and independent newsgroups offer the reader over 15,000 possibilities to choose from. Yes, multiple choices are allowed.

You use a newsreader to obtain news from a news server. Newsreaders take several forms, but generally all provide a list of available groups, a list of messages within each group, and may organize those messages into conversations or *threads*, as shown in figure 21.2. Threads become important when you want to follow a complete discussion from beginning to end, although you should realize that many newsgroup discussions may not have a beginning or end, but may go on endlessly, often rambling. Some newsgroups are more prone to this than others—generally alt newsgroups have the lowest signal to noise ratio (extraneous content often dominates), while technical subject areas, such as sci, tend to have the highest. Most newsreaders provide some way of following threads.

Another feature is the ability to select certain newsgroups as *subscribed*. This is somewhat of a misnomer, since it technically makes no difference, but it allows the newsreader to treat these groups differently. On a news server carrying 15,000 different newsgroups, you will have a very long list when you look at what's available. Subscribing to the newsgroups allows you to move your favorites to the top of the list. Some newsreaders will also retrieve more information on the groups you've subscribed to than on others.

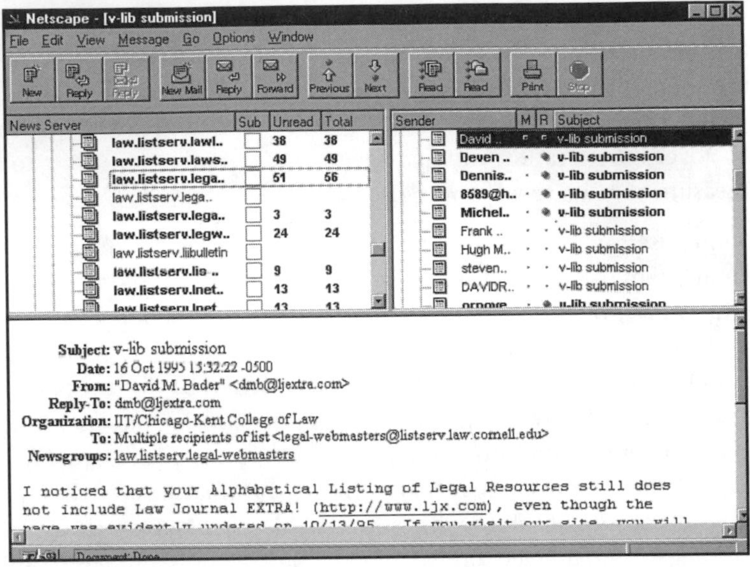

Fig. 21.2
Netscape's Newsreader is included with Netscape Navigator 2.0.

When you're reading articles posted in a newsgroup, you usually have three different options for how to reply to a message, and several important things to consider when addressing your reply. First, you can either reply to the message on the newsgroup or by e-mail. If you are discussing a salient point in an ongoing discussion, posting your reply to the group may be the best choice. If, however, you are making comments or asking questions which are not appropriate for general discussion, or which diverge from the subject at hand, replying by e-mail may be the best choice. If you simply want to make someone else aware of the posting, you can forward the message to them by e-mail.

You should be careful when addressing your replies, many messages are "cross-posted" to several different newsgroups, often inappropriately. When you reply, make sure you limit your response to those groups that are appropriate. Excessive cross-posting is one of the reasons that so many threads get out of hand—it's better to limit your postings and your replies to only the groups to which they are directly relevant.

Network Etiquette (Netiquette)

Newsgroups are probably the most common venue for breaches of Netiquette, simply due to the large number of people involved, and the nature of a public dialog. Some of the things you have to be careful to avoid are flaming and spamming.

Flaming is the common name given to loud, harsh, obscene, or offensive conduct. If someone posts a message that is inflammatory, several readers may post public replies condemning the original poster, and a long and loud argument usually ensues. This is known as a "flame war." If you feel a need to reply to an inflammatory posting, consider whether your remarks lend anything to the discussion at hand. If not, consider holding your tongue or making the comments privately. Some people actually post intentionally inflammatory statements in hopes of starting a flame war—this process is known as *trolling*. If you spot a troll, bear in mind that the best possible response is to ignore the posting.

Spamming is the act of posting a message to a large number of often unrelated newsgroups. This is normally someone advocating for a cause or advertising a product or service. When posting a message, make sure you only address it to the newsgroups to which it is directly appropriate. When replying to such a message, make sure you reply to the sender, and not to the hundreds (or even thousands) of newsgroups to which the message was originally posted. Rather than start a flame war online in response to spam, direct your action at the poster, the poster's system administrator, or the company whose product or services were advertised. While some people intentionally spam messages to thousands of newsgroups, most do so unknowingly. Those who act unintentionally usually change their techniques quickly when their mailboxes fill with complaints.

Using Telnet

When you need to log in to another computer system somewhere on the Internet, you'll probably use a Telnet application to do it. Basically, Telnet is a form of terminal emulator that works over the Internet, allowing you to log in to a remote system as if you were directly connected. Telnet is a common means of logging in to information systems, and also for playing certain types of games.

Whether you use Telnet to log in to government bulletin boards, or to play games in Multi-User Dungeons (MUDs), the application is much the same. Windows 95 includes a basic Telnet application, or you can seek out more powerful Telnet programs online. The beginning of your connection is the same, you specify the site you want to connect to, the TCP/IP port number, and what type of emulation you want to use. For most connections, the default VT100 emulation will be fine. Some systems or server programs will benefit from more powerful or specialized terminal programs, which provide added capabilities and features.

The following illustrations show two different applications of the same Telnet program. First, a business-type connection, as shown in figure 21.3 to a collection of U.S. Government bulletin boards, and second, as shown in figure 21.4, a connection to a role-playing game.

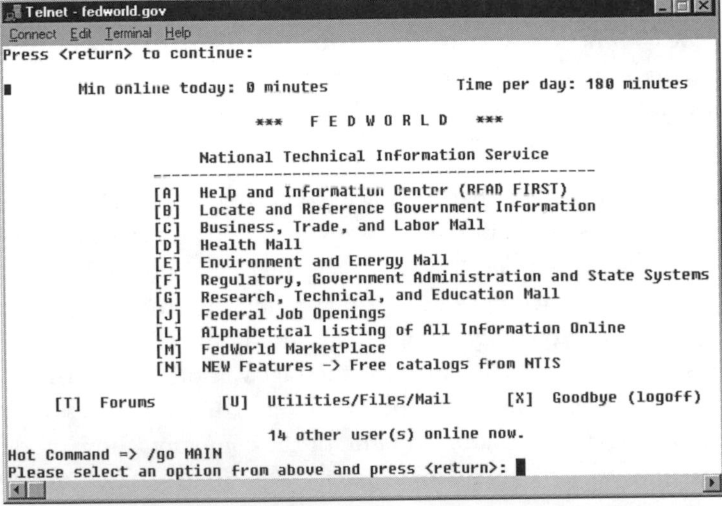

Fig. 21.3
You can use Telnet to connect to Internet-based bulletin boards.

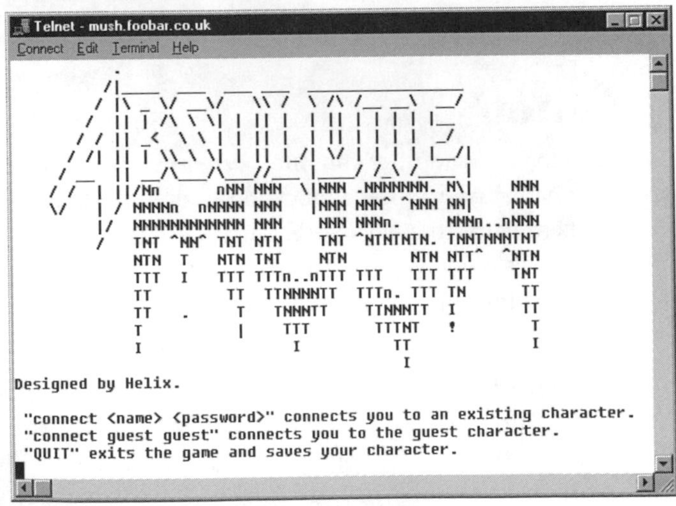

Fig. 21.4
You can also use Telnet to connect to Multi-User Dungeon games.

Telnet can literally be your window to the world. Telnet's level of interactivity sets it apart from the World Wide Web and other services. When you use Telnet and connect to another system, you are interacting with the remote system, not just browsing. In addition to the remote system, you also may be interacting with other users on the system, not just the system itself.

If you're looking for sites to telnet to, your best bet is to go searching on the World Wide Web (WWW) using one of the search tools listed later in this chapter. You may often find WWW pages that contain links to specific Telnet sites that contain lists of interesting sites.

Transferring Files with FTP

As you're building your software collection, or maintaining your existing programs, you'll need to get out on the Internet and download some files. To retrieve files from a remote location on the Internet, you'll use a File Transfer Protocol, or FTP, application. Think of an FTP application as a type of remote file manager program. FTP applications usually have two divisions: a window showing your local files, and a window showing the files on the remote system to which you have connected.

Some systems require you to have a defined user ID and password in order to connect or transfer files, and others support what is known as *anonymous FTP*. Anonymous FTP is a universally accepted method of allowing public access to an FTP server. Instead of requiring that each user have his or her own predefined user ID and password, everyone is allowed to connect with a user name of "anonymous," while using a password which is the same as their e-mail address. This removes most of the administrative burden, but still provides a record of who downloaded what, and when. Most of the time, you'll be using anonymous FTP.

Most FTP applications are similar in design. An initial window is presented to allow you to enter the site you wish to connect to, and to specify your login ID and password. You can also specify any special parameters, such as a different TCP/IP port setting (if it's non-standard) and what directory you want to look for files in. Once you connect, you'll usually see two different windows, one showing directories and files on your local system or network, and another showing directories and files on the remote system to which you have connected. You can now navigate the directories, select the files you wish to transfer, and send them over the wire. Depending on the system to which you've connected, this may work in both directions, or you may find that you can only retrieve files.

Microsoft includes a minimal FTP program with Windows 95, but most users will want to look elsewhere immediately. The FTP program that ships with

Windows 95, shown in figure 21.5, is a command-line, text-based, MS-DOS style program. You will need to become familiar with command line syntax, and several UNIX commands. You also give up the easy and intuitive Windows interface. If you're used to a UNIX system and doing everything from the command line, you'll feel right at home with the Windows 95 FTP program. Otherwise, you'll need to get an FTP program with a more friendly user interface, such as the one shown in figure 21.6 that makes working with files easier.

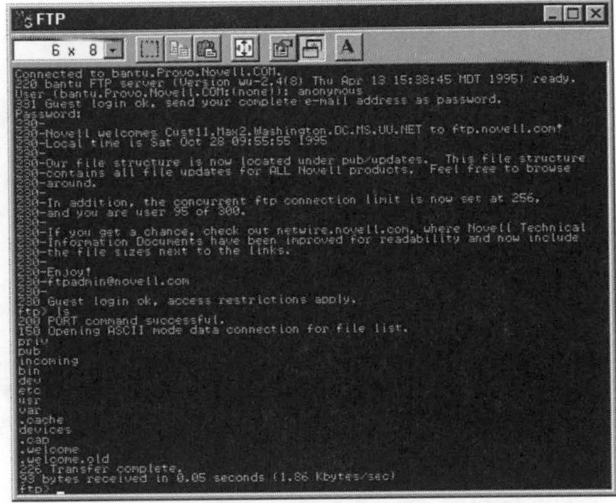

Fig. 21.5
The Windows 95 FTP program, with its text-based command-line interface, is hardly what most Windows users expect.

While the Windows 95 FTP program is indeed functional, it's anything but easy to use. Many alternatives are available, and most make quick work of presenting an attractive and intuitive interface. There are many versions available specifically for Windows 95 or Windows NT. Try several of these and choose the one you like best.

There are a lot of different FTP programs out there, some offering unique advantages or features. While many WWW browsers support FTP servers and offer minimal FTP capabilities, most users who use FTP frequently will want a dedicated program which simplifies the process.

When working with FTP programs, you are likely to encounter at least some pieces of the UNIX file systems. For starters, it is common for FTP servers to list subdirectories separated by forward slashes (/) instead of backslashes (\) as is common in MS-DOS and Windows 95. When navigating the directory structures, you will normally find publicly accessible files listed in the /pub directory. Many FTP clients allow you to specify the initial directories for both the local and remote systems when defining an FTP connection.

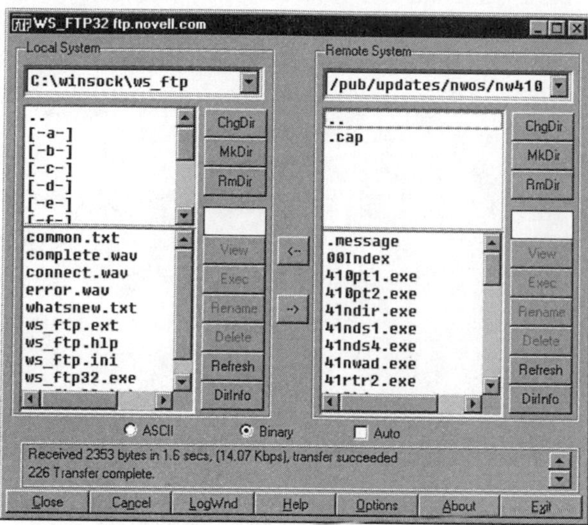

Fig. 21.6
John Junod's user-friendly WS_FTP program for Windows 95.

Search Tools and Strategies

The Internet shares its best and worst points. The best thing about the Internet is that practically everything is out there. The worst thing about the Internet is that practically everything is out there. The dilemma is that there is little or no organization to anything, and there is no such thing as a complete index or catalog.

Various different organizations provide a wide variety of search tools. Most operate for free, though some offer additional services for paid subscribers. Over time, you'll find one or several that work for you. Often, the secret is using several different searches, because different search tools will frequently turn up different results.

Let's take a look at some of the more popular search services: Yahoo, InfoSeek, Lycos, and WebCrawler.

Yahoo (http://www.yahoo.com/)

Yahoo is a searchable, browsable hierarchical index of the Internet. Yahoo is probably the largest and most popular index of what's on the Internet, with entries arranged by categories. Yahoo also provides a powerful search tool, which allows you to search across different categories for what interests you. Yahoo began as a project at Stanford University, and later went commercial. One of the largest and most frequently used search services, Yahoo is organized as a categorical index, as shown in figure 21.7, and search tools allow you to search within or across categories.

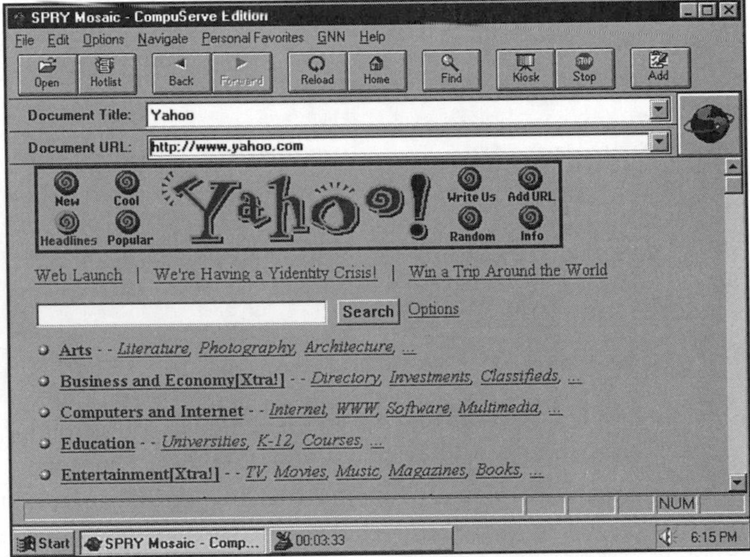

Fig. 21.7
Yahoo's home page and category list.

InfoSeek (http://www.infoseek.com/)

InfoSeek is a commercial service, but they allow two forms of free access. First, you can perform a search on the WWW for free. Second, you can sign up for a free 30-day trial for the full InfoSeek Professional search engine, as shown in figure 21.8, which provides quick access to continuous newswires, business, computer, scientific, and health publications, as well as Web pages, UseNet News, and more. This is one of the more powerful search tools available, even in its (temporarily) free form. There are few Internet search tools that are more powerful or broader in scope than the InfoSeek Professional search engine. And while limited, the free WWW search is still one of the most useful options available.

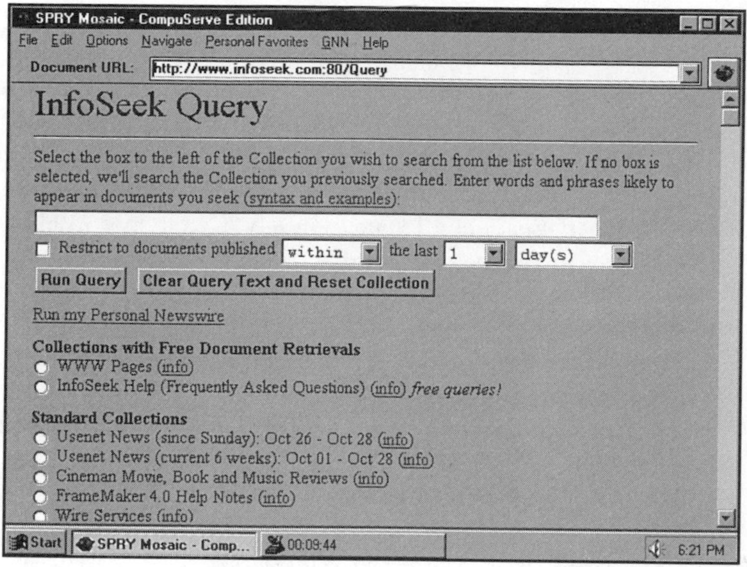

Fig. 21.8
InfoSeek's Professional search engine covers more than just WWW pages.

Lycos (http://www.lycos.com/)

Lycos, as shown in figure 21.9, advertises itself as "The Catalog of the Internet." Lycos has one of the more comprehensive indices of WWW pages, and offers a variety of categorical lookups as well. Lycos also provides a listing of the current "Top 250" sites, which is often an interesting starting point. Lycos has also acquired Point, which publishes its listing of the top 5 percent of the sites on the WWW.

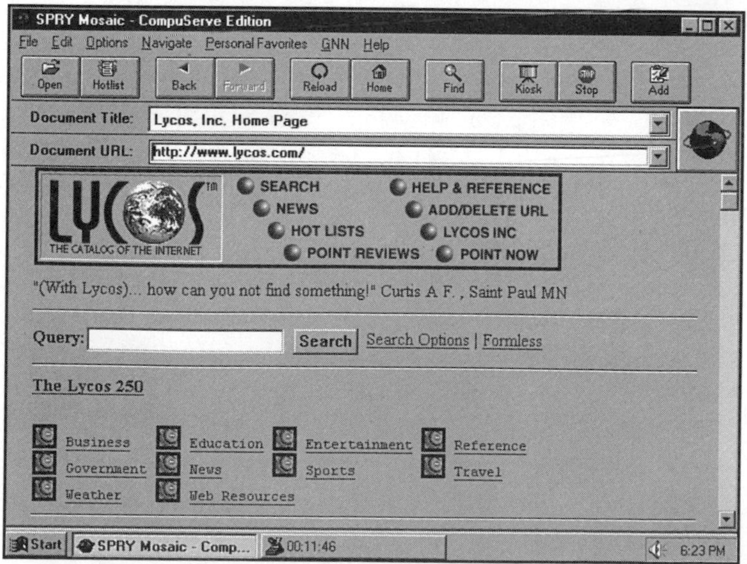

Fig. 21.9
Lycos' initial menu makes for a quick and easy search.

WebCrawler (http://www.webcrawler.com/)

America Online's WebCrawler is another WWW index, as shown in figure 21.10. One of the quicker and more comprehensive search engines, WebCrawler often offers the quickest WWW search. In experimenting, WebCrawler always returned the most "hits" on searches, but didn't provide any way to narrow or rank the search results. For some purposes, this makes WebCrawler less than useful, but if you absolutely need to find EVERY possible link, WebCrawler may be your best bet.

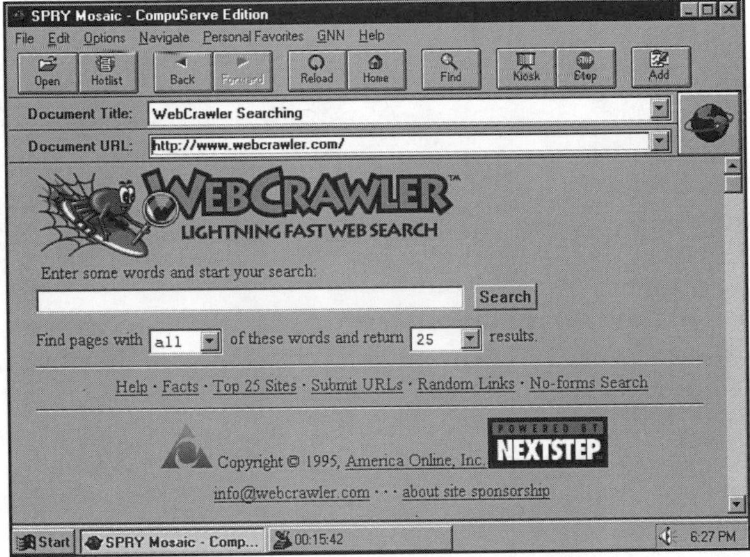

Fig. 21.10
The WebCrawler search engine may be slow, but turns up interesting results.

There are dozens, if not hundreds, of other search tools out there on the Internet. Over time, you'll develop a feel for those that yield the best results for various types of searches, and develop your own personal favorites. Most users will end up with a single favorite that they use by default, but they will use different tools under different circumstances when searching for specific types of data. The best suggestion is to try every different search tool you happen onto, and keep a list of those you find useful, and what they do best. ❖

CHAPTER 22

Using FTP, Ping, and Other Internet Tools

by Jim Boyce

Windows 95 includes many features that simplify accessing and using the Internet. Among these features are Internet utility programs that can help you configure and troubleshoot your TCP/IP connection, upload and download files, and more. This chapter explores some of the Internet tools in Windows 95 that are geared toward the typical user.

In this chapter, you learn how to

- Use FTP
- Use netstat
- Use Ping
- Use Telnet
- Use Winipcfg

Windows 95 includes additional TCP/IP utilities including arp, nbtstat, route, and tracert. It's unlikely that you will need to use these tools, so they are not covered in this chapter. For an explanation of these commands, consult the Windows 95 Resource Kit. Or, Telnet to a UNIX host and use the man command to view the manual pages for the commands (such as **man route**). Also, some third-party Internet applications provide graphical replacements for some of the Internet tools discussed in this chapter, particularly the FTP utility.

The TCP/IP tools covered in this chapter are installed automatically when you install TCP/IP. There are no configuration or setup steps needed to begin using the tools. To start each of the command-line programs explained in this chapter, first choose Start, Programs, and MS-DOS Prompt to start a command line session, then enter the desired command, along with any parameters.

Note

The command syntax examples in this chapter include square brackets ([ ]) to indicate optional parameters. These square brackets are intended only to identify the parameters in the syntax example—you do not include the square brackets when issuing the command.

Using FTP

File transfer is a major use for the Internet. This chapter explains the command line-based FTP (file transfer protocol) utility included with Windows 95. Although most Web browsing programs integrate FTP within the Web program itself, eliminating the need for the command line version, the command line version provides a finer degree of control over the transfer process, making it a useful tool. The Windows 95 FTP command-line utility enables you to connect to remote hosts to send and receive files.

◀ See "Transferring Files," p. 129

To transfer a file with FTP, you first must connect to the FTP host. You then can use many different FTP commands to change your current directory, specify the type of transfer, initiate the transfer, and so on.

Tip

You can open and use multiple FTP connections at one time in Windows 95, which enables you to upload and download files simultaneously with more than one FTP host. Naturally, working with multiple sites at one time slows down the transfer rate for each session.

The syntax of the FTP command is as follows:

```
ftp [-v] [-n] [-i] [-d] [-g] [host] [-s: filename]
```

You can use the following command parameters to start FTP:

- **-v.** This parameter suppresses the display of responses from the remote FTP server. Use the verbose command to turn on or off server response display after you have started FTP. (See "verbose" later in this chapter.)
- **-n.** This parameter suppresses autologon for the initial connection, which means that FTP will not automatically attempt to log on to the remote FTP server.
- **-i.** This parameter starts FTP in non-interactive mode, turning off interactive prompting. Use the prompt command to turn on or off interactive prompting when the FTP command is already running.

- **-d.** This parameter turns on debugging, which causes all FTP commands passed between the client and server to be displayed.
- **-g.** This parameter disables file name *globbing*. Globbing enables the use of wild card characters in local file and path names. Use the glob command to turn on or off file name globbing if FTP is already running.
- ***host.*** This parameter specifies the host name of the remote FTP server. You can enter a DNS-format name or IP address.
- **-s: *filename.*** This parameter specifies a script file to execute after FTP starts. You can use the script to automate FTP transfers.

Most often, you use FTP as an interactive program. After you start FTP, you enter various FTP commands to connect to a server, set options, access files, and control file transfer. If you specify a host with which to connect when you issue the FTP command, FTP establishes a connection with the host, prompting you for a password, if necessary. If you don't specify a host name when you start FTP, the program starts its command interpreter and waits for you to enter commands to configure FTP, run scripts, and perform other setup options. After starting FTP in this way, use the **open** command to establish a connection to a host.

Note

The parameters discussed previously are entered at the Windows 95 command prompt with the FTP command when you start the program. The following are FTP commands you enter on the FTP command prompt after FTP is running. When FTP is running, it displays an **ftp>** prompt, indicating it is waiting for command input.

The following sections explain each of the FTP commands.

! [*command* [*args*]]

The ! command invokes an operating system shell on your computer, which in the case of Windows 95, is a Windows 95 (DOS) command line. If you specify command arguments with the ! command, the first argument is interpreted as a command to run directly. Subsequent parameters are interpreted as arguments to that command. Essentially, the ! command without any additional parameters opens a Windows 95 command line, enabling you to execute DOS and Windows 95 commands. The FTP program is still running, however, even though the ftp> prompt is replaced by a standard Windows 95 command-line prompt (such as C:\WINDOWS). To close the shell and return to the ftp> prompt, type **exit** and press Enter.

If you include arguments with the ! command, FTP executes the command non-interactively and returns to the ftp> prompt. The following example displays the doc files in the current directory on the local computer and return to the ftp> prompt when completed:

```
ftp>! dir *.doc
```

Tip

The macdef or $ commands that are supported by UNIX FTP, which enable you to create and run FTP macros, are not supported by the FTP utility in Windows 95.

append *local-file* [*remote-file*]

This command appends a local file to a file on the remote host using the current file settings (type, format, mode, and structure). You must specify the local file name, but the remote file name is optional. The local file name is used if you omit the remote file name.

The following example appends the local file End.txt to the remote file Begin.txt:

```
ftp>append End.txt Begin.txt
```

Note

You must have write permission in the remote FTP directory to perform file creation actions in the remote directory, including appending a file. You also must have the necessary permissions to create and delete directories. You can determine your permissions for a file or directory from the last three characters of the file's or directory's permission mode.

ascii

The ascii command sets the file transfer type to ASCII (the default transfer type). Files you transfer when the ASCII file type is in effect are transferred as ASCII files. Use the ascii command to reset file type if it is set to binary, for example.

bell

The bell command causes a tone to play at the end of each file transfer. Issuing the bell command turns the bell on or off, depending on the current state. Using this command is helpful for long file transfer or series of transfers, enabling the computer to notify you when the transfers are completed.

binary

The binary command sets the file type to binary, enabling transfer of binary files. If you are transferring binary files such as exe, com, zip, arc, or others, you must use the binary command to transfer the files correctly.

bye

The bye command closes the connection to the remote host and terminates the FTP program. Use the close command if you want to close the connection but keep FTP running (for example, to connect to a different host). The quit command is synonymous with bye.

cd [*directory*]

The cd command changes the current directory on the remote host. Use a forward slash to separate directory names and file names on UNIX systems. Use a backslash to separate directory names and file names on DOS and Windows 95 systems. Use the dot (.) and double-dot (..) entries to specify the current and parent directories, respectively.

The following example changes the current directory on the remote UNIX host to the directory pub, located in the current directory's parent directory:

```
ftp>cd ../ftp-file
```

Tip

NT hosts support both the / and \ characters to separate directory names. You must use the UNIX / character for separating directory names on a UNIX host.

close

The close command closes the FTP session with the remote host, but doesn't terminate the FTP program. Use the close command to disconnect from a remote host, then use the open command to connect to a new host.

debug

The debug command turns on and off debugging. When debugging is on, each command sent to the remote host is echoed to the local screen, preceded by the characters --->. Debugging is off by default.

delete [*file*]

The delete command deletes files on the remote host. You can't use wild card characters to delete multiple files with one delete command, which means you can delete only one file at a time. You also must have the necessary permissions in the directory on the remote host to delete files. You must use the same case when specifying a file name on a UNIX host, because UNIX file and directory names are case-sensitive.

dir [*filespec*]

The ftp dir command is very similar to the DOS DIR command. dir displays a listing of the files and directories on the remote host. As with the DOS version of the command, you can use the dir command by itself or you can use file names, directories, and wild cards to display directory listings. Output of the dir command is similar to the output of the UNIX ls -l command, as shown in the following example:

```
ftp> dir
200 PORT command successful.
150 Opening ASCII mode data connection for /bin/ls.
total 35
drwxr-xr-x  3 jimb     members      1024 Mar 13 21:36 .NeXT
-r--r--r--  1 jimb     members       240 Mar  4  1992 .commanddict
-rw-r--r--  1 jimb     members       477 Sep 13  1993 .cshrc
-r--r--r--  1 jimb     members       885 Jul 15  1991 .indent.pro
-rw-r--r--  1 jimb     members     16384 Nov  7  1994 .index.store
-rw-r--r--  1 jimb     members       180 Sep 13  1993 .login
-rw-r--r--  1 jimb     members         6 Sep 13  1993 .logout
-rw-r--r--  1 jimb     members        19 Sep 13  1993 .mailrc
-r--r--r--  1 jimb     members        49 Jul 15  1991 .pipedict
-rw-r--r--  1 jimb     members       257 Sep 13  1993 .plan
-rw-r--r--  1 jimb     members       236 Sep 13  1993 .profile
drwxr-xr-x  2 jimb     members      1024 Sep 13  1993 Apps
-rw-r--r--  1 jimb     members       194 Feb 11 19:39 LIST.TXT
drwxr-xr-x  5 jimb     members      1024 Nov  7  1994 Library
drwx------  3 jimb     members      1024 Oct 20  1993 Mail
drwxr-xr-x  3 jimb     members      1024 Oct 22  1993 Mailboxes
-rw-r--r--  1 jimb     members        13 Jun 10 13:08 ftpscrip.txt
-rw-r--r--  1 jimb     members      2420 Apr  3 09:41 readme.txt
226 Transfer complete.
1142 bytes received in 0.77 seconds (1.48 Kbytes/sec)
```

Note

Refer to the ls command for an explanation of the information displayed by the dir command.

disconnect

The disconnect command is synonymous with the close command. It terminates a connection to a remote host without terminating the FTP program.

get [*file*] [*newname*]

The get command retrieves the file specified by the *file* parameter from the remote host. The current file type (ascii or binary) is used for the transfer, and the file is placed in the current directory on the local computer. Specify a file name for the *newname* parameter to cause FTP to rename the file on your system. The following example retrieves the file Readme.txt and renames it Readme.now:

```
ftp> get readme.txt readme.now
```

Note

The Windows 95 FTP command supports long file names. Enclose the long file name in quotes, such as **get readme.txt "Read this for more information"**, to name the file using a long file name.

The recv command is synonymous with the get command.

glob

Use of the glob command applies primarily to the mdelete, mget, and mput commands, which handle multiple files. The glob command turns on or off file *globbing*, which enables the use of wild card characters in local file and path names. Wild card characters are interpreted in the file and directory names as wild card characters when globbing is turned on. File and directory names are treated literally and are not expanded when globbing is turned off.

hash

The hash command turns on or off printing of # symbol hash marks to show the status of a file transfer. When hash marks are on, FTP prints one # symbol to the screen for each 2K bytes transferred. Using hash marks lets you monitor the status of a long file transfer. Hash marks are turned off by default.

You also can monitor the progress of the file transfer by double-clicking on the modem icon in the tray. Doing so displays the modem status dialog box shown in figure 22.1. As bytes are transferred, the value in the dialog box changes accordingly.

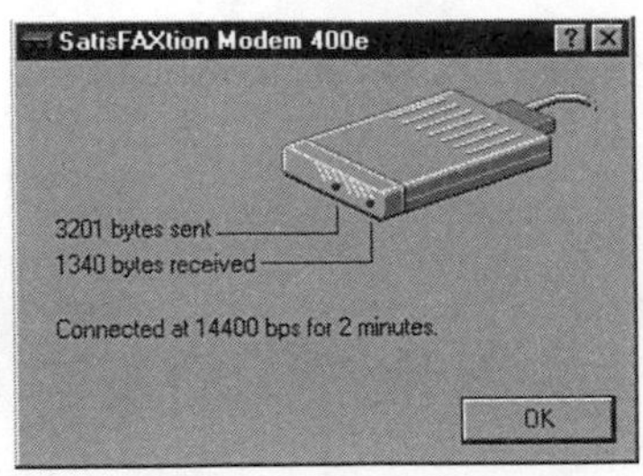

Fig. 22.1 You can monitor file transfer status with the modem status dialog box.

help

The help command lists FTP commands and their descriptions. The following is an example of the output of the help command:

```
ftp> help
Commands may be abbreviated. Commands are:

!          delete       literal    prompt       send
?          debug        ls         put          status
append     dir          mdelete    pwd          trace
ascii      disconnect   mdir       quit         type
bell       get          mget       quote        user
binary     glob         mkdir        recv       verbose
bye        hash         mls        remotehelp
cd         help         mput       rename
close      lcd          open       rmdir
```

lcd

The lcd command changes the current working directory on the local computer. Use lcd to change the current directory before initiating a file transfer to cause the file to be uploaded from or downloaded to the specified directory. The lcd command is similar to the DOS CD command. By default, the Windows folder, where the ftp.exe program file is located, is the current directory.

literal and quote

The literal command sends command line arguments to the remote FTP host verbatim, without interpreting the content of the command line. The remote FTP host returns a reply code in response. The quote command is synonymous with literal.

ls [-acdfgilqrstu1ACLFR] [*filespec*]

The ls command is similar to the UNIX ls command. It produces an abbreviated list of the contents of the directory based on the file pattern you specify with *filespec*. You can use a number of different command line options with ls, as indicated above. The most commonly used options are described in the following list:

- **-l.** This option uses long format to list the files, giving mode, number of links, owner, size in bytes, and time of last modification for each file. If the file is a special file, the size field will instead contain the major and minor device numbers. If the file is a symbolic link, the pathname of the linked-to file is printed preceded by "->".
- **-g.** This option includes group ownership of the file in the list.
- **-t.** This option sorts the listing by time modified (latest first), rather than by name.
- **-s.** This option lists the size in kilobytes of each file.
- **-r.** This option reverses the sort order for reverse alphabetic, or oldest first as appropriate.
- **-u.** This option displays the time of last access instead of last modification for sorting with the -t option and / or displaying with the -l option.
- **-i.** This option causes the output to include the i-number of each file in the first column of the report.
- **-F.** This option causes directories to be marked with a trailing "/", sockets with a trailing "=", executable files with a trailing "*", and symbolic links to files with a trailing "@". Symbolic links to directories are marked with a trailing "/", unless the -l option is also used.
- **-R.** This option recursively lists subdirectories (list the contents of all subdirectories encountered during the file list).
- **-1.** This option, which is the default, forces output to one entry per line.
- **-C.** This option forces multi-column output.

The mode listed with the -l option for each entry contains 11 characters. The first character can be any one of the following six characters:

d	directory
b	block-type special file
c	character-type special file
l	symbolic link
s	socket
-	a plain file

The remaining 9 characters in an entry's mode field are interpreted as three sets of three bits each. The first set of three indicates owner permissions. The second set of three indicates permissions to others in the same user-group. The last set of three indicates permissions for all others. The three characters in each set indicate permission respectively to read, write, or execute the file as a program. For a directory, execute permission provides the ability to search the directory. The permissions are indicated as follows:

r	read
w	write
x	execute
-	indicates permission is not granted

mdelete [*filespec*]

This command deletes multiple files on the remote host. To delete files on a remote host, you must have the necessary permission in the remote directory. (Use the delete command to delete single files.) Before using the mdelete command, use the glob command to turn on or off file globbing as necessary to specify file names. Remember that file names on UNIX hosts are case-sensitive, so you must use the same case when specifying files to delete.

mdir [*filespec*] [*filespec*]...[*localfile*]

The mdir command displays a list of a remote directory's files and sub-directories, which lets you specify multiple files. The *localfile* parameter is interpreted as the name of a local file in which to store the directory output. FTP prompts you to verify that the file name specified by *localfile* in interactive mode is on. The following example lists the files in the pub, lib, etc, and download directories, placing the output in a local file name output.txt:

```
ftp> mdir pub lib etc files output.txt
output to local-file: output.txt? Y
```

mget [*filespec*]

The mget command retrieves multiple files from the remote host with a single command. The current file transfer type (ascii or binary) applies. Use wild card matching to specify the names of multiple files. When interactive prompting is on, mget prompts you to verify the receipt of each file. To retrieve a large number of files, start FTP using the -i option or enter the prompt command at the ftp> prompt to turn off interactive prompting. The following example turns off interactive prompting and retrieves all files in the current directory on the host:

```
ftp> prompt
Interactive mode Off
ftp> mget *.*
```

mkdir [*dirname*]

The mkdir command creates the remote directory specified by the *dirname* parameter. As with other commands that manipulate the remote host's file system, you must have the appropriate permissions in the remote host directory.

mls [*filespec*] [*localfile*]

This command displays a list of the subdirectory and file names in the remote host's current directory using an abbreviated format. The output of the command is written to the file specified by *localfile*.

mput

The mput command copies multiple files from your computer to the remote host using the current file transfer type. FTP prompts you to verify the transfer of each file if interactive prompting is on. Start FTP with the -i parameter or use the prompt command to turn off interactive prompting if you want to transfer the files without any interaction. The following example would copy all of the files in the current directory on the local computer to the current directory on the remote host without interaction:

```
ftp> prompt
Interactive mode Off
ftp> mput *.*
```

open [[*host.domain*] or [*ipaddress*]]

The open command establishes a connection to a remote FTP host. You can specify a host name in DNS format or enter the remote host's IP address. A logon prompt is displayed if the remote host requires a logon, which requires you to enter a valid user name and password.

Tip

Many FTP servers allow you to log on using the user name anonymous and specify your email address as the password.

The following example opens a connection to Microsoft' FTP server, logging on as anonymous:

```
ftp> open ftp.microsoft.com
Connected to ftp.microsoft.com.
220 ftp Windows NT FTP Server (Version 3.51).
User (ftp.microsoft.com:(none)): anonymous
331 Anonymous access allowed, send identity (e-mail name) as password.
Password: jimb@tigers.k12.cfa.org
```

```
230-This is ftp.microsoft.com. Please see the index.txt file for more
information.
230 Anonymous user logged in as anonymous.
```

prompt

The prompt command turns on and off interactive prompting. Prompting is on by default. You might want to turn off prompting when using the mget, mput, and mdir commands so file transfers will occur without interaction from you. If prompting is on, you must verify the transfer of each file.

put [*file*] [*newfile*]

The put command copies a file from your computer to the remote host using the current file transfer type. To copy multiple files, use the mget command. Specify a new file name for the optional parameter *newfile* if you want the file renamed as it is copied. The following example copies the file Readme.txt from the local computer to the host, renaming the file Readme.now:

```
ftp> put Readme.txt Readme.now
```

The send command is synonymous with put.

pwd

Like its UNIX counterpart, this command lists the name of the current directory on the remote host. The following is a sample output of the pwd command:

```
ftp> pwd
257 "/Users/staff/jimb" is current directory.
```

remotehelp [*command*]

By itself, the remotehelp command displays the list of commands that are recognized by the remote FTP host. If you include a command name with the remotehelp command, the remote host responds with a syntax description of the command. The following example illustrates the use of the remotehelp command without a command parameter:

```
ftp> remotehelp
214-The following commands are recognized (* =>'s unimplemented).
   USER    PORT    STOR    MSAM*   RNTO    NLST    MKD     CDUP
   PASS    PASV    APPE    MRSQ*   ABOR    SITE    XMKD    XCUP
   ACCT*   TYPE    MLFL*   MRCP*   DELE    SYST    RMD     STOU
   SMNT*   STRU    MAIL*   ALLO    CWD     STAT    XRMD    SIZE
   REIN*   MODE    MSND*   REST    XCWD    HELP    PWD     MDTM
   QUIT    RETR    MSOM*   RNFR    LIST    NOOP    XPWD
214 Direct comments to ftp-bugs@tigers.
```

rename [*oldfile*] [*newfile*]

The rename command renames a file on the remote host from *oldfile* to *newfile*. The following example renames the file Readme.now on the host to Readme.txt:

```
ftp> rename Readme.now Readme.txt
```

rmdir [*dirname*]

The rmdir command removes a directory on the remote host. Two restrictions apply: the remote directory must be empty, and you must have the appropriate privileges for the directory to remove the directory.

status

The status command displays the current status of the FTP connection and parameters. The following is a sample output of the status command:

```
ftp> status
Connected to ftp.microsoft.com
Type: ascii; Verbose: On; Bell: Off; Prompting: On; Globbing: On
Debugging: Off; Hash mark printing: Off
```

trace

The trace command turns on and off packet tracing. Packet tracing displays the route and status of each FTP packet. Generally, trace is useful only for debugging, and it is unlikely you'll ever need to use it.

type [*filetype*]

The type command sets or displays the current file transfer type. If you omit *filetype*, the type command displays the current file transfer type as shown in the following example:

```
ftp> type
Using binary mode to transfer files.
```

Tip

Use the ascii and binary commands to set file transfer type, or enter **type ascii** or **type binary** to set the transfer type.

user [*username*]

The user command specifies the name by which you want to log on to the remote host. If you enter **ftp -n** to start FTP and turn off autologon, FTP won't automatically initiate the logon process. You then can use a variety of commands to configure FTP. When you're ready to log on, enter the user command to log on to the FTP server. If the remote system requires a password for the specified name, the remote FTP server will prompt you for a password, as in the following example:

```
C:\WINDOWS>ftp -n ftp.microsoft.com
Connected to ftp.microsoft.com.
220 ftp Windows NT FTP Server (Version 3.5 DEBUG).
ftp> user anonymous
331 Anonymous access allowed, send identity (e-mail name) as password.
Password: jimb@tigers.k12.cfa.org
230-This is ftp.microsoft.com. Please see the file index.txt for more
information.
230 Anonymous user logged in as anonymous.
```

The FTP server will prompt you to enter a user name if you omit the *username* parameter.

verbose

The verbose command turns on and off verbose mode. If verbose mode is on, all responses from the FTP server are displayed, and file transfer statistics are displayed when a file transfer is completed. Verbose mode is turned on by default.

Troubleshooting

I can connect with FTP to a remote server using the remote server's IP address, but FTP won't connect if I use the server domain name. How can I make the domain name work?

Either you're using the wrong domain name or your DNS server doesn't contain an entry for the domain name you're trying to use. Use the ping command as explained in the section "Using Ping" later in this chapter to determine the domain name of the server based on its IP address. If the domain names match, the problem is in your DNS configuration—either the domain name of the server isn't contained in the DNS server's database, or the IP address you've specified for your DNS server is incorrect. Try connecting to another FTP server using the server's domain name. If you can connect, add to your host's file the domain name that didn't work. If you can't connect to any other servers using a domain name, verify that you have specified the correct address for the DNS server in your TCP/IP configuration.

Using netstat

◀ See "Understanding TCP/IP," p. 410

The netstat program lets you monitor your connections to remote hosts and view protocol statistics for the connections. The netstat program also is useful for extracting the IP addresses of hosts to which you have connected using domain names. The syntax of the netstat command is as follows:

```
netstat [-a] [-ens] [-p protocol] [-r] [interval]
```

The following list describes the parameters you can use with the netstat command:

- **-a.** This parameter causes netstat to display all connections. Normally, server connections are not displayed.
- **-e.** This parameter causes netstat to display Ethernet statistics. Use the -e parameter in conjunction with the -s parameter (explained later).
- **-n.** This parameter causes netstat to display addresses and port numbers in numerical format instead of listing the names in host.domain format.
- **-s.** This parameter causes netstat to display statistics on a per-protocol basis. By default, netstat displays statistics for the TCP, UDP, ICMP, and IP protocols.
- **-p *protocol.*** This parameter displays connections for the protocol specified by the *protocol* parameter.
- **-r.** This parameter causes netstat to display the contents of the routing table.
- ***interval.*** You can specify an interval, in seconds, at which netstat will display the requested information. To terminate netstat's output, press Ctrl+C. If you don't include a value for *interval*, netstat displays the requested data only once and terminates.

If you want to determine the IP address of a remote host to which you're connected, use the netstat -n command. The following example uses netstat without any parameters to list the connected hosts, then issues netstat again with the -n parameter to derive the IP addresses. You can tell from the second output that the IP address of Microsoft's FTP server is 198.105.232.1.

```
C:\WINDOWS>netstat

Active Connections
  Proto  Local Address          Foreign Address        State
  TCP    tower:1283             ftp.microsoft.com:ftp  ESTABLISHED

C:\WINDOWS>netstat -n

Active Connections
  Proto  Local Address          Foreign Address        State
  TCP    198.87.118.72:1283     198.105.232.1:21       ESTABLISHED
```

In addition to using netstat for deriving an IP address from a host.domain name, you also can do the reverse: derive the host.domain name of a host to which you have connected using its IP address.

Using Ping

Ping is another TCP/IP diagnostic utility that made its way from the UNIX world to Windows 95. As its name implies, Ping is like TCP/IP sonar—you send a packet to a remote host and it bounces the packet back to you. If the packet doesn't come back, either the host is not available or there is something wrong with the connection. For troubleshooting connections, Ping is the single most useful TCP/IP utility.

Ping transmits Internet Control Message Protocol (ICMP) packets to a remote host and then waits for response packets to be received from the host. The version of Ping included with Windows 95 waits for as long as one second for the packets to be returned and prints the results of each packet transmission. Ping sends four packets by default, but you can use Ping to transmit any number of packets or transmit continuously until you terminate the command. The following shows a sample ping command and its output:

```
C:\WINDOWS>ping 198.87.118.1

Pinging 198.87.118.1 with 32 bytes of data:

Reply from 198.87.118.1: bytes=32 time=224ms TTL=14
Reply from 198.87.118.1: bytes=32 time=213ms TTL=14
Reply from 198.87.118.1: bytes=32 time=198ms TTL=14
Reply from 198.87.118.1: bytes=32 time=170ms TTL=14
```

In addition to helping test connections and determining when a host or router is not available, Ping enables you to test for routing and name resolution problems. If you can ping a host using its IP address but Ping fails to reach the host when you use the host name, the host probably is not listed in your DNS server or in your local host's file, you have specified an invalid DNS server, or the DNS server is unavailable. Add the remote host's name and IP address to the host's file to alleviate the problem.

Before you begin troubleshooting connection or routing problems, you should ping your own computer to verify that its network interface is working properly. To ping your own machine, use any of the following commands (for the third example, substitute your computer's IP address in place of *yourIPaddress*):

```
ping localhost
ping 127.0.0.1
ping yourIPaddress
```

The following is the syntax of the ping command:

```
ping [-t] [-a] [-n count] [-l length] [-f] [-i ttl] [-v tos] [-r
count] [-s count] [[-j host-list] ¦ [-k host-list]] [-w timeout]
destination-list
```

The parameters you can use with the ping command are described in the following list:

- **-t.** This parameter directs Ping to continue pinging the remote host until you interrupt the command by pressing Ctrl+C.
- **-a.** This parameter directs Ping not to resolve IP addresses to host names, and is useful for troubleshooting DNS and host's file problems.
- **-n *count*.** By default, Ping sends four ICMP packets to the remote host. You can use the -n parameter to specify a different number of packets to be sent.
- **-l *length*.** Use the -l parameter to specify the length of the ICMP packets that Ping transmits to the remote host. By default, Ping sends packets of 64 bytes, but you can specify up to a maximum of 8192 bytes.
- **-f.** This parameter causes Ping to include a Do Not Fragment flag in each packet, which prevents gateways through which the packet passes from fragmenting the packet.
- **-i *ttl*.** This parameter sets the Time To Live field to the value specified by *ttl*.
- **-v *tos*.** This parameter sets the Type Of Service field to the value specified by *tos*.
- **-r *count*.** This parameter records the route of the outgoing packet and the return packet. You must specify from 1 to 9 hosts using the *count* value.
- **-s *count*.** This parameter specifies the time stamp for the number of hops specified by *count*.
- **-j *host-list*.** This parameter enables you to use a route list to route the packets. You can separate consecutive hosts by intermediate gateways. The maximum number of hosts supported by IP is 9.
- **-k *host-list*.** This parameter enables you to route packets by means of the list of hosts specified by *host-list*. You cannot separate consecutive hosts by intermediate gateways. The maximum number of hosts supported by IP is 9.
- **-w *timeout*.** This parameter specifies the time-out value in milliseconds for packet transmission.
- ***destination-list*.** This parameter specifies the host to ping.

Troubleshooting

My TCP/IP connections don't seem to be working. I used the ping localhost command to test my TCP/IP configuration, but the ping command failed. How can I get my connections to work?

If you're unable to ping localhost, either you have the wrong entry in your host's file or your TCP/IP configuration is incorrect. Check the hosts file in the Windows folder and verify that the localhost domain name is associated with the IP address 127.0.0.1. Then, use the command **ping 127.0.0.1** to test your TCP/IP configuration. If the command still fails, your TCP/IP configuration is incorrect. Refer to Chapter 19, "Configuring TCP/IP," to correct your configuration.

Using Telnet

In previous sections of this chapter, you've read about command-line TCP/IP programs. The Telnet utility is one of only two Windows-based TCP/IP utility programs included with Windows 95. The other—Winpicfg—is explained later in this chapter.

▶ See "Using Dial-Up Networking," p. 495

Telnet is a terminal emulator program that enables you to connect to and log on to a remote host and perform tasks on the remote host, such as starting and running programs (see fig. 22.2). For example, you can use Telnet across your network to log onto a UNIX host and execute programs on the remote host. Or, you can use Dial-Up Networking to dial into a UNIX host or a remote LAN containing a UNIX host, then use Telnet across the Dial-Up Networking connection to log on to the host.

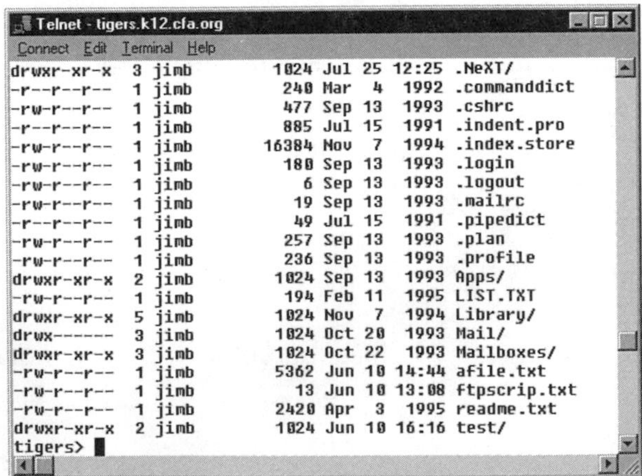

Fig. 22.2
Telnet enables you to connect to remote hosts.

The Telnet program is located in the Windows folder as the file Telnet.exe. Open the folder and double-click on Telnet.exe to start the program, or choose Start, Run, type **telnet** in the Run dialog box, and choose OK. You also can start Telnet from the command prompt. The syntax for starting the Telnet program is as follows:

```
telnet [host] [port]
```

The *host* parameter specifies the name or IP address of the host to which you want to connect. The *port* parameter specifies the port number to which you want to connect on the remote host. If you don't supply a port value, the default value of 23 is used. The *port* parameter is included primarily for compatibility with utilities such as gopher and Mosaic that require specific port connections.

Tip

If you want to create a shortcut to a host, first create a shortcut to the Telnet program. Then, open the property sheet for the shortcut and display the Shortcut property page. In the Target text box, enter the name of the host after the path to the Telnet program file, such as **c:\windows\telnet.exe host.domain.com**, substituting the desired host address.

If you specify a host name, Telnet will attempt the connection to the host, and if successful, will display the remote host's logon prompt. If you don't specify a host name or IP address on the Telnet command line, the Telnet window opens without a connection. You then can choose Connect, then Remote System to display the Connect dialog box (see fig. 22.3). In the Host Name combo box, enter the name or IP address of the host to which you want to connect, or choose a previous connection from the drop-down list. Use the Port combo box to enter or select a connection port. Use the TermType combo box to enter or select a terminal type.

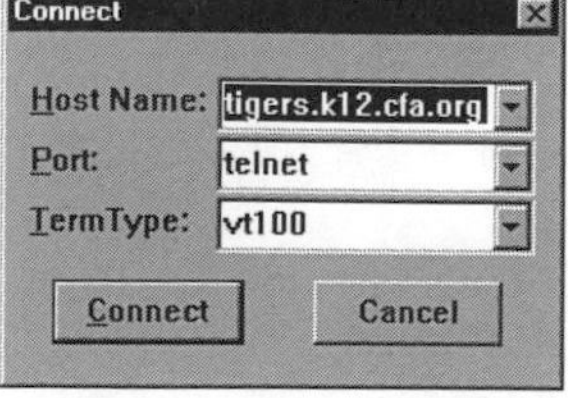

Fig. 22.3
Use the Connect dialog box to specify a host.

Tip

Typing error? To backspace characters that you enter on the remote host's command line, use Ctrl+Backspace.

Setting Preferences

Telnet supports a small number of preferences you can set to control the way the program functions. Choose Terminal, then Preferences to display the Terminal Preferences dialog box (see fig. 22.4) and set these preferences.

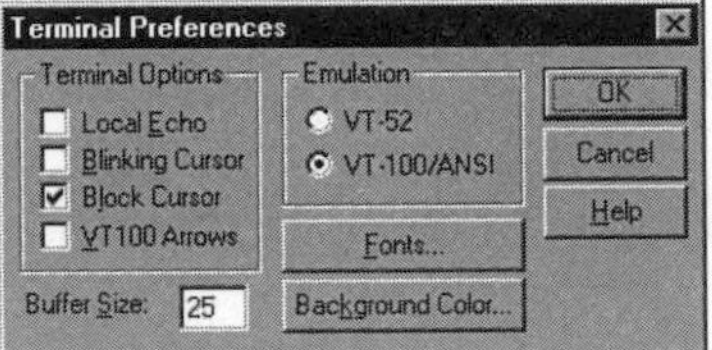

Fig. 22.4
Use the Terminal Preferences dialog box to set options.

The options on the Terminal Preferences dialog box are explained in the following list:

- *Local Echo.* Enable this check box to cause all of your keyboard input to be echoed to the terminal window.
- *Blinking Cursor.* Enable this check box if you want the cursor to blink, which can make it easier to locate the cursor.
- *Block Cursor.* Enable this check box to use a block cursor, rather than an underline cursor.
- *VT100 Arrows.* If you enable this check box, cursor key entries are treated as terminal keystrokes and are sent to the remote host. Disable this check box if you want the cursor keys to be treated as local application keys.
- *Emulation.* Select the correct terminal type based on the requirements of the remote system.
- *Buffer Size.* This setting specifies the number of lines Telnet will maintain in its line buffer.

Using a Log File

Telnet lets you maintain a session log of each connection. To turn on logging, choose Terminal, Start Logging. Telnet displays an Open log file dialog box you can use to specify a file name for the log file. After you choose Open,

Telnet will begin echoing all input and output to the log file. To turn off logging, choose Terminal, Stop Logging.

Using Winipcfg

The Winipcfg is a Windows 95 graphical utility that lets you view information about your Ethernet adapter and TCP/IP protocol settings. Winipcfg is located in the Windows directory in the file Winipcfg.exe. To run Winipcfg, choose Start, Run, enter **winipcfg** in the Open text box, then choose OK. Or, double-click on the Winipcfg.exe program in the Windows folder. A Winipcfg window similar to the one shown in figure 22.5 will appear on the display.

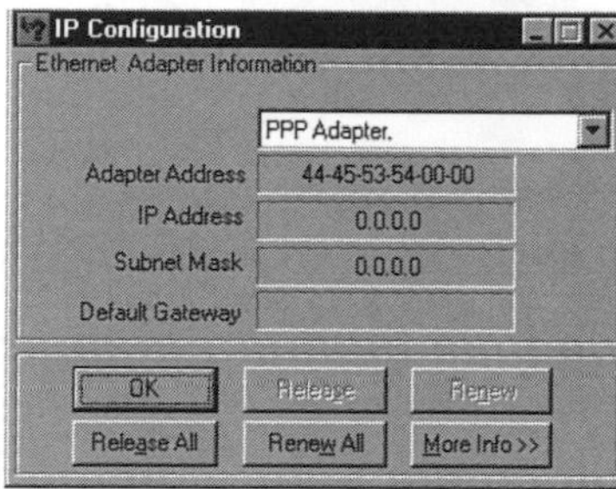

Fig. 22.5
Winipcfg lets you view TCP/IP configuration information.

The Winipcfg window shows the physical address, IP address, subnet mask, and default gateway settings of your primary TCP/IP adapter. If your computer contains multiple adapters to which TCP/IP is bound, you can select the other adapter(s) from the drop-down list to view their settings. If your PC contains a network adapter and you're also using Dial-Up Networking, for example, you'll be able to choose from the PPP dial-up adapter and the hardware NIC. To view additional information about the adapter and protocol settings, choose the More Info button to expand the dialog box to resemble the one shown in figure 22.6.

◀ See "Understanding Gateways and Routing," p. 413

Winipcfg displays additional information such as your computer's host name, addresses of DHCP and WINS servers (if used), and other data. To copy the data for use in troubleshooting or to place in a hardware log, open Winipcfg's control menu and choose Copy. Winipcfg copies the information in the Winipcfg window to the Clipboard, enabling you to paste the data into Notepad or other application to print or save. The following is a sample output copied from Winipcfg:

```
Windows 95 IP Configuration
   Host Name . . . . . . . . . . : tower.tigers.k12.cfa.org
   DNS Servers . . . . . . . . . : 192.217.242.2
                                   192.217.240.2
   Node Type . . . . . . . . . . : Broadcast
   NetBIOS Scope ID. . . . . . . :
   IP Routing Enabled. . . . . . : No
   WINS Proxy Enabled. . . . . . : No
   NetBIOS Resolution Uses DNS : Yes
Ethernet adapter :
   Description . . . . . . . . . : PPP Adapter.
   Physical Address. . . . . . . : 44-45-53-54-00-00
   DHCP Enabled. . . . . . . . . : No
   IP Address. . . . . . . . . . : 198.87.118.72
   Subnet Mask . . . . . . . . . : 255.255.255.0
   Default Gateway . . . . . . . : 198.87.118.1
   Primary WINS Server . . . . :
   Secondary WINS Server . . . :
   Lease Obtained. . . . . . . . :
   Lease Expires . . . . . . . . :
```

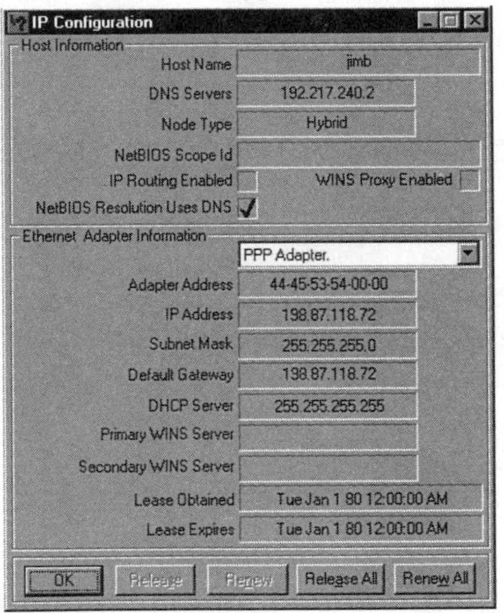

Fig. 22.6
You can expand the Winipcfg window to view additional information.

If your computer uses DHCP to receive an IP address from a host, the Release and Renew buttons enable you to release and renew the IP address, respectively. For more information on DHCP and TCP/IP, refer to Chapter 19, "Configuring TCP/IP."

Note

Winipcfg also works if you're using TCP/IP through a Dial-Up Networking connection.

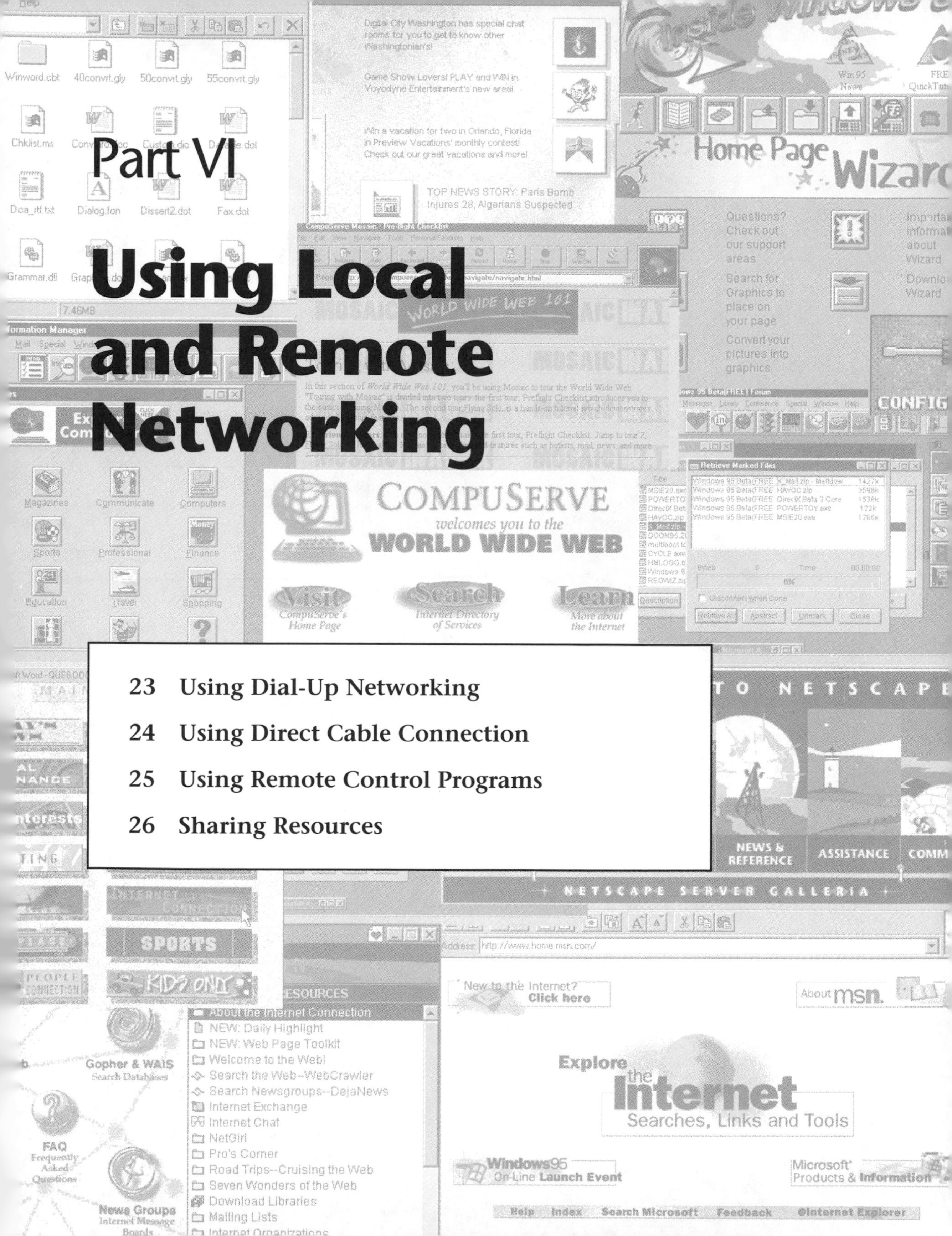

Part VI

Using Local and Remote Networking

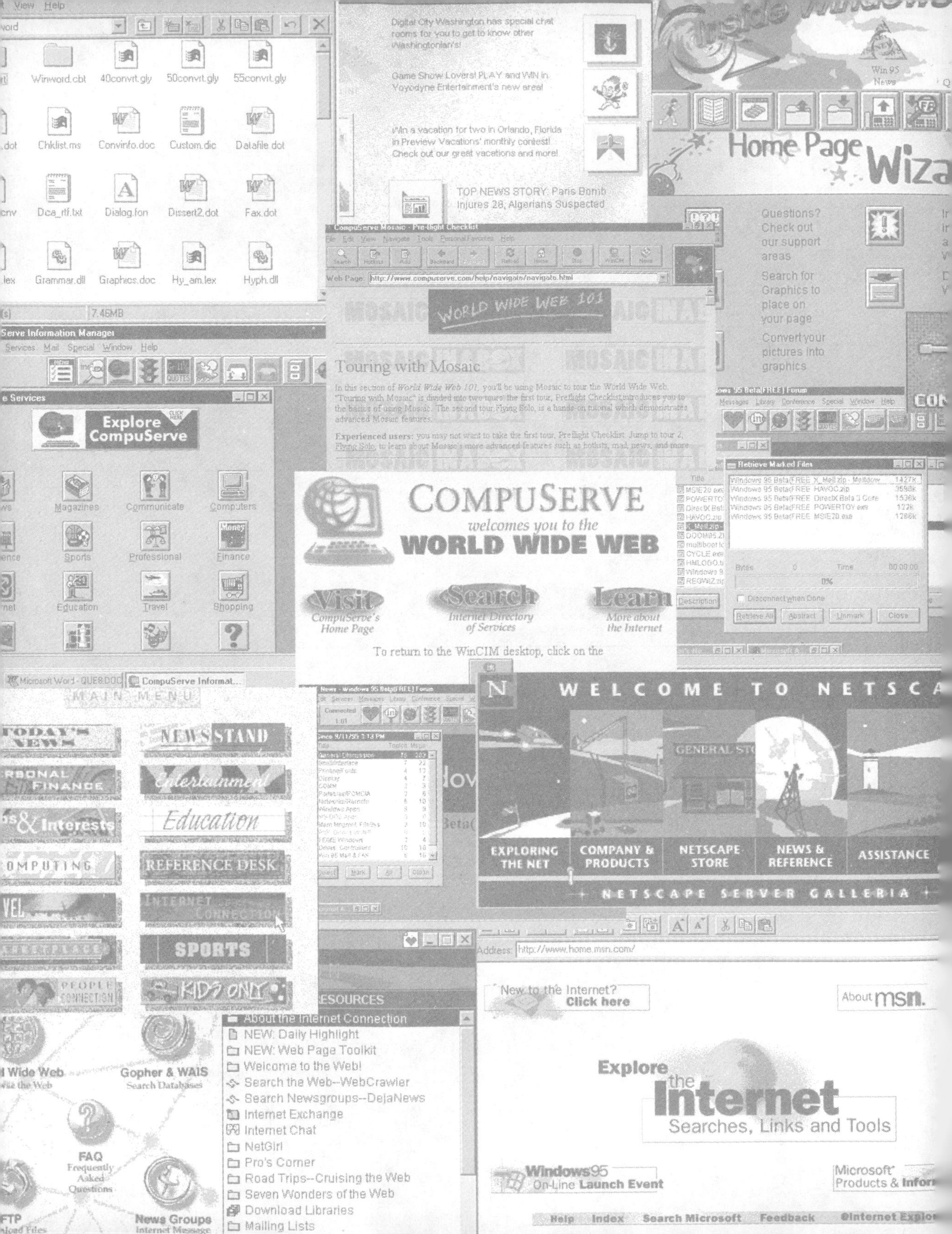

View Help
Winword.cbt
40convrt.gly
50convrt.gly
55convrt.gly
Chklist.ms
Convinfo.doc
Custom.dic
Datafile.dot
Dca_rtf.txt
Dialog.fon
Dissert2.dot
Fax.dot
Grammar.dll
Graphics.doc
Hy_am.lex
Hyph.dll
7.46MB
Digital City Washington has special chat rooms for you to get to know other Washingtonian's!
Game Show Lovers! PLAY and WIN in Yoyodyne Entertainment's new area!
Win a vacation for two in Orlando, Florida in Preview Vacations' monthly contest! Check out our great vacations and more!
TOP NEWS STORY: Paris Bomb Injures 28, Algerians Suspected
Win 95 News
Home Page
Questions? Check out our support areas
Search for Graphics to place on your page
Convert your pictures into graphics
CompuServe Mosaic - Preflight Checklist
Web Page: http://www.compuserve.com/help/navigate/navigate.html
WORLD WIDE WEB 101
Touring with Mosaic
In this section of World Wide Web 101, you'll be using Mosaic to tour the World Wide Web. "Touring with Mosaic" is divided into two tours: the first tour, Preflight Checklist, introduces you to the basics of using Mosaic. The second tour, Flying Solo, is a hands-on tutorial which demonstrates advanced Mosaic features.
Experienced users: you may not want to take the first tour, Preflight Checklist. Jump to tour 2, Flying Solo, to learn about Mosaic's more advanced features such as hotlists, mail, news, and more.
Services Mail Special Window Help
Explore CompuServe
Magazines
Communicate
Computers
Sports
Professional
Finance
Education
Travel
Shopping
COMPUSERVE
welcomes you to the
WORLD WIDE WEB
Visit
CompuServe's Home Page
Search
Internet Directory of Services
Learn
More about the Internet
To return to the WinCIM desktop, click on the
Retrieve Marked Files
Retrieve All
Abstract
Unmark
Close
Disconnect when Done
Microsoft Word - QUE8.DOC
CompuServe Informat...
MAIN MENU
NEWSSTAND
Entertainment
Education
REFERENCE DESK
INTERNET CONNECTION
SPORTS
KIDS ONLY
PEOPLE CONNECTION
News - Windows 95 Beta[FREE] Forum
WELCOME TO NETSCA
GENERAL STO
EXPLORING THE NET
COMPANY & PRODUCTS
NETSCAPE STORE
NEWS & REFERENCE
ASSISTANCE
NETSCAPE SERVER GALLERIA
Address: http://www.home.msn.com/
New to the Internet? Click here
About msn.
Explore the Internet
Searches, Links and Tools
Windows95 On-Line Launch Event
Microsoft Products &
Help Index Search Microsoft Feedback
Gopher & WAIS
Search Databases
FAQ
Frequently Asked Questions
News Groups
About the Internet Connection
NEW: Daily Highlight
NEW: Web Page Toolkit
Welcome to the Web!
Search the Web--WebCrawler
Search Newsgroups--DejaNews
Internet Exchange
Internet Chat
NetGirl
Pro's Corner
Road Trips--Cruising the Web
Seven Wonders of the Web
Download Libraries
Mailing Lists

CHAPTER 23

Using Dial-Up Networking

by Jim Boyce

One feature in Windows 95 that plays an important part in Windows 95 communications is Dial-Up Networking. You can use Dial-Up Networking to connect through your modem to a remote LAN, Internet service provider, another Windows 95 user's PC, and other remote systems. Dial-Up Networking also works in conjunction with Exchange's Remote Mail to enable you to send and receive e-mail through remote mail servers. Dial-Up Networking is an important part of the operating system because it supports so many other features and programs in Windows 95.

In this chapter, you explore Dial-Up Networking and learn how to

- Understand Dial-Up Networking
- Install and configure Dial-Up Networking
- Use a Dial-Up Networking session
- Use remote LAN resources
- Use SLIP and CSLIP connections
- Create Dial-Up scripts
- Set up a Dial-Up Networking server

Before you begin setting up Dial-Up Networking, you should have a basic understanding of how Dial-Up Networking works. The following section provides an overview.

Understanding Dial-Up Networking

In a Dial-Up Networking session, one computer acts as a *server* and another computer acts as a *client*. If you're connecting to a remote LAN, for example, the computer that you dial into is the server, and your PC is the client. So the server provides access to the client (see fig. 23.1).

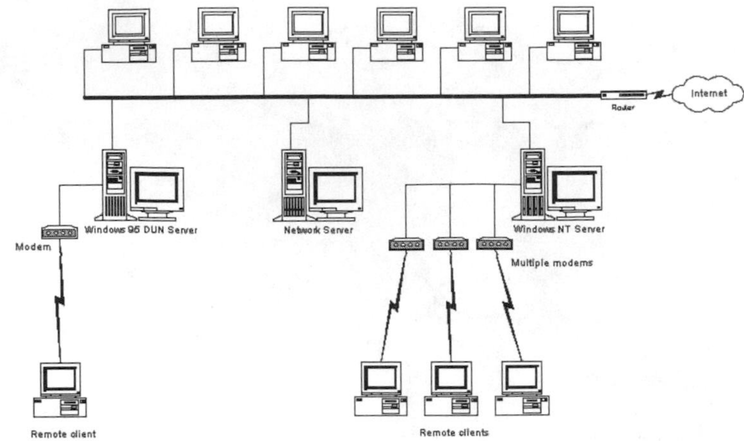

Fig. 23.1 Dial-Up Networking clients can connect to individual machines or networks.

Windows 95 includes the software you need to turn your PC into a Dial-Up Networking client. You can connect to a variety of remote servers, including NetWare and Windows NT servers, Point-to-Point Protocol (PPP) servers (many Internet service providers use PPP), and other types of dial-up servers. In addition, the Microsoft Plus! add-on for Windows 95 includes software that turns your PC into a Dial-Up Networking server, enabling other users to dial into your PC.

Tip

Dial-Up Networking is one of the best methods for connecting your PC to a friend's PC to share files over a modem. One of you must be running the Dial-Up Networking Server software, which is included with Microsoft Plus! for Windows 95.

As you can see in figure 23.1, a Windows 95 computer can act as a Dial-Up Networking server for one computer at a time, provided you install the Dial-Up Networking server software on the Windows 95 server. Windows NT, NetWare, and other remote access servers can support multiple modems and multiple dial-in users at one time.

▶ See "Using Remote Control Programs," p. 533

What can you do once you're connected to the remote system? To a degree, that depends on the server. If you're connecting to a remote LAN, you can access the shared resources on the LAN just as if you were sitting at a computer connected directly to the LAN. You can use files, send and receive mail, and print, although the speed at which you can perform these tasks naturally is slower because you're working through a modem connection. You can't run a program from the server, for example. For that, you need to use a remote control program.

If you're connecting to a Windows 95 computer running the Dial-Up Networking Server software, you can access that computer's resources, as well as the resources on the network to which the server is connected. A Windows 95 Dial-Up Networking server doesn't support the same number of protocols as other types of remote access servers, however (explained next).

The Windows 95 Client

The Dial-Up Networking software in Windows 95 includes a Dial-Up Adapter, which essentially is a driver that makes your modem work like a network card. When you install Dial-Up Networking, Windows 95 installs the Dial-Up Adapter software automatically.

With the Windows 95 Dial-Up Networking client, you can connect to remote access servers that support these protocols:

- *Point-to-Point Protocol (PPP).* PPP is supported by an increasing number of remote access servers, including many Internet service providers, Windows 95, and Windows NT 3.5x.
- *Novell NetWare Connect.* NRN is NetWare's proprietary remote access protocol that enables clients to connect to NetWare-based LANs.
- *Windows NT 3.1 and Windows for Workgroups 3.11 RAS.* These two operating platforms use asynchronous NetBEUI protocol, and a Windows 95 client can connect to remote access servers running either Windows NT 3.1 or Windows for Workgroups 3.11.
- *Serial Line Interface Protocol (SLIP).* The SLIP protocol originated in UNIX. Through its support for SLIP, the Windows 95 Dial-Up Networking client enables you to connect to a UNIX server. The SLIP software for the Windows 95 client is included on the Windows 95 CD.

Note

The Windows 95 Dial-Up Networking server software doesn't support SLIP. It supports only NetBEUI and PPP protocols. Therefore, a Windows 95 Dial-Up Networking server can't act as a gateway to the Internet because the server software doesn't support TCP/IP.

Tip

For expanded Windows 95 dial-up support, you can turn to third-party remote access products such as Shiva Corporation (617-270-8300, 800-458-3550, or **sales@shiva.com**). Shiva sells a variety of remote access products, including their NetModem and LanRover server modems. Shiva's products provide features not included with the Windows 95 Dial-Up Networking client, including:

- IPX/SPX, TCP/IP, and AppleTalk routing
- Support for Apple Remote Access dial-in
- Integrated ISDN support
- Modem pooling for sharing dial-out modems

Requirements for Dial-Up Networking

To use Dial-Up Networking in Windows 95, you need the following:

- A modem compatible with Windows 95
- Roughly 3M of available hard disk space to store the Dial-Up Networking software
- One of the file and printer sharing services (included with Windows 95) if you want to use the remote server's or LAN's resources.

As explained previously, only the Dial-Up Networking client software is included with Windows 95. You also need the Microsoft Plus! for Windows 95 add-on to use the Dial-Up Networking server software.

Installing and Configuring Dial-Up Networking

Adding and configuring Dial-Up Networking on your system requires two steps: install the Dial-Up Networking software, and then bind a protocol to the Dial-Up Adapter. The next section explains how to add the Dial-Up Networking software to your system.

Installing Dial-Up Networking

Setup gives you the option of installing Dial-Up Networking when you install Windows 95. If you didn't install Dial-Up Networking when you installed Windows 95, you can add the software through the Control Panel. Use the following steps to add Dial-Up Networking to your PC:

1. Open the Control Panel and double-click the Add/Remove Programs icon.
2. Click the Windows Setup tab to display the Windows Setup property page.
3. Click the Communications item in the list of installed components; then choose the Details button.
4. On the Communications dialog box, place a check beside the Dial-Up Networking item; then choose OK.
5. On the Add/Remove Programs Properties sheet, choose OK. Windows 95 then adds the Dial-Up Networking software to your PC, prompting you for the Windows 95 diskettes or CD if necessary. Follow the prompts to complete the installation process.

Adding Protocols

The next step in configuring Dial-Up Networking is to *bind* one or more network protocols to the Dial-Up Adapter. Binding a protocol associates it with the adapter and causes the adapter to use the protocol when communicating with the server.

To add a protocol to the Dial-Up Adapter, follow these steps:

1. Open the Control Panel and double-click the Network icon to display the Network property sheet (see fig. 23.2).

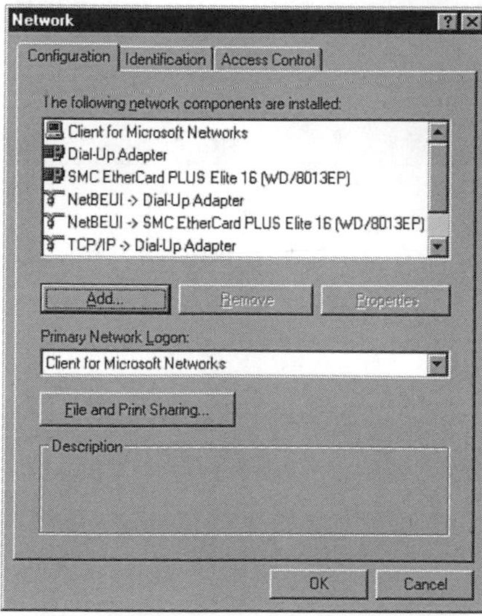

Fig. 23.2
Use the Configuration page to add a protocol to the Dial-Up Adapter.

2. Scroll through the list of installed services to determine if the protocol you need to use with the Dial-Up Adapter is already installed. If so, it should already be associated with the Dial-Up Adapter, and you can skip to step 6.
3. If the protocol you need is not yet installed, click the Add button.
4. From the Select Network Component dialog box, choose Protocol; then choose Add.
5. In the Select Network Protocol dialog box, choose the manufacturer and protocol you want to use; then choose OK.
6. When the Configuration page reappears, select the Dial-Up Adapter, choose Properties, and click the Bindings tab to display the Bindings page (see fig. 23.3).

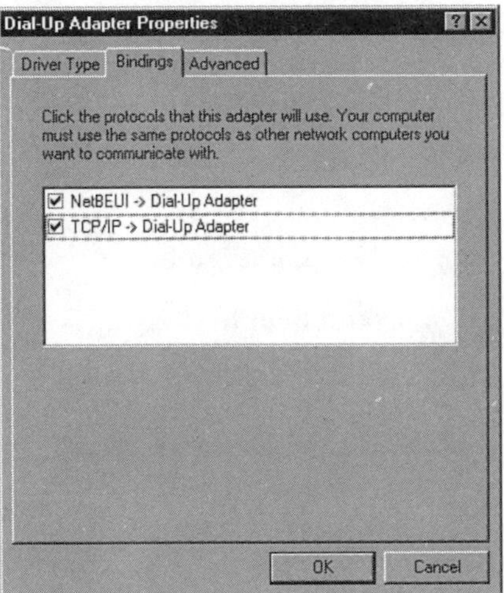

Fig. 23.3
Use the Bindings page to specify which protocols the Dial-Up Adapter will use.

7. Place a check beside each of the protocols you want the Dial-Up Adapter to use; then choose OK.
8. If you need to configure the TCP/IP protocol, refer to Chapter 19 to learn what settings you need to provide. When you finish configuring the protocol(s), choose OK. Windows 95 prompts you to reboot the system.

Tip

The Dial-Up Adapter requires a protected mode NDIS driver in order to work. While the Dial-Up Adapter property sheet is open, click the Driver Type tab and verify that the Enhanced mode option button is selected.

After the PC reboots, you're ready to start using Dial-Up Networking. Windows 95 creates a new folder named Dial-Up Networking in the My Computer folder. Windows 95 stores your Dial-Up Networking connections in this folder. Your next step, therefore, is to create Dial-Up Networking connections for the servers you want to access.

Do I Really Need a Client?

You don't need to use a network client with Dial-Up Networking, but you do need to use at least one network protocol. If you want to access shared resources on the remote computer or its LAN, you do need to use a network protocol. If you're connecting to a NetWare server, you should use the Client for NetWare Networks. Use the Client for Microsoft Networks if you're connecting to a Windows 95, Windows NT, or Windows for Workgroups server.

You install a client in much the same way as you install a network protocol. Use the steps listed previously for installing a protocol, but in step 4, choose Client rather than Protocol. Follow the prompts to select and install the client you need.

Using a Dial-Up Networking Session

When you choose a resource or feature available only by a Dial-Up Networking connection, Windows 95 automatically connects for you. You also can start a Dial-Up Networking session yourself. The next section explains how.

Creating a Dial-Up Networking Connection

To open the Dial-Up Networking folder, double-click My Computer; then double-click the Dial-Up Networking folder icon. Or choose Start, Programs, Accessories, Dial-Up Networking. At first, the Dial-Up Networking contains only one icon—the Make New Connection icon. Selecting the Make New Connection icon starts a wizard that helps you set up a Dial-Up Networking session. As you create various Dial-Up Networking connections, their icons appear in the Dial-Up Networking folder.

Use the following steps to run the Make New Connection Wizard and create your first Dial-Up Networking session:

1. If you haven't set up your modem yet, do so now. See Chapter 3 for an explanation of how to install a modem.
2. Double-click My Computer; then double-click the Dial-Up Networking folder icon to open the Dial-Up Networking folder.

3. Double-click the Make New Connection icon. The dialog box shown in figure 23.4 appears.

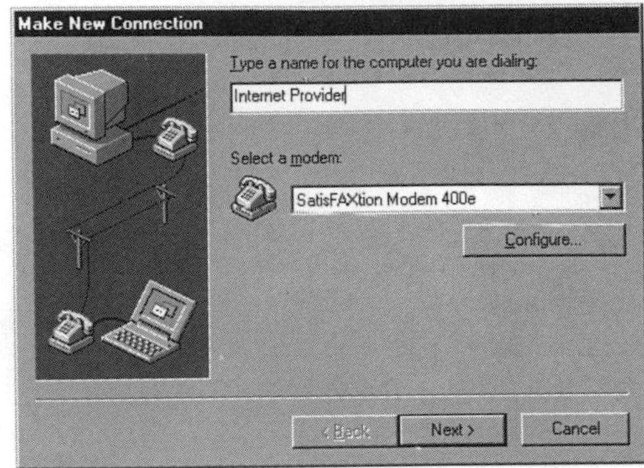

Fig. 23.4
The Make New Connection Wizard automates the process of creating a Dial-Up Networking session.

4. Type a name for the computer you're dialing in the text box provided. This is the name that appears under the session icon as its description. The name also appears in the list of available servers whenever Windows 95 prompts you to select a Dial-Up Networking connection for Remote Mail or other features or programs that use Dial-Up Networking.
5. From the Select a Modem drop-down list, choose the modem you want to use for the Dial-Up Networking connection.
6. If you need to set options for the modem, choose the Configure button to open the property sheet for the modem and set its properties (explained in Chapter 3).
7. After you have configured the modem, return to the Make New Connection Wizard and click Next.
8. The wizard next prompts you to provide the area code, phone number, and country code of the server you are dialing. Specify these items of information; then choose Next and Finish. Windows 95 adds the icon for the session to the Dial-Up Networking folder.

Connecting to a Remote Server

Connecting to a remote server is easy. Just open the Dial-Up Networking folder and double-click the icon of the session you want to use. Dial-Up Networking displays a Connect To dialog box similar to the one shown in figure 23.5.

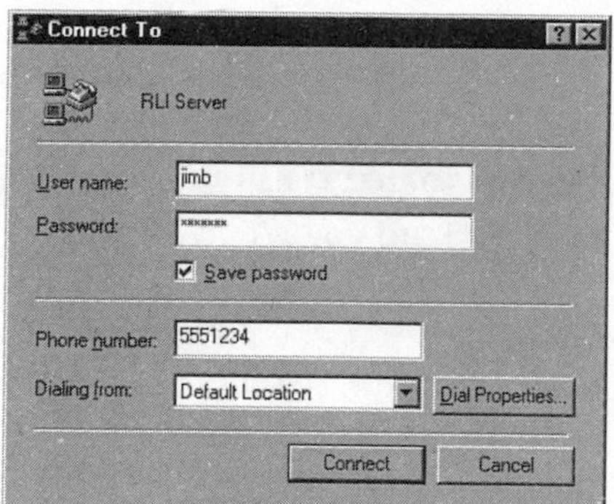

Fig. 23.5
The Connect To dialog box lets you set options before connecting.

In the User Name text box, enter the user name under which you want to log on to the remote server. In the Password text box, enter the password for your logon account. If you want Dial-Up Networking to save the password so that you don't have to type it next time, enable the Save Password checkbox. Dial-Up Networking stores the password in your password cache file.

If you want to change settings such as the phone number, dialing properties, or dialing location, use the controls in the Connect To dialog box to set them. Then click the Connect button. Dial-Up Networking dials the server and attempts to connect. After the connection is established, you can begin using the remote server's resources.

▶ See "Sharing Resources," p. 553

Dial-Up Networking is tightly integrated into the Windows 95 environment, enabling Windows 95 applications to use Dial-Up Networking automatically. Windows 95 itself uses Dial-Up Networking in the following situations:

- *No network.* If you attempt to use a remote resource or UNC (Universal Naming Convention) path name when no network is loaded, Windows 95 automatically uses Dial-Up Networking to establish a connection to the resource. A UNC name includes the name of the computer sharing a resource, as well as the name of the shared resource. The UNC name for a shared folder named Docs on a computer named Server is \\Server\Docs.
- *UNC name not on the LAN.* If you specify a UNC name and Windows 95 can't locate the specified machine on the network, it opens a Dial-Up Networking connection for the resource.
- *Remote OLE.* Activating a remote OLE object causes Windows 95 to open a Dial-Up Networking session to connect to the OLE resource.

In some cases, Windows 95 and applications use Dial-Up Networking to access resources without any interaction with you. Remote Mail, for example, can use Dial-Up Networking to connect to a remote mail server, download message headers and messages, and disconnect automatically.

Setting a Session's Properties

The Make New Connection Wizard doesn't give you much control over a Dial-Up Networking session's properties, but you can change the properties after you create the session. To do so, open the Dial-Up Networking folder and right-click the session's icon; then choose Properties from the context menu. Windows 95 displays a property sheet for the connection similar to the one shown in figure 23.6.

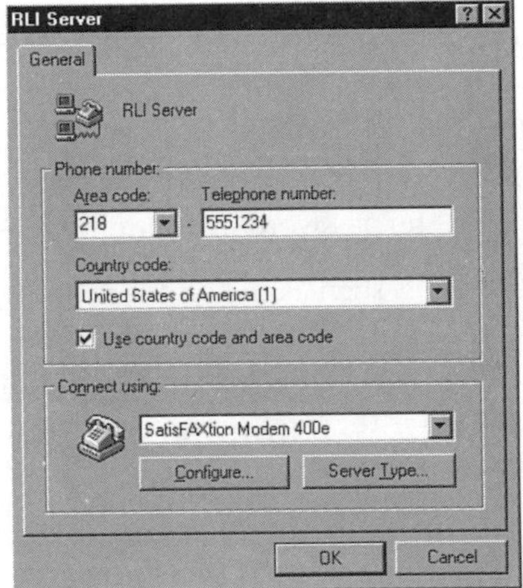

Fig. 23.6
Use the session's property sheet to control its settings.

As you can see in figure 23.6, you can change the area code, phone number, and modem for the session. You also can click the Configure button to configure the modem for the session. Enabling the Use Country Code and Area Code checkbox causes Dial-Up Networking to include the country and area codes in the dialing string. Clear the checkbox if the number is a local one.

Next, specify which protocol you want the session to use by clicking the Server Type button. Windows 95 displays the Server Types dialog box shown in figure 23.7.

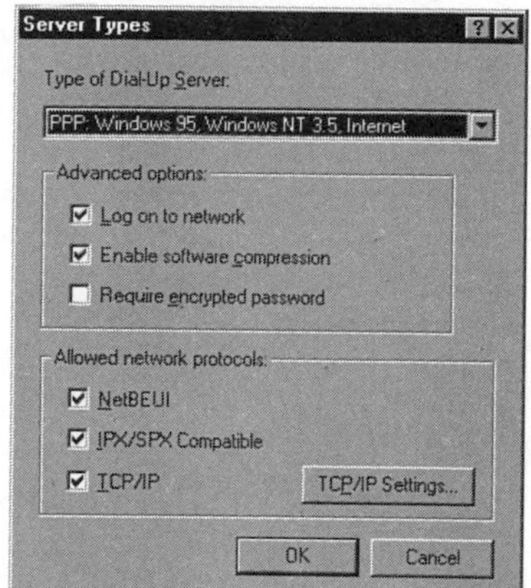

Fig. 23.7
Choose the type of protocol and other properties to use for the session.

The following list explains options you can set in the Server Types dialog box:

- *Type of Dial-Up Server.* From this drop-down list, select the type of server to which you're connecting. Choose NRN for a NetWare Connect server. Choose PPP for a Windows NT 3.5x or Windows 95 remote access server, or for a PPP-based Internet service provider. Choose Windows for Workgroups and Windows NT 3.1 to use asynchronous NetBEUI.
- *Log on to the Network.* Enable this checkbox if you want Dial-Up Networking to attempt to log on to the remote server using the user name and password you supplied in the Connect To dialog box.
- *Enable Software Compression.* Enable this checkbox if you want Dial-Up Networking to compress data as it is sent to speed performance. The server must also support software compression.
- *Require Encrypted Password.* Enable this checkbox to ensure maximum security for your password. With this checkbox enabled, Dial-Up Networking encrypts your password before sending it to the server. If the server doesn't support encrypted passwords, the password is sent unencrypted.
- *NetBEUI, IPX/SPX Compatible, TCP/IP.* Choose one or more of these checkboxes to select the network protocol you want to use for the connection. The server must support the protocol(s) you select.
- *TCP/IP Settings.* Click this button if you want to specify settings for the TCP/IP protocol different from the default settings stored in the Control Panel. Dial-Up Networking displays the dialog box shown in figure 23.8.

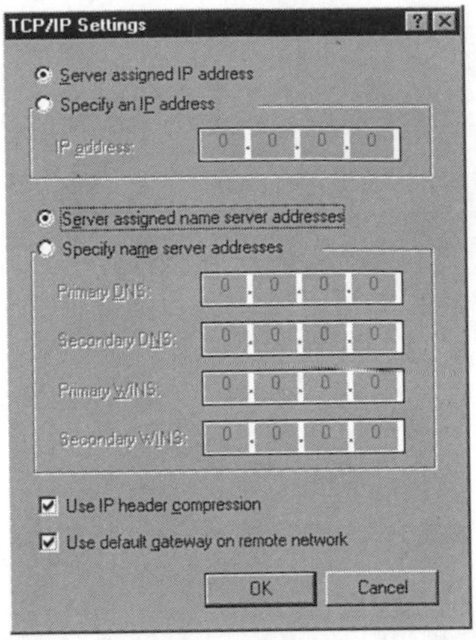

Fig. 23.8
Use the TCP/IP Settings dialog box to specify TCP/IP settings different from your Windows 95 default settings.

Tip

Each Dial-Up Networking session can use a different set of TCP/IP settings. For example, one server might require an explicit IP address, and another server might assign one to you when you log on. You can configure each session appropriately through the TCP/IP Settings dialog box.

Use the TCP/IP Settings dialog box to set the following properties:

- *Server Assigned IP Address*. Choose this option button if the server assigns an IP address to you when you log on.
- *Specify an IP Address*. Choose this option button to specify an explicit IP address. Enter the IP address in the IP Address box.
- *Server Assigned Name Server Addresses*. Choose this option button if you want the server to assign DNS and WINS server IP addresses to you when you log on.
- *Specify Name Server Addresses*. Choose this option button to specify explicit IP addresses of your primary and secondary DNS and WINS servers. Enter the appropriate server IP addresses in the boxes provided.
- *Use IP Header Compression*. If the remote server supports IP header compression, enable this checkbox to improve performance. If the server doesn't support IP header compression, clear this checkbox.
- *Use Default Gateway on Remote Network*. Enable this checkbox if you want the Dial-Up Networking to automatically route all your TCP/IP traffic to the remote network's default router.

After you specify the settings you want to use, choose OK to close the TCP/IP Settings dialog box. Then choose OK to close the Server Types dialog box. Choose OK a third time to close the property sheet for the connection.

Using SLIP and CSLIP Connections

Most Internet service providers offer PPP access, which means that you can use Dial-Up Networking's PPP support to connect to the service provider's server and access the Internet. Many UNIX systems, however, support Serial Line Interface Protocol (SLIP) for dial-up connections. Fortunately, Windows 95's Dial-Up Networking supports SLIP as well as Compressed SLIP (CSLIP). So you can use Dial-Up Networking to connect to a UNIX system through SLIP or CSLIP. You then can use whatever network transport protocol is required by the remote system, such as TCP/IP, to access the remote system's resources.

The SLIP driver for Windows 95 Dial-Up Networking isn't installed automatically when you install Dial-Up Networking. The SLIP driver is contained on the Windows 95 CD and on the CD-ROM Extras for Windows 95 update disk set, which is available from Microsoft (for people who have the floppy disk version of Windows 95). The following section explains how to install the SLIP driver from the Windows 95 CD.

Installing SLIP

Installing the SLIP driver is simple. Use the following steps:

1. Insert the Windows 95 CD into your CD-ROM drive. If insert notification is turned on, the CD autoplays, and its autoplay window appears on the display. Click the Add/Remove Software button.
2. If insert notification is turned off, the CD will not autoplay on insertion. Instead, open the Control Panel and double-click the Add/Remove Programs icon.
3. Click the Windows Setup tab to display the Windows Setup property page.
4. Click the Have Disk button to display the Install From Disk dialog box.
5. Click the Browse button; then select the CD-ROM drive from the Open dialog box.
6. Locate the file \ADMIN\APPTOOLS\DSCRIPT\RNAPLUS.INF on the CD and choose OK; then click OK in the Install From Disk dialog box.
7. Windows 95 then displays the Have Disk dialog box with the SLIP driver displayed in the Components list (see fig. 23.9). Place a check

beside the SLIP driver, and choose Install. Windows 95 copies the necessary files from the CD and installs the driver.

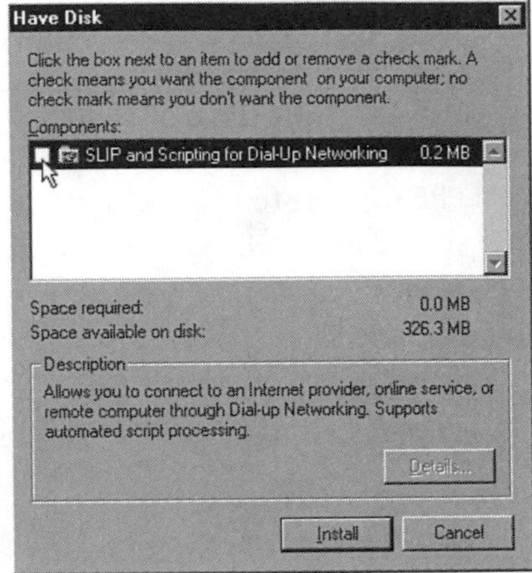

Fig. 23.9
Installing the SLIP driver also installs dial-up scripting.

> **Note**
>
> Installing the SLIP driver also installs dial-up scripting, which enables you to create dialing and logon scripts for use with the SLIP and PPP connection protocols in Dial-Up Networking. Scripting is explained later in the section "Creating Dial-Up Scripts."

8. Click OK to close the Windows Setup page.

Windows 95 doesn't have to reboot after installing the SLIP driver, but you do need to configure your Dial-Up Networking session(s) to use it. The next section explains how.

Using the SLIP Protocol

You use the Server Type dialog box described earlier in this chapter to configure a Dial-Up Networking session for a SLIP connection. Follow these steps to configure the SLIP connection:

1. Open the Dial-Up Networking folder as explained earlier in this chapter.
2. Right-click the icon whose session you want to configure for a SLIP connection; then choose Properties from the context menu.
3. Click the Server Type button to display the Server Type dialog box.

4. From the Type of Dial-Up Server drop-down list, choose SLIP: UNIX Connection to use SLIP, or CSLIP: UNIX Connection with IP Header Compression to use CSLIP; then choose OK.

> **Note**
>
> The SLIP and CSLIP protocols work only with the TCP/IP network transport protocol. You can't use NetBEUI or IPX/SPX protocols with a SLIP connection.

5. Choose OK on the session's property sheet.

To establish the connection, open the Dial-Up Networking folder and double-click the session's icon, just as you would for any other Dial-Up Networking session. Click the Connect button in the session's Connect To dialog box. Dial-Up Networking dials the remote server and opens a Terminal Screen window after the server answers.

Enter your user name and password in the terminal window. The server logs you on and assigns an IP address to you. Write down the IP address; then click Continue or press F7. Windows 95 then displays a SLIP IP Connection Address dialog box, prompting you to enter your IP address. Enter the IP address provided by the server; then choose OK to begin using the SLIP connection.

It might seem cumbersome to you to connect to a server using SLIP, and you're right. Fortunately, you can automate the process using Dial-Up Networking scripts. The next section explains scripting.

Creating Dial-Up Scripts

If you read the preceding section, you'll realize that it would be helpful to have a method of automating logon to a server. When you install the SLIP driver, Windows 95 also installs a dial-up scripting tool that lets you create and assign logon scripts to a Dial-Up Networking session. Even if you use PPP to connect to the server, you can still use dial-up scripting—you don't have to use a SLIP or CSLIP protocol.

To install the dial-up scripting tool, refer to the section "Installing SLIP" earlier in this chapter. The procedure explained in that section installs dial-up scripting for you.

Creating and Editing Scripts

You can use any ASCII text editor to create and modify dial-up scripts. Notepad works well, but you also can use WordPad or even your favorite word processor, as long as the program can save the file in ASCII format.

The script that you create automates such tasks as sending your user name and password to the server and retrieving your assigned IP address.

Every script must include a procedure named *main* that defines the starting point of the script. Usually, the main procedure contains the commands that automate the logon process. In fact, the main procedure can be the only procedure in the script if you like, performing all the tasks you want to automate.

The scripting commands supported by the dial-up scripting tool are similar to the scripting commands used by other communications programs. Fortunately, you don't have to know how to create a script to get started. The scripting tool includes four standard scripts that you can use as-is or modify to suit your needs. The best way to understand scripting is to look at an example. The following sample script included with the scripting tool automates logon to a SLIP server that uses a menu. The script sends the user name and password, selects an item from the server's menu, and retrieves the IP address for the session.

```
; This is a script file that demonstrates how
; to establish a SLIP connection with a host
; that uses a menu system.
;
; A script file must have a 'main' procedure.
; All script execution starts with this 'main'
; procedure.
;

; Main entry point to script
;
proc main

    ; Delay for 3 seconds first to allow host time
    ; to send initial characters.

    delay 3
    transmit "^M"

    ; Wait for the login prompt before entering
    ; the user ID

    waitfor "username:"
    transmit $USERID
    transmit "^M"

    ; Enter the password

    waitfor "password:"
    transmit $PASSWORD
    transmit "^M"
```

```
   ;
   ; This provider has a menu list like this:
   ;
   ;   1               : Our special GUI
   ;   2               : Establish slip connection
   ;   3               : Establish PPP connection
   ;   4               : Establish shell access
   ;   5               : Download our software
   ;   6               : Exit
   ;
   ;   annex:
   ;

   waitfor "annex:"
   transmit "2^M"       ; Choose SLIP connection
   set ipaddr getip 2   ; Get the second IP address and use it
endproc
```

If you scan the script, you see that it relies on a few variables to assign user name and password. These variables are as follows:

- *$USERID*. This variable corresponds to the user name you enter in the User Name text box on the Connect To dialog box.
- *$PASSWORD*. This variable corresponds to the password you enter in the Password text box on the Connect To dialog box.

The script also uses other commands, such as `getip`, that are explained later in the section "Script Command Reference." The next section explains how you can associate a script with a Dial-Up Networking session.

Using the Dial-Up Scripting Tool

A new item, the Dial-Up Scripting Tool, appears on your Accessories menu after you install the SLIP and scripting software. Selecting Start, Programs, Accessories, and Dial-Up Scripting tool displays the Dial-Up Scripting Tool dialog box shown in figure 23.10. Use this tool to view, edit, and assign scripts to a Dial-Up Networking session.

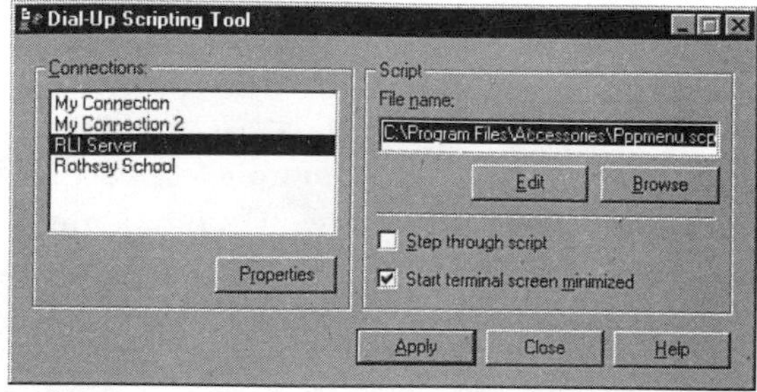

Fig. 23.10
Use the Dial-Up Scripting tool to edit and assign scripts.

To associate a script with a Dial-Up Networking session, first create the session. Then open the Dial-Up Scripting Tool and select the connection from the Connections list. Click the Browse button to display a standard Open dialog box and choose the script you want to use; then choose OK. Focus then returns to the Dial-Up Scripting Tool dialog box. Click the Edit button if you want to edit the script using Notepad. You also can set the following two properties for the script:

- *Step through Script.* Enable this check box if you want Dial-Up Networking to step through the script one command at a time as you verify each command. Enabling this option is helpful for debugging a script.
- *Start Terminal Screen Minimized.* Enable this check box if you want the terminal screen to open on the taskbar instead of as a window. If you don't need to enter any information in the terminal window, you probably don't need to see it unless you want to monitor the script's progress. Leave the check box cleared if you want to monitor the script's progress as it runs.

Click either Close or Apply to apply the changes to the connection.

Script Command Reference

The following sections describe the commands you can use in a Dial-Up Networking script.

proc <*name*>

This statement begins a script procedure. The *name* parameter specifies the name of the procedure. Each script must have a procedure named main as the entry point of the script. Processing of the script begins with the `proc main` statement and ends with the main procedure's `endproc` statement.

Example:

```
proc main
```

endproc

This statement ends a script procedure. Dial-Up Networking starts PPP or SLIP, depending on the server type selected for the connection, when the script reaches the endproc statement for the main procedure.

delay <*n* seconds>

This statement causes the script to pause for the specified number of seconds.

Example to delay three seconds:

```
delay 3
```

waitfor "<*string*>"

This statement causes the script to pause until it receives the specified string of characters. The waitfor statement is case-sensitive.

Example to wait for the string "Select menu item: ":

```
waitfor "Select menu item: "
```

transmit "<*string*>" | $USERID | $PASSWORD

This statement transmits a string to the server. You can use the transmit command to send your user name and password stored in the $USERID and $PASSWORD variables. These variable keywords correspond to the user name and password stored with the Dial-Up Networking connection's properties.

Example to transmit the string "2" and a carriage return, followed by your password:

```
transmit "2^M"
transmit $PASSWORD
```

Windows 95 appends a carriage return to the $USERID and $PASSWORD variables when transmitting them, so you don't need to append a carriage return to them.

set port databits <*integer*>

This statement sets the number of data bits in each data word (byte). Valid settings are from 5 to 8. Dial-Up Networking uses the setting specified by the Dial-Up Networking connection's properties if you don't specify a value for data bits.

Example to specify seven data bits:

```
set port databits 7
```

set port stopbits <*integer*>

This statement changes the number of stop bits for the port and can be either 1 or 2. Dial-Up Networking uses the port settings specified by the Dial-Up Networking connection's properties if you don't specify the number of stop bits with the set port stopbits statement.

Example to specify two stop bits:

```
set port stopbits 2
```

set port parity none | odd | even | mark | space

This statement specifies the type of parity checking used for the connection. Dial-Up Networking uses the parity method defined in the Dial-Up Networking connection's properties if you don't specify the parity method.

Example to specify odd parity:

```
set port parity odd
```

set ipaddr

This statement specifies the IP address of your node for the session. You typically use this statement after using the `getip` statement to retrieve your computer's assigned IP address from the server. So you use the `getip` statement to retrieve your IP address from the server, and then use `set ippaddr` to tell Dial-Up Networking to use that IP address for the session.

getip "<*delimiter*>"

This statement reads an IP address from the server. Specify with the *delimiter* parameter the character that separates the IP address from the characters that surround it. This enables Dial-Up Networking to parse the IP address from the string.

Example to retrieve the IP address when a comma is used to separate the address from other text:

```
set ipaddr getip ","
```

; (comments)

Text on a line following a semicolon is treated as a comment and is ignored by the script processor. To create a comment, start the line with a semicolon.

Example:

```
; This is a comment
```

Note

Include either ^M or <cr> in the transmit string, such as **transmit "CIS^M"**, to transmit a carriage return. To send only a linefeed character, use <lf> in the string, such as **transmit "<lf>"**. To transmit a carriage return and linefeed, use <cr><lf>, as in **transmit "<cr><lf>"**.

Setting Up a Dial-Up Networking Server

Windows 95 includes all the client software you need to dial into a remote access server with Dial-Up Networking. You also can set up your Windows 95 workstation as a Dial-Up Networking server, but you need the Microsoft Plus! for Windows 95 add-on to do it. Plus! includes Dial-Up Networking server software that lets other users dial into your PC to access your PC's resources, and to access the resources of your LAN if the PC is connected to a LAN.

The Windows 95 Dial-Up Networking server software supports NetBEUI and IPX/SPX protocols, enabling clients that use those protocols to dial in and use resources. The Windows 95 Dial-Up Networking server doesn't support TCP/IP or NetWare's NRN protocols, however, which means you can't connect with a NetWare dial-up client or use the Windows 95 server as a TCP/IP gateway. The Windows 95 server supports PPP and asynchronous NetBEUI (used by Windows NT 3.1 and Windows for Workgroups 3.11); but it doesn't support SLIP, CSLIP, or NetWare's NRN protocols.

The Windows 95 Dial-Up Networking server supports two types of security: *share-level* and *user-level*. With share-level security, shared resources are protected using passwords. Any user that has the correct password can access the shared resource. All Windows 95 workstations use share-level security to protect resources they are sharing.

User-level security provides greater security by requiring access to be handled through a Windows NT or NetWare security provider. When a user tries to access a resource, the request is directed to the security server. The server checks its security database to determine if the user is authorized to use the resource. If so, the security server grants access to the resource. Access is denied if the user doesn't have the necessary access privilege. Using user-level security requires that your Windows 95 Dial-Up Networking server be connected to a LAN that contains a Windows NT or NetWare server that can act as a security server.

Installing the Dial-Up Networking Server

To install the Windows 95 Dial-Up Networking server software, run the Setup program for your Microsoft Plus! product. In Setup, choose the Custom option to enable you to select which items to install. Select the Dial-Up Networking Server from the Options list; then follow the remaining instructions in Setup to complete the installation process.

Configuring the Dial-Up Networking Server

After you install the Dial-Up Networking server, you might not know it's there. The only real indication is a new item in your Dial-Up Networking folder's menu. Open the Dial-Up Networking folder and choose Connections, then Dial-Up Server. Dial-Up Networking displays a Dial-Up Server property page similar to the one shown in figure 23.11.

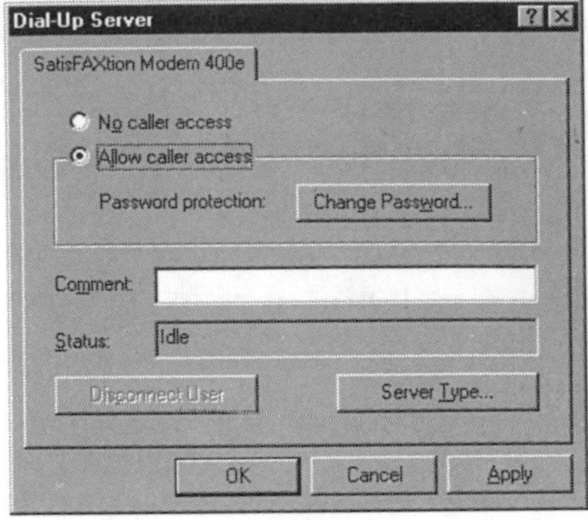

Fig. 23.11
Use the Dial-Up Server dialog box to enable callers to dial into your PC.

To allow others to dial into your PC, choose the Allow Caller Access option button. If you're using share-level security, you can assign a password for call-in access. Anyone calling in must provide the correct password to be connected. To assign the password, click the Change Password button to open a simple dialog box in which you specify the password for your PC.

If you're using user-level security, the Dial-Up Server dialog box is slightly different, as shown in figure 23.12. With user-level security, you must click the Add button and add each user who you want to have access. The list of available user names comes from the security server on the LAN. After you add names, they show up in the User Name list on the Dial-Up Server dialog box.

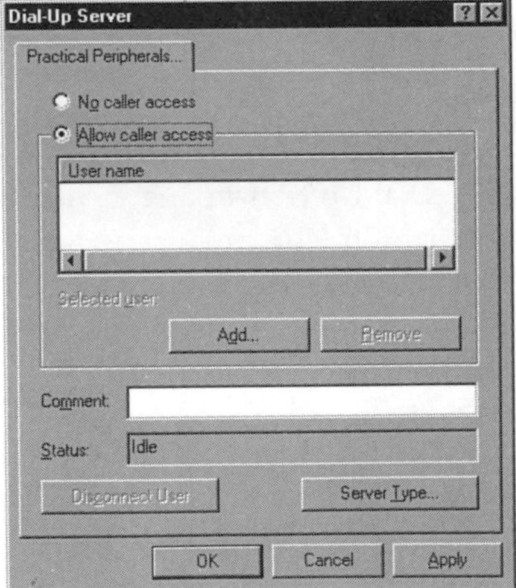

Fig. 23.12
You can use user-level security for your server.

Note

User-level security applies not only to dial-in users, but also to users on your local network who want to access resources on your PC. Share-level security is the default. To turn on user-level security, open the Control Panel, double-click the Network icon, and then click the Access Control tab of the Network property sheet. Select the User-level access control option button; then choose OK. Windows 95 restarts your PC to apply the change.

After you configure the security options, you need to specify the type of connection protocol your Windows 95 Dial-Up Networking server will use. On the Dial-Up Server dialog box, click the Server Type button to display the Server Types dialog box shown in figure 23.13.

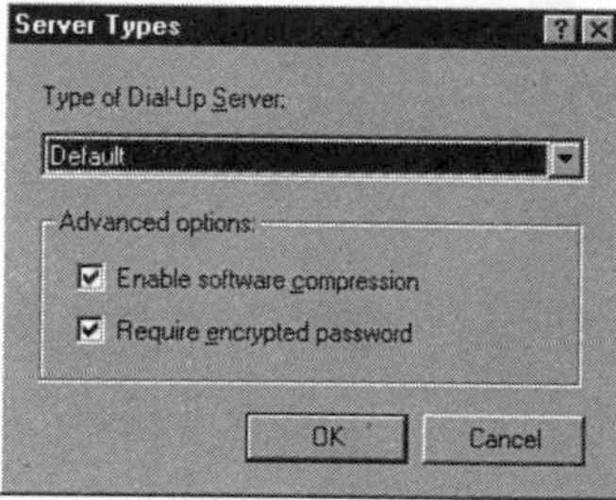

Fig. 23.13
You must specify the type of connection protocol to use.

If you select the Default server type, your Dial-Up Networking server attempts to use PPP to connect callers, and if the PPP connection fails, attempts asynchronous NetBEUI. If the NetBEUI connection fails, the call terminates. If you want to limit calls specifically to either PPP or NetBEUI, select the desired protocol from the drop-down list.

Two other options on the Server Types dialog box let you control the connection:

- *Enable Software Compression.* Enable this check box if you want the server to use software compression to improve data transfer speed. The remote user must also be using software compression. If not, the server connects without compression.
- *Require Encrypted Password.* Enable this check box to require the caller's client to transmit the logon password in encrypted format. If you clear this check box, the password is sent unencrypted.

Choose OK to return to the Dial-Up Server dialog box; then click OK to begin monitoring the port for incoming calls.

Terminating a User

Occasionally, you might need to terminate a user's connection to your Dial-Up Networking server. The user might have forgotten to log off and terminate the connection, for example, which is tying up the line and preventing other callers from connecting. Or, you might need to disconnect a user for security reasons.

To disconnect a user, open the Dial-Up Networking folder and choose Connections, Dial-Up Server to open the Dial-Up Server dialog box. Click the Disconnect User button. Dial-Up Networking prompts you to verify that you want to disconnect the current caller. ❖

CHAPTER 24

Using Direct Cable Connection

by Jim Boyce

One major improvement Windows 95 has over Windows 3.x is in connectivity. Windows 95 offers many different methods for you to connect two or more PCs to share files and printers. One of the easiest methods is Direct Cable Connection, which enables you to connect two PCs using a null-modem serial or parallel cable. Although Direct Cable Connection was designed to make it possible to share resources between notebook and desktop PCs, you can use Direct Cable Connection to connect any two PCs running Windows 95 to create a small network. You also can use Direct Cable Connection to connect a visiting PC (such as a notebook) to a LAN.

This chapter explains how to use Direct Cable Connection, including what type of cables to use.

In this chapter, you'll learn to

- Understand Direct Cable Connection
- Set up Direct Cable Connection
- Use Direct Cable Connection
- Make your own cable

Understanding Direct Cable Connection

Microsoft's Dial-Up Adapter enables Windows 95's Dial-Up Networking software to connect to a remote access server or other Windows 95 PC through a modem connection. The Dial-Up Adapter also serves another purpose: it enables you to connect two PCs using a serial null-modem cable or a parallel cable. Using the Direct Cable Connection software included with Windows 95, the two PCs can share files and printers, just as if they were connected by network cards and cables. Although transfer speed isn't as fast with Direct Cable Connection as with a standard network connection, the cost is minimal: less than $15 for the cable. There are no other gadgets or software to buy.

◀ See "Using Dial-Up Networking," p. 495

In a Direct Cable Connection between two PCs, one PC acts as a *host* and the other acts as a *guest*. The host system "listens" to the serial or parallel port, waiting for a guest to request a connection. When the guest makes that request, the host validates the connection, authenticating the logon password (if you've configured Direct Cable Connection to require one). Then, the guest can connect to resources shared by the host in the same way you connect to resources on a LAN—you can map resource IDs (such as drive letters) on the guest to resources on the host, or use the Network Neighborhood to browse for resources. You then can transfer files between the two PCs and print from the guest to the host PC's printer(s). Figure 24.1 illustrates Direct Cable Connection.

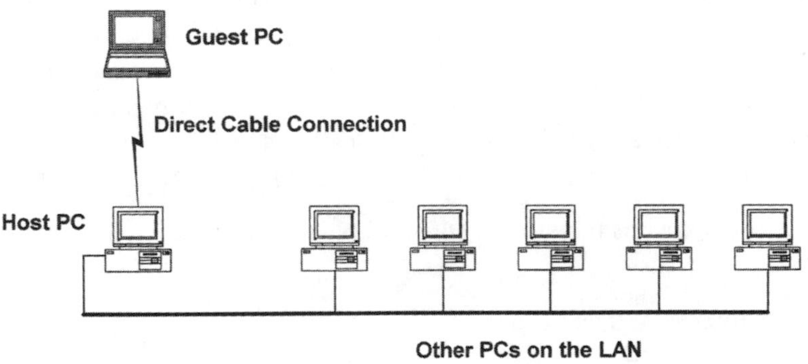

Fig. 24.1
You can network PCs using Direct Cable Connection.

Direct Cable Connection can also provide connectivity to your LAN. If the host PC is connected to a LAN, the guest PC will gain access not only to the host's resources, but also to the shared resources on the network. Essentially, the host computer acts as a gateway to the LAN for the guest.

> **Note**
>
> Direct Cable Connection doesn't support connection by computers on the LAN to the guest PC. The guest can access the LAN, but not the other way around.

Direct Cable Connection uses the same types of security as the Windows 95 network. You can access shared resources with user-level security or share-level security, depending on how the host and guest are configured. For this reason, access to the network using Direct Cable Connection is the same as it is with a PC connected directly to the LAN. You must either have the required share-level passwords to access a shared resource, or if user-level security is active, your user account must be validated by a security server on the LAN.

Note

If you want to connect your two PCs using a parallel cable, the parallel ports of both PCs must be configured as bidirectional ports. For best performance, the two ports should also be configured as ECPs (Enhanced Capabilities Ports). For more information on configuring your systems' parallel ports, refer to Chapter 4, "Configuring Parallel Ports."

◀ See "Setting Up a Dial-Up Networking Server," p. 514

▶ See "Sharing Resources," p. 553

Setting Up Direct Cable Connection

The first step in using Direct Cable Connection is to install the software. Like other Windows 95 components, Direct Cable Connection can be installed through the Add/Remove Programs object in the Control Panel. Use the following steps to add Direct Cable Connection to the host and guest PCs:

1. On the host PC, open the Control Panel and double-click the Add/Remove Programs icon.
2. Click the Windows Setup tab to display the Windows Setup page.
3. Select the Communications item, then click the Details button.
4. Place checks beside Direct Cable Connection and Dial-Up Networking (Direct Cable Connection requires the use of the Dial-Up Networking adapter).
5. Choose OK, then OK again to install the software on the host PC.
6. Repeat steps 1 through 5 on the guest PC.

The next step is to configure the Dial-Up Adapter, network protocol, and network client.

Note

You can install Direct Cable Connection when you install Windows 95 by using the Custom or Portable options. If you use the Compact or Typical options, however, you must install Direct Cable Connection through the Add/Remove Software object in the Control Panel.

Configuring a Protocol and Client

Like a real network adapter, the Dial-Up Adapter used by Direct Cable Connection relies on a network transport protocol and network client. Windows 95 adds the Dial-Up Adapter and associates with it the Client for Microsoft Networks, Client for NetWare Networks, NetBEUI protocol, and IPX/SPX protocol. If you're connecting to a NetWare-based system, these selections will work. If you're using a Windows 95- or Windows NT-based network, however, you can remove the NetWare components because they are not required to connect to Windows 95 and Windows NT-based networks. Removing them will simplify your network configuration and release a small amount of memory to Windows 95 and your applications. The following steps explain how to remove the NetWare components:

1. Open the Control Panel and double-click the Network icon.
2. On the Configuration page, click the Client for NetWare Networks, then click Remove.
3. Click the IPX/SPX-compatible Protocol, and then choose Remove.
4. Choose OK. Windows 95 prompts you to restart the system.

Tip

Although you can use TCP/IP for Direct Cable Connection, the host won't transport TCP/IP packets for the guest, which prevents the guest from accessing resources beyond the host (such as on the LAN). In other words, a Direct Cable Connection host will not act as a gateway for TCP/IP clients. Consider using NetBEUI instead, because a Direct Cable Connection host will serve as a gateway for NetBEUI and IPX/SPX clients.

For an explanation of how to add a protocol to the Dial-Up Adapter, refer to Chapter 23, "Using Dial-Up Networking." After adding a protocol, you must restart Windows 95 before using the protocol.

Configuring Sharing

◀ See "Adding Protocols," p. 499

In addition to configuring the necessary protocol, you also need to configure the PCs to share files and printers. The guest can access resources shared by the host, and the host can access the guest's shared resources, but only after you configure the two computers appropriately. It's important to note that you don't need to enable file and print sharing on a PC to access shared resources located on another PC. Adding the appropriate network client gives you that ability. If you want to share resources on a PC with other users, however, you must enable sharing on that PC.

To enable sharing on either the host or guest, follow these steps:

1. Open the Control Panel and double-click the Network icon.

   If a sharing service (such as File and Printer Sharing for Microsoft Networks) is listed on the Configuration property page, skip to step 7. Otherwise, proceed with step 2.

2. Click the Add button.
3. Select Service from the Select Network Component Type dialog box, and then choose Add.
4. From the Manufacturers list, choose Microsoft.
5. From the Network Services list, choose File and Print Sharing for Microsoft Networks if you're using the Microsoft client. Choose File and Print Sharing for NetWare Networks if you're using the NetWare client. Then, click OK.
6. On the Configuration page, click the File and Printer Sharing button to display the File and Print Sharing dialog box (see fig. 24.2).

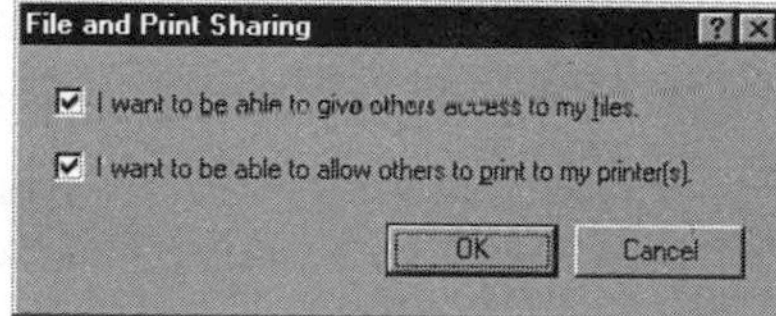

Fig. 24.2
You must enable file and print sharing on a PC before you can share its resources.

7. To enable the PC to share its files, place a check in the check box labeled I Want to Be Able to Give Others Access to My Files.
8. To enable the PC to share its printer(s), place a check in the check box labeled I Want to Be Able to Allow Others to Print to My Printer(s).
9. Choose OK to close the File and Print Sharing dialog box.
10. Choose OK on the Network property sheet. Windows 95 prompts you to restart the system. You must do so before the changes will take effect.

You can move files between the host and the guest if you only enable sharing on the host. However, you can only access files located in shared folders on the host, and you can only place files from the guest in those shared folders. If your host PC isn't connected to a LAN, consider sharing the root folder of each hard disk, which will enable you to access any host folder from the guest. If your host is connected to a LAN, you should take a different approach for security: share the root folders of each disk on the guest, then perform all your file operations from the host. The host will be able to copy files from the guest, and place files in any of the guest's folders.

Because Direct Cable Connection doesn't support access by other machines on the LAN to the guest, sharing the guest's entire file system doesn't place the files at risk for unauthorized access. Just remember to disconnect the guest when you're finished so no one else can sit down at your host PC and access its files.

Note

For a detailed explanation of how to share files and printers and ensure security for your data, refer to Chapter 26, "Sharing Resources."

Connecting the Cable

The next step in setting up Direct Cable Connection is to connect the cable between the two PCs. You can use a null-modem serial cable or parallel cable (see "Making Your Own Cable" later in this chapter). The only restriction (other than using a cable that's supported by Direct Cable Connection) is that you must use the same port on each computer. If you connect the cable to COM1 on the guest, for example, you must connect the cable to COM1 on the host.

Tip

It is unlikely that you will experience any problems connecting a serial or parallel cable to a running PC. There is the rare chance that something could be damaged, however, so I recommend you shut down and turn off the PCs before connecting them.

The following cables are compatible with Direct Cable Connection:

- Standard RS-232 serial null-modem cables
- 4-bit cables, including LapLink and InterLink cables that were available before 1992
- Extended Capabilities Port (ECP) cables, which work on ECP-enabled ports and allow data to be transferred more quickly than a standard cable
- Universal Cable Module (UCM) cable, which supports connecting different types of parallel ports; use UCM cables between two ECP ports for the best transfer speed

Be aware that not all serial cables advertised as null-modem cables will work with Direct Cable Connection. If you want to check your cable or make a cable that is compatible with Direct Cable Connection, see "Making Your Own Cable" later in this chapter for the appropriate cable pin-outs.

Troubleshooting

I only have one serial port on my notebook, and I have an external pointing device (mouse or trackball) connected to it. How can I use the pointing device and Direct Cable Connection at the same time?

You can't use the serial pointing device and a serial Direct Cable Connection at the same time, since you only have one port. You have two options. If your notebook includes a PS/2 mouse port (most do), you can connect the pointing device to the PS/2 port with an adapter that probably came with the pointing device. If you don't have such an adapter, check with your local computer store for one or contact the pointing device's manufacturer to see if one is available. The best option, however, is to use the parallel port instead of the serial port for Direct Cable Connection, because you'll experience better transfer speeds.

Using a Direct Cable Connection

After you configure and connect the two PCs, you can begin using Direct Cable Connection. The following section explains how to set up the host and guest.

Setting Up the Host and Guest

The first step in using Direct Cable Connection is to set the host to begin listening for a connection on the appropriate port. Then, set the guest to attempt a connection to the host. To start Direct Cable Connection on either the host or the guest, choose Start, Programs, Accessories, Direct Cable Connection.

The first time you run Direct Cable Connection, a wizard steps you through the process of configuring the PC as either a host or guest (see fig. 24.3). Select either the Host or Guest option button, then choose Next.

Next, the wizard prompts you to select the port to use for the connection (see fig. 24.4). Choose the appropriate port, then click Next.

If you're setting up the host, the wizard asks you if you want to use password protection (see fig. 24.5). If password protection is enabled, the guest must specify the correct password to connect to the host and use its resources. To enable password protection, place a check in the Use Password Protection check box, then click the Set Password button. The wizard displays a simple dialog box in which you enter and verify the connection password. When your password settings are ready, click the Finish button. Direct Cable Connection initializes the port and begins listening for a connection from the guest.

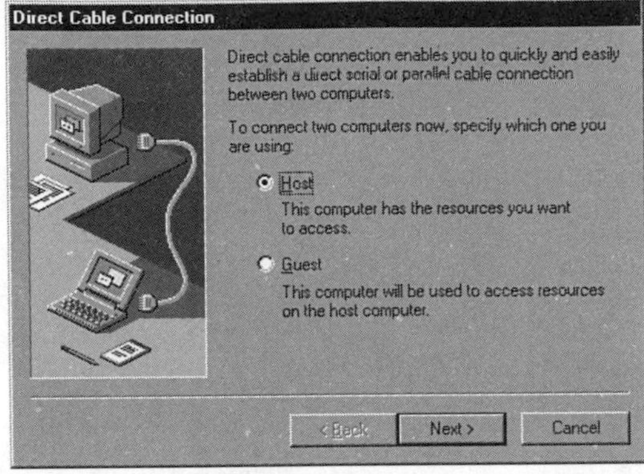

Fig. 24.3
Specify whether the PC will act as a host or as a guest.

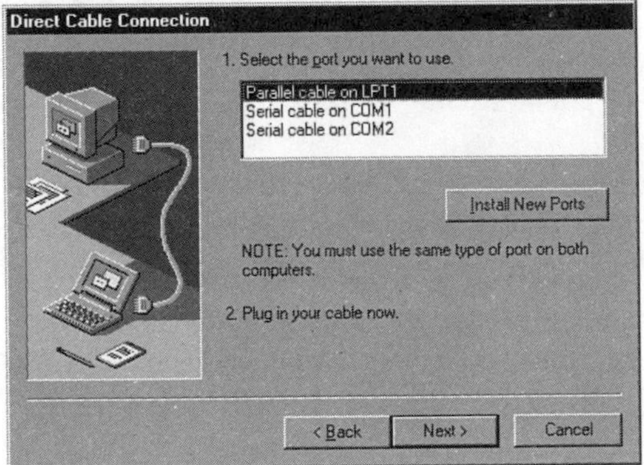

Fig. 24.4
Choose the port to which the cable is connected.

If you're setting up the guest, the wizard prompts you for the port to use, just as it does when setting up the host. After you select the port and click Next, click Finish to attempt a connection to the host. Direct Cable Connection initializes the port and attempts a connection to the host. While it's attempting the connection, you should see the message `Verifying user name and password` on the host as well as the guest. When the connection is established, the guest begins searching the host for shared folders. If no connection or browse errors occur, a window containing all of the shared folders appears on the guest (see fig. 24.6). The next section, "Using Shared Resources," gives you a brief explanation of how to use those shared resources.

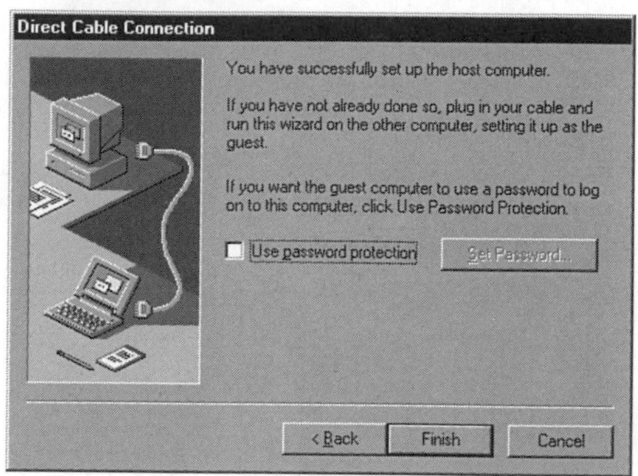

Fig. 24.5
You can enable password protection on the host.

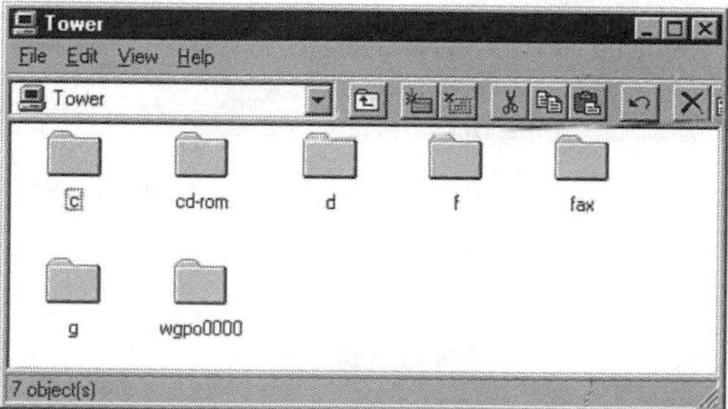

Fig. 24.6
Direct Cable Connection automatically browses the host for shared folders.

If Direct Cable Connection is unable to browse the host for shared resources, Direct Cable Connection on the guest PC opens a simple dialog box that prompts you to specify the name of the host PC. Type the name of the host computer, such as TOWER, then choose OK. Note that this is the PC's network name, not the "My Computer" name you see on the desktop of each computer.

Tip

If you close the shared resource window on the guest, you can cause Direct Cable Connection to browse the host again by clicking the View Host button on the Direct Cable Connection dialog box (see fig. 24.7).

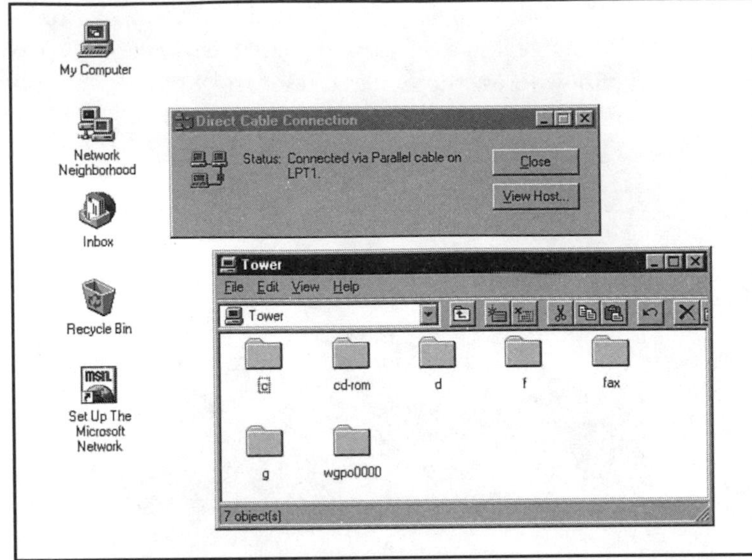

Fig. 24.7
Click the View Host button to browse for resources on the host PC.

Troubleshooting

When I try to connect to the host, the guest can't automatically browse for shared folders on the host. Direct Cable Connection prompts me to specify the name of the host. Is there some way to make it browse automatically?

If you have more than one protocol bound to the Dial-Up Adapter on the guest or the host, the multiple protocols could be preventing Direct Cable Connection from browsing the connection. Reduce the protocols for the Dial-Up Adapter on the guest to only the NetBEUI protocol, then try again (the system will have to restart after you change protocols). To remove a protocol, open the Control Panel and double-click the Network icon. Select the protocol from the list of installed components, then click Remove. Click OK to close the property sheet.

If reducing to one protocol on the guest doesn't enable the guest to automatically browse the host, try removing all but the NetBEUI protocol for the Dial-Up Adapter on the host, then try the connection again.

Direct Cable Connection is unable to connect, and I'm sure the cable is OK. What else could be wrong?

Open the Control Panel and double-click the Network icon. Verify that the Dial-Up Adapter is installed and has the right protocol bound to it (Microsoft strongly recommends NetBEUI). To do so, double-click the Dial-Up Adapter then click the Bindings tab to display the Bindings property page, on which the bound protocols are listed. Choose OK to close the property sheet. Then, verify that NetBEUI is defined as the default protocol for the Dial-Up Adapter. To do so, double-click NetBEUI -> Dial-Up Adapter on the Configuration page, then verify that the appropriate client is enabled on the Bindings page. Then, click the Advanced tab and place a check in the check box labeled Set this Protocol to be the Default Protocol. Close the property sheet and let Windows 95 restart. Then test the connection again.

Using Shared Resources

You can use folders on the host from the guest without mapping a guest drive ID to the remote folder. When Direct Cable Connection establishes the connection, browses for resources, and displays a window containing those resources, just double-click the shared folder you want to use. Its files and subfolders appear in a window just as if you were browsing through a folder on your own system.

If you want to associate a drive ID on the guest to the shared folder on the host, use one of the following techniques:

- Right-click a shared folder, then choose Map Network Drive. Windows 95 prompts you to choose the drive ID you want to associate with the remote folder (see fig. 24.8). From the Drive drop-down list, choose a drive letter. If you want the guest to try to reconnect to the shared folder each time the guest starts Windows 95, enable the Reconnect At Logon check box. Choose OK.

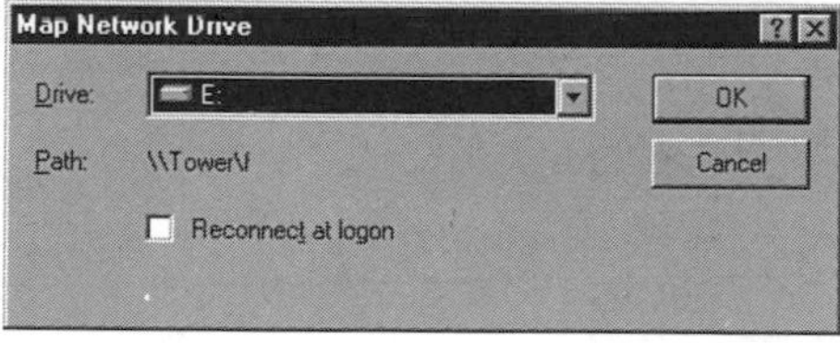

Fig. 24.8
Select the drive to associate with the resource, then choose OK.

- Right-click the Network Neighborhood folder and choose Map Network Drive. Windows 95 displays a dialog box similar to the one shown in figure 24.8, except the Path combo-box is not filled in for you automatically. In the Path combo-box, type the UNC name of the shared resource, such as \\DESKTOP\C, where DESKTOP is the name of the host computer and C: is the shared folder name. Or, click the drop-down button and choose a connection name you've previously used. Click OK.

For a more detailed explanation of how to share files and printers, read Chapter 26, "Sharing Resources."

Making Your Own Cable

You might have a cable you'd like to use with Direct Cable Connection, but you're not sure if it's the right type. Or, you might not have quick access to a location where you can buy a cable, but you can get the connectors and raw cable to make a Direct Cable Connection cable. If you have a cable and you're not sure if it will work with Direct Cable Connection, just hook it up and try it. If it doesn't work, you can check it against the diagrams shown in figures 24.9 and 24.10. Use a volt-ohm meter or set to check continuity (resistance) or an inexpensive continuity tester to determine if the wires are connected to the proper pins on each connector. You can find these types of meters at electronics stores, hardware stores, and retail discount chains. Or, you can use figures 24.9 and 24.10 as a guide to make your own cable.

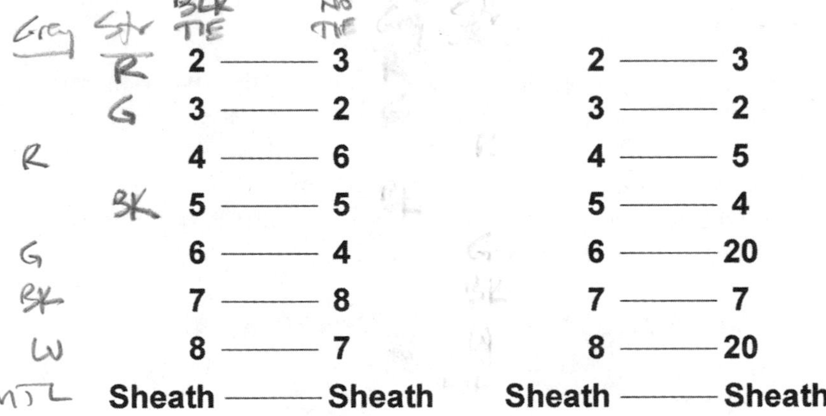

Fig. 24.9
These are the pin connections for a null-modem serial cable that works with DCC.

15 — 2
2 — 15
3 — 13
4 — 12
5 — 10
6 — 11
10 — 5
11 — 6
12 — 4
13 — 3
25 — 25
Sheath — Sheath

25-Pin Parallel Cable

15 — 2

Fig. 24.10
These are the pin connections for a parallel cable that works with DCC.

CHAPTER 25

Using Remote Control Programs

by Rich Castagna

The computing power that only a few short years ago commanded a desktop or more now fits neatly into a five-pound package. Add a high-speed modem about the size of a chubby credit card and you've got a full-featured office on the go. The challenge, though, is making the data you need to do business as mobile as you are.

This chapter describes remote control software and several of the more popular programs currently available. In this chapter, you learn

- Control versus Access—the features that distinguish remote control programs from remote access packages
- Some of the issues that you'll have to consider to get remote control to work for you
- Tips on selecting the program that best suits your needs
- Several suggested remote control applications
- What you'll need to do to set up for remote control—including hardware considerations
- Methods of connecting PCs for remote control operations
- Program features generic to most remote control software
- Overviews of three remote control programs for Windows 95

Access or Control

Remote access and remote control programs let you hook up to an unattended PC so that your data can catch up to you. Both of these communication methods require that you install software at both the unattended system—often called the host—and the remote PC. A physical link also is required. Most of these programs work over phone lines, or between two directly connected PCs linked by a network or a serial or parallel null-modem cable.

Remote access is somewhat more basic than remote control. Generally, remote access lets you access and use the host's resources, such as its hard disk or an attached printer. Remote control doesn't stop there. It gives you full control of the entire host system—just as if you were sitting in front of it. But you run the show remotely, with a keyboard or mouse and a display that could be thousands of miles away.

The toughest technical problem that remote control programs had to overcome to provide more functionality than the access applications is screen display and synchronization. Under DOS, this was a surmountable task because a couple of speedy modems could adequately handle shifting the character-based information back and forth.

With Windows, much of what is shown on the screen is graphical, which is far more complex and involves moving much more data. Using the early Windows remote control programs was often a lesson in patience and perseverance. Screens repainted at agonizingly slow speeds—even with fast modems—and the cursor often seemed a time zone or two behind your mouse movements. Today's crop of remote controllers use a variety of techniques to provide almost instantaneous response. They use more efficient data compression routines that cram more into the bits that stream across the line, and they tend to send only the information related to the parts of the screen that have changed. Coupled with lickety-split modems and high-speed serial ports, these programs can deliver the remote screen image almost as quickly as if you really were sitting at the host machine.

If you exercise your remote control mastery of another machine over a network or a direct link, you'll reap the rewards of the greater bandwidth those physical connections usually afford. The delays will be so significantly reduced that they're likely to be little more than a slight distraction.

How to Choose

Remote access programs are easier to install, learn, and use, simply because they do less than their control-minded brethren. When your needs are limited to just swapping files or updating information, remote access will suffice as long as those resources are currently available on the host.

But if you want more—much more—you'll need a remote control program which lets you do things like access and use all of the host's hardware peripherals—disk, CD-ROM drives, printers, or even another modem. You can run programs that you don't have on your machine but are installed on the host PC. You can even log in to the network that the host is connected to (more on that later). You have many more options and, consequently, more things to consider when setting up functional, secure remote environments (more on that later, too).

Applications

The simplest—and most obvious—application for remote control is getting your hands on what you need when you need it. If you work at home evenings or weekends, you don't have to load your briefcase with floppy diskettes and hope that you've taken all the files you'll need. A quick remote control link and you can download the data you need from the host. And when you're done doing your thing with the files, you can put them right back where you found them, on the host's hard disk.

But you can do a lot more than just fiddle with files, because you can run applications on the host. Maybe you may have the data you need, but not the program to massage the data and turn it into useful information. No problem, just run the program on the host and use your data. You can also run a host application to get information that you then download to the remote. For example, a sales rep might hook into a host, run a contact manager program and get a list of prospects for her next destination.

Mobile business people also can use remote control to synchronize files, so that they know that information that was updated back in the office is up to date on their machines as well. And because remote control puts you in the host's driver's seat, you can access any hardware peripherals, too.

Making the office-connection scenario probably accounts for the widest use of remote control programs; they do have some other equally serious applications. Support professionals can use remote control to get to the bottom of a user's problems without lengthy phone discussions. If a user called with a problem that appeared to be related to system files, the support technician could check the files, correct them, and then test the fix—without ever showing up on-site. Similarly, remote control can be used as a training platform as both instructor and student can see what's going on and can share control.

Another useful application is work collaboration. Two people can view and work on the same document simultaneously.

Setting Up for Remote Control

All remote control programs are actually two separate pieces of software. There's a program that you must install on the remote PC—the one that's doing the dialing or otherwise tapping in—and another that gets loaded on the host system, the one that receives the call. The remote software gets a kickstart whenever you need to make a connection, but the host side has to be up, running and ready already, although it's really just lurking in the background waiting to spring into action when a call from the remote gets its attention. For this reason, the host is typically a TSR, a tiny program that occupies little space and makes few demands on the system's RAM or other resources.

Remote control program publishers also take great efforts to keep the part of the program running on the remote end small, too, so that it doesn't gobble up valuable RAM. The idea is to make it as unobtrusive as possible, and keep it out of the way of other applications. The two sides of the remote control bridge end up acting like a pitcher and a catcher—neither wants to hold onto the ball for too long, so they do their best to keep it in play and keep the game rolling along.

As with any communications setup, there's hardware to consider. For remote control, you usually have a number of choices when selecting the hardware to complete the link between the two PCs, but it will be your application that is likely to determine the connection method and the hardware required to make it.

There are three basic ways of connecting PCs for remote control, generally related to the distance that the remote control process has to cover.

- For long distance connections, phone lines are preferred. To make a phone line link, in addition to available phone lines, you only need compatible modems on each end. Compatible doesn't necessarily mean identical, but the two units must be able to swap data at the same speed. If you have a fast modem on one end and a slower one on the other, the rate of data transfer will drop down to the speed of the slow modem.
- Remote control connections also can be made between two PCs over a network. If you're going to use a network hookup, then you don't have to worry about a physical link—it's there already, courtesy of your

network operating system, network interface cards, and the cable that holds the whole thing together. You should, however, make sure that the remote control software you're considering will work in your specific network environment.

- The third way of coupling two PCs for remote control is the direct connection. The most common direct connection is achieved using a null modem cable plugged into either your serial or parallel port. The null modem looks like a standard cable, but its pinouts are reversed. Obviously, this type of connection requires the two machines to be close—usually no more than six to twenty-five feet apart, depending on the cable used—so it's used mostly for file transfers and synchronization, rather than to take advantage of all the features of a remote control program.

There are other ways of establishing a channel of communications between remote PCs, but they require fairly new, sophisticated technology and are really just variations on some of the more familiar methods. For example, you can eschew the null modem for a close-quarters connection if both PCs are equipped with infrared ports. Infrared ports are far from common, but more and more notebooks are showing up with these ports, intended primarily for quick file transfers or to zap a few files to a similarly equipped printer. Other wireless methods to span greater distances are also available, but they, too, are not very prevalent and require special equipment, such as modems that can send data over cellular phone networks.

Features of Remote Control Programs

All remote control programs offer the basic features that let you make the connection, operate the remote PC, and sever the link when you're done. The differentiating factors among these programs include the depth of their feature sets, speed, and system considerations.

Remote control features can generally be arranged into two categories—ease of use and security. Again, every major remote control program has some of these features, and most have at least some variation of those listed here. When comparing features, it's often a subtle difference in how one program handles an operation that may tip the scales in its favor.

Among the *ease-of-use* features, some of the key program components to check out include a phone book, the ability to map remote drives, host rebooting, and scripting.

Save Connection Information in the Phone Book

When you use a remote control program, you'll always know where the host is, but you may not know where you'll be dialing in from. A phone book lets you set different dialing sequences, so that you can have all of the possible dialing scenarios preset and available. For example, you may want to set up an entry that uses a dialing prefix such as "9" for when you're in an office that has a PBX or for calling from a hotel room. Or maybe you use a telephone credit card, so you'll want to be able to include any required codes along with the number. With a phone book that allows for these situations, you won't have to fumble with your dialing setup each time you dial in from a different location.

If you'll need to dial into a number of hosts, you'll want a phone that cannot only accommodate an ample number of entries, but one that also lets you set communication parameters such as modem speed or transfer protocol.

Because many remote control programs also have terminal communications functions, you can use them for traditional communications activities such as point-to-point connections or access to bulletin board systems. If you plan on using your remote control software for these types of communications as well, the phone book can be invaluable—with all the phone numbers and specific setup requirements stored for each and just a click away.

Drive Mapping Sorts Out Local and Remote Routes

Drive mapping is a remote control feature that can make your sessions run smoothly and in the right direction. Drive mapping lets you make the host PC's disk drives look like local drives to the remote system. This helps avoid the confusion that is all but inevitable when you're dealing with a C: drive on one end and another C: drive on the other end. You can, for example, set the host's C: drive to look like your machine's (the remote) D:, or E:—or just about any letter—drive.

Tip

Try to use the same drive mappings for all remote control sessions. This will keep drives sorted out to sidestep slip-ups like copying files in the wrong direction. If your host is connected to a network, don't duplicate the drive designations of the network drives it can access.

Kickstart a Stalled Host with Remote Reboot

The ability to reboot a PC that might be thousands of miles away may seem like a rather arcane feature, but if you're on the remote end of a host that's dead in the water, it may be your only hope for restoring the remote control link. Remote host reboot lets you cold-boot the host machine from the remote and, in the process, reload the host's remote control module so that you can reestablish the connection. Rebooting a host will seem like a minor miracle the next time the host locks up just as you're about to download tomorrow morning's presentation.

Scripting

Some remote control programs include a scripting facility with which you can customize the software's interface and specific remote control operations. Scripting can be as simple as capturing keystrokes to create macros that can be saved, recalled, and reused. In other programs, the scripting process is far more sophisticated and you actually write program code using a programming language that typically bears a striking resemblance to the syntax used by BASIC, Visual Basic, or other popular programming environments.

Even if you're the type who doesn't lock the front door when you go away for a weekend, you *must* give *security* due consideration when using remote control software. Keep in mind that the host machine must be turned on and waiting when the remote PC rings up to tap in and complete the connection. Sure, you might have explicit trust in your coworkers, office visitors, building staff, but an ounce or two of prevention can remove temptation that may attract the curious. And it might not be malice that puts the kibosh on a remote control session—"I saw your PC going nuts while you were away so I shut it off for you."

Tip

Lead then not into temptation: Physical security can be used to complement the security features that your remote control program provides. If you can, lock the door to the office where the host is kept. And keep the host's keyboard and monitor out of view.

To make sure that the host PC is ready, remote control programs offer a number of security features that make disasters less likely to occur.

Host Keyboard Lock and Host Screen Blanking Eliminate the Sights and Sounds and Keep Away the Curious

With host screen blanking, the host PC doesn't display any images so it looks like it's turned off. With nothing to catch their eyes, passersby aren't likely to have their interest aroused to the point where they interfere with a remote session in progress. You also can disable the host's keyboard and lock them out.

Passwords: The Keys to a Safe Host

All remote control programs have provisions for passwords. When you define an acceptable remote connection on the host side, you can indicate a password that must be entered from the remote to start a remote control session. Passwording is the easiest and most effective form of security; you should *always* include a password in your remote setup.

Host Makes the Call with Dialback

For host PCs that are accessed regularly from the same remote locations, dialback can help ensure that only the phones at those locations can wake up the host and initiate connections. Dialback is easy to set up. On the host side, you define authorized users and associate a phone number with each. When the host receives a call, the remote user is identified by its password. The host then drops the connections before calling the user back at the preset phone number to restore the link. Some remote control programs offer a more dynamic version of dialback where you can call the host, use your password to establish that you're authorized to log in, and then leave a number where you can be reached.

Reading, Writing, and Other Rights: Directory Access

In conjunction with a password, you can also indicate what the remote caller can do with the host. Specifically, each authorized remote user can be limited to accessing certain directories on the host. This feature is especially useful when a single host serves a number of remote "clients."

Use Connection Time Limits to Ensure Host Availability

With a shared host, you may want to limit the time an individual remote user can connect. You can limit the length of each session, or set specific time periods when each user is allowed to log in. Even if you're the only one accessing the host, you add a small measure of security by locking any remote callers during the hours that you know you'll never want to connect. This lessens the likelihood of someone "hacking" his or her way in while you're snoozing in your hotel room.

Release a Tied-Up Host with Inactivity Timeout

If you don't use connection time limits, you can still make sure that an idle session doesn't tie up your host. An inactivity timeout will automatically sever a connection if nothing happens for a predetermined period of time. This not only frees up the host for another remote user, but it can save a bundle on phone bills when a connected remote PC is left unattended.

Performance, Drivers, and Other Considerations

Remote control programs use all different kinds of algorithms and methods to speed up the transfer between the two PCs. As a result, some will provide better *performance* than others, and some will work better for specific applications. Although the speed differences are generally minor with the current crop of programs, if you plan to run applications remotely or work with graphics a lot, the faster the better. In fact, for those cases, speed may be the main factor in choosing a program.

When you install remote control software, the program usually asks to choose the *modem* brand and model that you're using from a list. The list is usually quite long—*very* long in some cases—and will include just about every major modem on the market. But if you're using the very latest, fastest, hottest modem around or you've got a $19 Mighty Mickey Modem special, you should check with the software vendors before you buy to make sure that their programs support your modem.

One of the toughest technical issues that has plagued remote control is that some of the programs replace the *video driver* in your PC's setup. It's one of the ways that they pump up performance. But it can also leave your system's display looking awful at the end of the remote session. Today, some programs get around this bugaboo using a variety of techniques, such as interceding and controlling video signals during a session and then gracefully bowing out when it wraps up.

You also may want to use the remote control software for *other communications*, such as tapping into a BBS or the Internet. If you don't already have a favorite terminal emulation program to do this, this value-added feature may be the clincher when you're choosing your remote control software.

For remote setups over a *network*, you don't have to worry about modems, but you do have to be sure that the program will support the communication protocol that your network uses. Again, if you're running Novell NetWare or another popular network operating system, virtually all remote control programs will work with it. But if you ordered your network from the same catalog that you ordered your bedroom slippers, you'd better check with the software vendor first.

Remote Control Programs for Windows 95

These three remote control programs are among the earliest arrivals for Windows 95—no surprise, too, as all of them have long histories in both DOS and Windows 3.*x* versions. Functionally, they all accomplish the same thing, but the way they go about it differs as does their exploitation of Windows 95 ease-of-use features.

- pcAnywhere 7.0
- Carbon Copy 3.0
- CoSession 6.0

pcAnywhere 7.0 (Symantec)

Once a pioneer among DOS remote control programs, Symantec's pcAnywhere is again treading on new turf with a Windows 95 version. The program has a new look that suits its new environment well, but it hasn't left its trademark ease-of-use behind.

pcAnywhere: Wizards Everywhere

pcAnywhere's main screen is virtually a clean slate, with eight large buttons across the top; but before you get to see it for the first time, the program walks you through some basic setup steps, such as confirming that you will use the modem that the software found. That initial assistance represents your first encounter with pcAnywhere's wizards that are waiting in the wings and available at the click of the Quick Start button to help you get started with your other setup chores.

Six other buttons provide access to the program's four communication categories: host, remote, network connections, and on-line services. There's also a button for file transfers, another for gateway setup, and finally one to quit the program. When you click on one of the buttons for the four comm types, the screen below shows a series of icons representing different setups for different connections. It's easy enough to proceed from there, but you can always tap the Quick Start button and use a wizard to get started.

The program's interface is simple and clean so everything is straightforward and easy to do. When it's time to get down to the nitty gritty and deal with details, tabbed dialog boxes simplify those tasks. The dialogs are uncluttered, and have instructions and fill-in fields that are written in plain English. There's also a high degree of consistency from operation to operation; for example, when you have to define a connection the screens are essentially the same. So if you managed to do something before, the screens will be familiar enough to make new setup tasks seem old hat.

Be a Good Host

You can set up multiple hosts with pcAnywhere so that a single machine can manage sessions with a variety of remotes. You get to the host screen by clicking on the Be A Host PC button. Any hosts that have already been set up will be represented by icons alongside an icon to add a host. Double-clicking on that icon starts up a wizard that lets you name the host connection, pick the type of connection to use, and decide whether to run the host immediately. If you don't run the host right away, you can flesh out the setup details by right-clicking on the icon you just created and choosing Properties from the context menu.

The Properties sheet has tabbed pages where you can review and change the modem or connection type. Another page lets you disable the host's keyboard and mouse, and blank the host's screen. On the page labeled Callers (see fig. 25.1), you can define the caller access rights for the host setup: you can let anybody connect, or you can limit access to specific callers. If you select the latter, another wizard materializes to help you define callers' login names and passwords.

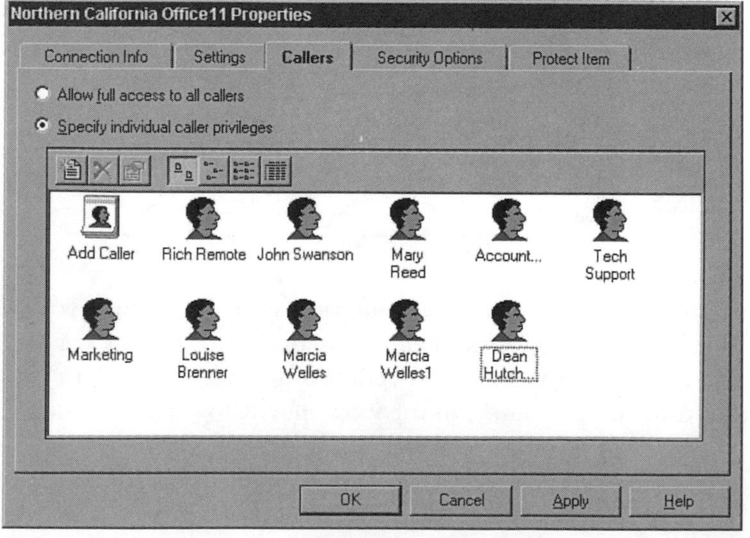

Fig. 25.1 pcAnywhere's host settings are adjusted in the Properties sheet. The Callers page makes the host available to all callers or to specific users.

On the Security Options page of the Properties sheet, you can choose to maintain a log of failed connection attempts, set a specific number of login attempts per call, limit the time it takes for a login to complete, and force a disconnect after a defined period of remote inactivity. The final page lets you password-protect all of the settings you just made.

When you've finished defining the host's properties, the program adds the new host's icon to those for other hosts. You can double-click the icon to launch the host and have it wait for an appropriate remote caller, or right-click it and select Launch Host from the context menu.

Remote Matters

The process of setting up remote connections is very much like that of host setup, but for remotes, you have a lot less to do as most of the controls that define remote rights and session characteristics are already established by the host. You can use pcAnywhere's Quick Start wizard to start setting up a new remote user (see fig. 25.2).

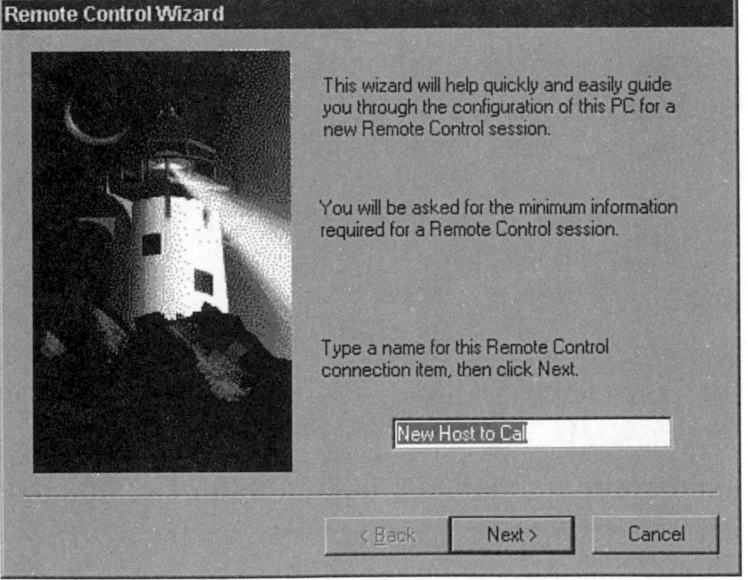

Fig. 25.2 pcAnywhere's Quick Start button will produce a wizard to help you complete the basic configuration for any connection.

The Remote Control screen looks like the Host screen, and when you select the icon to add a remote control item, a wizard appears to walk you through the brief basic steps. Again, the icon's context menu lets you adjust the more detailed settings of the remote. In the Properties dialog, you can enter the host's phone number and your login name and password. With this information, pcAnywhere will log you into the host automatically as soon as the connection is made.

Another page gives you the option of recording the events in a remote control session. The session can be saved to a named file and then played back at another time—a great time-saver if your remote control sessions consist of the same activities on a regular basis.

As with the host setup, the last page of the Properties sheet lets you protect all of your settings with a password.

Click Connect to Hook Up with a Host

With the host in a ready mode, a remote control session can begin. On the remote side, you just have to double-click on the appropriate icon on the Remote Control screen (or right-click on it and choose Connect from the context menu).

When the remote connects, you're first put into a terminal mode. In short order, the host requests your login name and password (assuming you haven't set up the remote for automatic login). If the host requires dialback to complete the connection, you're also notified that the host will call you back at the predetermined number or asked for a number that the host then dials.

Once connected, response is quick enough for most tasks although scrolling is somewhat slow. Response will be better if both machines are set at the same screen resolution. But if the host's screen resolution is at a higher setting than the remote's, you can use the vertical and horizontal scrollbars to navigate your way around the whole screen. Shifting a big screen around a smaller one can get tiresome, so you can click on an icon to resize the host screen to fit the viewing area at the remote.

Easy On, Easy Off

The best thing about pcAnywhere is how easy it is to use. You can set up both sides of the remote control session—with some very sophisticated controls—in a matter of minutes. And it's just as easy to make later adjustments to host-remote sessions to tweak security or other options.

Carbon Copy 3.0 (Microcom)

Like pcAnywhere, Carbon Copy has been around for a long time, dating back to the DOS days when it shared the remote control spotlight with its rival program, and the current version is among the first remote control programs for Windows 95. The latest edition of Carbon Copy—version 3.0—seems to be more concerned about settling comfortably into its new environment than about adding a slew of new features. The old stuff that worked well is still there, along with a handful of subtle, but welcome, enhancements. For example, more operations are now accessible via buttons.

Minimalist Menus

When Carbon Copy finishes loading its files onto your disk, it asks if you want to let its modem wizard poke around to find and identify your modem. The program has a list of 300 modem models so the odds are it'll find it, recognize it, and let you know the best communication speed to use for your remote control sessions. Then it restarts your system and you're on your way.

The installation program creates a folder with separate applications for either the host or remote—or in Carbon Copy's genteel terminology, the *guest*. Both the host and guest have minimalist main screens, consisting of only eight large buttons and a menubar (see fig. 25.3). The buttons are used to initiate connections and control operations once connected. To set up the specifics for remote sessions, you have to use the menubar options.

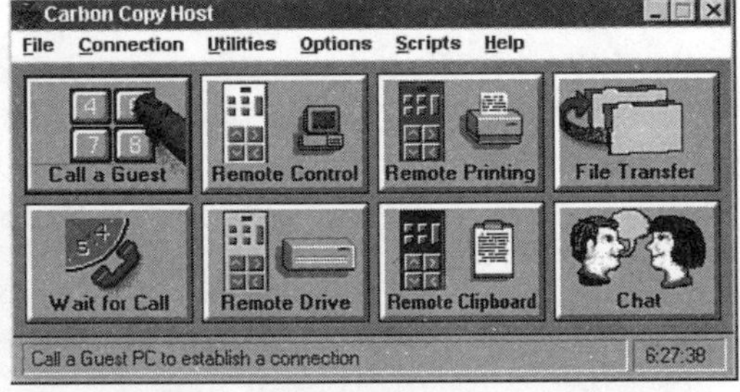

Fig. 25.3 Carbon Copy's host and remote main windows are simple and uncluttered. The host side shown here, has eight buttons for the most common operations.

Host, by the Book

To get Carbon Copy's host side set up, the first thing you have to do is create a phone book. The phone book is a simple affair; you just enter the names of authorized remotes with their phone numbers. Add a login name and password, and the entry's complete. Like pcAnywhere, Carbon Copy requires that you retype the password just to make certain that it's exactly the way you want it.

The Security selection on the Options menu (see fig. 25.4) lets you define the protection parameters for remote connections. You can require dialback to complete a connection and set the number of attempted logins allowed and the time to wait for a login to be completed. For busy hosts accessed by more than one remote, you set session time limits for inactivity timeouts. Carbon Copy also offers a couple of interesting security measures. One lets you prevent remotes from causing the host to exit Windows, and the other keeps roving remote eyes away from Carbon Copy's Host menu so that security or access rights can't be changed.

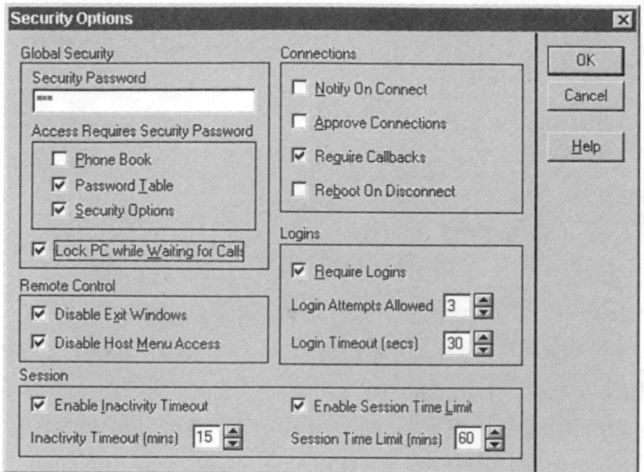

Fig. 25.4
Setting up security in Carbon Copy is a straightforward affair. In the Security Options sheet, you enable safeguards by simply clicking checkboxes for most of the options.

Remote Setup: Just Names & Numbers

On Carbon Copy's remote end, there's not much you need to do except enter the host's phone number and your login name and password. Like the host side of the equation, you can store the phone numbers and login information for each host that regularly connects to it in a phone book. In fact, many of the remote setup screens are identical to those of the host—a situation that can be confusing at times (see fig. 25.5).

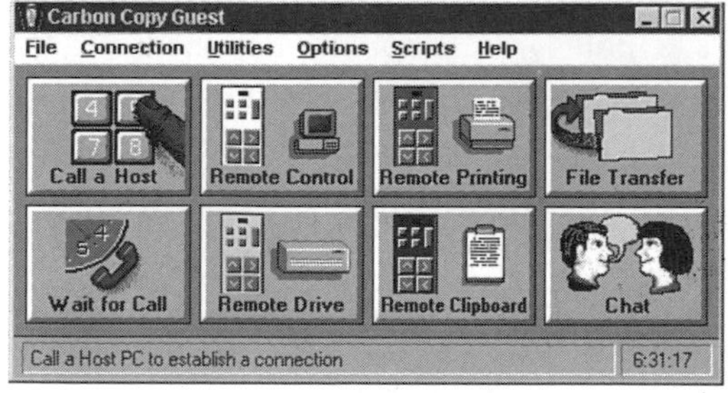

Fig. 25.5
Carbon Copy's remote side is similar to the host's. The buttons provide access to most frequently used functions, such as file transfer and remote clipboard.

One positive similarity is the ability to capture session activities on the remote end to save and play back as needed.

Click & Connect

For a connection to happen, the host has to be waiting for a call—and that's accomplished with a click on a button. Not much more effort is required on the remote end. You click on a button to dial out and then choose the appropriate host profile from the phone book. If you set up your connection with your login name and password, there's nothing left to do but wait for the two PCs to link.

If the host requires dialback, after you log in you will have to do one of three things as defined by the remote's profile in the host's phonebook. If your profile on the host was set up for *fixed* call back, all you have to do is wait—for the host to disconnect and then dialback using the phone number previously entered in your profile. It's also possible that your profile includes *roving* call back. This option simply means that the host doesn't know where you're going to be when you dial in, so it will ask you for a phone number to call back after you successfully login; then you wait again, while it calls that number. The final possibility is called *passthrough.* The passthrough call back option is like the roving choice, but the remote user can dispense with any call back at all by entering the letter "p" when a dialback number is requested by the host.

Once connected, you'll appreciate Carbon Copy's excellent performance. As with any other remote control program, you won't want to run applications from a distance regularly, but when you need to, you won't be frustrated by pokey screen redraws or poor cursor response.

The program's Remote Clipboard is useful for copying text or graphics from one end of the connection and pasting the information to the other. You can use Carbon Copy's Remote Drive feature to map the host PC's drives to the remote so they just look like local drives. File transfer is also a breeze, with drag-and-drop transfers among directories—and it's pretty quick, too.

Button Pusher's Paradise

Carbon Copy is not quite as easy to use as pcAnywhere, but it's not very hard, either. To its credit, its screen is minimal with simple, descriptive buttons to push for all major remote control activities. But the best part of Carbon Copy is its speed.

CoSession 6.0 (Triton Technologies)

CoSession's public face bears a striking resemblance to that of its rival, Carbon Copy. The remote and host sides of the software are neatly split, each with its own fairly minimal interface. CoSession also hangs its own moniker on its remote portion, which it calls the Viewer—perhaps not as cordial as Carbon Copy's Guest, still a lot warmer than plain old "remote."

When you install CoSession you may get the feeling that it doesn't trust you, but it just likes to sniff around and look for your modem itself. When it does find it, it compares what it's found to a list of popular modems and—if it matches up—identifies it. If your device isn't among CoSession's modems, you can enter its name yourself—but CoSession will still offer to check it out to determine the fastest and safest communication speed it can handle in conjunction with the software.

Interface

Like Carbon Copy, the main menus for CoSession's two sides are quite similar as well, with matching layouts and common operations in the same places. Each has a row of four big buttons in the top left of the window that provide access to the main remote control activities: Call, Wait for a Call, Stop Waiting (host) or Hang Up (remote) and Exit the program.

There's another row of buttons below the four on top, but this is where the host and viewer begin to differ. The host has two additional buttons: one to switch into Chat mode and another labeled Global Options. You click on Global Options to establish session settings that apply to all connection sessions.

The remote's second row is one button bigger than the host's. Like the host, the remote window has a button for Chat mode, but the other two apply strictly to the remote side of a session. The second—aptly title Remote Control—is used to toggle back and forth between the main window and the actual remote control session. The third button lets you transfer files between the host and the remote.

Shifting to the right side of the screen, the two sides look alike again. That place is occupied by the name and phone number of the currently selected connection profile. A button below that entry offers access to the phone book.

Host Setup

Setting up a CoSession host is essentially a two-step process. The Options selection under the Setup menu lets you make global host settings that will be applied to all sessions. For example, you can make passwords a requirement for all remote callers by clicking on a checkbox. You can choose to have the host's screen go blank and its keyboard be disabled upon connection with another click on a checkbox. Other global options that can be set in this window include an inactivity timeout and directory access restrictions for all remote callers.

The second step involves defining valid remote callers in the phone book (see fig. 25.6). Each entry can be customized for individual remote callers, but all should have the basics: a name for the entry with a short description, and the remote user's login name and password. You can also indicate the caller's file transfer privileges—send, receive, both, or none—and you can define the caller's directory access rights. You also use the phone book entry to indicate if dialback is required for a remote caller, in which case you must also enter the remote's phone number.

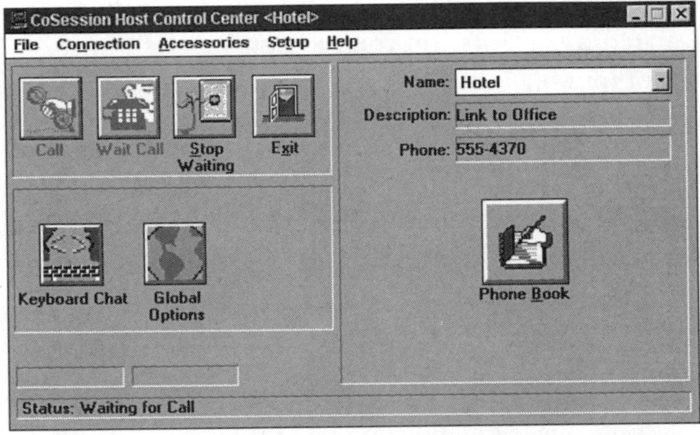

Fig. 25.6
Most of CoSession's key setup entries are made in the phone book, but settings that apply to all callers are made by clicking the Global Options button.

Remote

CoSession's remote setup is typical of most remote control programs. You don't have to do anything more than create an entry in the remote phone book for each host you wish to connect to. The entry is fairly rudimentary, too; all you need is the host's phone number and a login name and password that match what the host has in its phone book.

Connecting

With the host waiting, a connection can be initiated with a click on the Call button at the remote PC (see fig. 25.7). When the host and remote connect, the remote automatically sends its login name and password if the host requires these. When dialback has been enabled for a remote caller, the host will drop the line after a successful login and then reinitiate the connection by dialing the remote. Once you're finally connected, you'll see the host's screen in a resizable window.

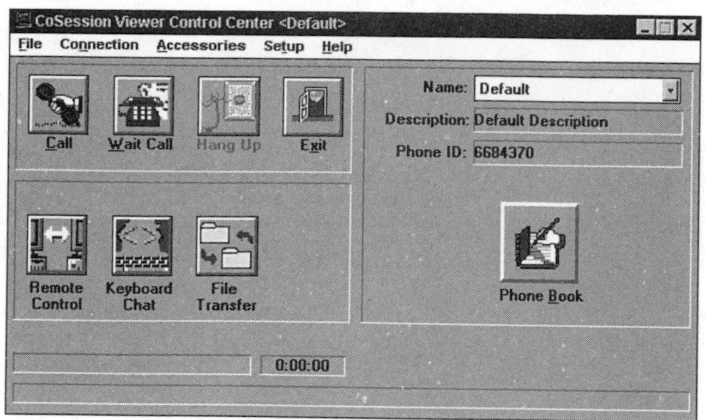

Fig. 25.7 CoSession's Remote Control button lets you toggle between the remote session and the control window, and the file transfer button.

During a session, from the remote end you can call up the Viewer window to switch operations. You can choose from standard remote control operations, file transfer, and chat—which lets you exchange keyboard messages with an attended host.

CoSession's capability to sniff out and test your modem helps get you up and running quickly. Like Carbon Copy, the similarity between its host and viewer screens and menus helps breed familiarity, but can still be confusing at times. But if you want to sidestep some of the more advanced features and just do some basic remote control, you're just a few clicks away from a connection. ❖

CHAPTER 26

Sharing Resources

by Jim Boyce

Many features in Windows 95 rely on Windows 95's peer-to-peer networking capability. Direct Cable Connection and Dial-Up Networking, for example, use Windows 95's peer-to-peer networking to enable PCs to share files and printers. *The Windows 95 Communications Handbook* doesn't explain how to install network cards and configure a network, but this chapter does teach you how to share resources such as files and printers between two or more PCs. In this chapter, you learn how to

- Share and use disk resources
- Share and use printers
- Secure your shared resources through share-level or user-level security to prevent unauthorized access

Note

Even though this book doesn't specifically cover how to install or configure a network adapter, many of the topics involved are explained in various chapters. For example, adding protocols, clients, and services is explained in Chapter 23, "Using Dial-Up Networking." And installing a network adapter is generally very easy. Just turn off the PC and install the adapter, and Windows 95 should recognize it automatically and step you through the process of configuring the clients, protocols, and so on. For more detailed information on installing and configuring network adapters, refer to *Windows 95 Installation and Configuration Handbook* and *Windows 95 Connectivity*, both from Que.

Sharing and Using Disk Resources

Windows 95 makes it easy to share a folder so that others can access the files in the folder. If your PC is connected to a LAN, for example, other users on the LAN can connect to your PC to access those shared resources, assuming that they have the appropriate access password or permission from a security server on the LAN (explained later in the section "Securing Your Folders"). Or you might share folders if others are connecting to your PC through Dial-Up Networking or Direct Cable Connection. In all cases, the first step is to set up your PC for sharing.

Setting Up for Sharing

You must use a file and printer sharing service on your PC to enable it to share its files and printer(s). You install the service through the Network icon in the Control Panel, and the service you use depends on the network client you're using. For the Client for Microsoft Networks, you should use the File and Printer Sharing for Microsoft Networks service. For the Client for NetWare Networks, you should use the File and Printer Sharing for NetWare Networks service. Use the following steps to add and enable file and print sharing on a PC:

1. Open the Control Panel and double-click the Network icon.
2. Scroll to the bottom of the list of installed components on the Configuration page and verify that the necessary file and print sharing service is not already installed.
3. If the required service isn't installed, click the Add button to display the Select Network Component Type dialog box.
4. Choose Service; then click Add to display the Select Network Service dialog box (see fig. 26.1).

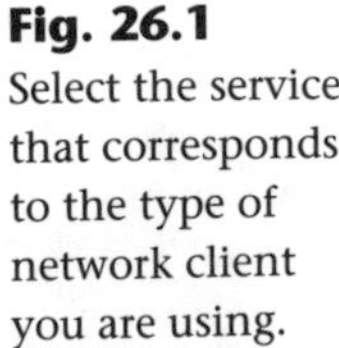

Fig. 26.1
Select the service that corresponds to the type of network client you are using.

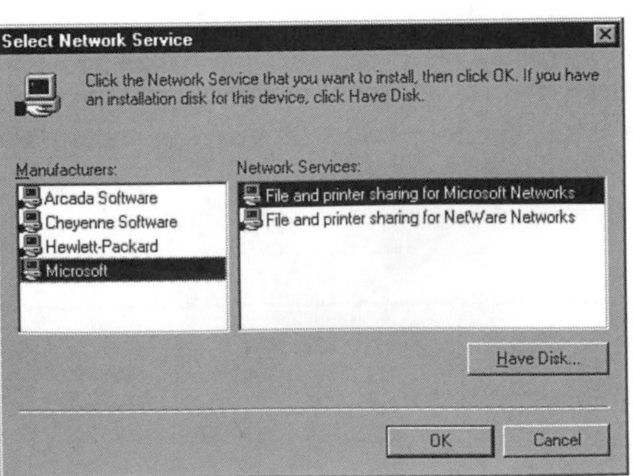

5. Choose Microsoft from the Manufacturers list; then choose from the Network Services list the file and printer sharing service that applies to your network client. Then choose OK.
6. When the Configuration page reappears, click the File and Print Sharing button to display the File and Print Sharing dialog box (see fig. 26.2).

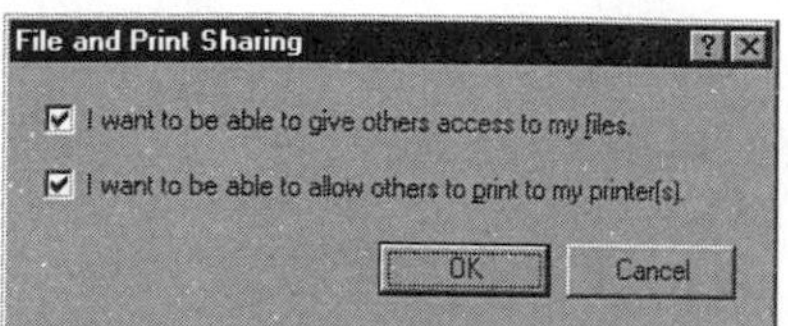

Fig. 26.2
Enable file and print sharing in the File and Print Sharing dialog box.

7. Place a check beside each of the types of resources you want to be able to share; then click OK.
8. Choose OK to close the Network property sheet. Windows 95 prompts you to let it restart the system. You must let the system restart before sharing will be enabled.

Note

If you have installed an appropriate network client such as Client for Microsoft Networks or Client for NetWare Networks, you don't have to install any additional network components to be able to access resources shared by other computers. You only need to install the file and print sharing service if you want to share your own file and print resources.

Sharing Folders

Before others can access a folder or the files it contains, you must share the folder. When you share a folder, all files and subfolders it contains become available to other users through the LAN, Direct Cable Connection, or Dial-Up Networking server. Therefore, if you share the root folder of a disk, the entire disk becomes available to other users, subject to the security restrictions you use (explained later in "Securing Your Folders"). If you don't want other users to access an entire disk, make sure that you share only those subfolders you want to make available.

You can share a folder from the Explorer, My Computer, or a folder window. In each case, the process is the same:

1. Locate the folder you want to share.

2. Right-click the folder to be shared, then choose Sharing from the context menu. Or select the folder and choose File, Sharing. Either action displays the Sharing property sheet for the folder (see fig. 26.3).

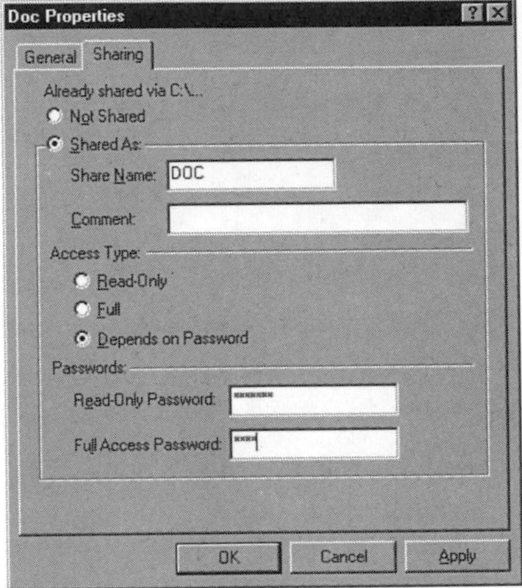

Fig. 26.3
Share a folder using the Sharing property sheet.

> **Note**
>
> The Sharing property sheet looks slightly different from the one shown in figure 26.3 if you're using user-level security. The primary difference is that instead of access type and password controls, the property sheet contains a list you use to define which users can access the folder (see fig. 26.4).

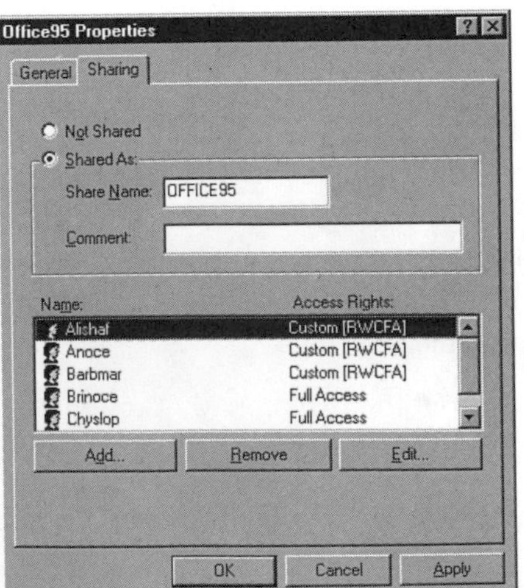

Fig. 26.4
The Sharing property appears similar to this when user-level security is enabled.

3. To share the folder, choose the Shared As option button.
4. The folder name automatically appears in the Share Name text box. You can leave the share name as it is, or type a different share name. Whatever name you use is the name by which other users see the shared folder.
5. Choose one of the three option buttons in the Access Type group (Read-Only, Full, or Depends on Password) according to the share-level security you want to use. The following list explains each option:
   - *Read-Only.* Others can read the files but cannot delete or modify them, nor can they create new files or folders in the shared folder.
   - *Full.* Others can read, delete, and modify files in the folder, as well as create new files and folders.
   - *Depends on Password.* This option lets you offer read-only and full access in the same folder. Users who provide the read-only password when connecting to the resource have read-only permission in the folder. Users who provide the full-access password have full access to the folder.
6. Enter passwords in the Read-Only Password and/or Full Access Password as desired. These are the passwords that other users must provide to access the shared folder.
7. Choose OK to close the property sheet and begin sharing the folder.

Troubleshooting

I right-click a folder to share it, but the Sharing command doesn't appear in the context menu? How can I share a folder?

If the Sharing folder isn't there, you don't have file and printer sharing enabled on your computer. Open the Control Panel and double-click the Network icon. In the Configuration property page, click the File and Print Sharing button. In the File and Print Sharing dialog box, enable both checkboxes to allow sharing of files and printers on your PC, then choose OK. Choose OK on the Configuration page to close the property sheet. You'll have to restart Windows 95 for the change to take effect.

Securing Your Folders

In most cases, share-level security as explained previously provides adequate security for your shared folders and the files they contain, but only as long as you understand the limitations of share-level security. Share-level security makes no distinction between one user and another. As long as the user provides the required password, he or she gains access to the shared folder and all subfolders contained in it. The type of access the user receives depends on whether you have enabled read-only, full, or both types of access, and which password is provided.

If you want to provide more detailed security levels and protect your folders and files on a user-by-user basis, you need to employ user-level security. Using this type of security requires that a security server (Windows NT or Novell NetWare server) be available on the network to process access requests. When a user attempts to connect to or use a resource on your PC that is protected by user-level security, your PC sends a request across the LAN to the security server to authenticate and validate the user's request to access the folder or file. If the user is included in the list of authorized users, the server indicates the level of access the user can have. This means that you can restrict access on a user-by-user basis, but also means that you have a much finer degree of control over what a user can do with a shared file or folder.

Tip

You can't use user-level security if you only use the File and Print Sharing for NetWare Networks service. You must use the Client for Microsoft Networks, as well as the File and Print Sharing for Microsoft Networks service.

Enabling User-Level Security

Before you can begin using user-level security, you must enable it (share-level security is the default). To turn on user-level security, follow these steps:

1. Open the Control Panel and double-click the Network icon.
2. Click the Access Control tab to display the Access Control page shown in figure 26.5.
3. Choose the User-level Access Control option button.
4. Click in the text box and type the name of the security server you want to use to authenticate user access requests. This can be the name of a Windows NT domain, Windows NT workstation, or NetWare server.
5. Choose OK. Windows 95 prompts you to restart the system to make the change take effect.

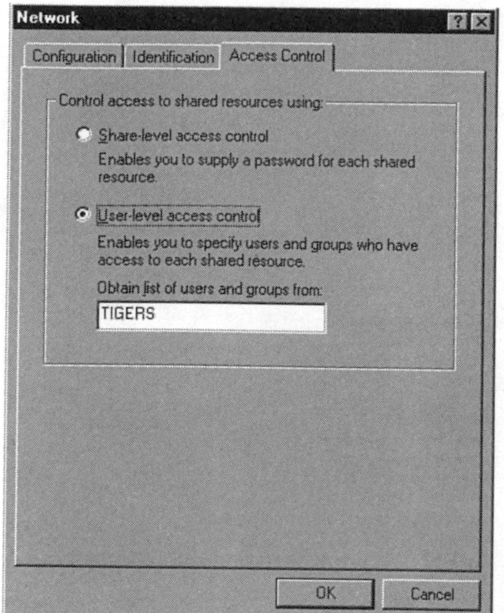

Fig. 26.5
Enable user-level security through the Access Control page.

Tip

Any folders currently shared with share-level security are removed from sharing when you enable user-level security. You must reshare them and assign user access to each one.

After the PC restarts, you can share a folder and define which users can gain access to it. The list of allowed users is stored on your PC, but their account information still resides on the security server. Although you must have system administrator privileges on the security server to create and modify user accounts, you don't need such privileges to specify which users can access your shared folders.

To specify the list of users, first right-click the folder you want to share and choose Sharing from the context menu to display the Sharing property page (similar to the one shown previously in figure 26.4). Click the Add button to display the Add Users dialog box shown in figure 26.6.

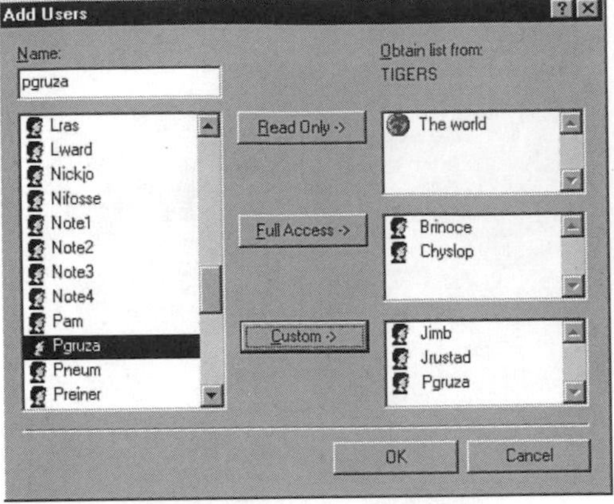

Fig. 26.6
Use the Add Users dialog box to define which users can access the shared resource.

You can assign read-only, full, or custom permissions to individual users or groups of users. Select the user or group from the list or type the user's account name in the Name text box. Then click the Read Only, Full Access, or Custom button depending on the type of access you want to grant to the user or group. When you're finished adding users, click OK. If you've specified Custom for any user, Windows 95 displays the Change Access Rights dialog box shown in figure 26.7.

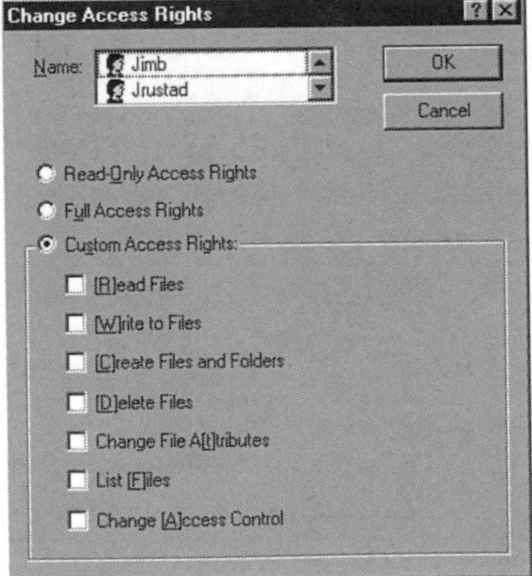

Fig. 26.7
Use the Change Access Rights dialog box to define custom access levels.

Place check marks in each checkbox according to the access level you want to grant to the user(s). Table 26.1 lists the various file access levels and what they mean. When the levels are set the way you want them, click OK.

Table 26.1 File Operations and Access Rights

File Operation	Access Rights Required
Change access rights	Change access control
Change directory or file attributes	Change file attributes
Copy files from a directory	Read, list files
Copy files to a directory	Write, create, list files
Create and write to a file	Create files
Delete a file	Delete files
Make a new directory	Create files
Read from a closed file	Read files
Remove a directory	Delete files
Rename a file or directory	Change file attributes
Run an executable file	Read, list files
Search a directory for files	List files
See a file name	List files
Write to a closed file	Write, create, delete, change file attributes

Tip

You can set access rights on individual files on NetWare and Windows NT systems. Because Windows 95 uses a FAT file system, however, you can't assign access rights to individual files. You can, however, assign user-by-user access to a folder. Access rights for a shared folder apply to all subfolders it contains.

If you want to change a user's or group's access rights, just select the user or group name from the Sharing property page and click the Edit button.

Using a Shared Folder

Windows 95 makes it easy to access and use folders shared by other PCs on a LAN, host (in the case of Direct Cable Connection), or remote server (in the case of Dial-Up Networking). Regardless of how your PC is connected to the other system(s), you access and work with shared folders using the same methods.

Using the Network Neighborhood

The first and perhaps easiest method to access a shared folder is to open the Network Neighborhood folder. The Network Neighborhood folder (see fig. 26.8) contains an icon for each of the other computers in your workgroup, as well as printers that are shared directly on the LAN (and not through a specific computer). The Network Neighborhood also contains the Entire Network icon, which gives you access to PCs, printers, and other resources assigned to other workgroups on the network.

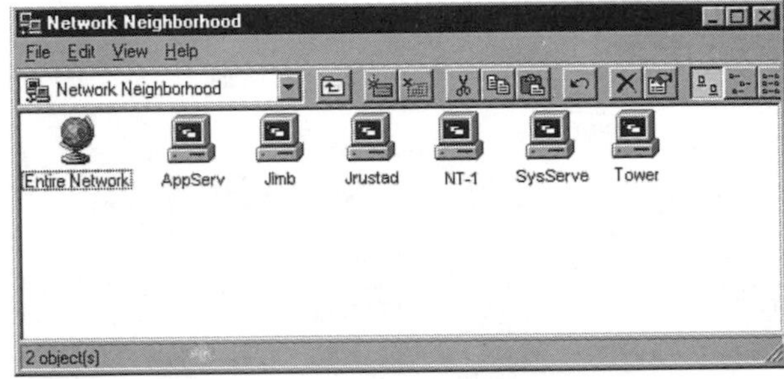

Fig. 26.8
The Network Neighborhood gives you quick access to shared resources.

To use a shared folder, just open the Network Neighborhood folder and double-click the icon of the computer that is sharing the folder. The Network Neighborhood folder changes to show all the resources shared by the selected computer, including folders and printers (see fig. 26.9).

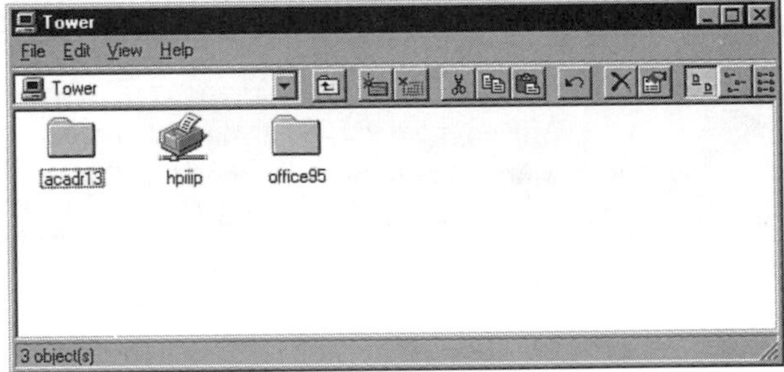

Fig. 26.9
A computer's folder shows all its shared resources.

To use a folder, double-click its icon as you would a folder on your own PC. Windows 95 opens a window to display the contents of the folder (see fig. 26.10). You then can start programs, open documents, and manipulate (copy, move, and so on) files to and from the folder, assuming that you have the appropriate access rights in the folder. If the folder is password-protected through share-level security, Windows 95 prompts you for the appropriate password before connecting you to the shared folder. The password is then stored in your password cache so that you don't have to enter it the next time you connect to the shared folder.

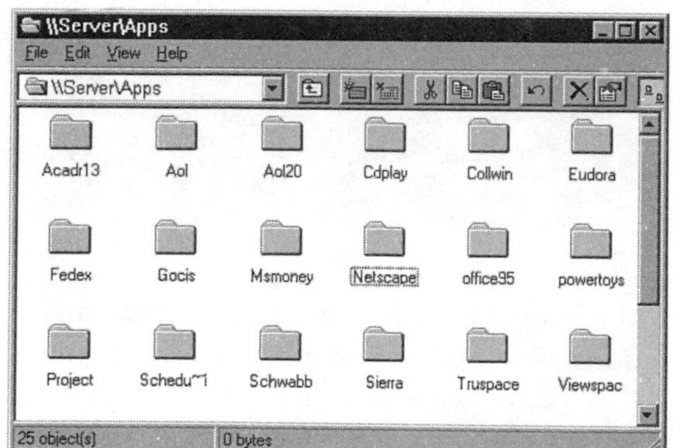

Fig. 26.10
Shared files appear just like local files.

Mapping to a Local Drive ID

You might want a more permanent connection to a shared folder, or you're working with a Windows 3.*x* or DOS application and need to access a file in the shared folder from the application. In both cases, you can *map* a local drive ID to the remote folder. For example, assume that your PC contains two hard disks, C: and D:, and a CD-ROM drive as E:. You want to make a connection to a folder named Documents on another computer. So you might map drive F: on your computer to the Documents folder on the other computer. After you map drive F: to the folder, an icon for drive F: appears in My Computer. Double-click the drive F: icon, and Windows 95 opens a folder window showing the contents of the remote shared folder. This means that you now have a local drive letter you can use to open files from the folder using your applications.

> **Note**
>
> The shared folder is mapped as the root folder of the drive. In this example, the Documents folder appears as the root folder of drive F:.

You have a couple of methods to map a local drive ID to a remote folder. If you want to associate a drive ID on the guest to the shared folder on the host, use one of the following techniques:

- Right-click a shared folder, and then choose Map Network Drive. Windows 95 prompts you to choose the drive ID you want to associate with the remote folder (see fig. 26.11). From the Drive drop-down list, choose a drive letter. If you want your PC to try to reconnect to the shared folder each time Windows 95 starts, enable the Reconnect At Logon checkbox. Then choose OK.

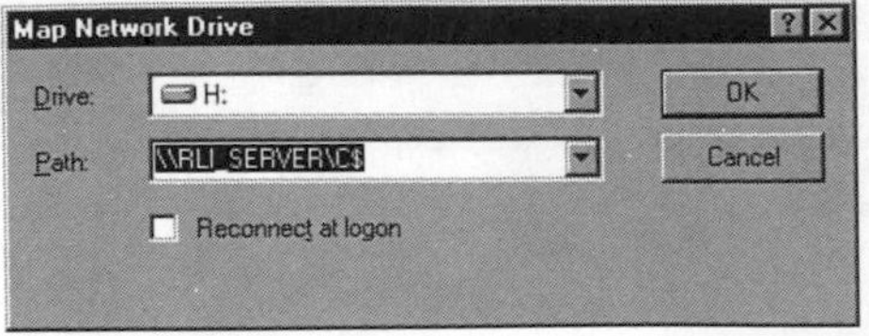

Fig. 26.11
Select the drive to associate with the resource; then choose OK.

- Right-click the Network Neighborhood folder and choose Map Network Drive. Windows 95 displays a dialog box similar to the one shown in figure 26.11, except the Path combo-box is not filled in for you automatically. In the Path text box, type the UNC name of the shared resource, such as ***DESKTOP*\C**, where *DESKTOP* is the name of the host computer, and C is the shared folder name. Or click the drop-down button and choose a connection name you've previously used. Then click OK.
- Locate in the Network Neighborhood the folder you want to use; then right-drag the folder to your desktop and release it. From the context menu, choose Create Shortcut(s) Here. Windows 95 creates a shortcut to the folder, and whenever you need to use it, you can simply double-click the shortcut icon. Windows 95 then opens the folder so that you can access its contents.

If you've mapped a local drive letter to a remote shared folder, you might at some point want to disconnect the remote folder from the drive ID. To disconnect from a shared folder, right-click the Network Neighborhood icon and choose Disconnect Network Drive. From the resulting dialog box, select the drive you want to disconnect; then click OK. You also can disconnect a network drive from a folder window or the Explorer. If you're using a folder window, click the Disconnect Network Drive button on the toolbar. In the Explorer, choose Tools, Disconnect Network Drive.

Using UNC Path Names

You can work with files in shared folders directly without having to go through the Network Neighborhood or map a local drive ID to the shared folder. For example, suppose that you want to open a document named Sales.doc, located in a shared folder named Documents on a computer named Marketing. In your application, choose File, Open to display the standard Windows 95 Open dialog box. In the File Name text box, enter the UNC path to the file, which in this case is **\\Marketing\Documents\Sales.doc**. Then click Open.

Tip

Windows 3.*x* applications are not UNC-aware. Therefore, you can only directly specify a UNC path to a document from a Windows 95 application. For Windows 3.*x* programs, you must map a local drive ID to the shared folder, and then use the mapped drive ID to access the file.

Troubleshooting

My PC is connected to a network, but I can't see any other computers in the Network Neighborhood. How can I view other resources on the network?

A handful of problems could be preventing you from seeing resources in the Network Neighborhood, all of which relate to your network configuration. Verify that you have installed the correct client and protocol for your network, and that they are bound to your network adapter. If your configuration is correct, you should see shared resources in the Network Neighborhood. If not, verify that you are using the correct workgroup name.

Sharing and Using Printers

You can share printers under Windows 95 in much the same way you share folders, even if you're connecting to the printer through Dial-Up Networking or Direct Cable Connection. Shared printers appear in a computer's folder when you open the computer's folder through the Network Neighborhood. And like remote folders and files, you can print to a shared printer without mapping a local printer port to the remote printer. Instead, you simply reference the remote printer's UNC (Universal Naming Convention) path name. Windows 95 still enables you to map a local printer port to a remote printer, however, to support printing from DOS and Windows 3.*x* programs.

Note

A UNC name consists of the name of a computer and a resource shared by that computer. For example, the UNC name of a shared printer named HP on a computer named Server is \\Server\HP.

Sharing a Printer

You share a printer through its Sharing property page. To share a printer, first set any required properties and make sure that the printer is working properly by printing a test page. Then open My Computer and double-click the Printers icon to open the Printers folder. Right-click the printer you want to share, and then choose Sharing. Windows 95 displays a Sharing property page similar to the one shown in figure 26.12.

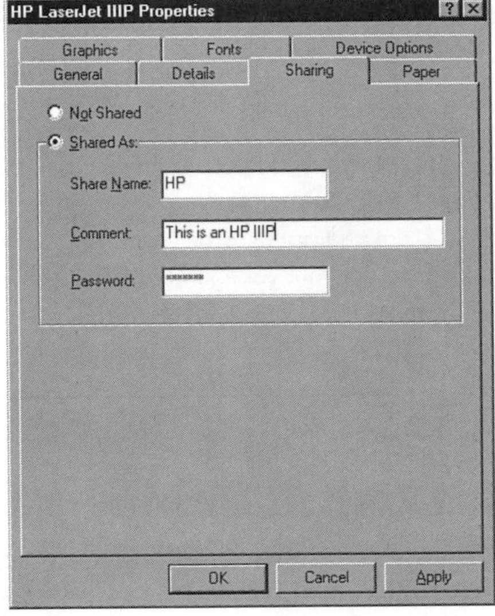

Fig. 26.12
Share a printer through its Sharing property page.

Choose the Shared As option button to enable sharing. In the Share Name text box, type the name by which you want the printer to be shared. This name appears under the printer's icon when other people browse your computer for shared resources. You also can enter an optional comment in the Comment text box. This comment appears in the Network Neighborhood beside the printer if the Network Neighborhood is configured for a detailed view (on the other users' computers).

If you want to protect access to the printer, type a password in the Password text box. Others then have to provide this password before they can print to your printer.

Tip

The Password text box appears only if you're using share-level security. You can't password-protect a printer when user-level security is active. Instead, the remote user's access rights are validated by the security server. Also, there are no varying levels of printer access as there are with folders. Another user can either print to your printer or not.

Using a Shared Printer

Windows 95 includes a feature Microsoft calls Point and Print that automates printer setup. Instead of requiring a confusing setup process, installing support for a remote printer only requires that you attempt to print to the printer. If the printer is not yet set up on your PC, Windows 95 recognizes that fact and automatically installs support for the printer. In many cases, Windows 95 can download the required driver files from the computer that is sharing the printer, rather than requiring you to have the Windows 95 distribution diskettes or CD.

Tip

Windows 95, Windows NT, and Novell NetWare all support Point and Print. Windows 95 can automatically install printers from a print server running any of these operating systems.

You have a variety of methods at your disposal to install a remote printer. The following three methods are the easiest:

- *Drag a document to the printer's icon.* Open the Network Neighborhood and locate the remote printer you want to use. You'll find the printer in the folder of the computer to which the printer is connected. Drag a document icon from a folder on your PC to the printer icon and release the document. Windows 95 recognizes that you don't have the printer installed yet and installs the driver for it, prompting you for the Windows 95 distribution diskettes or CD, if necessary.
- *Double-click the printer's icon.* Normally, this action opens a printer's queue window. When you double-click a remote printer that isn't installed yet, however, Windows 95 recognizes that the printer isn't installed and automatically starts the installation process for the printer.

- *Open the Printers folder and double-click the Add New Printer icon.* This starts the Add New Printer wizard, which steps you through the process of installing a printer. When prompted by the wizard, choose the Network Printer option button to direct the wizard to install a network printer. You can specify the UNC path to the printer in the form *computer**printer*, where *computer* is the name of the computer sharing the printer, and *printer* is the name by which the printer is shared. Or click the Browse button to browse the network for a printer (see fig. 26.13).

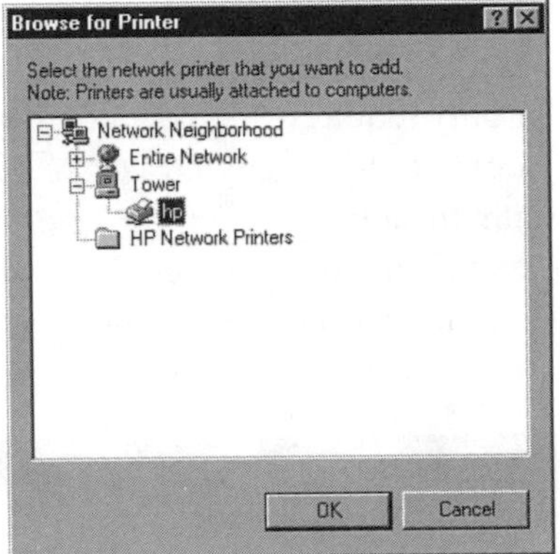

Fig. 26.13
Use the Browse for Printer dialog box to locate a shared network printer.

After the remote printer is installed, you can print to it by dragging documents onto its icon. In some programs, you can specify the printer's UNC name in the program's Print dialog box. However, in most programs, including Windows 95 programs, you must associate the printer with a local printer port. To do so, open the Printers folder and right-click the printer's icon; then choose Properties. Click the Details tab to display the Details property page (see fig. 26.14).

Click the Capture Printer Port button to display the Capture Printer Port dialog box. From the Device drop-down list, select the virtual port you want to associate with the remote printer. Note that you don't have to select a port that is physically present in your system. The port simply provides a logical handle that applications can use when printing. In the Path text box, type the UNC path to the printer. For example, the UNC path to a printer named HP on a computer named Aardvaark would be \\aardvaark\hp (the name is not case-sensitive). After you specify the path name, click OK; then click OK to close the printer's property sheet. You now can print to the printer by using the specified LPT port, just as you would for a local printer.

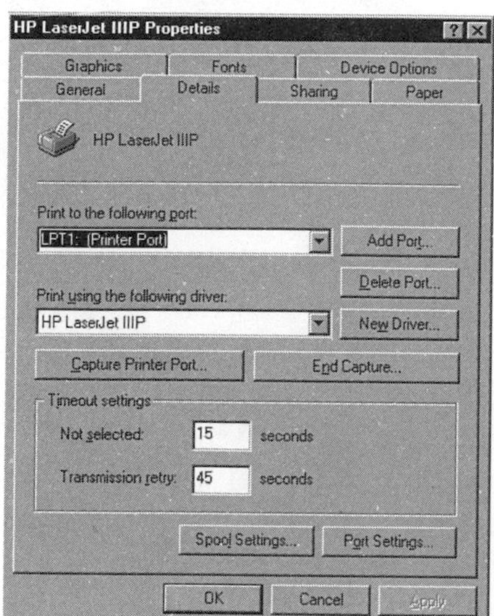

Fig. 26.14
Associate a local printer port with a remote printer in the Details property page.

Creating Shortcuts to Shared Resources

Although you can access shared folders and printers through the Network Neighborhood, it can take a lot of time to locate the resource, particularly if your network contains many computers or workgroups. Therefore, it's a good idea to create shortcuts to these resources, just as you create shortcuts to programs, documents, and other objects on your PC that you use regularly.

You create shortcuts to shared resources in much the same way you create shortcuts to objects on your own PC. Simply open the Network Neighborhood and locate the resource for which you want to create a shortcut. Then right-drag the shared folder or printer from the Network Neighborhood to a folder on your computer or to your Windows 95 desktop, release the icon, and choose Create Shortcut(s) Here from the context menu. Windows 95 then creates a shortcut to the remote shared resource. The next time you want to use the resource, just double-click its shortcut icon. Windows 95 connects to the resource (even if it is connected by a Dial-Up Networking connection) so that you can use it.

Part VII

Appendixes

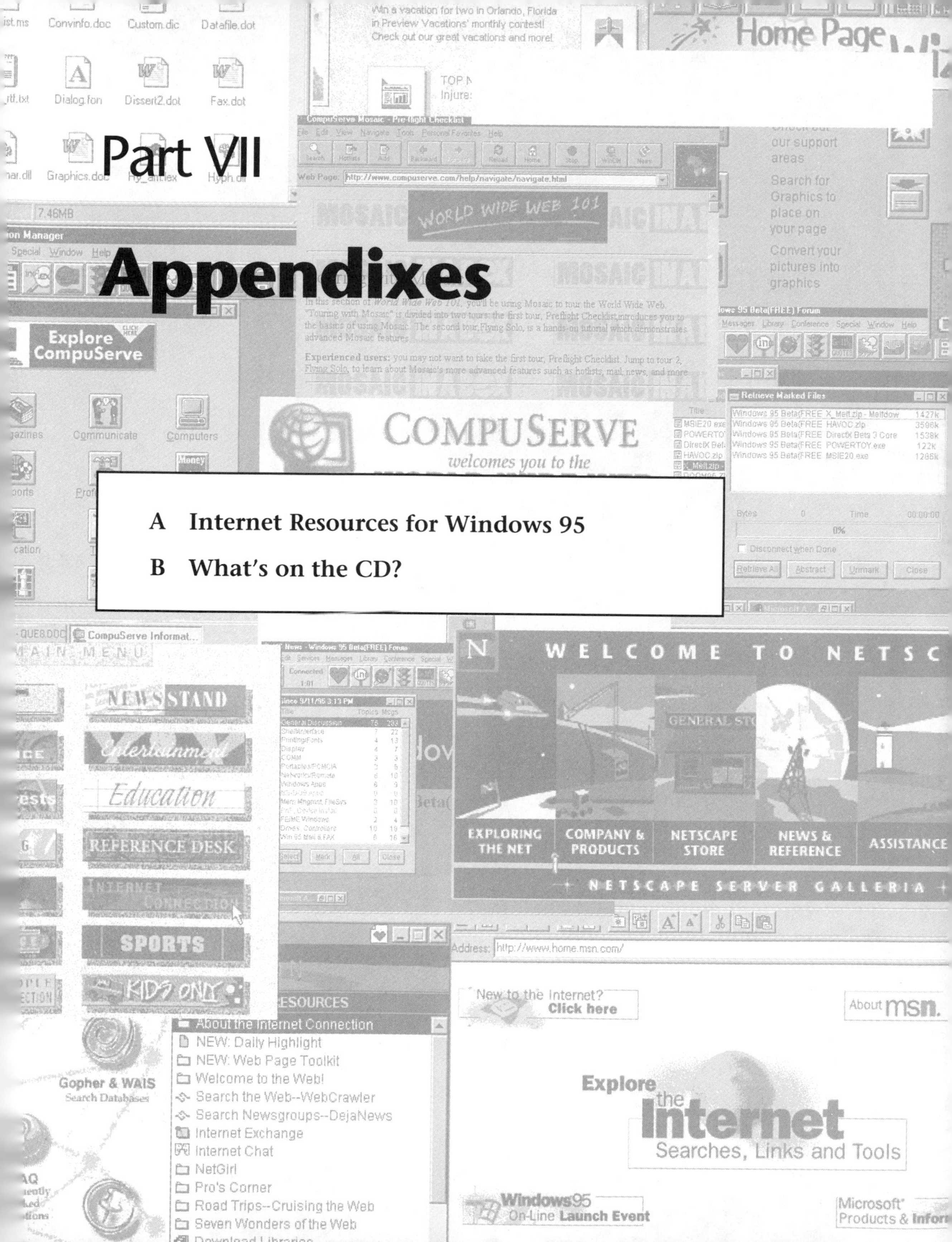

Yoyodyne Entertainment's new area!
tion for two in Orlando, Florida
Vacations' monthly contest!
our great vacations and more!
TOP NEWS STORY: Paris Bomb Injures 28, Algerians Suspected
Home Page
Questions? Check out our support areas
Search for Graphics to place on your page
Convert your pictures into graphics
Dialog.fon
Dissert2.dot
Fax.dot
Graphics.doc
Hy_am.lex
Hyph.dll
7.46MB
CompuServe Mosaic - Pre-flight Checklist
Web Page: http://www.compuserve.com/help/navigate/navigate.html
WORLD WIDE WEB 101
Touring with Mosaic
In this section of World Wide Web 101, you'll be using Mosaic to tour the World Wide Web. "Touring with Mosaic" is divided into two tours: the first tour, Preflight Checklist introduces you to the basics of using Mosaic. The second tour, Flying Solo, is a hands-on tutorial which demonstrates advanced Mosaic features.
Experienced users: you may not want to take the first tour, Preflight Checklist. Jump to tour 2, Flying Solo, to learn about Mosaic's more advanced features such as hotlists, mail, news, and more.
Explore CompuServe
Magazines
Communicate
Computers
Sports
Professional
Finance
Education
Travel
Shopping
COMPUSERVE
welcomes you to the
WORLD WIDE WEB
Visit CompuServe's Home Page
Search Internet Directory of Services
Learn More about the Internet
To return to the WinCIM desktop, click on the
Retrieve Marked Files
Retrieve All
Abstract
Unmark
MAIN MENU
NEWSSTAND
Entertainment
Education
REFERENCE DESK
INTERNET CONNECTION
SPORTS
KIDS ONLY
PEOPLE CONNECTION
WELCOME TO NETS
EXPLORING THE NET
COMPANY & PRODUCTS
NETSCAPE STORE
NEWS & REFERENCE
NETSCAPE SERVER GALLER
Address: http://www.home.msn.com/
New to the Internet? Click here
RESOURCES
About the Internet Connection
NEW: Daily Highlight
NEW: Web Page Toolkit
Welcome to the Web!
Search the Web--WebCrawler
Search Newsgroups--DejaNews
Internet Exchange
Internet Chat
NetGirl
Pro's Corner
Gopher & WAIS
Search Databases
FAQ
Explore the Internet
Searches, Links and Tools

APPENDIX A

Internet Resources for Windows 95

by Jerry Honeycutt

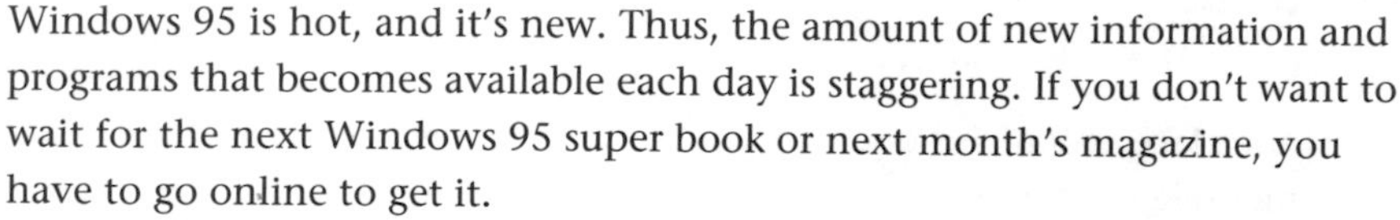

Windows 95 is hot, and it's new. Thus, the amount of new information and programs that becomes available each day is staggering. If you don't want to wait for the next Windows 95 super book or next month's magazine, you have to go online to get it.

You can get a lot of information through commercial online services such as CompuServe, America Online, or The Microsoft Network. You'll find more variety, and potentially more useful information on the Internet, however. That's where this appendix comes in to help you. It'll point you to some of the best resources on the Internet for Windows 95 information and programs. Here are the types of Internet resources you'll find in this appendix:

- *FTP Servers.* It's usually easier to find shareware programs on the World Wide Web, but this sample of FTP sites concentrates so many programs in a few areas that they're worth checking out.
- *Mailing Lists.* Sometimes it's just easier to let the information you want come to you, instead of going out onto the Internet to look for it.
- *UseNet Newsgroups.* Newsgroups are the place to look for quickly changing information. If you also need help, you'll find what you need here.
- *World Wide Web.* There's little doubt that the Web is the hottest resource on the Internet. You'll find a variety of Web pages dedicated to Windows 95, including personal and corporate Web pages.

FTP Servers

Tip

If you don't have a specific FTP program, you can use your Web browser to access FTP servers. Type **ftp://** followed by the FTP address in your Web browser's address bar.

The FTP servers in this section contain large collections of Windows 95 shareware programs. They are all well organized, so you can quickly find the program you're looking for.

Microsoft

FTP address: **ftp.microsoft.com**

This is the place to look for updated drivers, new files for Windows 95, and sometimes free programs. My favorite part of this FTP site is the Knowledge Base articles that answer common questions about most of Microsoft's programs. If you're having trouble finding your way around, look for a file called DIRMAP.TXT, which tells you what the different folders have in them. Here's what you'll find under each of the folders on this site:

- **/bussys.** Here you'll find files for business systems, including networking, mail, SQL Server, and Windows NT.
- **/deskapps.** You'll find files for all of Microsoft's desktop applications, including Access, Excel, PowerPoint, Project, and Word. You'll also find information for the Home series, including games and Works.
- **/develpr.** This is the place to look if you're a developer. There are folders for Visual C++, Visual Basic, various utilities, the Microsoft Developer Network, and more. If you subscribe to the Microsoft Systems Journal, check here to find the source code for articles.
- **/kbhelp.** This is Microsoft's Knowledge Base folder. A knowledge base, in this context, is a help file that contains common questions and answers about Microsoft products. This folder contains one, self-extracting, compressed file for each Microsoft Product. The Windows 95 knowledge base files are under yet another folder called **win95**.
  If you're having difficulty with a Microsoft product, download the appropriate file, decompress it, and double-click it to load it in Help.
- **/softlib.** This is the folder to check out if you're looking for updated drivers, patches, or bug fixes. This folder contains more than 1,500 files, though, so you need to check out INDEX.TXT to locate what you want.

- **/peropsys.** This folder is for personal operating systems. If you're looking for back issues of WINNEWS, look in the **WIN_NEWS** folder. There are other folders relating to all versions of Windows, MS-DOS, and Microsoft hardware.
- **/services.** This folder contains information about TechNet, Microsoft educational services, sales information, and so on.

Note

Many of the folders on the Microsoft FTP site have two files that you should read: README.TXT and INDEX.TXT. README.TXT describes the type of files you'll find in the current folder and any subfolders. It may also describe recent additions and files that have been removed. INDEX.TXT describes each file in the folder. It's a good idea to search for the file you want in INDEX.TXT before trying to pick it out of the listing. Note that Microsoft's site is constantly changing, so you'll want to check back here often.

The Oak Software Repository

FTP address: **oak.oakland.edu**

This is another large site of freeware and shareware programs sponsored by Oakland University in Rochester, Michigan. You'll find all the Windows 95 files in **/SimTel/win95**. Table A.1 shows the folders that you'll find for Windows 95. If you're still looking for DOS and Windows 3.1 files, you'll find those at this site, too. Take a look at README for more information about the files on this FTP site.

Table A.1 Folders under `/SimTel/win95`

animate	graphics
archiver	info
cad	multimed
canon	pgmtools
commprog	pim
desktop	sysutil
edit	txtutil
filedocs	virus
fileutil winword	

Walnut Creek

FTP address: **ftp.cdrom.com**

Tip

If you get onto this site, don't let yourself get disconnected by taking a coffee break; it could be a while before you get on again.

I consider myself lucky to get on this FTP site. It's incredibly popular. Walnut Creek is in the business of selling CD-ROMs that are packed with freeware and shareware programs. Files from these CD-ROMs are available from the Walnut Creek FTP site, too. Table A.2 shows you the folders that you'll find for Windows 95.

Table A.2 Interesting Folders under `/pub/win95`

cdextras	inetapps
demos	misc
drivers	multimedia
FAQ	patches
graphics	utilities
incoming	

WinSite (formerly known as CICA)

FTP address: **ftp.winsite.com**

This archive used to be managed by the Center for Innovative Computing Applications (CICA). It's created a new group called WinSite to manage the archive.

This could be the only FTP site that you need. It has the largest collection of freeware and shareware programs on the Internet. This could be the Internet equivalent of CompuServe's WinShare forum (a forum on CompuServe that contains shareware Windows programs). Table A.3 describes what you'll find in each of the folders on the CICA FTP server.

Table A.3 Folders under `/pub/pc/win95`

access	patches
demo	pdoxwin
desktop	pim
drivers	programr
dskutil	sounds
excel	sysutil
games	txtutil
icons	uploads
misc	winword
miscutil	wpwin
netutil	

Because everyone looks for files at this FTP site, you'll find it very crowded. At times, you won't be able to log on to the FTP server at all. Be patient and keep trying. If you give up, look at the log file that your FTP client program displays to see whether WinSite reported any mirror sites that you can use.

Mailing Lists

Windows 95-related mailing lists keep your mailbox full of messages. This section describes three of the most popular ones: **DevWire**, **WinNews**, and **WIN95-L**.

Microsoft DevWire

This is for Windows programmers. You'll find news and product information, such as seminar schedules and visual tool release schedules. To subscribe, send an e-mail to **DevWire@microsoft.nwnet.com** with **subscribe DevWire** in the body of your message.

Microsoft WinNews

This monthly newsletter keeps you up to date on the latest happenings at Microsoft. You'll also find product tips and press releases. To subscribe, send an e-mail to **enews99@microsoft.nwnet.com** with **subscribe winnews** in the body of your message.

WIN95-L

The WIN95-L mailing list is more like a forum. A subscriber posts a message to the list, and the list forwards the message to the other subscribers. Using this mailing list, you'll get Windows 95 help much faster than you'll get it through a support line or commercial on-line service. The answers are usually better, too. To subscribe, send an e-mail to **listserv@peach.ease.lsoft.com** with **subscribe winnews *your name*** in the body of your message.

> **Caution**
>
> WIN95-L floods your mailbox with hundreds of messages each day. If you want to receive four or five messages each day that contain 30 to 40 posts in each message, send an e-mail to **listserv@peach.ease.lsoft.com** with the text **set win95-l digest** in the body of your message.

UseNet Newsgroups

As of this writing, there aren't very many UseNet newsgroups dedicated to Windows 95, although the older Windows 3.1 groups are leaning in that direction. Table A.4 lists the newsgroups that you'll find useful. The only two that are dedicated to Windows 95, however, are **win95.misc** and **win95.setup**.

Table A.4 Newsgroups under `comp.os.ms-windows`

advocacy	programmer.graphics
announce	programmer.memory
apps.comm	programmer.misc
apps.financial	programmer.multimedia
apps.misc	programmer.networks
apps.utilities	programmer.ole
apps.winsock.mail	programmer.tools
apps.winsock.misc	programmer.tools.mfc
apps.winsock.news	programmer.tools.misc
apps.word-proc	programmer.tools.owl
misc	programmer.tools.winsock
networking.misc	programmer.vxd
networking.ras	programmer.winhelp

networking.tcp-ip	setup
networking.windows	video
programmer.controls	win95.misc
programmer.drivers	win95.setup

World Wide Web

Web pages aren't updated as often as UseNet newsgroups or mailing lists. There's potentially more information available on the Web, however, because it gets more attention from the media and corporate community. The Web pages in this section are only a sample. Each one contains links to other Windows 95 sites.

Microsoft Corporation

URL address: **www.microsoft.com**

> **Tip**
>
> Microsoft's Web site is now searchable. Point your Web browser at **www.msn.com/access/local.htm.**

Microsoft's Web site contains an amazing amount of information about its products, services, plans, job opportunities, and more. You'll find the two most useful Windows 95 Web pages by clicking the Windows 95 link or the Support link. Here's what you'll find on each:

- *Windows 95 link.* The Windows 95 Home Page contains general information about Windows 95, launch events, news, Microsoft Internet products, and the Microsoft Software Library. This Web page is constantly updated, so check in frequently.
- *Support link.* The Support Desktop Web page provides access to the Microsoft Knowledge Base, which you can search for articles based on key words that you specify. It also contains links to the Microsoft Software Library and Frequently Asked Questions Web pages.

Frank Condron's Windows 95 Page

URL address: **www.rust.net/~frankc**

This Web site was chosen as a ClubWin Web site. ClubWin is a collection of Web sites that have been recognized by Microsoft as providing outstanding

Windows 95 support and information on the Web. This page fits the bill. It has updated drivers, software, hints, and links to other ClubWin sites.

Stroud's CWSApps List

URL address: **cwsapps.texas.net**

> **Tip**
>
> Click the Windows 95 Section link to see a list that is limited to Windows 95 programs.

This Web site contains every Windows Winsock program available on the Internet. You'll find World Wide Web, FTP, e-mail, IRC, and UseNet client programs. You'll also find HTML editors and communication suites. In addition to the standard Winsock programs, this site contains all of the essential utilities that you'll need for Windows 95, such as WinZip 95 and ViruScan for Windows 95.

Windows 95 Annoyances

URL address: **www.creativelement.com/win95ann**

Is something in Windows 95 annoying you? You may find a way to fix it on this Web page. It contains a collection of fixes for things that Microsoft overlooked.

FedCenter

URL address: **199.171.16.49/fedcenter/fw95.html**

This Web page is sponsored by The InterFed Group. It contains information about Windows 95 events and shareware programs, as well as links to numerous other Windows 95 Web pages.

PC World's Windows 95

URL address: **www.pcworld.com/win95**

> **Tip**
>
> Sign up at this Web page for a free subscription to the Windows 95 tip-of-the-day mailing list.

Wow! This Web page has links to almost everything you need for Windows 95. It has articles about Windows 95 that you can search. *PC World* claims to have the largest collection of Windows 95 shareware on the Internet. They may be right.

Shareware.com

URL address: **www.shareware.com**

Shareware.com is a hot new Web site that indexes shareware and freeware products on the Internet. You can search for products by platform, category, and so on. You can also look at the top products based on the number of downloads or recent submissions. If you're looking for a shareware product, you don't need to log on to the on-line service anymore, you can find it here.

Windows 96

URL address: **www.cdrom.com/~brian**

This site boasts: "Enough upgrades, utilities, and other neat stuff to make Microsoft's Windows 95 seem like Windows 96." They're not kidding, either. This is easily one of the most extensive collection of freeware and shareware Windows 95 applications on the Web.

ZD Net Windows 95 Shareware Collection

URL address: **www.zdnet.com/~zdi/software/win95**

Ziff-Davis's site contains some of the best Windows 95 shareware on the Internet. You'll find applications, utilities, games, and communications programs. You'll also find some special utilities written by Ziff-Davis just for Windows 95 power users. ❖

APPENDIX B
What's on the CD?

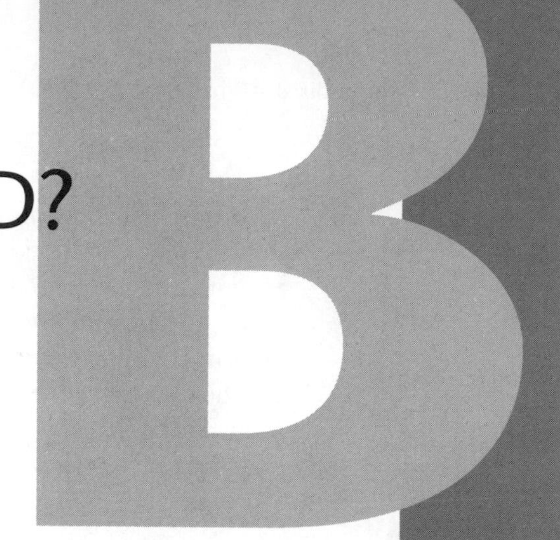

by Lisa D. Wagner

The CD-ROM that accompanies this book includes a wide variety of communications tools. We've made a special effort to offer a little something for just about every task you might want or need to accomplish: signing up for a commercial service, chatting with friends online, troubleshooting your modem or your connection, surfing the Web, using e-mail, and even exploring the exciting new world of VRML.

Using the *Windows 95 Communications Handbook* CD-ROM

Unlike some other CD-ROM bundles you may have run across, all of the software on this CD-ROM claims to work just fine with Windows 95; most of it, in fact, is 32-bit applications designed specifically to take advantage of the special features provided by Windows 95 and/or Windows NT.

Arranged by application type, this appendix briefly describes the products on the CD-ROM and how to access them. In addition, we've identified the *type* of program (shareware or freeware) so you'll know what to expect before you install it.

Important Information about Shareware

Shareware distribution gives users a chance to try software before buying it. If you try a shareware program and continue using it, you are expected to register. Individual programs differ on details—some request registration while others require it, and some specify a maximum trial period. With registration, you get anything from the simple right to continue using the software to an updated program with a printed manual.

Copyright laws apply to both shareware and commercial software, and the copyright holder retains all rights, with a few specific exceptions as stated below. Shareware authors are accomplished programmers, just like commercial authors, and the programs are of comparable quality. (In both cases, there are good programs and bad ones!) The main difference is in the method of distribution. The Shareware author specifically grants the right to copy and distribute the software, either to all and sundry or to a specific group. For example, some authors require written permission before a commercial disk vendor may copy their Shareware.

Shareware is a distribution method, not a type of software. You should find software that suits your needs and pocketbook, whether it's commercial or shareware. The shareware system makes fitting your needs easier, because you can try before you buy. And because the overhead is low, prices are low also. Shareware has the ultimate money-back guarantee—if you don't use the product, you don't pay for it.

Put another way, shareware is software that's publicly distributed, and paid for according to an honor system. Frequently innovative, always inexpensive, it represents one of the best sources of software for personal computers. If you use a shareware program, you're duty-bound to pay for it; if not, you simply uninstall it.

Tip

Generally, a shareware program will keep reminding you to register until you do. By sending in your fee, you'll usually get a registration number to enter so that the program will stop nagging you.

If the program doesn't make it painfully clear how to register, you can usually find the information in the readme.txt or similarly named file.

What Is Freeware?

This CD-ROM also includes some products known as *freeware* or *public domain software*. These programs may be used free of charge, courtesy of generous and public-spirited developers and contributors. In lieu of a monetary fee, the program's author might occasionally request that you make a donation to a favorite charity, perhaps mail a postcard to him or her from your city, or make some other kind of non-monetary contribution.

Accessing the Software

When you insert the CD-ROM into your CD drive, Windows 95 automatically runs the built-in installer interface. This installer automates the setup process for most of the applications offered here. After a short multimedia welcome, the installer presents you with a dialog box that enables you to choose which applications you want to install.

Commercial Online Service Sign-Up Kits

Among all the commercial services available, America Online and Prodigy are the most popular among the general population. Both offer a free month of service; try them both and decide which one you like best.

America Online

America Online is one of the largest and fastest growing commercial services. Its popularity is based on the ease of use for any user level, the wide variety of features and services offered, and its limited but adequate access to the Internet.

Type: Commercial subscription service; billed monthly

Provided by:

America Online
8619 Westwood Center Drive
Vienna, VA 22182
USA
1-800-827-6364

Prodigy

Another one of the "big three" services, Prodigy is known for its family-oriented content. It's also popular among do-it-yourself investors and stock market watchers.

Type: Commercial subscription service; billed monthly

Provided by:

Prodigy, Inc.
1-800-PRODIGY

Communications

This section features general communications tools you'll need from time to time, such as terminal emulation programs and some helpful faxing tools.

CRT 1.0 Beta 7

CRT stands for "Combined Rlogin and Telnet." CRT is a 32-bit Winsock terminal emulator that supports the rlogin and Telnet protocol as well as Telnet via a SOCKS firewall. CRT supports ZModem file transfer over Telnet (download only).

CRT's features include:

- Quality VT100/VT102 emulation
- Support for bold, underline, and reverse attributes (no blinking)
- User-configurable number of rows and columns
- User-defined foreground/background, number of savelines (scroll back), and keymaps
- Support for use from the command line or Web browsers
- Copy and paste

Type: Shareware

Provided by:

Van Dyke Technologies
PO Box 37457
Albuquerque, NM 87176
E-mail: **support@vandyke.com**
http://www.vandyke.com/vandyke/crt/

FaxMail 5.01

Includes four different installations, which support Microsoft Windows 95, Windows 3.1, Windows for Workgroups 3.11, and Windows NT. Supports most fax/modems, Group 3 CLASS 1, CLASS 2, and CLASS 2.0.

FaxMail for Windows will add a <Fax> button to all your Windows Programs, giving you access to all the fax/modems and fax machines in the world, making them become your printers. FaxMail attaches itself to and becomes a part of the actual Microsoft Windows environment, whereby it appends itself to all system menus thereby adding its features to all Windows Applications.

FaxMail has hundreds of useful features, such as Dynamic View/Edit Cover Page, FaxBook Import, Windows Dynamic All Class Fax/Modem Driver, and Technical Support. You can import up to 1,000 names and phone numbers into each FaxBook (phone book) at a time from any Xbase database program, and you can have as many FaxBooks as you want. FaxMail gives you laser-quality fax output, making it a great tool to send an occasional fax or large numbers of high-quality faxes from the background while you work on other tasks. No TSR, DOS, or real-time drivers required.

Type: Shareware

Provided by:

Jon Krahmer
ElectraSoft
3207 Carmel Valley Dr.
Missouri City, TX 77459-3068
Voice: 713-261-0307
Fax: 713-499-5939,11,11,11,11
E-mail: **JonK@blkbox.com**
http://www.blkbox.com/~jonk/

FaxModem Wizard

FaxModem Wizard will tell you what, if anything, is on each of your four COM-Ports and which IRQ each COM-Port is using, COM?-IRQ?. It will give you a written report about your Modem.

Type: Freeware (included with FaxMail for Windows just described)

Provided by:

Jon Krahmer
ElectraSoft
(see contact information under FaxMail for Windows)

Internet Chat

It might not be the first thing you do when you get hooked up to the Internet, but everybody does it eventually: real-time chat. The following tools should make your chat sessions as much fun as the real thing. (You remember that, don't you?)

Internet TeleCafé 1.99

The TeleCafé is an interactive, friendly place to socialize and chat on the Internet. It specializes in giving you the opportunity to talk to people from all around the world. The easy-to-understand interface and Windows client make this place the number one place to be on the Internet.

There are three types of TeleCafé users:

- Trial members have the opportunity to come into the TeleCafé and see what kinds of options it has to offer. If they are satisfied, they have the option to join as a Regular Member. NO FEE.
- Regular members have the opportunity to move freely through most of the rooms and options of the TeleCafé. NO FEE.
- V.I.P. members have the greatest options in the TeleCafé. To become a V.I.P. Member, you have to purchase an account ($29/yr U.S., $35/yr Canada).

Tip

If you want to briefly check out the TeleCafé before installing the software, Telnet to **telecafe.com:9000**.

Type: Shareware

Provided by:

The Internet TeleCafé
ComputerLink OnLine Inc.
5415 Dundas St. W. #301
Etobicoke, Ontario
M9B 1B5
E-mail: **admin@telecafe.com**
http://idirect.com/telecafe/

PowWow 1.7 beta 4

PowWow is a unique personal communications program for the Internet. It allows you to call your friends, chat with up to seven people by keyboard or voice, show a picture of yourself, send and receive files, play WAV format sound files, and browse the World Wide Web together as a group. All you need to know in order to reach other PowWow users is their e-mail addresses. PowWow will automatically connect with them, provided PowWow is running on their computers.

System Requirements:

- A World Wide Web browser is *not* required to use the chat and file transfer functions.
- PowWow does not require a sound card, but you will be unable to play sound files or voice chat with a Microsoft Windows-compatible sound card installed.
- A 486DX/33 or faster computer and at least a 28,800 bps Internet connection are required for voice chatting. Using a slower computer or Internet connection will result in an incoherent voice chat connection.
- In order to browse the World Wide Web with other people using PowWow, a World Wide Web browser such as Netscape Navigator Version 1.1N or later or MS Internet Explorer Version 4.40.308 or later must also be installed.
- In order to use the sound player and voice chat functions of PowWow, you will need a Microsoft Windows-compatible sound card with speakers and microphone.

Tip

Includes detailed instruction manual that you're likely to find very helpful. See the file named powwow.doc.

Tribal Voice is an organization run by Native Americans from many tribes who are dedicated to providing a Native American presence in the high-tech industry through free and low-cost computer software and services.

Type: Freeware

Provided by:

Tribal Voice
627 West Midland Avenue
Woodland Park, CO 80863
Voice: 719-687-0480
Fax: 719-687-0716
E-mail: **support@tribal.com**
http://www.tribal.com

WinTalk 32 1.2 beta 3

WinTalk allows Windows users who have the WINSOCK DLL installed on their system to participate in real-time conversations with remote users, using the popular UNIX ntalk and talk protocols. The program acts as both a talk client and server, responding to remote talk requests with a pop-up "ring" dialog box, an auditory ring, or both. Other features include:

- Command-line options: configurable .ini file location, auto-talk
- Daemon discovery: auto-detects OTALK or NTALK on remote machine
- Configurable timeout action for incoming talks
- User-editable hotlist of frequently called addresses
- A "system beep" option for users without sound cards
- Option for system-modal ring dialogs
- Automatic detection/warning of "questionable" Winsock configurations

> **Note**
>
> This program does not automatically install from the CD-ROM. See the README file for installation instructions.

Type: Freeware

Provided by:

Glen Daniels
ELF Communications, Inc.
1212 Boylston Street #221
Chestnut Hill, MA 02167
USA
Voice: 617-629-2323
E-mail: **gub@ELF.com**
http://www.elf.com/elf/home.html

WS-IRC

WS-IRC is a Windows client for the Internet Relay Chat network. It allows Internet users to chat electronically with each other in a group/channel using IRC servers. The advantage is that users can access the IRC network and converse with users worldwide. WS-IRC is Windows Sockets 1.1 compliant, and has been tested with NetManage's and Trumpet's WINSOCK.DLL TCP/IP protocol stack.

Type: Freeware

Provided by:

Caesar M. Samsi
E-mail: **csamsi@clark.net**, **72030.562@compuserve.com**
http://www.clark.net/pub/csamsi

E-Mail

The following programs either give you access to Internet e-mail, or provide enhancements to your existing e-mail program.

E-Mail Notify 1.01

e-Mail Notify is a Winsock-compliant Biff Internet e-mail client. It will connect to your POP3 server and retrieve the headers of any e-mail waiting there for you. You can configure e-Mail Notify very extensively to warn you about new mail.

If it runs in Windows 95 or Windows NT, it uses multithreading for smoother multitasking. You will hardly notice anything happens when it transfers headers, even on a PPP link. If it runs in Windows 95 or in NT 3.51 with the Shell Preview, it will add a small icon in the Windows 95 taskbar, where you will be able to control everything.

Type: Shareware

Provided by:

Ludovic Dubost
9 Av du Colonel Bonnet
75016 Paris, France
Voice: +33 1 42309069
E-mail: **zic@olympe.polytechnique.fr**
http://olympe.polytechnique.fr/~zic/english/email.html

Eudora Light for Windows 1.5.2

Eudora has long been a favorite among Internet e-mail users due to its robust features and ease of use. Although a commercial version is available, this freeware version might be all you need!

- IBM PC-compatible machine
- Windows Version 3.1 or higher
- Winsock v1.1-compliant TCP/IP stack
- Microsoft (or compatible) mouse (highly recommended)
- At least 750KB of free disk space (more depending on mailbox sizes)

Type: Freeware

Provided by:

Jeff Beckley
QUEST
QUALCOMM Incorporated
6455 Lusk Blvd.
San Diego, CA 92121-2779
USA
E-mail: **beckley@qualcomm.com**

Internet Idioms for Microsoft Exchange 0.2.2

"Heartily sick of staring at Arial 10 text in Exchange?" asks Ben Goetter. He was, so he wrote a utility to give Exchange signature capability and a configurable read-font, and in so doing make it a slightly more comfortable Internet mail client. Ben calls the extension "Internet Idioms," because that's what it contains: little bits to patch and otherwise band-aid Exchange into a semblance of a traditional, idiomatic Internet mail client.

The Exchange Internet Idioms package requires Microsoft Windows 95, with Exchange and MAPI installed, of course. Also requires MSVC 4.0 runtime files, which can be downloaded from http://www.halcyon.com/goetter/msvcrt40.zip.

Note

This product will not work with Office 95 Wordmail or with Windows NT 3.51.

Type: Freeware

Provided by:

Ben Goetter
Angry Greycat Designs
E-mail: **goetter@halcyon.com**
http://www.halcyon.com/goetter/widgets.htm

PageMaster 1.62

PageMaster is a Windows application that allows both manual and automatic paging to numeric and alphanumeric pagers. Users enter a list of pages, then selectively page single, multiple, or predefined groups at a time. PageMaster will monitor MAPI- and VIM-compliant e-mail (including Microsoft Mail and Lotus cc:Mail) and can send partial or entire e-mail messages to a pager. Mail filers allow the user to select which messages are sent to the pager by searching for keywords. In addition, PageMaster will monitor a telephone line for a predetermined number of rings. When the number of rings is received, PageMaster issues a page indicating a call has gone unanswered. Similar to the more expensive commercial paging systems you've seen.

Type: Shareware

Provided by:

Tom Carbone
Sales Representative
OmniTrend
E-mail: **72662.455@compuserve.com**
http://www/omnitrend.com

Pegasus Mail 2.23

Pegasus Mail is a full-fledged electronic mail system for use with Novell NetWare (versions 2.15A and later), and on stand-alone systems using the Winsock TCP/IP interface. You can use it without charge, restriction, or obligation on as many servers and machines as you wish. User manuals available for a fee.

Type: Freeware

Provided by:

David Harris
http://www.cuslm.ca/pegasus/

FTP

Finding Windows 95's FTP utility leaves something to be desired? Try one of these third-party programs instead. You might actually start looking forward to using FTP rather than dreading it.

CuteFTP for Windows 95

CuteFTP is one of very few programs that allow novice users to utilize the capabilities of FTP without having to know all the details of the protocol itself. The strongest point of CuteFTP is its ability to gather almost every available bit of information about files and directory structure of a remote system and present it to the user in an easy-to-use File Manager-like browsing screen. CuteFTP will also keep data transfers to a minimum by means of storing all the data it can to a temporary file.

Other features include:

- Full-screen, configurable, local, and remote directory browsing.
- Integrated handling of index files. No need to launch notepad to view file descriptions.
- Caching of already visited directories and index files for them. No need to transfer a directory list for a single directory a hundred times.
- Automatic directory tree downloading.
- Complete custom configurations for each remote system.
- Robust stop command. With CuteFTP you can cancel any operation in progress without loosing connection.

> **Note**
>
> Does not work with AOL Winsock or SunSoft PC-NFS.

Type: Shareware

Provided by:

Alex Kunadze
E-mail: **alex@sbk.trigem.co.kr**

FTP Icon Connection 95/NT 1.2

FTP Icon Connection is an Explorer-like graphic interface for FTP downloading and uploading. Files are shown as icons; you can view directories by small or large icons, by detail view, and more. The unregistered version has limited functionality, but more than enough to get you started. Some popular FTP connections are already set up for you.

Registering the program enables a wide range of very handy features, including:

- Shortcuts: Simply double-click the Profile Icon and fill in the blanks.
- Change Permissions: Graphically change the permissions on a remote system
- Icon to Application Association: Just double-click the Icon and load from a remote into the Associated Application
- Scheduler: Schedule a download/upload while you are away from your computer, or just send that all-important status report to the office
- Synchronize local Folder with Remote Folder, for those of us who work on multiple systems
- Complete Help file

Type: Shareware

Provided by:

Bill Jackson
PO Box 14334
Huntsville, AL 35815
E-mail: **billj@hiwaay.net**
http://fly.hiwaay.net/~billj/FTPic

Windows FTP Daemon

Windows FTP Daemon is a Windows program that allows you to set up your machine as an FTP site. It is easy to configure through Windows dialog boxes, and requires no direct editing of INI files or Registry databases.

WFTPD has the following useful features:

- RFC compliance to 959 & 1123 (in other words, it's a real FTP server).
- Multiple logins and simultaneous transfers allowed.
- Works with Mosaic/Netscape/Cello.
- Secured access by means of password authentication, address-based host authentication, and the ability to restrict users to named subtrees of your directory structure.
- Further security by means of user rights which may be set easily on any directories in your system—including those that don't yet exist.
- "Windows friendly": does not flash cursors while it is transferring, or hold up processing.
- Configurable logs of all logins, anonymous logins, gets, puts, commands, warnings, and so on.
- Logs to file that can be read by other applications, including session number, time, and date stamp. This information is also logged to the screen. Other Windows applications can read this log while it is open, and it can be transferred through WFTPD.
- Status bar displays count of users and number of sockets in use.

...plus many more features that are enabled when you register the software.

Type: Shareware

Provided by:

Alun Jones
E-mail: **alun@StarBase.NeoSoft.COM**

WS-FTP32

This application is a standard File Transfer Protocol (FTP) client application for Windows Sockets. The user interface for this FTP client is designed with the novice FTP user in mind. Thus, WS_FTP has become wildly popular among users of all levels—even the experts.

WS_FTP also provides for automatic downloads of files.

Type: Freeware

Provided by:

John A. Junod
Ipswitch, Inc.
81 Hartwell Ave.
Lexington, MA 02173
Voice: 617/676-5700
E-mail: **info@ipswitch.com**
http://www.ipswitch.com/

> **Note**
>
> Author says: For tech support, please use the CompuServe WINCON area. Please do *not* send "How do I use WS_FTP" questions to the author. Bug reports and suggestions may be sent to junodj@martinez.ipswitch.com or junodj@csra.net.

Gopher

Before the World Wide Web, Gopher was the most popular way of finding and retrieving information on the Internet. Of course, it's still a great tool, if not as visually stimulating as the Web. Try this tool to get started.

WSGopher

WSGopher's best feature is its excellent collection of gopher server bookmarks. Even if you don't know a lot about Gopher searches, this program can help you learn the basics in no time.

Type: Freeware

Provided by:

Dave Brooks
Brooks Internet Software, Inc.

410 N. Bellin Rd.
Idaho Falls, ID 83402-2352
USA
Voice: 208-523-6970
E-mail: **support@brooksnet.com**
http://brooksnet.com/

Newsreaders

With well over 10,000 newsgroups out there and hundreds more starting up every day, a good newsreader program is essential for keeping your favorite groups organized and manageable.

NewsXpress

NewsXpress is a Windows Sockets-compliant UseNet newsreader that uses the NNTP to access newsgroups and articles on a news server. It's an in-house favorite at Que Corporation.

Some of the key features of NX are:

- An integrated MDI application
- XOVER to access overview database from news server
- AUTHINFO for authorization
- XPAT for searching articles remotely
- Support for threads and signatures
- Built-in UUEncode and UUDecode
- Support for kill and auto-selection, accept regular expressions for specifying patterns
- Local folders for storing articles, and outbox for queuing posts and mails
- MIME-compliant, support for Base64 and Quoted-Printable

Type: Freeware

Provided by:

W.L. Ken, Ng.
Rm F, 5/F, Odeon Bldg.
26-28 Shu Kuk St., North Point
Hong Kong
E-mail: **kenng@hk.super.net**

WinVN 32-bit

File name: WV32_990.zip

WinVN is an NNTP newsreader for the Microsoft Windows family. You can use it to read and post UseNet News, and send e-mail via the SMTP or MAPI protocols. Its name stands for Windows Visual Newsreader. It can be used to select, view, write, sort, and print UseNet News articles. Articles can be saved locally, cut into the Windows Clipboard or forwarded to other individuals via e-mail.

WinVN offers a more visual approach to reading News than most other newsreaders. WinVN allows the user to easily navigate between newsgroups and articles via its point-and-click interface. It allows the viewing of multiple articles simultaneously and on multitasking systems such as Windows/NT; it even allows multiple simultaneous news server connections.

In addition to Windows and a TCP/IP connection, WinVN requires an NNTP News Server that supports either XHDR or NNTP extensions.

Type: Freeware

Provided by:

Sam Rushing
E-mail: **rushing@titan.ksc.nasa.gov**
Mail list: **WinVN-request@titan.ksc.nasa.gov**

Suites and All-in-One Packages

Rather than using one program for FTP, another for e-mail, yet another for news reading, and still another for Web access, some companies have developed integrated packages that let you do everything from one place. The following are among the elite.

NetCruiser

Not only is NETCOM a leading Internet Service Provider, but it's got its own Windows-based software to let you browse the Internet, FTP to different sites, surf the Web, read and post to newsgroups, and more. Part of NETCOM's popularity is due to this great software package. You have to use NETCOM as your service provider to use this software.

Type: Dedicated suite for Internet Service Provider

Provided by:

NETCOM
Voice: 800-983-5970
http://www.netcom.com/faq

Pipeline 2 version 1.2

Pipeline 2 is a video display terminal (VDT) emulation software package designed to run in the Windows environment. Pipeline 2 is made to replace your VDT and more by incorporating a VDT's features and functions on your PC, while providing for full compatibility with your application software. If you have been using DEC, Wyse, Falco, Televideo, or any of the other listed VDTs, a Pipeline 2-equipped PC is a direct replacement for your operating environment.

Pipeline 2 communicates to a local or remote host system via: serial connection, local and remote modem, local and wide area network connections, or a combination of all of these. Pipeline 2 also allows more complete system resource sharing through the use of local and remote peripherals access. You have to use Pipeline USA as your service provider to use this software.

Type: Dedicated suite for Internet Service Provider

Note

This program does not automatically install from the CD-ROM. See the README file for installation instructions.

Provided by:

PSI Net
510 Herndon Park Drive
Herndon, VA 22070
Voice: 703-904-4100
http://www.usa.pipeline.com

QVT/Net 4.0

About the only thing missing from QVT/Net is a Web browser. Everything else (FTP, news, terminal, network printing, mail services, Gopher client, RCP server, SMTP server, Telnet) is well integrated and easy to use.

Type: Shareware

Provided by:

QPC Software
E-mail: **chloe@qpc.com**

WinNET

WinNET Communications provides nationwide toll-free access to the Internet, as well as toll-free technical support from 9 a.m.–9 p.m., Monday through Friday. Its software supports offline e-mail and news reading, so you don't have to be connected during these tasks. You have to use WinNET as your service provider to use this software.

Type: Dedicated suite for Internet Service Provider

Provided by:

WinNET Communications, Inc.
330F Distillery Commons
Louisville, KY 40206
Voice: 502-589-6800
http://www.win.net

Telnet

If you're looking for some solid Telnet tools, either of these should make you happy.

QWS3270 Extra 2.4

QWS3270 Extra includes customizable screen, font, and default settings. Its strength lies in its support for IBM 3270 and Tektronix 4010 terminal emulation.

> **Note**
>
> QWS 3270 cannot run multiple sessions without reloading the program.

Type: Shareware

Provided by:

Jim Rymerson
Jolly Giant Software Inc.
1322 Channelview Road
Kingston Ontario Canada
K7L 4V1

Voice: 613-541-0740
Fax: 613-544-2459
E-mail: **jgs@fox.nstn.ca**

Trumpet Telnet

Trumpet Telnet is a no-frills program, but it's reliable. It works especially well as an external client for Web browsers and Gopher clients. VT100 terminal emulation is included along with cut-and-paste capabilities and a few font options.

Type: Freeware

Trumpet Software International Pty Ltd
GPO Box 1649
Hobart Tasmania 7001
Australia
Voice: 61 02 450220
Fax: 61 02 450210
http://www.trumpet.com.au

Other Internet Tools

In this section you'll find a little bit of everything else you'll need or want for working online: encoding/decoding, troubleshooting, time tracking, and, of course, the infamous Trumpet Winsock itself.

Connect Time Monitor for Windows 95 3.0.2

This nifty tool helps you keep track of your time online. You'll find this especially handy if you're new to the Internet—it is amazing how quickly the hours can pass!

Type: Freeware

Provided by:

Scott Craig
409 Jessie Drive
Nashville, TN 37211
USA
E-mail: **scraig@ix.netcom.com**

Finger32

Are you supposed to "meet" someone online at a certain time, but can't find him or her? Finger32 helps you find out the names of users logged on to a particular server. Easy-to-use freeware is unsupported.

Type: Freeware

Provided by:

Laurence Kahn
E-mail: **kahn@drcoffsite.com**

Grep 32 1.1.0

Grep 32 is a DOS command-line file search utility. If you're familiar with UNIX, you'll recognize this application as a hand-me-down of a very useful UNIX tool.

Type: Freeware

Provided by:

MarcNet
Marc Geist
945 Sparta Drive
Lafayette, CO 80026
Voice: 303-538-2653
E-mail: **mag@dr.att.com**

Here 32-bit 1.9b5

Here allows you to easily post your ever-changing dynamic PPP or SLIP Internet address to a Finger account, thereby allowing others to look up your current Internet address and contact you.

Here also includes a Finger client to allow you to easily check the PPP or SLIP address postings of other Here users.

Since other users will now be able to locate your current address, you will be able to use talk servers such as WinTalk; FTP servers such as WinQV/Net, Serv-U, and WFTPD; and HTTP servers such as HTTPD and ZB Server.

Type: Freeware

Provided by:

Everitt Beers
E-mail: **ebeers@usc.edu**

HotJava 1.0 Alpha 3

First, there was the Internet: plain, text-based. Lots of information, but not very much fun to look at. The World Wide Web added visual interest: graphics, colors, and better-looking text. Java takes it one step further, by making the World Wide Web a full-blown multimedia experience. This program from Sun Computing brings the exciting new world of Java to your computer.

To run this release of HotJava for Win32 you will need:

- An x86-based PC running Windows 95 (build 950 or greater) or Windows NT 3.5 (Pentium recommended)
- A supported multimedia sound device
- 256 colors

In addition to the documentation included in this release, the latest information about Java and HotJava is available from **http://java.sun.com**. This includes announcements about new releases, a FAQ, a known bugs list, links to Java applets developed at other sites, and much more. In addition, several mailing lists are maintained by the Java team.

> **Note**
>
> Does not work with Windows 95 beta build 450.

> **Note**
>
> This program does not automatically install from the CD-ROM. See the README file for installation instructions.

Type: Freeware

Provided by:

Sun Computing, Inc.
E-mail: **java@java.sun.com**
http://java.sun.com/mail.html

Internet Control Center 1.21d

This Internet front-end package is a must-have for the serious Internet user. It brings all your online applications together so you can be more productive:

- Manage twelve programs at once
- Run multiple instances of any application
- One-touch application switching
- Background applications automatically minimized
- Automatically starts and closes Winsock
- Works with any Winsock

> **Note**
>
> This program does not automatically install from the CD-ROM. See the README file for installation instructions.

Type: Shareware

Provided by:

John Foltz
President
UsefulWare, Inc.
3817 Bayside Passage
Acworth, GA 30101
USA
E-mail: **jfoltz@usefulware.com**
http://www.usefulware.com/icc.html

InterSnoop 1.01

InterSnoop is a powerful, fully integrated Winsock client application designed specifically for the Windows 95 and Windows NT 3.5x operating systems. InterSnoop embodies the functionality of three major Internet clients, namely Whois, Finger, and Ph. By embodying these three client services, InterSnoop allows you to retrieve various information on users and machines that are a part of the Internet. In addition, InterSnoop provides two more services that help you determine the IP Address of a machine from its Hostname (and vice versa) as well as determine whether or not a machine is currently online.

Type: Shareware

Provided by:

AKI Software Solutions
5901 Nicholson Street, Suite 100
Pittsburgh, PA 15217
USA
E-mail: **akiss@akiss.lm.com**
http://www.akiss.lm.com

LogTick

Another time-tracking utility you will thank yourself for installing when the ISP bill arrives each month.

Type: Shareware

Provided by:

Ton Martens
E-mail: **tmartens@pi.net**
http://www.pi.net/~tmartens

> **Note**
>
> Requires vbrun300.dll, which you can download from most sites that distribute Windows software.

Pping 0.3

Pping is a multithreaded console utility. It is similar to the Ping program that comes with operating systems that have TCP/IP.

Ping sends an ICMP message to the remote machine and waits for a response. The output of Ping is verbose and needs some explanation to a lay-person. Pping, on the other hand, gives a simple go/no-go type of response that is more suitable for checking if the remote machine is responding. Further, Pping accepts multiple remote machine names as well as wildcards for IP addresses.

Type: Freeware

Provided by:

Intellisoft, Inc.
Stoeckmattstr. 3
CH-5316 Leuggern
Switzerland
Fax: 41-56-455-14
E-mail: **raju@inso.pr.net.ch**
ftp.eunet.ch/customers/varghese/

Trumpet Winsock for Windows 95

Trumpet Winsock is the most widely used shareware Winsock package. The software supports modem and network connections. After copying this program to your hard drive, you need to provide IP address information. If you're using the program over a modem, you need to modify LOGIN.CMD to work with your service provider. You also might need to add the directory that contains Trumpet to your path statement in AUTOEXEC.BAT.

Type: Shareware

Provided by:

Trumpet Software International Pty Ltd.
GPO Box 1649
Hobart Tasmania 7001
Australia
Voice: 61 02 450220
Fax: 61 02 450210
http://www.trumpet.com.au

UpTime 1.0 for Windows

Use this ultra-simple utility to display how much free time has passed since a connection has been made. This is intended for use with a dial-up SLIP connection, although its uses are not restricted to it. Simply configure your SLIP dialer to launch UpTime when connected, and your UpTime will be displayed at the bottom of the screen. This is a Visual Basic 3.0 application, so you'll need the file VBRUN300.DLL to be in your Windows/System directory. If you don't have this file, you can get it on virtually any online service or bulletin board.

Type: Shareware

Provided by:

David A. Karp
CEO
Creative Element
P.O. Box 20024
Oakland, CA 94620-0024
U.S.A.

E-mail: **daaron@creativelement.com**
http://www.creativelement.com/

Wincode

Wincode is a great utility for UUEncoding and UUDecoding files. A couple of really nice features are the way the program handles multiple files and its capability to tie its menus to other programs. The program decodes many poorly encoded programs that other decoders can handle. Also supports BINHEX decoding.

Type: Freeware, but help file has $5 shareware fee

Provided by:

Snappy Software
E-mail: **feedback@snappy.globalone.net**

Winsock RCP/RSH for Win32

This is actually two applications: RCP, a remote copy utility, and RSH, which executes a command on a remote host and displays the results on your PC's screen or stores the output in a file. Both programs include a console and a windowing version. The windowing versions enable you to take advantage of Windows features such as cut, copy, paste, and scrolling.

Type: Shareware

Provided by:

Denicomp Systems
PO Box 731
Exton, PA 19341
E-mail: **71612.2333@compuserve.com**

WS-Archie

WS-Archie is a Winsock-compliant Archie program that allows you to connect to an Archie server and search for a file by using the familiar Windows interface. The program comes preconfigured with the locations of several Archie servers. You can configure WS-Archie to transfer files directly from the list of found files so that you don't have to open your FTP client manually and then reenter the address and directory information. The software doesn't work this way, however, with the current version of WS_FTP32.

Type: Freeware (optional registration fee)

Provided by: David Woakes
88 Spottiswoode St.
Edinburg, Scotland
E-mail: **david.woakes@dial.pipex.com**

WS-Ping

Ping is an uncomplicated Windows application used to test an Internet connection. The author wrote the program to test whether his two computers were connected on the Internet; you can do the same thing. The source code is included in the archive, and the author grants you permission to alter it, if necessary.

> **Note**
>
> Because Ping uses nonstandard Winsock calls, this application may not run on every Winsock stack.

Type: Freeware

Provided by: John A. Junod
Ipswitch, Inc.
81 Hartwell Ave.
Lexington, MA 02173
Voice: 617/676-5700
Fax: 617/676-5710
E-mail: **info@ipswitch.com**
http://www.ipswitch.com

WSFinger 1.5

WSFinger was developed to provide Finger and Whois client capabilities to computers using Windows and Winsock 1.1. Its simple features include command-line capabilities, address book, history of recent fingers, copy, save, and print features.

Type: Shareware

Provided by:

Jim O'Brien
Tidewater Systems
304 Jefferson Street
Salisbury, MD 21801
Voice: 410-860-0593
E-mail: **72713.1426@compuserve.com**

VRML

Fountain 0.9

Fountain includes 3D shape-creation tools as well as the extrusion of TrueType fonts. You can choose between infinite and local light sources, and you can paint not only entire objects, but also on individual faces and vertices.

Existing 3D geometry can be imported via DXF, 3D Studio, Wavefront, LightWave and Imagine filters, and the following 2D formats are supported: PostScript, BMP, and JPG. While Fountain is primarily an authoring tool, the ability to read VRML files allows you to take advantage of existing 3D resources on the Internet and to test VRML-specific features such as levels of detail, in-lining, and hyperlinks.

The minimum requirements for Fountain are a fast 486 with 8M of RAM. To access VRML worlds on the Web, a SLIP/PPP connection and a 14.4k modem are also required. To comfortably navigate through worlds with over a thousand polygons, we recommend a Pentium with a 64-bit graphics card (preferably with 3D acceleration). A 28.8k modem or ISDN connection are also recommended for accessing larger worlds.

Although you do not need an HTML browser to access VRML files across the Web, you will need one to display 2D formats such as HTML. Currently, only Netscape is supported.

Tip

If any problems are encountered with the 3DR installation, you may wish to try installing 3DR by itself—run SETUP.EXE in your target Fountain directory.

Type: Freeware

Provided by:

Caligari Corporation
Voice: 415-390-9600
Toll-free: 800-351-7620
Fax: 415-390-9755
E-mail: **sales@caligari.com**
http://www.caligari.com/

World Wide Web Browsers and Editors

HotDog Web Editor - Standard Edition 1.3.2

HotDog is an HTML editor for Windows. It helps you maintain and create documents for the World Wide Web. HotDog makes life simple for you by providing quick access to tags and attributes and dialog boxes to help you create complex elements. HotDog supports HTML 3 and Netscape revisions. Requires VBRUN 300.DLL, which can be downloaded from our Web site.

> **Note**
>
> Some of the HTML 3 elements are not yet supported by the Netscape Navigator.

Sausage Software recommends a 80486 computer with at least 8M of RAM.

Type: Shareware

Provided by:

Sausage Software
1/10 Stutt Avenue
Doncaster, 3108
Victoria, Australia
Fax: 613-9816-3922
E-mail: **hotdog-support@sausage.com**
http://www.sausage.com

Web HotSpots 1.6P

Web HotSpots is an image map editor.

> **Note**
>
> Requires the files mfc40.dll and msvcrt40.dll in your Windows\System folder. If you don't have them, you can download them from the HotSpots Web page.

Type: Shareware

Provided by:

1Automata
E-mail: **1auto@hooked.net**
http://www.cris.com/~automata/support.htm

MapEdit 1.5

MapEdit allows you to load your GIF image into a scrollable, resizable window and then draw polygons, circles, and rectangles on top of it, specifying a URL for each. It also allows you to go back and delete these "hot spots," set a default URL for clicks outside of the "hot" areas, and so on. In addition, it allows you to associate comments of arbitrary length with each object if you are creating an NCSA-format map. Features a Help system better than most.

Type: Shareware

Provided by:

Thomas Boutell
boutell.com
PO Box 20837
Seattle, WA 98102
USA
E-mail: **boutell@boutell.com**
http://www.boutell.com

> **Note**
>
> Mr. Boutell is also the author of the World Wide Web Frequently Asked Questions, With Answers (http://sunsite.unc.edu./boutell/faq).

MapThis! 32-bit 1.20

MapThis! is a program to create and edit World Wide Web image maps.

The "official" method (from NCSA's and CERN's HTTPD tutorial pages, two of the most widely used HTTPD servers) of creating image maps is to use a painting program, such as Paintbrush, XV, Lview, or whatever, to find the "points" that define the areas of the map. Then you have to write them down, and type them into a specially formatted text file to place on your server. Talk about a lot of work! Map This takes care of all the "where is this" stuff, in a graphical, user-friendly way. You can drag-and-plot your rectangles, circles, and polygons to your heart's content, reshape them, and then set up what they point to.

Type: Freeware

Provided by:

Todd C. Wilson
Molly Penguin Software
E-mail: **tc@galadriel.ecaetc.ohio-state.edu**
http://galadriel.ecaetc.ohio-state.edu/tc/mt

NouWeb 3.0

NouWeb is a Windows HTML editor with integrated access to and use of Web-related tools including converters, browsers, and publishers. It includes support for HTML 2.0 and the Netscape extensions, and provides template management and project management features.

Type: Shareware

Provided by:

Noumena, Inc.
3836 NE 63rd Avenue
Portland, OR 97213
USA
E-mail: **noumena@hevanet.com**
http://winftp.cica.indiana.edu

SoftQuad HoTMetaL 1.0+

SoftQuad HoTMetaL is an editor for the HTML files used on the World Wide Web. It runs on Sun SPARC systems with X11 or OpenWindows, and under Microsoft Windows. Use HoTMetaL to create new pages or to edit existing ones. Designed for and works best with NSCA Mosaic.

Note

A full-featured, supported commercial version called HoTMetaL Pro is available for purchase from SoftQuad or from your local reseller.

Type: Freeware

Provided by:

SoftQuad, Inc.
The MetaL-Workers
56 Aberfoyle Crescent
Toronto, Ontario,
MBX 2W4 Canada
Voice: 416-239-4801
Fax: 416-239-7105
E-mail: **hotmetal@sq.com**
http://www.sq.com

URL Grabber

URL Grabber is a small floating toolbar that resides in a corner of your MS Windows desktop. It enables you to easily grab and store URLs from news groups, e-mail messages, and other sources, as you are reading them.

With a click of the mouse, URL Grabber will automatically convert your collection of URLs to active WWW links on an HTML page.

With another mouse click, URL Grabber will bring up your favorite browser displaying your collected links so you can view Web pages, download files, and otherwise obtain information from the WWW almost instantly.

Type: Shareware

Provided by:

Brooklyn North Software Works
25 Doyle Street
Bedford, Nova Scotia B4A 1K4
Canada
E-mail: **harawitz@brooknorth.bedford.ns.ca**

Web Spinner 1.0

Web Spinner allows you to create World Wide Web pages without learning complicated HTML. Web Spinner has an easy-to-use interface and all tasks are completed by simply highlighting text and then using toolbars or menu choices. Web Spinner has numerous features to help the novice to the advanced user. Common tasks such as adding a link to a list are combined into a single task to simplify maintenance. Web Spinner includes a complete help file.

Type: Shareware

Provided by:

FLFSoft, Inc.
PO Box 306
Oak Creek, WI 53154-0306
E-mail: **flfsoft@execpc.com**
http://www.execpc.com/~flfsoft/flfsoft.html

Web Wizard 32-bit

Web Wizard is an HTML document creator that works like a Windows Wizard. You simply answer the questions asked by the Wizard, click Finish, and the Wizard creates the document for you. Great for beginners, or to use as a starting point for any HTML document.

Type: Freeware (optional $10 registration fee)

Provided by:

David Geller
Arta Software Group
15520 Mill Creek Blvd. #H201
Mill Creek, WA 98012
USA
E-mail: **davidg@arta.com**
http://www.halcyon.com/webwizard

WebWatch for Windows 95/NT 1.1

WebWatch is a tool for keeping track of changes in selected Web documents. Given an HTML document referencing URLs on the Web, WebWatch produces a filtered list, containing only those URLs that have been modified since a given time.

The input file can be the bookmark file of Netscape, the exported (to HTML format) hotlist of Mosaic, or any other standard HTML document edited locally or retrieved from the Web.

WebWatch generates a local HTML document that contains links to only those documents that were updated after the given date. You can load this document into any Web browser and use it to navigate to the updated documents.

WebWatch 2.0 for Windows 95 is currently in beta testing. You can download it from the provider's home page.

Type: Shareware

Provided by:

Joseph Janos, Director
Specter Communications
45 Selwyn Road
Belmont, MA 02178
Voice: 617-484-6512
Fax: 617-484-6512
E-mail: **webwatch@specter.com**
http://www.specter.com/

Multimedia Viewers and Editors

If you frequently download graphics or sound files, you need software to view or listen to these files. Although a commercial graphics program may have more power and versatility than the programs listed here, you sometimes may prefer to use a smaller, simpler program. You're not likely to use all of these programs, but we've included several with similar features to give you more choices. What's right in one situation might not be right in others.

Adobe Acrobat Reader

Adobe Acrobat Reader lets you view electronic documents that were originally created from a wide range of authoring tools and saved as .PDF files. For example, during tax season, you can save yourself a trip to the post office by downloading PDF versions of almost any income tax form you need; print them out using Acrobat Reader, and get to work. You don't need the original program the document was created in; you can view or print the document with the hardware and software you already have.

Type: Freeware

Provided by:

Adobe Systems Incorporated
1585 Charleston Road
Mountain View, CA 94039-7900
E-mail: **webmaster@adobe.com**
http://www.adobe.com/

ImgLib 1.2

ImgLib is a 32-bit DLL for developers who would like to support the reading, converting, and manipulating of all popular graphics image formats like BMP, JPEG, TIFF, PCX, Photo CD, and others as needed by today's multimedia applications.

Besides the ability to read the most popular raster image formats, ImgLib offers added functionality to modify the bitmaps in memory to aid in displaying them on all existing Windows-capable displays with best possible results and without sacrificing the image quality.

ImgLib supports the following file formats: Windows and OS/2 BMP, JPEG, PC Paintbrush (PCX), TIFF, Targa, Photo CD, MacPaint, FBM, Sun Raster, CMU WM Raster, Portable Bit Map (PBM, PGM, PPM), Faces Project, Utah RLE, X Window Dump, McIDAS areafile, G3 FAX, GEM Bit, X Pixmap, and X Bitmap.

Type: Shareware

> **Note**
>
> When you register the software, you'll receive a version that has been optimized for speed.

Provided by:

Adam Rybicki, Consultant
SimSoft
PO Box 4091
Redondo Beach, CA 90278
USA
Voice: 310-679-7222
E-mail: **arybicki@netcom.com**

JASC Media Center

If you have a large collection of multimedia files you have collected from the Internet, use this program to keep them organized. It supports 37 file formats internally (including GIF, JPEG, MIDI, WAV, and AVI), but you can still use formats that aren't supported if you have an external file filter for them.

Type: Shareware

Provided by:

JASC, Inc.
PO Box 44997
Eden Prairie, MN 55344
USA
Voice: 612-930-9171 (9 a.m. to 5 p.m. USA central time)
Fax: 612-930-9172 (24 hours)
E-mail: **jasc@winternet.com**

LView Pro for Windows 95

LView is one of the best all-around graphics viewers and utilities. NCSA recommends this viewer for both GIF and JPEG images with Mosaic. It also supports TIFF, PCX, and several other image formats. In addition to viewing these files, you can retouch images by adjusting their color balance, contrast, and many other attributes.

Type: Shareware

Provided by:

Leonardo Haddad Loureiro
MMedia Research
1501 East Hallandale Beach Boulevard, #254
Hallandale, FL 33009
USA
E-mail: **mmedia@world.std.com**

Paint Shop Pro

Paint Shop Pro is a powerful graphics viewing and editing utility. It supports about twenty different graphics file formats, including the common GIF and JPEG formats found on the Web. It has a host of features for editing and manipulating graphics, and rivals commercial packages with the number and variety of filters and special effects. It also includes a screen capture program.

Type: Shareware

Provided by:

JASC, Inc.
PO Box 44997
Eden Prairie, MN 55344
USA
Voice: 612-930-9171 (9 a.m. to 5 p.m. USA central time)
Fax: 612-930-9172 (24 hours)
E-mail: **jasc@winternet.com**

PolyView for Windows 95

PolyView is a BMP, GIF, JPEG, Photo-CD, PNG, and TIFF graphics viewer, file conversion, and printing utility for Windows NT and Windows 95.

Type: Shareware

Provided by:

PolyBytes
3427 Bever Avenue S.E.
Cedar Rapids, Iowa 52403
E-mail: **polybytes@kagi.com**

SnapShot/32

SnapShot/32 brings professional quality and convenient Windows 95 and NT screen captures to your fingertips. It was designed for ease of use, with powerful and useful features to aid the professional as well as support the needs of the occasional user.

Type: Shareware

Provided by:

Greg Kochaniak
3146 Chestnut Street
Murrysville, PA 15668, USA
E-mail: **gregko@kagi.com**
http://198.207.242.3/authors/gregko/gregko.htm

VMPEG Lite 1.7

MPEG files are highly compressed movie files, and VMPEG Lite is a great tool for working with them. This program offers a variety of features including high-quality stereo playback, high-speed performance, and a variety of display options. It even plays video CDs!

VMPEG is a fast software decoder for MPEG encoded video sequences. Both video and audio are decoded in real-time (with frame-dropping, if the processor is not fast enough) and output synchronously to the graphics card and sound card of the PC. There are currently two major application areas for MPEG-1 software decoding: Video CD playback and transmission of video via the Internet (e.g., World Wide Web). Video CD is by far the more ambitious task. You will need at least a Pentium 90, a PCI graphics card, and a 2x (better 4x) CD-ROM. Best results are obtained when using a DCI graphics cards accelerating some of the decoding steps with dedicated hardware.

Note

This release of VMPEG is a demonstration version. For this reason, audio and video CD playback are restricted to 60 seconds. The full commercial version is not yet available.

Type: Freeware

Provided by:

Stefan Eckart
555 W Middlefield Rd, Apt. K203
Mountain View, CA 94043
USA
E-mail: **stefan@chromatic.com**

VuePrint 32-bit

VuePrint is a program that lets you view, print, and convert graphics files, while playing sound and movie files at the same time. You can even convert your favorite graphics files to screen savers!

Some of the main features of VuePrint are

- Reads and writes six different types of graphics files
- Has a built-in screen saver
- Includes a slide show feature with more than a dozen options
- Supports all graphics displays, including 16-color laptops
- Supports copying to the clipboard, and pasting from the clipboard

Type: Shareware

Provided by:

Ed Hamrick
Hamrick Software
4025 E. Chandler Blvd.
Suite 70-F16
Phoenix, AZ 85044
E-mail: **support@hamrick.com**
http://www.hamrick.com/

System Utilities

The programs in this section are designed to help you keep Windows 95 in tip-top shape and running efficiently. Here you'll find programs for virus detection, uninstalling software, file compression, and other various system diagnostic/repair utilities.

Rosenthal UnInstall

Rosenthal UnInstall makes trying new software more attractive by eliminating the aggravation normally associated with removing unwanted software and restoring the system. Rosenthal UnInstall enables you to automatically remove unwanted Windows and DOS programs, files, directories and restore the system's AUTOEXEC.BAT, CONFIG.SYS, WIN.INI, SYSTEM.INI, and disk boot sector system tracks quickly and easily. Run Rosenthal UnInstall before you add anything new to your system. New programs can then be added and, at your option, kept, or deleted, and the system completely returned to normal.

Single systems as well as networks with multiple and even removable drives are supported. Rosenthal UnInstall maintains a map of your disk drives and records the appearance of each new installation. When you execute UNINSTAL.EXE before adding new software to your system, Rosenthal UnInstall can automatically remove it at some later date.

After you've tested the program, simply run UnInstall again to delete the program or update UnInstall's data.

> **Note**
>
> This program does not automatically install from the CD-ROM. See the README file for installation instructions.

Type: Shareware

Provided by:

Doren Rosenthal
Rosenthal Engineering
PO Box 1650
San Luis Obispo, CA USA 93406
Voice: 805-541-0910
E-mail: **doren@slonet.org**
http://slonet.org/~doren/

Software Manager

The Software Manager provides three wizards to help you manage the system and application software on your computer. The wizards eliminate the risk and guesswork associated with uninstalling software, maintaining Windows initialization (INI) files, and maintaining DOS configuration files (AUTOEXEC.BAT and CONFIG.SYS).

- The Uninstall Wizard simplifies the complex task of removing all traces of an existing application from your system. Using an expert system, the Uninstall Wizard guides you through the steps required to safely uninstall an application. Both manual and automated uninstalls are provided.
- The Installation Wizard guides you through the steps required to safely install new software, and creates a comprehensive report of changes made to your system by the installation process.

- The Configuration File Wizard provides a full-featured ASCII text editor to modify DOS and Windows configuration files. The text editor can handle larger text files than Notepad and Sysedit. An automatic backup is created when a configuration file is changed. Difference reporting allows review of changes between current and previous versions of a configuration file.

Type: Shareware

Provided by:

PCSoft
25 Mt. Lassen Drive
San Rafael, CA 94903
Voice: 415-492-0123
Fax: 415- 892-8950
E-mail: **72203.2310@compuserve.com**

ThunderBYTE Anitvirus for Windows 95

ThunderBYTE has been battling the virus hackers for some time now, and its comprehensive antivirus software is evidence of that fact.

Type: Shareware

Provided by:

ESaSS-ThunderBYTE Headquarters
PO Box 1380
6501 BJ Nijmegen
The Netherlands
Voice: 31 (0)24 642 2282
Fax: 31 (0)24 645 0899
USA Voice: 1-800-667-TBAV
E-mail: **int.tech@thunderbyte.com**

WinBatch 32

This critically acclaimed program helps you write your own Windows batch files. Dialog boxes, automatic program control, and powerful data manipulation let you control every aspect of your machine's operation. There are more than 350 different functions—a must for the power user. It can be set up to run in several different languages.

Type: Shareware

Provided by:

Wilson WindowWare
2701 California Ave. SW
Suite 212
Seattle, WA 98116
USA
http://www.windowware.com/wilson/pages/

WinBench 96 1.0

WinBench 96 is a subsystem-level benchmark that measures the performance of a PC's graphics, disk, processor, video, and CD-ROM subsystems in a Windows-based environment. WinBench 96's tests perform many of the same operations applications commonly execute. These applications cover top-selling Windows product areas, including database, business graphics and desktop publishing, spreadsheet, and word processing.

WinBench 96 returns five main results that provide an overview of a PC's graphics, disk, processor, and CD-ROM subsystems performance: the Graphics WinMark 96, Disk WinMark 96, the CPUmark16 and CPUmark32, and the CD-ROM WinMark 96. In addition, the benchmark includes full-motion video tests to measure the PC's video subsystem performance.

> **Note**
>
> You need Video for Windows to run any of the video playback tests.

WinBench 96's minimum hardware and software requirements include:

- MS-DOS 5.0 or later, Novell DOS 7, or OS/2 Warp
- Microsoft Windows 3.1 or later, Windows for Workgroups 3.1 or later, or Windows NT 3.5 or later
- An 80386 (or compatible) or higher processor
- 8M of RAM, when used with DOS and Windows 3.1, more for other configurations. WinBench 96 will run in less RAM, but it may produce invalid results due to paging activity
- 6M of free disk space for installation
- 58M plus the size of RAM on the PC as additional free disk space for the Disk WinMark 96 tests

- A CD-ROM drive if you're planning to run the CD-ROM or video tests
- A VGA resolution (640x480) or higher graphics adapter
- The Microsoft CD Extension software or equivalent
- A sound card
- Video for Windows (Windows, Windows for Workgroups, and OS/2 Warp PCs only)
- Win32s (version 1.25 for Windows and Windows for Workgroups; version 1.1 for OS/2 Warp)

Type: Freeware

Provided by:

Ziff-Davis Benchmark Operation
1001 Aviation Parkway, Suite 400
Morrisville, North Carolina 27560
Fax: 919-380-2879
CompuServe: GO ZDBENCH

WinPack 32 Deluxe 8

WinPack is a ZIP utility designed to eliminate the need to shell out to DOS equivalents. The developers felt the need for a ZIP package that would run completely under Windows, with all functions self-contained. WinPack Deluxe supports ZIP, GZIP, ARC, LHARC, ARJ, TAR, ZOO, COMPRESS, FREEZE, BINHEX, PACK, PACKIT, MIME, UUENCODE, DECODE, and a few others. WinPack is developed by AshSoft and distributed by RetroSpect.

Type: Shareware

Provided by:

RestroSpect
Voice: 405-482-0672
Fax: 405-482-0248
E-mail: **snow@retrospect.com**

WinZip 6.0 for Windows 95

WinZip brings the convenience of Windows to the use of ZIP files. TAR, gzip, UNIX compress, LZH, ARJ, and ARC files are also supported. WinZip features an intuitive point-and-click interface for viewing, running, extracting, adding, deleting, and testing files in archives. You can even use WinZip to temporarily install a program to see what it's all about. Optional virus scanning support is included.

Type: Shareware

Niko Mak Computing
PO Box 919
Bristol, CT 06011
USA
E-mail: **support@winzip.com**

ZIPExplorer 1.05 for Windows 95

ZIPExplorer is an extension to your Windows Shell that allows you to interact with compressed ZIP archives as if they were normal folders on your hard disk. You can open ZIP archives as you would any normal folder, and inside you will find the files and directories that were added to the archive by whomever originally created it.

Type: Freeware

Provided by:

Silicon Prairie Software
Suite N202
4771 148th Ave. NE
Bellevue, WA 98007
E-mail: **plummer@iceonline.com**
www.iceonline.com/home/plummer/zipexplr

Index of Common Problems

Installing Hardware and Software

Using Modems and Communications Programs

Using the Internet

Using Commercial Online Services

Using E-Mail and Faxing

Sharing Resources (Networking)

Index

Symbols

A

B

E

F

G

J

K

L

M

N

O

P

Q

R

S

T

W

X

Y

Z

GET CONNECTED
to the ultimate source of computer information!

The MCP Forum on CompuServe

online with the world's leading computer book publisher!
:millan Computer Publishing offers everything
need for computer success!

d the books that are right for you!

mplete online catalog, plus sample
·ters and tables of contents give
an in-depth look at all our books.
best way to shop or browse!

- Get fast answers and technical support for MCP books and software
- oin discussion groups on major computer ubjects
- nteract with our expert authors via e-mail nd conferences
- Download software from our immense ibrary:
  - Source code from books
  - Demos of hot software
  - The best shareware and freeware
  - Graphics files

Join now and get a free CompuServe Starter Kit!

To receive your free CompuServe Introductory Membership, call **1-800-848-8199** and ask for representative #597.

The Starter Kit includes:

- Personal ID number and password
- $15 credit on the system
- Subscription to *CompuServe Magazine*

Once on the CompuServe System, type:

GO MACMILLAN

for the most computer information anywhere!

CompuServe

Complete and Return this Card for a *FREE* Computer Book Catalog

Thank you for purchasing this book! You have purchased a superior computer book written expressly for your needs. To continue to provide the kind of up-to-date, pertinent coverage you've come to expect from us, we need to hear from you. Please take a minute to complete and return this self-addressed, postage-paid form. In return, we'll send you a free catalog of all our computer books on topics ranging from word processing to programming and the internet.

Mrs. ☐ Ms. ☐ Dr. ☐

st) ☐ (M.I.) ☐ (last) ☐

State ☐ Zip ☐

Fax ☐

Name ☐

dress ☐

: check at least (3) influencing factors for asing this book.

- ack cover information on book ☐
- pproach to the content ☐
- ness of content ☐
- reputation ☐
- 's reputation ☐
- er design or layout ☐
- able of contents of book ☐
- ook ☐
- fects, graphics, illustrations ☐
- ease specify): ______ ☐

lid you first learn about this book?

- acmillan Computer Publishing catalog ☐
- ended by store personnel ☐
- ook on bookshelf at store ☐
- ended by a friend ☐
- advertisement in the mail ☐
- lvertisement in: ______ ☐
- k review in: ______ ☐
- ease specify): ______ ☐

nany computer books have you ased in the last six months?

- only ☐ 3 to 5 books ☐
- ☐ More than 5 ☐

4. Where did you purchase this book?

- Bookstore ☐
- Computer Store ☐
- Consumer Electronics Store ☐
- Department Store ☐
- Office Club ☐
- Warehouse Club ☐
- Mail Order ☐
- Direct from Publisher ☐
- Internet site ☐
- Other (Please specify): ______ ☐

5. How long have you been using a computer?

- ☐ Less than 6 months ☐ 6 months to a year
- ☐ 1 to 3 years ☐ More than 3 years

6. What is your level of experience with personal computers and with the subject of this book?

	With PCs	With subject of book
New	☐	☐
Casual	☐	☐
Accomplished	☐	☐
Expert	☐	☐

Source Code ISBN: 0-7897-0557-5

7. Which of the following best describes your job title?

Administrative Assistant ☐
Coordinator ☐
Manager/Supervisor ☐
Director ☐
Vice President ☐
President/CEO/COO ☐
Lawyer/Doctor/Medical Professional ☐
Teacher/Educator/Trainer ☐
Engineer/Technician ☐
Consultant ☐
Not employed/Student/Retired ☐
Other (Please specify): ________________ ☐

8. Which of the following best describes the area of the company your job title falls under?

Accounting ☐
Engineering ☐
Manufacturing ☐
Operations ☐
Marketing ☐
Sales ☐
Other (Please specify): ________________ ☐

9. What is your age?

Under 20
21-29
30-39
40-49
50-59
60-over

10. Are you:

Male
Female

11. Which computer publications do you re[ad] regularly? (Please list)

____

Comments: ________________

Fold here and scotch

BUSINESS REPLY MAIL
FIRST-CLASS MAIL PERMIT NO. 9918 INDIANAPOLIS IN

POSTAGE WILL BE PAID BY THE ADDRESSEE

ATTN MARKETING
MACMILLAN COMPUTER PUBLISHING
MACMILLAN PUBLISHING USA
201 W 103RD ST
INDIANAPOLIS IN 46290-9042

NO POSTAGE
NECESSARY
IF MAILED
IN THE
UNITED STATES

License Agreement

This package contains one CD-ROM with software described in this book. See applicable chapters for a description of these programs and instructions for their use.

This CD-ROM contains shareware software, and the purchase of this book does not absolve the purchaser from any applicable software royalties due the software authors. See the individual product's documentation for more information.

By opening this package you are agreeing to be bound by the following:

> This software is copyrighted and all rights are reserved by the publisher and its licensers. You are licensed to use this software on a single computer. You may copy the software for backup or archival purposes only. Making copies of the software for any other purpose is a violation of United States copyright laws. THIS SOFTWARE IS SOLD AS IS, WITHOUT WARRANTY OF ANY KIND, EITHER EXPRESSED OR IMPLIED, INCLUDING BUT NOT LIMITED TO THE IMPLIED WARRANTIES OF MERCHANTABILITY AND FITNESS FOR A PARTICULAR PURPOSE. Neither the publisher nor its licensers, dealers, or distributors assumes any liability for any alleged or actual damages arising from the use of this software. (Some states do not allow exclusion of implied warranties, so the exclusion may not apply to you.)